Effective Training:

Systems, Strategies,
and Practices

Effective Training:

Systems, Strategies, and Practices

P. Nick Blanchard
Eastern Michigan University

James W. Thacker
University of Windsor

Prentice Hall, Upper Saddle River, New Jersey 07458

Acquisitions Editor: Stephanie Johnson
Assistant Editor: Shane Gemsa
Editorial Assistant: Hersch Doby
Editor-in-Chief: Natalie Anderson
Marketing Manager: Tami Wederbrand
Production Coordinator: Maureen Wilson
Managing Editor: Dee Josephson
Manufacturing Buyer: Diane Peirano
Manufacturing Supervisor: Arnold Vila
Manufacturing Manager: Vincent Scelta
Cover Design: Bruce Kenselaar
Cover Photo: David Madison/Tony Stone Images
Composition: Rainbow Graphics, LLC

Library of Congress Cataloging-in-Publication Data
Blanchard, P. Nick.
    Effective training : systems, strategies, and practices / P. Nick
Blanchard and James W. Thacker.
        p.   cm.
    Includes bibliographical references and index.
    ISBN 0-13-268160-9 (hardcover)
    1. Employees—Training of.   2. Occupational training.
I. Thacker, James W.   II. Title.
HF5549.5.T7B555 1998
658.3'124—dc21   98-13480
                                                                                        CIP

PRENTICE-HALL INTERNATIONAL (UK) LIMITED, *LONDON*
PRENTICE-HALL OF AUSTRALIA PTY. LIMITED, *SYDNEY*
PRENTICE-HALL CANADA INC., *TORONTO*
PRENTICE-HALL HISPANOAMERICANA, S.A., *MEXICO*
PRENTICE-HALL OF INDIA PRIVATE LIMITED, *NEW DELHI*
PRENTICE-HALL OF JAPAN, INC., *TOKYO*
PEARSON EDUCATION ASIA PTE. LTD., *SINGAPORE*
EDITORA PRENTICE-HALL DO BRASIL, LTDA., *RIO DE JANEIRO*

Printed in the United States of America

10 9 8 7 6 5 4 3

To Claudia, whose understanding, love, and support have nurtured and comforted me, and to Mike and Brandon, sources of pride and joy.

N.B.

To the women in my life: Gabrielle, my best friend (and wife); Helen, Chris, Wendy, and Karen, who have enriched my life in so many ways.

J.T.

Contents

Preface   xiii

CHAPTER 1   Overview of Training in Organizations   1

Learning Objectives   1

Overview of Training   3
  Terminology   4

The Role of Training in Organizations   9
  Training, budgets, and management responsibilities   10
  Strategy, training, and organizational development   12
  ISO 9000 and training   14

Structure of Training Organizations   14
  Training as part of the HR function   14
  The training organization   16
  Training in large and small businesses   17

A Training Process Model   19
  Open systems   19
  Training as an open system   20

Key Roles and Competencies   25
  Development of professional competencies   25

CHAPTER 2   Strategic Planning, Training, and OD   30

Learning Objectives   30

Overview   33

Strategic Planning Process   35
  Organizational mission   36
  Strategy   36
  Strategic contingencies   38
  Proactive and reactive strategy   41
  Matching internal to external strategy   42
  HR and HRD influences on competitive strategy   44
  What about small business?   50

HRD's Role in Supporting Strategy   53
  Developing an HRD strategy   53
  The training environment and amount of centralization   57
  Some strategic training alternatives   58

OD, Strategy, and Training   62
  OD and strategy   62
  Levels of internal change and resistance   67
  Training and OD   68

CHAPTER 3   Learning, Motivation, and Performance   80

Learning Objectives   80

A Few Words about Theory   83

Understanding Motivation and Performance   85
  Motivation: why do they act like that?   86
  Self-efficacy and motivation   94

Understanding Learning   95
  What is learning?   95

Two Integrative Theories of Learning   99
  Gagné's learning types   99
  Social learning theory   111

Why Are They Resisting and What Can I Do about It?   113
  Motivation to learn   114
  Training that motivates adults to learn   116

Individual Differences Related to Learning   117

CHAPTER 4   Needs Analysis   126

Learning Objectives   126

Why Conduct a Needs Analysis?   127

The Framework for Conducting a TNA   129
  Organizational analysis   131
  Operational analysis   136
  Person analysis   153
  Gathering TNA data   161

Outcomes of TNA   162
  Nontraining needs   162
  Training needs   164

Approach to TNA   165
  Proactive TNA   165
  Reactive TNA   169
  Reactive versus proactive   171

The Small Business   172
  Assistance for small business   173

TNA and Design   173

CHAPTER 5   Training Design   183

Learning Objectives   183

Developing Objectives   184
Identifying objectives   185

Advantages of Training Objectives   188
The trainee   188
The training designer   188
The trainer   189
Training evaluator   189

Organizational Constraints   189
Organizational/environmental constraints   190
Trainee population   191

Facilitation of Learning: Focus on the Trainee   192
KSAs (Individual differences)   192
Motivation of trainee   193
Classical conditioning and reinforcement (the environment)   197
Goal setting   197

Facilitation of Learning: Focus on Training Design   198
Attention/expectancy   199
Retention   200

Facilitation of Transfer: Focus on Training Design   203
Conditions of practice   204
Maximize similarity   206
Vary the situation   206
Other considerations to facilitate transfer   207

Facilitation of Transfer: Focus on Organizational Intervention   209
Supervisor support   209
Peer support   209
Trainer support   210
Reward systems   210
Climate and culture   210
What about the small organization?   211

Outcomes of Design   212

CHAPTER 6   Evaluation of Training   221

Learning Objectives   221

Rationale for Evaluation   222
Resistance to training evaluation   223
So we must evaluate   224

Types of Evaluation Data Collected   225
Process data   225
Outcome data   228

Evaluation: The Validity Issue   253
   Threats to internal validity   255
   External validity   257
   What does it all mean?   259

Evaluation Design Issues   259
   Basic designs   259
   More complex designs   262
   What design to use   265

What About the Small Organization?   266

Summing It All Up   269

CHAPTER 7   Training Methods   275

Learning Objectives   275

Overview of the Chapter   277

Matching Methods with Outcomes   277

The Lecture   278
   Straight lecture/lecturette   278
   Discussion method   279
   Strengths and limitations of lecture and discussion   279

Computer-Based Training   285
   Strengths and limitations of CBT   288

Games and Simulations   293
   Equipment simulators   293
   Business games   294
   In-basket technique   295
   Case study   297
   Role play   297
   Behavior modeling   299
   Strengths and limitations of G/S   300
   Training group characteristics   304

On-the-Job Training   305
   Job instruction technique (JIT)   306
   Apprenticeship training   308
   Coaching   308
   Training the trainer for OJT   309
   Strengths and limitations of OJT   309

Audiovisual Enhancements to Training   311
   Static media   312
   Dynamic audiovisual methods   313
   Strengths and limitations of audiovisuals   315

A Summary of Method and Learning Objective Match   322

CHAPTER 8   Development and Implementation of Training   330

   Learning Objectives   331

   Instructional Methods   332

      Lecture   332

      Computer-based training (CBT)   339

      Games and simulations   343

      Business games/in-basket/case study   343

      Role play/behavior modeling   348

      On-the-job training   351

      Trainers for OJT   356

   Audiovisual Enhancements   358

      Static media   359

      Dynamic media   361

   Facilities   366

      The training room   366

      Off-site training facilities   369

   The Trainer   369

      Trainer KSAs   369

      Trainer credibility   370

   Integrated Instructional Strategy   372

      Content: learning points   372

      Method of instruction   372

      Facilities, material and equipment, trainers   372

      The strategy   373

   The Alternative to Development   375

      Alternatives for the small business   376

   Implementation   378

      Dry run   378

      Pilot program   379

      Tips for trainers   380

CHAPTER 9   Management Development   389

   Learning Objectives   389

   Why Focus on Management Development?   390

      Managers get a lot of training   391

      Managers are accountable for success   391

      The manager's job is complex   391

   Our Approach to Management Development   392

   General Overview of the Managerial Job   392

      Managerial roles   393

      Organizational factors   395

      Integrating strategy, structure, and technology   395

General Characteristics of Managers   396
Management styles   396
Categories of management characteristics   397
Integrating managerial roles and characteristics   399

Integration: Strategies and Management Characteristics   401
Technical competence and context   401
Interpersonal competence and context   401
Conceptual competence and context   402
Personal traits and context   402
Management style and context   402

Management Development Implications   404
Understanding context   404
Self-awareness and diagnostic skills   404
The managerial person analysis   405

Sources of Knowledge/Skill Acquisition   407
Externally based training   407
Corporate universities   408
Types of management development programs   409

The Special Needs of the Technical Manager   412
History and experience   412
Skills   413
Traits   413
Leadership style   413
Strategies for development of technical managers   413

Index   419

Preface

This book is for those who wish to understand the process of developing human resources as well as for those who teach it. Our approach differs from that of other training books in that it places training activities in the context of organizational strategy. Whether you are a student or a practitioner, this book will be of both conceptual and practical value for developing training programs that meet strategic and tactical needs. At the same time an overarching model of the training process will guide you step by step through the training procedures, from initial needs analysis through the evaluation of training's effectiveness.

As human resource competencies have become a significant competitive advantage both in North America and globally, the pace and intensity of organizational training has increased dramatically. Training departments must demonstrate not only that their programs provide enhanced employee competencies, but that those competencies are of strategic value to the organization. Some organizations are including continuous learning, often called the "learning organization," as part of their strategy. As a company's strategies change, the types of management competencies and styles need to change as well, and Human Resource Development is responsible for this alignment. We address these and related issues because we believe that effective training practices are determined by the organizational context in which they occur.

Unique Characteristics of This Book

There are a number of things that set this book apart from others on the same topic. As was noted above, we integrate training into the strategic planning process. We set the stage for this process early (chapter 2), discussing how organizations approach strategic planning, and showing how input from the Human Resources function in general and the Human Resource Development function in particular can influence strategic direction. We then proceed to discuss how these functions develop internal strategies to support the overall strategic plan. We often refer back to this chapter to demonstrate how strategic issues drive human resource development decisions. We also provide an important link between organizational development (OD) practitioners and trainers, showing how the competencies of each of these disciplines complement and support the objectives of the other. In the remaining chapters we use an OD philosophy to address ways in which the training process and outcomes can be integrated into other organizational systems. This integration of the training process into a systems perspective provides the reader with an understanding of where training fits in the organization and how it operates.

Training books often prescribe what organizations should do to provide effective training. Often this "one best way" approach doesn't take into account the variety of constraints that individual organizations may face. We provide a contingency approach, suggesting alternatives and explaining the associated consequences. Thus the reader comes to understand that what is best depends upon the objectives of the organization and its unique constraints.

Another important difference in this book is the overarching model of the training process and its subprocesses. This model provides an understanding of the logical sequencing of training activities, from needs analysis to implementation and evaluation. This model demonstrates that training is a system and each of its processes are interconnected. Thus each chapter covering a phase of the training process (i.e., needs assessment, design, development, implementation, and evaluation) begins with a description of the types of input needed to complete that phase and the types of output produced. The bulk of the chapter provides a step-by-step description of how the input is transformed into the output.

In teaching training classes in the past we have found that two books were necessary: one to provide the theory and constructs and one to provide the hands-on, practical aspects of training. This book provides both. For example, on the topic of "methods of training," chapter 7 discusses the methods from a theoretical and conceptual basis, and chapter 8 explains how to use these methods when developing the training program. Throughout the book we attempt to provide the *why*, *what*, and *how to* components of training.

Most training books focus on large organizations that have access to many resources, ignoring the smaller companies with more limited resources. We have addressed the training issues faced by smaller businesses in two ways. First, the contingency approach provides alternative activities and procedures, some of them compatible with limited resources. Throughout the book we address the applicability of various approaches to the smaller business. Second, many of the chapters have sections directed at the small business; these sections provide possible alternatives and describe what some of the small businesses are actually doing in these areas. Unfortunately, the literature on small-business training practices is relatively sparse. If you know of small-business practices that have been successful, we would love to hear about them and include them in subsequent editions.

Learning objectives provide trainees with an understanding of what the training is trying to accomplish, and so they are an important part of the training process. Better learning is achieved if, at the beginning of training, people know where they should focus their attention. Therefore, at the beginning of each chapter we will identify its learning objectives, stating what the reader should be capable of doing after completing the chapter. (The value of learning objectives and the characteristics of good objectives are discussed in depth in chapter 5.)

Following the learning objectives is a case example to stimulate the reader to think about the issues that will be raised in the chapter. Throughout the chapter we refer back to the case to make specific points, asking the reader relevant questions about the case. Some of the cases are presented in totality at the beginning of the chapter; others are split into two parts, the first part stopping at a critical point, and the rest presented at the end of the chapter, so the reader can see how the issues were handled or what consequences resulted from the actions taken.

A number of applied examples are presented throughout the book, some highlighted outside the text and others integrated into the text. These help to make concepts come alive for the reader and make the reading more interesting, understandable, and easily remembered.

At the end of each chapter are discussion questions, cases, and exercises to enhance understanding. The instructor's manual provides more information about this material and offers additional ideas for teaching. It also includes sample course outlines and a test bank.

We know that there are an abundance of excellent teaching techniques, exercises, and research applications that we were unable to locate. Our goal is to improve this book continually so that it makes learning and teaching the joy that it can be. To that end we ask you to contact us with your thoughts, applications, exercises, and so on so that they can be shared with everyone. You can reach us at Nick.Blanchard@emich.edu or JWT@uwindsor.ca. Of course, any contributions will be acknowledged in future editions of this book.

Organization and Plan of the Book

We begin with an overview of training and a definition of key terms. The first chapter also discusses training's role in the organization, how training fits into the human resources (HR) function, and how the training function fits into the structure of large and small companies. Here we discuss training as a career. This chapter also presents the overarching training process model, which is used to outline the organization of the book and provide an overview of the content of the remaining chapters. The chapter ends with a discussion of the key roles and competencies of human resources development (HRD) professionals.

Chapter 2 discusses strategic planning and the roles Human Resources and HRD play in this process. This chapter shows how training is integrated into the competitive strategy of the company. The role of OD (change management) in the training process is also presented, as is a rationale for combining the activities in these disciplines. The case example provides a discussion point for many of the topics in this and subsequent chapters, allowing the student to walk through a case from the beginning of the strategic plan to the development of training.

Chapter 3 provides the theoretical and conceptual framework for understanding the training process. It begins with a short discussion of the practical application of theory. A model of the factors that determine performance (motivation, knowledge, skills, abilities, and environment) is followed by a review of theories of motivation and learning. These theories are discussed in terms of their application to training. There follows a discussion of resistance to learning and applications of adult learning theory to overcoming this resistance. The chapter concludes with a discussion of individual trainee differences and offers training alternatives that can address such differences. The concepts and principles developed here are referred to throughout many of the following chapters, tying particular practices to the theoretical rationale for those practices.

Chapter 4 addresses the first phase of the training model presented in chapter 1: needs analysis. An expanded graphic of this phase is presented and discussed at the outset so the reader will understand the organization of the chapter. The philosophy of needs analysis is discussed in terms of both its proactive use (as related to the strategic plan) and its reactive use (to deal with immediate concerns and changing conditions). The relationship between these two approaches is also explored. The steps involved in the needs analysis are discussed, along with the sources from which data can be gathered and to set training priorities.

Chapter 5 begins with the second phase of the training model: training design. The outcomes of the needs assessment phase are shown as inputs to this phase. The chapter then identifies the activities conducted in the design phase of training, from the development of the training/learning objectives to the identification of organizational constraints on training and factors that will facilitate learning. The learning facilitation factors focus separately on the trainee and the training design. Next, factors that facilitate the transfer of learning back to the trainee's job are discussed; these are broken down into training design factors and organizational systems factors back on the job.

One of the logical outputs of the needs assessment (chapter 4) and learning objectives (chapter 5) is the creation of training evaluation objectives. Because evaluation outcomes are defined in relation to objectives, the evaluation process begins at that point. In addition, the measurements used in determining training needs are likely to be a part of the evaluation systems. For these reasons, we have followed the design chapter with the evaluation chapter, reinforcing the fact that the evaluation process begins early in the development of training programs, even though the actual measurement of outcomes doesn't occur until after the training. Chapter 6 then addresses the issues and activities involved in the evaluation phase of the overarching training model.

Chapter 7 provides the conceptual framework for determining which methods to use when developing a particular training program. It begins with a discussion of the importance of matching training methods to the desired training outcomes. The various training methods are then described, along with their strengths and limitations. Included here are the relative costs; trainer versus trainee control over what is learned and how; effectiveness at developing knowledge, skills, or changing attitudes; and issues related to training group size and individual differences. The chapter concludes with a summary table of the various methods' effectiveness in meeting knowledge, skill, and attitude change objectives. Chapter 8 discusses the same methods, but in terms of how actually to use them in developing and conducting a training program.

Chapter 9 begins with a general overview of a manager's job, then discusses the types of competencies needed by managers. This discussion includes the conceptual, technical, and interpersonal knowledge and skills, as well as personal traits or styles. In addition to the traditional listing of various types of management development programs that address these areas of competency, the capacity of our readers is enhanced through a model that allows the training professional to determine what competencies a manager *in their organization* should have. The model integrates the competitive strategy, organizational structure, and technology literature into a continuum that describes the organizational context in which managers must operate. This context then determines the relative value to the company that various managerial competencies and characteristics (such as style) are likely to have. The chapter also discusses three important areas of managerial knowledge and competency: understanding of the organizational context, self-awareness and diagnostic skills, and adaptability. The chapter concludes with a discussion of the special needs of technical managers.

Acknowledgments

In a boat in northern Manitoba on a quiet sunny day, while the authors were catching their share of walleye, we conceived writing this book. From that time until now, many people have helped make the final product possible, and we are grateful to them. Of course any errors or omissions are ultimately ours, and we bear responsibility for them.

The people at Prentice Hall were especially helpful. Thanks to Natalie Anderson, the editor who accepted the project and got us off the ground; and our current editor, Stephanie Johnson, whose advice and help were ultimately responsible for its final form. Thanks to Maureen Wilson, production editor at Prentice Hall, for her timely feedback and assistance in turning the product into its final form. Thanks also to those anonymous yet most important people whose diligence and skill in copy editing and production create the final images, text, and layout that make reading and learning a pleasure. We would also like to thank Wendy Thomas for her developmental editing, particularly for repairing the fractures we imposed on the English language. Special thanks to Patricia Currie, who has been involved with this project from its beginning. She not only gathered research but also read each of the chapters many times and provided helpful comments. Heidi Kalyna Birmele contributed volumes of research for many chapters and deserves recognition and thanks for her scholarship and commitment. Also a heartfelt thanks to Gabrielle Thacker, who is able to detect the errors that everyone else misses, and does so often.

We would like to acknowledge the contributions of both the academics and practitioners who have shared their insights with us. Specifically, we would like to thank Mitchell Fields, University of Windsor, and Rick Camp, Eastern Michigan University. Lee Sanborn of Ford Motor Company and Greg Huszczo of Eastern Michigan University deserve thanks for demonstrating how effective training can be developed and delivered. The reviewers of the early drafts of this book whose feedback has really made a difference in shaping the form and content of the book are Talya Bauer, Portland State University; James Brown, University of Southern Colorado; Joseph Martocchio, University of Illinois at Urbana-Champaign; Jim Wanek, Boise State University.

Finally, for the number of times she had to retype chapters and renumber tables and figures, and did so with a smile, we wish to thank May Nhan. To Sean Way and John Farlinger, thanks for helping to gather research information for the book.

About the Authors

Nick Blanchard

Nick Blanchard completed his undergraduate studies in psychology at UCLA and his Ph.D. in industrial and organizational psychology at Wayne State University. He is currently a professor in the Management Department at Eastern Michigan University. His writings appear in both scholarly and applied publications. He is co-author of *Toward a More Organizationally Effective Training Strategy and Practice*, a training text published by Prentice-Hall in 1986. He has served as consultant and trainer to many organizations including Bethlehem Steel, Chrysler Corporation, Domtar Gypsum, Ford Motor Company, and various local and state government agencies.

James Thacker

Jim Thacker received an undergraduate degree in psychology from the University of Winnipeg, in Winnipeg, Manitoba, and his Ph.D. in industrial and organizational psychology from Wayne State University. He is currently a professor at the University of Windsor, Faculty of Business. His research has been published in both academic (*Journal of Applied Psychology*, *Personnel Psychology*, *Academy of Management Journal*) and practitioner (*Journal of Managerial Psychology*, *The Human Resource*, *Consultation: An International Journal*) journals. He also co-authored the first Canadian edition of the text *Managing Human Resources* with Wayne Cascio, published in 1994. He has been a consultant and trainer in the private sector (Michigan Bell, Ford, Hiram Walker's, Navistar, H.J.Heinz) and public sector (Revenue Canada, CanAm Friendship Canter). Prior to obtaining a Ph.D., Jim worked for a gas utility as a tradesman and served as vice-president of his local union (Oil, Chemical and Atomic Workers) for a number of years. This firsthand experience as a tradesman and union official combined with his consulting and academic credentials has provided Jim with a unique combination of skills.

Effective Training:

Systems, Strategies,
and Practices

CHAPTER 1

Overview
of Training
in Organizations

Learning Objectives

After completing this chapter, you should be able to:

- Define and differentiate among knowledge, skills, and attitudes

- Describe the similarities and differences among employee development, education, and training

- Describe the economic importance of training to business operations

- Describe various roles and expectations of training in large and small businesses

- Describe the components of a general open systems model and the corresponding components of the training processes model

- Describe the career options for trainers and the key roles and competencies associated with those options

- Describe the relationship between training, the Human Resources function, and line operations

Training a Key Factor in British Airways Turnaround

In the early 1980s British Airways (BA) was in serious trouble. It had lost £544 million (about $1.3 billion) in 1981–1982 and was continuing to lose money at the rate of about £200 a minute. The company had to face laying off about 20,000 employees, closing down unprofitable routes, and disposing of substantial assets just to stay in business. In 1983 the board of directors charged Colin Marshall with reestablishing the company as "the world's favorite airline," a title it had once worn proudly. By 1987 Marshall and his executive team had revitalized the company enough to merge with British Caledonian and be privatized. Since then British Airways has shown a steady rise in performance and profitability that has brought it back to world-class status. Training was a significant part of Marshall's strategy for revitalization. However, he recognized that just training people wasn't enough. He knew that employees' new skills and abilities had to be supported by the company's systems and procedures. Thus he insisted that the training be integrated with all the other "people" and business initiatives that were being developed.

The central focus of British Airways' strategy was a total dedication to the passenger. "Winning for Customers" was a core program in this strategy. It was required for all managers. It assessed their skills and identified areas for development. The carefully chosen title constantly reminded managers that the focus of their activities should be on what was best for the customer. Other human resources systems were redesigned to support this strategy in many ways.

- A program of performance feedback, used on a quarterly basis, measured strengths and weaknesses of managers via a framework of "key" management practices.
- "Managing Winners" was a series of programs developed to meet the training needs identified in "Winning for Customers."
- A number of customer-focused training initiatives were provided to all employees, beginning with a one-day meeting on service recovery (what to do when a service fails) and the value of customer retention.
- A new learning center, using state-of-the-art learning and training systems, was open to employees at all levels and was used for both independent learning and formal training.

Training programs at BA are a part of an integrated system in which each program builds on the learning achieved in earlier programs. The following systems have been developed to ensure that training is linked to the customer service strategy.

- Training consistency is ensured by a framework that specifies the skills to be developed in each training module.
- Professional capability performance standards (e.g., platform skills, content knowledge, and use of training methods) are set for trainers.
- Customer service training is compared to "best practices" both within British Airways and externally.

- Line managers are partnered with trainers to work out common language and concepts to ensure the practicality of training and its transfer to the job site.

These practices ensured that training would provide the maximum return to the organization. However, recognizing that training would not solve every customer service problem, BA used the following process to determine where problems existed and what solution was most appropriate.

1. Customer satisfaction analysis identifies areas where customer service needs improvement.
2. To identify the cause of the problem, an analysis determines if it stems from employees' abilities or from other factors such as motivation or work procedures.
3. Based on the cause, a training or nontraining intervention is developed. If it is a training intervention, an analysis of the learning objectives and possible training alternatives is conducted to determine the most practical and cost-effective training methods.
4. Both professional training staff and line personnel are used to ensure maximum learning.
5. A tangible value for the training investment is set before the training begins, reflecting how much improvement in customer satisfaction is to be expected if training is successful. Thus, the cost of training is justified, or not, by its potential benefits. The customer satisfaction problem area is then evaluated after the training as a measure of the training's effectiveness.

British Airways has become one of the most profitable airlines in the world. Not only has its approach to human resources development had a positive impact on the bottom line, it has established BA as a leader in customer service.

(This case is based on the reports and descriptions in *The 8 Practices of Exceptional Companies,* Fitz-Enz 1997.)

Overview of Training

As the British Airways case demonstrates, employee training enables companies to adapt to changing conditions and be more effective in the marketplace. This is accomplished by providing employees with opportunities to learn how to perform more effectively and by preparing them for any changes in their jobs. However, training doesn't always result in these outcomes. Training is an "opportunity" for learning, but what is learned depends on many factors: the design and implementation of the training itself, the characteristics of the trainees, and the learning climate of the organization. There are several basic things training professionals can do to maximize the effectiveness of training:

- Provide a supportive environment in which learning is facilitated
- Design training programs so that trainees are motivated to learn

- Work with others in the organization to identify and remove barriers to using the new knowledge and skills on the job

At its worst, training can be an isolated program of activities put together with no understanding of the needs of the business or the trainees and no attempt to determine the value of the training. When a training program is not well thought out, employees tend to discount its relevance to their jobs and realize little improvement. Training, at its best, is a set of processes aimed at continuously improving employees and organizational systems, including the training itself. The key word here is *processes.* When training is structured as a set of continuous processes that are integrated with other systems and business strategies, the connections between training and day-to-day business practices are apparent. In the British Airways case we saw that the training was tied closely to the core business strategy of customer service. Training was part of an integrated system in which performance was measured against criteria (best practices benchmarks) that were tied to strategic objectives. Employee performance was systematically reviewed and feedback was provided to them on a regular basis. Performance problems were analyzed to determine the cause, and solutions were developed on the basis of this analysis. Although many training programs were developed, they were integrated into a coherent whole with each program building on the learning from previous programs. Training was developed and implemented in partnership with line managers, so a clear link was created between what happened in training and what happened on the actual job. This continuity and integration illustrate training as a process and not just a program.

This text will take you through the complete training process as it would be conducted under ideal conditions. Unfortunately, for most organizations ideal conditions don't exist. There is often insufficient money, time, or training professionals. Recognizing these limitations, we have provided variations that while not ideal, will do a reasonable job of accomplishing training objectives. Of course, there is a price to pay for shortcuts, and we identify the major consequences associated with various alternatives. Thus we have tried to provide both "ideal" and more practical approaches to conducting training activities.

TERMINOLOGY

At this point we should review some of the terms and concepts that will be used throughout the book. It is important to have a good understanding of them at the outset.

Learning

Definitions for *learning* found in the literature vary according to the theoretical background of the authors. Unless otherwise indicated, the term **learning** in this text means a relatively permanent change in cognition (i.e., understanding and thinking) that results from experience and that directly influences behavior. This definition, of course, reflects our own theoretical assumptions. We will discuss this definition and others at length in chapter 3.

KSAs

Learning can be separated into different categories. Again, how these categories are defined differs according to the source. Traditionally, organizational psychologists have used the categories "knowledge, skills, and abilities" (KSAs) to label the different types of learning outcomes. One drawback to this categorization is that it is difficult to differentiate between skills and abilities. **Abilities** have been defined as general capacities related to performing a set of tasks that are developed over time as a result of heredity and experience (Fleishman 1972). **Skills** have been defined as general capacities to perform a set of tasks developed as a result of training and experience (Dunnette 1976). The only difference seems to be whether or not heredity is involved. To our knowledge, the existing scientific evidence suggests that skills are influenced by heredity as well as by experience. Sometimes skills are categorized as psychomotor (behavioral) while abilities are categorized as cognitive. However, if that is the case, how do abilities differ from knowledge? Our definition of *knowledge* covers both the facts people learn and the strategies they learn for using those facts. While some would argue that abilities can still be distinguished from knowledge and skills, we believe the distinction to be of minimal value. On the other hand, attitudes are relatively easy to distinguish from knowledge or skills. In addition, it is scientifically well established that attitudes influence behavior and that they are learned (Oskamp 1991). Thus attitudes must be part of any paradigm or model attempting to describe the categories of learning or outcomes of training.

In this text the acronym **KSAs** refers to the learning categories of "knowledge, skills, and attitudes." The three categories of learning are pictured in Figure 1.1. The way these three types of learning occur and the way they manifest themselves are interrelated, but quite different. We will be discussing these in depth throughout the text (notably in chapters 3, 4, and 7).

Knowledge   This category of learning refers to the information we acquire and place into memory, how it is organized into the structure of what we already know, and to our understanding of how and when it is used. Thus knowledge can be seen as composed of three distinct but interrelated types: declarative, procedural, and strategic (Kraiger, Ford, and Salas 1993).

Declarative knowledge is a person's store of factual information about a subject matter. Facts are verifiable blocks of information such as the legal requirements for

FIGURE 1.1 Classification of Learning Outcomes

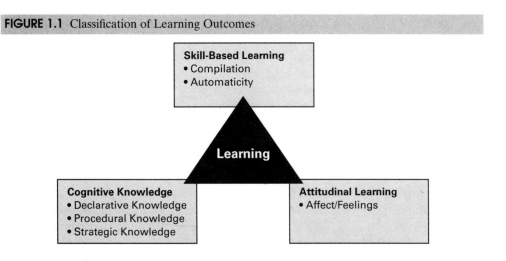

hiring, safety rules, and the like. Evidence of factual learning exists when the learner is able to recall and/or recognize specific blocks of information.

At a higher level is the person's understanding about how and when to apply the facts that have been learned. This is referred to as **procedural knowledge.** It assumes some degree of factual knowledge, since some information must be known about an object or activity before rules for its use can be developed. For example, one could not know when to apply steps in problem solving (procedural knowledge) if she did not know what the steps were (declarative knowledge). Procedural knowledge includes the underlying relationships among facts and procedures (e.g., business strategy or machine troubleshooting). It allows trainees to understand the underlying rationale and contingencies surrounding potential courses of action so they can apply their factual knowledge appropriately. This type of knowledge reflects how the facts are stored in memory and what types of linkages are formed with other knowledge the trainee has acquired.

The highest level of knowledge is **strategic knowledge.** This is used for planning, monitoring, and revising goal-directed activity. It requires acquisition of the two lower levels of knowledge (facts and procedures), which are internalized as complex mental models. Strategic knowledge consists of the person's awareness of what he knows and the internal rules for accessing relevant facts and procedures to be applied toward some goal. When this type of knowledge is the focus of training or education, it is often called a "learning how to learn" program.

Skills   We use Dunnette's definition of **skill** as the capacities needed to perform a set of tasks that are developed as a result of training and experience (Dunnette 1976). A person's skills are reflected by how well she is able to carry out specific actions such as operating a piece of equipment, communicating effectively, or implementing a business strategy. Skills are dependent on knowledge in the sense that the person must know "what" to do and "when" to do it. However, there is a difference between knowing what to do when, and how well one is actually able to "do" it. A skill is a proficiency at doing something, beyond just knowing something about it.

Two levels of skill acquisition—*compilation* (lower level) and *automaticity* (higher level)—reflect differences in the degree to which a skill has become a routinized behavior pattern. When a person is learning a particular skill or has only recently learned it, he is in the **compilation** stage. Here he needs to think about what he is doing while he is performing the skill.

After a person has mastered the skill and used it often, she has reached the **automaticity** stage. Here she is able to perform the skill without really thinking about what she is doing. In fact, thinking about it may actually slow her down. Learning how to play tennis is a good example of the different stages of skill development. When you are first learning to play, you must constantly think about each aspect of hitting the ball, such as where to stand on the court, and so on. Gradually, changes in how you grip the racket and your movement on the court become automatic, and thinking about them may actually reduce your effectiveness.

Attitudes   **Attitudes** are reflections of employee beliefs and opinions that support or inhibit behavior (Oskamp 1991). In a training context, we are concerned about employees' attitudes that are related to job performance. Examples would be employee beliefs about management, union, empowerment, training, and how satisfying various aspects of the job are. These beliefs and opinions create associations between objects and events that can modify positive or negative feelings (called *affect*) that the person attaches to the objects and events. Thus changing a person's beliefs or opinions can change how she feels about a particular object or event, making it more or less desirable. For example, if an employee has positive feelings about her supervisor, those positive feelings are likely to become associated with the employee's job. If she learns from a coworker that the supervisor has said negative things about her, her job satisfaction is likely to be reduced, even though nothing about the job itself has changed.

Attitudes are important issues for training because they affect motivation. Motivation is reflected in a person's selection of goals and the amount of effort expended in achieving those goals. Goals and effort are influenced by how the person feels about things related to the goal (i.e., attitudes). Because of the relatively strong relationship between a person's attitude and his behavior, attitudes that motivate employees to perform or learn more effectively need to be addressed by training. For example, Lockheed Corporation began to have concerns about the security of company products and product development processes. They realized that they would have to either significantly increase their security force (which was not financially feasible) or include security in the job descriptions of all employees. They chose the latter approach and instituted employee security awareness orientations (and annual reorientations). The sessions were designed to change employees' attitudes (beliefs and opinions) about their jobs, so that all employees saw workplace security as part of their responsibility rather than only the responsibility of the security department. By 1990, five years after the start of the program, the number of reports of "suspicious incidents" had increased by 700 percent (Chuvala, Gilmere, and Gillette 1992). Training in Action 1.1 on page 8 illustrates the importance of examining not only attitudes, but each of the three learning categories (KSAs) when designing training programs.

Training, Development, and Education

The terms *training, development,* and *education* have been used in various ways by various authors. *Training* is often described as focusing on the acquisition of KSAs needed to perform more effectively on one's current job. *Development* is used by many to refer to the acquisition of KSAs needed to perform in some future job. While we see some value in distinguishing between KSA acquisition for a current job and a future job, we feel that the use of the terms *training* and *development* create confusion, because the creation of KSAs is largely the same regardless of when the KSAs will be needed. One cannot develop KSAs without some form of training or educational experience. We use the terms *training* and *development* here to refer to distinct but related aspects of learning: Training is a set of activities, and development is the desired outcome of those activities. **Training** is the systematic process of attempting to develop KSAs for current or future jobs; **development** refers to the learning of KSAs. That is, training provides the opportunity for learning, and development is the result of the learning.

What used to be called "training departments" and "management training" are now called Human Resource Development (HRD) departments and management development, respectively. The change in terminology reflects the change from a focus on the process (training) to a focus on the outcome (development).

Training Needs in the Student Registration Office

The president's and provost's office at a large university were receiving many complaints about the registration office being nonresponsive to student problems during registration for classes. The director of registration felt that, because of the high turnover in customer service representatives (CSRs), who handled student problems, most CSRs did not know the proper procedure. The director wanted to initiate training in registration procedures immediately and called in a consultant to assist in developing and conducting the training.

After listening to the director's description of what she wanted, the consultant said, "You're probably right. Of course, we could conduct a training needs analysis to clarify the exact nature of the performance problem." The director was concerned about the time required for a needs analysis and wanted to get training started right away. However, since she agreed that the needs analysis would determine specific problem areas, she said, "Okay, do the analysis, but let's get started on training right away. I want them to know exactly what they are supposed to do."

The needs analysis revealed the steps and procedures that an effective CSR was required to complete in dealing with an unhappy customer. For example, one of the first steps was to identify and clarify the customer's problem. To do this, the CSR was first to acknowledge the feelings the customer was displaying (e.g., anger or frustration) in a friendly and empathetic manner. Once these feelings had been acknowledged, the CSR was to determine the exact nature of the customer's problem through nonevaluative questioning (i.e., determining the facts without placing blame for outcomes).

Interviews with the CSRs established that they all knew the correct procedure and most could quote it word for word. However, observation of the CSRs at work showed very marked differences in how the procedure was carried out. Further analysis of each of the CSR's skills in performing these tasks revealed that low skill levels and CSR attitudes were the primary causes of unsatisfactory performance. While nearly everyone "knew" what to do, some were not very good at doing it. Others didn't believe it was important to follow every step. One CSR said, "Hey, if they get their problem solved, what do they care if I acknowledged their feelings?"

Certainly training was required in this case, but not the "knowledge" training the registration director thought was necessary. For those CSRs who lacked the behavioral skill to carry out the procedures, demonstrations and practice sessions with immediate feedback were provided. For those CSRs who had the skill but didn't understand the importance of all the procedures, attitudinal training sessions were conducted in which the CSRs reevaluated their attitudes through various educational and experiential activities.

Education is typically differentiated from training and development by the types of KSAs developed. Whereas training is generally seen as the development of job-specific KSAs, **education** is viewed as the development of more general KSAs, related (but not specifically tailored) to a person's career or job. This is a satisfactory distinction, but we want to caution the reader that many activities labeled "training" are educational in nature. Thus education shouldn't be thought of as something that is done only outside the organization. For example, many organizations provide literacy training for their employees. This training isn't tailored to the specific job requirements of these employees but is directed at developing general reading and writing skills.

The Role of Training in Organizations

Most moderate to large organizations have a centralized training area, often called a Human Resource Development (HRD) department. Training is typically part of the Human Resources (HR) department, along with other human resources activities, such as recruiting, selection, and compensation. The role of the HRD department is to improve the organization's effectiveness by providing employees with the KSAs that will improve their current or future job performance. The focus is on the development of job-related KSAs. At the same time, effective training must address the personal needs of employees, helping them to learn, to grow, and to cope with the issues that are important to them. Focusing on KSAs that don't meet the needs of the organization will not be productive. Likewise, unless the new KSAs are seen as relevant and important by the employees, they won't transfer back to the employee's job and will waste company resources. Truly effective training strategies and practices are those that meet the needs of the organization while simultaneously responding to the needs of individual employees.

Some examples that illustrate this point are demonstrated in Training in Action 1.2 (page 10) and 1.3 (page 11).

In these two examples, training was successful in developing new knowledge and skills, but it failed to take into account the needs of the organization or the employees. This failure prevented the knowledge and skills from becoming integrated into the day-to-day operations. In the first example, training met the needs of the supervisors but was rendered unusable by the organization's new policy. Because of past problems in the performance appraisal system, the organization felt a need to put in place a new system that included reviewing and documenting the formal appraisal. A more careful needs analysis would have identified this systems conflict, leading to more appropriate training or an intervention to prevent or modify the change in policy. In this case they might have developed "periodic, informal appraisal interviews" so when it came time to do the formal interview there were few surprises and little "selling" required. Or they might have intervened to change the new system so that the face-to-face interview could take place before the appraisal was finalized. This would have allowed for a more integrated approach to both the feedback and documentation aspects of the performance appraisal system. The British Airways case presented at the beginning of this chapter demonstrates the value of integrated personnel systems.

In the second example, training met the organization's need for developing problem-solving and team-building skills in employees but failed to recognize the employee's issues of (1) fair workloads, (2) recognition, and (3) peer acceptance. As a re-

---

Selling Performance Appraisals

The supervisors in a large electronics company had been badgering the training director for years to help them do a better job of conducting performance appraisal interviews. Most supervisors were using a "tell and sell" approach. They would tell the employee the problems they had observed and try to sell the employee a corrective action plan. The supervisors and employees would constantly argue about the accuracy of the appraisal and the value of the corrective action plan.

Finally the training director put together an off-site workshop focusing on performance appraisal interviewing skills. The seminar emphasized a "problem-solving" approach, in which the supervisor and employee come to agreement on the "problem" and identify ways to solve it. The workshop cost the company a significant amount of money, and evaluations taken immediately after the workshop showed that the supervisors liked the approach and understood the steps and processes involved. They believed their problems with appraisal interviews were now solved. Unfortunately, follow-up evaluations, taken a few months after the workshop, showed that none of the supervisors were using the problem-solving approach.

Further investigation revealed that a few weeks after the workshop, the HR department had issued a policy modifying the performance appraisal procedure. The new policy required that the official evaluation documents, with the supervisor's signature, be forwarded to HR before any formal, face-to-face feedback sessions between supervisor and subordinate took place. Thus the supervisor's appraisal, without input from the subordinate, became official. Once HR had received and filed the document, the supervisor was required to provide formal, face-to-face feedback to the subordinate. All supervisors were using the "tell and sell" approach under the new policy *because they had already submitted their official appraisals to HR* and they now had to convince the subordinate that the appraisal was accurate.

---

sult, implementing what was learned did not last very long back on the job. Had a more thorough needs analysis been conducted, the needs of both the organization and the employees could have been dealt with in the design of the training. Chapter 3, on learning, motivation, and performance, discusses the many causes of performance problems and shows that training is a solution for only some of them.

TRAINING, BUDGETS, AND MANAGEMENT RESPONSIBILITIES

Managers are accountable for the performance of the entire area they manage. The capabilities of their employees play a significant role in their ability to achieve the objectives set out for the area. Thus managers need to participate in determining their subordinates' training needs and the type of training to meet those needs. After the

---

Training in Action 1.3

Team Building Sizzles Then Fizzles

The director of a city utilities department felt that creating employee problem-solving teams would improve the quality of his operations and improve the efficiency of the department. All employees were provided the opportunity to participate in team building and problem-solving training. About 60 percent of the employees, including the director and his management group, signed up for the training. Three-hour training sessions took place once a week for ten weeks. Employees, working on a common process within their department, were grouped into teams for three weeks of team building training and seven weeks of problem-solving training.

At the beginning of the problem-solving training each team identified a problem in its area of operation and worked through this problem as it went through each step of the training. The team members were delighted to be learning new skills while working on a real problem. By the end of training, each group had actually solved or had made significant progress toward solving the problem it was working on. Evaluations taken at the conclusion of training indicated that trainees enjoyed the training and understood the steps, tools, and techniques of team building and problem solving. The director was pleased with the results and submitted a report to the city manager documenting the successes of the training.

Follow-up evaluation conducted six months later showed only one team still in operation. Other teams had fallen apart because work loads prevented their setting aside time for meetings, little recognition was given when problems were solved, nontrained employees resisted making changes in work processes, and/or teams were ridiculed by those who had not participated in training.

---

training has been completed, managers should judge its effectiveness. They also need to be involved in managing their own training and development. Clearly, training is a manager's responsibility, whether it is explicitly stated to be so in his job description or just implied from his objectives.

As organizations streamline operations and cut costs to become more competitive, many managers and supervisors will be asked to do some of the training themselves. This can take the form of on-the-job coaching or more formal classroom sessions as topic area experts. This can happen in any sized business but especially in smaller businesses where resources don't allow for full-time HRD professionals. Familiarity with effective training practices and strategies will make a manager more valuable in any function or at any level in the organization.

U.S. organizations employing 100 or more employees budgeted a total of $59.8 billion for training (*Training* 1996), continuing an upward trend from $43.2 billion in 1991. Smaller to midsized firms, employing 100 to 499 people, averaged $140,040 per company for training; these companies make up about 78% of the Dun & Bradstreet data base of 146,837 U.S. organizations. Those employing between 500 and 999 people, about 10% of the data base, planned to spend about $237,600 each. The largest companies, those with 10,000 or more employees (1% of the data base), had training budgets that averaged well over $15 million. Educational services companies spent the least on training, and companies in transportation, communication, and utilities spent the most. Of the nearly $60 billion, $42.1 billion was spent for HRD staff salaries, and another $14.7 billion was allocated for outside services (seminars, conferences, materials, etc.). Similar trends exist in Canada. IBM Canada, for example, with 12,000 employees, spent more than $36 million a year for training (Cascio and Thacker 1994), or about $3,000 per employee.

Obviously, organizations see training as an important investment and are devoting substantial amounts of cash to training activities. Whether you are part of the training staff or a line manager, it makes sense to understand a part of the organization that commands this sort of financial attention. While most training departments do not charge internal clients for their services, 38% of the companies say they do have a charge-back system, whereby departments must use part of their budget to pay for training services. This practice is most common in manufacturing, wholesale/retail trade, and public administration but is becoming increasingly common. Companies using this practice no longer view training as just a cost to the organization. Executives and managers in these companies expect a return on their training dollar investments. HRD departments that are not able to document the value of their products and services may find their internal customers going to outside vendors for services. The HRD departments that can document favorable cost/benefit ratios will continue to get their fair share of budget dollars. An example of this situation is Scepter Manufacturing (Le Gault 1997), a plastic product supplier. In 1992 the company's training budget totaled $6,000 and covered about 150 employees. A change in company strategy necessitated training all employees in various new technical areas and cross-training in the other jobs within their work area. Performance measures after the training and the implementation of new systems showed that scrap had been reduced by 50% and defective parts were reduced from 5% to 0.1%. Was training worth it? "Yes," said the plant manager, who indicated that the training budget is now $60,000. Although it is somewhat time-consuming and complex to document how new KSAs have resulted in increased operational profitability, the Scepter example shows it is both feasible and practical to do so. Chapter 6 (on evaluation) discusses methods for documenting and evaluating training results.

STRATEGY, TRAINING, AND ORGANIZATIONAL DEVELOPMENT

Today's competitive environment is more intense than ever before. Significant and rapid changes are affecting the business environment. One only has to think about the remarkable changes in technology, political boundaries and treaties, population demographics, and consumer preferences in the last decade to appreciate how turbulent the business environment has been. Businesses that are able to develop strategies that match their internal strengths to meet the demands of the external environment will find themselves at a competitive advantage. Because the business environment is so unstable, most businesses must continually evolve their competitive strategies. As strategies change, mechanisms are required to enable the organization's structure, systems, processes, and people to change with them. Organizational development and training are becoming preferred options for managing these internal changes.

Organizational development (OD) is a set of processes designed to improve the ability of an organization to adapt its internal characteristics to the demands of its environment, while meeting the needs of its members, through planned interventions (Bennis 1969; Beckhard 1969; Alderfer 1977; Beer & Walton 1990). These OD interventions apply behavioral science concepts to facilitate the change of beliefs, values, attitudes, procedures, systems, and structure in an organization to match more closely requirements imposed by external forces (e.g., markets, competitors, technology, etc.). Another way of saying this is that OD is a set of planned activities to change systematically the way an organization operates to conform to the conditions it faces.

Training, of course, is one method of changing employee capabilities in the workplace. Effective training practitioners are also OD practitioners. They are concerned with more than just the delivery of a set of KSAs; they are concerned with how employee KSAs will impact the effectiveness of the organization and the individual. They understand the processes and systems of the organization and how these will either support or inhibit the employee's use of KSAs on the job. When the systems and processes (structure) inhibit the employee's performance, the training practitioner must intervene to secure appropriate change. Had the practitioner at the electronics company in Training in Action 1.2 intervened, the training could have been more effective and the organization more productive. The training director should have been aware of the proposed policy changes for performance appraisals. With this information the director could have modified the policy to reflect the problem-solving approach. Failing that, the training could have been modified to provide supervisors with techniques for conducting the appraisals in ways that were consistent with the policy. If you were a consultant to the director of the utilities department in Training in Action 1.3, how could you have intervened to make the department's systems and processes more conducive to team problem solving?

Ken Hansen, Motorola University's Director of Strategic Information, believes that the success of most businesses will depend on whether they can continually adapt to constant change (Filipczak 1994). Hansen sees HRD departments providing organizations with a critical piece of the change and adaptation process that will make the organization competitive. When business conditions change, employees must change the way they carry out their responsibilities or acquire new responsibilities. Simply providing the knowledge and skill is not enough. The organizational structure (i.e., design, systems, and processes) must change to support the changes expected in employee performance. Similarly, when organizations change their processes or systems, employees must be provided with the knowledge and skills to operate effectively within those systems.

This is not to say that all OD interventions are within the training practitioner's scope of responsibility or that all trainers actually do apply OD techniques and principles. Rather, we are pointing out that there is a large amount of overlap between OD goals and activities and those of training, so the effective trainer needs to have a basic understanding of organizational development. Helping organizations and employees change to become effective is at the heart of the training enterprise. Therefore, organizational development concepts are used frequently throughout this book as we discuss the various training strategies and practices. Chapter 2 is devoted to exploring the relationships among business strategy, OD, and training.

ISO 9000 AND TRAINING

ISO 9000 is a series of standards to ensure consistency in product quality. Developed by the International Organization for Standardization (ISO) in Geneva, Switzerland, in the late 1980s for the European Common Market, it has since expanded into the United States, Canada, and more than 50 other countries. It consists of a number of stages (Fattal 1996):

Preaudit:	Assessing how you are doing now
Process mapping:	Documenting the way things are done
Change:	Developing processes to improve the way things are done to reach a desired level of quality
Training:	Training in the new processes
Postaudit:	Assessing how well you are doing after the changes

Training, then, is built into the standards for certification. Once certification has been granted, there are additional audits from time to time to ensure that the company is still in compliance with ISO 9000 procedures.

Companies involved in the ISO process find that it results in better-trained personnel, improved efficiency and internal communication, cost reductions, and the ability to document quality control processes to their customers (Dolack 1996). Glen Black, president of the Process Quality Association in Canada, has compared ISO certified to noncertified companies (Williamson 1997) and has found that the certified companies are six times less likely to experience bankruptcy, average 76% lower warranty costs in customer-discovered defects, and have 36% less bureaucracy within their company structure. These benefits do not come free, however. Once the company makes the decision to seek certification, it must be prepared to engage in a substantial amount of training. For example, in the process of becoming certified, Carolina Fluids Components in the United States provided every one of their employees with 120 hours of training on all aspects of the business (Wisnia 1997). Furthermore, training is only a part of the overall cost. Each business must determine whether the costs of ISO certification are justified by the benefits.

Structure of Training Organizations

TRAINING AS PART OF THE HR FUNCTION

Understanding the training function as an open system makes it easier to see how training fits into an organization's structural systems. In most organizations training is part of the Human Resource function. A typical HR function is depicted in Figure 1.2. While HR functions differ to some degree across large organizations, most have the components listed in the figure. The descriptions of the positions are necessarily broad, but they convey the differences in the types of activities performed.

Each of the functional areas within HR needs to integrate its goals, systems, and activities with the other areas. Thus the training area needs to understand what the other HR areas are doing to ensure that everyone is moving toward a common goal. When that does not happen, issues such as those depicted in Training in Action 1.1, 1.2, and 1.3 will occur. HRD management that is closely involved with all HR pro-

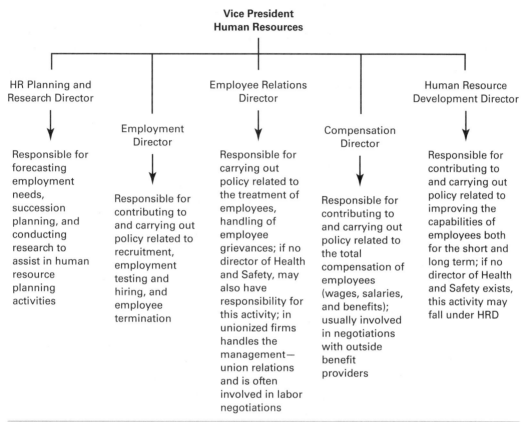

FIGURE 1.2 Organization Chart for Human Resource Function

grams and interventions will understand what needs to be done to improve employee competencies.

The relationship of training to the other HR activities is fairly clear. The attitudes of employees toward their organization affects employee motivation and performance. HRD staff must understand this point to determine training needs. Training itself can play a role in how positively or negatively employees view the organization. The employment activity controls the number of employees entering and leaving the organization. The influx and outflow of employees changes the capability mix within the organization. New employees have special needs such as orientation training, as do those leaving the organization (e.g., retirement seminars or outplacement workshops). HR planning and research are extremely important to the HRD area as organizational employment models and succession plans identify the future KSA needs of the organization. In addition, the research aspect of this HR function can assist the HRD area in understanding current organizational and employee needs. HRD, then, is one aspect of the organization's overall human resource strategy. The overall HR strategy is developed in conjunction with the organization's competitive strategy. For the HR strategy to be effective, each of the specialized activities within HR must understand its role in carrying out the strategy and must have its activities integrated with those of the other areas.

THE TRAINING ORGANIZATION

HRD or Training Departments vary considerably in how they are constructed. We will provide here an example of how a training department in a large organization might be organized and the types of activities it might be engaged in.

Within the HRD department, activities are often divided into Management Development, Employee Development, and Organizational Development. Each of these areas might be further divided into more specialized activities. For example, the Employee Development area might contain Customer Service Training, Employee Orientation, Health and Safety Training, and a separate training area for each of the organization's major operations. If the company is very large, it might also have specialists working in evaluation and research, program design, materials development, and needs analysis. The customer service training coordinator, for example, would work with specialists in these areas to do the following:

- Determine the customer service training needs in the organization
- Develop training programs to meet those needs
- Develop materials to support the instructional methods to be used in the programs
- Evaluate the effectiveness of the programs

Entry-level positions in a large company's HRD department are usually at the specialist level. Thus a new hire with little experience but a good education in the training area could start out as a materials designer or a stand-up trainer, depending on her KSAs. In a large organization a career path might look like the one shown in Figure 1.3. The early rotation through the various specialist positions provides the novice trainer with solid, firsthand experience in all aspects of the training system. When a person has a solid grasp of the system (i.e., how it is "supposed" to work and how it "actually" works), she is able to supervise one of the specialist areas. A supervisor must make sure not only that her area is running properly, but also that her area's activities are fully integrated with what other areas are doing. The only way to do this is to have a realistic understanding of the other areas' goals and how they operate. Some large companies also require their HRD specialists to spend time in a line position, to understand better the needs of line personnel. Thus at some point in the career ladder pictured in Figure 1.3 (probably between the supervisor and managerial positions) the training practitioner could find himself supervising or working in a line operation for a period of 6 to 12 months, although this requirement is still fairly unusual.

In general, the smaller the organization, the more activities each individual is asked to perform. In a medium-sized company, the HRD activities of employee, management, and organizational development may all be carried out by a small group of people under the guidance of an HRD manager. Each individual is expected to perform all (or most) aspects of each of the activities. Smaller companies may not have an HRD or Training Department at all. Instead, a single individual may be responsible for

Director HRD

↗

Rotation through other HRD management positions

↗

Manager, Training Support Services

↗

Supervisor of Materials Development

↗

Rotation through other specialist positions

↗

Entry-level specialist position (e.g., training materials developer)

FIGURE 1.3 Possible Career Path in HRD

all training activities. In even smaller businesses many of the HR responsibilities, including training, are decentralized out to the line managers. Human Resources may consist of only one or two people who handle the core HR activities and act as consultants and facilitators for the line managers in carrying out their HR responsibilities.

Another career path for a training and development professional is as a member of a training or consulting firm. Generally, entry-level positions require a minimum of several years of experience working in different areas of training. This is because most training or consulting firms are relatively small (1 to 15 people), and the staff must be capable of performing many activities, not just one specialty. In addition, the financial resources of these firms generally will not support a long and extensive training period. Employees are expected to be able to "hit the ground running," with only a minimum of orientation to the firm's philosophy, product, and service lines. Some very large training or consulting firms do hire specialists in certain areas such as instructional design, materials development, and evaluation. However, these firms also prefer employees to have several years of experience as well as advanced degrees. Generally, they are able to recruit a sufficient number of applicants who meet the experience and education requirements, because their compensation package is typically much better than that of the smaller firms, although compensation levels vary considerably from firm to firm.

TRAINING IN LARGE AND SMALL BUSINESSES

Most business texts, especially those covering human resource management (HRM), focus on medium- to large-size businesses. There are many reasons for this, including the following:

- Research typically requires a larger number of employees.
- Larger firms have the budgets to support research.
- Policies and procedures are more formalized, thus easier to track.
- The techniques described in HR texts usually require a formal HR function containing multiple areas of specialization, such as compensation, HRD, selection, and so on.

When small businesses are ignored, a major component of the economic engine that runs North America is missed. Small business firms created more than six million jobs in the United States during the 1980s while large companies reduced their number of employees by over a million (Holt 1993). Almost all businesses (98%) in the United States employ fewer than 100 employees, and 87.5% employ fewer than 20 people. Over half of the U.S. workforce work at companies employing fewer than 100 people. By contrast, only 0.1% of the companies have 1,000 or more employees and only about 13% of the workforce is employed by these companies (Griffin and Ebert 1996). Similar numbers are true for Canada (McKay Stokes 1995), where 93% of the businesses have fewer than 20 employees.

There is no size criterion that is accepted in the literature for categorizing a business as large or small. Some use fewer than 500 employees (Deshpande and Golhar 1994), some 200 or fewer employees (Banks, Bures, and Champion 1987), and others 100 or fewer (Szonyi and Steinhoff 1983). We generally use the term **small business** here to refer to organizations with fewer than 100 employees, but we will on occasion use examples with about 150 employees. Our main criterion is that the company does not have a formalized Human Resources Department.

The model of the training process that we will present is applicable to both large and small businesses, but the ways in which it is implemented can differ dramatically with the size of the company. One difference is the number of employees that need to be trained. Because larger companies train greater numbers of employees, they must use a more systematic and controlled method of determining what training needs exist. In smaller companies the owner or president can have a close working knowledge of each employee and his or her training needs. Another difference is in developing training programs. The smaller business can easily determine what types of training are more or less important to the company's objectives and can design training accordingly. In larger companies, again, a more systematic and formal approach will be needed because the firm's strategies and objectives are more complex. In larger companies economies of scale can be obtained if common training needs across the workforce are identified. This reduces the per person cost of training but a more rigorous approach to identifying needs is required. Another difference is that smaller companies can use less costly and formalized methods of evaluating training's effectiveness, because the results are more easily seen. Throughout the following chapters, where applicable, we have identified strategies and practices that might be more appropriate for the smaller business. Where research has been done, we will highlight its implications. When research is not available, we will offer logic and applied examples.

Although many differences exist between smaller and larger firms in the way they deal with training, owners of small businesses have the same concerns as big businesses. They identify as their number one concern the ability to obtain, develop, and retain a high-quality workforce (Hornsby and Kuratko 1990). They recognize that training is a critical component to increasing the quality of their workforce. So, while training is just as important to the small business as to the medium or large business, the methods and practices they use are different. The differences discussed above suggest that there is no "one best way" to determine training needs, design a training program, or evaluate the effectiveness of training. Nevertheless, there are a set of processes that are tied to training effectiveness regardless of organizational size, and they are the focus of the following section.

A Training Process Model

OPEN SYSTEMS

Figure 1.4 shows a general systems model that has long been in use as a description of business organizations (Katz and Khan 1978). This model is called the **open-systems model.** Open systems have a dynamic relationship with their environment.

As Figure 1.4 indicates, the system is open to influences from its environment and, in fact, depends on the environment for input. The system takes inputs from the environment and transforms them into outputs. Outputs enter the system's environment and may or may not influence future inputs into the system. A business is a social-technical system and operates in the same fashion as any other open system. Its environment consists of many factors such as customer markets, other businesses that are competitors and suppliers, local and global economics, political and legal systems, and others.

The system (business organization) must be responsive to the needs and demands of its environment, because the environment provides the input needed for the system to replenish itself. For example, if a business is responsive to the needs of society by providing valued goods and services (output), it receives valued input from society in the form of financial and goodwill credits. These are used by the business to continue operating. If the business doesn't provide sufficient value to its environment, it will fail because the environment will not provide the input necessary for the system to replenish itself. While the business must meet the needs of its environment, it must also protect itself from aspects of the environment that are harmful to the system.

The barrier between the system and the environment is represented by a dotted line in Figure 1.4 to indicate that this is a semipermeable barrier allowing components of the environment (input) and system (output) to cross over. The semipermeable barrier represents the organization's policies, systems, and procedures that are designed to allow only certain components of the external environment to enter the system. For example, the company must hire employees (input), but it doesn't hire just anyone. It wants to hire only those who can make a contribution to the organization's goals (desirable input). Therefore it sets up criteria for selecting employees from the labor pool, allowing only those with the proper qualifications to enter the organization. On the other hand, the company must comply with the laws set up by society or face sanctions (undesirable input), and some of those laws address the criteria that can be used in selecting employees (e.g., equal employment opportunity and affirmative action). Thus input from one area of the environment (the law) influences the nature of barriers that allow input from another area of the larger system (the labor pool). It is the organization's policies, systems, and procedures that allow it to exam-

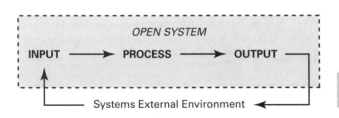

FIGURE 1.4 General Open Systems Model

ine and analyze the environment to determine which components of the environment to respond to and what response is most appropriate. These topics are covered in more depth in the next chapter, in the discussion of strategic planning and organizational development.

TRAINING AS AN OPEN SYSTEM

The environment of most open systems is another open system. In this view, most systems can also be thought of as subsystems of a larger system. For example, a product assembly system is a subsystem of a manufacturing system, which itself is a subsystem of the business, which is a subsystem of the industry, and so on. In the open-systems model, training can be seen as one subsystem within the larger system of HR, which is a subsystem of the company. Figure 1.5 illustrates some of the exchanges that take place between the training system and the larger organizational system. The organization's mission, strategies, resources, and the like all represent sources of input into the training subsystem. Of course, if the training department is part of a larger HR function, then these inputs would be filtered through that system. These inputs are translated by the training subsystem into usable input in the form of organizational and employee needs, training budgets, staff, equipment, and so forth. This input is then utilized to produce the output of the training system (improved KSAs, job performance, and so on). This illustration shows how interconnected the training activities are with what is happening in the organization as a whole. Unless training takes into account and meets the expectations of the business, the business will institute sanctions on the training system (e.g., reduced budgets, staff, and other resources) rather than providing it with more desirable inputs. Training in Action examples presented earlier demonstrate the consequences of a poor match between the training system and the organizational environment. The British Airways case provides an example of how a training system can be designed to ensure that training staff appropriately analyze and respond to the organizational environment. In the next chapter we will take a closer look at the training environment.

FIGURE 1.5 Training as a Subsystem within the Organizational System

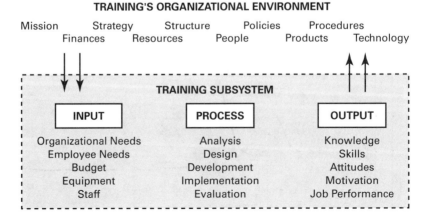

TRAINING'S ORGANIZATIONAL ENVIRONMENT

Mission   Strategy   Structure   Policies   Procedures
      Finances   Resources   People   Products   Technology

TRAINING SUBSYSTEM

INPUT	PROCESS	OUTPUT
Organizational Needs	Analysis	Knowledge
Employee Needs	Design	Skills
Budget	Development	Attitudes
Equipment	Implementation	Motivation
Staff	Evaluation	Job Performance

Training: A Set of Processes

Another point inferred from the open-systems model of training is that training is a process, not just a set of discrete programs. To be sure, training does consist of programs. When a particular training need is identified, a training program may be developed to address that need. However, when this is done through a set of integrated processes in which organizational and employee needs are analyzed and responded to in a rational, logical, and strategic manner, the environment (i.e., organization) is more likely to respond with desired inputs. When each training program is tied in to an overall plan, it provides output of maximum value to the organization for its investment in training.

It is the training system adopted by an organization that determines the degree to which training programs are tied to the company's strategic objectives and provide a reasonable return on investment. Recall that British Airways developed standards for training outcomes, for consistency in the training approach, and for the trainer's professional capabilities. This evaluation of both process and outcomes allowed British Airways to improve not only their customer service, but also the effectiveness and efficiency of their training. Such an approach creates a continuous improvement process for training that is integrated with the continuous improvement of other organizational systems. Our model of the training system, depicted in Figure 1.6, reflects this approach.

FIGURE 1.6 Training Processes Model

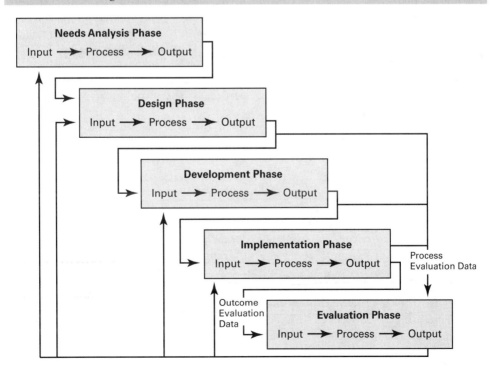

We view training as one of several possible solutions to organizational and individual performance problems. Whether training is the right solution depends on the cause of the problem and the cost-benefit ratios of the other alternatives. Thus training processes are similar to problem-solving processes. Most problem-solving processes include the following steps:

- Identifying organizational problem areas (those in need of improvement)
- Determining the cause(s) of the problem
- Identifying, selecting, and implementing the best solutions
- Evaluating the effectiveness of the solution

By comparing this list with Figure 1.6, you can identify how our model of training processes serves as a problem-solving tool. The **Needs Analysis Phase** identifies the problems and identifies their cause(s). Training becomes a solution when the problem is caused by inadequate KSAs. Once training is identified as a solution, the **Design, Development,** and **Implementation Phases** result in a training program for the appropriate employees. The **Evaluation Phase** assesses both the training processes and the training outcomes. Figure 1.6 is merely an overview of the process; a more detailed figure for each phase is provided at the beginning of the relevant chapter, where the input and output of each process is described in considerably more detail. For now we will briefly describe the phases and their inputs and outputs.

Analysis Phase   An effective business is one that is able to scan its environment and determine the products and services it can provide to meet customer or market needs. Similarly, in the ideal training system, the training process begins with a determination of needs. These needs show up as either current or anticipated performance deficiencies. A current deficiency would be evidenced by documentation of things such as profitability short falls, low levels of customer satisfaction, or excessive scrap. An anticipated deficiency would exist when information suggests that objectives are not likely to be realized unless changes are made. For example, when the ISO 9000 certification standards first came out, organizations wishing to do international business had an anticipated performance deficiency. They would lose business unless they were able to achieve certification by a certain date. On an individual level, when a manager has been targeted for promotion, the difference between her current capabilities and those she will need after the promotion would be anticipated performance deficiencies.

Once performance deficiencies are identified, the cause must then be determined. If the deficiency is caused by inadequate KSAs, then training becomes a way to satisfy the need. Since not all performance problems are due to KSA deficiencies, those problems for which training will be beneficial must be culled from those for which training is irrelevant. Performance deficiencies that are caused by motivation or equipment, for example, require a different solution. The performance deficiencies that are to be addressed by training are then prioritized.

The process of data gathering and causal analysis to determine which performance problems should be addressed by training is termed **training needs analysis (TNA).** Information from three sources serve as inputs to the analysis process: the organization as a whole, operational areas where problems exist, and the people within the operational areas.

The output of the Analysis Phase consists of identification of the training and nontraining needs and their priorities. Nontraining needs become inputs to organizational systems outside the training system. Training needs become the inputs to the Design Phase, where the **training objectives** are developed.

Design Phase   The training needs (employee KSA inadequacies) that have been identified in the TNA serve as the major input to the Design Phase. However, additional inputs are derived from the organizational and operational analyses. These constitute both the constraints placed on training and areas of expected support. Constraints and support occur in relation to things such as organizational plans, resources, and business cycles. Another set of inputs is derived from theory and research on learning; these are used in the design of training programs to facilitate learning and the transfer of the learning back to the work site.

Training objectives, that is, the outcomes a particular training program is to achieve, are developed by examining training needs in relation to the identified organizational constraints and support. These objectives specify what the employee will be capable of doing and the conditions under which it can be done at the conclusion of training.

The second part of the design process is identifying the factors that are needed in the training program to facilitate the learning and its transfer back to the job, including identifying alternative methods of instruction. Finally, the training objectives provide the foundation for the evaluation objectives. In fact, they become some of the criteria used in evaluation, although there are more evaluation criteria than just the training objectives.

The factors needed to facilitate learning and transfer and the alternative methods of instruction become inputs to the Development Phase of the training system. The evaluation objectives become inputs to the Evaluation Phase. As you might have noticed, the evaluation process begins after the evaluation objectives have been identified and is conducted concurrently with the other phases of the training system.

Evaluation Phase   Traditionally we think of evaluation as occurring at the end of a process, but for many reasons it is important to think about it during all the phases. Although the outcomes of training are a principal focus of evaluation, no improvement in the process is possible unless the process itself is evaluated. In addition, designing the evaluation of a training program's outcomes must be completed well in advance of the implementation of that program. For these reasons, we have placed the evaluation chapter immediately after the design chapter. A close look at the training process model indicates that some type of evaluation can occur at each training phase.

The model indicates two types of evaluation that are useful for training: process evaluation and outcome evaluation. **Process evaluation** is a determination of how well a particular process achieved its objectives (i.e., outputs). Each phase of the training process model constitutes a process with inputs and outputs. For example, in the Analysis Phase a process evaluation would be concerned with the accuracy and completeness of the organizational, operational, and person data collected. It would also determine if the data had been interpreted accurately, whether the cause of performance discrepancies had been identified accurately, and if the training objectives reflected all the key training needs that were feasible to address. Logical rather than statistical analysis is used for this type of evaluation. Collecting and analyzing process data can provide early warning of potential problems in the training program.

Outcome evaluation is conducted at the end of training and is a determination of the effects that training has had on the trainee, the job, and the organization. Outcome evaluation is based on the training objectives. The processes and instruments used are typically created sometime between the Design and Implementation Phases, although they are not used until the training has been completed. Outcome evaluation can also be used to improve training processes. Outcome evaluation data by themselves do not provide enough information for program improvement, but in combination with process evaluation data they serve as a powerful tool for improving programs. By examining outcome evaluation results from the first presentation of the course, you can determine if all the training objectives were achieved. If they were, you can be fairly comfortable that the training processes are working as they should be. However, if one or more objectives are not achieved, the training process evaluation data can then be used to identify where problems exist and corrective action can be taken.

Development Phase   Program development is the process of formulating an instructional strategy to meet a set of training objectives. The instructional strategy consists of the order, timing, and combination of elements that will be used in the training program. Inputs into this phase are provided by analysis of the various instructional methods and the required design factors. The Design Phase provides the information relating to learning facilitation and transfer. In chapter 7 instructional methods are described and discussed in terms of the types of learning for which they are best suited.

All elements of a particular training program are determined during the Development Phase. The specific content, instructional methods, materials, equipment and media, manuals, and facilities are integrated into a training plan designed to achieve the training objectives. These outputs of the Development Phase serve as inputs to the Implementation Phase.

Implementation Phase   All the aspects of the training program come together during the implementation phase; however, it is a mistake to assume that everything will happen as planned. Therefore, it is useful to conduct a dry run of the training, similar to a dress rehearsal for a play, allowing the trainer to become familiar with the facility, equipment, and materials with no trainees actually being present. A useful next step in the implementation process is a pilot training group, consisting of a small number of trainees who are representative of the larger population. Although the trainer is usually not at liberty to make major deviations from the training plan, there are many opportunities to influence the effectiveness of the training. A pilot group allows the trainer to see where improvements can be made before the training becomes generally available. Trainee reactions to the training, how much they learn, and process evaluation data allow the trainer to identify areas of self-improvement. In addition, improvements to the training strategy can be identified from the pilot group evaluations. Once these refinements have been made, the training is ready for full implementation.

The output of the Implementation Phase is the trainees' response to training, their learning, their behavior back on the job, and its effect on key organizational outcomes. These outcomes combined with process evaluations are fed back to the appropriate constituencies within the training area and the rest of the organization, thus completing the Evaluation Phase.

Key Roles and Competencies

The American Society for Training and Development (ASTD 1983) has identified 15 key roles required of training and development professionals. These roles have remained relatively stable over time. Many of the skills and competencies required of training and development professionals are similar to the knowledge and skills required of managers in general. Several additional "lists" of these skills have been developed over the years (Lippitt and Nadler 1967; McLagan 1989). Table 1.1 (page 26), a sampling of competencies culled from these lists, identifies many of the competencies that HRD professionals must master in their different roles. It provides a glimpse of what is required to be an effective training professional.

Specialists may be required to have expertise in only one or a few of these areas. However, training generalists such as training managers and supervisors must have developed competencies in all of these areas. We will discuss these and other competencies throughout the text as we examine various phases of the training process.

DEVELOPMENT OF PROFESSIONAL COMPETENCIES

How do HRD professionals acquire the knowledge and skill bases required for entry or advancement in the field? Some have received formal college training. Bachelor's, Master's, and Ph.D. programs are available to those seeking formal education credentials. The ASTD publishes the *Academic Directory of Programs in HRD* (1993), listing many of these programs. HRD degrees are typically housed within schools of business, psychology, or education. Those in business schools usually require students to acquire core competencies in business (e.g., accounting, marketing, finance) as well as training and development. Another source for developing HRD competencies is professional associations, which offer conferences, workshops, and seminars covering basic and advanced HRD topics.

Many with training responsibilities find they must learn on the job as training assignments are handed to them. The best of these individuals learn through independent study, observation of other trainers, and personal tutoring from training professionals. Line managers, for example, are increasingly being asked to assume responsibility for training their staff. Managers in some companies are also routinely rotated through training as a part of their developmental activities. Many have been successful, many others have not. Companies should carefully think through the implications of placing personnel untrained or inexperienced in HRD in the position of providing training to others, even though they may be experts in their technical specialty area. Problems associated with using such employees as trainers have been well documented for some time (Clement, Pinto, and Walker 1978). They include the following:

- Lack of professional training expertise to carry out the assignment
- Violation of confidences where information gained in the training process is used outside of training
- Dishonesty regarding training outcomes
- Use of programs mismatched with the needs of trainees
- Inappropriate trainer behavior that abuses trainees

TABLE 1.1 Professional Trainer's Roles and Competencies

Domain	Role	Competency
Technical	Evaluator/	Measurement
	Analyst	Test development
		Data analysis, drawing inferences
		Research methods
	Instructor	Learning theory (focus on adults)
		Communication skills (see Communicator role)
		Capturing the interest of trainees
		Subject matter knowledge
		Training methods/techniques
		Platform skills
	Career Development Facilitator	Knowledge/application of career models
		Career counseling
		Job counseling
	Instructional Technologist	Knowledge of equipment and software related to self-paced learning
	Program Designer/ Developer	Writing training objectives
		Literature review
		Model building
		Materials development
		Media capabilities
		Training methods/techniques
	Facility Manager	Logistics
		Equipment setup
		Materials/equipment acquisition
		Facility maintenance
Business	Management	Cost/benefit analysis
		Delegating
		Organizational behavior/development
		Project management
		Records management
		Strategic planning
		Creating alliances
		Negotiating
	Marketer	Promotion
		Distribution
		Development of customer focus
Interpersonal	Communicator	Processing group reactions
		Providing constructive feedback
		Presentation skills
		Interviewing
		Relationship building
		Writing (announcements, reports, memos, etc.)

This is not to say that these problems don't occur in the ranks of professional trainers, or that those without professional training credentials can't possibly be good trainers. Rather, the risk of these negative outcomes is higher when those without proper HRD training and experience are put into those roles. When organizations do find it necessary to use nonprofessionals as trainers, they should receive appropriate train-the-trainer training. We will discuss this topic in more depth when we discuss on-the-job training in chapter 7.

Those seeking to enter the field of HRD far outnumber the positions available. Unfortunately, no commonly agreed-upon system (such as that in law or medicine) exists for certifying that a person has the KSAs necessary to be an effective training professional. The Society of Human Resource Management (SHRM) conducts certification exams for human resource management, one portion of which deals with training and development. However, this exam is designed to meet the broader scope of the HR manager. Successfully completing this exam is a definite advantage, but not a requirement. The ASTD has been developing a certification exam for HRD professionals, but a complete set of standards has yet to be agreed upon. For now, as in the past, a training professional's credentials consist of one's formal education, HRD training, professional experience, and references. Those seeking to enter the field of HRD will need to acquire firsthand experience to supplement their educational credentials. Most degree- and certificate-granting programs offer co-ops and internships that provide their students with opportunities to gain experience in the field.

This book will provide you with much of the knowledge needed to be a successful HRD professional. However, no book in itself will provide you with all the KSAs you will need. Firsthand experience is a necessity. If you are reading this book as part of a course, your instructor will probably facilitate the development of your skills and attitudes through experiential exercises and projects. Other courses in your program of study can sometimes further develop your KSAs related to HRD. These will serve as a solid base for the most significant learning experience: actually doing HRD work under the guidance of a training professional.

Key Terms

- Abilities
- Attitudes
- Automaticity
- Compilation
- Declarative knowledge
- Design Phase
- Development
- Development Phase
- Education
- Evaluation Phase
- Implementation Phase
- ISO 9000
- Knowledge
- KSAs

- Learning
- Needs Analysis Phase
- Open-systems model
- Organizational development (OD)
- Outcome evaluation
- Procedural knowledge
- Process evaluation
- Skills
- Small business
- Strategic knowledge
- Training
- Training objectives
- Training needs analysis (TNA)

Exercises

1. Conduct a search of recent newspaper and magazine articles that address needs for corporate training. Summarize your findings.
2. Describe your vision of where you will be in your career five years from now. How will training play a part in that career?
3. In small groups, discuss the training responsibilities of supervisors and managers who are not part of the HRD department. Prepare a list of what those responsibilities might be and a rationale for your choices.
4. Conduct an interview with a small business owner or manager. Get a good understanding of how they approach training in their company. What differences do you see in how this company approaches training and what has been described in this chapter? What are the reasons for this difference?

Questions for Review

1. Pick one of the following jobs that most appeals to you: training manager, instructional designer, training instructor, training evaluator. What are the range of roles an individual could play in that job (identify at least four different roles)? Describe why that job is especially appealing to you and why.
2. Describe the relationship between the HR and the HRD functions in a large organization. How might a small organization handle the responsibilities of these two areas?
3. Define and provide an example of the following:
   a. Each of the three types of knowledge
   b. Each of the two levels of skills
   c. An attitude
4. Below is a problem-solving model. Describe how the training process model is or is not consistent with this model.
   a. Define and understand the problem.
   b. Determine the cause of the problem.
   c. Identify potential solutions to the problem.
   d. Select the solution that provides the most benefits for the least cost.
   e. Develop an action plan for putting the solution in place.
   f. Implement the solution.
   g. Evaluate and, if necessary, modify the solution.

References

Alderfer, C. P. 1977. Organizational Development. *Annual Review of Psychology* 28:197–223.

American Society for Training and Development. 1983. *Models for Excellence: The Conclusions and Recommendations of the ASTD Training and Development Competency Study.* Washington, DC: ASTD.

ASTD. 1993. *Academic Directory of Programs in HRD.* Washington, DC: ASTD.

Banks, M., A. Bures, and D. Champion. 1987. Decision making factors in small business. *Journal of Small Business Management,* January, pp. 19–26.

Beckhard, R. 1969. *Organizational Development: Strategies and Models.* Reading, MA: Addison-Wesley.

Beer, M., and E. Walton. 1990. "Developing the competitive organization: Interventions and strategies." *American Psychologist* 45:154–61.

Bennis, W. G. 1969. *Organization Development: Its Nature, Origins, and Prospects.* Reading, MA: Addison-Wesley.

Cascio, W., and J. Thacker, 1994. *Managing Human Resources.* Toronto: McGraw-Hill Ryerson.

Chuvala, J., J. Gilmere, and T. Gillette. 1992. The new kid on the training block. *Security Management,* August, pp. 65–72.

Clement, R. W., P. R. Pinto, and J. W. Walker. 1978. How do I hurt thee? Let me count the ways: Unethical and improper behavior by training and development professionals. *Training and Development Journal* 32:10–12.

Deshpande, S., and D. Golhar. 1994. HRM practices in large and small firms: A comparative study. *Journal of Small Business Management,* April, pp. 49–56.

Dolack, P. 1996. ISO 9000 comes of age. *Chemical Marketing Reporter* 249:7–8.

Dunnette, M. 1976. Aptitudes, abilities and skills. In *The Handbook of Industrial and Organizational Psychology,* edited by M. Dunnette. Chicago: Rand McNally.

Fattal, T. 1996. Quality is what ISO 9000 is all about. *Computing Canada* 22:30.

Filipczak, B. 1994. Industry Report. *Training,* October, pp. 67–74.

Fitz-Enz, J. 1997. *The 8 Practices of Exceptional Companies.* New York: AMACOM.

Fleishman, E. 1972. On the relation between abilities, learning, and human performance. *American Psychologist* 27:1017–32.

Griffin, R., and R. Ebert. 1996. *Business.* 4th ed. Upper Saddle River, NJ: Prentice Hall.

Holt, D. 1993. *Management Principles and Practices.* Upper Saddle River, NJ: Prentice Hall.

Hornsby, J., and D. Kuratko. 1990. Human resource management in small business: Critical issues for the 1990s. *Journal of Small Business Management,* July, pp. 9–18.

Katz, D., and R. L. Khan. 1978. *The Social Psychology of Organizations.* New York: Wiley.

Kraiger, K., J. Ford, and E. Salas. 1993. Application of cognitive, skill based and affective theories of learning outcomes to new methods of training evaluation. *Journal of Applied Psychology* 78(2):311–28.

Le Gault, M. 1997. In house training that gets results. *Canadian Plastics,* February, pp. 14–18.

Lippitt, G., and L. Nadler. 1967. Emerging roles of the training director. *Training and Development Journal* 21:2–10.

McKay Stokes, D. 1995. Small business: A force to be reckoned with. *Profits,* Spring, pp. 1–2.

McLagan, P. A. 1989. Models for HRD practice. *Training and Development Journal* 41(9):49–59.

Oskamp, S. 1991. *Attitudes and Opinions.* 2d ed. Upper Saddle River, NJ: Prentice Hall.

Szonyi, A., and B. Steinhoff. 1983. *Small Business Fundamentals.* Toronto: McGraw-Hill Ryerson.

Training. 1996. 1996 Industry report: Training budgets, October, pp. 41–49.

Williamson, D. 1997. ISO rating the sign of the times. *Windsor Star,* July 16, p. F1.

Wisnia, S. 1997. Running to the rescue. *Industrial Distribution* 86:120–23.

CHAPTER

2

Strategic Planning, Training, and OD

Learning Objectives

After reading this chapter, you should be able to:

- Describe the strategic planning process, its components, and their relationships

- Distinguish between an organization's external and internal strategies and describe the value of each

- Describe the benefits of using an HRD perspective in strategy development

- Describe the characteristics and major components of a learning organization

- Describe the differences, similarities, and relationships among competitive HR and HRD strategies

- Identify and describe external and internal factors influencing HRD strategy

- Identify possible HRD strategic alternatives and situations in which they might be appropriate

- Describe the field of Organizational Development and its relationship to training activities, including the value of cross training between the two

Strategic Planning at Multistate Health Corporation (MHC)

As you read this case think about the relationship among MHC's competitive strategy, the HR function, and HRD. The case is real, but the corporation has asked that its name not be used.

Multistate Health Corporation (MHC) is a U.S.-based health care provider owned and operated by a religious order. MHC owns 30 hospitals and four subsidiary corporations, employing over 10,000 people. The headquarters is in Michigan and the hospitals are located in 17 states scattered across the country. The overall organizational structure and the corporate HR structure are depicted in Exhibits 2.1 and 2.2.

In line with their mission, which is rooted in the tenets of their religion, MHC has focused on providing care to the indigent and less able members of the community. They have been reasonably successful, but the health care industry has undergone considerable change due to new governmental regulations and insurance procedures. Hospitals are now reimbursed on the basis of a preset, standardized price for treatment, regardless of the cost of the actual procedures. The federal and state governments are putting increasing pressure on health care institutions to reduce costs.

In addition, new medical technologies and procedures are continually being developed. These are expensive to acquire and operate. MHC has recently acquired some subsidiary corporations to develop these new procedures and technologies. These subsidiaries are responsible to work in partnership with the regions to implement any new procedures and technology.

MHC has lost money each of the last six years. Currently there is an oversupply of bed space in most of the communities in which MHC has hospitals. Projections indicate that need for inpatient services will decline while the need for outpatient services will increase. Nontraditional health-related services are also projected to increase (e.g., services in which patients and their relatives are

EXHIBIT 2.1

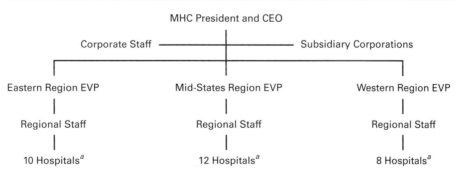

aEach hospital has a CEO reporting to the regional executive vice president (EVP). Hospitals are referred to as divisions within MHC and have a CEO as well as a functional staff (including HR) for conducting divisional operations. Corporate HR is included as part of corporate staff, as described in Exhibit 2.2.

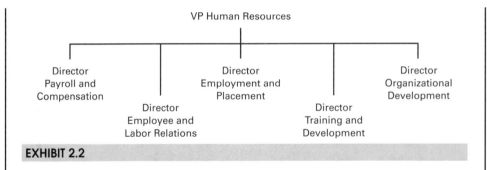

EXHIBIT 2.2

trained in self-care or care of relatives). In short, the market has become much more competitive while products and services are rapidly changing.

MHC has just finished its corporate strategic planning process and has planned to develop a two-pronged market strategy to deal with its changing business environment. One major area of focus was technology. The strategic planners decided to be a leader in the development of new health care technology and procedures. They felt the new developments would allow quicker recovery times, thus reducing the hospitals' costs. In addition, the technology could be marketed to other health care providers, generating more revenue. The drawback was that new technologies and procedures were expensive to develop and often had long waiting periods before being approved by the insurers and government agencies.

The second prong of the strategy was to improve efficiencies in basic health care and outpatient services. Doing this would allow them to continue to provide for the basic health care needs of the less fortunate. The substantial governmental fees, grants, and other revenues tied to this population would provide a profit only if efficiencies could be developed throughout the corporation.

Carrie Brown, hired six months earlier as corporate vice president of Human Resources, had listened to several days of strategy discussion, without participating much. She now felt it was time to address the human resource implications of these strategies.

"While I agree that these are good strategies," Carrie said, "I don't know if we have the right people in the right places to carry them out. A few of our regional and divisional executives are already doing some of the things you're talking about, but most of them have grown up in the old system and don't know how to go about cost cutting in a way that doesn't diminish the quality of our service. Many of our divisions are in rural areas and haven't kept up with technology. We do have some middle- to upper-level managers who are up to date in cost cutting and technology implementation, but they are scattered throughout the organization."

Mitchell Fields, president and CEO of MHC, suggested, "Why don't we just move those people who have the capabilities to implement our strategies into positions where they have the power to make it happen?"

"Unfortunately," Carrie said, "we have no accurate data about which of our people have the capabilities. It would be a mistake to move forward unless we're sure that we have the knowledge and skills on board to be successful. What I've discovered in the short time I've been here is that we have grown too large for our human resource information system. We're still doing most of the data collection on paper, and the forms used are different in each of the divisions, so we can't consolidate information across divisions, and even if we could it would take forever to do it by hand. We have different pay scales in different divisions, and you can't get a VP in Boston to take a CEO position in Iowa because he'd have to take a cut in pay. Basically, what I'm saying is that we don't have a coherent HR system in place to give us the information we need to put the right people in the right places.

"Another issue is that our current structure isn't very conducive to setting up partnerships between the subsidiary corporations and the regions. The corporations developing the technology are seen as pretty distant from the regions and divisions. While the subsidiary corporations will bear the developmental costs, they are going to want to pass those along to the regions and divisions. The divisions will then have to bear the costs of implementing the new technology and working out the bugs. Once all the kinks are worked out, the subsidiaries will be selling the technology to our competitors at lower prices because of the volume. Our current systems don't let all of our businesses come out winners."

"I understand what you're saying," Mitchell said. "Our competitive strategy is for the long term. If this HR thing is going to be a problem, then we have to fix it right away. We also are going to have to work out some way for both the subsidiaries and the divisions to come out winners in moving new medical technology forward. Assuming we are able to put our HR house in order and get the right systems in place so our subsidiaries and divisions want to do business together, are there any other concerns about adopting our strategies?" Hearing no additional objections, he said, "Okay, then, let's get to work on putting an implementation plan together, and first on the list is our HR system."

Overview

Most people understand the value of having a plan of action before starting a project. Though planning requires additional time at the beginning of a project, it can save considerable time by preventing mistakes and ensuring that important steps are not skipped. In fact, the cornerstone for most quality programs is a "plan-do-check" cycle to ensure that desired outcomes are reached in the most effective manner. Whether for a large organization or a single department, planning is a key to organizational success.

Strategic planning is the development of relatively long-term objectives and plans for pursuing an organization's mission. It sets the direction for all other organizational activities. For example, the HRD department determines which KSAs are and which are not important to develop by referencing the strategic plan. The strategic plan not only provides direction to the various functional areas of an organization, but it is also influenced by them. Functional areas provide valuable input that shapes the development of strategies, while a strategy provides guidelines and parameters for the activities of the functional areas. Thus HR and the HRD function are both directed by organizational strategies and may also influence their content.

This chapter explores the relationship among HR, HRD, **Organizational Development (OD),** and strategic planning. In general we use the terms *HRD* and *training* synonymously. However, in this chapter, just for the sake of clarity, the term *HRD* will refer to the functional area of an organization responsible for managing training activities, and *training* will refer to the activities (i.e., training processes) being managed by the HRD area.

In the MHC case, did Ms. Brown's HRD department need to be involved in shaping MHC's strategy? Are there training implications to these strategies? HRD can be (and should be) involved with strategic planning at three levels. First, at the organizational level, HRD has much to contribute in the shaping of the organization's competitive strategy, though this role may not be obvious. In the MHC case the divisional staff's ability to carry out the strategy was seen as a problem. MHC decided to go ahead with their strategy, but would they have been better served by adopting a strategy that better fit the KSAs of their staff? Perhaps MHC has enough time to identify who the right people are for the key positions and get them in place. If there aren't enough people with the desired competencies, what are the alternatives? Hire people from the outside? Train high-potential insiders? The answers to these questions help to define the tactics that will be used in pursuing the organization's competitive strategy.

The second strategic role for HRD is influencing the organization's HR strategy. The **HR strategy** is one level below the organization's **competitive strategy** and is the set of tactics HR will use to support the competitive strategy. In the MHC case the HR strategy appears to be one of promoting from within and "moving the right people into the right positions." This assumes that there are and will be enough of the "right" people to fill all the positions that need to be filled and that these people can be identified. To implement this strategy, the HR function will need to create a succession planning process and a corresponding executive development program for those identified as successors. Before committing to this strategy, Ms. Brown should consult with her HRD manager to determine the probable cost and time parameters of such a program. Of course, this and other HR programs will be dependent upon a Human Resource Information System (HRIS) that provides accurate and meaningful data necessary for HR planning.

The third strategic role for the HRD function is developing and implementing its own strategy. **HRD strategies** are the set of tactics that will be used to support the achievement of the business and HR strategies. When viewed from an organizational level, HR and HRD strategies are tactics, containing considerably more detail about actions to be taken than is provided in the organizational strategy.

Figure 2.1 illustrates the relationships between competitive strategy and the tactics of individual units in carrying out the strategy. However, when these are viewed from within the HR or HRD unit, they provide only general direction and themselves require supporting tactics. In this way, plans providing direction for fulfilling the organization's mission are developed and coordinated throughout the organization. The

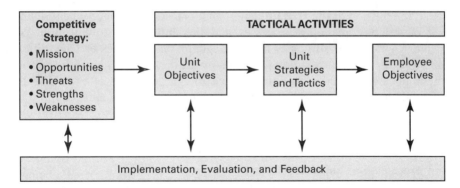

FIGURE 2.1 Linkage between Strategy, Tactics, and Objectives

process of developing strategic plans is similar whether the strategy is being developed for the entire organization or for some subunit. What differs is the type of information that is collected and analyzed in developing the strategy and the level of detail provided in directing actions.

Assuming MHC continues its current strategic direction, what are the implications for HRD strategy? How does MHC determine the competencies of its executives? Assuming they conduct a needs analysis, how will they store and review the information? Clearly the development of the HRIS is an important first step. If they decide to develop their current executives, should these executive development programs be centralized at corporate HR or decentralized to the regions and divisions? Should they be developed in house or farmed out to firms specializing in executive development? How does executive development fit into the culture of the organization? The answers to these kinds of questions provide the content of an HRD strategy.

Strategic planning and strategy implementation involve change. So HRD must understand the change process, which involves principles and concepts of *Organizational Development (OD)*. OD refers to the research base and set of techniques related to organizational improvement and to management of change. As the organization's objectives and strategies change, the KSAs required of employees change as well. However, it is not enough simply to provide new KSAs. The organization's systems and procedures must change to support the use of the new KSAs if the desired change in performance is to occur. In the MHC case, what types of systems and procedures must change if the strategies are to be successful? The reward system? The way MHC is organized? The HRD process? The field of OD provides processes for identifying when systems and procedures need to change and how to manage the change. In the discussion of OD in this chapter we will focus on the strategic planning process and the ways HRD and OD can support each other. However, throughout the book we will also be addressing other OD issues as we discuss the training process.

Strategic Planning Process

While the objectives and strategies of HRD departments have many similarities across organizations, there exist as well many differences related to the unique competitive strategies and planning processes of each organization. In order to understand the mission of the HRD function and its tactics, you need a general understanding of strategic planning processes and the implications of different competitive strategies. Different strategies and strategic planning processes have different HRD implications. The following discussion explains the strategy development process and the implications of differing competitive strategies as they relate to HRD. Some additional discussion of competitive strategy is provided in the management development chapter.

ORGANIZATIONAL MISSION

An organization's **mission** statement is a general statement of why the organization exists and the commitments it is making. The mission is the focal point for strategy development because it outlines what the strategies are designed to achieve. Here are examples of mission statements from two very different types of organizations.

> **MISSION OF "OZONE HOUSE" (A SOCIAL SERVICE AGENCY)**
> Ozone House is a community-based, not-for-profit agency that seeks to help youth lead safe, healthy, and productive lives through intensive prevention and intervention strategies. (Ozone House, 1995)

> **MISSION OF FORD'S "WINDSOR ENGINE PLANT," WINDSOR, ONTARIO, CANADA**
> Our mission is to continually improve our products and services to meet our customers' needs, allowing us to prosper as a business and provide a reasonable return for our stockholders.

These statements, though different, have many similarities. A good mission statement is a fairly general description of what the organization seeks to accomplish. It describes the products or services the organization provides, who it provides them to, and what it wishes to accomplish. Do both of these mission statements do that?

STRATEGY

The mission describes what the organization wants to accomplish; strategies define how the organization will go about doing so. There are numerous definitions of **organizational strategy** (Bower 1982; Chandler 1962; Jamison 1981; Tichey, Fombrun, and Devanna 1982), but they all include the following:

> Strategies attempt to optimize the match between the organization's mission, what is occurring or is projected to occur in the external environment, and the organization's internal operations. Strategies include (1) setting short- and long-term business objectives for the organization, (2) setting courses of action necessary to achieve those objectives, and (3) allocating the resources needed to carry out those actions.

Competitive Strategy

The literature dealing with strategy contains a great many categorizations and terms that refer to different types and levels of strategy. For simplicity we have chosen one, *competitive strategy,* to demonstrate the relationship between organizational strategy, HR, and HRD. What most companies call their competitive strategy has to do with positioning themselves in the marketplace. This, their most important strategy, includes the set of interrelated internal and external choices made by the company to improve or retain its competitive position. Competitive strategy also has the added benefit of a documented relationship to many aspects of managerial and organizational behavior (Gutpa and Govindarajan 1984; Jackson, Schuler, and Rivero 1989) as is demonstrated below.

Three market positioning strategies illustrate the ends and middle point of a continuum of possible competitive strategies: Market Leader, Market Follower, and Cost Leader. We will briefly discuss all three but will concentrate on the two ends of the continuum (Market Leader and Cost Leader) to illustrate the strategic planning process and implications for developing HR and HRD strategies. The descriptions below reflect a combination of internal (i.e. technology and structure) and external (i.e., market) factors that must be addressed in the organization's competitive strategy.

Market Leader organizations, also labeled "prospectors" (Miles and Snow 1978) and "innovators" (Miller 1987), find and exploit new product and market opportunities. Success depends on their capacity to survey a wide range of environmental conditions, trends, and events and move quickly into windows of opportunity. Market leaders typically use multiple types of technology that are capable of being used in many different ways.

The **Market Follower,** also labeled "analyzer" (Miles and Snow 1978, 1986) and "differentiator" (Miller 1987), minimizes risk and maximizes profit opportunity by moving into a market after its viability has been established by others. The success of the Market Follower depends on copying and improving upon products that have established a market. Such organizations must be able to respond once markets have been proven, but at the same time maintain operating efficiency in the market and product areas already established. These firms represent the middle portion of the competitive strategy continuum.

The **Cost Leader** (Porter 1980), similar to what Miles and Snow (1978) refer to as a "defender," represents the opposite end of the continuum from the Market Leader. Its main goal is to be the low-cost provider in the industry. Its success depends on its pricing competitiveness and having a product that is acceptable to the market (not necessarily the best). It achieves this by producing a standardized product or service efficiently, by using economies of scale, low-cost labor, and perhaps by introducing innovative production methods.

There are a number of ways (strategies) to pursue a mission, and each organization must decide which among the feasible alternatives is best for it. Strategies are the choices the organization makes from among these sometimes contradictory ways of pursuing its mission. For example, in a cost leader strategy (one prong of the MHC strategy), the goal is to provide the lowest priced products and services to the market. One way to do this is to keep the cost of materials to a minimum. A tactic for keeping cost low is to aggressively pursue competing bids from as many suppliers as possible and accept the lowest bids from as many suppliers as needed to meet quantity requirements. Another tactic could be to develop long-term relationships with a few suppliers, guaranteeing sole supplier status in return for their meeting a specified price target. Either tactic could achieve the same result (reducing the cost of supplied materials) but they have very different impacts on the purchasing activities of the organization and on supplier relationships. Which will be "best" depends on how the organization addresses its other strategic contingencies.

STRATEGIC CONTINGENCIES

The success of a competitive strategy will depend on how well it addresses the important external and internal factors the organization must deal with. Two major internal factors that are strongly related to strategy are the organization's structure and its technology. These must be matched to the demands of the external environment the organization operates in. We use a relatively simple model to represent the relationship of environment, strategy, structure, and technology (Chandler 1962; Miles and Snow 1978). As Figure 2.2 illustrates, the environment and the mission of the organization are the major factors determining strategy. However, the choice of strategy may change the environment in which the firm operates, so the arrow shows influence in both directions. Strategic choice can also be influenced by the core technology of the organization (how the principle products or services are created). Thus strategies are created to maximize the match between environmental demands and core technology and are then implemented through the structure and core technology of the organization. Therefore core technology, like the environment, both influences and is influenced by strategy. In summary, strategies for pursuing the mission depend on the nature of the organization's environment and its core technology. These strategies have direct implications for the structure of the organization and its core technology.

External Environment

An organization's **external environment** consists of elements outside the organization that influence the organization's ability to achieve its mission. Competitors, the economy, societal norms and values, laws and regulations, raw materials, suppliers, and technological innovation are examples. The degree to which they need to be addressed in a strategic plan depends on how much impact they are likely to have on important organizational outcomes. What kinds of environmental factors were important in the MHC case? Certainly governmental regulations, technology, and MHC's competitors would seem to be important areas to be addressed by their strategies.

An environmental factor that is important to one organization may or may not be important to another, even if they are in the same industry, because organizations differ in their mission, internal resources, and operations. Each organization must determine the environmental factors that are important to what it does and seeks to accomplish.

The success of a competitive strategy can be significantly influenced by the uncertainty of the external environment. **Environmental uncertainty** is determined by

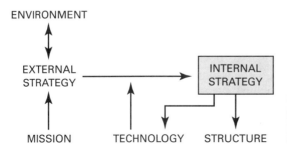

FIGURE 2.2 Mission, Strategy, Technology, Structure Relationship

two factors: complexity and stability. **Complexity** refers to the number of factors in the environment and how interrelated they are. **Stability** is the rate at which key factors in the environment change; the more rapid the change, the more unstable the environment. When the environment is more complex and unstable, it is more uncertain. When it is simpler and more stable, it is more certain. Table 2.1 depicts this relationship.

In more uncertain environments, the organization must become more flexible and adaptable in order to respond effectively. A market leader strategy is consistent with this situation. In more certain environments there is less need for flexibility, and more rigidly defined operating methods can minimize costs and maximize profitability, a situation consistent with the cost leader strategy. Uncertain environments generally favor strategies using more decentralized decision making, whereas centralized decision making is usually more effective when the external environment is more certain. How would you characterize MHC's environment? Is it complex or simple, stable or unstable? What type of strategy has it adopted? Is that appropriate for the environment in which it is operating?

The chosen competitive strategy also influences the environment. A decision to adopt a market leader or a cost leader strategy places the organization into a more or a less uncertain environment. Given two similar organizations, the one choosing the market leader strategy will by definition compete in the more uncertain environment. This is true for a number of reasons, but most obviously because the cost leader is competing only in established and more stable markets. This environment may be more hostile, but it most likely has a slower rate of change (Duncan 1972). Thus choice of strategy is in many respects a choice of environment. At the same time, the state of an organization's external environment can influence strategy decisions. For example, in an industry such as telecommunications, rapid changes in electronic technology and the regulatory environment have influenced many firms to shift their market position strategies more toward the market leader end of the continuum (Dowling, Boulton, and Elliot 1994). While these generalizations are somewhat simplified, the concepts are generally supported by others and serve here as a heuristic for understanding the contingent nature of the relationship between strategy and environment.

TABLE 2.1   Factors Influencing Environmental Uncertainty

		COMPLEXITY High	COMPLEXITY Low
STABILITY	Low	High Uncertainty	Moderate Uncertainty
STABILITY	High	**Moderate Uncertainty**	**Low Uncertainty**

Core Technology

By *technology* we mean how the work gets done in the organization. Each unit in the organization has a technology for how it accomplishes its tasks. The **core technology,** the term used in this section, refers simply to the main activities associated with producing the organization's principle products and services. Categorizations of technology have been provided by many authors (Perrow 1970; Thompson 1967; Woodward 1965). Taking some liberties with these, we will simply use a continuum of "routine" to "nonroutine" technologies. The **routine technology** label is applied to tasks that have a high degree of predictability of outcomes or results, few problems occurring, and well-structured and well-defined solutions when problems do occur. A high-volume assembly line, such as a garment factory or some automobile plants, would exemplify a routine technology. Such operations are highly specialized and have well-defined rules for the coordination of activities. The decision-making processes are typically centralized and highly formalized. The routine technology is most typical of the cost leader strategy.

A task using **nonroutine technology** is characterized by task outcomes or results that are difficult to predict, problems occurring often and unexpectedly, and solutions to problems not being readily available and needing to be developed on a case-by-case basis. With this type of technology, the organization needs to provide managers and workers with more decision-making authority to meet the challenges that are encountered. The organization's task is further complicated by the fact that this type of technology involves a great deal of task interdependence, creating higher needs for coordination and integration. Managers and workers need decision-making authority within their own areas but, their activities must also be coordinated with the activities of others. Thus, employees must be given clear goals and parameters for their work outcomes but be allowed to determine the best way to meet those expectations. This type of technology is more typical in organizations with market leader strategies. Leading-edge computer software developers, such as Microsoft, are examples of such companies.

Structural Implications of Strategy

Organization structure refers to how a firm is organized (i.e., how labor has been divided) and the policies and procedures used for coordinating the various activities. This structure is utilized to carry out the strategy and must be adapted to the environmental conditions and the technology available. There are many aspects to an organization's structure, but we are interested primarily in three components: organizational design, decision-making autonomy, and division of labor.

Design   **Organizational design** is a component of how the organization is structured. It refers to the number and formality of rules, policies, and procedures designed to direct the behavior of organizational members. Any organization's design can be characterized as existing somewhere on a continuum ranging from mechanistic to organic (Burns and Stalker 1961). A highly **mechanistic design** reflects an organization that has highly defined tasks, rigid and detailed procedures, high reliance on authority, and vertical communication channels. The highly **organic design** reflects an organization that is flexible in its rules and procedures, has loosely defined tasks, is highly reliant on expertise, and places a high reliance on horizontal communication channels.

Design decisions about these elements determine the relative emphasis placed on the human versus other organizational resources. The organic design places more emphasis on human resources and the mechanistic less. In the mechanistic design, employees' technical and interpersonal skills and behaviors are prescribed, whereas in the organic design these skills and behaviors are permitted to evolve (within broad parameters) in order to supplement and complement the unit's structure and technology. The organic design is most appropriate for nonroutine technologies, whereas the mechanistic design is more appropriate for routine technologies (David, Pearce, and Randolf 1989).

Decision Autonomy   **Decision autonomy** (Perrow 1970) relates to the amount of authority employees have in deciding how to complete a task and the degree to which they are able to influence goals and strategies for their work unit. Individual or small group decision-making autonomy is a function of whether decisions are centralized or decentralized. Cost efficiencies are associated with more centralization, whereas flexibility/adaptability is associated with decentralization (Mintzberg 1979; McDonough and Leifer 1983). Thus centralized structures are more appropriate for cost leader strategies and decentralization for market leaders.

Division of Labor   The way in which the work is divided up and organized is called **division of labor.** There are many ways in which labor can be divided. One such division is line and staff; another is management and labor. Some organizations are organized by products, others by customers or geography. Some have divided the work into functional areas while others have organized work around the processes in their core technology. For the purposes of our discussion the focus will be on how specialized the duties and responsibilities are within the organization. In general, the more specialized the duties and responsibilities, the more centralized the decision making and the more mechanistic the organization must be. That is so because of the need to coordinate the activities of employees whose scope of responsibility is fairly narrow. In organizations in which duties and responsibilities are relatively broadly defined, a more organic and decentralized structure is appropriate, allowing the employees to coordinate their activities less formally and providing more flexibility and adaptability for the organization.

PROACTIVE AND REACTIVE STRATEGY

Formalized strategic planning is a proactive process used to decide how best to meet the demands of the environment in the near (e.g., next year or two) and long term (e.g., next five to ten years). Strategy that is developed via a formalized process typically involves sophisticated analytical and decision-making tools, which assist the strategists in determining the current and probable future state of the environment and the organization. It is *proactive* because it is a deliberate process of determining how the organization should respond to the anticipated business environment. Its purpose is to create a good fit between the organization and its future environment.

However, strategy can also develop in a more *reactive* fashion, evolving in reaction to short-term business conditions. Here there is less formal analysis and planning and more focus on the immediate future. Mintzberg (1987) suggests that both reactive and proactive strategies are necessary for an organization to be effective. The formalized strategic planning process uses a best guess about what the future will bring; the day-to-day operations confront what the future has actually brought. A strategic plan that positions the firm for long-term expectations but is modified by the firm's experience as it moves forward is preferable to a rigidly held long-term plan or merely reactions to short-term experience.

In the proactive strategy development, the organization typically identifies its strengths and weaknesses (internal focus) and compares them to the mission-related opportunities and threats (external focus) posed by the environment. This SWOT analysis (strengths, weaknesses, opportunities, and threats) is used to identify the organization's business objectives (e.g., market share, volume, profit) and its strategies (e.g., market penetration, product mix, pricing), which are aimed at minimizing threats and weaknesses while taking advantage of the opportunities and strengths. Do you think that MHC engaged in SWOT analysis prior to developing their strategic direction? It seems as if they developed their strategy, then discovered the human resource deficiencies. Once a plan has been developed, it becomes difficult to say, "Let's back up and start over again."

When the strategy is allowed to evolve in a more reactive form, the same processes take place but there is typically less formal analysis and fewer people are involved in the decision making. Organizations that engage in both proactive and reactive strategy formulation typically use the reactive approach as an ongoing fine-tuning of the strategic direction.

MATCHING INTERNAL TO EXTERNAL STRATEGY

Organizational strategy needs to be both externally and internally focused. As Figure 2.2 indicated, an organization's strategy is related to its external environment, the technology used to produce its products and services, and the structure of the organization. Technology and structure are internal factors, and environment is external. The role of strategy is to make the best possible match between the internal and external factors.

The competitive (market positioning) strategy is external. It is concerned with such factors as what products or services markets are or will be demanding and what competitors are doing. It attempts to position the organization to take advantage of opportunities and avoid threats. **Internal strategies** address issues such as organizational culture, structure and design, division of labor, resource allocation, and innovation. Internal strategies aim to maximize the strengths and eliminate the weaknesses of the organization. Together, the internal and external strategies are integrated to form the organization's total competitive strategy. The development of internal and external strategies is an interactive process with each being more or less dependent on the other. For example, a cost leader strategy would require strength in areas such as production efficiency (e.g., economy of scale), purchasing (e.g., supplier leverage), and labor cost (e.g., number of employees). If a firm is weak in these areas, adopting a cost leader strategy is difficult because the firm will have to transform its weaknesses into strengths. It is easier to adopt a strategy that is consistent with its existing strengths.

On the other hand, the environment may compel an organization to abandon its current strengths to pursue opportunities and avoid threats. Suppose a company has developed moderate strength in areas supporting a cost leader strategy, but it has

---

Training in Action 2.1

Back from the Brink

In the early 1980s Hewlett-Packard Canada was considered to be a slow-moving, inefficient company compared with its new competitors in the computer equipment business. Although it had state-of-the-art printers and other computer-related equipment, it was slow to get these to the market and its price was comparatively high. Business results were poor and projected to get worse. Furthermore, a recession was in full swing. A rethinking of the competitive strategy was necessary. Top management performed the normal strategic planning activities, but, they also formed teams to target companies in need of computer equipment and to determine what HP Canada needed to do to win their business. After analyzing their environment and internal strengths and weaknesses, the HP strategic planning team adopted a strategy combining elements of both quality and cost leadership.

To address the internal weaknesses related to this strategy, HP Canada cut staff and streamlined operations. The sales force, for example, had been organized into separate groups specializing in one or a few products. Under the new structure the groups were merged into a sales force organized around customers but familiar with all products. HP Canada also relied on developing economies of scale in the production of its printers, pricing them competitively rather than taking large profit margins on their popular models. This strategy of getting a smaller unit profit from a larger volume of units combined with improvements in product quality has vaulted Hewlett-Packard Canada back into a market leadership position. Profits increased in spite of a continued Canadian recession. By the late 1980s HP Canada had positioned itself to be one of the toughest competitors in a very competitive industry.

Source: Information in part derived from Yoder 1991.

---

many competitors who are also strong in these areas (threats) and few or none who are strong in product leader characteristics. If the analysis indicates strong opportunities for those developing new products, these factors may suggest that the firm develop a product leader strategy. Doing so would then require an internal strategy to develop the necessary strengths. Training in Action 2.1 describes the experience of Hewlett-Packard Canada in strategy reformulation. The point is that whatever external strategy is adopted, it must be supported by internal strategies that bring the structure and core technology into proper alignment. HR and HRD are typically key players in the development of these internal strategies.

The match between the external and internal strategies is critical to achieving the organization's business objectives. What might an organization that adopts a market leader (product innovation) strategy do to make sure that its internal processes and systems support this strategy? Here are some of the internal strategies that might be required:

- Restructuring to increase the size and influence of the product development and market research functions
- Increased flexibility of production technology (i.e., ability to shift from product to product quickly)
- Increased interaction between product development and market research (structure)
- Increased creativity within product development (structure)
- Corporate culture supportive of innovation (structure)
- Increased knowledge base of employees (technology and structure)

HR AND HRD INFLUENCES ON COMPETITIVE STRATEGY

As was noted in chapter 1, the HR function is responsible for acquiring and maintaining the human resources needed by the organization. This is accomplished through systems such as staffing, human resource planning, performance appraisal, compensation, health and safety, employee and union relations, and, of course, training. Each of these activities has important influences on the organization. Integrated under the HR umbrella, they can enhance the organization's ability to mobilize the necessary human resources to carry out a competitive strategy. The organization's HR function is also a critical contributor to the analysis of organizational strengths and weaknesses. Analysis of information related to current employee capabilities is important in developing external strategies (e.g., market position) and the corresponding internal strategies (i.e., structure, technology).

Increased Importance of HR

For many years HR's only role was to support organizational strategies, but in the early 1980s organizations began to recognize the importance of HR issues in making business decisions. Strategic HR management is now fairly commonplace, and the practice of using HR strategies to gain competitive advantage is increasingly evident. Fundamental changes have occurred in the business environment over the last two decades, making HR issues more central to long-term business success. Table 2.2 lists many of these changes and their corresponding HR issues.

A common thread running through all these changes and issues is environmental uncertainty. To be competitive in this environment, organizations must respond more quickly, flexibly, and intelligently. A rapidly changing business environment requires constant adaptation and flexible use of resources. Employees must be more competent, and the organization must institute systems using that competence more effectively.

There is an interesting dilemma here. Just as organizations are requiring their employees to have higher levels of knowledge and skill, the supply of entry-level employees with these characteristics is shrinking. Evidence indicates that almost 30% of U.S. high school students fail to graduate and that between 20% and 30% lack basic reading, writing, and arithmetic skills (Stone 1991). Even graduates of schools and colleges of business are found to lack basic business skills (Howard 1986; Porter and McKibbin 1988; Whetten and Cameron 1995). A report commissioned by the American Assembly of Collegiate Schools of Business (AACSB), the business school accrediting agency, states, "The corporate sector gives Business School graduates relatively low ratings in terms of their leadership and interpersonal skills" (Porter and McKibbin 1988). Using assessment center methodology, a study of approximately 350 students from four

TABLE 2.2 Conditions Increasing the Importance of HR Issues	
High rate of change in market demand	Requires employees who can develop or adapt products and services quickly
High level of uncertainty in market demand	Requires employees who can forecast more accurately and react more flexibly
Rising costs combined with competitive pressures on profit margins	Requires employees with wider range of KSAs so fewer people can do more things well
High rate of technological change	Requires employees who are more technologically literate and current
More complex organizations (number and type of products, technologies, locations, customers, etc.)	Requires employees who can process and analyze complex information from a variety of sources
More diverse labor pool	Requires employees who can interact effectively in many cultural and ethnic contexts
Smaller labor pool	Requires more effective use of existing employees and better recruiting of new employees

schools found minimal skill improvement from the start to the completion of their undergraduate course work (AACSB *Outcome Measurement Project* 1987).

While both the public school systems and business schools are working hard to correct these problems, businesses can't wait for the solutions. The general decline in the KSAs of the labor pool combined with a projected shrinking of the total labor pool spell problems for business. Organizations that place a high priority on employee competencies will also need to place a high priority on internal strategies for human resource development and/or staffing. The "learning organization," which is described later in this chapter, is one example of such an internal competitive strategy.

In addition to contributing to the development of the organization's competitive strategy, HR activities must support those strategies once they are adopted. Decisions about competitive strategy need to be reflected in HR strategy and vice versa. For example, if the company's operations are labor intensive and it has a strong union that consistently demands high wages and restrictive work rules, it would be foolish to adopt a cost leader strategy without addressing these issues first. Similarly, once the company makes the decision to adopt a cost leader strategy, HR must develop its own strategies for supporting cost leadership. Figure 2.3 (page 46) reflects this relationship and some of the factors involved in developing an HR strategy. As this figure illustrates, HR strategy and competitive strategy must be coordinated, and each influences the other. Both, for example, must take account of the technology used for production. Let's assume a cost leader strategy required a change in production technology (e.g., more automation); this could be accomplished only if HR was capable of staffing the new technology. HR's input into the strategy formulation process might be the identification of what it would take to staff the proposed technology and the likelihood of being able to do so. Failure to address the HR side of the strategy could lead to the purchase and installation of a new technology that, among other things, proved

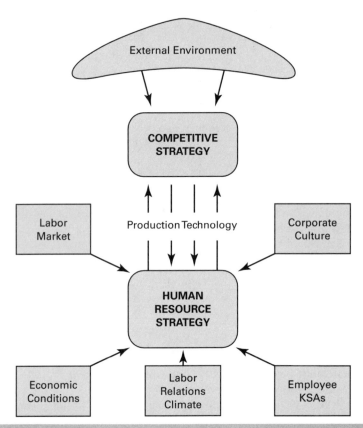

FIGURE 2.3 Relationship between Competitive and Human Resource Strategies

too costly to staff, created labor conflict, produced conflicts in the existing culture, or required lengthy training, thus delaying the implementation of the technology. Might these things happen at MHC?

HRD, Staffing, and Strategy Development

Throughout this text we emphasize that HRD is in the business of supporting the organization's strategies, goals, and objectives. In this supporting role, HRD contributes to the organization's competitive position in several ways. It ensures that employees have the necessary competencies to meet strategic performance demands, and it identifies barriers to desired performance. In addition, HRD has much to offer in the development of organizational strategies.

Since the focus of training is improving employee competencies, the HRD area needs to be involved in discussions of strategies that depend on the competencies and knowledge base of the organization. It is imperative that the capabilities of current employees to carry out a strategy be assessed and factored into decisions. However, many organizations don't think of HRD in this strategic sense. Product innovation or cost leadership strategies are often formulated with little consideration of employee capabilities, and it is only after implementation problems surface that HRD considerations may arise. These problems often result in costly delays in implementing the strategy, perhaps even dooming the strategy to failure.

Think back to the MHC case. What would have happened if Carrie Brown had not been invited to participate in the strategic planning session? Even with her input, will the plan be successful? It's clear there are a number of issues that HR must deal with before the competitive strategy can be put in place.

Training is not the only way of improving the competency base of the organization. Another option is staffing. The company must examine the feasibility of the various alternatives, including making rough estimates of the time and costs involved. This information is supplied by the HR function. Tradeoffs in these areas are something Carrie Brown will have to examine at MHC.

In the staffing approach, competencies would be imported through recruitment and hiring. HRD would need to be involved in orientation of new employees and any other "new employee training." Adding competencies through new hires implies other aspects of the staffing function. If the existing employees don't have the competencies to implement the competitive strategy, termination and/or reassignment of these employees must be considered and factored into the feasibility equation.

In the training approach, the various methods of raising the competencies of existing employees would need to be examined. It would have to be decided whether to do the training in house or to use a training vendor. This decision will determine how long it will take before employees are ready to implement the strategy and the amount of resources required. This information is provided to the strategic planning group so it can determine the most appropriate strategy.

The Role of Competencies in Strategy Development

We are not suggesting that HR issues are, or should be, the only influence on the strategic direction taken by an organization; nevertheless, it should be part of the equation. The relative importance of strategic variables such as technology, financial assets, product, and human resources varies from one context to the next. Likewise, the importance of HRD issues to competitive strategy depends on how central employee expertise is to business success and the value of using current employees compared with acquiring new ones. For firms that compete in markets where technical innovations are continuous and the rate of knowledge growth is high (e.g., electronic communications), employee expertise is a strategic asset. For firms in which change is slow or nonexistent or where markets are less knowledge-intense (e.g., food processing), HRD may have less strategic importance. However, any organization operating in a highly competitive market should consider giving employee competencies a high strategic value. Because technology continually improves and continuous quality improvement has become standard in most industries, strategies for increasing employee competence can provide a competitive advantage.

In formulating the firm's competitive strategy the value of input from HR and HRD lies in the information they possess about the organization's ability to carry out different strategies. Organizations in market leadership positions, especially, must find ways to sustain their innovation advantage. Human resources are ultimately the only resource that has the capability to adjust continually to changing market conditions. The development of human resource expertise provides a potentially inexhaustible supply of new ideas and creative approaches to the demands of the environment. Using employee knowledge as a major component of company growth and competitive advantage has only recently begun to be appreciated in strategy formulation (Senge et al. 1994; Nevis, DiBella, and Gould 1995).

Once the competitive strategies have been formulated, HR and HRD adopt the more traditional role of supporting those strategies. Before we move to HRD's role in supporting organizational strategy, let's examine an internal strategy that is directly tied to both HR and HRD.

The Learning Organization: An Internal Strategy

As was indicated earlier, external strategies require supportive internal strategies. The *learning organization* is an example of an internal strategy for improving the competency base of the organization. This is a relatively new phenomenon and has both advocates and critics. Because it is a very amorphous strategy, there is some difficulty finding an agreed-on definition. The goal of a learning organization is to stimulate and capture individual learning in ways that allow the learning to be spread across the organization.

Defining the Learning Organization   There are many definitions of the **learning organization** (e.g., Garvin 1993; Senge 1990; Shaw and Perkins 1991), and we have attempted to combine the commonalities among them in our definition. The learning organization builds a sense of common understanding among individuals, enhancing their capacity to create the results they want to create through continually learning how to learn, together. Its systems support employees in creating, acquiring, and transferring knowledge to others. In a learning organization employees modify their behavior to reflect new knowledge. It is part of an overall competitive strategy in which knowledge is the competitive advantage. It requires large investments in time, energy, and people. While it is an obvious fit with a market leader strategy, in which innovation separates winners from losers, it also has applications to every organization, including those that adopt cost leader strategies.

Creating a learning organization is a challenging process. The components of the learning organization are listed in Table 2.3. Organizational learning requires a focused support system and an infrastructure that can capture and deploy learning to those who seek it. Upper management must provide the appropriate climate and reinforcement, demonstrating commitment to the strategy even through the difficult initial stages of implementation.

> The primary responsibility of management, and the focus of management practices in a learning organization is to create and foster a climate that promotes learning. Management's task is not to control or be a corporate cheerleader or crisis handler; it is to encourage experimentation, open communication, promote constructive dialog, and facilitate the processing of experience. (McGill and Slocum 1993)

HRD's Role in the Learning Organization   HRD systems and employees are critical to the success of the learning organization strategy. They not only must know their field and craft very well, but also must fully understand the organization and its strategic direction. They must be able to fashion learning experiences for employees that fit the culture, systems, and values of the organization. Learning organizations often require fewer employees because line managers have learned how to integrate many of the staff functions into their daily routine. This is especially true for the HR function.

TABLE 2.3   Components of a Learning Organization

Personal mastery	This involves the continual clarification and deepening of one's personal vision. It connects personal learning with organizational learning.
Mental models	These are the deeply ingrained assumptions and generalizations that influence how we understand the world. Until these are brought to the surface, little learning takes place that doesn't conform to these models.
Building a shared vision	This sets up a creative tension that pulls the visions of individuals into a common future that all desire, thus galvanizing a group toward goal accomplishment.
Team learning	Teams are the learning blocks of organizations. If the team doesn't learn, the organization doesn't learn.
Systems thinking	This is a framework for seeing the interrelationships rather than the things that are related.
Systematic problem solving	There is a reliance on the scientific method rather than guesses or hunches. Data, rather than assumptions, are used for decision making. People are skilled in the use of basic statistical techniques for analysis.
Experimentation	This is distinguished from problem solving in that its focus is on expanding knowledge rather than responding to current difficulties. Failure of experiments is accepted as a way of gaining knowledge.
Learning from experience	The lessons of experience are documented in a form that employees find accessible and understandable.
Learning from others	Knowledge is gained from what others do and how they do it, rather than from the results they have achieved. Benchmarking and similar practices are encouraged.
Transference of knowledge	For the organization, rather than just individuals, to learn, knowledge must be documented and made transferable quickly and easily.

For example, the selection process is traditionally an HR activity, but in learning organizations this process might be handled by an autonomous work team that has learned how to perform this activity. Those inside HR in such organizations have learned how to improve HR processes so that fewer dull, routinized tasks are required, and thus staff and clerical support needs are reduced. HRD staffs, however, have shown dramatic increases in learning organizations. The HRD professionals are doing less stand-up training but are creating more learning situations, opportunities, and systems. James DeVito (1996), vice president of Educational Research and Services for Johnson & Johnson, has described their former role as learning stonemasons and their new role as learning architects. As stonemasons they were responsible for providing the content and the process of learning; as architects they are designing systems that allow individuals and groups to identify what they need to know and the best way of learning it. The learning organization radically changes the focus and core competencies required of HRD professionals. They now have the responsibility of empowering employees to identify and meet their training needs.

Electronic information systems are critical to the success of this strategy. There is no organizational learning if there is no capacity to store learning compactly and cheaply and to transmit it quickly and easily. Self-directed training delivery systems such as satellite broadcast systems, video discs, and networked learning libraries make it possible for people to learn what they need to know when they need to know it. This capability changes the paradigm for how the training function meets the training needs of the organization. Rather than directing the learning experiences of employees, training entails helping employees learn how to learn on their own and also developing the means for that learning to happen. Organizations such as Xerox, Samsung, and Corning have implemented these systems with much success. Corning, for example, set a company-wide goal that 5% of each employee's annual workload would be spent in job-related training. A few years later, in 1991, *Business Week* recognized Corning as a prime example of an effective competitor (Marquardt and Reynolds 1994). Corning attributes their success to their commitment to employee and organizational learning.

At this point you might be wondering, "If this strategy is so difficult to implement and requires so much time, money, and commitment, why would a company decide to do it? Isn't there a fairly high risk of failure?" The answer is that the potential advantages are so large that companies are willing to take the risk. Let's assume the learning organization strategy is successful and allows a company to jump ahead of its competitors who are using a traditional training system. By the time this fact becomes apparent, the company already has a substantial knowledge lead on the competition. Because of the difficulties in moving to a learning organization strategy, it will take the competitors some time to put this strategy into place. Meanwhile, the company is continuing to improve the competencies of its employees and increasing its competitive advantage. Because of its head start, competitors probably couldn't catch up for a long time; perhaps some never would.

Although the learning organization strategy is still young, it shows great promise. It also presents traditional training organizations and training professionals with a significant threat. If the above scenario proves correct, the focus and technology of HRD and training professionals will have shifted dramatically. Those who don't keep up will go the way of buggy whips and computer punch cards.

WHAT ABOUT SMALL BUSINESS?

We have noted that strategic planning provides direction to the HRD department about the amount and types of training that are valuable to the organization. But is it necessary for small businesses to get involved in strategic planning in order to be successful? Strategic planning has been shown to be positively related to small business performance (Ackelsberg and Arlow 1985; Bracker, Keats, and Pearson 1988). In spite of this benefit, Wheelen and Hunger (1995) note that many small business owners and managers do not engage in strategic planning for the following reasons:

Not enough time:	Too busy with day-to-day operations. Concern about tomorrow is the excuse for not planning for next year.
Unfamiliarity with it:	Unaware of strategic planning or do not see its value. See it as limiting flexibility.
Lack of skills:	Do not have the skills nor time to learn them. Do not wish to spend money to bring in consultants.

Lack of trust: Want to keep their key information to themselves. Do not wish to share this information with other employees or outsiders.

What can be done to encourage small businesses to become more involved in such planning? First, education about the advantages of such efforts would be useful. Even large organizations use the excuse that they are so busy fighting fires they don't have time for planning. However, if they spent time planning, there might not be so many fires. Bringing small business owners and managers in touch with those who have used strategic planning successfully in their small business is a good start for this education.

The skills issue can be addressed by using a less formal and rigorous process. Evidence indicates that small businesses that use a more informal strategic planning process can be more effective than those using more formal processes (Ackelsberg and Arlow 1985; Buchele 1967; Gilmore 1971). Additional evidence suggests that, at the very least, a formalized process produces no better results (Kargar and Blumenthal 1994). The emphasis on structured written plans in strategic planning may be dysfunctional for the small business. A less formal strategic planning process for the small business is provided in Table 2.4.

What about the issue of lack of trust? Research suggests that when faced with threats (SWOT analysis), small firms benefit by going outside the organization for help. Unlike large organizations, they are unlikely to have the necessary internal resources to address these threats (Lang, Calantone, and Gudmundson 1997). If there is no one they trust, they will simply not obtain the necessary information or assistance. Lang et al. (1997) suggest that small businesses should seek out possible resources and establish appropriate relationships in "good times" so that they can be drawn on for help in "bad times." The small business owner can evaluate the relationship during times when threats don't create a crisis.

Will an increase in strategic planning result in a corresponding increase in the attention small businesses give to training? We believe it will focus attention on the "right" training. Training is often ignored as a strategic initiative because owners and managers do not have a clear model for making decisions about whether training activities will lead to a competitive advantage (O'Neal and Duker 1986). Involvement in strategic planning will provide such direction. As we discussed earlier, when the need for training emerges from the strategic planning process, it is clearly tied to the mis-

TABLE 2.4 Questions for the Strategic Planning Process in a Small Business

1. Why are we in business?
2. What are we trying to achieve?
3. Who is our competition and how can we beat them?
4. What sort of ground rules should we be following to get the job done right?
5. How should we organize ourselves to reach our goals and beat the competition?
6. How much detail do we need to provide so everyone knows what to do?
7. What are the few key things that will determine if we make it? How should we keep track of them?

Training in Action 2.2

Stories along the Road to ISO

Rivait Machine Tools, which provides electrical discharge machining of steel, employs 14 people. The president, James Rivait, made an important strategic decision to diversify into the aerospace industry. To even be considered as a supplier in this industry, a company must be ISO 9000 certified. Eighteen months later and $100,000 poorer, Rivait achieved certification. (Williamson 1997)

Early in 1993 Grace Specialty Polymers set out in a new strategic direction that required ISO 9000 certification. The strategic plan set a target of achieving certification for four separate locations by the end of 1994. To accomplish this, an executive steering committee was set up consisting of the general manager and employees who reported directly to him. They were to provide the direction, commitment, and resources. Next an ISO implementation team was set up. This seven-member, cross-functional team was made up mostly of department managers. While successful, the members of the team indicate it is not an easy process. Their assessment was that a company must be committed to getting it done. You can't have less than a full effort. (Benson and Sherman 1995)

Reelcraft industries embarked on an ISO certification program to improve processes. It took the company two years to achieve certification, and the paperwork it produced was awesome. The main difference is that Reelcraft now "builds quality in rather than inspecting errors out." Among the chief benefits are increased knowledge and skills and communication. (Bible 1996)

Cavalier Tool & Manufacturing examined the ISO process and determined that it did not make strategic sense for them at that time. Sometimes a customer has a short run emergency and needs a "down and dirty mold." "If we were ISO 9000 certified, we would not be allowed to take on that business. All your work must follow the ISO process, and so I would have to turn down this customer. I am not ready to do that," president Rick Jannisse said. Furthermore, he is not disposed toward the discipline required to be ISO certified. Examining the external environment, he realizes that he may be forced to become certified eventually, but not now. At least he is aware of the implications of the decision he is making. (Williamson 1997)

---

sion and objectives of the small business. For example, in companies that include ISO 9000 certification in their strategy, training is clearly value added, since the certification won't be granted without it.

One final point should be made about small businesses. Because they are small, communicating a strategic direction and implementing the plan should be considerably easier than with a large firm. In fact, Kargar and Blumenthal (1994) have provided evidence that, in implementing strategic plans, small companies had to anticipate and prevent fewer problems than larger firms. Some problems still do exist, however. For example, the small business that seeks to become a preferred supplier to a company doing business in Europe must receive ISO 9000 certification. Many small companies have used the strategic planning process to determine if becoming certified is worthwhile. The planning process allows them to see how certification fits their overall competitive strategy. Training in Action 2.2 shows how different companies used the strategic planning process to make the decision.

HRD's Role in Supporting Strategy

It is not enough for the organization to develop competitive strategies—these strategies must be followed with action, typically referred to as tactics. Figure 2.1 illustrated the links between an organization's competitive strategy and **tactical activities.** The strategies are implemented through a tactical action plan, which consists of the required actions and the unit(s) responsible for those actions. The process begins with assigning objectives to the different work units of the organization. The units must then develop strategies and implementation tactics to achieve the objectives. Eventually, they are translated into individual employee objectives. The objectives for the HRD unit, as for all functional areas, must be tied directly to organizational strategies. Of course, for HRD these will be filtered through the strategies the HR unit has developed to achieve its objectives.

DEVELOPING AN HRD STRATEGY

Without a strategic plan, training is likely to be managed in a haphazard manner, its resources underutilized and its full strategic value not realized. At the most basic level the training function must make strategic decisions about where it will focus its resources and energies. This will depend in part on the environment in which training operates, the resources available (financial, material, and personnel), and the core competencies contained within the training function. Analysis of these areas leads to strategic decisions about the technology that should be used to develop needed employee competencies. An organizational analysis will provide the bulk of the data necessary for creating the training strategy. This analysis and sources from which data can be obtained are detailed in chapter 4, on needs analysis.

The Training Environment

Just as the organization must align its competitive strategy with the demands of its environment, so too must the training function. The environment of the HRD function consists of the organization itself and its business strategies as well as some aspects of the organization's external environment. HRD must also help to shape and support the strategies adopted by the HR function. Figure 2.4 (page 54) illustrates key factors in the selection of a training strategy. In any given organization the importance of these factors will vary and additional factors may exist. However, in general, these factors should be important determinants of the training strategy for most organizations.

Factors External to the Organization   As Figure 2.4 indicates, factors outside the training function influence internal operations. Some of these external factors are outside the organization, and others are outside the training function but internal to the organization. Factors outside the organization may exert their influence on the training function directly or through other parts of the organization.

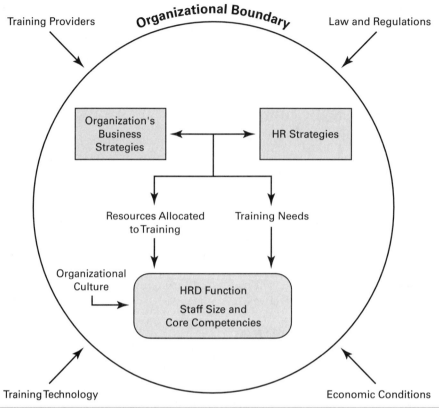

FIGURE 2.4 Environmental Factors Affecting the Selection of a Training Strategy

External training providers. Training providers such as private training and consulting firms, professional associations, and colleges and universities can be seen as either threats to or opportunities for the training function.

They can be threats in several ways. Most obviously, they can be seen as competitors, providing similar products and services. In this sense their threat is to the size and perhaps even the existence of the training function. If their products and services are viewed as higher or equivalent in quality but less costly, the organization may decide to reduce or eliminate internal training. In addition, the external providers are threats to the extent that they provide competitors with competencies. Thus the training function needs to constantly monitor the activities of external training providers as benchmarks against which to judge their own performance.

On the other hand, these external training providers can be seen as opportunities. They can be used as resources for products and services that are not cost effective to develop internally or for which internal resources or capabilities are lacking. Some of the primary uses for external training providers are in new program development, specialized program development, needs analysis, and evaluation. These all require specialized competencies that may not be used on a continual basis. By going to outside providers, the company avoids the expense of narrowly focused full-time employees who are needed only on occasion. Additionally, development costs for new training programs are relatively high. However, an outside provider who specializes in the training program area will have lower development costs that can be spread over many clients, further lowering the cost to any one company.

Law and regulations.   Some training is either mandated by laws and regulations or strongly encouraged by the nature of the legal system. Mandated training focuses primarily on health and safety programs. Equal employment opportunity laws place restrictions on how training can be used, who has access to it, and who must be included in various types of training. Some types of training are encouraged because they reduce the employer's exposure to lawsuits. For example, in the mid-1980s sexual harassment was rarely mentioned as a training content area, but today nearly all medium- to large-size firms provide such training, even though it is not required by law. Employers who provide such training to their employees reduce their liability exposure if an employee brings a sexual harassment suit against them.

The training function needs to keep abreast of the laws, regulations, and legal practices related to training because they affect important organizational outcomes and can have a profound impact on the demands placed on the training function.

Training technology.   Training technology refers to the tools, methods, and media through which learning opportunities are created and put into effect. For example, during the past decade we have seen tremendous changes in the capabilities of interactive, multimedia, computer-based systems. In addition to hardware and software development, advances in learning theory, educational practices, and training facilities are all part of the technology of training. As these technologies change, training professionals must assess their implications for training strategy. For instance, a firm with a given set of training needs and a defined set of resources to meet those needs must make a strategic decision about how the resources will be used to meet the needs. Investment in new training technology typically requires fairly large amounts of capital, reducing the firm's ability to meet some training needs in the short term. But failure to make the investment will result in higher training costs and perhaps less effective training over the long run. If the technology is developing rapidly, an investment now may lead to quick obsolescence (as in computer hardware and software). However, it may also provide better and less costly training across a wide range of training needs, so this early investment can lead to a competitive advantage, even if the technology has to be replaced in a few years. This is a dilemma faced by many training departments. For example, should a company invest in CD-ROM technology, allowing it to integrate all aspects of training onto an easily portable disc, or stay with the more traditional videocassette technology? The start-up cost for the CD-ROM system is about $100,000. A state-of-the-art video system costs about $1,000. Is the advanced technology worth the additional cost? The answer depends on how well it will allow the training function to meet its strategic objectives. Thus the advances in training technology must be viewed with regard to the opportunities and threats they pose to HRD's mission and objectives.

Economic conditions.   Certainly economic conditions are critical in the development of the organization's strategic plan, and, therefore, on HRD's strategies. The economy also has other direct implications for the development of a training strategy.

When the economy is robust, organizations tend to grow, and growth increases the demands on training (e.g., new employees need orientation and job training, employees need to change KSAs). This generally means larger training budgets and more difficulty attracting highly qualified staff (while full employment may be desirable for society, it means a tighter labor market for employers). It also means there is less time available for training, since everyone is working hard to take advantage of the "good" times. In times of economic downturn, the reverse is true.

From a training perspective, there are positives and negatives in any phase of the economic cycle. Economic booms may be the best time to invest in new training technologies. It will be difficult to schedule training then, the budget is larger, and the immediate training needs will be for those who are trying to cope with the growth in customer demand, staffing, and the like. Economic downturns, on the other hand, typically place different demands on training. With reductions in workforce, those remaining are likely to be asked to do more with less and to do it better. New systems and procedures may be implemented to improve efficiencies, and all of this requires training. Some organizations, rather than downsizing in times of economic recession, choose to use production downtime to upgrade employees' skills, as North American automobile manufacturers did during the mid to late 1980s. Regardless of the organization's competitive strategy, HRD is well advised to take economic forecasts into consideration when developing its training strategies.

Factors Internal to the Organization   HRD must develop its strategy within the context of the strategies adopted by the HR function as a whole, which, in turn, are dependent on the competitive strategies of the organization. Together they will determine the resources available and the training needs that must be addressed. At the same time, training strategies must take into account the culture of the organization, in particular the training climate.

Organizational and HR strategy.   The adoption of a competitive strategy has wide-ranging implications for the human resources function.

Because the "market leader" strategy depends on innovation, employee knowledge and skills are critically important. Highly skilled and knowledgeable people must be hired and developed, and they need to work under a structure that allows them latitude in how they go about their work. Reward and feedback systems must focus on long-term rather than short-term performance. Some amount of failure must be expected as employees try out new ideas. The failure of an experiment can be positive if it brings the organization closer to realizing its objectives through the learning that occurs. If failure is punished, employees will be reluctant to attempt new things. Hewlett-Packard, Raytheon, and PepsiCo illustrate this philosophy (Schuler and Jackson 1987) by selecting highly trained and skilled employees, being committed to their long-term development, and developing systems that evaluate and reward employees for their contributions to the company's objectives.

"Cost leader" organizations, in contrast, emphasize tight fiscal and management controls. Because their leadership position is dependent on their ability to produce high volumes at low cost, efficiencies and productivity are critical. Strategies for reducing costs include reducing the number of employees, reducing wages and salaries, using part-time and contract labor, and improving work methods. Conforming to standardized procedures is emphasized in these organizations, and training helps to ensure conformance. On-the-job training (OJT) techniques are used more frequently for line employees. It is only at the middle-management levels and above that more autonomous decision making occurs and that higher level competencies are emphasized. In these organizations, training is more likely to be focused on management.

The two strategies described above illustrate the extreme positions, but there is a vast array of strategic positions between them. Also there are a myriad of HR implications in any given strategy. The important point is that the organization's competitive strategy and the supporting HR strategies determine the strategic goals training must focus on. Specifically, they identify the employee competencies that need to exist, and this information is used to identify the organization's training needs. This part of the process is reflected in Figure 2.4 by the arrows leading from organizational strategy to HR strategy and then to training needs.

Organizational and HR strategies each have additional implications for the type of training strategy adopted. The competitive strategy determines the structure of the organization, the policies and procedures, budgets, and so on. The HR strategy determines the structure of the HR function, its policies, procedures, and budgets. HRD's training strategy must take these constraints into account. Figure 2.4 shows the resources allocated to training flowing from both HR and business strategies. These resources affect the feasibility of various training strategies.

Organizational culture.   An organization's culture is made up of the shared beliefs and basic assumptions its employees have adopted as they adapt to the organization and its demands. The culture is reinforced and transmitted through formal statements, materials, policies, procedures (formal and informal), stories (real or invented) about key individuals and events, and the actions that have been rewarded and punished. The culture of an organization determines what is valued. The training must fit within the culture of the organization, unless part of the organization's strategic plan is to change the culture. For example, companies sometimes decentralize training by using experts within each of the work units to provide training. This policy will not be successful if the culture devalues these experts. Likewise, training itself can be devalued by the culture because of a widely shared belief. Training directed at attitudes and attitude change would be applicable in this case. These cultural values must be taken into account when training strategy is developed.

THE TRAINING ENVIRONMENT
AND AMOUNT OF CENTRALIZATION

The number of factors in the HRD environment and their stability determine the degree of uncertainty faced by HRD in developing a training strategy. Remember, the level of environmental uncertainty is determined by two factors: rate of change and degree of complexity. Further, because each environmental factor influences not only the training function but also one another, more complex environments create more uncertainty: It is more difficult to predict how three things will interact than it is to predict how two things will interact.

The amount of environmental uncertainty has strong implications for centralization in the HRD organization. In predictable environments, where training needs and budgets are known quantities for the foreseeable future, the training systems should be more centralized and under more formalized controls so that the most efficient means of meeting the training needs can be realized. In uncertain environments, training systems should be more decentralized and flexible so as to adapt to changing conditions.

At extreme levels of centralization, all training is developed and provided by a central training function (e.g., corporate training). In an extremely decentralized training strategy, each of the separate units of an organization would acquire its own training. On-the-job training is an example of a decentralized training strategy, since each area's management is responsible for providing (or delegating) the development and implementation of OJT.

Different levels of centralization have both advantages and disadvantages. More centralization results in greater assurance of common content and method, greater economies of scale for development costs, and higher competencies in those who develop and deliver training. On the other hand, decentralization increases the relevance of training to each specific area of the organization, creates more commitment to training, and ensures that training occurs where it is most needed (Carnevale, Gainer, and Villet 1990; Tovar, Rossett, and Carter 1989). Furthermore, because local managers are involved in the training, learning is more likely to be used on the job (transfer of training), and barriers preventing transfer are more easily addressed. Decentralization also results in managers' being more involved in the development of subordinates. Aspects of centralization are discussed in the strategies described below. As you read this section, think about how the strategies would apply to the MHC case.

SOME STRATEGIC TRAINING ALTERNATIVES

The strategic alternatives discussed here deal primarily with whether training is developed and implemented in house or purchased from the outside, and the amount of centralization in making training decisions. The three strategic alternatives discussed below are each labeled in terms of the HRD function's role. In the primary provider strategy HRD provides all training. The manager/middleman strategy uses the HRD function as a purchaser, manager, and monitor of training provided by outside sources. The mixed strategy is a combination of these. These represent only a few of the many strategic issues HRD might consider; they serve merely to illustrate how training strategy varies according to the organization's competitive strategy and the environment in which HRD operates. These alternatives were selected because they are not unique to a particular strategic plan but rather can be applied to any company. Budget requirements and core staff competencies are discussed in general terms.

Primary Provider

In this strategy all, or nearly all, training is developed and provided "in house" by the HRD department. Each phase of the training process is handled by specialists. The types of training needs that will be addressed, the development of programs to address those needs, and the evaluation of those programs are determined by a centralized HRD function. Because it is most effective in a stable environment where training needs do not change rapidly, it is most appropriate for cost leader companies. The principal advantages of this strategy are the control over the training content, consistency in delivery across the organization, and reduced training costs. It is more effective in larger organizations where a single training program can be applied to many groups of employees. Because the cost of development can be spread across a large number of employees, the cost per employee is reduced. Since a single program is developed to meet a particular training need, the content is consistent across the organization. Because the content and design of the program are developed by in-house specialists, it is tailored to the company's needs.

This strategy requires a fairly large centralized training staff. Core competencies for HRD departments using this strategy include all those necessary to identify training needs, design and develop training programs, conduct the programs, evaluate the programs, and manage the training processes and systems. Because of the resource requirements, it is usually adopted only by the largest companies.[1]

A way to reduce centralization while reducing costs is to have training developed by the corporate HRD staff but conducted by other employees. This system places a higher reliance on train-the-trainer and self-learning methods (e.g., videos and computer-based training). In this approach, after the training programs are developed by the HRD area and then shipped out to the various business units, the training is completed by the trainee alone or facilitated by a business unit representative (e.g., supervisor or in-house technical expert). Those conducting the training will need to go through a train-the-trainer course to familiarize themselves with the content and methods. Even so, problems can develop in the effectiveness of training throughout the organization.

Suppose MHC identified "listening skills" as a problem area for hospital staff who must deal with patients and their families. In response, HRD developed a listening skills training program and also decided to decentralize the training and have it conducted by unit managers within the division. Because this type of training includes many experiential exercises and some behavior modeling, these managers would have to demonstrate effective listening skills, be familiar with the exercises and skilled at facilitating them, and be skilled at providing constructive feedback. Because of differences in managers' training capabilities, different locations would receive different levels of training. For this reason, evaluation would become even more important.

Often the strategic KSAs that training is intended to provide are subverted through modifications in the training content and design at the work unit level. One solution to this problem is to provide extensive training and develop reward systems that motivate the work unit trainer to be consistent in presenting the material and applying the methods that have been built into the training. However, doing this can substantially reduce the cost advantage.

Manager/Intermediary

This strategy has all or almost all training activities provided by outside training venders. The training function's role is to select and manage training suppliers. Suppliers may be training firms, consultants, professional seminars, college/university courses, and the like. A full commitment to this strategy would have outside vendors conducting all aspects of the training process from the training needs analysis through evaluation.

---

[1] This doesn't mean all large companies adopt this strategy, only that they are more capable of adopting it. Many large companies have successfully adopted a decentralized training strategy, and others have been successful with a centralized strategy (Gerber 1987; Lee 1988).

For small businesses and organizations with a small or nonexistent training function, the manager or intermediary strategy is most typical. It is adopted primarily for
budgetary reasons. Because these organizations employ a relatively small number of
people, it is more economical to pay a vendor than to pay the salaries of a professional training staff.

This strategy is also appropriate for larger organizations whose training needs
vary dramatically over short periods of time. Thus market leaders and those HRD departments that operate in very uncertain environments will find many advantages in
this strategy. It provides a flexible way of meeting changing and diverse training needs
with professionally developed and administered programs. It also fits well with a decentralized HRD structure. A small central HRD staff is involved in the budgeting
process, monitoring of training-related policies, and providing consultation and support to the various units. For example, compilation of lists of approved vendors, payment of vendors, and mandated training are decisions that might be made by the central HRD group. Then the different units of the organization (business units, divisions,
geographical units, and the like) are free to select the vendors and programs best
suited to their needs and within their training budget.

The core competencies required of the HRD function in this strategy revolve
around the selection and management of training providers. Because a large number
of firms and individuals offer training services, the manager must carefully screen potential providers. Obviously, cost is one factor to consider. However, cost is also related to quality. Typically, the low-cost providers are those that have just entered the
field. However, the fact that a provider is more expensive or experienced doesn't
mean its quality is higher. Within your budgetary limits, the primary criteria should be
the ability to provide the desired KSAs to your employees. Some key questions for
making this determination are listed in Table 2.5. Of course, these are not sufficient to
evaluate the provider fully, but they are a good start for making comparisons. These
issues will be discussed more completely in chapter 8.

Managing the training providers requires typical management competencies. The
provider must be given clear direction—that is, the goals and expectations must be

---

TABLE 2.5   Questions to Assess Training Provider Capabilities

What is their background (education, experience, etc.)?

Have they ever provided these particular training programs or services before?

Have they conducted formal evaluations of their results? If so, what have been the results?

Can they give you the names of people in these companies who could speak knowledgeably
about the trainer's products and services?

Can they give you names of those who were recipients of the service and those who brought
the training provider into the organization and oversaw the training or the service?

Can they provide an outline of their approach and/or process? How do they go about
developing a program, delivering training, or providing a training service?

If they are providing training they have already developed, can they show you materials, such
as handouts, exercises, and videos?

Since these are not specific to your organization, how will they alter them to make them
appropriate for your situation?

clearly spelled out. The various training providers and their programs must be organized in a logical flow and with minimal disruption to the activities of the company. The providers' activities must be monitored to ensure they are going according to plan and evaluated to be sure goals are met. An open communication system must be established between the training function and the training providers so that both parties have access to the information they need.

Under the manager/intermediary strategy, HRD staff costs are minimized because the actual training activities are contracted outside the organization, so there are substantial savings on employee salaries, benefits, and taxes. The cost per training session is usually higher, though, because the hourly or daily cost for training vendors is almost always higher than the comparable rate for in-house training staff (even including benefits and taxes). However, the training provider is paid only for the time spent actually providing the service. The contract ends once the service has been provided. With this strategy there are no layoffs or staff relocations when the need for training slacks off. Also, since these outside firms have already developed training programs, the company pays less for program development. Although these costs are often built into the consultant's fee, they are typically lower because the training provider can spread them over many companies. Even when the training provider creates a customized program, much of the developmental work has already been done. Thus the total costs for training can be substantially less than when using full-time employees. However, this is true only during times of rapid change and when training needs are very diverse. Under more stable conditions, moderate- to larger-sized organizations can meet a given set of ongoing training needs more consistently and at less cost via in-house training staff.

To reduce costs further, a train-the-trainer approach can be used with the manager/intermediary strategy. In this case, a training provider (rather than HRD staff) will train one or more employees to use the program the provider has developed. For example, it may be too costly and disruptive for a small business (of, say, 15 employees) to send all its employees to a customer service seminar and workshop. Instead, the company may send the general manager to the workshop, followed by a train-the-trainer session conducted by the workshop provider. While the company would likely pay a fee for using the materials, when the general manager returns to the company, she can train the rest of the employees as time allows and for little additional cost. The general manager can also modify the training, customizing it for the specific needs of the organization.

The Mixed Strategy

Most firms use some combination of the above two strategies, providing some training internally and contracting some to external providers. Decision making is centralized for some training activities and decentralized for others. There are different philosophies about where centralization should take place and what training should be developed and/or conducted internally. One approach is to conduct ongoing training internally and contract to external providers all new training. New training is usually required when some aspect of the environment has changed. This strategy allows the firm to be adaptable to changing aspects of the environment while focusing its internal efforts on ongoing training. If there is uncertainty about the training that is required or how quickly the need will change, this strategy puts the company in a more flexible position to respond. In addition, less of the development costs of new training are borne by the company. A negative aspect, however, is that training developed by outside vendors can be less directly relevant to the employees and additional resources may need to be allocated to tailor the training to the organization. Also if the training need becomes ongoing, plans should be developed to provide it internally, an action that will require agreement from the external provider.

Another approach is to develop all new training internally and contract out ongoing training. This strategy reduces the size of the organization's training staff. Typically, trainers are individual consultants who are willing to work as contract employees for the firm. This strategy ensures the fit between the training and the training needs, but the organization has to shoulder all the development costs. However, these costs may be offset by reduced staffing needs. A careful break-even analysis would determine if reduced staffing would adequately compensate for increased development costs.

The more strategically important training is and the more likely it is to be needed on an ongoing basis, the more likely it is to be developed and conducted internally. Specialized training such as that required for software developers is typically outsourced because it is difficult and expensive to develop and maintain the needed expertise internally. Training associated with obtaining certification or professional credentials is also typically obtained from external providers for similar reasons.

The mixed strategy may also be appropriate for organizations with training needs that are extremely diverse from one sector of the organization to another. MASCO Corp., a home improvement and building products company with over $3 billion in sales in 1996, is a good example. MASCO consists of an assortment of divisions, each producing different products and services. The corporation has adopted elements of both the market leader and cost leader strategies, and the training needs of the different divisions vary substantially. For this company to hire a centralized HRD staff that could handle the training needs for all the divisions would be very expensive. Because there is little overlap in the training needs, it makes more sense for the HRD function to be decentralized to the divisions. On the other hand, MASCO is in the process of redefining its culture after a period of strong growth. As a part of this redefinition, the company is instituting an executive development program in which key executives are given the opportunity to earn an MBA. This is a centralized program that is provided by an outside vendor (Eastern Michigan University). Thus MASCO centralizes some of its training and decentralizes others. It uses internal staff for training unique to its divisions and external vendors for the training of its executives.

OD, Strategy, and Training

Organizational development (*OD*) is the field of study that deals with creating and implementing planned change in organizations. Obviously, strategic planning involves change—both in the way the organization interacts with its external environment and in how it manages its internal operations. Although many organizations fail to take advantage of OD in the development and implementation of strategic plans, we believe it has much to offer.

OD AND STRATEGY

Whether an organization's strategies are developed proactively, reactively, or both, they require support from the internal systems. Organizational change is an inherent part of the processes of developing and implementing strategy. There are three core issues that organizations must resolve in developing and implementing strategy (Tichey 1983; Tichey, Fombrun, and Devanna 1992):

- *Technical design issues.* These arise in relation to how the product or service will be determined, created, and delivered.
- *Cultural/ideological issues.* These relate to the shared beliefs and values that employees need to hold for the strategy to be implemented effectively.
- *Political issues.* These occur as a result of shifting power and resources within the organization as the strategy is pursued.

These three issues must be addressed because they will determine the organization's ability to achieve its objectives. During the strategy development process, the decisions that are made about what products to develop and how they are produced determine what parts of the organization gain or lose resources. Cultural/ideological and power issues determine the support for, or resistance to, adopting a particular strategy. During strategy implementation, the business units will also face these change issues.

Organizational development provides a research base and a set of techniques that allow these decisions to be made and implemented in a more objective and well-thought-out manner. OD uses an open-systems, planned-change process that is rooted in the behavioral sciences and aimed at enhancing organizational and employee effectiveness. A model of a generic planned-change process is provided in Table 2.6.

The strategic planning process, if done properly, is an OD approach to change. The first step, establishing a compelling need for change, is what occurs in strategic planning during the environmental scanning phase. The need for change is made apparent when the strategic planners identify the threats and opportunities in the external environment and compare that information with what the organization is currently doing. When a gap exists between what the organization is doing and what the external environment requires (or will require), a need for change is established. Next the company's business objectives are set (step 2 in the change model). The company's current strengths and weaknesses are analyzed to determine what internal

---

TABLE 2.6 Steps in a Generic Planned Change Model

1. A compelling need for change is established.
2. Goals are developed and agreed to by the concerned parties.
3. The cause of the need for change is determined.
4. Alternative approaches for addressing the cause are identified and evaluated.
5. An approach to addressing the cause is selected.
6. The approach is carried out.
7. The results of the approach are evaluated.
8. The results are fed back to the organization.
    - If results are favorable, go to step 9.
    - If results are unfavorable, go back to step 4.
9. The change becomes internalized. The changes that have been made become routine and normal ways the organization conducts its business.

changes are necessary (step 3). This information then provides the compelling need for internal change, and internal strategic objectives are developed for these areas. The rest of the steps in the OD model concern the development of tactical plans that are used to achieve the strategic objectives.

Examples of OD Techniques

Although there is not space in this chapter to catalog OD's many techniques and their variations, it will be useful for us to get a flavor of the types of things OD practitioners do to achieve long-term, planned change. The techniques briefly described here represent fairly typical OD approaches to change. As you read through them, try to pick out the ways in which training would be useful to the technique and/or ways the technique could be useful to the training function.

Diagnostic and Planning Interventions (Macro)   These interventions attempt to help groups identify the current state of the organization, facilitate decisions about where the organization should be in the future, and develop plans for how to get there. They will be highlighted because they are of particular relevance to training needs analysis, design, and evaluation. Some of the most popular techniques in this area are **survey feedback, organizational confrontation meetings,** and **force-field analysis.**

Survey feedback.   *Survey feedback* begins with the design and administration of instruments for capturing employee attitudes, perceptions, and beliefs about various aspects of their work life. This information is then analyzed and fed back to various constituencies in the organization. The process provides a snapshot of how employees view the organization. The value of this approach is that, done properly, it provides objective data that can be used to implement change that addresses the problems and issues identified in the survey. This technique capitalizes on the participatory nature of OD because everyone has the opportunity to provide input. Thus, the data are "owned" by everyone.

Once the data have been analyzed, the results need to be fed back to those who participated in the process. Feeding back the data requires well-developed specialized skills. The results must be presented in a form that is understandable to the audience and in a manner that doesn't threaten them or make them defensive. At the same time it must convey the nature of the problem. One very popular strategy for providing feedback is the "waterfall." In this method, the consultant first gives the results to the leadership group, which in turn presents the results to the people who report to them, and so on throughout the organization. What kind of training would be useful for those who will be presenting feedback to others? Obviously, they will need the appropriate presentation skills. Since feedback and subsequent planning sessions are done in group formats, skills in facilitating group discussions and problem solving will be desirable. Can you think of others?

Organizational confrontation meeting.   The *organizational confrontation meeting* is a technique designed to mobilize the resources of the organization in identifying problems and developing action targets and action plans. It is particularly useful when a gap exists in the understanding between leadership and the rest of the organization (such as when a new top manager is hired) and when the organization is in a state of stress. It was originally developed for upper management and professional staff but has been used effectively with many types of line and support groups.

Representatives from each of the organization units (e.g., functions) are selected to participate as a member of a group. On a given date all the groups assemble and each is asked to identify problems it is facing. Since groups are made up of people from different parts of the organization, the problems are representative of what is going on across the total organization. The problems are compiled onto a master list that is shared with everyone. Each of the problem areas is discussed and categorized; participants are re-formed into problem-solving groups. The new groups rank the problems and agree on action plans with time lines for solving the problems. These are reported to the entire group, discussed, and perhaps modified. Follow-up meetings are held periodically to report progress and plan future actions.

How does training relate to this intervention? Participants would likely need training. To be effective, they require skills in listening, conflict management, negotiations, group problem solving, providing feedback, and group dynamics.

Force-field analysis. *Force-field analysis* is another technique OD practitioners use for helping groups understand a problem or situation and develop action plans. The underlying concept is that any situation can be explained by the sets of counterbalancing forces that are holding it in place (Lewin 1969). *Force* refers not only to physical forces but also to psychological forces that influence individual behavior. For example, if you wanted to understand why a work group isn't following the new company procedures, you would need to examine the forces acting within and outside the group in order to change the members' behavior. Tradition and group norms are forces that often exert strong pressure on group members, preventing them from trying new ways of doing things. Other forces that can influence group behavior are economic factors; individual KSAs; stereotypes of race, gender, and religion; and group conflict.

To understand a particular situation, you must first identify all the factors that exert influence on that situation. Then you must determine if each factor is exerting force either for changing the situation (drivers) or against change (restraining).

The force-field model is displayed in Figure 2.5. The arrows show forces that are driving and restraining change. In this figure the restraining forces are more numerous and larger than the driving forces, a combination that would create resistance to change in the people operating within the force field. The line of interaction, where these forces meet, symbolizes the current state. This means that the current array of forces on each side of the line have resulted in the current situation you are trying to change. Thus, for change to occur, actions must be developed to shift the force fields so that the forces for change are larger than the restraining forces. This model helps groups and individuals understand what actions are necessary to overcome resistance to change.

The steps for using the force-field analysis are listed in Figure 2.5 (page 66). Research has shown that change in force fields occurs more smoothly and quickly if the forces that are restraining change are reduced while driving forces are increased. Simply increasing the driving forces often results in escalated conflict before change can be achieved.

Techno-structural Interventions   These interventions address the structural configuration of the organization and its technological processes (how the work is done). Techniques in this area include job redesign, enrichment, rotation, and enlargement;

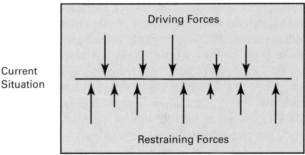

1. Identify the current state of the situation.
2. Envision the desired state.
3. Identify the forces restraining change.
4. Identify the forces that support or encourage change.
5. Assess the strength of the forces.
6. Develop strategies to:
   reduce the forces restraining change
   increase the forces for change (or capitalize on existing drivers).

FIGURE 2.5 Force-field Analysis Model

collateral organizations; organizational restructuring; and responsibility charting. Programs such as Total Quality Management, Organizational Reengineering, and the like are forms of techno-structural intervention. They are used to change how the work is done, the responsibilities assigned to individuals or groups, reporting relationships, and communication channels.

While each of these techniques addresses a different set of issues, they all deal with how the organization transforms raw materials into finished products and services, and thus go to the heart of what the organization is all about. These techniques use behavioral science and business operation models to assess the current state of the organization's technology and work systems. The objective is to analyze current systems and processes and design ones that are more effective in meeting the needs of the organization and the individual employee.

As you might expect, changes in these areas generate a great deal of conflict and resistance. To reduce this resistance, it is important to involve those who will be affected by the potential changes. Generally, a task force is formed with representatives from affected work areas, and the representatives are responsible for communicating from and to their respective areas. Rarely do more than a few individuals know all the critical information about the entire work process, so the first step is for individuals from various areas to educate one another about their operating processes. Once the group understands the entire process, it attempts to redesign the process so that it is improved and the needs of the employees are better met. The open-systems perspective is used to connect these changes in the operating system with other parts of the organization. Often the changes in the socio-technical system require the redesign of other parts of the organization.

Once the changes have been agreed on, an implementation plan must be put in place identifying who will do what by when. This procedure is typically called responsibility charting. As was mentioned earlier, whenever changes are made to the structure or work system, those affected will need to receive training to understand the changes and develop the KSAs to be able to function effectively.

LEVELS OF INTERNAL CHANGE AND RESISTANCE

Whenever internal change is planned in organizations, three levels should be addressed in the plan:

1. *The organization itself:* The way the organization is put together (what we call structure and design) must be examined to ensure that work is allocated appropriately and organizational systems are supportive of the change. This level of analysis identifies how labor is to be divided and what rules and procedures will govern operations.
2. *Groups and their interrelationships:* The way work is performed in the organizational units (i.e., the socio-technical systems) and how the outputs of the various units are integrated is the focus of this level of analysis. The issues here have to do with the design of jobs within units of the organization and the interrelationships of the jobs to one another.
3. *Individuals within groups:* The changes in performance that will be required of employees must be identified and mechanisms put into place to enable the desired performance to occur. This includes facilities, machines, equipment, and KSAs.

Resistance to change is a common occurrence. Without sufficient motivation to change, resistance is natural. Change requires effort, new learning, and possible shifts of resources and outcomes. Often those satisfied with the status quo can create enough resistance to derail the change effort, even to the point that the business fails. A major factor in this resistance is the failure of the change process to address all three levels of change. For example, instituting a work-team system in the organization without addressing the performance-appraisal system will naturally cause resistance to the new approach. People ask, "Why should we work as a team if we're getting evaluated as individuals?"

To achieve successful change at one level, then, requires analysis and possibly interventions at all three levels. Consider the impact a change in the organizational structure would have. Work would be allocated differently, so that some units might get work they hadn't done before while others might have certain jobs taken away. The affected units would need to change their work processes because they would have different amounts and/or types of work to do. These changes would require OD interventions at the group level. Here the OD practitioner is involved in the design or redesign of jobs and work systems and the associated interpersonal relationships. In addition, changes in how these work groups interact with others would be required, because they would now be producing something different. Employee resistance to new procedures would need to be addressed as jobs were being redesigned. At the individual level employees would also have to acquire the knowledge and skills necessary to perform their redesigned jobs.

You might think that these three levels of change are intertwined only if the change occurs at the organizational level. However, they are integrated no matter where the initial change takes place. That's why it's important to take a systems perspective. For example, at the individual level you might want employees to increase their skill levels in some aspect of the job (e.g., integrating quality control [QC] into their production work). You might regard this as just a training issue. However, even if employee KSAs are developed, the job itself and the organizational systems must support the use of those KSAs. You will need to ensure that the design of the job supports the performance you want from your employees. For example, the equipment and tools might need to be changed. If employees feel that QC is just a way for management to eliminate their jobs, they may resist this intervention. If so, simply providing new KSAs will not be enough. Work group norms (i.e., attitudes) will need to be changed to be consistent with QC objectives. At the organizational level, reward and appraisal systems would need to reflect the desired performance outcomes and work procedures. If the focus of the old appraisal system was quantity and it remained so, employees would not be likely to sacrifice quantity for quality. Change in the appraisal system to reflect the importance of quality would need to be made. The point is that the components of the organization (structure and design, jobs and employees) are interdependent, and changes in one need to be addressed as part of the overall change effort. The training needs analysis process (chapter 4) provides a model for determining not only what training is needed, but also what other changes are necessary to support the training.

Another important point is that most change carries with it the need for changing employee attitudes. This is the central focus in overcoming resistance to change. It is most effectively accomplished through involving employees in the change process and through education and training. Involving employees develops commitment to the change for several reasons:

- They are intimately familiar with the current system and can make valuable contributions to the change effort, increasing its chances of success.
- They become knowledgeable about what will happen as a result of the change (reducing fear of the unknown).
- They are acting in a way that is supportive of the change by being part of the process, and their beliefs about the change become more positive.

Educating employees about the need for change also affects attitudes by allowing the employee to understand the consequences of not changing and the benefits that change can bring. Training allows employees to develop the knowledge and skills to be successful under the new conditions. Training in Action 2.3 provides an illustration of why change management must deal with all three levels.

TRAINING AND OD

Using the principles of change management inherent in OD allows strategic plans to be implemented more effectively. Since training also focuses on change, the principles are applicable to training efforts as well. By including an analysis of organizational problems as an integral part of the training needs analysis, the organization ends up not only with training programs that address critical competencies but also an increased awareness of what problems need to be solved by other means. Trainers can also use organizational information to design better programs so that potential appli-

---

Training in Action 2.3

Self-Managed Work Groups at the Ypsilanti Ford Plant

The Ypsilanti Ford plant is part of the Ford automotive parts manufacturing system. In 1987 the plant was divided into three manufacturing areas (Areas A, B, and C). The Area B manager, after some initial research, decided to install self-managed work groups (SMWG). An outside consultant was brought in to assist in the change. The following activities were carried out in the order presented:

1. A steering committee was formed consisting of the UAW plant bargaining committee chairman, two other UAW representatives, the area manager, the plant industrial relations manager, two area superintendents, and the consultant. This group developed and managed the change process.

2. An analysis of Area B employees, supervisors, and productions systems was conducted to identify areas for piloting the SMWG concept. Three production processes were selected on the basis of employee and supervisor interest and on the ability of the production process to create natural groupings of employees. Although the way work was assigned in the team concept would change, the equipment would remain the same.

3. Training as described below was provided, with length indicated in parentheses.

   - General orientation to self-managed work groups was provided to all employees in Area B. This included an overview of the changes that would occur in the pilot groups, the process of determining how those changes would occur, the role of staff support functions (e.g., engineering, accounting, etc.), and a question-and-answer period. (2 hours)

   - Supervisors and line employees in the SMWGs were provided with the following:

     - A more in-depth orientation, including the goals, roles, and expectations for the SMWGs and the salaried coordinator (formerly supervisor). In addition each SMWG developed a team mission and set team goals. (4 hours)

     - Basic team skills: interpersonal communication, interpersonal relations, conflict management, and problem solving. (16 hours)

     - Team building training for each group. This consisted of both instruction and trainer-facilitated application. After each component of training (e.g., development and assignment of roles) the team would apply that area to themselves. For example, after presentation of the team procedures material, the team would develop an "operating plan" for their work group describing how work would be assigned, how team meetings would be conducted, how coordination between shifts would occur, etc. (20 hours)

     - Training in information management, group facilitation, meeting management, and stress management, to prepare supervisors for their new roles as salaried coordinators. Time was also provided for them to identify problems in carrying out their new roles and to develop potential solutions. (8 hours)

     - Ongoing consultation for SMWGs and salaried coordinators for a year after completion of the training.

This applied example demonstrates elements of effective change management at the group and individual level. However there were problems at the organizational level.

Group Level: All SMWGs had been informed of why the change was desirable, understood what the change would mean to them personally, and what would be the benefits to Area B and the plant. They had representatives on the steering committee (line employees had UAW representatives and supervisors had their management), so their voices could be heard. Each work group helped to shape the way the change was implemented in their group by developing the team mission statement, goals, operating procedures, and so on.

Individual Level: Prior to implementation each individual had a choice of remaining in the work group or moving to a different work group in the plant. Only a few individuals chose to leave their work groups. Extensive training provided each individual with the KSAs needed to be successful in the SMWG concept.

Organizational Level: This effort ran into problems in two areas. First, no changes were made in the performance appraisal system, so salaried coordinators were still evaluated on the criteria used for supervisors. Thus coordinators began reverting to their old supervisory behaviors, telling SMWGs what to do rather than helping the groups learn what to do. Second, no changes were made in support systems such as engineering and accounting. Accounting would not furnish the SMWGs with cost and operating efficiency information in a form they could understand. Without this the SMWGs were unable to determine if they were meeting their goals. Equally troublesome was the relationship with engineering. Engineers were used to coming into an area and telling the employees what was wrong and how to fix it. The new system required them to work with the SMWG to determine both the problem and the solution. Engineers saw this as a waste of their time, since they already knew what to do. As a consequence, engineers would frequently not show up at SMWG meetings or would dominate the meeting. Since engineering didn't report to the area manager, he had little control over how the engineers interacted with the SMWGs.

These problems could have been prevented if organizational systems had been addressed as a part of the steering committee's change management plan. The plant manager needed to be a part of the steering committee, because he was the only one with authority to make systemwide changes.

cation problems are included in the training rather than becoming surprises after training has begun.

In spite of the seemingly obvious advantages of collaboration between OD and training professionals, a gulf sometimes seems to separate the two. An article in *Training* (Rossett 1996) gives the following examples:

- An executive complains that his training and OD people can't seem to work together.

- A training staff complains at length about a manager they consider unreasonable, attributing her faults to her background in OD.
- A training staff objects strongly when told that training needs analysis data could be used to identify performance problem solutions other than training.

One of the reasons for conflict between OD and training professionals lies in their perceived role and power base. OD practitioners are typically strategic, and executives are usually their clients. Trainers are typically tactical, and their clients are lower in the hierarchy. It is the nature of the OD practice to challenge assumptions underlying organizational practices. Trainers typically take organizational practices as givens and try to make people more effective within those practices. For example, suppose the needs analysis data show that the problems in a work unit are due to its manager acting inconsistently and arbitrarily. More OD professionals than training professionals would be willing to be guided by the data and confront the manager. Training professionals may be willing to say that there were no employee training needs identified, but less likely to tell the manager that it is his behavior that needs to change. OD professionals, however, are much more likely to get tagged with the "analysis paralysis" label than trainers, who are seen as "doers." Yet despite these stereotypes, there are so many connections between the two fields that one wonders why such divisions exist.

Why Trainers Need OD Competencies

Trainers can benefit from using OD if only because its planning procedures help to clarify what is needed in a given organizational situation. We believe that training programs will benefit from the application of many elements from the field of OD. OD's emphasis on participative approaches to problem solving suggests that training is better when trainees have an active role in the selection of their training opportunities and in the training itself. When involved in the planning stages, they are less likely to demonstrate resistance. This learner-focused orientation opens the communication channels and results in higher levels of motivation during the training program. A participative orientation also ties line managers directly to the training process by involving them in assessing their employees' needs, developing the training, and developing support systems for applying the training back on the job.

In the training needs analysis and training design chapters we emphasize an open-systems approach. The needs analysis chapter focuses on understanding training needs in the context of organizational systems. The design chapter emphasizes connections between the training program and other organizational systems. These connections help to ensure transfer of the training to the job. Furthermore, connecting the training to these other systems legitimizes it. Many trainers have entered the field on the strength of their platform skills, but those skills are not sufficient to develop effective training or provide enriching experiences for the trainees. Many trainers have told us of their frustrations when trainees were excited about what they learned but at the conclusion of training nothing had changed.

OD can also help trainers enrich their own jobs. If they view themselves as part of an assembly line in which they are simply putting on one piece of the product, they will not see how their work relates to the final product. OD suggests that trainers need to understand why the training has been developed, what the trainees are expected to do back on the job, and the obstacles they will face when trying to apply the training. When they understand the organizational context, having full knowledge of how what they do affects the desired outcomes, their job becomes more meaningful.

Why OD Professionals Need Training Competencies

Over the last several decades OD has been generally successful, but it has experienced some glaring failures (Golembiewski, Proehl, and Sink 1982; Nicholas 1982), many of which could have been avoided with a well-designed and -implemented training program. Earlier we identified the types of training required as a prerequisite or supplement to various OD techniques. OD interventions nearly always involve groups of employees in structured activities such as planning, problem solving, and intergroup conflict management. It is naive to assume that one can bring people together in new relationships to solve new problems, in a new situation with a new process, without prior training. These employees need to (1) have a common knowledge and skill base in these areas, (2) understand group dynamics and be skilled in working in groups, and (3) understand and be skilled at using a common problem-solving model.

If OD practitioners are not skilled in designing and implementing training programs, they must develop collaborative relationships with trainers who are. Doing so can provide an excellent opportunity for involving internal training resources in the change efforts and is especially helpful when an OD consultant has been retained from outside the organization. However, the external change agent must be familiar with good training practice. When these two areas work together in a collaborative fashion, they will go a long way toward defusing any conflict between external consultants and the HR function.

If OD is to be a long-term effort, the change must be institutionalized into the way the company does business. One study found that only about a third of the OD efforts examined lasted more than five years (Goodman and Dean 1983). This study suggested, and we agree, that training is a critical component to institutionalizing the change. Three situations are identified as key times for training:

1. When the OD process is started, training is needed to provide education about the change process and to provide the necessary KSAs.
2. After the process has been in place for a while, some retraining or upgrading of KSAs is required to sustain the process.
3. As new employees enter the organization, they need an understanding of the process and the KSAs.

While most organizations provide the initial training, few conduct follow-up training or modify their new employee training to include the new process and the related KSAs.

Integrating Training and OD

While it is true that trainers and OD professionals have legitimate differences in the nature of the change they are responsible for, their interests are intimately connected, and each can provide valuable service to the other. Nonetheless, as we have seen, they often are at odds with each other. One analysis (Rossett 1996) suggests the division between them occurs because companies typically organize around their different functional activities and OD and HRD departments are often separated. This separation increases the differences in perspective, role, value of services, clients, and so on. An obvious solution, then, is to house them together in something like a Performance Improvement Department within HR. This is a classic example of an organizational change effort requiring attention to the critical change management issues. For example, such a department would need to have different measures of success than either currently has. It could be measured by its contribution to business results rather than the number of bodies passing through training courses or the number of teams built and facilitated by OD staff. This overarching goal would require trainers to identify system deficiencies that are likely to interfere with training and ODers to identify KSA deficiencies that are likely to interfere with system changes.

Companies such as Anderson Consulting—Education, AT&T Universal Card Service, and the United States Coast Guard have made these changes and improved their business operations (Rossett 1996). These companies have found that integrating OD and training activities requires sponsorship from the top HR and other executives. One way toward full-scale integration of these activities is to develop pilot collaborations focusing on a particular business problem. This approach allows staff from each discipline to learn more about how the other operates and where the synergy exists. In addition, the HR executive needs to encourage people in both disciplines to learn as much as possible about the other. Another process that should lead to better integration of training and OD activities is having the staff in both areas work together to identify barriers to collaboration and identify ways to remove the barriers. This activity not only creates familiarity but also uses the OD principle of involving those affected by the change in the change process. By integrating the two activities, the organization also receives the potential benefit of cross-functional training, increasing the KSAs of both groups.

Key Terms

- Competitive strategy
- Core technology
- Cost Leader
- Decision autonomy
- Division of labor
- Environmental uncertainty
- Environmental complexity
- Environmental stability
- External environment
- Force-field analysis
- HR strategy
- HRD strategies
- Internal strategies
- Learning organization
- Levels of internal change
- Market Follower

- Market Leader
- Mechanistic design
- Mission
- Nonroutine technology
- Organic design
- Organizational confrontation meeting
- Organizational development (OD)
- Organizational strategy
- Organization structure
- Proactive strategy
- Reactive strategy
- Resistance to change
- Routine technology
- Strategic planning
- Survey feedback
- Tactical activities

Case Analysis

The first part of this case was presented at the beginning of the chapter (page 31). The following reflects HR's response to Mr. Field's directive.

MULTISTATE HEALTH CORPORATION: HR Follow-up to Strategic Planning

MCH had determined that it needed to address the human resource implications of the new climate in health care and that some type of planning system was in order, so it hired an outside consulting firm. The consultants agreed that some type of system would likely be appropriate, but they were not ready to stipulate what that system would look like. They conducted some initial diagnostic interviews, lasting one to two hours, with all of the divisional CEOs, the regional EVPs, the corporate CEO, and the corporate vice presidents, including the VP of human resources and the VP of organizational development. The interview format is shown in Exhibit 2.3.

EXHIBIT 2.3

Agenda and Clarification of Issues for HRPS

I. What is the purpose of this meeting?

To enhance and develop the objectives of the Human Resource Planning System (HRPS).

II. What is HRPS?

HRPS is a business planning system designed to provide quality data to enhance individual and organizational decision making in all aspects of human resource management.

III. Why was I asked to participate in this meeting?

As you are a key decision maker, we want to ensure that HRPS fits the needs of your organization.

IV. What specific information should I provide?

We want your input regarding the following:

1. Should administrative access to the data in HRPS be local, regional, or only at the corporate level?
2. Who in your organization would use and benefit most from this system?
3. What, if any, problems are there with current information used in human resource management decisions (i.e., recruiting, training, appraising, etc.)? For example, do you lack information as to which people are capable successors for certain jobs, and/or do you know what recruiting sources produce the best employees?
4. What values of the corporation should be incorporated into HRPS? How might these values be incorporated?
5. As you see it, ideally what job responsibilities will change in your organization as a result of HRPS?

The following information was obtained from the interviews.

The current HR activities conducted at the corporate level are:

1. To collect and store résumé-type information for all employees. This information includes demographic data, employment history, and performance evaluations.
2. To select divisional CEOs, regional EVPs, corporate officers, and staff professionals, and to give assistance at the regional and divisional levels for selection of management-level employees. This is accomplished primarily through posting the position and through word-of-mouth about who is competent and available.
3. To sponsor occasional management development programs at the corporate level, although no system is in place to determine whether these are perceived as valuable or necessary. Most management development is done externally with tuition reimbursement, and some is done by individual divisions.

The interviewees expressed varying degrees of dissatisfaction with the following:

1. No system for comparing internal candidates for positions. Performance evaluation is decentralized.
2. No system for making known the criteria for positions. People do not respond to posted openings, because rejection is a block to future promotion. Recommendation from a higher-up is known to be necessary. A related complaint was that many CEOs will not recommend their best people, either because they rely on them or because the bright young people might eventually be competition.
3. No system for evaluating the KSA required of a CEO in one part of the corporation compared to that of another. For example, the CEO in Grand Rapids has different responsibilities compared to a CEO in Detroit, but no one at corporate knows what the differences are.
4. No corporate human resource philosophy/strategy that would guide the organization in its HR activities.

Individuals at the corporate, regional, and divisional level had slightly different perceptions of the priority of needs for a human resource planning system (HRPS). See Exhibit 2.4.

Exhibit 2.4

Rank Order of Top HRPS Objectives by Organizational Level

Organizational Level	Improve Selection/ Search Process	Develop a Succession Plan	Forecast Critical Human Resource Skills	Develop Critical Human Resource Skills	Create and Utilize Career Development
Corporate	2	4	3	5	1
Regional	1	3	4	5	2
Divisional	1	5	4	3	2

Although monitoring equal employment and affirmative action is in the company's mission statement, it was considered important by only one respondent. The various levels disagreed on what job classifications should be in the HRPS: Corporate and regional personnel preferred to include only executive-level personnel, and divisional personnel wanted to include data down to the first-level supervisor. As an interviewee stated, "The MHC value statement says that we respect the dignity of all individuals. To exclude people below the executive level tells them they are worth less." On the issue of control and administration of the HRPS, corporate and regional executives preferred corporate- or regional-level administration, while divisional executives had a strong preference for direct access. Some expressed concern that corporate administration would reduce divisional autonomy in human resource decision making. The degree of centralization had been a sore point for several years. The divisions had always operated individually as profit centers, but corporate headquarters had increasingly been discussing the need for a more integrated approach.

After reviewing the consultants' report and meeting with the consultants, the Executive Committee (representing the three levels of management) arrived at consensus on the following HRPS objectives:

1. Improve the selection/search process for filling vacant positions.
2. Develop a succession plan.
3. Forecast critical skill/knowledge and ability needs.
4. Identify critical skill/knowledge and ability deficiencies.
5. Identify equal employment and affirmative action concerns.
6. Create a career development system that reflects the organizational mission.

The following HR philosophy was developed and was then approved by the Board of Directors of MHC:

As an employer committed to the value of human life and the dignity of each individual, we seek to foster justice, understanding, and a unity of purpose created by people and organizations working together to achieve a common goal. Therefore, we commit ourselves to the following beliefs:

1. People are our most important resource.
2. The human resource needs of the organization are best met through the development of employees to their maximum potential.
3. Justice in the workplace is embodied in honest, fair, and equitable employment and personnel practices with priority given to the correction of past social injustices.

CASE QUESTIONS

1. How would you characterize the fit between MHC's environment, competitive strategy, structure, and technology? Indicate any issues with this fit that might influence the success of the strategy.
2. How could HRD have influenced the shaping of the competitive strategy?

3. In what ways will OD and training have to collaborate to maximize the effectiveness of the strategy? What forces are currently operating that drive or act to restrain the new strategy? Which of those need to change?

4. Given the strategy, how can HR support the strategy? What type of structure should the corporate HR function adopt to match the competitive strategy?

5. Given the facts of the case, what would you suggest as an HRD strategy? Provide specific tactics that can be used by HRD to support the competitive strategy.

6. What sources of support and resistance are likely to exist in creating and implementing the new HRPS? What tactics could be used to reduce or eliminate the resistance?

Exercises

1. Conduct an environmental analysis of HRD's environment at the company you work for (if you're going to school and don't work, use the school's environment). What are the opportunities and threats to HRD in that environment? What demands is the environment making on the HRD department?

2. Form groups of three to five people, one of them having been provided with training by their employer within the last two years. Have this person explain the company's mission to the rest of the group. Then have the person describe the type of training he or she received. The group's task is to try to determine the linkage between the training and the mission.

3. Identify two organizations that have different environments and core technologies. Describe what these differences are. Indicate how the HRD strategies of these companies might be similar or different. Provide a rationale for your conclusions.

Questions for Review

1. What factors might inhibit HRD managers from developing a strategic planning approach to training? How might these factors be overcome?

2. Think of possible strategic training alternatives other than those described in the text. Under what conditions would these be important in developing a training strategy?

3. Identify (through personal knowledge or research) an organization that has utilized HRD as a part of their competitive strategy. What role does HRD play in their strategy and how is HRD involved in the implementation of the strategy?

References

AACSB (American Assembly of Collegiate Schools of Business). 1987. *Outcome Measurement Project, Phase III.* St. Louis: AACSB.

Ackelsberg, R., and P. Arlow. 1985. Small businesses do plan and it pays off. *Long Range Planning* 18:61–66.

Benson, R., and R. Sherman. 1995. A practical step-by-step approach. *Quality Progress,* October, pp. 75–8.

Bible, R. 1996. Implementing ISO has made us better. *Industrial Distribution,* April, p. 128.

Bower, J. 1982. Business policy in the 80's. *Academy of Management Review* 7:630–38.

Bracker, J., B. Keats, and J. Pearson. 1988. Planning and financial performance among small firms in a growth industry. *Strategic Management Journal* 9:591–603.

Buchele, R. 1967. *Business Policy in Growing Firms.* San Fransisco: Chandler.

Burns, T., and G. Stalker. 1961. *The Management of Innovation.* London: Tavistock.

Carnevale, A., L. Gainer, and J. Villet. 1990. *Training in America.* San Francisco: Jossey-Bass.

Chandler, A. 1962. *Strategy and Structure.* Cambridge: MIT Press.

David, F., J. Pearce, and W. Randolf. 1989. Linking technology and structure to enhance group performance. *Journal of Applied Psychology,* April, pp. 233–41.

DeVito, J. 1996. The learning organization. *The ASTD Training and Development Handbook.* 4th ed., pp. 77–103.

Dowling, M., W. Boulton, and S. Elliot. 1994. Strategies for change in the service sector: The global telecommunications industry. *California Management Review,* 36(3):57–88.

Duncan, B. 1972. Characteristics of organizational environments and perceived uncertainty. *Administrative Science Quarterly* 17(3).

Garvin, D. 1993. Building a learning organization. *Harvard Business Review,* July–August.

Gerber, B. 1987. It's a whole new ball game at BC Tel. *Training,* no. 24:75-81.

Gilmore, F. 1971. Formulating strategy in smaller companies. *Harvard Business Review* 49:71–81.

Golembiewski, R., C. Proehl, and D. Sink. 1982. Estimating the success of OD applications. *Training and Development Journal,* April, pp. 86-95.

Goodman, P., and J. Dean. 1983. Why productivity efforts fail. In *Organizational Development: Theory, Practice, and Research,* edited by W. French, C. Bell, and R. Zawacki. Plano, TX: Business Publications.

Gutpa, A., and V. Govindarajan. 1984. Business unit strategy, managerial characteristics, and business unit effectiveness at strategy implementation. *Academy of Management Journal* 27:25–41.

Howard, A. 1986. College experiences and managerial performance. *Journal of Applied Psychology Monographs* 71(3):530–52.

Jackson, S., R. Schuler, and J. C. Rivero. 1989. Organizational characteristics as predictors of personnel practices. *Personnel Psychology* 42: 727-86.

Jamison, D. 1981. The importance of an integrative approach to strategic management research. *Academy of Management Review* 6: 601–8.

Kargar, J., and R. Blumenthal. 1994. Successful implementation of strategic decisions in small community banks. *Journal of Small Business Management,* April, pp. 10–21.

Lang, J., R. Calantone, and D. Gudmundson. 1997. Small firm information seeking as a response to environmental threats and opportunities. *Journal of Small Business Management,* January, pp. 11–21.

Lee, C. 1988. Where does training belong? *Training* 25:53–60.

Lewin, K. 1969. Quasi-stationary social equilibrium and the problem of permanent changes. In *The Planning of Change,* edited by W. Bennis, D. Benne, and R. Chin. New York: Holt, Rinehart and Winston.

Marquardt, M., and A. Reynolds. 1994. *Global Learning Organization.* New York: Irwin.

McDonough III, E., and R. Leifer. 1983. Using simultaneous structures to cope with uncertainty. *Academy of Management Journal,* December 727–35.

McGill, M., and J. Slocum. 1993. Unlearning the organization. *Organizational Dynamics,* vol 22, Autumn 67–79.

Miles, R., and C. Snow. 1978. *Organizational Strategy, Structure and Process.* New York: McGraw-Hill.

Miller, D. 1987. The structural and environmental correlates of business strategy. *Strategic Management Journal,* Jan.–Feb., pp. 55–76.

Mintzberg, H. 1979. *The Structuring of Organizations.* Upper Saddle River, NJ: Prentice Hall, pp. 272–85.

———. 1987. Crafting Strategy. *Harvard Business Review,* July–August.

Nevis, E., A. DiBella, and J. Gould. 1995. Understanding organizations as learning systems. *Sloan Management Review* 36(2):73–85.

Nicholas, J. 1982. The comparative impact of organizational development interventions on hard criteria measures. *Academy of Management Review,* October, pp. 531–42.

O'Neal, H., and J. Duker. 1986. Survival and failure in small businesses. *Journal of Small Business Management,* January, pp. 30–37.

Ozone House, Inc. 1995. *Strategic Plan.* Ypsilanti, MI.

Perrow, C. 1970. *Organizational Analysis: A Sociological View.* Belmont, CA: Wadsworth.

Porter, L. W., and L. E. McKibbin. 1988. *Management Education and Development: Drift or Thrust into the Twenty-First Century.* St. Louis: AACSB.

Porter, M. 1980. *Competitive Strategy: Techniques for Analyzing Industries and Competitors.* New York: Free Press.

Rossett, A. 1996. Training and organizational development: Separated at birth? *Training,* April, pp. 53–59.

Schuler, R, and S. Jackson. 1987. Linking competitive strategies with human resource management practices. *Academy of Management Executive* 1(3): 207–19.

Senge, P. 1990. *The Fifth Discipline.* New York: Doubleday Currency.

Senge, P., C. Roberts, R. Ross, B. Smith, and A. Kliener. 1994. *The Fifth Discipline Fieldbook.* New York: Doubleday Currency.

Shaw, R., and D. Perkins. 1991. Teaching organizations to learn. *Organizational Development Journal,* Winter: 1–12.

Stone, N. 1991. Does business have any business in education? *Harvard Business Review* 69(2): 46–62.

Thompson, J. D. 1967. *Organization in Action.* New York: McGraw-Hill.

Tichey, N. 1983. *Managing Strategic Change: Technical, Political and Cultural Dynamics.* New York: Wiley.

Tichey, N., C. Fombrun, and M. Devanna. 1982. Strategic human resource management. *Sloan Management Review* 22:47–60.

Tovar, R., A. Rossett, and N. Carter. 1989. Centralized training in a decentralized organization. *Training and Development Journal* 43: 62–65.

Wheelen, T., and J. Hunger. 1995. *Strategic Management and Business Policy.* New York: Addison-Wesley.

Whetten, D. A., and K. S. Cameron. 1995. *Developing managerial skills.* New York: HarperCollins.

Williamson, D. 1997. ISO rating: The sign of the times. *Windsor Star,* July 16, p. F1.

Woodward, J. 1965. *Industrial Organization: Theory and Practice.* London: Oxford University.

Yoder, S. 1991. A 1990 reorganization at Hewlett-Packard already is paying off. *Wall Street Journal,* July 22: AI, AID.

CHAPTER 3

Learning, Motivation, and Performance

Learning Objectives

After reading this chapter, you should be able to:

- Identify the major factors determining human performance and their relevance to training

- Explain what motivates people and describe the factors influencing motivation

- Describe the cognitive and behavioral approaches to learning and their contradictory implications for instructional practices

- Describe different types of learning and how they relate to one another

- Identify a learning theory that integrates cognitive and behaviorist perspectives and describe how its processes and components relate to training

- Describe the causes for resistance to learning

- Explain why different people need different training methods to learn the same things

- Identify the characteristics of training design that motivate learning and accommodate trainee differences

The Wilderness Training Lab

Claudia, a successful 33-year-old corporate marketing executive, found herself in the mountains of New Mexico preparing to climb a rope ladder attached to a tree. When she reached the top of the ladder, she would fall off backwards. It wouldn't be an accident. No, she wasn't suicidal or deranged. She was participating in an executive development program called Wilderness Training Lab.

At the corporate office in Michigan, she was known as an independent, smart, and tenacious businesswoman. She had moved quickly up the corporate ladder from product research assistant to brand manager. Claudia had a reputation for micromanaging her subordinates and being a loner. When asked about these issues, Claudia replied:

"When I was in college, I had a lot of group projects. At first I went along with group decisions and trusted others to do a good job, even though I felt anxious about putting my grade in the hands of someone else. It seemed to be a good way to get along in the group. Those projects received mediocre grades, and I'm only satisfied with being the best. Then I started to take over the leadership of every group I was in. I developed the plan, decided who would do what and what the time lines were, and always took on the most difficult and complex parts myself, all the time making sure the others were doing what they were assigned. From then on my group projects always got an "A." I carried those lessons with me into the work place and I've had good success here too. Maybe it rubs some people the wrong way, but it works for me. The only trouble I'm having is keeping up with all my projects. Some of the other brand managers want to work with me on joint projects, but I don't have time. Besides, they probably just want me to do their work for them or steal my ideas. The VP of marketing will be retiring soon and only one of the seven brand managers will get that job. What's in it for me if I collaborate with them? Let each of us sink or swim on our own merits."

A few months ago, the VP of marketing, Sandy Cines, sat down with Claudia to discuss career plans. Sandy had always praised and encouraged Claudia's work, but this time he was a little reserved. He suggested, in rather strong terms, that she attend a Wilderness Executive Development Program. Claudia hesitated, because of her workload and upcoming deadlines. Sandy said, "Well, I'll leave the decision up to you. The director of training and I have looked at your strengths and what you'll need for the next level as an executive. Technically you're very strong, but more important at the next level is building good interpersonal relationships. The training director recommended this program for you. But, as I said, I'll leave the decision up to you."

Claudia wondered what he thought was wrong with her interpersonal relationships. She had great relationships with customers, with outside vendors, and in her personal life. Relationships with her subordinates and peers had to be different. She had to be firmer and less flexible with them, didn't she? She didn't think she had bad relationships with her subordinates or peers. They never complained to her. However, Claudia decided it was pretty clear that Sandy wanted her to attend the Wilderness program.

In New Mexico she found a diverse group of men and women executives from all around the United States. Many confided that they had been sent by their organizations to "learn how to be more effective in groups." Most of them indicated they were interested and eager, but a little nervous about what was expected of them. They soon found out. They were divided into groups of ten and taken out on the "course."

The first training exercise was climbing the "trust ladder." Doug, the program director, explained that the group members would have to rely on each other quite a bit during the coming week. To demonstrate that the group could be trusted, each person was to climb to the top of the ladder and fall backward into the group, who would catch the person in a proper manner. Doug showed them how. After everyone had completed the exercise, they discussed risk taking, building and trusting one's support systems, being part of a support system, and communicating one's needs.

Then came more challenging exercises: building and using rope bridges to cross a stream, white-water rafting, and—the most physically challenging of all—scaling a 13-foot wall. The front of the wall was sheer and smooth. On the other side was a platform on which two people could stand at about waist level with the top of the wall, and from which extended a ladder to the ground. Everyone had to scale the wall and no one could stand on the platform until he or she had scaled the wall. The event was timed, and the groups were in competition with each other. The first thing a group had to do was develop a plan. Strong and tall people were needed to boost the others to a point where they could pull themselves over. Some had to stand on the platform and help those who were not strong enough to pull themselves over. It was clear the first people over also had to be strong. Another problem was the last person over. Everyone except the last pair would have "spotters" in case of a fall and also the last person would have no one left to boost him or her to the top. Someone would have to act as a human rope, hanging down from the top so the last person could climb up him and over the wall. Therefore the last person would have to be light but strong enough to boost the second-to-last person up and to climb over the human rope.

In order to determine the order, the group members needed to share with one another their strengths and weaknesses. Claudia wanted to be the last person so she could make sure everyone was doing what they were supposed to, and also because, as the last person over the wall, she would represent the group's successful completion of this exercise. Two of the strongest men in the group confessed to having injuries that would hamper them. Claudia realized that her tennis elbow would be a great liability. When it came to her turn to discuss her strengths and weaknesses, she was honest about her injury and indicated she would fit best somewhere in the middle where there were many people to help her.

When Claudia's turn to climb came, she called out to those on top what to expect—where she couldn't put much strain, and how she would indicate that someone was pulling too hard. Then she was being pushed up with spotters all around her, and the next thing she knew she was over the wall.

Later, when the members discussed the event, Claudia asked what impact her limitations had caused the group. Those who had been pullers replied "None." They said that because she told them about her problem ahead of time, they knew what they had to do to adjust to it.

While getting packed to go home, Claudia thought about how much she had learned about herself and her relationship to other people, especially at work. She recognized that she had not trusted others to do their part and so she was not being as effective as she could have been. Her success had been at a very high price to herself because of the extra workload she imposed on herself. In addition, she wondered, "What was the price paid by my subordinates? How have my actions affected their attitudes and performance? Do I need to be so competitive with my peers? Is that really in my or my company's best interests?" She knew she would have a lot to think about on the trip home.

A Few Words about Theory

Theories are speculative road maps for how things work. In fact, most of us develop our own theories to explain how the world around us works. "Good" theories assemble a number of facts, show the relationship among those facts, and develop a logical rationale for what is likely to be true, given those facts. From theory, predictions or hypotheses can be generated and tested. If the tests show the predictions are correct, the theory is supported. If the new facts are inconsistent with the predictions, the theory must be revised or discarded. This process of developing, testing, and reformulating theory is the basis of science. It is how new knowledge is created. Because a good theory explains facts in as simple a manner as possible and predicts future events, it provides practical applications. It also suggests what can be done to change a situation or to prevent undesirable things from happening.

Thus theories are abstractions that allow us to make sense out of a large number of facts related to an issue. Effective training practices have been developed from theories and theoretical constructs that describe how learning occurs, how and what motivates people, and what influences their behavior. This chapter addresses those models, concepts, and issues and thus is necessarily somewhat abstract. Unfortunately, some people may see little value in wading through the frequently complex logic and rationale of theories. Perhaps if one were going to follow a set of instructions, like a recipe, it would be possible to ignore theory. Unfortunately, in training, as in business, a single recipe won't work the same way for everyone in every situation. Each organization is unique, with different missions, strategies, environments, technologies, and people. The interaction of these elements creates a different "chemistry" in each organization, making a "one best way for everyone" approach impossible. Recipes require standardized ingredients—businesses don't have them. Theories, however, provide the guidelines, principles, and predictions that allow organizations to navigate through different environmental conditions. Successful people in business pay attention to theory.

Firms in all industries from manufacturing to telecommunications, from energy production to health care (e.g., Ford, 3-M, Microsoft, Motorola, Toshiba, Toyota, and Xerox), have jumped ahead of the competition because they have understood and applied theories. Some of these theories have to do with the product, others with how the product is made, and others with how the firm is managed. Rather than copying others, these companies understood the underlying theories related to what they were trying to do and applied them to their goals. As the quality guru W. E. Deming (1986) indicated, experience teaches nothing without theory. He warns that unless you understand the theory behind someone's success, copying can lead to chaos (Dobyns and Crawford-Mason 1991). Supporting this view is a survey of Fortune 1000 companies engaged in programs to improve quality (e.g., TQM, ISO 9000) and involve employees in decision making. The companies that applied the underlying models and theories correctly were getting the best results; those that simply put programs into place were getting the worst results (Lawler, Mohrman, and Ledford 1995).

Let's consider this discussion in regard to HR systems. Suppose you know of a company that pays its employees on the basis of how much they produce (i.e., a piece-rate system). The company is very successful and the employees make a high wage. Therefore you decide to institute the piece-rate system in your company. Will it work? It might, but it might not. Its success will depend on your total reward system, what you are trying to accomplish, and what your employees value. For example, your employees may turn out a high volume of the product but at the cost of many problems with quality. Consider also social pressures in the workplace. Piece-rate systems often create a "norm" in the work group that prohibits them from producing more than a specified amount (to avoid increases in the product/money ratio or to protect slower workers). In other words, the success of the piece-rate system is affected by the differences in the people and work environments.

Once you understand motivational theory, you can see that in improving employee performance levels, each organization must apply the principles of motivation to its unique circumstances. The same is true with training. Whether someone else's training program will work for you will depend on the needs of your company, your employees, and the training system you use. Copying without understanding is like taking someone else's prescription drugs. Even though they may have made someone else better, they could kill you.

What theories are important to the success of the training enterprise? If trainees don't learn, training has failed. Thus theories of learning are important. If trainees learn but don't attempt to transfer the learning to the job, training has failed. This is a motivational issue. If the trainees learn and also attempt to transfer the learning to the job site, but obstacles in their work environment prevent them from making the transfer, training again has failed, in this case because it didn't take into consideration the changes in the work environment needed to support the desired behavior. Thus in order to design and implement effective training programs, you need to understand how people learn, what motivates learning and performance, and how the learning and work environment affects motivation and performance. That's what this chapter is about. The theories, models, and concepts discussed here serve as a foundation for the rest of the book. These theories and their implications for training will be referred to throughout the text, because they are related to each phase of the training process.

Understanding Motivation and Performance

An employee's *job performance*, or behavior in general, is a function of what he knows and believes (KSAs). If employees don't have the KSAs, they can't perform. However, additional factors are important in determining employee performance. A general model of performance is depicted in Figure 3.1. This model indicates that a person's performance depends on the interaction of the person's motivation, KSAs, and environment. *Motivation* arises from your needs and your beliefs about how best to satisfy those needs. Both motivation and KSAs are part of your memory and thinking systems (i.e., **cognitive structure**). **Environment** refers to the physical surroundings in which performance must occur. This includes barriers and aids to performance, as well as objects and events (cues) that you might see as indicating that your performance will be rewarded or punished.

Think back to the Wilderness Training case. What KSAs did Claudia have that allowed her to reach her current position? Her boss felt she lacked the interpersonal skills necessary for developing good relationships. Did she lack these skills or was she not motivated to use them? Apparently she had the skills, because she was able to develop good relationships with others she wasn't directly working with. The training director probably understood this fact, because he suggested the Wilderness Training rather than an interpersonal skill-building workshop. The Wilderness Training didn't teach people how to develop good interpersonal relationships as much as it broke down barriers that prevented those relationships from developing. The program worked on the motivation and attitudes of the trainees. Are there any barriers in Claudia's work environment to developing these relationships? How about the upcoming retirement of the VP and that open position? What criteria could be used in evaluating managers that would encourage them to develop positive relationships with peers and subordinates?

Each of the factors M, KSA, and E in Figure 3.1 can influence performance, but it is the combination of these factors that actually determines the person's performance. This means that the likelihood of engaging in any activity is limited by the weakest factor. For instance, no matter how knowledgeable or skilled you are, if you're not motivated to perform the activity—or worse, are motivated not to perform it—then you won't. If the environment doesn't support your engaging in the activity or prevents you from doing so, then it doesn't matter how motivated or knowledgeable you are—you won't do it. For example, if necessary tools, materials, or other equipment is

FIGURE 3.1 Factors Determining Human Performance

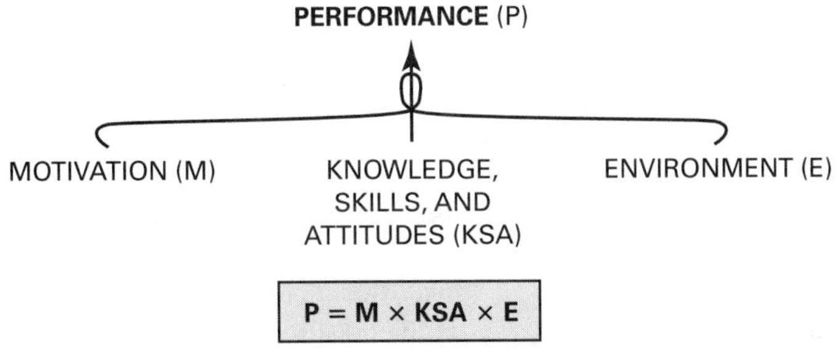

PERFORMANCE (P)

MOTIVATION (M)   KNOWLEDGE, SKILLS, AND ATTITUDES (KSA)   ENVIRONMENT (E)

$$P = M \times KSA \times E$$

broken or missing, you won't attempt the activity. Likewise, if the environment is sending signals that a certain type of performance will be punished, you won't perform. In Claudia's case, she seemed to want to stay at work and not attend the training. However, her boss gave strong indications that staying would be viewed negatively. Her environment had changed, signaling that old ways of performing wouldn't be rewarded and new ways would.

This model of performance is particularly important in determining employee training needs. It helps us understand whether poor job performance is due to KSAs or other factors. It is also very important in the design of training. When putting together the learning modules and training methods, the trainer must consider how they will affect the trainees' motivation to learn. Similarly, when selecting the training facility and materials, we must consider how they will interact with trainee motivation. When we ask trainees to use their new knowledge and skills back on the job, we must make sure the environment there is supportive of this new way of performing. A deeper understanding of the three determinants of performance will increase your ability to design and implement effective training programs. First we'll look at motivation, presenting the most prominent theories and clarifying their relationship to the training enterprise.

MOTIVATION: WHY DO THEY ACT LIKE THAT?

Motivation is part of a person's cognitive structure and is not directly observable. Thus it is typically defined in terms of its effects on behavior, which *is* observable. Most of the scientific literature defines **motivation** as the direction, persistence, and amount of effort expended by an individual to achieve a specified outcome. In other words, the person's motivation is reflected by what need she is trying to satisfy, the types of activity she does to satisfy the need, how long she keeps doing it, and how hard she works at it. Motivation is goal directed and is explained by both the needs that people have and the decision processes they use to satisfy those needs. Theories have evolved separately to describe the relationship between needs and motivation and between decision processes and motivation. **Needs theories** attempt to describe the types of needs people have, their relative importance and how they are related to each other. **Process theories** attempt to describe and explain how a person's needs are translated into actions to satisfy the needs.

Needs Theory

Our needs are the basis of our motivation, the reason for almost all of our activity. Understanding a person's needs helps you to understand his behavior. From earlier work by Maslow (1954, 1968), Clayton Alderfer (1969) developed a needs theory of motivation, called **ERG theory.** ERG is an acronym representing the three basic needs of the theory: existence, relatedness, and growth. **Existence needs** correspond to Maslow's lower-order physiological and security needs. These are the needs people have to sustain life—needs for food, shelter, and the like—as well as the need for some security about future ability to have a safe and healthy life. **Relatedness needs** are similar to Maslow's belonging and love needs. This area reflects people's need to be valued and accepted by others. Interpersonal relationships and group membership (work, family, friends, etc.) act to satisfy these needs. **Growth needs** combine Maslow's esteem and self-actualization needs. Needs in this domain include feelings of self-worth and competency and achieving one's potential. Recognition, accomplishment, challenging opportunities, and a feeling of fulfillment are outcomes that can satisfy these needs. While some disagreement exists in the scientific community about the relationships among these needs and their relative importance at any given point in life, there is little disagreement that these needs exist for everyone.

Because people work to satisfy their needs, understanding the types and strength of employee needs is important to the training process. It can help to identify some of the causes of poor performance and therefore determine training needs. Consider the employee who has strong relatedness needs but whose job is structured so that he must work alone most of the time. He may not be getting the required quality and quantity of work completed because he spends too much time socializing with others in the workplace. Additional technical KSAs will do little to improve his job performance. Some other type of training (perhaps time management) or some nontraining intervention (such as job redesign or counseling) would be more likely to result in performance improvement.

Understanding needs is also important in designing training programs and facilities. Trainers need to make sure that the environment and training methods—that is, how the training is conducted and where it takes place—meet the trainee's physical, relationship, and growth needs. We will discuss these issues in depth in the chapters covering training design, development, and implementation. To get a sense of how training methods, materials, and environment influence trainee motivation, think back to the Wilderness Training case.

Although Claudia was motivated to attend the training because of her boss's pressure, was she motivated to learn when she first arrived or was she skeptical about the value of the training? What if she had been given a series of lectures on the importance of developing strong interpersonal relationships instead of the outdoor group experiences? Would she have been as motivated to absorb the lessons and apply them to her work? How strong do you think Claudia's relatedness needs were? Do you think training that focused on showing her how changing her behavior would result in increased acceptance by her peers would be effective? It seems apparent that Claudia did have high growth needs. The outdoor training presented her with a series of physical and psychological challenges, fitting in with her growth needs and motivating her to become an involved participant in the training.

The few empirical studies that have been conducted tend to support Alderfer's notion that people can experience needs in all three areas simultaneously (Alderfer 1969; Schneider and Alderfer 1973). Which are more important depends on the relative satisfaction level in each area. Unsatisfied needs motivate us, and motivation decreases as needs in an area are satisfied. However, needs in these three basic areas tend to renew themselves, and needs in an area can expand. Though you may have a good job that provides you with food, shelter, and security, you can start to feel the need for better food, a larger and more comfortable home, a larger savings account or investment portfolio. Similarly, while your relationships with family, friends, and co-workers may at first satisfy your relatedness needs, you may begin to feel that you would like the relationships to be better or closer, or that you want to develop additional relationships.

Sometimes our needs may conflict with one another, or one type of need may become more important than the others. Then we feel we must choose one over the other. This is what happened with Claudia. We can't be sure how strong her relatedness needs are, but we do know that she saw them as conflicting with her ability to satisfy her growth needs at work. The wilderness training was designed to satisfy the trainees' needs for growth and relationships at the same time. Step by step the training demonstrated how building strong interpersonal relationships could not only satisfy relationship needs, but also make greater accomplishment possible.

This illustrates a central point about motivating trainees to learn. The best training incorporates opportunities to satisfy all three categories of needs. Existence needs are addressed, in part, through the training facility and accommodations. The trainees' physical comfort, level of hunger, and so on will make a difference in how much is learned. Demonstrating how the training will improve the trainee's competencies should also show how the learning can increase his security, another aspect of existence needs. Relatedness needs can be addressed through building a network of positive relationships among trainees and between trainees and the trainer. Growth needs can be addressed by using methods that provide challenging experiences that lead to the attainment of the target KSAs. By making sure your training program addresses all three categories of needs, you will go a long way toward motivating all trainees, because you have something for everyone.

Need theory has implications for the training process even after training has been completed. Trainers need to make sure that the trainees are able to see the links between their learning and the satisfaction of their needs. In Claudia's case, her boss has provided some of that linkage by telling her how important relationship building is to her current and future job success (i.e., security needs). What could the trainers at the Wilderness Training Lab have done to create these links? We will discuss this more in the next section, because these links are the focus of the process theories.

Process Theories

Needs are only part of the motivation equation. The other part is the process of deciding how to go about satisfying those needs. Process theories of motivation describe how a person's needs get translated into action. Although there are many types of process theories, we will focus on the two that have the most direct implications for training: reinforcement theory and expectancy theory.

Reinforcement Theory—The Environment   *Reinforcement theory* is relatively simple on the surface but can be difficult to apply. Although it does not provide all the answers for how needs are translated into action, its major points are essential for understanding human behavior. The foundation for reinforcement theory comes from the work of E. L. Thorndike (1905, 1913, 1932). Thorndike's **law of effect** states that behavior followed by satisfying experiences tends to be repeated, and behavior followed by annoyance or dissatisfaction tends to be avoided. This principle was used by Skinner (1953, 1968) in developing the operant conditioning model and reinforcement theory.

Reinforcement theory is closely related to the operant conditioning theory of learning. In fact, it is difficult to discuss this theory without discussing learning, because reinforcement theory and operant learning theory are part of the same theoretical package. The basic components of learning in **operant conditioning** are illustrated in Figure 3.2. A person is faced with an object or event in the environment (stimulus) and behaves in a certain way (response). That behavior results in an outcome (conse-

Stimulus ⟶ **Response** ⟶ **Consequence**

FIGURE 3.2 Behaviorist
Model of Learning

quence) to the individual that is positive or negative. In the illustration the child sees
the pot with steam rising out of it on the stove (environmental stimulus). The child
reaches up to grab the pot (response). You can imagine the consequence. Thus, the environment provides both stimuli that elicit behavior and consequences that reinforce
or punish the behavior.

The consequences of past behavior have an effect on future behavior in similar
situations. What will the behavior of the child in Figure 3.2 be around stoves in the
near future? Skinner would say the child learned to avoid stoves. A person's motivation (i.e., direction, magnitude, and persistence of her behavior), then, is a function of
her reinforcement history. Unfortunately, reinforcement theory provides no explanation of the processes involved in storing, retrieving, or using the reinforcement history.
The model leaves us wondering *how* future behavior becomes influenced by previous
reinforcement history. Nevertheless, the theory does predict very well the various effects on future behavior caused by the consequences of past behavior.

Skinner identified four types of consequences that can result from behavior:
(1) positive reinforcement, (2) negative reinforcement, (3) punishment, and (4) extinction. When behavior results in either positive or negative reinforcement, the likelihood of that behavior occurring in similar circumstances in the future is increased.
Positive reinforcement occurs when the person's behavior results in something desirable happening to her—either tangible, such as receiving money, or psychological,
such as a feeling of pleasure, or some combination of the two. **Negative reinforcement**
occurs when the person's behavior results in removal of something she finds annoy-
ing, frustrating, or disliked. This valued outcome increases the likelihood of the behavior occurring in the future. For example, if you have a headache, you take an aspirin
and the headache goes away, the "aspirin-taking response" is negatively reinforced.
There is nothing inherently desirable about taking the aspirin; its reinforcing power

comes from its ability to remove the pain. Positive and negative reinforcement can be provided by some element in the environment or by the person himself. For example, when a person is paid for work he has done, the positive reinforcement (pay) is provided by the environment. When a person feels a sense of pride and accomplishment after completing a task, the person is positively reinforcing himself.

When your behavior results in something undesirable happening to you, the outcome is considered **punishment,** and it decreases the likelihood of the response occurring in the future. Like reinforcement, punishment can be tangible or psychological or both and can come from the environment or be self-administered. In Figure 3.2 the environment will provide the punishment. On the other hand, when we do things that violate our personal values and beliefs and therefore experience negative feelings, we are self-punishing that behavior. Punishment can be in the form of some damage, harm, or unpleasantness, or in losing something desirable. The latter form of punishment is called **extinction.** For example, you may have been buying books by a certain author because of the positive feelings you experienced as you read them. However, while reading the last two books by this author you didn't experience those positive feelings. Therefore, you stop buying this author's books. When the person's behavior (like buying and reading the books) no longer produces the desired outcomes, the behavior is less likely to occur in the future. Figure 3.3 depicts the various types of behavioral consequences.

These definitions can be confusing or misunderstood, so let's look at a couple of examples. First think back to the Wilderness Training Lab case. What kind of reinforcement history did Claudia have in doing work in groups? Her first group experiences in college resulted in the negative outcomes (for her) of mediocre grades. Because her cooperative behavior in groups was punished, she stopped it. When she changed her behavior to become more directive, monitoring and doing more of the important work, two consequences resulted: (1) she was positively reinforced by good grades; (2) she avoided the negative feelings of anxiety about having other group members not do their assignments well and the resulting mediocre grades. Her new group behavior was both positively and negatively reinforced over a number of years. It is no wonder then, that she continued to work in groups this way. Is it possible she avoided working in groups with her peers because she couldn't control those groups in the same way she could her subordinates? The training she received provided her with new group situations in which she was positively reinforced (e.g., recognition, accomplishment) for using a new set of group behaviors.

	DESIRABLE CONSEQUENCES	UNDESIRABLE CONSEQUENCES
TRAINEE RECEIVES	Behavior Positively Reinforced	Behavior Punished
TRAINEE LOSES	Behavior Punished (Extinction)	Behavior Negatively Reinforced

FIGURE 3.3 Types of Consequences That May Follow Behavior

In another example, suppose Jon, a machinist, after working for a few hours, suddenly hears a loud, unpleasant screeching noise coming from the exhaust fans near his work area. He finds the electrical switch and turns the fans off, then later switches them on again, after which they work for the rest of the day. The same thing happens the next two days. The fourth day, after the fans have been running for a few hours, when he takes his break he shuts them off before the noise begins. When he returns from his break, he turns them on and they operate normally for the rest of the day. This becomes a daily habit with Jon. What Jon doesn't know is that plant maintenance repaired the fan the evening before he began his "shutting it off at the break" behavior. Jon maintained this behavior because it was negatively reinforcing. By "giving the fans a rest," he avoided the loud, unpleasant noise. Because this worked every time, it was self-reinforcing. This is how many workplace habits and "superstitious behaviors" develop.

Reinforcement versus Punishment   Punishment reduces the future likelihood of a behavior. However, there are several problems that make it undesirable as a management or training tool.

- It doesn't motivate people to do things, only *not* to do things. It doesn't indicate what the desired behavior is, only what is not desired.
- If the undesired behavior is punished only sometimes, people will learn the situations in which they can get away with it. The saying "While the cat's away the mice will play" neatly captures one problem with this technique: It implies that punishment requires constant vigilance on the part of a supervisor and encourages efforts to "beat the system."
- If a person's undesired behavior is rewarding to him, the punishment must be severe enough to offset the behavior's reinforcing properties. Escalating negative outcomes to employees raises ethical, moral, and common-sense objections.
- Someone must do the punishing. This person becomes someone to be avoided.

Positive and negative reinforcement are better tools for motivating and especially training employees. Negative reinforcement can cause the desired behavior to become self-reinforcing, like Jon's turning off the fans. When the person continually performs the desired behavior (avoiding the undesired behavior), negative outcomes are avoided. If the desired behavior is then also positively reinforced, the person not only avoids the negative outcome but receives a positive outcome. As with Claudia in the opening case, the result is a very strong maintenance of the behavior.

With reinforcement, the person doing the reinforcing doesn't always have to be present for the desired behavior to occur. The employee actively seeks to make the reinforcing agent (e.g., supervisor or trainer) aware of her behavior. When punishment is used as the motivational or learning mechanism, the employee attempts to hide behavior so as to avoid the consequences. Obviously, a trainer or supervisor's job is much easier when employees are attempting to communicate what they are doing rather than hiding it.

Thus either positive or negative reinforcement is preferred over punishment as a strategy for motivating learning and behavior change. Used in combination, positive and negative reinforcement appear more effective than either used alone (Skinner 1953, 1968). We will discuss this technique later in the chapter when we review Gagné's learning types and "shaping" behavior. For those interested in finding out more about how to implement positive, humanistic, and effective work environments, we would encourage you to read Dick Grote's *Discipline Without Punishment* (1995).

Reinforcement theory suggests that any training must be concerned not only about the KSAs that are to be learned, but also about the consequences that are attached to (1) the learning process, (2) the old way of doing the job, and (3) the new way of doing the job. These will play a key role in determining how much is learned and how much is actually used back on the job.

As was mentioned, there are many unanswered questions when using reinforcement theory to describe the motivational process. **Expectancy theory,** however, provides some additional explanation and has many more implications for training.

Expectancy Theory   In 1964 Victor Vroom published a theory of work motivation called expectancy theory. This theory describes the cognitive processes involved in deciding the best course of action for achieving one's goals (i.e., satisfying one's needs). A **cognitive process** is a mental activity such as information storage, retrieval, or use. Thinking and decision making are cognitive processes. In its most basic form, the theory proposes that a person's motivation can be explained by the relationship among three conceptually distinct elements:

1. The level of success expected by the individual (e.g., how well she will be able to do what she set out to do). This is termed *Expectancy 1.*
2. The individual's beliefs about what the outcomes will be if she is successful. The expected outcomes and their likelihood of occurrence make up *Expectancy 2.*
3. The individual's feelings about the various outcomes' positive or negative value. An outcome's subjective value is referred to as its **valence.**

In combination, these elements determine the individual's motivation (i.e., effort) to engage in a particular course of action. When situations allow different courses of action, as most do, the one with the highest motivation level is chosen. The motivation level for a particular course of action can be calculated mathematically with the formula below:

$$\text{EFFORT} = \text{Expectancy1}_i \times \Sigma_{ij}(\text{Expectancy2}_{ij} \times \text{Valence}_{ij}).$$

Although this formula is useful for those conducting research on motivation, it is not very useful in the day-to-day activities of most people. It does, however, have some important implications for training and learning, which we will discuss shortly.

To get a better understanding of the expectancy theory framework, let's go back to Claudia at the point where she was trying to decide whether to attend the executive development seminar her boss suggested to her. Today is the last day she can register for the seminar, which starts in two weeks. She has postponed the decision as long as possible and now must decide. She feels confident about her ability to complete this training successfully but she has some doubts about whether it will teach her anything useful about running her marketing operation or working more effectively in a group. She knows that during the week she will be in training the marketing strategies for five important accounts will arrive on her desk and she will need to review and finalize them before forwarding them to top management. They are due by the Wednesday following training. In addition, her normal work will continue to pile up. Claudia is faced with choosing between incompatible performance goals and courses of action. Her cognitive processes, in expectancy theory terms, are illustrated in Figure 3.4.

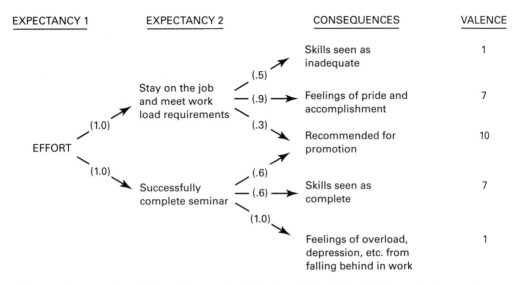

EXPECTANCY 1	EXPECTANCY 2	CONSEQUENCES	VALENCE

Valence values: a value of 5.5 would be neutral. Numbers below this reflect increasingly negative outcomes. Numbers above it reflect increasing desirability.

FIGURE 3.4 Illustration of Expectancy Theory

Examining Claudia's situation in terms of expectancy theory, we see that her expectations of success (Expectancy 1) are high for both behaviors. The expectancy of 1.0 means she is 100% sure that she would successfully be able to complete either course of action. The Expectancy 2 links reflect the outcomes that Claudia anticipates if she successfully completes the seminar or stays at the office and completes her workload. If she turns down the training and stays on the job, she believes there is a 50% chance her boss will see her skills as inadequate. It would be higher, but she believes if she can do a superior job on these strategies, he won't think those relationship skills are so important. She believes it's 90% likely she will have feelings of pride and accomplishment for getting all her work completed on time. However, if she turns down the training, she believes there's only a 30% chance her boss will recommend her for promotion.

On the other hand, if she goes to the training, she believes there is a 60% likelihood that her boss will evaluate her as having a more complete set of managerial skills. However, she will fall behind in her work, and it is a certainty (1.0) she will feel harried, overloaded, and depressed. Yet she sees the chances of being recommended for a promotion increasing to 60% if she goes to training. As the valences in Figure 3.4 shows, she values her boss's recommendation for promotion the most. She views having her boss evaluate her skills as being inadequate and the feelings associated with being behind in her work as the least desirable of the outcomes.

Using the formula to calculate Claudia's motivation to turn down training and stay on the job, we come up with a force of 9.8. This is arrived at by multiplying each Expectancy 2 by its respective outcome valence, summing the values, and then multiplying the total by the Expectancy 1 value. Using the same procedure for the alternative goal, attending the seminar, we find a force of 11.2. Thus for Claudia the motivation to stay at work is less than the motivation to attend the seminar. While the actual values of expectancies and valences are interesting from a scientific perspective, from a practical standpoint it is the relationships among the elements of the model that are useful.

This example illustrates the cognitive processes that link a person's goals, possible courses of action, and likely outcomes. These connections determine the person's motivation, and these connections are what is missing from the reinforcement theory. Of course, we have simplified the situation considerably from what Claudia would actually face in the real work setting. Many other alternatives were available to her. She could have delegated someone to cover most of the normal work coming across her desk (though she wasn't too comfortable with delegating). She could have had the marketing strategies sent to her in New Mexico and worked on them at night, after training, and on the weekend. Each of these alternatives would have its own expected outcomes and associated valences.

Faced with the situation Claudia faced, what would you do? It is unlikely that you would place the same value (valence) on the outcomes or give them the same likelihood of occurring. You might have identified more or fewer outcomes. One of the things that makes this theory so useful is that it takes into account the fact that people view the world differently and are motivated by different things.

Few people would consciously go through the formal math or mapping of expectancy theory, but it is interesting to note that most training programs that teach decision making use a model similar to this. More typically, we go through these processes unconsciously and in a less systematic fashion. We choose a particular way of behaving because of our expectations about the costs and benefits of that action. Relationships between our past behavior and its consequences are combined with current information to make inferences about the consequences of our future behavior. There are some rather obvious implications for training here.

First, a person must believe he or she has a reasonable chance of being successful. Expectancy 1 has the most influence on our behavior. We don't waste our time trying to do things we know or believe we can't do. Sometimes this belief is what makes people reluctant to go to training. The trainers must demonstrate that success is likely for the participants. Second, and this relates to needs and reinforcement theory, trainers must make sure the right outcomes are attached to the successful completion of training. Trainees should be able to make clear connections between the content of training and important organizational and personal outcomes. Third, the training outcomes must be made as desirable as possible for the trainees rather than just the organization, the supervisor, or the trainer.

SELF-EFFICACY AND MOTIVATION

Feelings about one's own competency are reflected in the concept of **self-efficacy,** which is one of the better-researched constructs related to motivation. High self-efficacy is associated with a belief that one can and will perform successfully. Those with low self-efficacy are preoccupied with concerns about failure (Bandura 1977b). Research supports the belief that the higher the self-efficacy, the better the performance (Gecas 1989; Gist 1987; Manz and Simms 1981). Not only is performance better, but in difficult situations those with high self-efficacy try harder while those with low self-efficacy tend to reduce effort or give up (Locke, Lee, and Bobko 1984).

Several factors combine to provide employees with an estimate of their ability to be successful:

- *Prior experience*: The person's past successes and failures and their consequences.
- *Behavioral models*: Successes and failures of others who have been observed attempting the behavior.
- *Others' feedback*: The encouragement or discouragement provided by others.
- *Physical and emotional state*: The physical and/or emotional limitations that are believed to impact ability to perform.

Self-efficacy, therefore, plays a large role in the person's Expectancy 1 evaluation. The employee's feelings of self-efficacy then are translated into behavior. If success is expected, the employee works harder, longer, and more creatively in anticipation of the positive consequences of a successful effort. If failure is expected, the employee acts to minimize the negative consequences of failure. For example, withdrawing from the activity (refusing to try) moves the person away from proven failure to simply "I didn't try." It also allows the person to say "At least I didn't put a lot of energy into it" or other forms of rationalization. The point is that the employee's self-efficacy sets up the person's behavior to fulfill the self-efficacy beliefs. In expectancy theory terms, if I don't believe I can successfully do something, then I won't exert the effort to do it, I'll do something else.

Training can improve self-efficacy either directly or as a by-product. If the employee has low self-efficacy regarding his or her abilities to perform the job, but evidence indicates he or she has the requisite KSAs, a program of improving self-concept and confidence is needed. If, however, the low self-efficacy is due to a true lack of required KSAs, attaining competency in these KSAs should increase the employee's self-efficacy if the training allows the trainee to demonstrate mastery on a continuous basis.

In any event, it is useful to assess trainee self-efficacy before and during training, because self-efficacy beliefs seem to be a good predictor of both learning in the training environment and transfer of the behavior to the job (Kraiger, Ford, and Salas 1993).

Understanding Learning

Learning has been probed and prodded by scientific inquiry since the late 1800s. The resulting theories have led to practical application in both educational and industrial settings. The range of theoretical perspectives has varied widely over the last century. Examining the rise and fall of the various theories, though intellectually fascinating, is beyond the scope of this chapter, and indeed of this book. Rather we will examine the essential elements of learning theories and identify their relationship to training. Specific applications of the theories are provided in subsequent chapters.

WHAT IS LEARNING?

To understand the differences among learning theories, it helps to understand the difficulties of just defining the concept of learning. Learning is not directly observable, but it is something that almost everyone says they experience. People can "feel" that they have learned. Scientists assure us that it occurs physically, yet they are not sure how. It is clear from physiological evidence that learning is related to changes in the physical, neuronal structure of the brain and its related electrochemical functioning (Schacter 1996; Squire, Shimamura, and Graf 1985; Squire and Zola-Morgan 1991). Unfortunately, much is still unknown about how or why these electrochemical changes take place. Learning, of course, is closely tied to memory: Whatever is learned must be retained if it is to be useful. Electrochemical changes created during learning apparently create a relatively permanent change in neural functioning that becomes what is commonly termed *memory*. Again, relatively few definitive answers exist about how or where learning is stored in the central nervous system.

Two Definitions of Learning

Since we can't actually observe learning occurring or determine its physical existence, how do we know that learning has occurred? We must use something we can observe that is influenced by learning. That is, we must infer that learning has occurred by looking at its observable effects. What are the things that learning influences that we can observe? The answer is that we are pretty much limited to observing the learner's behavior. For instance, in school you are often given tests to determine if you have learned. The behavior being observed is the way you answer the questions. In the workplace your supervisor might look for ways you perform your job differently after training. In science, concepts, events, and phenomena are given an operational definition; this means that the concept is defined in terms of how it is measured. Since learning is measured in terms of relatively permanent changes in behavior, these changes have become the operational definition of learning for many theorists. *Behaviorists* in particular have adopted this definition.

Cognitive theorists on the other hand, insist that while learning can be inferred from behavior, it is separate from the behavior itself. By examining the ways in which people respond to information and the ways in which different types of behavior are grouped or separated, they have developed theories of how information is learned. For cognitive theorists, learning represents a change in the content, organization, and storage of information (see the section "Example of Cognitive Theory"). The term used to refer to the mental processing of information—mental representation of objects and events, their characteristics, and their relationships to other objects and events—is **cognition.** For many of these theorists, learning is defined as a relatively permanent change in cognition occurring as a result of experience. These theorists discuss learning in terms of mental infrastructures or schema rather than in terms of behavior. Learning is seen as the building and reorganization of schema to make sense of new information. Bruner (1966), Gagné (1965), and Piaget (1954) are among the cognitive theorists.

Implications of Behaviorist versus Cognitive Approaches

At first the differences in the definition of learning may not seem to be important. It seems like a simple difference of whether learning is synonymous with behavior or with how information is processed, organized, and stored. However, these differences have created widely different approaches to how education and training are conducted.

One obvious and important difference is where control of learning is believed to occur. The behaviorist approach suggests that learning is controlled by the environment. Certain external stimuli are present, the person responds to them, and certain consequences result. This is the model of learning implied in Figure 3.2 (page 89) and discussed earlier as part of reinforcement theory. In the behaviorist approach, the trainer controls learning by controlling the stimuli and consequences that the learner experiences. The learner is dependent on the trainer to elicit the correct associations between stimulus and response. Note that this model does not include the brain or any mental activity. B. F. Skinner (1971) is the best-known of the contemporary behaviorists. His explanation of learning will perhaps clarify why he was sometimes referred to as a radical behaviorist. He defined learning as "a relatively permanent change in behavior in response to a particular stimulus or set of stimuli." He proposed that "we learn to perceive in the sense that we learn to respond to things in particular ways, because of the contingencies of which they are a part." To paraphrase Skinner: We perceive things a certain way because of the consequences of perceiving them that way. Skinner viewed the brain in much the same way as he viewed the body, as just another organ in which certain neural activities are conditioned to occur, or not occur, in a given situation, depending on the past history of consequences for those activities. Learning occurs when new consequences are experienced.

In contrast, the cognitive approach suggests that learning is controlled by the learner. Prospective learners come to training with their own set of goals and priorities. They possess a set of cognitive structures for understanding their environment and how it works. They have even developed their own set of strategies about how to learn. The learners decide what is important to learn and go about learning by applying the strategies they have developed and with which they feel comfortable. For cognitive theorists, the learner controls what is learned and how. The trainer and the learning environment will facilitate that process to a greater or lesser degree.

Adoption of one approach or the other has implications for how training is conducted and the atmosphere of the training environment. Table 3.1 lists some of the instructional implications of these two positions. For some learning situations, a behaviorist approach is better, and for others a cognitive approach works better (Knowles 1984, 1989). We will discuss this issue again later in the chapter.

TABLE 3.1 Some Training Implications of Cognitive and Behaviorist Learning Theory

Issue	*Cognitive Approach*	*Behaviorist Approach*
Learner's role	Active, self-directed, self-evaluating	Passive, dependent
Instructor's role	Facilitator, coordinator, and presenter	Director, monitor, evaluator
Training content	Problem or task oriented	Subject oriented
Learner motivation	More internally motivated	More externally motivated
Training climate	Relaxed, mutually trustful and respectful, collaborative	Formal, authority oriented, judgmental, competitive
Instructional goals	Collaboratively developed	Developed by instructor
Instructional activities	Interactive, group, project oriented, experiential	Directive, individual subject oriented

Example of Cognitive Theory The developmental psychologist Piaget identified two cognitive processes that are critical for learning: accommodation and assimilation. **Accommodation** is the process of changing our construction ("cognitive map") of the world to correspond with our experience in it. Piaget indicated that accommodation occurs through the creation of new categories, or schema, to accommodate experience that doesn't fit into existing categories. **Assimilation** is the incorporation of new experience into existing categories. In cognitive map terms, accommodation changes the map whereas assimilation fills in the detail.

These two processes are most clearly evident in young children but exist in adults as well. Suppose Mike (age eight) is in the rear seat of the car with his younger brother Brandon (almost two and learning to talk) as Dad is driving through some farmland. As they pass a pasture where horses are grazing, Mike points and says, "Look, Brandon, horses." Brandon responds hesitantly, "Horsies?" Mike excitedly replies, "Yes, that's right, horsies!" Dad glances back and says, "Good work, Brandon, you now know a new word!" Brandon is very pleased and repeats the word several times to himself. As they continue driving, they pass another pasture that has cows grazing. Brandon yells, "Look, Mike, horsies!" Mike or Dad is now faced with teaching Brandon the difference between horses and cows.

What is the learning process that took place? Brandon started out with no understanding of horse or cow. When presented with a new perceptual experience and a label, Brandon created a new cognitive category that might have included the following parameters: "large, four-legged, brown, moving thing with a tail." So when Brandon saw the cows, they fit enough of the parameters that he attempted to assimilate this new experience into the category "horsies." If Mike and Dad do a good job of teaching Brandon the differences between horses and cows, he will learn to discriminate between these two and create a separate category for cows (accommodation). What he doesn't know yet is that later in life he will be taught to create new categories such as mammals and species and that both horses and cows are included in some categories but not in others.

The process of assimilation and accommodation reflects the way we organize our experience and the meanings we attach to the world as we encounter it. Our behavior will depend on how we have accommodated or assimilated previous stimuli.

Integration of Cognitive and Behavioral Approaches

Both the cognitive and behaviorist approaches have provided insight into the process of learning and furnished practical tools for increasing the effectiveness of training. We believe that the cognitive and behavioral approaches must be integrated to provide a full definition of learning. **Learning,** as we use the term throughout this text, is defined as a *relatively permanent change in cognition, resulting from experience and directly influencing behavior.* A fairly obvious implication of this definition is that changes in cognition and related behavior that result from things other than experience (e.g., effects of drugs, fatigue, and the like) would not be considered learning.

The definition also implies that changes in cognition and behavior that are short-lived have not been learned. For example, memorizing a phone number long enough to walk from the telephone directory to the phone and dial the number would not fit into our definition. However, learning the mnemonic techniques that allow you to do that could fit the definition if they were retained over a relatively long period of time.

Practice, which is discussed in more depth later in this chapter, enhances learning and usually makes it more permanent.

Learning, as defined here, is not dependent on behavior. Relatively permanent cognitive changes (new KSAs) can occur even without the occurrence of an observable behavior, but in that case only the individual who has learned would know that the learning has taken place. For example, think of courses you have taken in which the material was presented in a lecture or audiovisual form. If it was effective, you changed your way of thinking about the topic and/or had a deeper understanding of the material—even though you did nothing other than pay attention and think about what was being presented. However, until you engage in some activity related to the topic, no one other than yourself would know that learning had taken place. This phenomenon could also happen with skills. Suppose you are a chef and you are attending a seminar on preparing a dish. You observe the presenter enhancing the flavor of a dish using a technique of which you had no previous knowledge. You could go back to your kitchen, try the technique, and be successful on the first try. You would have acquired the "flavoring" skill through observation rather than behavior. However, you might not be sure you had acquired the skill until after you engaged in the behavior. Additionally, the more you used the technique, the more permanent (i.e., resistant to forgetting) it would become. Thus behavior is both an important measure of learning and a means of learning.

The debates between learning cognitivists and behaviorists have been going on for some time, but the gap between the two positions is continually narrowing. It has been pointed out that:

> To show that behavior is determined only by cognition, one would have to find a control group consisting of individuals who cannot think. Similarly, to provide empirical support for the argument that behavior is due to environmental consequences alone, one would have the impossible task of forming a control group for which there was no environment. (Latham and Sarri 1979)

Each of the two approaches has produced valuable insights about learning. Learning theories that have integrated the substantiated aspects of both approaches explain learning more completely than either singly. We'll discuss two of these next.

Two Integrative Theories of Learning

The two learning theories presented here capture critical elements of both the behavioral and the cognitive approaches and weave them together in a coherent and compelling fashion. The first, Gagné's approach, is somewhat more behavioral. The second, Bandura's social learning model, includes more cognitive processes. Each, however, incorporates concepts and principles of both theoretical perspectives. We begin with Gagné, because he provides a systematic explanation of learning from the most elementary, associative form to higher-level problem solving.

GAGNÉ'S LEARNING TYPES

According to Robert Gagné (1962, 1965, 1974), there are different types of learning that can be categorized in terms of the events required for the learning to occur. The eight types are presented in Table 3.2 on page 100. All but Type 1 (signal learn-

TABLE 3.2 Summary of Gagné's Eight Learning Types

Learning Type	Description
1. Signal learning	Learning a general response to a specific signal. Pavlov's classical conditioning falls into this category.
2. Stimulus–response (S–R)	Learning a single response to a stimulus situation. Basic forms of operant conditioning fall into this category.
3. Shaping	Chaining together of two or more S–R associations. Originally termed *chaining* by Gagné, we have called it *shaping* to avoid confusion with other parts of the text.
4. Verbal association	A chain of two or more verbal associations. Basically the same as shaping, but the application to language makes this a special case since it involves internal links to language capabilities.
5. Multiple discrimination	Ability to make different but appropriate responses to stimuli that differ to greater or lesser degrees.
6. Concept learning	Typically called *generalization* learning. Reflected by the ability to make a common response to a class of stimuli having some common characteristic or relationship but otherwise differing to greater or lesser degrees.
7. Principle learning	Represented by a chain of two or more concepts characterized by the development of a formal logical relation between concepts similar to an "if A then B" formulation, where A and B are concepts.
8. Problem solving	Involves the retrieval of two or more previously learned principles and their combination to produce a novel (to the learner) capability reflecting a higher-order principle.

ing) and Type 2 (stimulus–response learning) require competence at the preceding levels of learning. Type 1 is simply a different type of learning and Type 2 learning is not dependent on it. The other types of learning have a hierarchical dependency on the lower types. For example, Type 4 (verbal association) requires competence at Type 3 learning (shaping).

Both the behavioral and the cognitive approaches to learning are embodied in Gagné's learning hierarchy. It should be clear from reviewing the table that the behavioral approach provides greater explanation for simpler forms of learning and serves as the foundation for more complex forms of learning. As learning becomes more complex, there is an increasing reliance on cognitive constructs and processes. Thus, which approach is "better" depends on the type of learning you are focusing on.

Type 1: Signal Learning

Signal learning is the association of a generalized response to some signal in the environment. This typically involves learning to emit a nonvoluntary response to some signal that in the past did not produce that response. For example, when an optometrist examines your eyes, she may put you in front of a machine that blows a puff of air into your eye. This puff of air causes you to blink your eye. If a red light came on just before the puff of air, you would probably learn to associate the puff of air with the red light and begin blinking when the red light came on. At that point you would have learned to blink (generalized response) in response to the red light (signal).

Behaviorist approaches to learning have their roots in the early signal learning research. Pavlov's (1897, 1912) principles of the conditioned reflex (classical conditioning) are perhaps the most widely known. Pavlov wasn't studying learning, he was examining the physiology of digestion. He was studying the amount of salivation produced by various substances placed on the tongues of dogs. As the story goes, Pavlov observed that the dogs began to salivate upon his entering the lab, thus playing havoc with his desire to determine the amount of saliva produced by various substances. He speculated that over time his entrance had been followed so often with substances placed on the dogs' tongues, that the dogs had learned to salivate on his entrance.

Table 3.3 shows how the classical conditioning, or signal learning, process works. Step 1 reflects the state of affairs before conditioning has taken place. Certain things in the environment (unconditioned stimuli) produce automatic responses in animals and people (unconditioned responses). If we placed an unconditioned stimulus such as meat powder on a dog's tongue, an unconditioned response would be the dog's salivation. That is, the dog doesn't have to be trained (conditioned) to salivate when meat powder is put on its tongue. However, this salivation response doesn't occur to every stimulus that might be in the dog's environment, such as a buzzer. If, however, you sounded that buzzer just before putting meat powder on the dog's tongue, over a number of trials, the buzzer would become a conditioned stimulus. The dog is learning (being conditioned) to associate the buzzer with the meat powder. However, you're still putting meat powder on the dog's tongue, so the salivation is really a response to the meat powder and remains an unconditioned response. This situation is reflected in Step 2 of Table 3.3.

In Step 3 you stop putting meat powder on the dog's tongue after sounding the buzzer. If the dog salivates at the buzzer, you have created a conditioned response (salivation) to a conditioned stimulus (the buzzer). This response can be extinguished (removed) by continually sounding the buzzer without offering the meat powder. Over time, the conditioned response gradually disappears. Through conditioning, a response to one stimulus can be transferred to another, unrelated stimulus.

TABLE 3.3 Classical Conditioning Process

STEP 1	**Unconditioned Stimulus** (Meat powder)	$\longrightarrow$	**Unconditioned Response** (Salivation)
STEP 2	**Conditional Stimulus paired** **with Unconditioned Stimulus** (Buzzer followed closely in time, over many trials, by meat powder)	$\longrightarrow$	**Unconditioned Response** (Salivation)
STEP 3	**Conditional Stimulus** (Buzzer alone)	$\longrightarrow$	**Conditioned Response** (Salivation)

Signal learning occurs frequently in the workplace, though it typically receives little attention. The noon whistle blows at the factory and the digestive juices of the workers begin to flow. Sparks fly from the welding machine and your eyes blink, even though you are wearing goggles. Signal learning is the most rudimentary form of learning and has some relevance for skill development. However, most skill development requires a more complicated sequencing of behavior than can be explained by the pairing of unconditioned and conditioned responses. Operant conditioning and reinforcement theory (learning types 2 to 5) provide a more compelling explanation for skill development.

Type 2: Stimulus–Response Learning

Stimulus–response learning, like classical conditioning, is elementary but forms the basis for more complex types of learning. Essentially, it is the association of a single response to a single stimulus. This differs from type 1 learning since the response in type 2 learning is considered voluntary. In signal learning the unconditioned response becomes conditioned to occur to a stimulus that doesn't innately produce it. In stimulus–response learning the association occurs as a result of the consequences of the response. This type of learning has also been called *operant conditioning* (Skinner 1938) and *instrumental learning* (Kimble 1967). Reinforcement theory is a part of the stimulus–response learning paradigm. It is very difficult to observe this type of learning in adults, or even young children, because they have already developed millions of these types of associations and integrated them into more complex behavior patterns. The relevance of this type of learning to more advanced forms is the underlying nature of how these stimulus–response relationships are formed. This was addressed earlier as part of the reinforcement theory discussion.

Stimulus–response learning is the foundation for all skill development. By itself it is generally too elementary to be of much value in organizational training programs. The principles of reinforcement and punishment are, however, quite relevant for the more complex types of learning that follow.

Type 3: Shaping and Chaining

Any complex behavior can be broken down into a set of simple behaviors, arranged in chronological order. **Shaping** refers to the process of learning to link the appropriate behaviors to one another (the behavioral set) and learning the reinforcing consequences that are linked to the behavioral set. It establishes the learning of complex behaviors through what is called "reinforcing successive approximations" to the desired end behavior. That is, the person learns the first part of the behavioral sequence and it is reinforced. When that has been learned, the next part of the sequence is learned and reinforced. This continues until the desired combination of simple behaviors (stimulus–response connections) are integrated into a coordinated set of behaviors. The end result is that the person has learned to perform a more complex behavior.

When using shaping during training, you would first break the complex behavior that must be learned into smaller, simpler behaviors that are well within the trainee's capabilities. The trainee is shown how to order the behaviors and asked to perform them in the proper order. You would reinforce the trainee each time his behavior moves closer to the standard than the previous attempt. After demonstrating that he has learned a part of the sequence, he is no longer reinforced for that but only for learning more of the sequence. At the conclusion of training, only the complete set of behaviors that demonstrates learning of the complex behavior is reinforced.

The following example illustrates the shaping process and resulting learning. Suppose a production supervisor is frustrated by a machinist who consistently turns out a high volume of product but whose work area is always littered with debris and oil. This mess not only is a potentially hazardous environment for the machinist, but causes a half hour delay for the operator on the next shift, who must clean up the area before beginning work. The supervisor speaks to the machinist about this problem, and the next day the machinist stops work a half hour early to clean up the area. The half hour of lost production results in the machinist's turning out less product than required. When the supervisor discusses this with him, the machinist replies, "What do you want, high volume or a clean area?"

Here we have a complex behavior pattern that the supervisor needs to change. The supervisor has consistently given praise for producing at a high volume. The machinist values the praise and perhaps even sees it as related to some future reinforcement (such as a raise or a promotion). The machinist has learned to operate his machine continuously except for his two fifteen-minute breaks and during lunch. While the machine is in operation, debris and oil accumulates on the work surface and floor. During a work shift the debris and oil are scattered and pushed around the work area. By observing the machinist's sequence of behaviors, the supervisor can identify changes that will produce both the high volume of production and the clean work area. The machinist's current pattern of behavior is shown in Figure 3.5 as Machinist's Initial Behavior.

If the machinist were to spend a small amount of time keeping the work area clean throughout the shift, there would be less scattering of debris and oil, and less overall time devoted to cleaning. The supervisor will need to modify the machinist's pattern of behavior to something like that shown as Machinist's Modified Behavior in Figure 3.5, where the number of times the machinist cleans the work area is increased.

The supervisor can discuss the behavior pattern with the machinist and get his agreement to try the new approach. Discussion and agreement will not be enough, however. The supervisor must, in the beginning, also be diligent in visiting the machinist's work area just prior to breaks, lunch, and quitting time to supply the necessary reinforcement for keeping the work area clean throughout the shift, and he should continue

FIGURE 3.5 Machinist's Behavior Patterns before and after Modification

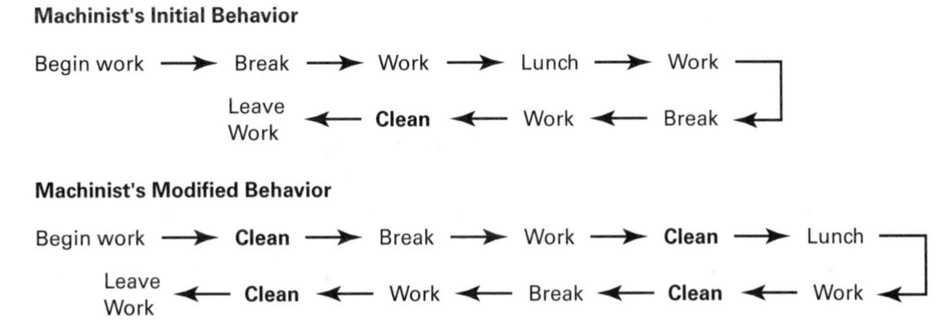

Machinist's Initial Behavior

Begin work → Break → Work → Lunch → Work ⌐
Leave Work ← **Clean** ← Work ← Break ⌐

Machinist's Modified Behavior

Begin work → **Clean** → Break → Work → **Clean** → Lunch ⌐
Leave Work ← **Clean** ← Work ← Break ← **Clean** ← Work ⌐

doing so until the desired behavior pattern is established. Because the machinist is learning a new, more complex behavior pattern, the supervisor must accept that at the start there will be times when productivity is high and cleanliness is low and other times when the reverse will occur. Because the machinist already knows how to produce high volume, the supervisor should withhold praise for high productivity unless it is accompanied by a clean work area. In the beginning, the supervisor should praise even small improvements in the cleanliness of the work area as long as productivity remains at an acceptable level. For example, if some attempt at cleaning the area was made prior to the first break, the supervisor might say, "Well, the area is looking better. I see you're trying to keep it cleaner." However, praise should be withheld (but encouragement given to do better) if cleanliness has not improved just prior to the lunch break. At this point the supervisor might say, "I know it's hard to keep the area clean and concentrate on running the machine, but I'm sure you'll be able to do better after the lunch break."

The key to shaping is to reinforce movement in the direction of the desired behavioral pattern and to withhold reinforcement when behavior moves away from that pattern. Behaviorists call this technique *reinforcing successive approximations.* In our machinist example, any time the machinist is able to improve the cleanliness of the work area and maintain acceptable production levels, it would constitute an approximation to the ultimate desired behavior pattern of maintaining high productivity levels and a clean work area.

The second operant conditioning concept important to training is **chaining.** This process describes how the outcomes of behavior come to acquire their reinforcing or punishing properties. A fundamental assumption of chaining is that all outcomes acquire their positive or negative value through association with the feelings produced by their physical effects. Food is usually valued positively because it produces physical effects that are subjectively experienced as "good." Money is also a positively valued outcome, yet it has no direct physical effects; it acquires its positive value because it is associated with things that do create those physical effects. The reinforcement value of money, then, is chained to the reinforcement value of the things that money can acquire. While food is a **primary reinforcer** because it is directly linked to physiological effects, money is a **secondary reinforcer** because its value comes from its links to primary reinforcers.

Primary reinforcers are sometimes used in the training environment; such as refreshments provided at the start of the program and at other times throughout the program. The trainees begin to associate the reinforcing properties of the refreshments (a primary reinforcer) with the training. Training starts on a positive note because it has been chained to the positive value of the refreshments. This association has become so strong in some companies that trainees become upset if refreshments aren't provided.

Chaining affects training in other ways as well. Because of chaining, it is often difficult to know whether a particular outcome will be seen by the trainee as positive or negative. For example, public praise is often believed to be a positive reinforcer. Sometimes, however, public praise from the trainer can be punishing because of the norms of the work group. Peers may see a person receiving praise from the "boss" as being an "apple polisher" and may ridicule or make sarcastic remarks to the person. Rather than reinforcing the person's behavior through praise, the trainer has unknowingly punished the behavior.

The trainer must understand as clearly as possible how trainees will perceive the outcomes with which the training is linked. This relates to Expectancy 2 and valence concepts of expectancy theory. The work unit norms and the culture of the organization will strongly influence whether training is chained to positive or negative outcomes. Shaping and chaining can be useful for understanding employee work performance and for improving trainee motivation and attention in the design of training.

Type 4: Verbal Association Learning

Among the primary focal points of education and training is the acquisition of knowledge, concepts, principles, and problem-solving ability. However, underlying all these is the ability to make appropriate associations among various objects and actions that are symbolized by the learner's vocabulary. Nearly all training involves the communication of fact and meaning through verbal symbols, written or spoken. Though the exact process remains largely a mystery, it is clear that objects, events, and actions are placed into memory along with corresponding verbal symbols. These verbal symbols are the language we use to communicate with each other.

The most elementary **verbal association learning** is the pairing of a verbal response to an object or event in the environment. Mechanically, the process is similar to that of operant conditioning. A fundamental difference is that the stimulus (object or event) becomes internalized as language. Thus the word *house* is associated with the various stored experiences the person has had with houses, and he differentiates this word from other words (e.g., *tent*). The labeling of objects and events is required before the person is able to form concepts by associating two or more language symbols. As with stimulus–response learning, the consequences of verbalizing the associations will enhance or discourage their use in the future. In this way, verbal sequences become memorized, either intentionally or unintentionally.

Obviously, one measure of learning is the degree to which the person is able to identify and use the language of the subject matter appropriately. For example, we cannot easily determine a manager's decision-making process by simply observing the decision or watching the manager as she makes the decision. The decision itself, whether right or wrong, doesn't indicate how or why it was chosen. However, the manager's ability to describe the factors and processes that led to the decision will indicate the level of both subject matter knowledge and decision-making skill. This information can be used to design training to meet the subject matter and/or decision-making skill needs of the trainee. If, however, the manager is not able to verbalize these factors and processes, training must begin at the verbal association level, to provide the trainee with the vocabulary necessary to describe relevant subject matter factors and decision-making processes.

Often it is assumed that if the person can't communicate effectively about a particular subject, he lacks the knowledge and skill to behave effectively in the area. However, the person may know the principle or concept but be unable to express it in language that is understood by the trainer or those in the job environment. What is missing is a common set of language symbols. While the person may be able to perform the task, he is unable to communicate effectively about it; that is, he lacks communication skills.

Of course, in training it is also important not to use unnecessarily complex phrases or words. We have observed one company in which the line employees were given training that had been designed for middle- and upper-level managers. The line employees complained that they had never heard of many of the terms used, and even when they understood the words, the sentences made no sense to them. You must start your training at the verbal association level of the trainees. This common language can then be used to develop understanding of the more complex language. When terms or phrases are complex but are integral to effectively communicating about a subject, by all means use them, but not until your audience understands them.

The following example will be used to illustrate verbal association as well as each of the remaining types of learning. Imagine you are conducting a management training seminar for first- and second-level managers. You are attempting to teach them to use the best management style for a given situation. You want to train them to identify important differences among situations and to apply the appropriate management behaviors in each situation. Ultimately, you would like them to be able to determine on their own how to interact with their employees in ways appropriate for the particular situation. To do this, the managers must first understand the critical aspects of the situation and their behavior in those situations. This understanding begins with the appropriate verbal associations for the terms, concepts, and principles that will be used.

We will focus here on only two aspects of the situation: (1) the structure of the work itself, called task structure, and (2) the subordinate's need for independence. The trainees must understand the meaning of these terms if they are to learn how to identify the situation correctly. If the trainees are provided with a definition of the term *task structure,* they can use the verbal associations in the definition to form an abstract foundation for the term. A typical definition of task structure might be:

> The degree to which the process of production, the rules of the work unit, and other factors outside the direct control of the worker determine what, when, how, and where the work will be done.

If the trainee can reliably associate the above definition with the term *task structure,* this would be an example of complex, verbal, paired association learning. The difference between high and low task structure can be described by following the above definition with a statement such as, "The more discretion the employee has in determining what, when, how, and where the work is done, the less structured the job is." Providing verbal examples is also useful in building an understanding of new terms. You might give the following example: "An assembly line job, for example, is typically more structured than a vice presidency." The trainer should use terms, examples, and concepts already known by the trainee as a base from which to work.

In most cases the training objective is not merely to have trainees use, recall, or recognize appropriate words and phrases. Rather, they must usually demonstrate the ability to do something when it is appropriate to do it and not do it when it is inappropriate. The next two sections (discrimination and concept learning) deal with these types of learning.

Type 5: Multiple Discrimination Learning

Discrimination learning occurs when the person learns to identify the key aspects of a specific situation that indicate a particular response is appropriate. As was stated in the previous section, the relevant verbal associations must be acquired first.

Training people to distinguish among different parts of their surroundings must begin at simpler levels and advance to more complex. In simple multiple discrimination learning, only one aspect of the situation changes to signal that a different response is appropriate. Thus each aspect of the situation that is to be associated with different response patterns must be presented separately, so that the linkage to behavior can be established for each one. In our example, we will deal with only the two situational factors described above and two types of managerial behavior. We want to teach trainees to discriminate among higher and lower levels of the situational factors and the managerial behaviors. We will only use the extremes here, although in real training we would have to show the full range of situations and managerial responses. The two situational factors are "task structure" and "employee need for independence." The two types of managerial behavior are (1) initiating structure and (2) participative management.[1] Our goals are for the managers to learn that:

- When task structure is high, the manager's initiating structure should be low.
- When task structure is low, the manager's initiating structure should be high.
- When the subordinate's need for independence is high, the manager should become more participative in setting goals.
- When the subordinate's need for independence is low, the manager should become more directive in setting goals.

This pattern is set out in Table 3.4.

As Table 3.4 suggests, the learner needs to discriminate not only between the situational factors of "task structure" and "subordinate need for independence" but also between the high and low levels. The same is true for the response categories "initiating structure" and "participation." The supervisor must be able to identify when an initiating structure or participative management style is being used as well as the extent to which the style is being used.

TABLE 3.4   Supervisor Behavior Patterns Recommended for Two Levels of Two Environmental Stimuli

Task Structure	Subordinate Need for Independence	
	High	Low
High	Low initiating structure High participation	Low initiating structure Low participation
Low	High initiating structure High participation	High initiating structure Low participation

[1] Initiating structure occurs when the manager provides direction to the employees regarding what, when, and how things are to be done. When using a participative management style, the manager seeks the involvement of employees in making decisions about what, when, and how things are done.

For now, we are trying to teach the managers to discriminate between situations based on structure being high or low, or based on employee independence being high or low, so they can identify the appropriate managerial style. Training would focus on one factor at a time. A single type of situation would be used in which only the task structure or employee need for independence varies. We would try to use a job situation that everyone would be familiar with. If the trainees come from different areas of the organization, some of them may not be familiar with the job, so it will have to be explained. Only one job is used because if we vary both the job and the amount of task structure, the trainees may become confused about what they should be responding to. Once they have learned to discriminate among the factors, we can move to the next level, concept learning. There we will use several jobs.

At first trainees are reinforced for recognizing aspects of the job that indicate something about its task structure. Once they can reliably recognize structural elements, they are asked to determine whether the information indicates that task structure is high or low. Reinforcement is no longer applied for just recognizing an element as related to task structure, but only for recognizing both the element and its impact on task structure. Can you see how the shaping concept is used even at higher levels of learning? Once the managers can correctly identify the level of task structure, they are ready to move on. Next we might ask them to indicate whether they would provide any initiating structure in the situation. We would follow the same procedure as before until they were consistently indicating the appropriate amount of task structure to use in the situation. The same procedures would be used for participation. The cycle would be repeated for situations involving employee need for independence. When all these are mastered, the trainees will be ready to learn to generalize their learning across multiple situations. This is called concept learning.

Type 6: Concept Learning

Concept learning is defined as the ability to use a *common abstract property* to respond correctly to a variety of situations that differ widely in appearance. Whereas in discrimination learning the trainee learns to apply different responses to a single changing situation, here the trainees must generalize those responses across many situations. However, the supervisor trainees are not yet ready to apply the appropriate managerial behavior to both the task structure and employee need for independence. Again, we must teach one concept at a time. In the next type of learning, principle learning, these concepts can be combined into an integrated behavioral pattern. For now we are simply creating an understanding of each concept (task structure, employee need for independence) so that they can be recognized across different situations.

In the management training example, you want the trainees to generalize from the situations they encounter in the training environment to those they might find in the work environment. Suppose the trainees were managers and supervisors from production, sales, information systems, and accounting. You might have used an assembly job to demonstrate a highly structured task because the technology, the programmed decision making, and the formal procedures best exemplified a highly structured work situation. Further, you might have used a job in new-product engineering as a clear example of tasks with low structure, since this job has a great deal of latitude in decision making, the tasks are usually new and nonroutine, and the duties are broadly defined. While the trainees might do very well discriminating high from low task structure in the training environment, this ability will not transfer back to their jobs unless they can generalize the concept of task structure to any job. When the trainees are able consistently to identify the level of task structure across a sequence of novel and distinct stimulus situations, the trainer can say that they have learned the task structure concept.

Although trial-and-error learning can be used to establish a concept, this is usually not the best method. A systematic approach moving from simple to more difficult learning tasks is typically more efficient and leads to better retention. The trainer might begin with concrete examples that trainees can test to see if their understanding corresponds with what is desired by the trainer. The best situations are those that have reference to the trainees' experience. They can be real situations or hypothetical situations that are experienced vicariously (e.g., some case studies, simulations, or demonstrations). Once this experiential foundation has been mastered, trainees must apply it to concrete situations that are different from their experience but that contain the elements of the concept to be learned. In our example, this would be situations that the trainee had never experienced but that contained information about how structured a job is or how much independence employees desire. This is what was done in our example above; jobs in assembly and new product engineering were used to demonstrate the different levels of task structure, and trainees then had to generalize the concepts back to the areas that they were managing. When the trainee is consistently able to ignore elements unrelated to the concept and respond appropriately to elements of the concept across the novel situations, the concept has been learned.

Concept learning applies to skills as well as to knowledge. In our example, we are interested in more than just the trainees' ability to know *what* initiating structure and participative management are, we want them to know *how* to do these things. Thus we use a similar approach, but this time linking behavioral rather than just verbal responses to situational cues. The trainee must learn to display the range of behaviors that would constitute appropriate learning of the concept. Observational and experiential training methods such as videos combined with role playing are useful here. Again we would apply reinforcement for successive approximations to shape the trainees' ability to behave in ways consistent with the concept (e.g., high and low initiating structure). When both the verbal and behavioral concepts have been mastered, the trainer is ready to move on to principle learning.

Type 7: Principle Learning

Principles are chains of concepts. Learning that occurs with types 3–6 reflects what we have called declarative knowledge. **Principle learning** is required for development of procedural and strategic knowledge. The statement "Low initiating structure in a high task-structure work environment increases employee job satisfaction" represents three distinct concepts: (1) initiating structure, (2) task structure, and (3) job satisfaction. In order to learn this principle, the trainee must have already learned each of the three concepts. Again, memorizing the verbal chain in no way implies learning the principle, the discriminations, or the concepts. Learning the principle is demonstrated by its appropriate use in specific situations. Presenting the trainees with novel situations in which all the various factors and many irrelevant factors may be present, and determining if they can apply the appropriate managerial behavior, will demonstrate whether they have learned the principle.

In our continuing example, we would need to present trainees with situations in which varying levels of both task structure and need for independence were present. If the training objective was only on knowledge of the principle, we would ask them to indicate how they would respond to the situation. If skill development was also an objective, we would place them in these situations with instructions to demonstrate the appropriate managerial style. Role plays and some types of simulations are useful for this. As always, starting with the concrete and progressing to the abstract while reinforcing successive approximations to the desired response pattern will strengthen the learning and reduce the likelihood of forgetting.

Type 8: Problem Solving

Problem solving integrates and applies more than one principle to produce a novel response or capability that results in a higher-order principle previously unknown to the learner. In our example, suppose you have successfully fostered the learning of the principles matching participative management and initiating structure with the situational variables of task structure and employee need for independence. You might now present a videotape of an employee characterized as being low in self-esteem. While this employee tested well in the selection process, she hasn't been on the job long enough to know how well she's doing; nonetheless, she feels she is not performing well and is thinking of leaving the job for one that is not as demanding. None of the principles learned is directly applicable to this situation.

The ability to problem-solve would be evident in trainees who were able to generalize from the existing principles to develop a higher-order principle such as "managerial behavior that compensates for mismatches between employee characteristics and the work situation is effective." In this instance, providing support and reinforcement to the low self-esteem employee would compensate for the employee's low opinion of her work. Other managerial behaviors that provided similar support would also be appropriate.

By getting the trainees to share what they would do in the situation and why, the trainer can develop and reinforce the problem-solving capabilities of the trainees. The key in teaching trainees to problem-solve is to provide them with situations in which the existing principles do not directly apply but, if integrated, will provide a higher-order principle that will allow them to solve the problem.

When a problem has been solved, something has also been learned in the sense that the capabilities of the problem solver have been enhanced in a relatively permanent way. The higher-order principle becomes a part of the trainee's knowledge. Of course, higher-order principles may be learned in the same fashion as regular principles. The difference is in the process of discovery, or the amount and nature of the guidance provided. In typical principle-learning situations, the trainer will cue and even model the higher-order principle in combination with appropriately reinforcing trainee responses that more or less demonstrate acquisition of the principle. The problem-solving type of learning occurs when the trainee is able to discover the new principle without (or with minimal) help. Research indicates that this latter type of learning produces a highly effective capability that is extremely resistant to being forgotten (Ausubel 1963, Gagné and Dick 1983). It is in the ability to solve problems that strategic knowledge is developed.

SOCIAL LEARNING THEORY

Albert Bandura and his associates (Bandura 1977a, 1977b; Kraut 1976) developed a model of learning that has come to be known variously as *observational learning, vicarious learning,* and most often, **social learning theory.** One of its most important contributions to the science of learning was demonstrating that learning could occur without any overt behavior by the learner. That is, the learner didn't have to do anything except observe what was going on around her. No behavior pattern was produced and no reinforcement was given.

The basic premise of the theory is that events and consequences in the learning situation are cognitively processed before they are learned or influence behavior. It is the processing of information that leads to learning and changes in behavior. Certainly the consequences of behavior (reinforcement or punishment) influence the likelihood of that behavior in the future, but they do so as a result of how they are perceived, interpreted, and stored in memory. Thus one can learn by observing the behavior of others and the consequences that result. This theory is at odds with the strict behaviorists, who claim that learning can occur only as a result of one's own behavior and the resulting consequences. The cognitive processes that are a part of social learning theory are *motivation, attention, retention,* and to some extent *behavioral reproduction.* Figure 3.6 illustrates the relationships among these cognitive processes.

Motivation

Although we have discussed motivation at length earlier in this chapter, it is useful to see how it fits in with social learning theory. As the model indicates, motivation both influences and is influenced by the other processes. The learners' needs determine what things receive attention and are processed for retention. As is depicted in the model, social learning theory incorporates the operant conditioning concept of behavioral consequences affecting the likelihood of future behavior. However, whereas operant conditioning principles stipulate that the consequence can only be learned through learner behavior-consequence pairings, social learning theory sug-

---

FIGURE 3.6 The Cognitive Processes Involved in Social Learning

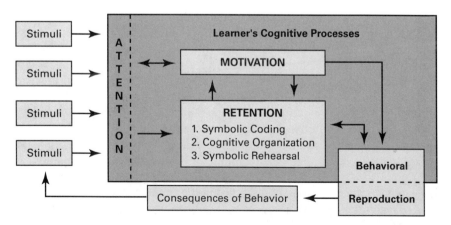

gests that behavioral consequences can be acquired through **anticipatory learning.** Anticipatory learning occurs when a person learns what consequences are associated with a behavior (or set of behaviors) without actually engaging in the behavior or receiving the consequences. By observing someone else's behavior, the observer can learn something about how to perform the behavior and also something about the consequences of the behavior. Thus this theory provides a model for learning through observation alone. That's why it is often referred to as a theory of observational or vicarious learning. The model of learning processes illustrated in Figure 3.6 is more than just observational learning, however. It combines cognitive and behaviorist concepts into a comprehensive set of integrated processes that are applicable to all types of learning, providing another set of tools for designing and implementing training. Additional motivational issues are discussed later in the motivation-to-learn section.

Attention

The learning process begins with the learner's **attention** becoming focused on particular objects and events in the environment (stimuli). Of the great multitude of objects and events in the typical environment, we notice many of them but pay attention to only a portion of these. The things we pay attention to are those that stand out for some reason (loud, bright, unusual, etc.) or those that we have learned are important (e.g., lead to need satisfaction). This reaction is reflected in the fact that we are more likely to model the behavior of someone who is spotlighted in some way (highly publicized, unusually attractive, very popular, etc.) than someone who isn't. Similarly, we are more likely to model someone who seems to receive a lot of reinforcement than someone who receives little.

The concept of attention is important in training. Making key learning points stand out so that the trainees will focus their attention on them improves learning. Eliminating extraneous objects like cell phones and beepers keeps trainees from becoming distracted during training. Making learning exercises fun and interesting will keep attention focused on the learning topic. However, exercises that are fun but don't relate to the learning objectives will draw attention away from what you want trainees to learn, making the training less effective. These issues and others related to capturing trainee attention are addressed in the training design chapter.

Retention

Once attention has been focused on an object or event, the incoming information is processed for possible retention. Some of the information will be retained, some will be lost. The more that training can facilitate the **retention** processes, the more learning that can occur. The initial phase of retention is the translation of the information into symbols meaningful to the individual. This is called **symbolic coding.** It typically takes the form of reducing the external objects and events into internal images and verbal symbols. These symbols are then organized into the existing cognitive structure through associations with previously stored information. This process, **cognitive organization,** can be facilitated in training by asking the trainees to provide examples of how the new information relates to what they already know. This exercise serves two purposes. It allows the trainee to code more easily and store the information, and it allows the trainer to see if the desired associations are being made. Other ways in which training can facilitate retention are discussed in the training design chapter.

To facilitate the retention process, the learner should "practice" the learned material through **symbolic rehearsal.** This means visualizing or imagining how the knowledge or skill will be used. If the focus is on skill building, the trainee imagines using the skills in different situations. This is usually fairly easy to do since the skill helps to define the situations. When the focus of learning is knowledge, it is sometimes more difficult to imagine how it can or will be used. For example, think back to when you were learning the multiplication tables. Most of us had to memorize these through constant repetition over many months, and that repetition provided us with the experience of using multiplication to solve problems; Each year as we advanced to the next grade, we were given more problems to solve that required multiplication. In contrast, storing information without any associations with personal use—in other words, just memorizing—typically results in only short-term retention. Students who have crammed for an exam are probably familiar with this phenomenon. Thus associating information with its uses enhances the storage and retrieval process. The symbolic rehearsal process can be thought of as mental practice. Observing others use the knowledge or skill provides additional opportunities for symbolic rehearsal, because as you watch them you can put yourself in their place. Symbolic rehearsal also increases the ability to generalize the learning to novel situations. The training design chapter discusses other ways to enhance retention through symbolic rehearsal.

Behavioral Reproduction

Behavioral reproduction is repeated practice. The more practice a person has using new information, the more it is learned and retained. The effectiveness of practice depends on how the practice is designed and reinforced, as we will discuss in detail in the training design chapter. Figure 3.6 shows the behavioral reproduction process as being a part of both the learner's cognitive processes and the external environment. This duality reflects the fact that behavior is initiated by the person's cognitive processes—the person must retrieve the appropriate behavior from storage and direct the body to perform the appropriate actions—and then the behavior itself actually occurs in and becomes part of the environment.

We have already spent considerable time discussing the importance of behavioral consequences. One additional point is worth making, however. If consequences are to affect behavior, the individuals must be aware of these consequences. For example, assume a supervisor recommends an employee for a bonus but hasn't yet told the employee. Subjectively for the employee, this is not a consequence of behavior, even though objectively it is. Even when the person is aware of a consequence, she may misinterpret its value. The supervisor who is disappointed in an employee's performance and sarcastically says, "Really nice job" may be misinterpreted by the employee as giving praise. Thus the person must be aware of and correctly interpret behavioral consequences if those consequences are going to have the desired effect. Effective training programs need to call attention to the desirable consequences of learning and of using the learning back on the job.

Why Are They Resisting and What Can I Do about It?

Learning, like eating, is one of the most fundamental processes of survival, yet trainers and managers continually complain about trainees who don't pay attention, are disruptive, and generally demonstrate a resistance to the training they are receiving.

Often the older the trainees or the higher their education, the more resistance they show. If learning is a basic human process, why are there so many complaints like this?

The first step to understanding **resistance to learning** is viewing learning as a performance outcome. Most learning isn't something that happens automatically or unconsciously. It's an activity we decide to do or not do. From the performance model discussed earlier (see Figure 3.1 on page 85), we know that learning performance is determined by a person's motivation, KSAs, and learning environment.

MOTIVATION TO LEARN

Most trainees arrive at training with an elaborate and highly integrated cognitive structure. They already know a lot about themselves, their work, their company, and many other things (Baltes and Willis 1976; Griffith et al. 1980; Knowles 1984, Pierce et al 1989). The objective of training is to change some part of that cognitive structure so that the trainee's performance will be improved. Change creates anxiety, however, for the following reasons:

Fear of the unknown:	"Right now I know how things work, but I don't know how this training will affect things."
Fear of incompetence:	"I don't know if I'll be able to learn this stuff."
Fear of losing rewards:	"What will happen to my pay, status, perks, etc.?"
Fear of lost influence:	"Will this training make me more or less valuable?"
Lost investments:	"I've spent a lot of time and energy learning to do it this way. Why change?"

These concerns deal with the trainees' needs, current competencies, and how training will change their current outcomes. These factors are addressed by expectancy theory, and the trainees' motivation to learn will depend on the answers to these questions. To the degree that the answers indicate that learning is worth the effort, the individual will be motivated to learn.

Even when trainees acknowledge the value of the training, they may believe the effort required to master the learning is just not worthwhile. The reluctance of many experienced managers to learn how to use computers is one example of this attitude. They are often bright and competent in other aspects of their jobs, but they continue to use their old ways of communicating and calculating, even though they see that the computer could increase their capabilities. Their already well-developed cognitive structures can make it seem too difficult to change all they already know and learn the new KSAs. The more difficult a task is, the more resistance there is likely to be, usually in the form of withdrawal or avoidance. That's because the benefits of doing a difficult task must be much higher than the costs to induce the person to do it. Why is it that learning is more difficult for those with more extensive and developed cognitive structures?

In Piaget's terms, it is the accommodation process (developing new cognitive categories) that is the most difficult, while assimilation (adding new things to existing categories) is relatively easy. This is so because accommodation requires one to create new categories, which then need to be linked to other, related categories. The more categories that exist and the more developed they are, the more difficult the learning. When assimilating, the learner has only to add new elements and rearrange associations among elements within a single category. When accommodating, not only must learners create a new category and place elements into that category, they must also associate this category with other categories and modify the elements within those categories to create the network of associations that appropriately incorporates the new information.

This is the type of situation that occurs whenever a company changes the paradigms it uses for conducting its business. For example, think about what supervisors face when companies move from a traditional, centralized, hierarchical, autocratic decision-making process to a team-based, flexible, more consensus-based, employee-involvement system. From their experience and training in the traditional system, the supervisors have developed a cognitive structure for how to get things done. They have learned how to make all the decisions for their subordinates, and have developed a system for communicating those decisions and ensuring that they are carried out effectively. These strategies have probably been reinforced over many years. A new piece of equipment or a change in the work process brings new procedures that are learned and assimilated into the supervisor's decision-making structure relatively easily. But, under the new, team-based, employee-involvement decision making, the whole process of making decisions must be relearned because the underlying organizational assumptions have changed. For the supervisor, the focus is no longer on the quality of his decisions, but on his ability to facilitate quality decisions by the team. While some aspects of the supervisor's old decision-making process might still be useful, his cognitive structure must be changed to incorporate the new concepts, and the useful aspects of the old concepts must be reorganized and integrated with the new. This is why learning the new system will be much harder for supervisors with a lot of experience than for a newly hired supervisor with little experience in the traditional system.

Resistance to learning also comes from defensiveness. The more experienced a person is, the more she has already learned and the more developed, integrated, and complex her cognitive structure will be. A great deal of effort has gone into creating that cognitive structure. Training can, in a sense, be seen as an attack on a person's competence, especially if the training is mandatory. Trainees in this situation can also feel they are being told that the trainer knows more about how to run their area than they do. In these cases, they are likely to try to show the trainer, and the other trainees, that the training and/or the trainer is inadequate or irrelevant or that their current KSAs are better than what training has to offer.

This is not to say that older, more experienced people cannot learn new things or discard old beliefs. They frequently do. As adults mature, they appear to go through periodic episodes of cognitive reorganization, in which concepts or principles of long standing are reevaluated (Geddie and Strickland 1984; Leibowitz, Farren, and Kaye 1986). During these cognitive reorganizations, knowledge that is of little functional value is discarded and new KSAs are discovered and integrated into their cognitive structure. This is especially true in times of transition such as job or career changes. For adults, the key factor in discarding old learning and acquiring new is its practical usefulness. Training that seems abstract, theoretical, or otherwise unrelated to doing the job will likely be ignored or resisted. Training that can demonstrate its value and practical utility will find trainees eager to learn.

TRAINING THAT MOTIVATES ADULTS TO LEARN

Learning occurs quite frequently in adults when it is seen as having practical application immediately or in the near future (Knowles 1978, 1984; Tough 1979). For example, IBM sales representatives were found to average more than 1,100 hours a year in "learning episodes." (A learning episode was defined as a deliberate attempt to gain and retain some significant knowledge or skill for problem solving or personal change.) Professors, by contrast, averaged slightly more time (1,745 hours) on fewer episodes (12).

Training Relevance, Value, and Readiness to Learn

Clearly, adults are not resistant to learning if they perceive the learning to be of practical value. Some of the reasons most often mentioned for adult learning are problems on the job, job/occupational changes, home and personal responsibilities, and competency at some hobby or recreational activity. In the study referred to above, about two-thirds of the learning episodes were job related. Knowles (1984) suggested that the need to know and the readiness to learn are critical aspects in the success of adult learning programs. The *need to know* refers to the value of the knowledge to the learner. Westmeyer (1988) found that adults most often seek to learn when the learning is life-, task-, or problem-centered. *Readiness to learn* refers to the amount of prerequisite knowledge (KSAs) the trainee possesses and the trainee's belief in his or her ability to learn the material. This aspect is consistent with the principles of self-efficacy and expectancy theory. People's motivation to learn a particular knowledge or skill set will be directly influenced by their belief that if they put forth the effort, they will be successful in their learning (Expectancy 1). Beyond this they must feel that the benefits of learning the KSAs outweigh the benefits of not learning them (Expectancy 2).

The challenge faced by organizational training is to provide instruction in a context that overcomes the natural resistance of adult learners to changing their cognitive structures. Making the relevance and value of the learning clear, as it relates to the trainee's and organization's goals, addresses one source of resistance to learning. A second source can be addressed by ensuring that the trainee believes she can successfully master the training content. Over time, adults have developed feelings of low self-efficacy in certain areas and feelings of high self-efficacy in others. For those with a low self-efficacy for learning in general or for the specific content area of the training, the trainer needs to change the self-efficacy beliefs before learning can occur. Doing so requires a careful match between the trainee's characteristics (KSA level, learning style preferences, etc.) and the design of the training. By demonstrating that learning in this subject area can be as easy as in areas in which trainees have high self-efficacy, trainers can overcome a significant type of resistance to learning.

Allowing Trainees Control over Their Learning

As we have pointed out, trainees walk into training with well-developed cognitive maps that reflect their experiences. Because these experiences differ from person to person, any given training group is likely to differ considerably in the KSAs they possess and in their learning strategies. Trainees often view these differences as hindrances to their learning and resist training with others who are dissimilar. However, these differences can be viewed as a learning resource if the trainees are willing to share their experiences and strategies and if the training environment supports such an exchange. In fact, adult learners prefer sharing their learning experience with others if the environment is supportive. While adults have been found to prefer to plan their own learning projects and to adopt a self-directed approach to learning, this preference doesn't imply a desire to learn in isolation. Rather, it reflects a desire to set their own pace, establish their own structure for learning, and have flexibility in the learning methods. More often than not, adults seek learning assistance from others. In short, they don't mind learning from others, but they want to maintain some control over the learning experience. These characteristics suggest training that has individualized components and also makes use of shared, relevant experiences that will be most effective at overcoming resistance to learning.

While it is true that many adults will be able to learn new competencies even when they are not told the significance or usefulness of the training, they are much less likely to be able to apply these new competencies to their job. For example, trainees receiving instruction on how to perform a set of skills showed improved performance at the end of training, but they failed to use the skills on their own or to generalize the skill usage to similar situations (Belmont and Butterfield 1971; Brown and Palicsar 1982). Training that provided instruction on the "how to" and included the "why and when" resulted in improved performance as well as independent maintenance of the skill across appropriate situations (Borkowski 1985; Kendall, Borkowski, and Cavanaugh 1980; Walker 1987).

Involving Trainees in the Process
Training, then, should take into account the motivational and cognitive processes that influence the trainee's readiness and willingness to learn. Many writers have emphasized the importance of participation, choice, personal experiences, critical reflection, and critical thinking as key characteristics of adult learning (Brookfield 1987; Knowles 1984; Marsick 1987). This boils down to involving the trainees in the learning process from needs assessment to design and evaluation. This involvement is a key part of overcoming resistance to change. You may remember, from the discussion of OD principles in chapter 2, that involving those who are affected by change in planning and implementing the change creates a sense of ownership. The result is increased commitment to the change, as well as better implementation. Supervisors as well as trainees should be involved in determining the training needs, since both are affected by the change. Supervisors have a clearer understanding of why new KSAs are necessary, how they fit in with the overall plans for the work unit, and the consequences of their employees having or not having the new KSAs. The trainees in turn see what KSAs they need to improve and understand why those KSAs will be of value. Involving trainees in needs analysis and other parts of the training process will be discussed in more depth in the relevant chapters.

Individual Differences Related to Learning

While we have indicated that it is desirable to consider diversity among trainees as an opportunity, this is true only up to a point. For example, trainees who are substantially less knowledgeable than others can create significant problems. They may not be able to keep up with the material, or if the material is presented at a pace they can keep up with the more knowledgeable trainees are bored to tears. It's not just differences in KSAs that can create problems in a training group. A fairly recent paper provides a

TABLE 3.5 Dimensions for Trainee Assessment Prior to Training	
1. Instrumentality	Desire for immediate applicability of the material to be learned
2. Skepticism	Need for logic, evidence, and examples
3. Resistance to change	Fear of unknown or personal consequences of change related to feelings about self-efficacy and locus of control orientation
4. Attention span	Amount of time before attentiveness is substantially diminished
5. Expectation level	Trainee's quality/quantity requirements of training
6. Dominant needs	Intrinsic and extrinsic motivators that drive the trainee
7. Absorption level	Pace at which trainee expects and can absorb new material
8. Topical interest	Trainee's personal (job-relevant) interest in the material

contingency approach to adult learning (Newstrom and Lengnick-Hall 1991) that considers certain characteristics of trainees that can make a real difference. This approach suggests that significant differences on the characteristics listed in Table 3.5 will require different approaches to training and development. At the very least, the authors suggest that these are areas that need to be assessed prior to training.

While the logic of this approach makes some sense, research in many of these areas is sparse or nonexistent. Currently, research in the areas of resistance to change, absorption level, and topical interest provide some substantiation for providing different training designs to different populations. For example, those with low self-efficacy should have training that first addresses the self-efficacy issue; for those with a high sense of self-efficacy, this training would seem not only irrelevant, but probably demeaning. Of course, providing different training designs becomes more complex and more costly for the organization.

While it is true that differences in learning characteristics can have important consequences for training, providing separate training sessions may not always be the most practical or cost-effective way to achieve the organization's HRD goals. Thus training programs need to be designed so that they can accommodate a sufficiently large group of trainees while at the same time considering individual differences. Training design issues are discussed in more detail in a later chapter. However, training professionals should consider the following nine principles in developing training programs for their employees (adapted from Gordon, Morgan, and Ponticell 1995):

1. Identify the types of individual learning strengths and problems and tailor the training around these.
2. Align learning objectives to organizational goals.
3. Clearly define program goals and objectives at the start.
4. Actively engage the trainee, thus maximizing attention, expectations, and memory.
5. Use a systematic, logically connected sequencing of learning activities so that trainees have mastered lower levels of learning before moving to higher levels.
6. Use a variety of training methods.
7. Use realistic job- or life-relevant training material.
8. Allow trainees to work together and share experiences.
9. Provide constant feedback and reinforcement while encouraging self-assessment.

By applying these principles to training programs, the trainer can address the diversity of characteristics trainees bring to training within the context of a group learning environment.

Key Terms

- Accommodation
- Anticipatory learning
- Assimilation
- Attention
- Behavioral reproduction
- Chaining
- Cognition
- Cognitive organization
- Cognitive process
- Cognitive structure
- Concept learning
- Discrimination learning
- Environment
- ERG theory
- Existence needs
- Expectancy theory
- Extinction
- Growth needs
- Law of effect
- Learning
- Motivation
- Needs theory
- Negative reinforcement

- Operant conditioning
- Performance model
- Positive reinforcement
- Primary reinforcer
- Principles
- Principle learning
- Problem solving
- Process theories
- Punishment
- Relatedness needs
- Resistance to learning
- Retention
- Secondary reinforcer
- Self-efficacy
- Shaping
- Signal learning
- Social learning theory
- Stimulus–response learning
- Symbolic coding
- Symbolic rehearsal
- Theories
- Valence
- Verbal association learning

Case Analysis

RICK'S NEW JOB

Rick recently received an MBA. At college he was known as a smart, hardworking, and friendly fellow. His good grades landed him an internship with Peterson Paper Products to head up their sales department. Near the end of the internship Val Peterson, the president and founder of the company, asked Rick to meet him after work to discuss the future.

PETERSON PAPER PRODUCTS

Peterson Paper Products, or PPP, was founded 17 years ago by Val Peterson. It purchases raw paper of varying grades and produces paper stock for business and personal stationery and greeting cards. It has annual sales of about $15 million and employs 80 to 90 people depending on demand. Sales have gradually declined over the last two years after steady and sometimes spectacular growth during the previous seven years. Competition has increased markedly over the last three years, and profit margins have dwindled. PPP has been known for the high quality of its products, but consumers have been shifting from premium-priced, high-quality products to products with higher overall value. Through all of this PPP has maintained a very close-knit family culture. At least half of the employees have been with the company since the beginning or are friends or relatives of the Petersons or Mr. Ball, Val's partner.

Val Peterson, 53, holds the majority of stock in this privately held company that he founded. He began working summers in a paper company during high school. He supervised a shift at a paper plant while he went to college at night. After graduation he worked at increasingly higher management levels, occasionally switching employers for a promotion. Eighteen years ago he quit his vice presidency with a major paper product manufacturer to start his own company. Employees see him as charismatic, even tempered, and reasonable. He spends most of his time and energy on company business, putting in 12-hour days.

Rosie Peterson, 50, is Val's second wife and has been married to him for 21 years. She is the controller for the company and holds 5% of the company stock. Rosie never went to college, and her accounting methods are rather primitive (all paper and pencil). Nonetheless, she is always on top of the financial picture and puts in nearly as many hours as Val. She has a great deal of influence in the operations and the direction of PPP.

Walter Ball, 61, is both Mr. Peterson's friend and business partner. He owns 25% of the stock and has known Val since before the start of PPP. He is VP of Operations, which means he oversees the computer information systems that run the paper production process and handles the technical side of the business. He is not very current on the latest computer or manufacturing technology, but he loves the paper business. He says he will probably retire at 65, but most people say they'll believe it when they see it.

Diane Able, 41, is the customer service manager and is married to Steve Able, the chief engineer. Diane has worked her way up in the company over the last ten years. She is often asked to assist Mr. Peterson with projects because of her common sense, and he trusts her to keep information to herself.

RICK'S OFFER

When Rick met Mr. Peterson to "discuss the future," he was nervous. He knew Mr. Peterson liked his work so far, but didn't know if it was enough to extend his internship another six months. So far he had worked only with Mr. Peterson on special projects and didn't know the rest of the management group very well. He was flabbergasted when Mr. Peterson said, "I was thinking that you might like work here at PPP full time and help us out with our sales department."

The two of them discussed the problems in the sales area and talked about what could be done to boost sales. Rick agreed to start the next Monday. During this conversation Rosie walked in, and she suggested they all go out to dinner. At dinner Rosie emphasized to Rick that PPP was a family operation, very down to earth and informal. "You probably shouldn't try to change things too quickly," she warned. "People need to have time to get used to you. You have to remember, you're an outsider here and everyone else is an insider." Then Val moved the conversation back to what the future could be like at PPP.

RICK'S AWAKENING

The first few days at work Rick spent in getting to know the plant and operations, meeting all the employees, and familiarizing himself with the problems in sales. He met with Val each morning and afternoon. He also met with the key managers, not only to introduce himself, but to convey his desire to work collaboratively with them in addressing the problems in sales. He was conscious not to flaunt his college education and to convey that he recognized he was a newcomer and had a lot to learn. In the middle of his second week, Val told him that his reception by the other employees was going very well. "Your enthusiasm and motivation seem to be contagious. Having you join us shows them that things need to change if we're going to reach our goals."

Rick had noticed, however, that the managers always went out in groups, and he hadn't been invited along. He also wasn't included in the informal discussion groups that formed periodically during the day. In fact, the conversation usually stopped when he approached. Everyone was very friendly, he thought; maybe it would just take a little more time.

By his third week Rick had identified some of the problems in the Sales Department. There were only four salespeople and their morale and productivity were moderate to low. He was unable to find any sales strategy, mission, or objectives. The records showed that Val was by far the leading salesman. The others indicated that Mr. Peterson "always works with us very closely to make sure we do things right. If he senses there might be a problem, he steps in right away." After formulating a plan, Rick discussed it with Mr. Peterson. "First, I would like to institute weekly sales meetings so we keep everyone up to date. I also want to create a centralized sales data base," he told him. Mr. Peterson smiled and agreed. Rick felt he was finally a manager. He did feel that he should have mentioned his idea for creating a sales department mission and strategy, but recalled Rosie's caution about not moving too fast.

Rick discussed with Mr. Ball the possibility of using the centralized computer system to run word processing and spreadsheet software on terminals. Mr. Ball was concerned that the data in the spreadsheets could be accessed by outsiders. Anyway, he didn't think the system could handle that since its primary function was production. Puzzled, Rick asked if there was a PC that could be allocated to him. Mr. Ball said that no one in the company had one.

"Well," Rick thought, "I'll just have to bring mine from home." The next Monday Rick walked through the office carrying his computer. Several of the other managers looked at him quizzically. Making light of it he said, "I'm not smart enough to keep everything in my head and I don't have enough time to write it all down on paper." As he was setting up the computer he got a call from Val. "Rick, that computer you brought in has caused a heck of a ruckus. Can you lie low with it until I get back late this afternoon?" Rick thought he sounded very strained, but chalked it up to overwork. He agreed and left the computer on his desk, partly assembled. Five minutes later Rosie walked into his office.

"Do you think it's funny bringing that thing in here? What are you trying to prove—how backward we all are? How much better you are with your big initials behind your name? You're still an outsider here, buster, and don't forget it."

Rick tried to explain how much more productive the Sales Department would be and that he had tried to use the company's computer system. However, Rosie wasn't listening. "Did you think about checking with me before bringing that in? With Val or even Walter? Don't you think we have a right to know what you're bringing in here?" Rick knew argument would do no good, so he apologized for not checking with everyone first. He said he had a meeting with Val for later to talk about it. Rosie said, "Good, talk to Val. But don't think he calls all the shots here."

At the meeting with Val, Val agreed that the computer would certainly help solve the problems in sales. "But, you have to be sensitive to the feelings of Rosie and the other managers. It would be best if you didn't use the computer for a while until things calm down."

The next day Walter walked into Rick's office. He told Rick he had moved far too fast with the computer. "That's not how it's done here, son. Maybe you're spending too much time listening to what Val says. He isn't really the one to talk to about these kinds of issues. Next time you just ask old Uncle Walter."

Without his computer, Rick spent the next few weeks building the data base by hand and conducting sales meetings with his staff. He had tried to set up meetings with Mr. Peterson, but Val was usually too busy. One day, Rick asked Diane Able about not being able to see Mr. Peterson and she said, "You know, you monopolized a lot of his time early on. Those of us who had worked closely with him before you came were pushed aside so he could spend time with you. Now, it's your turn to wait."

"Are you the one who's been spending all the time with him?" Rick asked.

"Well, it's been me and some of the other managers. We've really been taking a beating in sales so we have to figure out how to reduce our costs," Ms. Able answered.

A few weeks later Rick was called in to Val's office. Val began, "Rick, you know we've been going through some bad times. We're reducing head count and I'm afraid you're one of the people we're going to let go. It has nothing to do with your work. You haven't really been here long enough to have either succeeded or failed. It's just that we had unrealistic expectations about how quickly things in sales would turn around. I feel terrible having to do this and I'll do everything I can to help you find another job."

After packing his things and loading up the car, Rick sat in his car and stared out the window. "Welcome to the real world," he thought to himself.

CASE QUESTIONS

1. Why do you think Rick was let go? How does reinforcement theory apply to this situation?
2. Explain Rosie's and Walter's reaction to Rick's computer in terms of resistance to change.
3. Explain Rick's inability to "fit in" using social learning theory. Where did the breakdowns occur?
4. If Val hired you to develop a management training program for the senior managers at PPP, how would you go about designing the program? Provide appropriate theoretical rationale to support your position.

Exercises

1. Implementing a social learning strategy:
   a. In consultation with a friend, co-worker, or fellow student, identify a target behavior the person doesn't currently have but would like to have.
   b. Develop a social learning strategy for the person to acquire that behavior.
   c. Implement the strategy.
   d. In small groups or with the entire class describe what you tried to do and what happened.

2. In discussion groups of four to six people, identify the differences among you that would impact the kind of training you would prefer. Use Table 3.5 on page 118 to start your discussion, but don't limit it to just those characteristics. What accounts for the differences and similarities among your group?

3. Observe an introductory course in computer science or mathematics. Then observe an introductory course in art or music. Which course uses a more behavioral and which a more cognitive approach to learning? If possible, interview the instructors to find out why they use the approach they do. Describe the match between the instructional approach and the subject matter.

4. Class motivation:
   a. In a small group discuss the most important outcome you want to achieve in this class (it may or may not be a letter grade). Have each person indicate how valuable that outcome is to him or her using a scale from 1 = "not at all desirable" to 10 = "extremely desirable."
   b. After a person has described his most important outcome, have him indicate how motivated he is to achieve this compared with the other things he wants to do this term (use a scale of 1 = "not at all motivated" to 10 = "extremely motivated").
   c. Then have the person describe the things he will have to do (performance level) in order to achieve that outcome.
   d. Next, have him indicate his Expectancy 1 level (his belief that he will reach the performance level). Then have him describe his Expectancy 2 (the likelihood that successful performance will result in the outcome). Use probabilities (e.g., .1 = "very unlikely," .5 = "50% chance of happening," .9 = "very likely") to reflect expectancies.
   e. After everyone has completed step D, examine the expectancy linkages to see how well they conform to the person's level of motivation. Discuss any discrepancies and why they exist.

Questions for Review

1. Explain the behavioral and cognitive approaches to learning. Which is most relevant to training. Explain your answer.
2. List an example for each of Gagné's learning types 3–8 showing how it can be used in training. Use examples that have not been used in the text.
3. You're a trainer who is explaining expectancy theory to a group of managers so they can better understand and deal with employee motivation problems.

One of the managers says, "I don't have time for this theory stuff. I want real world training that helps me in my job." How would you respond to the trainee? What is your rationale for your response?

4. Explain why different people need different training methods.
5. How can training be designed to motivate learning and accommodate trainee differences?

References

Alderfer, C. 1969. An empirical test of a new theory of human needs. *Organizational Behavior and Human Performance,* 4(2): 142–75.

Ausubel, D. P. 1963. *The Psychology of Meaningful Verbal Learning.* New York: Grune and Stratton.

Baltes, P. B., and S. L. Willis. 1976. Toward psychological theories of aging. In *Handbook on Psychology of Aging,* edited by J. E. Birren and K. W. Schaie. New York: Reinhold-Van-Nostrand.

Bandura, A. 1977a. *Social Learning Theory.* Upper Saddle River, NJ: Prentice Hall.

———. 1977b. Self-efficacy: Towards a unifying theory of behavioral change. *Psychological Review* 84:191–215.

Belmont, J., and E. Butterfield. 1971. Learning strategies as determinants of memory deficiencies. *Cognitive Psychology* 2: 411–20.

Borkowski, J. 1985. Sign of intelligence: Strategy generalization and metacognition. In *The Growth of Reflection,* edited by S. R. Yussen. New York: Academic Press.

Brookfield, S. 1987. *Developing Critical Thinkers.* San Francisco: Jossey-Bass.

Brown, A., and A. Palicsar. 1982. Inducing strategic learning from texts by means of informed, self-control training. *Learning and Learning Disabilities,* April, pp. 1–17.

Bruner, J. S. 1966. *Toward a Theory of Instruction.* New York: Norton.

Deming, W. 1986. *Out of the Crisis.* Massachusetts Institute of Technology.

Dobyns, L., and C. Crawford-Mason. 1991. *Quality or Else.* Boston: Houghton Mifflin.

Gagné, R. M. 1962. Military training and principles of learning. *American Psychologist* 17: 83–91.

———. 1965. *The Conditions of Learning.* New York: Holt, Rinehart and Winston.

———. 1974. *Essentials of Learning for Instruction.* Hinsdale, IL: Dryden Press.

Gagné, R. M., and W. Dick. 1983. Instructional psychology. *Annual Review of Psychology* 34:261–95.

Gecas, V. 1989. The social psychology of self-efficacy. In *Annual Review of Sociology,* edited by W. R. Scott and J. Blake. Palo Alto: Annual Reviews, Inc., 15:291–316.

Geddie, C., and B. Strickland. 1984. From plateaus to progress: A model for career development. *Training,* June, pp. 56–61.

Gist, M. 1987. Self-efficacy: Implications for organizational behavior and human resource management. *Academy of Management Review,* July, pp. 472–85.

Gordon, E., R. Morgan, and J. Ponticell. 1995. The individualized training alternative. *Training and Development,* September, pp. 52–60.

Griffith, G., A. Tourgh, W. Barnard, and D. Brundage. 1980. *The Design of Self-Directed Learning.* Toronto: Ontario Institute for Studies in Education.

Grote, D. 1995. *Discipline Without Punishment.* New York: AMACOM.

Kendall, C., J. Borkowski, and J. Cavanaugh, 1980. Metamemory and the transfer of an interrogative strategy by EMR children. *Intelligence* 4:255–70.

Kimble, G. A. 1967. *Foundations of Conditioning and Learning.* New York: Appleton.

Knowles, M. S. 1978. *The Adult Learner: A Neglected Species.* Houston: Gulf Publishing.

———. 1984. Adult learning: Theory and practice. In *The Handbook of Human Resource*

Development, edited by D. A. Nadler. New York: Wiley.

———. 1989. *The Making of an Adult Educator.* San Francisco: Jossey-Bass.

Kraiger, K., J. Ford, and E. Salas. 1993. Application of cognitive, skill-based, and affective theories of learning outcomes to new methods of training evaluation. *Journal of Applied Psychology* 78(2):311–28.

Kraut, A. J. 1976. Behavior modeling symposium: Developing managerial skills via modeling techniques. *Personnel Psychology* 29:325–28.

Latham, G. P., and L. M. Sarri. 1979. Application of social learning theory to training supervisors through behavioral modeling. *Journal of Applied Psychology* 64:239–46.

Lawler, E. E., S. A. Mohrman, and G. E. Ledford. 1995. *Creating High Performance Organizations: Practices and Results of Employee Involvement and Total Quality Mangagement in Fortune 1000 Companies.* San Francisco: Jossey-Bass.

Leibowitz, Z. B., C. Farren, and B. L. Kaye. 1986. *Designing Career Development Systems.* San Francisco: Jossey-Bass.

Locke, E. A., E. F. Lee, and P. Bobko. 1984. Effect of Self-Efficacy, Goals, and Task Strategies of Task Performance. *Journal of Applied Psychology,* May, pp. 241–51.

Marsick, V. 1987. *Learning in the Workplace: Theory and Practice.* London: Croom Helm.

Manz, C. C., and H. P. Simms. 1981. Vicarious learning: The influence of modeling on organizational behavior. *Academy of Management Review* 6:105–13.

Maslow, A. H. 1954. *Motivation and Personality.* New York: Harper & Row.

———. 1968. *Toward a Psychology of Being.* 2d ed. New York: Van Nostrand Reinhold.

Newstrom, J. W., and M. L. Lengnick-Hall. 1991. One size does not fit all. *Training and Development Journal* 45(6):43–48.

Pavlov, I. P. 1897. *Lectures on the Principle Digestive Glands.* St. Petersburg, Russia: Kushnereff.

———. 1912. Principle laws of the activity of the central nervous system as they find expression in conditioned reflexes. As reported by G. Murphy and J. Kovach in *Historical Introduction to Modern Psychology.* New York: Harcourt Brace Jovanovich.

Piaget, J. 1954. *The Construction of Reality in the Child.* New York: Basic Books.

Pierce, J., D. Gardner, L. Cummings, and R. Dunham. 1989. Organization based self-esteem: Construct definition, measurement, and validation. *Academy of Management Journal,* September, pp. 622–48.

Schacter, D. 1996. *Searching for Memory: The Brain, the Mind and the Past.* New York: Basic Books.

Schneider, C. P., and C. Alderfer. 1973. Three studies of measures of need satisfaction in organizations. *Administrative Science Quarterly,* December, pp. 489–505.

Skinner, B. F. 1938. *The Behavior of Organisms.* New York: Appleton-Century-Crofts.

———. 1953. *Science and Human Behavior.* New York: Macmillan.

———. 1968. *The Technology of Teaching.* New York: Appleton-Century-Crofts.

———. 1971. *Beyond Freedom and Dignity.* New York: Bantam/Vintage.

Squire, L., A. Shimamura, and P. Graf. 1985. Independence of recognition memory and priming effects: A neuropsychological analysis, *Journal of Experimental Psychology—Learning, Memory, and Cognition.* 11 (January):34–44.

Squire, L. and S. Zola-Morgan. 1991. The medial temporal lobe memory system. *Science,* 253 (September 20):1380–86.

Thorndike, E. L. 1905. *The Elements of Psychology.* New York: Seiler.

———. 1913. The psychology of learning. *Educational Psychology,* vol. 2. New York: Teachers College, Columbia University Press.

———. 1932. *Purposive Behavior in Animals and Men.* New York: Appleton-Century-Crofts.

Tough, A. 1979. New conclusions on why and how adults learn. *Training,* January, pp. 8–10.

Vroom, V. 1964. *Work and Motivation.* New York: Wiley.

Walker, C. 1987. Relative importance of domain knowledge and overall aptitude on acquisition of domain related information. *Cognition and Instruction* 4:25–42.

Westmeyer, P. 1988. *Effective Teaching in Adult and Higher Education.* Springfield, IL: Charles C Thomas.

CHAPTER 4

Needs Analysis

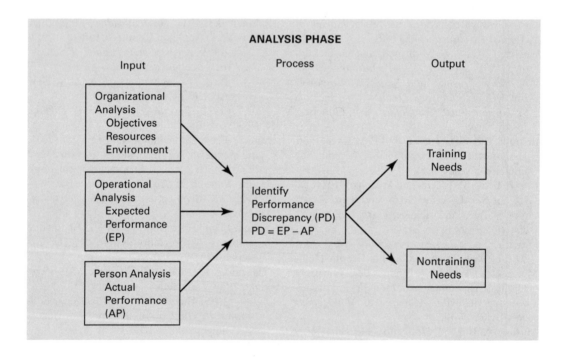

ANALYSIS PHASE

Input	Process	Output
Organizational Analysis Objectives Resources Environment		
Operational Analysis Expected Performance (EP)	Identify Performance Discrepancy (PD) PD = EP – AP	Training Needs
Person Analysis Actual Performance (AP)		Nontraining Needs

Learning Objectives

After reading this chapter you should be able to:

- Describe the purpose of a needs analysis

- Explain the difference between proactive and reactive needs analysis

- List and describe the steps in conducting a needs analysis

- Develop criterion measures appropriate for needs analysis

- Describe the relationship between needs analysis and the design and evaluation of training

---

Developing a Training Package at Westcan

Chris, a human resource manager at Westcan, was called into her boss's office one morning. "I just saw an old training film called *Meetings Bloody Meetings,* starring John Cleese. It deals with effective ways of running meetings. They showed it at the executive development seminar I'm attending," said Irven, the new vice president of Human Resources. Irven, a competent and well-liked engineer, had been promoted to vice president three months earlier. Although he had no HR expertise, he had been an effective production manager, and it was hoped that he would provide a measure of credibility to the HR department. In the past, HR had been seen as the department that forced its silly ideas on the rest of the company with little understanding of how to make these ideas work.

"With the number of team meetings we have company wide, I think we need some training on how to conduct effective meetings," Irven said. "Everyone can use this. It will be high profile and we can begin to gain the respect we need to be effective. What do you think?" "Well," said Chris "I . . . ." "Oh yes," Irven interjected, "I talked to a few managers this morning and they were enthusiastic about it. It's the first time I have ever seen managers enthusiastic about any type of training. Do we have such a training package available?" "No, I don't believe so," Chris replied. "Well," said Irven, "we need a one-day training session. It must be interesting, useful, generalizable to all managers. Okay?" With that, Irven stood up, signaling that the meeting was over.

Chris went to work designing the training. She began by examining some books that dealt with meetings. Then she called Larry, a friend at Satellite Systems, to see what he had. He faxed over a copy of a lecture he had given on the do's and don'ts of an effective meeting. It was nicely broken down into three parts: premeeting, meeting, and postmeeting. That information and a simulated meeting (to provide hands-on practice) could make up the one-day training program. Chris had never written a simulation and would need some help. She put in a call to one of her subordinates, Karen, a recent university graduate who had majored in HR. Karen would surely be able to help develop a simulation.

Why Conduct a Needs Analysis?

The main objective of training is to improve the performance of both the individual and the organization (Rummler 1987). Sometimes employees do not meet their job performance requirements. Recall from chapter 1 that a training needs analysis (TNA) is a systematic method for determining what needs to be done to bring performance in a particular job or set of jobs to the expected level. In some cases the needs analysis determines that employees lack necessary KSAs to do the job, and training is required. In other cases employees have the requisite KSAs to do the job, but roadblocks to effective performance are discovered that need to be removed. Training professionals make sure the right training is being provided to the right people by conducting needs analysis. The Westcan case illustrates a situation that often occurs in organizations.

At this point in the case, Chris is overlooking a critical part of the training process. She has not completed a TNA, instead relying on her boss's telling her what type of training is needed. She has jumped directly to the training design phase. As you go through this chapter, you will discover that if she had first conducted a TNA, she could have accomplished several important things:

- Increased the chances that the time and money spent on training would be spent wisely
- Determined the benchmark for evaluation of training
- Increased the motivation of participants
- Provided an essential component in the implementation of the strategic plan

Why spend thousands of dollars on a training program no one may have needed in the first place? With increased concern about costs in organizations today, it is important that all departments, including human resources, justify expenses.

A TNA provides a benchmark (premeasure) of the skills trainees have before training. This can be compared to a measure of the skills acquired in training (postmeasure). With pre- and postmeasures, it is possible to demonstrate the cost savings or value added as a result of training (Cascio 1991a, 1989). Although some evaluation designs do not require them, pretests provide a logical benchmark for evaluation. The needs analysis provides that pretest.

Regarding motivation, a TNA ensures that training focuses on KSAs the trainees really need. When training is perceived as relevant, it is more likely to create interest. In contrast, employees who are sent for training but do not need it are not going to take the training seriously. Their lack of interest may at a minimum be distracting to those who need the training or, worse, may cause the other trainees not to take it seriously. The needs analysis also allows the trainer to present a logical explanation, at the start of training about what's not happening now (but should be) on the job, and how the training will be useful. A good needs analysis not only ensures that only those who need the training are included, it also provides the data to show why the training is needed.

As we discussed in chapter 2, implementing a strategic plan requires careful analysis of the organization's human resource capabilities. A TNA is the process for determining the degree to which employees have the competencies to carry out the strategies.

Conducting a TNA is not always necessary. For example, when an organization is trying to convey a new corporate message or instill a new culture (attitude change), it would be advisable to educate *all* its employees. Consider a company's concerns regarding sexual harassment. To be sure everyone is aware of how seriously top management considers breaches of their "sexual harassment" policy, company-wide education on this issue would be the best choice. Sending everyone to a workshop on sexual harassment would ensure that management's expectations regarding this issue are clear. It would also demonstrate to the courts the employer's position should an employee consider a sexual harassment lawsuit.

Another situation in which a TNA might not be necessary is when team-building skills are needed for new teams. Here the goal is to build the dynamics of the team so that the members work together cohesively and effectively, as well as to provide the relevant KSAs. Everyone on the team must be part of the training, even though he or she may already possess many team KSAs.

For most types of training, however, a needs analysis will increase the relevance and effectiveness of training. For example, team building for teams that have been working together for a while would benefit from a TNA. In this case the needs analysis would focus on the team, not the individuals. Only teams that demonstrate problems in effectiveness or cohesion would go through training. Teams that are already functioning effectively wouldn't need to attend, so the overall cost of training is reduced.

The Framework for Conducting a TNA

A TNA is generally made up of three distinct but closely interrelated components: organization analysis, operations analysis, and person analysis (McGehee and Thayer 1961). Figure 4.1 provides a model of these three components.

Organizational analysis involves looking at the internal environment of the organization[1] and determining its fit with organizational goals and objectives. It is also an examination of how these factors affect job performance. Finally, the organizational analysis identifies constraints on training. For example, the small business owner who employs unskilled assembly-line workers may wish to move to a more team-oriented approach, but if none of the workers is able to read above third-grade level, there is a

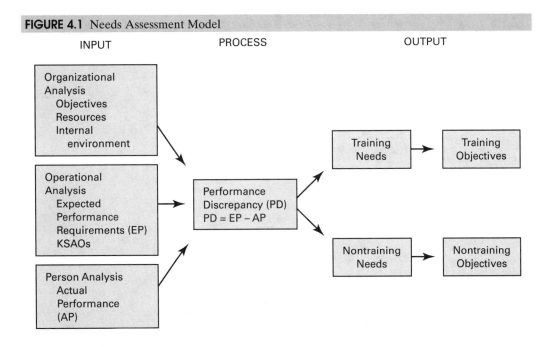

FIGURE 4.1 Needs Assessment Model

---

[1] The term *internal environment* refers to all influences that could affect employee performance (e.g., structure, policies and procedures, job design).

FIGURE 4.2 Model of Process When Performance Discrepancy Is Identified

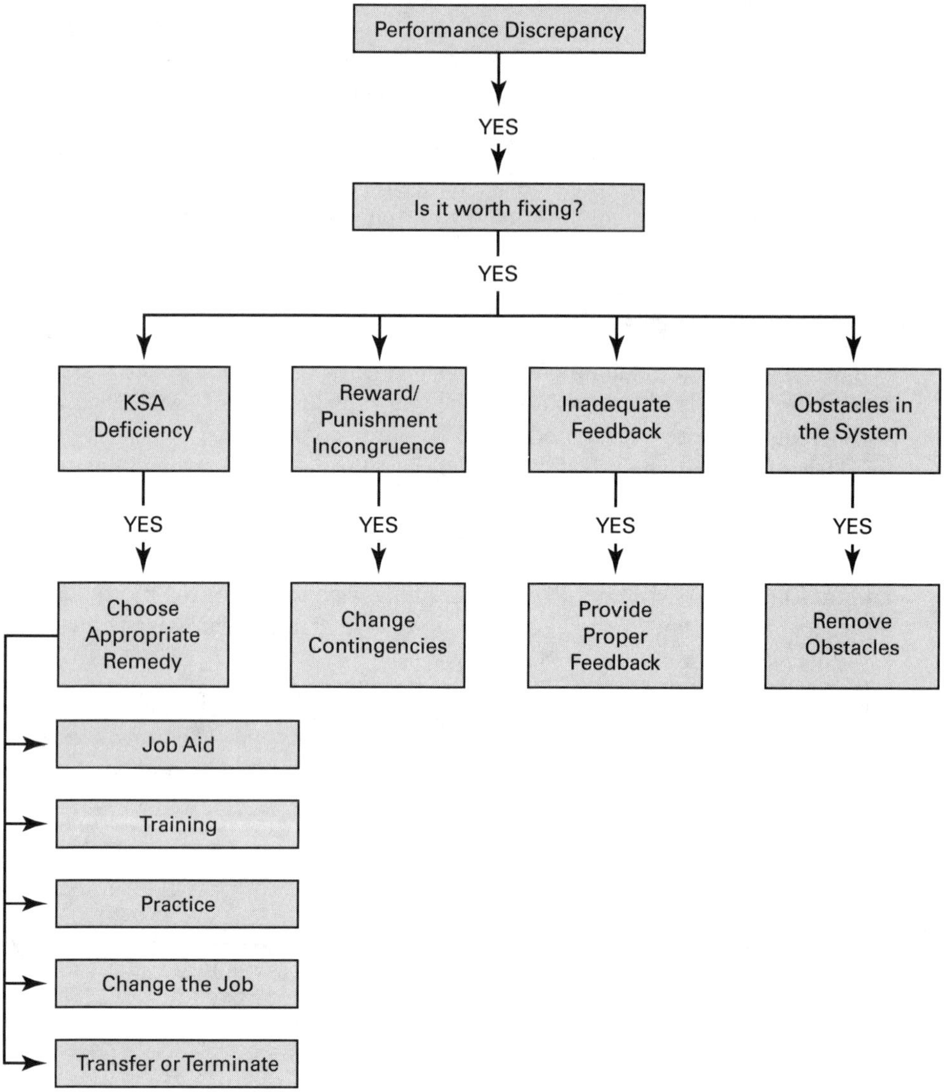

Performance Discrepancy

↓ YES

Is it worth fixing?

↓ YES

KSA Deficiency	Reward/ Punishment Incongruence	Inadequate Feedback	Obstacles in the System
↓ YES	↓ YES	↓ YES	↓ YES
Choose Appropriate Remedy	Change Contingencies	Provide Proper Feedback	Remove Obstacles

- Job Aid
- Training
- Practice
- Change the Job
- Transfer or Terminate

Source: Adapted from Michalak and Yager 1979.

constraint on the training, because it usually requires some reading. Of course, a solution would be first to develop the employees' reading skills. Alternatively, it might be possible to develop training that would not require reading.

Operational analysis examines specific jobs to determine the requirements (KSAs) that are necessary to get the job done (i.e., expected job performance).

Finally, **person analysis** examines those who occupy the jobs to see if they have the required KSAs to do the job. Here we first measure the actual job performance of those on the job, to see if they are performing at an acceptable level.

These three parts to a TNA are conceptually distinct, but in practice much of the information is gathered at the same time and is closely interrelated. For example, information related to all three types of analysis can be collected from the job incumbents. Questions would include: "Are there any particular procedures or rules you must follow that negatively affect your job performance?" (organization analysis); "Describe for me the tasks you perform when you first arrive at work" (operational analysis); "Are there any skills you believe you are lacking that, if you had them, might enhance your ability to perform at a higher level?" (person analysis).

When the standards for the job (operational analysis) do not match an employee's performance (person analysis), a **performance discrepancy** exists. In such a case, several questions must be answered (see Figure 4.2). If the performance discrepancy is worth fixing, the rest of the steps in Figure 4-2 are followed to determine the cause of the discrepancy. The figure details all the issues that could be considered in a TNA. The degree to which these would actually be included will depend on the scope of the performance issues being addressed. In a large undertaking such as "determining the ability of the organization's human resources to carry out the strategic plan," all of them would probably be addressed. To deal with a performance discrepancy in a single department would require addressing fewer performance issues.

ORGANIZATIONAL ANALYSIS

An organizational analysis conducted for strategic planning is a major undertaking. The mission and relevant strategies that have been identified in the strategic plan are an indication of where the organization wishes to be, and the organizational analysis indicates where the organization currently is. The discrepancy between these two (desired and actual) is a performance discrepancy. Once the organizational analysis determines where this discrepancy is located, we can focus our attention there and ask: Is the identified discrepancy worth fixing? If yes, then we know where to do our operational and person analysis. Consider the organization that has made the decision to become totally team oriented. At present it has working teams only at the management level. The organizational analysis indicates the management teams are operating effectively, but there are no teams operating at the shop floor. The shop floor, therefore, becomes the area of focus.

Organizational analysis done in response to a particular performance discrepancy is usually of less magnitude than that done for strategic planning. Such an analysis could occur when a unit fails to meet its objectives. This organizational unit becomes the focus of attention. Now you begin looking for the causes of the discrepancy.

McGehee and Thayer (1961) suggest that an organization analysis should focus on the strategies of the organization, the resources in the organization, and the allocation of these resources. More recently, organization analysis has been reconceptualized to include the total internal environment. This process looks at structures, policies and procedures, job-design work-flow processes, and other factors that facilitate or inhibit an employee's ability to meet job performance expectations (Tannenbaum and Yukl 1992). This expansion was necessary to help identify the cause of discrepancies, and specifically to determine if discrepancies were, in fact, training issues. According to Nancy Gordon, a TNA analyst at Ameritech, about 85% of all requests for training turned out to be related to issues that could not be addressed by training.

They were, instead, incongruencies in the organizational environment that inhibited or prevented the appropriate work behaviors (see Training in Action 4.1 below).

An organizational analysis, then, should include the following:

- An examination of the mission and strategies of an organization
- An examination of the resources and allocation of the resources, given the objectives
- An analysis of the factors in the internal environment to determine if they are causing the problem
- If training is required, the impact of those environmental factors on providing training and transferring the training to the job

Mission and Strategies

In the organizational analysis, an examination of the mission and strategies will help the analyst place the training in a particular context. Consider the Ford Engine Plant mission statement presented in chapter 2. A strategy that arose from that mission statement was to focus on the team approach for continuous improvement. One type of training to support this strategy would be training in problem solving. This type of training requires openness and trust to be effective and is therefore in line with the team approach. If the workers in the plant were offered training in traditional negotiations skills, would this be in line with the team approach? Perhaps not, because traditional negotiations training often suggests that it is useful to not reveal all your information, but instead hold back and attempt to get the best deal for your-

---

Training in Action 4.1

Incongruities in the Organizational Environment

A bank manager decided that in order to increase profits, he would send all his tellers to a training workshop about the products and services the bank offered. He wanted the front-line employees (tellers) to provide such information to customers who came into the bank. This practice would increase the amount of products and services sold.

The manager developed a method of tracking the number of products and services sold so he would have a measure of the success of the training. After a time he noticed there was no increase in sales. Training had not resulted in an increase in sales. What had gone wrong?

Analysis revealed that when tellers returned from training, they also returned to the same appraisal system that was in place before. Performance assessment was based largely on the number of customers the teller was able to process. Why would a teller risk receiving a low performance rating in order to spend time telling customers about the products and services being offered by the bank?

Source: Adapted from Johnson 1995.

self (or your department). To offer such training would at best not reinforce an environment of openness and trust, and at worst actually counteract it.

The organizational mission and strategies provide the priorities for training. Training resources are always finite, so decisions must be made as to where to spend the training budget. If, for example, "Quality is job one" at Ford, the analyst knows that development of KSAs relating to quality should receive priority. Thinking back to the MHC case in chapter 2, can you identify how the company's priorities would be related to training needs?

Resources

Capital Resources   When the term *resources* is used, issues of finance, equipment, facilities, and the like usually come to mind. Recall in chapter 2, during the strategic planning phase, decisions were made as to where money would be spent. Perhaps it was decided that a large expenditure would be made on new equipment for the machinists, or toward becoming ISO 9000 certified. These strategic decisions will determine the priorities for the HRD department.

At the TNA level we examine the resource issue to see where the organization's priorities are. In the case of purchasing new equipment for the machinists, you would concentrate on the assessment of the machinist position, based on the financial decisions made at the strategic level. Relevant training would need to be provided to the machinists so they can operate the new machinery. Choice of the ISO 9000 certification would indicate to the HRD department to concentrating on providing the necessary support in that area. In this case, all employees who would be involved need to be identified in order to determine if any performance discrepancies will exist. Once the discrepancies are identified, decisions about relevant training would need to be made.

The other main concern for HRD is based on its own budget. Decisions as to how to provide the required training is a function of the money HRD has to spend. Hiring external consultants versus developing its own training depends on a number of issues, not the least of which is the cost. In the Westcan case, the "meetings training" will have to be designed around the total training budget. Hiring a consultant to provide the training might result in very effective meeting skills for the managers, but Chris would have to weigh that against other training needs at Westcan, given her limited budget.

Human Resources   It is important to clarify once again the difference between examining human resources for the strategic needs assessment and for the training needs assessment. At the strategic level, HRD would provide top management with the skill levels and potential of the current human resource contingent to support various strategies.

At the TNA level, the HR strategies provide you with priorities for where you should focus your efforts. From this, you focus on those employees who have been identified as facing performance discrepancies in these areas. Providing them with the training and support they require to eliminate future performance discrepancies would be a priority for the HRD.

Organizational Environment

The other main objective of the organizational analysis is to examine the various structures (e.g., mechanistic or organic) and designs (e.g., pay systems and reward policies) operating in an organization to determine how congruent they are with the performance objectives of the unit in which the discrepancies have been identified. Identifying these incongruencies early, and changing them, will help ensure that when training is complete, it will transfer to the job.

Consider two scenarios.

> An organization has decided to move toward a more team-oriented approach. The mission and objectives reflect this recent change in company policy. Among the present procedures is the use of an employee suggestion box, which provides rewards for individual suggestions for improving company performance.

> An organization's mission and objectives can be summed up as "quality is most important." One of the organization's policies is that performance appraisals for first-line management provide a measure of how well these managers meet productivity quotas, but they measure nothing related to quality.

In the first scenario, does the individual incentive system reinforce or hinder the team approach? If, after training and implementation of the team approach, no innovative ideas were forthcoming, would that mean the training was not effective? You can't really tell. The skills may have been learned but not transferred to the job. Consider the reward/punishment incongruence (see Figure 4.2) between rewarding for individual ideas (suggestion box) and instituting a team approach. Identifying this incongruence and removing it before instituting the team approach would facilitate transfer of the training. Training in Action 1.2 (page 10) and 1.3 (page 11) also show where organizational analysis would have identified a reward/punishment incongruence, which would need to be addressed in order to facilitate transfer of training.

In the second scenario, would you expect training in quality issues to be effective or is training even needed? The results may be attainable by simply redesigning the performance appraisal to emphasize quality. These examples illustrate the value of conducting an analysis of the organizational environment as it relates to performance deficiencies.

One other point should be made here. The analysis at the environment level should not be conducted until you have an idea what jobs are targeted either for their performance deficiencies or because of future changes. This targeting will allow a certain degree of focus when you are conducting the analysis; you would gather data that were relevant to those jobs only. Otherwise you would gather enormous amounts of information that may be irrelevant and therefore a waste of valuable time.

Where to Collect Data

There is no one best way to perform an organizational analysis. Interviews with individuals at different levels in the organization, surveys, archival data such as grievance levels, productivity, and quality measures are all appropriate indicators of how the organization is operating and where problems are arising. It is useful to obtain information from many different sources. Table 4.1 provides a list of sources for gathering such data.

Data sources 4 to 9 provide information about areas of performance discrepancy. Note that the data sources in Table 4.1 are reflected to a certain extent in Figure 4.1 on page 129. The organizational goals and objectives in Table 4.1 are identified as objectives in Figure 4.1. Resources (Figure 4.1) are reflected in the second and third data sources. The climate indices in Table 4.1 can result from any of the inputs of organizational analysis in Figure 4.1.

TABLE 4.1 Data Sources for Organization Analysis		
Data Source Recommended	*Training Need Implications*	*Reference(s)*
1. Organizational Goals and Objectives and Budget	Where training emphasis can and should be placed. These provide normative standards of both direction and expected impact, which can highlight deviations from objectives and performance problems.	McGehee and Thayer (1961); Morano (1973); Patten (1971); Odiorne (1970); Proctor and Thornton (1961); Johnson (1967); Bass and Vaughan (1966); Goldstein (1974)
2. Labor Inventory	Where training is needed to fill gaps caused by retirement, turnover, age, etc. This provides an important demographic data base regarding possible scope of training needs.	McGehee and Thayer; Morano; Proctor and Thornton; BNA (1962); Goldstein
3. Skills Inventory	Number of employees in each skill group, knowledge and skill levels, training time per job, etc. This provides an estimate of the magnitude of specific training needs. Useful in cost/benefit analysis of training projects.	McGehee and Thayer; Johnson; Wessman (1975)
4. Organizational Climate Indices	These "quality of working life" indicators at the organization level may help focus on problems that have training components.	McGehee and Thayer; Goldstein; Hellriegel and Slocum (1974); Schneider (1975)
a. Labor–management data, strikes, lockouts, etc.	All these items related to either work participation or productivity are useful both in discrepancy analysis and in helping management set a value on the behaviors it wishes improved through training once training has been established as a relevant solution.	McGehee and Thayer; Lawrie and Boringer (1971)
b. Grievances		McGehee and Thayer; BNA (1962); Morano
c. Turnover		McGehee and Thayer; Morano
d. Absenteeism		McGehee and Thayer
e. Suggestions		McGehee and Thayer
f. Productivity		McGehee and Thayer
g. Accidents		McGehee and Thayer
h. Short-term sickness		
i. Observation of employee behavior		
j. Attitude surveys	Good for locating discrepancies between organizational expectations and perceived results.	McGehee and Thayer; Bellman (1975)
	Valuable feedback; look especially for patterns and repeat complaints.	Lawrie and Boringer
k. Customer complaints		

(continued)

TABLE 4.1 Data Sources for Organization Analysis *(continued)*

Data Source Recommended	Training Need Implications	Reference(s)
5. Analysis of Efficiency Indices	Cost accounting concepts may represent ratio between actual performance and desired or standard performance.	McGehee and Thayer; BNA (1962); Goldstein; Proctor and Thornton
a. Costs of labor		McGehee and Thayer
b. Costs of materials		McGehee and Thayer
c. Quality of product		McGehee and Thayer
d. Equipment utilization		McGehee and Thayer
e. Costs of distribution		McGehee and Thayer
f. Waste		McGehee and Thayer
g. Downtime		McGehee and Thayer; Lawrie and Boringer
h. Late deliveries		McGehee and Thayer
i. Repairs		McGehee and Thayer
6. Changes in System or Subsystem	New or changed equipment may present training problem.	Warren (1969); BNA (1969); Johnson
7. Management Requests or Management Interrogation	One of the most common techniques of training needs determination.	Mahler (1974); Proctor and Thornton; BNA (1962); French (1974); Prieve and Wentorf (1970); Glueck (1974); BNA (1969); Otto and Glaser (1970)
8. Exit Interviews	Often information not otherwise available can be obtained, especially in problem areas and supervisory training needs.	Kirkpatrick (1971)
9. MBO or Work Planning and Review Systems	Provides performance review, potential review, and long-term business objectives. Provides actual performance data on a recurring basis so that base-line measurements may be known and subsequent improvement or deterioration of performance can be identified and analyzed.	Odiorne (1970)

OPERATIONAL ANALYSIS

Once the organizational performance discrepancies have been analyzed and the areas of the discrepancies located, it is necessary to perform an operational analysis in these areas. As Figure 4.1 indicates, operational analysis consists primarily of an examination of the tasks required to do a particular job effectively. It requires an examination of what tasks are to be performed, at what level they must be performed, and what KSAs are necessary to perform them. It also requires an analysis of any roadblocks employees face in doing an effective job. Note that this is a point where operational analysis and organizational analysis overlap,[2] as they both examine factors that contribute to a deficit in performance. Table 4.2 (page 138) provides a number of sources for obtaining such information. Techniques for obtaining task and KSA data are usually some type of job analysis.

Analyzing the Job

The following steps are worth considering when you are about to analyze a job.

What Is the Job   The first step is to determine exactly what job is going to be analyzed. In today's environment, a common job title can mask real differences in the tasks that are done. In an extreme example, at Honda Manufacturing everyone's job title is "associate," from the line worker to top management. Other organizations have the same job title for employees who do different tasks, because they work in different departments, geographical locations, and so on. Therefore, it is important to define clearly the parameters for the job to be analyzed. Welding discrepancies in the Honda shop, for example, should have you examining the job of associate in the welding shop only. Once the job is defined, it should be clear how many employees work in the target job and where they are located.

Whom to Ask   In analyzing the job, the analyst needs to know what tasks are performed on the job. For this information you ask incumbents and supervisors. Incumbents are asked for two reasons. First, they are the employees who do the job and know exactly what tasks are being performed. Also, any training that develops will have more ownership from those who have been part of the data collection. In selecting incumbents, it is important to choose a cross-section based on tenure on the job[3] (Landy and Vasey 1991), because often the tasks required vary with an incumbent's experience.

Data should also be gathered from the incumbents' supervisors. This information provides a different perspective and helps yield a well-rounded concept of exactly what is required on the job. When there are discrepancies between what the supervisor and the incumbents say, an investigation into the reason for the discrepancy can provide useful information. One of the reasons we suggest that trainers need OD skills is that they provide the trainer with an effective way of resolving such differences in how the job should be performed.

One way to avoid conflicting beliefs between subordinates and supervisors is to implement the job expectation technique (Dayal and Thomas 1968). This requires subordinates and supervisors to meet to discuss the job responsibilities of the subordinates in order to clarify job expectations. Although this process sounds simplistic, it requires trust and respect between supervisors and their subordinates. In reality, many job incumbents learn about their job through working with other incumbents and through trial and error.

---

[2] To demonstrate the interrelatedness, compare data source 5 in Table 4.1 (organizational analysis) with the technique for obtaining job data (9) in Table 4.2 (operational analysis).

[3] Assuming there is more than one incumbent.

TABLE 4.2 Data Sources for Operational Analysis

Sources for Obtaining Job Data	Training Need Implications	Reference(s)
1. Job Descriptions	Outlines the job's typical duties and responsibilities but is not meant to be all-inclusive. Helps define performance discrepancies.	McGehee and Thayer (1961); Goldstein (1974); Kirkpatrick (1971); BNA (1962); Lawrie and Boringer (1971); DePhillips et al. (1960); Johnson (1967); Wessman (1975)
2. Job Specifications or Task Analysis	List specified tasks required for each job. More specific than job descriptions. Specifications may extend to judgments of knowledge and skills required of job incumbents.	McGehee and Thayer; Kirkpatrick; DePhillips et al.; Goldstein; Wessman; Johnson; Proctor and Thornton (1961)
3. Performance Standards	Objectives of the tasks of job, and standards by which they are judged. This may include base-line data as well.	McGehee and Thayer; Goldstein; Odiorne (1970)
4. Perform the Job	Most effective way of determining specific tasks, but has serious limitations in higher level jobs because performance requirements typically have longer gaps between performance and resulting outcomes.	McGehee and Thayer; Goldstein; Bass and Vaughan (1966)
5. Observe Job—Work Sampling		McGehee and Thayer; Goldstein; Proctor and Thornton; BNA (1969)
6. Review Literature Concerning the Job a. Research in other industries b. Professional journals c. Documents d. Government sources e. Ph.D. theses	Possibly useful in comparison analyses of job structures, but far removed from either unique aspects of the job structure within any *specific* organization or specific performance requirements.	McGehee and Thayer; Bass and Vaughan Lawrie and Boringer; Glueck (1974) Lawrie and Boringer Lawrie and Boringer Lawrie and Boringer Lawrie and Boringer
7. Ask Questions about the Job a. Of the job holder b. Of the supervisor c. Of higher management		McGehee and Thayer; Finnegan (1970) Kirkpatrick; Otto and Glaser (1970)
8. Training Committees or Conferences	Inputs from several viewpoints can often reveal training needs or training desires.	Patten (1971); Bass and Vaughan; Talbot and Ellis (1969); Prieve and Wentorf (1970); BNA (1962); Finnegan; Johnson; Goldstein; Proctor and Thornton; BNA (1969)

Sources for Obtaining Job Data	*Training Need Implications*	*Reference(s)*
9. Analysis of Operating Problems	Indications of task interference, environmental factors, etc.	Bass and Vaughan; Johnson; Glueck (1974)
		Proctor and Thornton
a. Downtime reports		McGehee and Thayer; Lawrie and Boringer
b. Waste		
c. Repairs		McGehee and Thayer
d. Late deliveries		McGehee and Thayer
e. Quality control		McGehee and Thayer
10. Card Sort	Used in training conferences. "How to" statements sorted by training importance.	McGehee and Thayer Johnson; Patten

If There Are No Incumbents   In today's environment of fast-changing technology, jobs are under constant change. In some cases new technology creates new jobs that require very different skills than the jobs they are replacing. For example, at a large food-processing plant in Ontario, management ordered a "state-of-the-art" machine to make a particular product that had previously been made with low-technology equipment. This new machine required new skills. The question was: How do you perform a job analysis for this job when there are no incumbents to ask? Dr. Mitchell Fields, a professor at the University of Windsor, was approached by the company to assist in determining the selection and training requirements for the new job. Table 4.3 (page 140) describes the steps Dr. Fields took in determining these requirements.

Who Should Select Incumbents   The selection process should be done by the job analyst, not the supervisor or a manager. If supervisors or other managers determine who should be selected, a biased sample may result, but perhaps more important, the incumbents may question the real purpose of the assessment and provide inaccurate data.

How Many to Ask   Different jobs in any organization have different numbers of incumbents. One incumbent makes the decision easy. When there are large numbers of incumbents, the more individuals you obtain information from, the better picture you will have of the job. Furthermore, the more involved in this process incumbents are, the more committed to the training they should be. At a minimum, talk to a representative sample of incumbents covering all aspects of the job. How you choose this sample is discussed under the next heading.

Exactly how many would be determined by your method of data gathering and the amount of time you have. Let's say there are 80 incumbents, 20 in each of four levels within the job. You have chosen to interview in small groups. You could have four interview sessions, each with five or six incumbents from each level. If time allowed, you might want to have two groups from each level, for increased participation and a more representative sample.

TABLE 4.3 Job Analysis When There Are No Incumbents

The food-processing company was unionized, and the union contract stipulated that new jobs go to existing employees. The company wanted to be sure those selected would have the KSAs to do the job. Most of the employees did not have much formal education, and their reading level was very low, so it was important to determine the level of skill required to perform the job. It was decided to use a selection test, but employees whose reading level affected their ability to take a test were not to be disqualified unless reading was an important part of the job. Dr. Fields outlines how he conducted the job analysis below.

1. Contacted the manufacturer of the new equipment and asked if that or similar equipment was being used elsewhere, so that data could be obtained from another company. In this case, the setup was customized for the company and no other application existed.

2. Obtained specifications and operating manuals for the new machinery. The manuals were incomplete and difficult to understand. In fact, they were more complex than they needed to be. As a result, initially it was thought that a high level of reading comprehension would be necessary.

3. Interviewed engineers who were responsible for designing the new machinery. This is where I received important information as to its operation. However, the engineers tended to overestimate the level of aptitude required. They believed that operators would be making modifications to the programming software. Further discussions revealed that for the operator's job, reading requirements were minimal. The operating manuals were needed only for maintenance and repair.

4. Obtained blueprints and layouts of the physical equipment, as well as flowcharts of the operating software. This material indicated that the operators would be required to interface with a user-friendly, icon-driven software package (far less than the complex programming tasks envisioned by the engineers).

5. Identified two main tasks. First, the operators would be required to keep track of the mechanical operations of a number of different (but integrated) assembly operations. It was determined, therefore, that mechanical aptitude was necessary. Second, the operators had to look at a VDT (video display terminal) display (two dimensional) and make decisions about the assembly-line operation (three dimensions). Having skill in spatial relations, therefore, would also be important.

6. On the basis of the skills identified, I suggested two subtests of the Differential Aptitude Test for use in selection of employees: mechanical comprehension and spatial relations tests. All operators were selected from current employees. The major advantage to these two tests is that reading level (which was determined not to be important) is not a factor.

How to Select   The best way to select the participants is through representative sampling of all those incumbents who are performing "adequately or better" on the job. The incumbents need to be placed into subgroups based on relevant characteristics, such as their level in the job (e.g., mechanic 1, mechanic 2). Once the categories have been developed within the job, the job analyst should choose within these categories on the basis of other factors, such as years in the category, gender, and so on, in order to ensure that different views of the job are obtained. Note that we do not advocate random sampling. Random sampling is effective only when you have large numbers of incumbents who are similar, which is seldom the case in a particular job in an organization. More will be said about this issue in chapter 6.

One other consideration: If the organization operates in more than one location, particularly in different cities, you need to have input from different locations.

Where to Collect Data   As Table 4.2 indicates, there are a number of sources from which to gather data. The decision to choose one over the other has to do with issues such as time, cost, number of incumbents in the job, and similar types of factors.

What to Ask About   There are a number of **job analysis** techniques available for gathering information about a job. Two main categories are worker-oriented and task-oriented approaches.

Worker-oriented approach.   The **worker-oriented** approach focuses on the KSAs that are required on the job, rather than the tasks or behaviors. Figure 4.3 provides an example of questions from a worker-oriented approach. In this example, the Position Analysis Questionnaire (PAQ) was used. A drawback of the PAQ is that task statements are not available to provide a link with the KSAs.

Task-oriented approach.   The **task-oriented** approach, as the name implies, identifies the various work activities required to perform the job. Whereas the worker-oriented method focuses on the KSAs used to do the job, this method focuses on the tasks required to get the job done. To understand the difference between the two approaches, note the different results that would be obtained using each of these methods, depicted in Table 4.4 on page 142.

One example of a task-oriented approach is the **job-duty-task** method (Mills, Pace, and Peterson 1988). The process is depicted in Figure 4.4 (page 142). Note that first the

---

FIGURE 4.3 Information Input

Note on Rating "Importance to This Job":

Each of the items in the questionnaire that uses the "Importance to This Job (1)" scale is to be rated on how important the activity described in the item is to the completion of this job. Consider such factors as amount of time spent, the possible influence on overall job performance if the worker does not properly perform this activity, etc.

Code Importance to This Job (1)
N   Does not apply
1   Very minor
2   Low
3   Average
4   High
5   Extreme

1. | Far visual differentiation (seeing differences in the details of the objects, events, or features *beyond arm's reach;* for example, operating a vehicle, landscaping, sports officiating)

2. | Depth perception (judging the distance from the observer to objects, or the distances between objects as they are positioned in space; for example, operating a crane, operating a dentist's drill, handling and positioning objects)

3. | Color perception (differentiating or identifying objects, materials, or details thereof on the basis of color)

4. | Sound pattern recognition (recognizing different patterns or sequences of sounds; for example, those involved in Morse code, heartbeats, engines not functioning correctly)

5. | Sound differentiation (recognizing differences or changes in sounds in their loudness, pitch, and/or tone quality; for example, piano tuner, sound system repairman)

TABLE 4.4 A Comparison of the Outcomes for Worker- and Task-Oriented Approaches to Job Analysis

Job	Task-Oriented Approach	Worker-Oriented Approach
Garage Attendant	Checks tire pressure	Obtains information from visual displays
Machinist	Checks thickness of crankshaft	Use of a measuring device
Dentist	Drills out decay from teeth	Use of precision instruments
Forklift Driver	Loads pallets of washers onto trucks	High level of eye–hand coordination

job is identified, then each of the duties is written out.[4] The writing out of the duties should provide a stimulus to generate tasks and subtasks for each of these duties.

Another step in the process is to determine how critical each of the tasks is, and how important it is to be able to perform the task at the time of hire. To obtain this information, have those providing information rate each of the tasks on a scale such as the one depicted in Table 4.5 (pages 144–145). This not only documents the importance of the tasks, but also provides valuable evidence for why certain KSAs are required for selection or training. Finally, the KSAs necessary to perform each of the important tasks and subtasks are identified. These too should be rated for importance to the job and importance at the time of hire.

FIGURE 4.4 Form for Recording Task Analysis Results Using the Job-Duty-Task Method of Job Analysis

Job Title: _____   Specific duty: _____

Tasks	Subtasks	Knowledge and Skills Required
1. _____	1. _____	_____
	2. _____	_____
	3. _____	_____
2. _____	1. _____	_____
	2. _____	_____
	3. _____	_____
3. _____	1. _____	_____
	2. _____	_____

Source: Adapted from Mills, Pace, and Peterson 1988.

----

[4] It is also possible to list all duties first, then tasks and subtasks for each duty, then go back and identify the KSAs for each of the tasks and subtasks. It is equally appropriate to go through each duty, determine the subtasks, then identify the required KSAs before moving to the next duty.

Identifying the duties, tasks and subtasks is done by examining (through interview, observation, etc.) incumbents' behavior (i.e., what they do). Systematically examining each duty and inquiring about the tasks required yields the list of tasks necessary to do the job. Identifying the required KSAs is not as obvious, but they are still relatively easy to obtain, by examining each task and asking the question, "What knowledge, skills, and/or attitudes are necessary to perform a particular task?" Once you are involved in the job analysis, it becomes apparent that incumbents and supervisors are able to determine the required KSAs. Using the form from Figure 4.4, an example of an analysis of the job of a Human Resource Professional is depicted in Figure 4.5 on page 146.

What is the process for conducting a large-scale operational analysis? Table 4.5 provides the process used to identify the tasks and KSAs for salespeople at a large computer firm in the United States with offices in a number of states. Because of the breadth of the job—many different types of equipment (hardware) were sold—and the many different locations, the needs analysis was a major undertaking. The effort was worthwhile, however, because important information was obtained. For example, it was determined that irrespective of type of hardware sold (cash register or computer), very similar tasks and identical KSAs were required. It was also determined that the job was the same in Los Angeles as it was in Detroit. Finally, from the importance scale, it was determined that there were a number of tasks and KSAs that, although performed, were not critical to effective job performance. For example, "knowledge of computer operations," "knowledge of program language," and "ability to write simple computer programs" were nice to have but not necessary, because there was a process for obtaining such support in the field.

From these data the company was able to refocus its selection procedures to include the KSAs necessary at the time of hire, and to provide its training department with a clear picture of the training that would be necessary after the salespeople were hired.

What You Should Get from the Job Analysis (Expected Performance)

The job analysis should result in a list of all the important tasks and KSAs required to perform the job. Both sets of information are necessary. The task information is important for identifying the expected behavior, developing actual training programs, and making subsequent evaluations of the training (McCormick 1979). The KSAs are discussed in the following sections.

Knowledge All jobs require some type of knowledge. This is often "declarative knowledge," as discussed earlier. The job analysis should provide a list of tasks that, when examined, will point to the knowledge requirements necessary to be successful. For example, if one of the tasks identified is to edit manuscripts using WordPerfect, then an inferred knowledge requirement would be knowledge of the editing functions in WordPerfect software.

An alternative approach. Assessing the need for declarative knowledge is possible using the traditional job analysis just discussed. Some have argued, however, that with the increased complexity of jobs, analysis of tasks alone is not sufficient; we need to determine the knowledge requirements at the procedural or strategic levels (Kraiger, Ford, and Salas 1993). The concern is that if the job is reduced to individual tasks, the interrelatedness and complexity of the job is lost.

TABLE 4.5   Assessment Procedure Followed by a Large U.S. Computer Firm

1. **Define the job in question.** The analyst met with management to discuss the scope of the assessment. It was determined the assessment would include all salespeople in the company.

2. **Who to ask.** Because of possible differences between what was being done in offices in different states, incumbents who work in each state would need to provide input. Furthermore, because of the different types of equipment being sold by different salespeople, it would be necessary to have a representative number of incumbents from these subgroups.

3. **What method to use.** Because of the need to include a large number of incumbents who were located in different geographical regions and sold different equipment, the questionnaire method was chosen. This would allow a large number of incumbents to provide input that could be easily analyzed.

4. To develop a questionnaire relevant to the job, the analyst obtained job descriptions from the various locations and for the different types of hardware being sold. He then met with incumbents (in small groups) as well as supervisors (in separate small groups) to obtain input on what tasks were done. After the tasks were identified, he asked them to indicate the KSAs they believed were necessary to do the tasks. The small-group interviews were scheduled so that out-of-state incumbents who were to be at the head office for other reasons were able to attend, thus providing input from the various states.

5. The questionnaire was developed and included all the tasks and KSAs that had been identified. Two ratings were requested for each task and KSA. The first related to how important the task (KSA) was to successful job performance (see below).

How Important Is the Task

1 NOT VERY IMPORTANT	POOR PERFORMANCE ON THIS TASK WILL NOT AFFECT THE OVERALL PERFORMANCE OF THE JOB.
2 SOMEWHAT IMPORTANT	POOR PERFORMANCE ON THIS TASK WILL HAVE A MODERATE EFFECT ON THE OVERALL PERFORMANCE OF THE JOB.
3 IMPORTANT	POOR PERFORMANCE ON THIS TASK WILL HAVE AN EFFECT ON THE OVERALL PERFORMANCE OF THE JOB.
4 VERY IMPORTANT	POOR PERFORMANCE ON THIS TASK WILL HAVE A SERIOUS EFFECT ON THE OVERALL PERFORMANCE OF THE JOB.

The operational analysis for higher levels of knowledge would be accomplished by examining the mental models of experts.[5] These types of analysis would be useful when more advanced training is required.[6]

Skill   A list of all the skill requirements to perform the job successfully will result from the job analysis. Consider the computer salesperson. One task for this job would be to "make presentations to groups," which would require presentation skills. Another would be to "deal with an irate customer," which would require conflict resolution skills. The outcome from the job analysis will result in a number of such skills be-

---

[5] Here an "expert" could be a high-performing incumbent or someone who performs the same job in another context (e.g., computer programmer).

[6] Techniques such as multidimensional scaling (Shoben 1983) and link-weighted methods such as pathfinder (Schvaneveldt, Durso, and Dearholt 1985) can be used to identify such structures. Space does not permit us to explore this area in detail, but those interested in this approach should consult Ford and Kraiger (1995), Goldsmith and Johnson (1990), Cooke and McDonald (1987), and Champagne et al. (1981).

TABLE 4.5   Assessment Procedure Followed by a Large U.S. Computer Firm *(continued)*

6. The other rating was related to how important it was to be able to do the task successfully at the time of hire. The scale for that rating is below.

Importance at the Time of Hire

1 A PERSON REQUIRES NO SPECIFIC CAPABILITY IN THIS AREA WHEN HIRED. TRAINING WILL BE PROVIDED FOR AN INDIVIDUAL TO BECOME PROFICIENT IN THIS AREA.

2 A PERSON MUST HAVE ONLY A BASIC CAPABILITY IN THIS AREA WHEN HIRED. EXPERIENCE ON THE JOB OR TRAINING IS THE PRIMARY METHOD FOR BECOMING PROFICIENT IN THIS AREA.

3 A PERSON MUST SHOW CONSIDERABLE PROFICIENCY IN THIS AREA WHEN HIRED. THERE IS TIME OR TRAINING AVAILABLE ONLY TO PROVIDE "FINE TUNING" ONCE THE PERSON IS ON THE JOB.

4 A PERSON MUST BE COMPLETELY PROFICIENT IN THIS AREA WHEN HIRED. THERE IS NO TIME OR TRAINING PROCEDURE AVAILABLE TO HELP AN INDIVIDUAL BECOME PROFICIENT IN THIS AREA AFTER BEING PLACED ON THE JOB.

7. The questionnaire was sent to all incumbents and their immediate supervisors.

8. Returned data were analyzed to determine if there were any differences between states and between salespeople who sold different hardware.

9. Those tasks that came up with a mean rating of 2.5 and above were placed in the relevant quadrants (see below).

	IMPORTANCE AT TIME OF HIRE	
	Below 2.5	At or above 2.5
At or above 2.5	TRAINING	SELECTION
Below 2.5	NOT IMPORTANT	

ing identified. The complete list of required skills would provide the needs analyst with an understanding of all the job requirements.

Attitude   What are the attitudinal outcomes from the job analysis? The job analysis gives an understanding of the tasks that must be done. For each task required, knowledge and skills are inferred. The same is true for attitudes. Asking the question, "Can you think of any attitudes or feelings a person could have that might facilitate or inhibit an employee from doing any part of this job well?" should generate some ideas. Consider a job that requires working in teams to solve problems. A response to the above question might be, "A person should have a positive attitude toward the team approach" or "The person should have a positive attitude toward working with others." These responses provide the analyst with information on what needs to be addressed in training.

Just such an issue was of concern in the new Ford assembly plant (see Training in Action 4.2). Here, incumbents were unavailable because the plant was not open yet. The needs analysis was conducted using their supervisors, who had been brought on board early to prepare the plant for opening.

FIGURE 4.5 Applying the Job-Duty-Task Method to the Job of Human Resource Professional

Job Title: __HRD Professional__   Specific duty: __Task Analysis__

Tasks	Subtasks	Knowledge and Skills Required
1. List tasks	1. Observe behavior	List four characteristics of behavior Classify behavior
	2. Select verb	Have knowledge of action verbs Have grammatical skills
	3. Record behavior	State so understood by others Record neatly
2. List subtasks	1. Observe behavior	List all remaining acts Classify behavior
	2. Select verb	State correctly Have grammatical skill
	3. Record behavior	Record so it is neat and understood by others
3. List knowledge	1. State what must be known	Classify all information
	2. Determine complexity of skill	Determine if skill represents a series of acts that must be learned in a sequence

Source: Adapted from Mills, Pace, and Peterson 1988.

Duty to Accommodate   Legislation in both Canada and the United States makes it unlawful, when hiring or training, to discriminate on the basis of a person's disability, whether physical or mental, if it does not prevent him from doing the job. By doing a job analysis and identifying the important tasks and KSAs, you can determine if the disability is relevant to the job. If the potential employee has the requisite KSAs, the choice should be clear. The problem is that often the disability results in the person's not being considered for the job in the first place, irrespective of his or her KSAs.

Consider the hearing-impaired person who is able to speak and read lips. He applies for the job of accounting clerk. A thorough job analysis identifies all the important tasks and KSAs, and he meets all those qualifications. However, although not identified as a critical task, the job does require the person to use the phone from time to time. Can the employer use this fact not to hire and/or train him? Although each case must be looked at individually, on the face of it the employer can't legally use this to exclude the person. The company can purchase a special phone for the hearing impaired. This type of requirement is called a **duty to accommodate.**

Training in Action 4.2

Changing Attitudes toward the Team Approach

Some of the Ford plants have moved toward a team approach to producing their product. Such was the case with the new Windsor Engine Plant. Because it was a new plant, there was an agreement with the Canadian Auto Workers that employees from other plants had first choice of the new jobs.

Employees transferred from other plants for many reasons: cleaner plant, closer to home, old job being phased out. Few if any transferred because of the potential for working in a team environment. In fact, it is well-known that the Canadian Auto Workers traditionally oppose such efforts, but in the case of the Windsor Engine Plant they made an exception.

In a determination of the skills needed, it became evident that many of the employees would be older, and the concern was that they would be set in their ways (generally against the team approach). The training program consisted of traditional skills training necessary for a team approach (communication skills, effective meeting skills, problem solving skills), but another component was added that was designed to influence attitudes toward the team approach.

This "other component" consisted of an orientation to the process of the team environment. Modules were designed to show the advantages of the team approach for the company and workers. An exercise called "Best Job Worst Job" allowed trainees to see that their own description of what a "best job" would look like was the type of job a worker would have in a team environment. The training also provided a six-hour session on individual growth and self-fulfillment. It was assumed that helping employees to focus on these issues would improve their attitudes toward the team approach.

Did the training have a significant impact on attitudes? No one knows for sure. After all the time and money spent on the training, there was no formal evaluation of the process. This omission should not be a surprise, as you will see in chapter 6.

Now the person is employed with the organization. Is he stuck in that position forever? Opportunities for promotion or lateral moves are often facilitated by the types of training (development) an employee receives over the years. To prevent this hearing-impaired person from taking advantage of temporary assignments (training opportunities) or developmental training that would help him become qualified for future jobs is also illegal.

You should conduct a job analysis and determine the importance of the KSAs required for each job so you can determine, for example, which jobs the hearing-impaired person could qualify for and assist in his developmental needs in those areas.

The Criterion

The operational analysis will identify the "type" of behavior expected in order for the job incumbent to be successful. As was mentioned earlier, this information will be used in evaluating the training. The standards used in evaluations are called criterion measures. Since the needs analysis process develops this information, it is important to understand the issues that relate to the developing of good criterion measures.

A **criterion** is defined as a standard by which a decision or judgment can be made. In developing a criterion, you need to be concerned about the reliability and validity of the measure. An examination of the issues related to reliability and validity of the criterion measure will help you understand the complexity of developing sound criteria for assessing the effectiveness of a training program.

Reliability   **Reliability** is a measure of the consistency of an outcome and is often measured using a correlation coefficient. It can be measured two ways: across similar measures (split half), and across time (test retest).

For the split half method, let's assume that 100 multiple-choice questions are used to test your knowledge on this course. To determine the reliability of the test, the instructor could consider the even-numbered questions and the odd-numbered questions as separate tests. Even though the 100 questions were given at the same time, adding up the score of the odd-numbered and even-numbered questions would provide two scores for each student. By correlating the two scores, he would determine how reliable the test was. A high correlation would suggest that the test was highly reliable.

In the test retest method, the instructor would give you the test today (all 100 questions) and again in three days. Then he would correlate student scores from the two time periods. Again, a high correlation between the two sets of scores would indicate a reliable test.

Highly reliable criterion measures are very important. Consider one possible criterion for a machinist who has completed training: He must produce a shaft exactly 4 centimeters thick. A test is constructed that requires the trainee to produce a shaft with the correct specifications. To pass the test, the trainee must produce a shaft whose measurement can be off by no more than 2/1,000ths of a centimeter. The evaluator measures the shaft with a micrometer (a measurement instrument able to detect differences in thousandths of centimeters). She finds it 1/1,000ths of a centimeter too large. If she measured it tomorrow, she would find the same results. If another instructor measured it using the same procedure, he would find the same results. This is a highly reliable criterion. If a ruler is used instead of a micrometer, the results may still be reliable, but less reliable because the less accurate ruler makes judgment errors in reading the scale more likely. Developing well-designed instrumentation, therefore, is important to obtaining a reliable measure, whether it be for a machinist or a measure of interpersonal skills.

Although developing a reliable instrument is important, of equal importance is the reliability in the use of the instrument. Both the instrument and the procedure used in applying it affect the reliability of the results. Consider the micrometer discussed above. Without training, the evaluator would not know how much to tighten the instrument around the shaft before obtaining the measurement. If one evaluator tightened it as much as he could and another tightened it just until she felt the first sign of resistance, the difference in results could be more than the 2/1,000ths of a centimeter tolerance allowed.

Relationship between Reliability and Validity   Reliability is the consistency of a measure, and **validity** is the degree to which you are measuring what you want to measure. As an example, imagine that a rifle manufacturer has two new rifles he wishes to test for their ability to hit the bull's-eye. He places the first rifle in a vise-like mechanism to prevent deviation, which might occur if a person were doing the shooting. For the purpose of this discussion, we will change the terminology for *validity* slightly. We will say validity is "doing what you want it to do" rather than "measuring what you want to measure." Conceptually, these notions are the same. In the vise, the first rifle is aimed at a target 50 yards away, and five shots are fired. Each shot hits the target (see Figure 4.6A). Is the rifle (instrument) consistent (reliable)? As you can see, the five bullets struck the target but they are all over the place. The rifle is not reliable. Nor is it valid (doing what you want it to do: hit the bull's-eye). There is no point in attempting to make the rifle valid (doing what you want it to do) because it has no reliability. You need reliability before you can have validity. The next rifle is placed in the vise. This time the five shots are all in the upper left-hand corner of the target (Figure 4.6B). Is the rifle reliable? Yes, since it consistently hit in the same place for all five shots. Is it valid? No, it did not hit the bull's-eye. We now adjust the sight and fire; all five hit the bull's-eye (Figure 4.6C). Is this rifle reliable? Yes, the bullets were all in relatively the same place (consistent). Is it valid? Yes, all five hit the bull's-eye as well.

From this example it should be clear that you can have a reliable test that is not valid (Figure 4.6B), but you cannot have a valid test that is not reliable (Figure 4.6A). You need consistency of a measure before you even consider expecting all the bullets to hit the bull's-eye. Reliability, therefore, is a primary concern, but only because you need it to have validity.

Validity   As we have said, *validity* is the degree to which you are measuring what you want to measure. It is more difficult to assess validity than reliability. Consider the question, "Has training resulted in learning?" Learning is a physiological process that takes place in the brain. We are unable to assess this process directly, so we test individuals and, on the basis of their scores, we infer learning has or has not taken place. This is not a direct measure of the learning process but an inference based on behavior.

To better understand the issues here, let's examine the *ultimate criterion* (Thorndike 1949). The **ultimate criterion** is what we would like to be able to measure if it were possible to do so. It would include the exact indicators of success. However, we are never able to measure the ultimate criterion, for it is simply a theoretical construct. We must settle for what we are able to measure: the *actual* criterion (Blum and

FIGURE 4.6 A Comparison Reliability and Validity

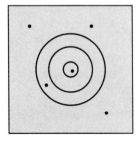
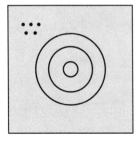
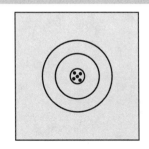

A   B   C

Naylor 1968). Examining the relationship between the ultimate criterion and the actual criterion provides us with insight into the problems associated with criterion development. The actual criterion can be thought of in terms of its relevance, deficiency, and contamination in relation to the ultimate criterion (see Figure 4.7).

Criterion relevancy.   The **criterion relevancy** is the portion of the actual criterion that overlaps the ultimate criterion (see Figure 4.7). This would be the true validity of the actual criterion. However, given that we can never measure the ultimate criterion, an empirical measure of this validity (a correlation between the ultimate criterion and actual criterion) is not possible. This problem illustrates the need for logical and rational analysis in developing the actual criterion to obtain an approximation of the ultimate criterion.

Let's look at an example in which training is designed to improve interpersonal relationships. Raters evaluate the learning by rating a trainee's behaviors in a scripted role play. The degree to which the raters are trained, to which the scales to be used in rating are well developed, and to which examples of acceptable and less acceptable behavior are clear to the raters are all factors that contribute to the validity (overlap of actual with ultimate) of the criterion. Because these will never match the ultimate criterion perfectly, there will always be deficiencies and contamination (see below). But the more rigorous the development of criterion measures and processes, the more the actual criterion will approach the ultimate criterion.

Criterion deficiency.   **Criterion deficiency** is the part of the ultimate criterion that we miss when we use the actual criterion, or the degree to which we are not measuring important aspects of performance. The factors that make up a trainee's ability to produce parts with a tolerance of a few thousandths of a centimeter are more complex than simply being able to do it under ideal testing conditions. Factors such as noise in the plant, the different types of parts that need to be machined, climate in the plant, and supervisor–subordinate relationships contribute to making a machinist successful. Our measure of success (producing one part in a training room) will obviously be deficient when compared with an ultimate measure of a successful machinist (the ultimate criterion).

Criterion contamination.   Just as any measure will miss some important aspects of true success (criterion deficiency), so will it contain some part that measures aspects not related to the true measure of success **(criterion contamination)**. This is the part

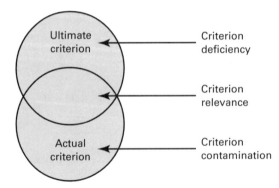

FIGURE 4.7 Diagram Illustrating the Criterion (Constructs) of Deficiency, Relevance, and Contamination

of the actual criterion that does not overlap with the ultimate criterion (Blum and Naylor 1968).

The two main categories of contamination are error and bias. **Error** is random variation in the scores on the criterion. It is, by definition, not correlated with anything. Error is, therefore, not as great a concern as bias. Although it lowers validity, it does not cause misrepresentation of the data. However, if error is too large, it can result in the criterion becoming invalid. A high error content could be caused by poor training of the evaluator, poorly developed instrument, or other factors.

When the contamination is **bias** rather than error, it is correlated with other measures. This can result in spuriously high correlations between the criterion and these measures of success. Four sources of such bias are opportunity bias, group characteristic bias, bias in ratings, and knowledge of predictor (Blum and Naylor 1968).

Opportunity bias occurs when certain individuals have some advantage that provides them with a higher level of performance, irrespective of their own skill level. For example, the criterion used to determine transfer of training is the number and quality of parts turned out by the machinist on the job. To determine if training is effective in transferring learned skills to the job, it is decided to correlate the scores on the training exam with performance one year later. In other words, the learning measured in the training evaluation is used as a predictor of future performance on the job. Analysis of this data indicates that those who scored highest on the test in training also produced the most and best quality (i.e., there was a high correlation between success in training and overall success after training). But what is not known is that those who scored the highest in training received as a reward the newest and best machines to work on. The relationship between the two scores was contaminated by the fact that the better trainees received the better machines, and it could be these that provided the opportunity for success.

Group characteristic bias occurs when something about the group creates higher (or lower) performance irrespective of an individual's capability. What if the trainees who did well were placed with supervisor A, who was very progressive and participative in her approach, and those who did less well in training were placed with a more authoritarian supervisor who would "keep an eye on them"? Once again, those who did better in training may produce more and better-quality products as a function of the climate created by the supervisor. Those working for the authoritarian supervisor could in fact be restricting output in protest.

Another possible contaminant of the criterion is **bias in performance ratings.** The measure of transfer of training is often determined by the supervisor. The subjective ratings of supervisors are often used even in areas where objective data are available. This is so because the objective data are often flawed—some workers have better territories (sales), better equipment (machinist), or a better environment (clean, well lit). In many cases the supervisor does not take these issues into account when rating subordinates. The **halo effect,** another type of rating bias, is a powerful force in rating subordinates. This occurs when a supervisor rates a subordinate on all dimensions of performance on the basis of knowledge of only one dimension. For example, Susan is well organized, so she is a great performer; Bill is excellent at running a meeting so he must be excellent at organizing, decision making, and interpersonal skills. To be effective in rating subordinates, supervisors need to rate each of the dimensions of the job separately and carefully so as not to allow one particular dimension to influence others.

The final possible contaminant is **knowledge of predictor bias.** The criterion for success in training could be thought of as a predictor of later performance on the job; successful training should contribute to successful performance. If, however, the supervisors were aware of the level of success in training, this information could influence their performance ratings.

Development of Criteria   It may seem that developing sound criteria is impossible, but this is not the case. As we discussed previously, the operational analysis identifies the level of acceptable performance. From this, criteria can be developed. Once criteria are established, the next step is to carefully develop instruments to measure the criteria. The instruments should leave as little as possible to the judgment of the rater.

Consider cognitive (declarative) knowledge. For the job of internal auditor, one of the tasks (expected behavior) is to know which reference books to use for each of the auditing issues. A part of the knowledge required to accomplish this is to know what is in the various reference manuals. Training would require the trainee to learn what was contained in the various reference books. A criterion for success would be demonstrating this knowledge.

In developing a measure of the criterion, the goal is to have it as objective as possible. In this case, a multiple-choice test of the material would be an excellent choice. The advantage of a well-designed multiple-choice test is that minimal judgment is necessary, so no matter who scores the test, the outcome will be the same (highly reliable). Given that well-designed multiple-choice tests can accurately measure any cognitive (declarative) knowledge (Nunnally 1978), we strongly suggest their use when possible.

Developing sound criteria for skills may be more difficult, and they may not be as reliable. However, instruments to measure skills, if carefully developed, could still meet reliability requirements.

With skill development, the trainee begins to learn more and more procedural, rather than declarative, knowledge. Procedural knowledge is more difficult to recall (Kraiger, Ford, and Salas 1993). Furthermore, the appropriate criterion measure should be behavioral. The internal auditor may have as an expected behavior "Calm an irate department head." The expected behavior is to be able to calm someone down who becomes irate. The skill required to accomplish this could be "active listening skills." A measure of the criterion would be how a trainee behaves in a role-play situation in which the role player becomes angry at something the auditor says.

In the case of measuring the criterion of "calming an irate department head," it is critical to develop clear rules and examples of what is and is not acceptable. Also it is important to train raters in the use of the rules and to provide examples. The more familiar the raters are with good, average, and poor responses, the more reliable the measure can be.

Validity in such instances is primarily what is called **content validity.** It is obtained when an expert examines the criteria on the basis of her knowledge of the TNA (Blum and Naylor 1968). It is important, therefore, to conduct a good TNA, for everything that follows from it (both training content and evaluation instruments) is based on that analysis.

The time and effort spent developing a sound criterion are critical to the training process. Once developed, the criterion is used to determine several things:

- The expected level of performance (operational analysis)
- Whether the incumbent can reach it (person analysis)
- The training needs for those who cannot reach it (a training objective)
- A measure of training effectiveness for those taking the training (measure of success)

PERSON ANALYSIS

Once the tasks and KSAs required to meet performance expectations are clear (operational analysis), the needs analyst must determine who is not meeting these expectations. A *person analysis* identifies those incumbents who are not meeting these performance requirements. Recall from Figure 4.1 that the resulting information provides a performance discrepancy (expected performance – actual performance = performance discrepancy). A *performance discrepancy* is generally thought of in the reactive sense, that is, as the difference between expected behavior and actual behavior. In the proactive sense, however, the expected behavior is a performance level expected in the future, and actual performance is the current performance level.

One other way of viewing this concept is the **developmental discrepancy,** which occurs when an employee or the organization desires development but not for any particular job. Here, expected performance is the performance level that the employee would like to achieve in the future. Consider the case of Bill, an accountant who is currently a high performer. He would like to move into management, a position that requires supervisory skills. Bill has a developmental performance discrepancy in the range of supervisory skills he does not have (e.g., interviewing, giving feedback, budgeting).

Where to Collect Data (Actual Performance)

Sources available to obtain person analysis information are shown in Table 4.6 (pages 154-155). Three of the more commonly used sources will be discussed in detail: performance appraisal, performance data, and proficiency tests (cognitive, work sample, assessment centers). Another source that will be discussed, one that is less commonly used, is the attitude survey.

Performance Appraisal   It is important to admit at the outset that many performance appraisals conducted regularly may not be of much value in determining an incumbent's needs. In theory, traditional performance ratings identify who has and who has not been meeting performance expectations. If performance appraisals accurately identified these employees, along with their strengths and weaknesses, there would be little need for any other assessment method. As a criterion measure, however, performance appraisals often suffer from a lack of reliability and validity for a number of reasons, such as lack of appraisal training, lack of opportunity to see performance, rater errors, and poorly defined appraisals. Performance appraisals can be a valuable source of this information, however, provided they are completed in a manner that is useful.

Supervisor ratings.   Performance appraisals are almost always completed by supervisors (Bernardin and Beatty 1984), and there are both political and interpersonal reasons why these appraisals are less than accurate assessments of the incumbents' KSAs (Benedict and Levine 1988; Longenecker, Sims, and Gioia 1987). This is less

TABLE 4.6　Data Sources for Person Analysis

Data Sources for Obtaining Data	*Training Need Implications*	*Reference(s)*
1. Performance Data or Appraisals	Include weaknesses and areas of improvement as well as strong points. Easy to analyze and quantify for purposes of determining subjects and kinds of training needed. These data can be used to identify performance discrepancies.	McGehee and Thayer (1961); Patten (1971); Warren (1969); Talbot and Ellis (1969); Kirkpatrick (1971); Goldstein (1974); Prieve and Wentorf (1970); DePhillips, et al. (1960); Renton (1969); Bass and Vaughan (1966); Lawrie and Boringer (1971); BNA (1969); Proctor and Thornton (1961); Finnegan (1970); Wessman (1975); Johnson (1967)
a. Productivity		
b. Absenteeism and tardiness		McGehee and Thayer
c. Accidents		McGehee and Thayer
d. Short-term sickness		McGehee and Thayer; Glueck (1974)
e. Grievances		McGehee and Thayer
f. Waste		McGehee and Thayer
g. Late deliveries		McGehee and Thayer
h. Product quality		McGehee and Thayer
i. Downtime		McGehee and Thayer
j. Repairs		McGehee and Thayer
k. Equipment utilization		McGehee and Thayer
l. Customer complaints		McGehee and Thayer
2. Observation—Work Sampling	More subjective technique but provides both employee behavior and results of the behavior.	Lawrie and Boringer
3. Interviews	Individual is only one who knows what he (she) believes he (she) needs to learn. Involvement in need analysis can also motivate employees to make an effort to learn.	McGehee and Thayer; Renton; BNA (1969); Johnson; Goldstein; Finnegan; Patten; Warren; Rose (1964); Talbot and Ellis McGehee and Thayer; Renton; Goldstein; Otto and Glaser (1970); Lawrie and Boringer; BNA (1962); Talbot and Ellis; Patten; Warren; Kirkpatrick; Johnson; Proctor and Thornton; BNA (1969)

Data Sources for Obtaining Data	*Training Need Implications*	*Reference(s)*
4. Questionnaires	Same approach as the interview. Easily tailored to specific characteristics of the organization. May produce bias through the necessity of prestructure categories. Can be tailor-made or stand-ardized. Care must be taken so that they measure job-related qualities.	McGehee and Thayer; Bellman (1975); Bass and Vaughan; Kirkpatrick; Patten; Finnegan; Rose; BNA (1962); Talbot and Ellis; Wood (1956); Johnson; BNA (1969)
5. Tests		
a. Job knowledge		McGehee and Thayer; Johnson; Wessman; Bass and Vaughan; Proctor and Thornton
b. Skills		McGehee and Thayer; Patten; Kirkpatrick; Rose; Prieve and Wentorf
c. Achievement		McGehee and Thayer; Kirkpatrick McGehee and Thayer; Rose
6. Attitude Surveys	On the individual basis, useful in determining morale, motivation, or satisfaction of each employee.	McGehee and Thayer; Johnson; Kirkpatrick; Morano (1973); Talbot and Ellis; Wessman; Prieve and Wentorf; Glueck
7. Checklists or Training Progress Charts	Up-to-date listing of each employee's skills. Indicates future training require-ments for each job.	McGehee and Thayer; Proctor and Thornton; Rose; Johnson; Goldstein
8. Rating Scales	Care must be taken to ensure relevant, reliable, and objective employee ratings.	McGehee and Thayer; Patten; Finnegan
9. Critical Incidents	Observed actions that are critical to the successful or unsuccessful performance of the job.	McGehee and Thayer; Johnson; Goldstein; Wessman
10. Diaries	The individual employee records details of his (her) job.	McGehee and Thayer; Talbot and Ellis; Goldstein
11. Devised Situations	Certain knowledge, skills, and attitudes are demonstrated in these techniques.	McGehee and Thayer
a. Role play		McGehee and Thayer
b. Case study		McGehee and Thayer; Johnson

TABLE 4.6 Data Sources for Person Analysis *(continued)*

Data Sources for Obtaining Data	Training Need Implications	Reference(s)
c. Conference leadership training sessions		McGehee and Thayer
d. Business games		McGehee and Thayer; Johnson
e. In-baskets		Johnson
12. Diagnostic Rating	Checklists are factor analyzed to yield diagnostic ratings.	McGehee and Thayer; Wherry (1959)
13. Assessment Centers	Combination of several of the above techniques into an intensive assessment program.	Wessman
14. Coaching	Similar to interview— one-to-one.	Wessman
15. MBO or Work Planning and Review Systems	Provides actual performance data on a recurring basis related to organizational (and individually or group-negotiated standards) so that base-line measurements may be known and subsequent improvement or deterioration of performance may be identified and analyzed. This performance review and potential review are keyed to larger organizations' goals and objectives.	Odiorne (1970); Humble (1970); Goldstein

likely to occur where performance appraisal information is gathered specifically for general development of the employee, and where the climate (Payne and Pugh 1976) in the organization fosters such development. The problem is that this is more often not the case.

There are things that can be done to minimize problems with supervisor ratings. First, the appraisal system should be relevant to the job (sometimes appraisals are too generic to be appropriate) and acceptable to both supervisor and employee (Cascio 1991b). Also the supervisor must have access to relevant information to make accurate appraisals (Herbert and Doverspike 1990). Finally, to increase the supervisor's motivation to provide accurate ratings, the performance appraisal should be for the TNA only (some companies have an appraisal in place that is used only for developmental purposes). As Murphy and Cleveland (1991) note:

> . . . it is likely that a supervisor experiences little conflict when information from a performance appraisal is being used for providing feedback to employees on their strengths and weaknesses and to recommend employees to training programs.

Furthermore, it stands to reason that an incumbent is more likely to accept ratings when she stands to benefit from the evaluation by receiving appropriate training.

A method being used by some large companies to identify training needs is called Work Planning and Review. The supervisor has periodic meetings with subordinates to assess whether they have met particular goals set earlier, what problems they are having meeting these goals, and what, if any, training would be useful. Corning Glass, for example, identifies 14 dimensions of performance and lists 3 to 6 behaviors within each of these. These behavioral statements become the goals. Supervisors are asked to read each behavioral statement and provide written examples of how the subordinate did or did not behave in the described manner (Table 4.7). If the subordinate is having problems meeting these objectives, the supervisor works with him to help him reach the goals. One way of helping is to provide relevant training, when applicable.

Even in the most progressive appraisal system, when supervisors rate subordinates, other concerns need to be taken into account. Various types of rater bias such as halo (Thorndike 1920) and leniency (Bass 1956) should be considered. This undertaking requires commitment from upper management to provide the supervisors with training necessary to deal with these type of errors. Another concern is that for some jobs, such as teaching and sales, supervisors do not often get to see the employee in action. Sometimes the supervisor is unfamiliar with the job details. Perhaps the best way to deal with these concerns is similar to that suggested for dealing with gathering job analysis data: the more perspectives, the better the picture. For this reason it is useful to consider others as potential raters of an employee's performance.

Self-ratings. Self-ratings are a possibility for determining the needs of employees. Much of the research on self-ratings suggests that the individual tends to overrate himself (Harris and Schaubroeck 1988). However, evidence also indicates that the inflated ratings are a function of the rating instruments rather than the individual attempting to sound better (Farh and Dobbins 1989). Williams and Levy (1992) further noted that when self-raters understand the performance system, they are more likely to agree with supervisor ratings. These findings suggest that self-ratings may be accurate where subordinates are more involved in the development of the appraisal process.

McEnery and McEnery (1987) examined self- and supervisory ratings gathered for a needs analysis related to training. They noted that self-ratings were inflated, but were also more discriminating in identifying different needs than were supervisory ratings. Furthermore, the results suggested that supervisory assessment of "subordinate needs" more closely resembled the needs of the raters themselves.

What does all this mean? The answer seems to be that both supervisory ratings and self-ratings should be gathered. Both parties need to be involved in the assessment

TABLE 4.7   Work Planning and Review at Corning

Dimension	Behavioral Statement	Written Example
Applying quality principles	Sets high standards for self and others: puts a great deal of emphasis on error-free work	Developed written requirements for all suppliers on the Stafford project and encouraged others to do the same.

process. As McEnery and McEnery (1987) suggest, the supervisor also provides a perspective on the needs of the subordinate. The subordinate gains insight into his needs through discussion with the supervisor. This process will also improve communication between the supervisor and subordinate and serves to improve the accuracy of the assessment. An example of such a process is found in Training in Action 4.3. Note that for Corning, both the supervisor and subordinate are involved in the process, and the process is continually examined and modified to meet the needs of the company.

The 360-degree performance review.   Generally, the more sources used to gather information, the higher the reliability and validity of the results. This is a good argument for using the 360-degree performance review (London and Beatty 1993), by which an individual rates himself on a number of dimensions and receives ratings on these dimensions by his supervisor, peers, and subordinates. The resulting information is fed back to the individual. The broader view provided by this method takes pressure off the supervisor, especially when others in the loop agree more with the supervisor than with the individual. These data provide a springboard for dialogue between the supervisor and subordinate regarding the subordinate's needs.

The advantages of this process are that the various groups see the person under different conditions, have different relationships with the individual, and also have different expectations regarding performance. Furthermore, as has been noted, the more sources of information, the better. The disadvantage to the 360-degree performance review is the amount of time it takes and the cost of implementing it. Also, for it to be effective, there has to be clear support from top management.

In summary, those performance processes designed to focus on development (e.g., WP&R) are more likely to provide accurate data. Also data from many sources (e.g., 360-degree performance appraisal) are likely to be more accurate than supervisor appraisals alone. If the traditional performance appraisal is considered alone, it would be wise, at a minimum, to gather self-appraisal information to provide a balance.

Performance Data   Many different measures of performance are used, depending on the nature of the job. In some production jobs, the amount of scrap, the number of units produced, and quality are all measures that could be used. For management performance, the number of projects completed on time as well as consistency in meeting objectives could be measures. One approach to using such performance data suggested by Camp, Blanchard, and Huszczo (1986) is to examine the causes of a performance discrepancy. This is done by looking at consensus and distinctiveness as they relate to the deficiency. **Consensus** refers to the degree to which the performance discrepancy is limited to a few (low consensus) or observed in many individuals (high consensus). **Distinctiveness** refers to the degree to which the discrepancy is specific to one area of the person's performance (high distinctiveness) or is present across a number of areas (low distinctiveness).

These two issues need to be considered jointly. The four possible combinations are charted in Table 4.8 (page 160). High consensus and high distinctiveness mean that the discrepancy occurs in a number of the incumbents and is specific to one dimension of performance. For example, say that the incumbent does not meet his quota of selling notebook computers, but this is also true of 70% of the other incumbents (high consensus). He does meet his quota for selling full-size computers, monitors, and software, so it is only the notebook computers that seem to be a problem (high distinctiveness).

Corning Glass: The Process Continues

In the mid-1960s Corning Glass did not have a formal performance system. The result was a great deal of discontent as to how incentives were administered.

To address the problem, management by objectives (MBO) and work planning and review (WP&R) procedures were developed (see Cascio 1995, pp. 287–88, for descriptions of these two appraisal methods). The MBO was the results-oriented approach and the WP&R was the developmental process. The two procedures would be conducted at different times. Training was provided for both methods. Both supervisors and subordinates attended the training, emphasizing that they were to use the process together, particularly the WP&R.

The WP&R consisted of a 76-item questionnaire (containing behavioral statements) that tapped into 19 key areas of behavior (e.g., formal communication, team building, openness to influence). The data were presented on a computer printout profiling the subordinate's strengths and shortcomings as deviations from the subordinate's own mean.

The WP&R part of the performance appraisal became the strongest and most widely used. The computer-generated profile was felt to be unnecessary and became optional. Subordinate and supervisor now completed the form separately and then discussed each of the ratings.

Plans were made to incorporate career planning into the process. Although upper management was using the system, they found the behavioral statements not very applicable to their jobs.

Revision of the WP&R resulted in 14 rather than 19 competency areas being defined, each of which had 4 to 6 behavioral statements to be measured. The total number of behavioral statements had been reduced from 76 to 67.

WP&R is now tied to career planning in that strengths and weaknesses are compared not only against the job the incumbent is in, but also against those she is considering in the future.

WP&R information is sent to a newly developed corporate human resource information system (HRIS). The computer profiles no longer exist.

Top management uses the WP&R, but rather than using the behavioral statements, they write a narrative. A list of what needs to be covered in the narrative is presented in the instructions for using the performance development and review.

THE NEXT STEP

Corning is presently designing a succession planning process which will incorporate their HRIS.

Source: Adapted from Cascio and Thacker 1994.

TABLE 4.8 Likelihood of Deficiency Being a Training Issue

		Distinctiveness	
		Low	High
Consensus	High	Unsure	Low
	Low	High	Unsure

This would suggest that it is not a KSA deficiency, but rather a deficiency elsewhere (e.g., the product is not competitive or the commission is too low on the product).

Low consensus and low distinctiveness suggests that the discrepancy may be a KSA concern, because others in the department do not seem to have the same problem (low consensus), and the incumbent also has trouble on other facets of the job (low distinctiveness). However, keep in mind that there still may be other causes for the discrepancy, such as a difficult sales territory. The distinctiveness/consensus categorization is meant only as a guide.

When consensus and distinctiveness are opposite (high/low or low/high), it is less clear whether the performance deficiency is a KSA issue or due to some other factor. In these cases, you would need to examine the incumbent more closely to determine the cause of the performance deficiency.

Proficiency tests. Rather than rely on ratings of job performance, an alternative is to test the individual under controlled conditions. Two types of proficiency testing are cognitive and behavioral.

Cognitive tests measure levels of knowledge. Plumbers need to understand government regulations for installing water and drainage systems in a house, supervisors need to understand the procedures for assigning overtime, salespeople need to understand the procedures for accepting returned merchandise. Any job has a certain amount of knowledge attached to it, and a test to measure that knowledge can be developed.

Tests of declarative knowledge can be paper-and-pencil tests. A concern of using such tests is that they will reflect the reading level when reading is not an important skill for the job. If you have a concern about the knowledge level of incumbents (and if reading is not a KSA), paper-and-pencil tests would not be appropriate, unless they were given orally (see Table 4.3 on page 140 for a description of an example where this occurred).

There are many advantages of paper-and-pencil tests.

- They can be given to large numbers of individuals at once.
- They can be scored easily.
- They provide an effective method of determining areas where there is a lack of knowledge.

There are also disadvantages.

- Time and effort are required to develop a comprehensive test that is both reliable and valid.

- If the test is other than true–false or multiple choice, developing effective scoring keys takes a great deal of time.

Recall from the operational analysis discussion (and chapter 3) that higher levels of knowledge could be assessed through measures of mental models. For an example of a traditional test for declarative knowledge and a test of higher levels of knowledge, see Figures 6.3 (page 236) and 6.4 (page 237) in chapter 6.

Behavioral tests measure skills. These are an important means of determining an employee's needs related to skills required on the job. These tests can incorporate work samples, which are simply work situations designed to reflect what actually happens in the workplace. Standardized rating methods are developed so everyone is presented with the same situation and measured according to preset criteria. For example, a welder may be required to measure and cut three pieces of channel iron, then weld them at right angles to make a U; a salesclerk may be required to respond to an irate customer who provides standardized antagonistic responses to the salesclerk's handling of a situation; a manager may be required to make a presentation to a boss on the advantages of going global.

Assessment centers are an expansion of the work sample approach. They often involve a number of work samples and a number of assessors who evaluate the individuals in different situations. Although assessment centers are costly to develop and administer (they often require two to three days off-site), they provide a comprehensive analysis of needs, especially for managerial positions.

Surveys   Attitudes are an important part of organizational effectiveness. If, for example, the team approach is an organizational objective, then attitudes toward this approach are important. Surveys of various attitudes are conducted routinely in some organizations. In such a situation, a scale related to the attitude toward teamwork could simply be included. If this practice does not exist, it might be useful to consider instituting one. At the very least, organizations could survey trainees before training to determine how they feel about teams and teamwork (if this was what training was about).

Developing attitude scales requires a great deal of skill, and it is much better to use well-developed scales found in the literature. Texts such as *Assessing Organizational Change* (Seashore et al. 1983) and *The Experience of Work* (Cook et al. 1981) contain a number of attitudinal measures. Another source that publishes such scales is the Institute for Social Research at the University of Michigan (Robinson, Athanasiou, and Head 1976).

GATHERING TNA DATA

It has been useful to divide the TNA into three distinct factors—organization, operation, and person—for a conceptual understanding of the types of data required. Practically, however, when conducting such an analysis, you will find they are all highly interrelated and often conducted at the same time. If you look at the sources for each (Tables 4.1, 4.2, and 4.6), you will see a great deal of overlap. If you were interviewing incumbents regarding operational analysis, for example, you can at the same time obtain information regarding roadblocks to getting the job done (organizational analysis). In the person analysis, when you examine performance data and compare consensus and distinctiveness, you can determine if there is a structural reason for the poor performance (organizational analysis) rather than a KSA problem.

Once the operational analysis data has determined the KSAs for the job, the person analysis defines whether each of the relevant employees has these KSAs. For those who do not, the discrepancy between what is required and what the employee has serves as the impetus for developing the necessary training.

For the TNA to be effective, it is important that the development of employees is of high concern to both the individual and the organization. This is more likely to occur when an organization (1) has procedures in place that allow for developmental appraisals to take place regularly and separate from other appraisals, (2) allows the individual to provide input into the process (self-appraisal), (3) places a high value on developing subordinates (such as by rewarding supervisors who spend time doing so), and (4) provides opportunities for employees to receive the training and mentoring necessary for development.

However, having these procedures in place is not enough! There are numerous stories of supervisors who simply go through the motions of a performance appraisal and employee development, then get on with the "real work." Such attitudes are likely to undermine any system. Subordinates' perceptions of the process must be positive, and they must believe training will be useful in their development. This is particularly important when self-assessment is being used in the TNA (Ford and Noe 1987).

Outcomes of TNA

From a TNA you will be able to determine what caused (or will cause) a performance discrepancy. Review Figure 4.2 on page 130. Imagine you have identified a performance discrepancy in Job "X." From the needs assessment, you can determine what needs to be done to alleviate the discrepancy.

NONTRAINING NEEDS

Through organizational and operational analysis, the reward/punishment incongruence, inadequate feedback, and obstacles in the system can be examined as they relate to Job "X."

First the reward/punishment incongruencies: Are there actual punishments to working at the expected level of performance for some or all those working in a particular job? As Training in Action 4.4 indicates, the answer can be yes. The punishment/reward situation can be even less obvious. Suppose an employee who works much harder than the others notices he is treated exactly the same as those who just do the bare minimum. It may not be long before he stops making the extra effort. In such cases, training this employee is not going to help. This does not suggest that training is not the answer. In fact, what may be required is supervisory training on how to motivate all employees. Clearly what is needed in this situation is for the supervisor to know how to provide rewards to the employees based on their performance, and be motivated to do it.

Another nontraining need may be feedback. There are numerous examples of employees believing they are good performers and their supervisors believing otherwise. Supervisors generally dislike providing negative feedback (Fisher 1979). In fact,

Training in Action 4.4

Punishment for Performance

At a Canadian gas utility, one of the tasks required of repairpersons was to change gas meters in residences. Each meter was taken in to be tested every six years. Most employees changed 15 per day. When the system became computerized, it allowed management to send a service person to one or two streets in a particular area to change meters, instead of having calls all over the city. Management believed that because of the lower amount of time now necessary to drive between the homes, productivity would increase substantially. It did not. In fact, for the majority of employees it remained at 15.

What was the problem? Was there punishment for doing more than 15? Yes, a norm had been set by the service people. Very few would change more than 15 meters, a standard that had been set by the majority. Those who violated the standard suffered ridicule and shunning by the rest of the service staff. Because they all unloaded their meters at the same time and at the same location, those who were breaking the norm were easily spotted and punished.

it has been suggested that it is the most disliked of all managerial activities (Carrol and Schneier 1982). Once again the problem is not a training issue for the subordinate, but it could be for the supervisor.

Obstacles in the system is a third reason the performance may not be at the required level. Receiving material too late, using worn-out machinery, and being constantly interrupted are but a few of the possibilities that could hinder performance. Once identified, these roadblocks need to be removed, a task that can be very complex and in some cases may require high-level support. Suppose a supervisor has too many reports to file each week and this responsibility takes her away from helping her subordinates. The reports are requested (and believed to be important) by middle management. The only way to reduce the amount of paper work (if that is the answer) is to request that middle management reduce the number of reports they receive or find another way to generate the reports (see Training in Action 4.5, page 164). This is not an easy task.

As Figure 4.2 indicates, KSA deficiencies have a number of possible solutions, only one of which is training (Michalak and Yager 1979).

A job aid is one solution. This is a set of instructions, diagrams, and the like, which are available at the job site to provide guidance to the worker. This is useful if the task is complex, if it requires a number of steps, or if it is dangerous to forget a step. Airline pilots use job aids—a list of things they must do prior to takeoff—so they do not forget any of the steps required. General Motors Electromotive Division in Chicago provides workers with a job aid in the wiring of the locomotives. It is simply a diagram that shows where the wiring runs, which colors branch off, and where to connect them. Because of the number of wires in the harness, memorizing their locations would be very difficult. Following the diagram makes a complex task very manageable.

Self-Managed Barrier Removal

A telephone company department manager had a number of computer-generated reports he was required to examine, provide input on, and send to higher-level management each month. He never knew what was done with the reports, but they took a great deal of his time away from other, more important work. After discussions with a consultant he had hired to do a needs assessment for other purposes, he decided to stop sending two of the reports. A few months later he heard nothing about the reports being late. He decided to stop sending a third report. Two days after the third report was due, he got a call asking where it was, and he sent it.

Six months later he had still not heard about the first two reports he had stopped sending. He shared this information with his other district-level managers, and they stopped sending the reports as well. The consultant left the organization a few months later and still no one had asked for the reports.

Certainly a more progressive approach would be to ask higher management whether the reports were necessary. The concern by the manager was that the answer would be yes even though the reports were not used.

Practice can also solve the problem. For important tasks that are infrequent, it is possible to forget or become less proficient at the skill. That is why police officers are required to practice on the firing range each month. Schools conduct fire drills as practice for an important task that may never occur. In these cases, you are providing the practice to prevent a performance discrepancy. If you discover a performance discrepancy in an infrequent task, you might want to institute practice sessions periodically to ensure that these discrepancies do not continue to occur, particularly when their occurrence can have serious consequences.

Changing the job itself may seem extreme, but it is sometimes worth considering. A number of years ago salespeople in automobile dealerships were responsible for the total job of selling a car. The most difficult part of selling is "closing the deal," which requires certain KSAs that are difficult to impart through training. As a result, many car salespeople did not last long in the business. This discrepancy led the dealers to change the job. They provided the salesperson with the skills to show the car, discuss various options, and negotiate to a certain extent. But when it came to closing the deal, the salesperson had the option of sending the customer to the sales manager. Thus the job was changed so that the salesperson no longer needed that skill.

Finally, if these options or training is not possible, the decision may have to be to transfer or terminate the individual.

TRAINING NEEDS

If training is required, the next step is to develop a clear and unambiguous list of the KSAs that require training. The method of doing this is to develop training objectives. This will be discussed in detail in the next chapter.

Approach to TNA

The training literature takes two general approaches to TNA, based on where they begin in the assessment process. One begins before a need has been identified, and one after a need has been identified (Sleezer 1992). We classify the former as *proactive* and the latter as *reactive*. Both methods use the same three components: organizational analysis, operational analysis, and person analysis. The analysis process is the same for each approach; the difference is the focus. Proactive assessment focuses on what potential needs will be, given the future direction of the organization. The reactive assessment focuses on a specific problem.

PROACTIVE TNA

The **proactive TNA** focuses on future human resource requirements. As chapter 2 described, the HR function needs to be involved in the development of a strategic plan (SWOT analysis). From the resulting unit objectives, HR must develop unit strategies and tactics (see Figure 2.1 on page 39) to be sure the organization has the required KSAs in each of the critical jobs based on the future KSA requirements. There are two ways of planning for this: (1) preparing employees for promotions/transfers to different jobs, and (2) preparing employees for changes in their current jobs.

Regarding the first way, an important activity that is tied directly to proactive TNA is **succession planning,** the identification and development of employees who are perceived to be of high potential. Organizations that have a proactive focus generally have a succession plan in place.

The first step is to identify key positions in the organization. These are positions that, if left vacant for any length of time, would have a significant negative impact on organizational functioning. In practice, these positions often are high-level management positions such as vice president finance, but they could be at any level (e.g., moldmaker if the position is key to the operation and difficult to fill). Once the positions are identified, employees who have potential to fill these key positions are identified. Information is then provided on the employees' readiness to fill the position if it becomes vacant. This becomes the TNA.

Regarding the second way, it is important that the TNA identify the changes that are expected in current jobs, based on strategic objectives. Once this is determined, you can identify the new KSAs that will be required for that job. These future KSAs can be compared with the incumbent's current KSAs, and the resulting discrepancy (if any) can then be prepared for through training.

Organizational Analysis

The proactive approach starts with the strategic plan and objectives. As in any other organizational analysis, the analyst examines the environment in the organization to determine if there are barriers to expected performance. The difference in the proactive approach is that the focus is on what performance expectations will be when the strategic objectives are met. The analyst is trying to determine the best fit between the organization's current internal environment (structures, policies, procedures, etc.) and the future expectations. Questions regarding the formal structure might include the following:

- Are pay practices (e.g., hourly wage) congruent with the new direction taken by the company (which was to treat departments as individual enterprises)?
- Is the emphasis of the new priorities (e.g., "quality is job 1") congruent with the performance appraisal system (is quality an important performance measure)?
- Is the strategy (e.g., desire for a cooperative union/management relationship) congruent with the current practices (e.g., the grievance procedure)?
- Are there a sufficient number of employees to be able to accomplish the objective (e.g., improve quality to meet ISO 9000 standards)?

Regarding the informal procedures, questions could include these:

- Are there norms that would restrict output?
- Will workers believe that changes in performance are required?
- What formal procedures are short-circuited by informal procedures, and what are the implications (perhaps the formal procedure is inappropriate)?

The above questions should be asked at all levels in the organization, but specifically at the departmental level, because this is where more meaningful data will be found. Often those in higher levels of management have a very different view of the impact of various policies on behavior.

Operational Analysis

Being truly proactive requires not only a systematic examination of jobs to determine how they are done and what KSAs are necessary now, but also an examination of the changes expected in the jobs, and the KSAs that will therefore be necessary in the near future.

Jobs have always been dynamic, changing over time. Today, however, the changes in some jobs are much more dramatic than in the past. Employees need to be prepared for these changes. The job analyst must gather information not only on what tasks are done, but also on what tasks will be done in the future. This **strategic job analysis** is defined as identifying the KSAs required for effective performance in a job as it is expected to exist in the future. The process has been described by Schneider and Konz (1989). Data gathering is identical to that in traditional job analysis, with the addition of a section called "gather information on the future." For this section you need to look at changes in areas of societal values, political/legal issues, economics/market/labor, technology, and others, and how those changes would affect the job in question. In this case, you need input from more than just incumbents and supervisors. Schneider and Konz (1989) have suggested considering inclusion of the following:

- At least one person responsible for corporate strategy and closely tied to the job in question
- Someone who is aware of how the competition structures the job (technologically and from a human resource standpoint)
- An efficiency expert (internal technology/communication expert)
- Someone who has worked his or her way up through the job in question
- A forward-thinking incumbent (one willing to suggest new ideas)

The list is not exhaustive but serves only as a guide. Once you have gathered these data, you will complete a revision of the tasks and KSAs based on these changes. The training function then uses this information coupled with person analysis to determine future training needs.

At first this seems like a horrendous task—and if the organization is doing this for the first time, it is. Clearly the first step is to identify the critical jobs. For example, if the primary function of the organization is writing software, the computer programmers' job will be more critical to the effectiveness of the organization than the file clerks' and should be examined first. Likewise, if the organization is making parts for the automotive industry, moldmaking might be a critical job.

Person Analysis

Assessment of the person (does she have the required KSAs?) is identical for the proactive or reactive TNA, and so the information presented earlier on person analysis is applicable.

Let's Do It

Let's go back to the Multistate Health Corporation (MHC) in chapter 2. The strategic plan was outlined, and from it arose a number of potential unit objectives for HR as related to developing an HRPS. Let's examine these as they affect a critical position, that of the CEO. No clear documentation exists of the required KSAs for the 30 CEOs of the hospitals; as a result no one knows the KSAs that are needed in order for someone to be promoted to CEO. To deal with this (and other positions in the organization), the MHC executive committee has developed six objectives. The first step in addressing these objectives (as they affect the position of CEO) would be to conduct an operational analysis of the CEO position. Recall how the job analysis was conducted for the large computer firm (Table 4.5 on page 143). A similar process could be used here, although questionnaires may not be necessary, given the small number of incumbents. You could interview all incumbents (four or five small group meetings) or, as we will do here, have one meeting with six CEOs: two from each region, one from the largest and one from the smallest hospital in that region. At the meeting you would have the group list all the tasks and subtasks they perform. Then, using a scale similar to the one in Table 4.5, ask each of them to rate the importance for the job, and importance at time of hire, for each task. Those that are important you will classify as shown in Table 4.5 as being a selection or training issue. If any differences are noted in the tasks for CEO between regions (or between large and small hospitals), you would document these as well. To organize these tasks, it is useful to combine similar ones under the classification of a duty (see below).

Next you need to identify the KSAs necessary to perform each task. These will be used to make selection and training decisions; publishing them during the recruitment process should make the selection criteria clear to all. The information also identifies what is required to be an effective CEO at the present time.

A team of subject matter experts on the position of CEO (see the discussion of strategic job analysis in the "Operational Analysis" section above) should be consulted to develop the strategic part of the job analysis (how the job might look in five years). This information, when compared with the above information on current requirements, highlights what the future requirements would be.

From the job analysis, one duty might be defined as the "development of subordinates." You might identify these tasks related to that duty:

- Initiates action to identify developmental needs
- Provides timely feedback to help subordinates improve
- Provides subordinates with the opportunities to develop
- Meets with subordinates to discuss performance and development
- Coaches subordinates in a manner that allows them to improve their skills

There would, of course, be a number of duties (and relevant tasks) that would be identified. Finally the KSAs necessary to perform the tasks would be identified. From the above list of tasks, some KSAs that would be relevant are:

- Knowledge of the performance review process
- Knowledge of basic coaching skills
- Skill at providing feedback in an effective manner
- Skill at interviewing
- Positive attitude toward the participative approach to problem solving
- Positive attitude toward helping others

These may all be required training for the CEOs, based on the assessment of the 30 CEOs' skills. This assessment is accomplished by the person analysis.

For the person analysis, let's just focus on the specific KSAs necessary to appraise performance. Here you would want to know about CEOs' knowledge of the appraisal process, skill in providing effective reviews, and attitude toward these reviews. This information could be obtained in part by asking CEOs directly (a subpart of your job analysis meeting). If managers have no confidence in a performance appraisal system, they will have no compunction about telling you that "it's not worth the time" or "it's never used anyway so why bother." If they simply do not believe they have the skill, they might also tell you that. Another place to obtain such information is from the CEOs' subordinates. You might get information from subordinates such as: "She really tries to do a good job but is constantly telling me what I need to do and never asks my opinion" or "He tells me I have a bad attitude. I'm not sure what he means but am in no mood to ask either." These types of comments strongly suggest a lack of skills on the CEO's part, but the CEO could simply have a negative attitude toward the process because she does not believe the performance appraisal to be useful. You could also use behavior tests to assess their skills. Put them in a role-play situation where they must provide feedback to an employee.

With regard to organizational analysis, some of this information has already been gathered from interviews conducted by the consultants. One of the objectives based on findings was the inclusion of a succession plan. This will provide the mechanism for having instant information on whom should be considered for the next promotion, rather than relying on individual CEOs to make that determination. Of course, you need a standardized performance review system in place to make such determinations.

The job analysis will provide the relevant data for developing the standard performance appraisals needed to make both promotion and developmental decisions. With such a system in place, each CEO would be responsible for completing performance reviews on his subordinates and providing developmental plans for them. This process would help to deal with the lack of interest by some CEOs in recommending their subordinates. Although not explicitly noted above, one important measure on the CEOs' performance appraisal would need to be how well the CEOs prepare and develop their subordinates for promotion. This, as part of their performance review specifically, along with the use of a succession plan in general, will serve to encourage all CEOs to work toward developing their subordinates for promotion.

REACTIVE TNA

Whereas the proactive model requires a determination of where discrepancies might exist in the future, the **reactive TNA** begins with an existing discrepancy in job performance. In this sense, Figure 4.2 represents a more complete picture of the reactive process. First there is a realization that a discrepancy exists between what needs to be done and what is actually getting done. A middle manager may notice that production is dropping, a supervisor may see that a particular employee's performance has declined, or human resources may note an increase in grievances from a department. Once you identify a discrepancy, you need to determine whether it is worth fixing. Although this decision may be based on financial implications, it does not have to be. For example, the company notes that one department has lower ratings of supervisory consideration (as rated by subordinates) than the organization expected. The cost of this lower rating would be difficult to assess. It may take a long time (if ever) to notice any significant impact on the company. But if the company has a strong commitment to developing a good employee–management relationship, it may decide to try to alleviate the problem.

In the reactive TNA, you still conduct the organizational analysis, operational analysis, and person analysis, but the distinction among them is even more blurred because (1) the focus is primarily on the one department, (2) those who demonstrate the discrepancy (and their peers and subordinates) are the key persons to be interviewed about all three components, and (3) the discrepancy focuses the issue on a particular part of the job (e.g., interactions with subordinates as noted above).

Organizational Analysis

Organizational analysis deals with the three issues identified to the right of the KSA deficiency in Figure 4.2. A complete analysis of all four aspects of Figure 4.2 is necessary whether or not it is determined that the issue is a KSA problem. This is so because even if a lack of KSAs is identified as a problem, there could still be other roadblocks in place that will prevent the appropriate behavior even if it is learned.

Operational Analysis/Person Analysis

In the reactive approach, the performance discrepancy has already been identified, because it is the trigger for the analysis. This determines where the focus of the TNA will be. From this initial discrepancy, an examination is needed to flush out the cause of the discrepancy, as described earlier.

Let's Do It

When there is a performance discrepancy, it is best to work from the discrepancy and deal only with those issues indicated from the analysis of the discrepancy. Instead of moving step by step through this analysis, let's look at one that was actually done (see Training in Action 4.6 on the following page).

Training in Action 4.6

Where Do You Start When You Have a Performance Discrepancy?

Students in a training and development class decided that for their class project they would like to determine why some professors are so boring whereas others are interesting and informative. The needs analysis of this performance discrepancy (PD) would help to determine whether the issue is training or something else.

They examined the PD using operational analysis (expected performance) and person analysis (actual performance). As is noted in Table 4.2, one way of obtaining expected performance data is to observe the job. The group of students had observed the job (lecturing) of professors (both good and bad) for two years, and also using data from other students they interviewed, they developed a list of behaviors they believed made lectures interesting and informative.

For person analysis (actual performance), the students used observation and performance data (see Table 4.6). Using the observation method, the students identified six professors who were considered as having a performance discrepancy. These data were compared with performance data (published student surveys) about the professors' teaching skills, which verified the observations. An attempt to verify this information further was made by asking the dean to provide student (customer) complaints about professors over the past two years. The dean declined to provide such information.

The organizational analysis was then conducted. Because of the nature of the discrepancy (only business school professors were identified), the organizational analysis focused primarily on the business school. Examining the university-wide mission and other documents was not necessary. From Figure 4.2, questions about the reward/punishment incongruence, inadequate feedback, and obstacles in the system were examined. This was done through an interview (management interrogation as noted in Table 4.1) with the dean of the business school. Questions related to adequate feedback were (1) Are there other performance ratings of professors? (2) Do the professors receive feedback on their performance? The dean's answer was that the only measure of their teaching performance is student surveys and any unsolicited complaints from students. Regarding feedback, the professors receive the student evaluations along with a ranking of themselves and all other faculty members based on these data. Any student complaints would also be made available to the professor. The dean noted that the same professors tended to be rated low each year but again declined to provide specifics. A question related to reward/punishment incongruence was: What happens to those who are rated high and low. The answer was nothing; there are no extrinsic rewards or punishment for being a good or poor teacher. Finally, in response to a question about obstacles in the system, the dean emphasized the pressure for publications. "Publish or perish" were the words he used. Promotions, tenure, travel, and other rewards were all provided to those who were publishing on a regular basis. These were the overall findings of the needs assessment.

From the information provided in Training in Action 4.6, will training help? You cannot really determine that yet. If you were to talk to the professors about the problem (something the students were reluctant to do), you might be able to determine if there was a skill deficiency and whether training would be of value. Even if they did not have the skills, they might also not have the motivation to change.

Let's suppose you did talk to the professors and they told you that they have always taught this way and suggested that their job was not to entertain but to teach. Through some subtle questioning, you determined that they do not seem to understand some basic skills about making a lecture interesting and effective. They evaded questions about how an effective overhead should be set up, how questions can be used to obtain interest, and so on. Thus they do require training. Would training alone be enough? It might. If the training were designed in a way that was interesting and motivated the professors, those professors might go back to the classroom willing to try some different ideas. But their cooperation would be more likely if there were other changes made to encourage them to improve. For example, when they reached an average response rate of 3.5 on a 5-point scale, the professors could be offered a bonus (in the form of travel money or computer equipment if a cash bonus were not possible). Changes in the way pay increases are offered, with heavier emphasis on teaching, would help. If these professors are not full professors with tenure, more emphasis on the importance of student evaluations in getting tenure and/or promotion could be used. Even personal interest by the dean could be effective. The dean might meet with the professor and indicate she is not happy with the performance; they could set goals for improvement and they could meet on a regular basis to encourage the change. All these changes would increase the motivation to try the newly learned skills. On top of that, having a well-designed training program that would also motivate the professors should result in an improvement.

REACTIVE VERSUS PROACTIVE

From a systems perspective, it makes sense that a proactive approach would be better than a reactive approach. Obviously, anticipating needs is better than waiting until they cause problems. Companies that have integrated the training function with strategic objectives are more readily able to respond to the rapidly changing technology and business conditions that have become an everyday part of corporate life (Casner 1989). However, even when operating proactively, there will be times when the organization will need to react to something happening in the environment; strategic plans are not meant to be cast in concrete. Using a combination of proactive and reactive strategies is necessary for an organization to be most effective (Mintzberg 1987).

In reality, however, many organizations operate from a reactive perspective when it comes to training. It is, in fact, possible that a proactive approach is more important for market leader organizations than for cost leader organizations (Burns and Stalker 1961). Market leaders need to be much more aware of their environment and anticipate how they will respond to that environment, otherwise they will not survive.

The Small Business

It has been argued that the small business is not simply a miniature large organization, but a unique entity in itself (Keats and Bracker 1988). This may be true, but many of the procedures necessary to be effective are similar. Because these businesses *are* small, the procedures that management decides to implement may be even more important, because errors in judgment (such as the building of the Edsel car by Ford) could destroy them. Therefore, the proactive approach to training would seem to make sense for the small business. Furthermore, it would seem logical that in smaller organizations it would be easier to integrate a proactive approach because fewer employees are involved.

It is usually top management of a small business (president or owner) that is responsible for any training (Banks, Bures, and Champion 1987). This setup creates a problem, because this individual usually does not understand how a proactive approach to training can be advantageous (Fairfield-Sonn 1987). In fact, much of the dissatisfaction with training in the small business sector is a function of the reactive approach, which responds to a crisis with a "quick fix." The small business owner/manager needs to realize that sound training practices tied to the strategic plan will in the long run pay off, as Metro Tool and Die has discovered (see Training in Action 4.7).

There is evidence that more small manufacturing businesses are undertaking TNA. Many want to become ISO certified. David Alcock works for the Canadian Plastics Training Center (CPTC) in Toronto, which provides training to many of the small mold-making companies in the region. He says that because of the investment required in becoming ISO certified, companies are requesting a TNA to obtain the

---

Training in Action 4.7

Training: Where Is the Return?

Metro Tool and Die of Mississauga, Ontario, has 42 employees, most of whom have little education or training. Mr. Panteno, the owner, was interested in improving the quality and efficiency of his shop. He contacted Fabian Hogan, a consultant with the Ontario Skills Development Ministry. After an assessment, Mr. Hogan suggested that all employees receive education in basic literacy skills and training in blueprint reading and instrumentation die setup. Doing this would entail a considerable expense, but the consultant convinced Mr. Panteno that the investment was, in the long term, a good one. At 3:30 every day training sessions were held on company premises and company time. Was this commitment to training worthwhile? Since completion of the training, rejects dropped from 7,500 per million to 325 per million. The company won the prestigious Xerox quality award in a worldwide competition. It recently provided one of its customers with a $9,600 cost savings. In the owner's own words, "Training has paid for itself. There is no tool and die company like us. We are a small company using big-company tactics."

Source: Adapted from MacKinnon 1992.

maximum effect for their training dollars. He noted that in the last few years more than half of the company's customers (which are mostly small businesses) have requested that the TNA be done.

ASSISTANCE FOR SMALL BUSINESS

Small-business owners have access to resources to aid them in training their employees. The different levels of government assist in various ways to help fund training. For example, in California customized training programs that have assisted companies in becoming ISO 9000 certified are available from the California State Department of Education at no cost. Instructors with factory experience conduct a TNA and develop training based on the analysis, making the training organization-specific. As a result, employees can see its advantages to their job. The major hurdle to these programs is convincing management of their value. Also the training must be integrated into the overall plan of the organization, or it is not successful (Kuri 1996).

In Canada the Federal Business Development Bank (FBDB) is set up to assist small businesses in various ways, one of which is to provide training seminars on topics important to them. The main problem with these resources is that many small businesses do not take advantage of them. One of the authors was recently talking to Arnold Gavel, a small business owner from Winnipeg who was being sued for wrongful dismissal. The owner was amazed that the terminated employee was able to sue. When asked if he had ever attended the various types of seminars offered by the FBDB, the owner replied that he had seen advertisements for them but never thought they were of interest. Was there one related to training managers how to discipline and discharge? Probably.

As was noted in the Training in Action example, when the small business does not have the time or expertise, government-sponsored consultants such as Mr. Hogan can provide support. Furthermore, in most universities, graduate students in psychology or business would welcome the opportunity to become involved. These individuals often operate under the watchful eye of highly trained professors and are willing to do the work at a fraction of the cost a professional would charge. In fact, if there were research possibilities, the project might be done for free. For those who argue that small businesses simply do not have the time to do a comprehensive TNA, we argue the opposite; they cannot afford not to. Furthermore, it is better to do something rather than nothing, as Training in Action 4.8 (page 174) shows.

TNA and Design

We return now to the opening case, Westcan. As you read the rest of the case (on page 175), think about the things you have learned about conducting a TNA. You will note the TNA Westcan uses are much simpler and less formal than some we have discussed. However, the value of doing the TNA is quite obvious.

The needs assessment shows that training was required at Westcan. However, that training is much different than what Chris had first imagined. Her problem was that she didn't have enough information to understand the types of needs her managers had. Without this information, she began to design what she thought would be a good "effective meeting" training session. What would have happened if she had gone ahead with her original plan? After conducting the TNA, she is now in a much better position to design an appropriate training program. The next step is to develop a clear

---

Needs Analysis for a Small Business:
How Complicated Does It Have to Be?

A business that manufactures trailers is only eight years old and has 52 employees, 36 of whom work on the shop floor under one job classification. The company had recently installed a computer-based process for tracking the various costs associated with its manufacturing. The first thing that was noticed was that 9 of the 36 workers took much more time building trailers than the rest. This was true for all trailers—custom, large, and small. Do these 9 need training?

WHAT WAS DONE

The owner asked the supervisor about these employees and the supervisor suggested that they were "not our best employees." He said he would watch them to see if they performed better. The supervisor monitored their work for about two weeks, during which time three of the nine quit and one simply stopped coming to work. The other five remained, but their work performance did not change. In fact, it seemed to deteriorate. Finally, the owner, in talking informally with one of the other employees, asked him what he thought the problem might be. "Too much pressure is being put on them lately," he said. "Before, when they were building a trailer, if they had a problem they would come to one of us to ask for help. Now that Mike [the supervisor] watches every move they make, they are afraid to come and ask."

It turned out that these employees had trouble reading the blueprints and seven or eight times a day needed to ask someone what to do next, which adversely affected their performance. When they were being monitored, they were afraid to admit they did not know how to read the blueprints, so four simply left and the performance of the other five got worse.

WHAT SHOULD HAVE BEEN DONE

Recall that low distinctiveness (the nine build all trailers more slowly than others do) and low consensus (only nine have such a problem) suggest a training problem. With this knowledge, further needs assessment could be done by simply asking the nine what the problem is. It is important to frame the questions as helping: "I have noticed you are not able to build the trailers as fast as many of the other employees. Are there some parts of the job you particularly have trouble with? If so, we could provide you with some training to alleviate it." Another possibility would be to have observed the employees unobtrusively (rather than monitoring, which scared them). This action would have revealed their constant asking for help reading the blueprints.

Notice that this is not a full-blown needs analysis. It is, however, much better than not doing anything at all, for had it been done, the employer would not have needlessly lost four employees.

set of training objectives that will drive both the design and evaluation of training. The importance of sound training objectives cannot be overstressed. The next chapter provides a step-by-step procedure for developing these objectives and meshing them with training design constraints and issues.

Developing a Training Package at Westcan

Chris told Karen about the conversation with Irven and what she had put together. Chris said, "What remains is to develop the simulation. Can you help?"

"Sure," said Karen, "but it's too bad you are so far along. I may have been able to help you in developing the training." Chris indicated she had not put a great deal of time into developing the training and was open to any suggestions.

Karen suggested that Chris consider using a needs analysis. "In a way, you have completed a partial operational analysis by determining what is required in running an effective meeting. What we don't know is where the managers are deficient; we call that a person analysis. One way to obtain that information is simply to ask the managers to describe how their meetings currently run and the areas they see as ineffective. Their answers should reflect the areas in which they are deficient. Also by asking the managers what training they want, we could ensure the training was relevant. Another method might be to sit in and observe how they run their meetings. This would allow us to identify deficiencies they might be unaware of," said Karen. Karen noted that in her brief time at Westcan, it seemed that premeeting information was well distributed and understood. There were always agendas, notice of meetings always contained the relevant information, and so on.

"You might be right," said Chris. "I simply never thought of asking them." Together they developed a questionnaire asking questions related to effective meetings such as "What would you like to see contained in a one-day effective meeting workshop?" "How well do the meetings with your staff stay on track?" They also got permission to sit in on a number of meetings.

The returned surveys and meeting observations suggested that most managers understood the rules of effective meetings. All had at one time or another attended a lecture or read material on running an effective meeting. The problem was that they had never been able to turn the knowledge into action. They knew what to do, just not how to do it. They wanted practice with feedback from a professional. They also wanted the training to be for the intact teams they continually operated in. This would mean that management and nonmanagement from a team would attend the same training and learn the behaviors required for effective meetings together. After going through the TNA with Karen and documenting all the information, Chris said to Karen. "Well, it looks like the training I was going to provide was way off the mark compared with what we now know they need. I owe you a dinner."

Key Terms

- Behavioral test
- Bias
- Bias in performance ratings
- Cognitive tests
- Consensus
- Content validity
- Criterion
- Criterion contamination
- Criterion deficiency
- Criterion relevancy
- Developmental discrepancy
- Distinctiveness
- Duty to accommodate
- Error
- Group characteristic bias
- Halo effect
- Job analysis

- Job-duty-task
- Knowledge of predictor bias
- Operational analysis
- Opportunity bias
- Organizational analysis
- Performance discrepancy
- Person analysis
- Proactive TNA
- Reactive TNA
- Reliability
- Strategic job analysis
- Succession planning
- Task oriented
- Ultimate criterion
- Validity
- Worker oriented

Cases

Case 1

Fred had just become a manager at a local hardware store that employees about 6 managers and 55 nonmanagement employees. With the coming of the larger chains such as Builders Square to the area, the owner is concerned about losing many of his customers because he cannot compete with regard to price. The management team met and discussed its strategic response. It was determined that the hardware store would focus on particular items of hardware and make personalized service the cornerstone of its effort. Fred's responsibility was to train all nonmanagement employees in good customer relations skills; he was given a budget of $70,000. The owner gave Fred a number of brochures that had been sent to the company over the past few months.

One of the brochures boasted, "Three-day workshop; $35,000. We will come in and train all your employees (maximum of 50 per session) so that any customer who comes to your store once will come again."

Another said, "One-day seminar on customer service skills. The best in the country. Only $8,000 (maximum participants 70)."

A third said, "Customer satisfaction guaranteed on our customer satisfaction training for sales clerks. Three-day workshop, $25,000. Maximum participants 25 to allow for individual help."

Fred liked the third one, because it provided personalized training. He called the company in to talk about its offering. The consultant said that by keeping the number small, he would be able to provide actual work simulations for each of the trainees to practice. He also indicated he would tailor the simulations to reflect the hardware store. Fred noted they would need two sessions and asked the consultant if he could take a few more per session to accommodate the 55 employees. The consultant agreed. The training went ahead, and the cost was under the budget by $20,000.

CASE QUESTIONS

1. Do you agree with Fred's choice? Why?
2. What else could have Fred done before choosing a training package?
3. If training went ahead as indicated above, how successful do you think it would be?

Case 2

You are the HRD manager of a large electronics manufacturing firm (LEM) and have 14 people who report to you (see HRD organizational chart). LEM manufactures radios and pilot information systems for passenger aircraft manufacturers. It has about 250 salaried employees and about 1,400 hourly paid employees, operating out of a single plant that is highly mechanized. Many of the operations are automated, with highly sophisticated robotics and sensing equipment. About half the hourly paid employees operate this type of equipment. They monitor the equipment's performance, make adjustments as necessary, and occasionally perform routine maintenance. Repairs and major maintenance are done by the maintenance department. The other half of the hourly paid workforce is engaged in manual operations such as wiring, assembling component boards, and assembling product housings. The salaried workforce is divided between engineers and management administrator types.

The structure of the organization is depicted in Exhibit 1.

EXHIBIT 1

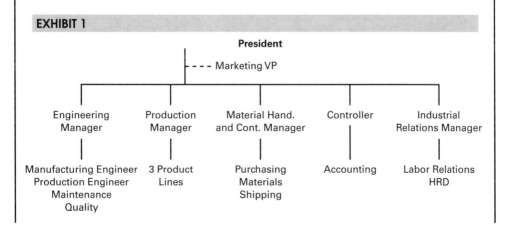

The pace of change for both product and manufacturing technology is increasing dramatically, so much so that within two years a new process will be installed that will reduce the need for the hourly workforce by one-third. The reduction will come primarily from the manual operations and will reduce the need for salaried supervisors by a proportional amount. Currently, the union representing the hourly workers is resistant to "team" approaches. However, it has yet to be made aware of the new manufacturing process or the proposed reduction in force. In spite of the union's formal posture, management has instituted two experiments in work redesign in which small work groups determine work procedures, monitor their quality, and do their own interfacing with Materials and Shipping. These experiments have gone a long way toward improving the quality of these products, and the hourly employees have become quite attached to this way of doing business.

Competition is quite fierce in this industry, yet the marketing vice president and president have recently secured two new contracts. One is to produce a new and highly secret passive restraint sensing system, which if successful will reduce passenger injuries in a crash by at least 50%. The second is a radar interpretation system that is asserted to be state of the art and will provide warning to pilots of air disturbance and air traffic and simplify existing radar interpretation. Putting these products on line will require dropping one of the old product lines (probably the radio) because of space limitations.

The training organization has been seen by management as useful in acquiring financial resources to support professional development opportunities, obtaining certification/recertification in various disciplines, and providing several in-house seminars/workshops that were very well received. The hourly paid workforce has a different view of training. Their training has focused on machine/equipment operation, safety, and literacy. Some seminars and workshops in teams and quality were not well received at all. In fact, the only program that has been well received by the hourly paid workforce is the literacy program that HRD strongly pushed. After two years in existence, this program is well thought of by both rank-and-file and union leadership.

EXHIBIT 2

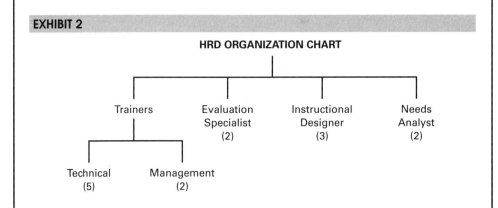

HRD ORGANIZATION CHART

You, the HRD manager, and the industrial relations manager will meet with the president and vice presidents to discuss the strategic plan for LEM over the next two years. The industrial relations manager has given you several questions to consider in preparation for the meeting. (See Case Questions below.)

CASE QUESTIONS

1. Based on the information provided here, what recommendations would you make regarding how human resources will be used over the next two years?

2. What are the short-term KSA needs for human resources, both hourly and managerial? Provide your rationale.

3. What are the long-term human resource needs of LEM, both hourly paid and managerial? Give your assumptions about the business's environment and technology.

4. Assuming your recommendations in item 1 are accepted, what is your strategic plan for training and development? Identify which HR needs will be met by HRD and which by other HR systems. For those needs that are addressed by HRD, what is your implementation plan? What contingencies have you built into your plan?

Exercises

1. Get a small group of students together and analyze the job of "student." What are the duties and tasks required? From these tasks, list the KSAs that students need. Are any in your group deficient in any of these KSAs? Now examine the list of workshops offered to students to help them be successful. Are these relevant to the KSAs you identified in general? Are there now some you could recommend be offered?

2. Do the same job analysis for students in another faculty and compare it with yours. Are the KSAs the same for a student in science and arts? In law or engineering? What (if anything) is different?

3. Examine the mission at the institution you are attending. Examine the one for your faculty (if it has one). Do the two relate? On the basis of the mission and objectives, do a SWOT analysis through interviews with administration or using your own expertise. What major changes are indicated? How will they affect the way courses will be taught? What training might be necessary to meet these changes?

4. Talk to someone you know who is currently working and see if it would be possible to do a TNA on a particular job classification or on his or her job. Even interviewing only a few employees would provide enough information to give you an idea of how to conduct the TNA.

Questions for Review

1. What is the purpose of a TNA? Is it always necessary?
2. What is the difference between proactive and reactive TNA? When is proactive better?
3. What is the difference between reliabil-

ity and validity? Which is more important?

4. Describe how you would go about analyzing the future training needs of your university.

5. What is the ultimate criterion? Describe in detail the factors that prevent us from ever reaching it.

6. Considering criterion development is not as simple as it might seem. What questions would you ask and of whom to determine "amount of scrap," "supervisory performance appraisal," and "work sample test" as a means of measuring training success.

References

Banks, M., A. Bures, and D. Champion. 1987. Decision making factors in small business: Training and development. *Journal of Small Business Management,* January, pp. 19–26.

Bass, B. 1956. Reducing leniency in merit ratings. *Personnel Psychology* 9:359–69.

Bass, B. M., and J. A. Vaughan. 1966. *Training in Industry: The Management of Learning.* Belmont, CA: Brooks/Cole.

Bellman, G. 1975. Supervising your supervisory training needs. *Training and Development Journal,* February, pp. 25–33.

Benedict, M. E., and E. L. Levine. 1988. Delay and distortion: Tacit influences on performance appraisal. *Journal of Applied Psychology* 73:507–14.

Bernardin, H. J., and R. Beatty. 1984. *Performance Appraisal: Assessing Human Behavior at Work.* Boston: Kent—Division of Wadsworth.

Blum, M. L., and J. C. Naylor. 1968. *Industrial Psychology: Its Theoretical and Social Foundation.* New York: Harper & Row.

Bureau of National Affairs. 1969. Training employees. *Survey No. 88.* Washington, DC: Personnel Policies Forum.

Bureau of National Affairs. 1962. Training rank and file employees. *Survey No. 66.* Washington, DC: Personnel Policies Forum.

Burns, T., and G. M. Stalker. 1961. *The Management of Innovation.* London: Tavistock.

Camp, R., P. Blanchard, and G. Huszczo. 1986. *Toward a More Organizationally Effective Training Strategy and Practice.* Upper Saddle River, NJ: Prentice Hall.

Carrol, S., and C. Schneier. 1982. *Performance Appraisal and Review Systems.* Glenview, IL: Scott Foresman.

Cascio, W. 1989. Using utility analysis to assess training outcomes. In *Training and Development in Organizations,* edited by I. L. Goldstein. San Francisco: Jossey-Bass.

———. 1991a. *Costing Human Resources: The Financial Impact of Behavior in Organizations.* Boston: PWS Kent.

———. 1991b. *Applied Psychology in Personnel Management.* Upper Saddle River, NJ: Prentice Hall.

———. 1995. *Managing Human Resources.* New York: McGraw-Hill.

Cascio, W., and J. Thacker. 1994. *Managing Human Resources.* Toronto: McGraw-Hill.

Casner, J. 1989. *Successful Training Strategies.* San Francisco: Jossey-Bass.

Champagne, A. B., L. E. Klopfer, A. T. Desena, and D. A. Squires. 1981. Structural representations of students' knowledge before and after science instruction. *Journal of Research in Science Technology* 18:97–111.

Cook, J., S. Hepworth, T. Wall, J. Toby, and P. Warr. 1981. *The Experience of Work: A Compendium and Review of 249 Measures and Their Use.* New York: Academic Press.

Cooke N. M., and J. E. McDonald. 1987. The application of psychological scaling techniques to knowledge elicitation for knowledge based systems. *International Journal of Man-Machine Studies* 28:533–50.

Dayal, I., and J. Thomas. 1968. Operation KPE: Developing a new organization. *Journal of Behavioral Science* 4:473–506.

DePhillips, F. A., W. M. Berliner, and J. J. Cribben. 1960. *Management of Training Programs.* Homewood, IL: Richard D. Irwin.

Fairfield-Sonn, J. 1987. A strategic process model for small business training and development. *Journal of Small Business Management,* January, pp. 11–18.

Farh, J., and G. Dobbins. 1989. Effects of self-esteem on leniency bias in self-reports of performance: A structural equation analysis. *Personnel Psychology* 42:835–50.

Finnegan, J. 1970. *Industrial Training Management.* London: Business Books.

Fisher, C. 1979. Transmission of negative and positive feedback to subordinates: A laboratory investigation. *Journal of Psychology* 64:533–40.

Ford, J. K., and K. Kraiger. 1995. The application of cognitive constructs and principles to the instructional systems model of training: Implications for needs assessment, design and transfer. In *International Review of Industrial and Organizational Psychology,* edited by C. L. Cooper and T. J. Robertson, 10:1–48.

Ford, J. K., and R. A. Noe. 1987. Self-assessed training needs: The effects of attitudes toward training, managerial level, and function. *Personnel Psychology* 40:39–53.

French, W. 1974. *The Personnel Management Process,* 3rd ed. Boston: Houghton-Mifflin.

Glueck, W. F. 1974. *Personnel: A Diagnostic Approach.* Dallas: Business Publications, Inc.

Goldsmith, T. E., and P. J. Johnson. 1990. A structural assessment of classroom learning. In *Pathfinder Associative Networks: Studies in Knowledge Organization,* edited by R. W. Schvaneveltd. Norwood, NJ: Ablex.

Goldstein, I. L. 1974. *Training: Program Development and Evaluation.* Monterey, CA: Brooks/Cole.

Harris, M. M., and J. Schaubroek. 1988. A meta analysis of self–supervisor, self–peer, and peer–supervisor ratings. *Personnel Psychology* 41:43–62.

Hellriegel, D., and J. W. Slocum. 1974. Organizational climate: measures, researches, and contingencies. *Academy of Management Journal* 17:225–280.

Herbert, G., and D. Doverspike. 1990. Performance appraisal in the training needs analysis process: A review and critique. *Public Personnel Management* 19:253–70.

Humble, John W. 1970. *Management by Objectives in Action.* London: McGraw-Hill.

Johnson, C. 1995. Making your training stick. *HR Magazine,* May, pp. 55–60.

Johnson, R. B. 1967. "Determining Training Needs." In *Training and Development Handbook,* edited by R. L. Craig and L. R. Bittel. New York: McGraw-Hill.

Keats, B., and J. Bracker. 1988. Toward a theory of small firm performance. *American Journal of Small Business* 4:35–43.

Kirkpatrick, D. L. 1971. *Supervisory Training and Development.* Menlo Park: Addison-Wesley.

Kraiger, K., J. Ford, and E. Salas. 1993. Application of cognitive, skill based, and affective theories of learning outcomes to new methods of training evaluation. *Journal of Applied Psychology* 78:311–28.

Kuri, F. 1996. Basic skills training boosts productivity. *HR Magazine,* September, pp. 73–79.

Landy, F., and J. Vasey. 1991. Job analysis: The composition of SME samples. *Personnel Psychology* 44:27–50.

Lawrie, J. W., and C. W. Boringer. 1971. Training needs assessment and training program evaluation. *Training and Development Journal,* pp. 6–9.

London, M., and R. Beatty. 1993. 360-degree feedback as a competitive advantage. *Human Resource Management* 32:353–72.

Longenecker, C. O., H. P. Sims, and D. A. Gioia. 1987. Behind the mask: The politics of employee appraisal. *Academy of Management Executive* 1:183–93.

MacKinnon, D. J. 1992. Training days at Metro Tool. *Toronto Star,* April 22, pp. C1–C2.

McCormick, E. 1979. *Job Analysis.* New York: AMACOM.

McEnery, J., and J. McEnery. 1987. Self-ratings in management training: A neglected opportunity? *Journal of Occupational Psychology* 60:49–60.

McGehee, W., and P. W. Thayer. 1961. *Training in Business and Industry.* New York: Wiley.

Michalak, D. F., and E. G. Yager. 1979. *Making the Training Process Work.* New York: Harper & Row.

Mills, G. E., R. W. Pace, and B. D. Peterson. 1988. *Analysis in Human Resource Training and Organizational Development.* Reading, MA: Addison-Wesley.

Mintzberg, H. 1987. Crafting strategy. *Harvard Business Review,* July–August, pp. 66–75.

Morano, R. 1973. Determining organizational training needs. *Personnel Psychology,* 26: 479–87.

Murphy, K. R., and J. N. Cleveland. 1991. *Performance Appraisal: An Organizational Perspective.* Boston: Allyn & Bacon.

Nunnally, J. 1978. *Psychometric Theory.* New York: McGraw-Hill.

Odiorne, G. S. 1970. *Training by Objectives: An Economic Approach to Management.* New York: Macmillan.

Otto, C., and R. Glaser. 1970. How to prepare and present a training forecast. *Training and Development Journal,* pp. 75–81.

Patten, T. H. 1971. *Manpower Planning and the Development of Human Resources.* New York: John Wiley.

Payne, R., and D. Pugh. 1976. Organizational structure and climate. In *Handbook of Industrial and Organizational Psychology,* edited by M. Dunnette, pp. 1125–73.

Prieve, E. A., and D. A. Wentorf. 1970. Training objectives: philosophy or practice. *Personnel Journal,* March, pp. 235–40.

Proctor, J., and W. Thornton. 1961. *Training: A Handbook for Managers.* New York: American Managers Association.

Renton, M. 1969. Developing in company training courses. *Training and Development Journal* 9:90–97.

Robinson, J., R. Athanasiou, and K. Head. 1976. *Measuring of Occupational Attitudes and Occupational Characteristics.* Ann Arbor: Institute for Social Research.

Rose, H. 1964. *The Development and Supervision of Training Programs.* New York: American Training Society.

Rummler, G. 1987. Determining needs. In *Training and Development Handbook,* edited by R. L. Craig. New York: McGraw-Hill.

Schneider, B. 1975. Organizational climates: an essay. *Personnel Psychology* 28:447–79.

Schneider, B., and A. Konz. 1989. Strategic job analysis. *Human Resource Management* 28:51–63.

Schvaneveltd, R. W., F. T. Durso, and D. W. Dearholt. 1985. *Pathfinder scaling with network structures.* (Memorandum in Computer and Cognitive Structures, MCCS-85-9). Las Cruces, NM: State Univ. Computing Research Laboratory.

Seashore, S., E. Lawler, P. Mirvis, and C. Cammann. 1983. *Assessing Organizational Change.* New York: Wiley.

Shoben, E. J. 1983. Applications of multidimensional scaling in cognitive psychology. *Applied Psychological Measurement* 7:473–90.

Sleezer, C. 1992. Needs assessment: Perspectives from the literature. *Performance Improvement Quarterly* 5:34–46.

Talbot, J. R., and C. Ellis. 1969. *Analysis and Costing of Company Training.* London: Gower Press.

Tannenbaum, S., and G. Yukl. 1992. Training and development in work organizations. *American Review of Psychology* 43:399–441.

Thorndike, E. L. 1920. A constant error in psychological ratings. *Journal of Applied Psychology* 4:25–29.

Thorndike, R. L. 1949. *Personnel Selection: Test and Measurement Technique.* New York: Wiley.

Warren, M. 1969. *Training for Results.* Menlo Park: Addison-Wesley.

Wessman, F. 1975. Determining the training needs of managers. *Personnel Journal,* February, pp. 109–113.

Wherry, R. J. 1959. An evaluative and diagnostic forced choice rating scale for serviceman. *Personnel Psychology* 12:227–236.

Williams, J., and P. Levy. 1992. The effects of perceived system knowledge on the agreement between self ratings and supervisor ratings. *Personnel Psychology* 45:835–47.

Wood, W. F. 1956. Identification of management training needs. Ph.D. Thesis, Purdue University, June.

CHAPTER 5

Training Design

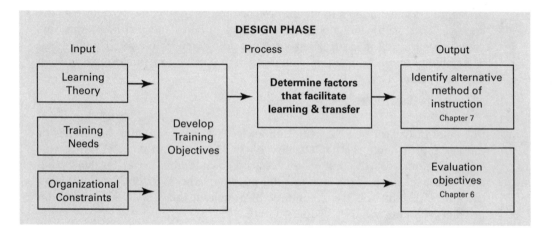

DESIGN PHASE

Input	Process	Output

- Learning Theory
- Training Needs
- Organizational Constraints

Develop Training Objectives

Determine factors that facilitate learning & transfer

Identify alternative method of instruction
Chapter 7

Evaluation objectives
Chapter 6

Learning Objectives

After reading this chapter, you should be able to:

- Describe the purpose of instructional objectives, the criteria for evaluating such objectives, and the advantages of developing these objectives

- Write an instructional objective that meets the criteria for a good objective and accurately reflects needs analysis data

- Describe the motivational, KSA, and learning environment factors that will act to facilitate trainee learning

- Appropriately apply principles derived from learning theory to design a training session

- List and describe the factors that will make it likely that learning gained during training will transfer back to the trainee's job

---

The Real World of Training . . . what is wrong here?

CASE 1

At a large training establishment operated by the government, a course was once offered in which trainees were to learn how to operate and repair a large, complex electronic system. The goal of the course was simply stated: to be able to operate and maintain the electronic system. It was impossible to provide every trainee with his or her own system to practice on, but the instructor decided to increase the amount of troubleshooting experience by providing classroom exercises on troubleshooting. The instructor would pose various problems for the students to solve. For a specific problem such as a burned-out capacitor, he would ask the students to identify the symptoms that would appear (e.g., the control board would not operate). After the training, the instructor was surprised to learn that many trainees were not doing well on the job. They seemed to be able to operate the equipment, but when it came to troubleshooting, they were not performing well.

CASE 2

The chief instructor of a 32-week military course was examining the grades of the last four groups to complete the course. He noted an unusual trend. Students did poorly on the first exam, then did considerably better on the second and third exams. Then the students did poorly on the fourth but got better on the fifth and sixth. This trend continued throughout the 32 weeks, even for the brightest students. What was going on here?

At this point in the training process, you have moved from conducting a TNA to identifying training needs (KSAs). Once it is clear which KSAs are needed in a particular situation, the next step is to translate those needs into training objectives. These objectives are then used to determine the design of training (content, methods, materials, etc.). Decisions about training design integrate what we know about "how people learn" (learning theory) with "what they need to learn" to develop the appropriate training, that is, how the training needs will be addressed. Of course, the plan must take into consideration any constraints (money, time, facilities, etc.) the organization may have. On the basis of all this information, a particular design is created and a training program is developed. This chapter discusses the design issues and provides an understanding of the process.

Developing Objectives

In this text, we use the term **training objectives** to refer to all the objectives that have been developed for the training program. Some of the most important types are presented in Table 5.1. The term **trainee reaction objectives** refers to the objectives that have been set for how trainees should feel about the training and their learning environment. The training's **learning objectives** describe the KSAs that trainees are ex-

TABLE 5.1   Types of Training Objectives

1. Trainee Reaction Objectives	Describes the desired trainee attitudinal and subjective evaluations of training
2. Learning Objectives	Describes the type of behavior that will demonstrate the learning, the conditions under which the behavior must occur, and the criteria that will signify that a sufficient level of learning has occurred
3. Transfer of Training Objectives	Describes the job behaviors that will be affected by training, the conditions under which those behaviors must occur, and the criteria that will signify that a sufficient transfer of learning from training to the job has occurred
4. Organizational Outcome Objectives	Describes the organizational outcomes that will be affected by the transfer of learning to the job and the criteria that will signify that organizational outcome objectives have been achieved

pected to acquire throughout the training program, and the ways that learning will be demonstrated. **Transfer of training objectives** describe the changes in job behavior that are expected to occur as a result of transferring the KSAs gained in training to the trainee's job. **Organizational outcome objectives** for the training describe the outcomes the organization can expect from the changes in the trainees' job behavior due to the learning. Ideally, a training program would develop objectives in all four areas.

IDENTIFYING OBJECTIVES

As was noted in the previous chapter, the TNA is a critical part of determining what the objectives of training should be. To summarize briefly: The result of integrating the organization, job, and person analyses is the identification of performance deficiencies and their negative effect on organizational outcomes, and also identification of the cause of the deficiencies (i.e., motivation, KSAs, environment). With this information you then determine (1) which performance deficiencies can and should be addressed by training, and (2) which KSAs need to be learned in order to change job behavior so that the performance deficiencies are reduced or eliminated.

Deciding which performance deficiencies to address and which KSAs to provide in training determines the learning objectives, the transfer of training objectives, and the organizational outcome objectives. Trainee reaction objectives can be linked to the person analysis but may also include areas not addressed in the needs analysis.

While the content of the various types of objectives differ, the structure and process of developing good objective statements is the same. Objectives are statements about what is expected to be accomplished. A good objective has three components (Mager 1975).

Desired outcome: What should be expected to occur?
Conditions: Under what conditions is the outcome expected to occur?
Standards: What criteria signify that the outcome is acceptable?

It is difficult to write good objectives. You must be careful to ensure that the three components are specified in unambiguous terms and the full range of expectations are addressed.

Writing a Good Learning Objective

We will focus attention on the writing of learning objectives, for several reasons. Learning objectives are often more difficult to write than other types because learning can be observed only through its influence on behavior. Thus when you are writing learning objectives, think not only about what will be learned, but also how learning will be demonstrated.

Another reason for focusing on learning objectives is that learning is at the heart of the training enterprise. If the trainer isn't clear about what is to be learned, the appropriate learning is not likely to occur and the other objectives will not matter and will not be achieved. For example, it doesn't matter to the trainees' supervisor or the CEO if a terrific learning environment is created and trainees enjoy the training if the trainees don't learn what they need to learn. If they don't, then performance deficiencies won't be corrected and the organizational outcome objectives are not likely to be met. Thus clearly articulated learning objectives are a critical first step in developing an effective training program.

Desired Outcome: Behavior   The desired behavior must be clearly and unambiguously worded. Anyone reading the objective should be able to understand what will be required by the learner to demonstrate she has learned the KSA. A learning objective that states: "to understand fully how to splice electrical wire" is ambiguous. It fails to specify what the trainee will be able to do. What behavior will indicate that she "understands fully"? A clearer learning objective would be: "will be able to splice electrical wires of any gauge." This indicates what the learner should be able to do at the end of training.

Consider another example: "The trainee will be able to differentiate (by sorting into two piles) between computer chips that are within specification and those that are outside of specification." Here it is clear *what* is expected, but not *how* the trainee is expected to differentiate between the computer chips.

Conditions   Explaining the conditions under which the behavior must occur further clarifies exactly what is required. In the above example, it is not clear how the trainee is to determine if the computer chips are within specifications. Is it a visual examination, or is a tester used? Providing the conditions makes the objective even clearer: "*Using an ohmmeter and chart,* the trainee will be able to differentiate (by sorting into two piles) between computer chips that are within specification and those that are outside of specification."

A description of the conditions (assistance or barriers) under which the desired behavior will be performed should be provided. For example, the statement "Using an ohmmeter and chart" indicates the help that is provided. If the objective began with the phrase "Without the use of reference material," it is clear that the trainee must discriminate between the chips without using any aids.

Writing in conditions is necessary in some cases and not in others. In the following example, it is critical to know that the pie charts must be developed using a specific software package: "present the results of an accounting problem in pie chart form, *using the Harvard Graphics software."* Conditions should be included only if they help clarify what is required.

Standards   Standards are the criteria for success. Three potential standards are represented by accuracy, quality, and speed. For example, a learning objective might define accuracy as being "able to take a reading off an altimeter with an error of no more than 10 feet." A quality standard might be indicated by the statement, "is within engineering specifications 99.9% of the time." Or if speed is a critical concern, "will be completed in 15 minutes or less."

The Formula for Writing the Objective   The outcome specifies the type of behavior, the conditions state the where, when, and/or what tools will be used, and standards describe the criteria that will be used to judge the adequacy of the behavior. Remember that a learning objective should clearly state what must be accomplished after training. To accomplish this, take one step at a time.

- Write out the "desired behavior." Here the verb needs to describe clearly what will be done: a "doing" verb such as *count, place, install, list, solve, replace, sort, recite* is used to indicate some action.
- Now add the conditions under which the behavior must be done. Remember that the use or nonuse of aids such as "a meter" or "reference material" needs to be indicated.
- Finally, it needs to be clear what standards for success will be used. How will the trainee know he has successfully completed the training? What level of accuracy is required? Is quality or speed an important part of success?

Now to test whether you have written a sound training objective, have someone read it and explain exactly what she believes she needs to do, under what conditions, and how she will know if she is successful. If she can do this, you have written a good learning objective.

The other three types of training objectives listed in Table 5.1—reaction, transfer of training, and organizational outcome objectives—require similar components. For example, a transfer of training objective might read as follows:

After completing training, participants, at their regular job station and using an ohmmeter and chart, will be able to separate acceptable (within specifications) from unacceptable (outside specifications) computer chips with an accuracy of 99.99% while sorting a minimum of 10 chips per minute.

Attitudes   Sometimes attitudes as well as knowledge and skills are the focus of training. You might ask, "How do you write a learning objective for an attitude?" When the goal of training is attitude change, the focus of training activities is to provide the trainees with information that contradicts inappropriate attitudes and supports more appropriate attitudes. Thus, training does not focus on changing attitudes specifically, but rather providing new knowledge. This might consist of alternate views and information related to the attitudes. Learning objectives for attitude change, therefore, should focus on acquisition of the relevant information rather than the resulting attitude change.

Consider training that is attempting to improve attitudes toward teamwork in a group of trainees who have all scored below the mid-point on a TNA teamwork awareness survey. In this case the learning objective might read as follows: Trainees will demonstrate an increased awareness of the positive aspects of teamwork (new knowledge) as demonstrated by a 50 percent improvement on the team awareness survey to be administered at the end of training.

Recall that the reason we want to have an impact on an attitude is to influence behavior. In this example, we want trainees to have positive attitudes so that once they are back in the workplace they will participate fully in team meetings and provide input. The transfer of training objective in this case might be "After completing training, the participants will attend all team meetings (assuming participation is voluntary) and, using the skills taught, provide ideas and suggestions in those meetings." Another might be "After completing training, the participants' performance rating in team meetings (as completed by all team members) will average one point higher than before training."

Advantages of Training Objectives

Obviously, developing good training objectives takes time, effort, and careful thought. Why devote resources to this activity when it's the actual training that will determine if trainees acquire the KSAs? Doesn't the trainer know what the trainee needs to learn? Although this may be true, training objectives do benefit the trainer. In addition, training objectives provide value to the trainee, the training designer, and evaluators of the training program. In discussing this, once again we will focus on the learning objectives.

THE TRAINEE

Trainees benefit from training objectives in a number of ways. First, by seeing these objectives at the beginning of training, the trainee understands exactly what will be required at the end of training. Knowing what is expected up front can serve to reduce the stress of the training. It also provides a context for focusing trainee attention, and attention is the first step in the learning process. Thus from a learning theory perspective, it is important to let the trainee know what the performance expectations are and to refer to them throughout the training. Also, as was indicated in the chapter on learning, this information will assist the learner in both focusing attention and cognitively organizing the new information.

Another benefit of training objectives is that they increase the likelihood that the trainees will achieve the objectives. This notion is supported by goal-setting research (Locke et al. 1981), which indicates that when specific and challenging goals are set (such as would be set by the training objectives), there is a higher probability that these goals will be achieved than if there is no goal or an instruction to "do the best you can" (Latham and Yukl 1975).

THE TRAINING DESIGNER

The learning objectives help guide the designer of the training or the purchaser of a training package. With clear objectives, you can check the training methods and content against the objectives to ensure that they are consistent.

Suppose the designer is told that she needs to "design training to provide sales-people with skills in customer service." Does she design a course in interpersonal skills so salespeople learn how to be friendly and upbeat? Does she design a course in product knowledge so the salesperson can provide information about the various products and their features to customers? Does she design a course in technical expertise so salespeople can assist customers in getting the product to work effectively? By having a learning objective available that reads "After completing training, participants will, using active listening skills (standard), be able to respond to an angry customer (conditions), to calm him down (desired outcome)." This learning objective provides a clear, unambiguous goal for the designer. She will design a course in active listening, with the focus on dealing with angry customers. Without that guidance, the training may not have been on track.

THE TRAINER

With clear learning objectives, the trainer can facilitate the learning process more effectively. Clear, specific objectives allow the trainer more readily to determine how well the trainees are progressing and make the appropriate adjustments. In addition, the trainer is able to highlight the relationship of particular segments of the training to the objectives.

TRAINING EVALUATOR

Evaluating training becomes much easier when there are objectives, because these objectives define the behaviors expected at the end of training. If there is no clear indication of what training was supposed to accomplish, there is no way to evaluate whether it was effective. It is analogous to the army sergeant who tells the private, "Dig a hole here." The private starts to dig and the sergeant walks away. After digging a few minutes, the private begins to worry because he knows he's in trouble. He doesn't know how deep the hole should be, how long, or wide, or anything else. When the private sees the platoon leader walk by, he asks him, "How am I doing on this hole, sir?" The platoon leader, of course, says, "How should I know?" When good objectives have been developed, the evaluator simply needs to assess whether the stated outcomes and standards have been met.

Training objectives are only one factor in the design and development of a training program. Two other components need to be factored into the design: learning theory and organizational constraints. Learning theory was discussed at length earlier. Its application to training design is covered following our discussion of organizational constraints.

Organizational Constraints

In a perfect world it would be possible to develop the perfect training program for every training need that has been identified. Reality prevails, however, and, in fact there are many constraints around which training must be designed. Many of these constraints can influence the type of training you are able to offer. Table 5.2 (on page 190) provides a list of some of these constraints and various ways of approaching the design of training. This obviously is not an exhaustive list and serves primarily as an example of the ways in which organizational constraints affect the methods and approaches used to meet the training needs.

TABLE 5.2 Constraints and Possible Ways of Dealing with Them	
Constraint	*Suggestion for How to Handle*
Need high level of simulation because:	
Law (fire drills)	
Task is critical to the job (police firing gun)	Incorporate a longer lead time to prepare simulations/role plays.
Mistakes are costly (airline pilot)	Purchase simulators.
Trainees vary in amount of experience	Consider modularization.
Trainees have large differences in ability levels	Use programmed instruction. Have high level of trainer–trainee interaction.
Mix of employees and new hires trained on a new procedure	Consider different training programs, because there may be negative transfer for employees but not for new hires.
Long lag between end of training and use of skill on the job	Distribute practice through the lag. Provide refresher material and/or models for the employees to follow.
Short lead time	Use external consultant or packaged training.
Bias against a type of training (role play, etc.)	Develop proof of effectiveness into the training package.
	Use another method.
Few trainees available at any one time	Use programmed instruction.
Small organization with limited funds	Hire consultant/purchase training. Join consortium.

We will discuss two major categories of constraints: organizational/environmental and trainee population. Each has an impact on whether to train and the type of training you will be able to offer.

ORGANIZATIONAL/ENVIRONMENTAL CONSTRAINTS

Because budgets are generally limited, you might have to make choices about who gets trained and what type of training they receive. One way of doing this is to follow the strategic direction the organization has taken. The strategic planning process, when completed, provides a rationale for determining who gets how much of what kind of training. Recall the MHC case presented in chapter 2 and discussed again in chapter 4. Its HR philosophy was that people were the most important resource and that HR needs are best met through employee development. This provides a guideline for training choices. The case suggests that management training in using the new performance appraisal process should be done before money is spent on developing a succession plan. A common performance appraisal process is necessary before effective succession planning can be introduced. Once a succession plan is developed, the choice might be whether to spend money on training managers to use the succession plan or on developing their interviewing skill for the selection process. Once again, although both are necessary, the strategic plan would indicate that if only one can be done at this time, it should probably be developing the interviewing skills.

Even if the organization does not have a clear strategic plan in place, it is a good idea for the top managers in HR to develop their own mission and goals for the HR area. This would be accomplished by meeting with top management to discuss their priorities. Such meetings would help define HR priorities and determine how to put resources in line with the wishes of top management. A side benefit is that the process may stimulate top management to engage in strategic planning.

Decisions about training priorities must also follow the law. Certain training requirements are mandated by The Occupational Safety and Health Act in the United States and provincial health and safety regulations in Canada. For example, employers must tell employees what hazardous waste they are exposed to, educate them about the risks, and provide them with the KSAs to handle the waste in a safe manner. Training in this and other safety areas should have high priority. There are other laws (e.g., unfair discrimination, sexual harassment) where training is advisable but not mandatory. These will need to be weighted against other priorities.

The technological sophistication of the organization will have an impact on the type of training you are able to offer. If, as in the MHC case, you are dealing with a number of locations and have little or no access to computer networks, videoconferencing, or video recorders, you will be severely constrained in the type of training you can offer.

TRAINEE POPULATION

If the needs analysis identifies two or more subgroups that have the same training objectives but different levels of KSAs, it is difficult to design a single training program that would meet all their needs. However, training could be designed in a modular manner in order to provide only the relevant modules to each subgroup. Training will then focus on the needs and interests of each subgroup.

Sometimes the needs analysis identifies a wide variability in the KSAs of the target population. In this case, the training design could provide individualized instruction, accomplished through computer-based or video instruction, although both take a long time to develop. Another alternative would be to allow for small classes and a high level of interaction between each trainee and the instructor.

In some instances trainees have very negative feelings about a particular training technique. If this attitude is known during the design stage, a different technique can be considered. Alternatively, the design could build in attitude-change modules at the beginning. We have found, for example, that many managers do not want to role-play in training. We often hear arguments such as "This is silly" or "These never work." One way to handle this resistance is simply to call it something different. The term *play,* for some, suggests it is not serious learning. Sometimes when we present the technique, we suggest it is time for some "behavioral practice." This simple change in terms causes the exercise to be received more positively. The point here is that if, through the needs analysis, you discover a particular method of training is disliked because of past experience or word of mouth, you need to include in the training design a method of changing the perception or use another method when possible.

Facilitation of Learning: Focus on the Trainee

Recall from Figure 3.1 the factors influencing performance ($P = M \times KSA \times E$). Many issues exist within each of these factors that will make it easier or more difficult for the trainee to achieve the learning objectives.

KSAs (INDIVIDUAL DIFFERENCES)

The needs assessment supplies not only information on the *need* for training, but also on the trainees' *readiness* for such training. Let's take the example of employees who have been recently hired or promoted. They have been selected because of their KSAs, but they will need some initial training to learn the specifics of this particular job at this company. Perfect selection techniques will ensure that those hired have the requisite KSAs to be successful in training. However, few selection techniques are perfect. Even the best selection practices result in a certain number of individuals who are selected but subsequently are not successful. If these "false positives" can somehow be identified as part of the TNA, the design of training might be able to address the issues that would prevent them from being successful.

For example, some who are identified as in need of training may not have the requisite KSAs to make use of the training methods and materials that would be effective for 90% of the other potential trainees. Providing a remedial training module for this group, prior to the regular training, may increase their likelihood of successfully completing training.

As we have just indicated, the selection process sets some sort of minimum criteria (based on a job analysis) which individuals must meet in order to be selected. There are still individual differences in abilities. Some individuals have higher levels of the KSA. Some may not have the minimum skills (e.g., false positive). Needs assessment data that show large differences among the potential trainees indicate that the training design must be adjusted to address the differences.

Just how important is the individual difference issue? Consider the following (Cascio 1995; Cascio and Thacker 1994):

- More than half the U.S. workforce now consists of racial (nonwhite) and ethnic minorities, immigrants, and women.
- In Canada visible minorities will represent 70% of the new immigrants by the year 2000.
- In the United States more than 20 million Americans were born in another country.
- In Canada the unemployment rate for aboriginals is 30%, and both federal and provincial legislation encourages their being hired into the workforce.
- In the United States white males will make up only 15% of the increase in the workforce over the next decade.
- New technology and government legislation in North America is making it easier for the disabled to enter the workforce.

These facts suggest a very different workforce emerging in North America. With this increase in diversity will come an increase in individual differences in more than just KSAs. Different cultures and ethnicities will mean very different ways of viewing the workplace and its norms and values. Care in the needs assessment to understand the special requirements of some individuals will help tremendously in designing a successful training program.

Cronbach and Snow (1977) have noted that individual differences may result in differences in how individuals learn. This issue is reflected in Figures 5.1 below and 5.2 (page 194). Note in Figure 5.1, the training design A produces better results for those at all levels of the particular trait. This suggests that training design A is the method of choice. In Figure 5.2, however, this is not the case. Design A provides positive results for those high in the trait, but not for those low in the trait. In contrast, training design B provides positive results for those low in the trait, but not those high in the trait. Here, those low in the trait should receive training design B, whereas those high in the trait should receive training design A.

The individual difference issue is very complex, and interactions are not very generalizable to different situations (Goldstein 1980). It usually makes more sense to think of additional rather than different training for employees who differ in KSAs.

When clear differences do exist in learning style preferences, two options are available. All trainees can receive the same training, but it needs to be designed so that all trainees' learning style preferences are used. In this situation, different methods of instruction would be incorporated into each learning topic. This method has the advantage of covering the same learning point in different ways, facilitating the learning process for everyone. A disadvantage is that it increases the time to complete training.

An alternative is to create separate training programs designed around the learning style preferences of each group. Here the training is tailored to the preference of the training group, but multiple training programs need to be designed, developed, and implemented.

MOTIVATION OF TRAINEE

As the performance formula ($P = M \times KSA \times E$) indicates, if motivation is lacking, no learning is likely to occur. Thus training should be designed not only to provide KSAs, but also to motivate trainees to learn those KSAs and apply them to their jobs.

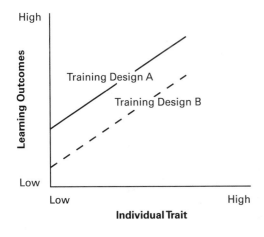

FIGURE 5.1 No Trait and Treatment Interaction

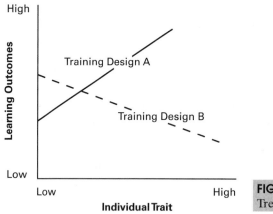

FIGURE 5.2 A Trait and Treatment Interaction

Expectations Toward Training

Those who come to a training program with positive expectations seem to be more successful. Trainees who tend to agree with such statements as

- "Even if I fail, this training will be a valuable experience"
- "I will get more from this training than most people"
- "I have a better chance of passing this training than most others"
- "If I have trouble during training, I will try harder"

are more likely to meet the training objectives than those who do not (Ryman and Biersner 1975). The reason is that those with positive expectations are more motivated.

Taking this idea one step further, it could be argued that if such expectations could be determined during the needs assessment, an intervention could take place for those with unfavorable expectations. It is important to socialize the trainee to training, just as it is important to socialize the new employee to the organization (Sanders and Yanouzas 1983). By (1) showing the trainee that he or she has the ability to complete training, (2) clarifying the outcomes associated with completed training, and (3) showing that positive outcomes are more likely to occur if training is completed, we can change unfavorable expectations to be more positive.

Consider the supervisor who has poor relations with her subordinates. Sending her to training to provide her with better interpersonal skills for dealing with subordinates will be fruitless unless she sees the value in such training. If in the needs assessment it is determined that she has low expectations and sees no value in the training, she could be asked to attend a pretraining workshop, designed to show the advantages of a positive relationship between supervisors and subordinates. The workshop would also preview the training, showing that participants could learn the skills if they put forth the effort. When the actual training begins, this supervisor would more likely be motivated to learn the skills.

Expectancy Theory Implications

Let's review the relationship between trainee motivation and performance in relation to expectancy theory. If the trainee believes successful completion of training will lead to outcomes he values (Expectancy 2), and if he believes that if he tries hard he has a reasonable likelihood of succeeding in training (Expectancy 1), then he will be motivated. Note that "positive expectations" discussed above relate to both Expectancy 1 (I have a better chance of passing this training) and Expectancy 2 (I will get more from this training than most people).

No one consciously goes systematically through all the steps suggested in expectancy theory to make a decision, but unconsciously such a process does occur. If you understand the process, you will be able to consider the various areas where you might influence someone's motivation by changing his expectancies or by identifying positive outcomes. Some examples will illustrate the point.

Bill is going to an interpersonal skills training workshop on active listening and other skills designed to teach supervisors how to interact better with subordinates, peers, and superiors. Will he be motivated to learn these skills? Let's look inside Bill's head, as represented in Training in Action 5.1 on page 196. Will Bill be motivated to learn? According to expectancy theory, he will not. By multiplying Expectancy 1 with Expectancy 2 and the valence of each of the outcomes, we note that the total for being motivated to learn is 10.9:

$$.5[(.2 \times 7) + (.6 \times 8) + (.7 \times 6) \text{ etc.}].$$

Motivation not to learn is much higher at 27.0

$$1.0 [(1.0 \times 10) + (1.0 \times 8) + (1.0 \times 9)].$$

What can be done to influence Bill to learn? There are a number of things. First, recall from chapter 3 that expectancies are beliefs about the way things are. They can be influenced in a number of ways (e.g., past experience, communication from others). If Bill heard from other supervisors that the training was not difficult, he might change his belief about how difficult it would be to pass the training (Expectancy 1). If supervisors who were successful in training were promoted more often than others, this situation might influence Bill's belief that if he completed training he would get promoted (Expectancy 2). If those who go to training generally receive higher pay raises and Bill is not aware of this fact, you can either make him aware of such an outcome (higher pay raise), or demonstrate the relationship between training and the raise (Expectancy 2).

There are other ways that Bill's motivation to try to learn can be influenced. Camp, Blanchard, and Huszczo (1986) provide some steps to enhance Expectancies 1 and 2 and to clarify the types of outcomes that will result from successful training. They suggest that prior to training, Bill and his supervisor should have done several things.

- Discussed his job performance and job-related goals and agreed that he needs to improve some set of KSAs in order to achieve those goals. Providing focus on goals presents specific outcomes the trainee may not have considered.
- Agreed that this particular training program is the best alternative available for achieving the desired improvement (Expectancy 1).
- Agreed that demonstrated improvement in the identified KSA area will result in desirable outcomes for him (Expectancy 2).

These steps should result in Bill's realizing the advantages of successful training and make his attitude more positive. In the design of any training, therefore, it is im-

---

Training in Action 5.1

What are the outcomes and the attractiveness (valence) of these outcomes for Bill (on a scale of 1 to 10) if he is successful in training versus if he is unsuccessful?

Outcomes If Successful	Valence	Outcomes If Unsuccessful	Valence
Promotion	7	Does not have to change behavior	10
Better at job	8	Employees still afraid of him	8
Less tension between Bill and subordinates	6	Not ridiculed by co-workers for being a nice guy	9
Less feeling of stress	4		
Better relationship with union	7		
Fewer grievances	9		

How likely is it that if Bill is successful or unsuccessful, these outcomes will actually occur (Expectancy 2)? These expectancies are based on Bill's belief that they will occur and range from 0 (not at all likely to occur) to 1.0 (guaranteed to occur).

Outcomes If Successful	(Exp. 2)	Valence	Outcomes If Unsuccessful	(Exp. 2)	Valence
Promotion	.2	7	Does not have to change behavior	1.0	10
Better at job	.6	8			
Less tension between Bill and others	.7	6	Employees still afraid of him	1.0	8
Less feeling of stress	.8	4	Not ridiculed by co-workers for being a nice guy	1.0	9
Better relationship with union	.4	7			
Fewer grievances	.6	9			

How likely does Bill think it is that he could learn the new skills if he really tried (Expectancy 1)? This is also expressed in a probability (0 to 1.0).

In this case, Bill believes the skills are rather hard to learn, and he also believes that "leopards cannot change their spots." Therefore, Bill believes that if he really tries, there is only a .5 chance he will be successful. On the other hand, if he does not try, there is a high probability (1.0) he will not learn or change his behavior.

---

portant to include pretraining interventions such as these. An integral part of the design might be working with the supervisors to ensure that the above discussions take place.

In large organizations with well-organized human resource functions, the trainee–supervisor discussions might take place in the formal performance review. A portion of any thorough review is the developmental aspect. As was noted in chapter 4, this is a useful tool the supervisor can use with subordinates for determining training needs and increasing the motivation to learn.

CLASSICAL CONDITIONING AND REINFORCEMENT (THE ENVIRONMENT)

Classical Conditioning

Recall from chapter 3 that classical conditioning can take place without awareness. We salivate when we smell something cooking that we like, because of prior learning. Similarly, if a trainee has had bad experiences in school and the training room is set up like a school classroom, he may develop a negative response on entering the room. Trainees who have high stress in their jobs become conditioned to feel stressed when they arrive at work. Seeing the building begins to create the stress because the two events have been so often paired. Having someone in such a state does not make for a conducive learning environment. One value of off-site locations for training is that they create a fresh environment. Consider, however, the salesperson who spends many lonely nights in hotels while on the road selling. Having the sales staff attend training sessions that require more lonely nights in a hotel room may not be appropriate.

To have trainees attentive and motivated, it is necessary to provide an environment conducive to a focused but relaxing and enjoyable experience.

Operant Conditioning

We explained in chapter 3 that if a particular behavior is immediately followed by a reward, that behavior is likely to be repeated. In the same way, punishment that immediately follows a particular behavior will decrease the likelihood of that behavior continuing. Training should be designed to offer trainees the opportunity to practice what they learn and receive some sort of reinforcement for the effort.

We have mentioned how reluctant some trainees are to role-play. It is useful, however, to have participants practice behaviors and gain experience. If role plays are incorporated into the training design, it is important also to design a procedure for ensuring that positive reinforcement rather than punishment follows. For example, you might have someone volunteer to do a simple role play, and when she is finished you and the trainees applaud her for her efforts. Of course, this is successful only if the applause is seen as reinforcing.

GOAL SETTING

Goal-setting research (Latham and Locke 1979; Locke et al. 1981) has consistently demonstrated that specific, challenging goals result in higher performance levels than do no goals or the goal of "do the best you can." Specific goals direct the individual's energy and attention toward meeting the goal and also provide the focus for directing this energy.

More specifically, Locke et al. (1981) indicated a number of specific conditions related to goal setting that affect performance.

- Individuals who are given specific, hard, or challenging goals perform better than those given specific easy goals, "do the best you can" goals, or no goals.

- Goals appear to have more predictable effects when they are given in specific terms rather than as vague intentions.
- The goals must be matched to the ability of the individual so that the person is likely to achieve it. Being able to achieve the goal is important for the individual's self-efficacy, for that is how the individual will judge his ability to perform well on the tasks. This means that the analyst will need to design intermediate goals that reflect progress.
- Feedback concerning the degree to which the goal is being achieved is necessary for goal setting to have the desired effect.
- For goal setting to be effective, the individual has to accept the goal that is set.

What is the application of this research to training? Well, what better way to capture the interest and attention of trainees than to provide them with individual goals? Learning objectives, which were discussed earlier, are a form of goal setting and could provide challenging, specific goals. It is also important to provide "how you are doing" feedback to trainees throughout the training.

So far we have examined issues related to getting and keeping trainees interested in the training. What remains is how to facilitate the learning process. In this regard, there are a number of important factors to address when you are designing a training program. These will be presented under two headings: facilitation of learning, and facilitation of transfer. Obviously, facilitation of transfer also helps facilitation of learning.

Facilitation of Learning: Focus on Training Design

Trainers can make use of the social learning model by designing specific training events to correspond to the specific learning processes as illustrated in Table 5.3.

TABLE 5.3 Learning Processes and Corresponding Training Events	
Attention/Expectancy	Learning environment, pretraining communications, statement of objectives and process, highlighting of key learning points
Retention	
Activation of memory	Stimulation of prior related learning
Symbolic coding and cognitive organization	Presentation of various encoding schemes and images, associations with previously learned material, order of presentation during training
Symbolic rehearsal and cues for retrieval	Case studies, hypothetical scenarios, aids for transfer of learning (identical elements and principles)
Behavioral Reproduction	Active and guided practice (role plays and simulations)
Reinforcement	Assessment and feedback (positive and/or negative)

ATTENTION/EXPECTANCY

As social learning theory (see Figure 3.6 on page 111) indicates, the trainee's motivation influences where attention is directed. Trainees will attend to things in the environment that are most important to them. Thus the environment and process should be structured so that the most important things are the learning events and materials. Attention detractors need to be removed and creature comforts attended to.

Eliminating Distractions

The room should be at a comfortable temperature, not too hot or too cold. People are generally comfortable at a temperature between 71 and 73 degrees Fahrenheit, with humidity level around 50%. The walls should be a neutral but pleasant color, free from distracting objects (e.g., posters, notices, and pictures unrelated to training). The room should be soundproof and have no view to the outside. If the room has windows, close the shades or curtains. Ideally, the learning facility will be away from the workplace so that trainees can concentrate on learning rather than be sidetracked by what might be going on at work. If the training must be conducted at the work site, establish a rule that no interruptions are allowed (from bosses, subordinates, or others who "just need a few minutes with . . ."). This also means no phones, beepers, or other communication devices while training is being conducted. Because communicating with the work area can be important, the training facility should have a system for having messages taken for trainees and delivered to them during breaks and after training has been completed.

The seating should be such that trainees will not become uncomfortable over a two-hour period, but not become so comfortable that they must fight off sleep. A comfortable, flexible, cloth-covered chair with armrests should be chosen. Trainees will also need a surface to place their training materials on and for writing.

Schedule training activities with the following rule in mind: "The brain can absorb only as much as the seat can endure." Thus breaks should be scheduled so that trainees do not have to sit for too long at one time.

Provide refreshments if trainees are likely to be hungry at the start of or during training. There is nothing like a growling stomach to take the trainee's mind off the learning. If lunch is provided, it should be light and not contain large amounts of carbohydrates, which tend to make people drowsy. Also avoid turkey, because it is very sleep-inducing. Remember how you feel after a turkey dinner? Obviously, alcohol should be avoided.

Attracting Attention

The first steps in motivating the employees and setting their expectations are to notify them that they will be participating in the training, inform them of the nature of the training, and explain its job-related benefits. This communication should, at a minimum, indicate the training objectives and agenda.

State the objectives again at the outset of training, and review them at strategic points throughout. Doing this helps to keep the focus of training on the desired outcomes and attention on the important training activities. However, it is not enough for the trainer simply to state the objectives from time to time. The trainees must accept those objectives. To this end, you might have them describe how accomplishing the objectives will lead to resolving job-related problems. This exercise not only focuses trainees' attention on the training objectives, but builds commitment that will facilitate the transfer of new KSAs back to the job.

In addition to accepting the training objectives, trainees must also feel that the objectives are achievable. This principle comes directly from both expectancy theory and goal setting. Here's how achievable goals can be designed into the training. At the start of training, the overall objective may seem very difficult if not impossible to achieve. You should point out that the overall objective is just the final step in a series of obtainable subobjectives. Research on goal setting (Latham and Locke 1979; Locke et al. 1981) suggests that following these procedures will result in higher levels of trainee learning. Suppose the overall objective of a one-day seminar was "To calm an irate customer without giving in to his request using the conflict resolution model." The thought of calming an irate customer using a method (conflict resolution model) that the trainees know nothing about could create a high level of anxiety. An intermediate objective that stated "Respond to a single angry comment using active listening" does not seem as imposing and would provide a view of one of the steps toward reaching the overall objective.

Finally, the trainee's attention should be focused on the critical aspects of each step in the learning process. Techniques for highlighting the important points should be built into the learning activities so that the appropriate material is processed into permanently stored information (Klatzky 1975; Lindsay and Norman 1972). The method of highlighting will vary according to the instructional method (e.g., case study, lecture). In the example of conflict resolution training discussed above, suppose the training included a videotape of the correct steps. As the video progressed through the various stages of the conflict resolution model, these steps would flash on the bottom of the screen. This model begins with active listening, so as the video was showing the person using active listening, "Active Listening" would be flashed on the bottom of the screen. This device would give the trainee an idea of how to perform each step and how the steps integrate into the total model.

RETENTION

To be able to retain something you've been taught, you go through four stages: activation of memory, symbolic coding and cognitive organization, and symbolic rehearsal and cues for retrieval.

Activation of Memory

Remember from social learning theory that information that has been attended to is transformed into symbolically coded (typically as language) long-term memory. From there it is called up when the appropriate cues are present (Anderson and Bower 1972; Bandura 1977; Melton and Martin 1972). Before the **symbolic encoding** process can begin, relevant prior learning must be stimulated, so connections between the new information and the old can be established. This process can be facilitated by the trainer through stimulating the recall of the relevant prerequisite learning and/or prior supportive learning.

An illustration of this process is the management development example in chapter 3,[1] in which we wanted managers to examine the structure of the subordinate's

---

[1] The management development example referred to begins under Type 4 (verbal association learning) of Gagné's learning types.

work and need for independence. Here we will focus on the subordinate's characteristics. Recall there are different ways of treating employees, depending on their work environment. Assume the trainer wants the management trainees to learn the "relevant employee characteristics" for matching managerial behavior to the needs of the subordinate. The trainer can stimulate the recall of the prerequisite learning by asking the trainees to "try to remember the names of the relevant employee characteristics and what things differentiate them from irrelevant characteristics." Recalling supportive, prior learning can be stimulated by asking the trainees to draw on related experience. In this case the trainer might say, "Think back to employees you've dealt with in the past. How would you determine which of their characteristics would be relevant to the management style you adopt with them?" This activity would recall information supporting the new learning, providing a context for the new learning to occur.

Symbolic Coding and Cognitive Organization

Once the appropriate prior learning has been recalled, the trainee is ready to encode the new information. The trainer can facilitate the encoding process through the technique of **guided discovery.** Typically the trainer makes statements and then asks a question. Let's assume the trainees had just watched a video of a supervisor and a subordinate discussing the subordinate's work outcomes. Following the video the trainer might say, "Remember, certain employee characteristics are more closely related to how the employee approaches the work situation. In the video, how did the employee approach the work situation and what characteristics are most likely to influence this approach?" The statement is intended to stimulate relevant prior learning, and the question is designed to allow the trainee to discover the appropriate rule from the cues provided. The question shouldn't contain all the information needed for the answer but should suggest a strategy for discovering the answer. Engaging in guided discovery helps the trainee develop a coding scheme that relates the new learning to prior learning.

Encoding can also be enhanced through the use of images. In addition to being coded as verbal propositions, information can be coded as a verbal image. When symbolic coding incorporates both verbal propositions and images, retention of the information is improved (Anderson and Bower 1973), probably because image retention and language retention occur through different cognitive channels. Thus, the addition of visual material in support of the oral and written language increases the trainees' ability to remember the information.

Cognitive organization is intimately tied to symbolic coding. The way information is organized during training, and the prior learning that supports learning the new information, shape the way the new information is organized into the cognitive structure. Likewise, the visual images that are used in training provide suggestions for how information fits together. When you are developing the materials and the flow of a training program, you should make sure the new learning builds on relevant older learning. The flow of training should help the learner organize the new material by providing various organizational strategies.

Symbolic Rehearsal and Behavioral Reproduction

Symbolic rehearsal and behavioral reproduction are types of practice. **Symbolic rehearsal** is practicing symbolically, as when the trainer asks the trainees to imagine a hypothetical situation and discuss how they would behave. At this point, the trainees

TABLE 5.4 Comparison of Traditional and Strategic Knowledge Training

Traditional Training	*Strategic Knowledge Training*
Step 1 **Declarative knowledge (what) is presented** Workers are told that the materials are designed to teach them to read and interpret quality control charts used throughout their organization.	**Step 1** **Declarative knowledge is presented the same way as in traditional training.**
	Step 2 **The context of the procedures (why and when) is added by instructing workers about the importance of the skill and the appropriate time for its use.** It is explained that if the assembly line workers could read and interpret quality control data, mistakes would be caught earlier and the product saved because traditionally quality control measures are taken after a specific number of items have been produced.
Step 2 **Procedural knowledge (how) is presented.** Workers are assisted in recalling specific math skills. Then stimulus materials and information required to master the task are presented. Examples of charts with various readings are provided, and the workers are shown how to record charts during production and interpret the data.	**Step 3** **Procedural knowledge (how) would be presented the same way as in traditional training.**
Step 3 **Workers practice using the charts and interpreting the results.**	**Step 4** **Workers practice using the charts and also practice determining when and why to use them.** Workers are provided opportunities for rehearsal and reinforcement of both conditional and procedural knowledge.
Step 4 **Workers are given feedback.**	**Step 5** **Workers would be given feedback (same as in traditional training).**

Source: Adapted from Schmitt and Newby 1986.

aren't actually doing what they have learned to do—they're thinking, talking, or writing about it. Case studies provide one form of symbolic rehearsal. Trainees read about a situation and describe how they would handle the situation.

Behavioral reproduction is the transformation of the learning into actual behavior. Pilot training provides a clear example of the difference between these two types of practice. Pilots go through an extensive training process in learning how to fly a new aircraft. They read manuals, attend lectures, watch videos, and engage in computer-assisted, self-paced learning modules. Once a sufficient amount of learning has occurred, the pilot trainees demonstrate their knowledge of procedures through discussions with the trainer and one another about what they would do in specific situations. They are given written or visual scenarios and asked how they would respond. All of this is symbolic rehearsal. When they have demonstrated sufficient cognitive command of the aircraft's systems, procedures, and capabilities, they are put into flight simulators, which allow them to practice flying the aircraft. After they have demonstrated competence flying the aircraft in simulation, they fly the actual aircraft under the supervision of an experienced pilot. The simulation and supervised flights are behavioral reproduction activities.

Strategic Knowledge

In the past, training has been designed to provide trainees only with the KSAs needed for their particular job. Many organizations have found that more broadly based training leads to greater organizational effectiveness. For example, a study by Arthur Anderson, a large management consulting firm, found that in Canada's best-managed companies the use of management teams was a common approach (Cascio and Thacker 1994). To be effective in the team approach, employees must have a broad understanding of how their jobs interact with other jobs. In these companies job specific training is supported with information about the job's relationship to other parts of the organization. This type of training incorporates aspects of **strategic knowledge development** because it allows trainees to understand when and why to use their new KSAs.

Strategic knowledge development increases the breadth of what is learned (Schmitt and Newby 1986) by extending the training content to include learning when and why KSAs are appropriate and developing strategies for their use. The strategies that are developed revolve around the planning, monitoring, and modifying of behavior. The trainee would not only learn how to perform the task but also how to behave strategically and adaptively. Table 5.4 compares a traditional skills training format with a format that includes training in strategic knowledge. You can see that the main difference is that the strategic knowledge training provides information as to when the skill is used and why it is important. Trainees are also provided with practice sessions in determining when to use the skill.

Facilitation of Transfer: Focus on Training Design

Transfer of training refers to how much of what is learned in training transfers to the job. Cascio (1995) suggests that there are three possibilities regarding transfer of training: (1) a higher level of job performance **(positive transfer),** (2) no change in job performance **(zero transfer),** or (3) a lower level of job performance **(negative transfer).** The goal is to have training result in positive transfer to the job.

Research into factors that influence transfer of training has focused on three areas: conditions of practice, identical elements, and stimulus variability. The research also provides evidence that the nature of feedback, the strategies used for retention, and goal setting can influence how well the training is transferred back to the job.

CONDITIONS OF PRACTICE

There are a number of ways to design opportunities for trainees to practice. Each will facilitate the transfer of training more or less effectively depending on the nature of the KSAs to be learned.

Massed versus Spaced Practice

Which is more effective—having trainees practice continuously for four hours, for one hour on four different days, or for a half hour on eight different days? Research has demonstrated that material learned under the latter approach, **spaced practice,** is generally retained longer than material learned under the first approach, **massed practice** (Naylor and Briggs 1963). Because retention is necessary for transfer to occur, spaced practice would seem to be most appropriate. However, it requires a longer training cycle and management generally resists it. Training departments need to become more creative in developing their training to allow for spaced practice. Instead of the traditional one-day workshop, eight one-hour sessions at the beginning of the workday might be possible. Instead of a five-day workshop, consider once a week for five weeks. This also gives trainees time to think about and even practice the knowledge or skill on their own.

Massed and spaced practice can be used together, and this combination is especially effective for training in difficult and complex tasks. Tasks that are difficult and complex seem to be performed better when massed practice is provided first, followed by briefer sessions with more frequent rest intervals (Baldwin and Ford 1988).

Whole versus Part Learning

Which is better, **part learning** or **whole learning?** Whether trainees should learn parts of the task separately or learn the whole task all at once depends, of course, on whether the task can be logically divided into parts. Adams (1987) has indicated that it is difficult to design part task training devices in many situations. Whole training devices are much easier because the design can be modeled after the real device (e.g., pilot training simulators). Even when the task can be divided into parts, the whole method is still preferred when (1) the intelligence of the trainee is high, (2) the training material is high in task organization but low in complexity, and (3) practice is spaced rather than massed (Naylor and Briggs 1963). **Task organization** relates to the degree to which the tasks are interrelated (highly dependent on each other). For example, in driving a car, the steering, braking, and acceleration are highly interdependent when you are turning a corner (high organization). Starting a standard-shift car, however, requires a number of tasks that are not as highly organized (pushing in the clutch, putting gear shift in neutral, placing foot on accelerator, turning key to start). **Task complexity** relates to the level of difficulty of performing each task (Blum and Naylor 1968).

In the design of training, many times it simply is not practical to attempt to subdivide the task into meaningful parts. If it *is* possible to subdivide them, you would still need to use the whole method if the task organization were high; if task organization were low, however, you would use the part method.

As an example of high task organization, imagine training a backhoe operator to dig a hole by first having her practice raising the boom, then practice moving the outer arm, and finally moving the bucket. This simply does not make sense. Ultimately the trainee has to learn how to open each of the valves concurrently and sequentially in the digging of a hole. An example of low task organization is the maintenance of the backhoe. Here there are a number of tasks (check the teeth on the bucket, check the hydraulic oil, inspect boom for cracks) that are not highly organized, so each could be taught separately.

A third option, **progressive part training,** can be used when tasks are not as clear in their organization. Consider the training of conflict resolution skills. Imagine there are four steps to the model that will be taught (actively listen, indicate respect, be assertive, and provide information). These tasks are interdependent, but might also be taught separately. In this case a combination of the two types may make sense. First the trainees learn and practice active listening; then active listening and indicating respect; then active listening, indicating respect, and being assertive; and finally the whole model. In this way, the trainee learns each step but at the same time learns the integration of the adjoining step.

Whole, part, and a combination of the two (progressive part) learning are represented in the diagram.

			Phases		
Training Type	*Phase 1*	*Phase 2*	*Phase 3*	*Phase 4*	*Phase 5*
Whole	A+B+C+D	A+B+C+D	A+B+C+D	A+B+C+D	A+B+C+D
Part	A	B	C	D	A+B+C+D
Progressive Part	A	A+B	A+B+C	A+B+C+D	A+B+C+D

Overlearning

McGhee and Thayer (1961) define **overlearning** as the process of providing trainees with continued practice far beyond the point at which they have performed the task successfully. We have discussed this with relation to the concept of automaticity. The more a task is overlearned, the greater the retention (Atwater 1953; Hagman and Rose 1983; Mandler 1954).

Overlearning is particularly valuable for tasks that are not used frequently or if the opportunity to practice them is limited. Schendel and Hagman (1982) studied three groups of soldiers assembling and disassembling their weapons. One group (the overlearning group) received extra trials equal to the number of trials it took them to learn the task; another was a refresher group, who received the same extra number of trials as the overlearning group, but at a later date; the final group was the control group, who received no extra trials. The overlearning and refresher groups outperformed the control group, but the overlearning group also retained more than the refresher group.

When trainees practice a skill beyond the ability simply to do the task, the responses become automatic and do not require thinking. This is why overlearning is most valuable for tasks that will be performed in high-stress situations such as emergencies, or, in baseball, when the bases are loaded and the count is 3 and 2. One of the authors, when in pilot training in the air force, recalls that numerous times during initial training the instructor would pull back the throttle of the aircraft and yell, "Emergency!" He did this frequently, and soon the author discovered that thinking was not even required—the emergency procedures became automatic, important in a situation where correct responses are critical.

In chapter 1 we defined the concept of automaticity; a closely related concept to overlearning. This could be thought of as an outcome of overlearning; although it could also occur after a great deal of on-the-job practice. It implies a shift to a point where performance of a task is fluid, requires little conscious effort, and, as the name implies, is "automatic" (Kraiger, Ford, and Salas 1993; Shiffrin and Schneider 1977). Automaticity, through overlearning, should be designed into training when the task will be performed in high-stress situations or those that are encountered infrequently.

MAXIMIZE SIMILARITY

Maximizing similarity is also known as **identical elements.** The more the elements in the training design are identical to the actual work setting, the more likely it is that transfer will occur (Thorndike and Woodsworth 1901). Two areas of similarity are possible: the tasks to be performed, and the environment in which they are to be performed. For example, a newscaster reading the news on television must use a teleprompter (the task) while someone is talking to him via an earphone (environment).

After the basic skill has been learned, to ensure transfer, you need to allow some opportunities for trainees to practice the skill in an environment similar to their actual workplace environment. A machinist should be exposed to the background noise of the factory floor and the interruptions he will receive back on the job. The secretary should be exposed to the office noise he will be faced with as well as the interruptions that occur in the office.

VARY THE SITUATION

It is much easier to use the concept of identical elements for motor or technical skills, where most of the elements required for learning are in the job situation (Camp, Blanchard, and Huszczo 1986). When conceptual or administrative skills are required, as in management training, there is often a great deal of variability in situations, and the use of identical elements simply is not effective. In such cases, the general principle approach is more useful (Camp, Blanchard, and Huszczo 1986).

General Principles

For much of management training, it is impossible to provide specific training for what to do in every situation that might arise. It is necessary, therefore, to provide a framework or context for what is being taught. This is what strategic knowledge training attempts to do. Training through general principles will better equip trainees to handle novel situations.

Imagine you were teaching managers how to motivate employees and you simply told them that praise was a good motivator. The managers would go back on the job and begin praising their workers. If some of the employees did not become motivated (and in some cases became less motivated), managers would be at a loss. If, however, the managers were taught some general principles about motivation, they would understand the responses they were getting and alter their own behavior. The principles related to expectancy theory suggest that certain things are attractive to some and not to others. Furthermore, it indicates that praise must be a function of performance to be motivating. The manager could think through these principles and identify what change was required in order to motivate those not responding to the praise. For some of these employees the attractive outcome may be for the manager to say nothing and stay away when they perform at an appropriate level.

OTHER CONSIDERATIONS TO FACILITATE TRANSFER

Knowledge of Results

Providing feedback **(knowledge of results)** to a trainee is important to learning and transfer of training. As Locke and Latham (1990) indicate, feedback performs three functions: (1) it tells trainees whether their responses are correct, allowing for necessary adjustments in their behavior; (2) it makes the learning more interesting, encouraging trainees to continue; and (3) it leads to specific goals for maintaining or improving performance. When you provide such feedback, it is better to indicate that the level of performance can be controlled by the trainee. Sometimes inexperienced trainers will try to be supportive by suggesting that the task is difficult so any problems in mastering it are understandable (Martocchio and Dulebohn 1994). This tends to reinforce low self-efficacy. Feedback that indicates that a trainee *can* master the task improves a person's self-efficacy, and trainees with high self-efficacy tend to be more motivated and achieve more (Bandura 1991).

Frequent opportunities to provide feedback should be part of the training design. This may take the trainer a rather long time if the group is large, because the trainer needs to get to all trainees and monitor improvements. To help overcome this problem, other trainees can be used to provide feedback. The authors, for example, use three-person groups in much of their interpersonal skills training. One of the three acts as an observer of the behavior and provides feedback to the person who is practicing.

Provide Relapse Prevention Strategy

A major reason that training does not transfer to the job is that, once back on the job, the trainee is faced with many of the same pressures that caused her to behave in her more traditional way. As a result, she may relapse into the old ways. Marx (1982) instituted a system of **relapse prevention** modeled after a successful approach to assisting addicts to resist returning to their addictive behavior (Brownell et al. 1986). The strategy of relapse prevention and a rationale for each step is depicted in Table 5.5 on page 208. The strategy sensitizes trainees to the fact that relapse is likely, prepares them for it by having them identify high-risk situations that will result in relapse, and finally has them develop coping strategies to prevent such a relapse. The advantage to this approach is that it uses both cognitive and behavioral components to facilitate long-term maintenance of the newly learned behaviors (Wexley and Baldwin 1986). Trainees leave the training expecting that relapse is a strong possibility but possessing a repertoire of coping responses to deal with it. An additional factor to ensure transfer is making the process of transfer public and monitoring it.

Goal Setting

Wexley and Baldwin (1986) noted that relapse prevention without goal setting did not seem to work. The main difference between the two interventions was that for goal setting, the trainees were required to meet with fellow trainees to discuss the goals and how they were going to accomplish them. Furthermore, trainees were re-

TABLE 5.5 Relapse-Prevention Strategies for Management Training

Strategy	*Purpose*
1. Awareness of the relapse process	1. Helps manager to understand how self-control strategies can enhance maintenance
2. Identification of high-risk situations	2. Heightens manager's sensitivity to specific situations that have previously resulted in difficulty
3. Development of coping responses	3. Enables manager to learn appropriate skills to overcome environmental hurdles
4. Enhancement of self-efficacy	4. Assists manager in maintaining personal worth, despite imperfect performance
5. Expectation of the positive effects of the activity	5. Counters manager's short-term positive expectations of the ineffective behavior
6. Abstinence violation effect (AVE)	6. Helps manager reduce guilt and avoid self-blame for having failed to implement a newly trained behavior
7. Apparently irrelevant decision (AID)	7. Strengthens awareness of seemingly minor decisions that culminate in a slip or relapse
8. Should/want ratio	8. Helps manager to maintain a balance of personal satisfaction in daily activities
9. Lifestyle interventions	9. Proposes physical and emotional coping skills to buffer manager from stress-induced relapse
10. Programmed relapse	10. Provides manager with monitored failure experiences that can be analyzed to avoid future relapse

Source: Adapted from Marx 1982.

quired to keep a record of their goal accomplishments, return these records to the trainer, and had to promise to meet at a later date to discuss these accomplishments publicly. This public commitment—through documentation of behavior, discussions with fellow trainees, and monitoring by trainers—may need to be incorporated into the relapse-prevention strategy. Wexley and Baldwin (1986) note that Marx has begun to include such steps in his relapse prevention.

This relapse-prevention strategy coupled with goal setting has been a successful mechanism for increasing the transfer of training in organizational settings (Saks and Haccoun 1996).

Much as setting goals in training facilitates the successful completion of training, setting goals for the transfer of training to the workplace will facilitate the transfer (Feldman 1981; Wexley and Baldwin 1986). An important part of the process seems to be the public commitment to the goals as indicated above. Having participants set such goals and providing them with a method of recording their accomplishments does seem to result in the successful transfer of training (Wexley and Baldwin 1986).

Facilitation of Transfer: Focus on Organizational Intervention

In chapter 4 we noted that once a performance deficiency was identified, the organizational analysis assessed the degree to which the deficiency was a function of KSAs or forces within the organization. Recall that many of these deficiencies (as noted by Nancy Gordon from Ameritech) were a function of organizational forces and not a lack of KSAs. Just as these forces can interfere with effective performance, they can also interfere with new learning and inhibit transfer. To enhance the possibility of transfer, therefore, it is useful to harness as much help as possible back on the job to assist in positive transfer.

SUPERVISOR SUPPORT

One of the key determining factors for the transfer of training is supervisory support (Baldwin and Ford 1988). Supervisors need to be cognizant of the behaviors being trained and must provide support for trainees who demonstrate the appropriate behaviors. These supports will go a long way toward facilitating transfer.

Supervisors can affect their employees' learning and transfer of training in other ways as well. Noe and Wilk (1993) demonstrated that those employees who are motivated to learn are more interested in improving themselves (more involved in their own development), and furthermore, support from supervisors for such developmental activity enhanced this motivation. Other research has indicated that motivation to learn can be enhanced when employees have realistic information regarding the benefits of development activities (Hicks and Klimoski 1987). Two other factors they identified that increased motivation to learn were the opportunity to attend what employees perceive to be relevant training, and alleviation of adverse working conditions (work that piled up) that can result from attending training. These two factors can also be controlled to a great extent by the supervisor.

PEER SUPPORT

Social learning theory is useful in understanding transfer of training. If the trainee is the only one from his department who is receiving training, there may be no peers back on the job to provide social support. In some climates this situation could result in pressure from more experienced peers to "forget all that stuff." With the right climate, however, peers can provide the proper support to use the training. What is the right climate? Learning must be considered an integral aspect of the organization's ongoing operation, becoming part of the employees' and managers' responsibilities. If everyone is involved in the learning process, it continues beyond the classroom. Most important, all employees must understand and support overall organizational objectives. In this way, the peer pressure will be to support company goals and objectives.

With this type of climate, it is possible to use peer support in a more formalized manner. Peers could be considered potential coaches. Although it is the supervisor that is generally thought of as a coach who helps recently trained employees transfer their skills to the workplace, Bergman (1993) suggests that this role can be accomplished by experienced peers. The peers would receive training as coaches and be provided with specific checklists to evaluate trainees periodically on their performance.

In addition, they would be role models willing to answer questions and provide advice, guidance, and support to remedy poor work habits.

We will discuss strategies for dealing with different climates in a later section. For now, it is sufficient to note that it is the responsibility of the training department to inform upper management of the advantages of creating such a climate if the goal is to encourage transfer of training.

TRAINER SUPPORT

Conventional wisdom has been that the trainer's job is done when training is over. More recent research, however, demonstrates the value of continued trainer involvement in the transfer of training. Trainees who commit to meet the trainer and other trainees at some later date to discuss transfer of training use the training more effectively (Wexley and Baldwin 1986). Thus there is value in the continued involvement of the trainer, who can be a useful resource in helping trainees work through any problems encountered in the workplace.

Stark (1986) has proposed that trainers offer to monitor trainees at some point after training to assess how they are doing and provide feedback. He calls these efforts **sit-ins.** The trainer sits in and observes the trainee in a situation where the trainee is required to use the trained behavior. To be effective, the sit-in must be voluntary on the part of the trainee, must be confidential between the trainer and trainee, and must be used only for developmental purposes, not administrative. Furthermore, the trainer must not interrupt the interaction between the trainee and others during the sit-in but provides feedback only after the session is over. Stark argues, "Who is better to be coaching the trainee on behaviors that were learned in training than the trainer?"

Using the trainer in a follow-up to facilitate transfer of training might spread the trainers rather thin. However, it is important to consider the investment already made in training. If transfer does not occur, the investment is lost.

REWARD SYSTEMS

As was noted earlier, operant conditioning is a powerful regulator of behavior. Employees are quite adept at determining which behaviors can get them in trouble, bring them rewards, or result in their being left alone. If trained behaviors are not reinforced, then there is little likelihood that such behaviors will be exhibited.

CLIMATE AND CULTURE

In a systems approach to training, as many forces as possible in the organization need to be focused on reinforcing the learned behaviors in order to ensure transfer. Although supervisor, peers, and reward systems all influence an organization's climate and culture, climate and culture need to be mentioned in their own right.

Climate has been conceptualized as the perception of salient characteristics of the organization (Schneider 1990). Tracey, Tannenbaum, and Kavanaugh (1995) suggest that such salient characteristics as company policies, reward systems, and management behaviors are important in determining the organizational climate and that organizational climate has an impact on the transfer of training. Supervisor support, peer support, and so forth all are part of the total climate that will reinforce the use of the trained skills, but they alone do not make up an organization's climate. Clearly, company policies and the attitudes reflected by upper management regarding training will also support or inhibit the transfer of training.

Culture is defined as a pattern of basic assumptions invented, discovered, or developed by a group within the organization. It can be considered a set of shared understandings about the organization (Schein 1985). One type of culture, a continuous learning culture—reflected by the shared understanding that learning is an important part of the job—has been shown to have a positive impact on the transfer of training (Tracey, Tannenbaum, and Kavanaugh 1995). A continuous learning culture is influenced by a variety of factors such as challenging jobs, social support (peer and supervisor), and developmental systems that allow employees the opportunity to learn continuously and receive appropriate training. Our discussion of the "learning organization" in chapter 2 described how such a culture is formed.

Influencing Climate and Culture

Given the importance of climate, what can be done if the climate is nonsupportive or neutral regarding training? Changing climate and culture in an organization is a long and difficult process and must be done from the top. Issues related to the incongruence of the training goals and organizational climate and culture should surface in the organizational analysis part of the needs analysis. This information would then be provided to the top HR manager.

There is evidence in North America that the human resource department of an organization now has more influence in organizational decision making than in the past (Cascio 1995), and employees in these departments are better trained in human resource issues (Thacker and Cattaneo 1992). With this increased influence and training, HR professionals are responsible for helping the company leadership to understand and resolve conflicts between organizational strategies and objectives and the existing climate and culture.

WHAT ABOUT THE SMALL ORGANIZATION?

Small businesses seem to have more sophisticated human resource policies today than in the 1980s (Hornsby and Kuratko 1990). In fact, a recent study suggests that many of their policies and practices are not much different from those of large businesses (Deshpande and Golhar 1994). In another study, Ahire and Golhar (1996) noted that in a comparison of small and large companies who had implemented Total Quality Management, they were equally involved in human resource activities such as training, and equally successful in producing quality products. This finding suggests that the small business is beginning to realize the importance of sound human resource practices. The major difference between small and large business is the impact successful training can have on the organization as a whole.

Much of what has been discussed earlier is relevant for any size organization. Ensuring that employees are highly motivated to learn and presenting interesting and relevant training is the same no matter the size of the company. As has been noted, the major problem in many training programs is not the learning of the skills, but the transfer of these skills to the job. To our mind, given the requirements necessary for transfer of training, the small business has a definite advantage. We have seen that climate and a continuous learning culture go a long way toward ensuring transfer of

---

Training in Action 5.2

Real Support

The Sandwich Community Health Center is a service-oriented organization with about 35 employees located in the community of Sandwich. The executive director and assistant executive director of the organization wanted to integrate the two areas of the organization (clinical and health promotion) as well as develop a team approach to much of the community care they were offering. After the issue was discussed with a consultant, a needs assessment was conducted, and training was provided on communication skills and conflict resolution. Everyone attended training, even the executive director. This involvement by top management sends an important message about the importance of the training. Top management also insisted that the training be evaluated. Knowing that an assessment will be made at some future date helps keep everyone focused on the need to change.

Finally, although no formal culture assessment was made, from the interviews conducted in the needs assessment, it was clear that a climate of continuous learning existed.

---

training. Although any organizational change is difficult, a small organization should be able to accomplish climate and culture change faster and more easily than a large one. Furthermore, in the small business, top management's commitment should be easier to obtain and to demonstrate. In many of the large company interventions conducted by the authors, top management provides written or verbal support for the intervention, but little else. Most of our dealings are with the human resource manager rather than the CEO or president. Although we stress the continued involvement of upper management, we often have little interaction with top management once the intervention has begun. Top management typically feels that they have more important things to do. In the small firm, it is often the CEO or owner who makes decisions about the type of training and development that will be provided (McRae et al. 1987). Access to these individuals is much easier and the ability to influence them is therefore greater. Because of their greater involvement they develop a clearer understanding of their role in making training successful. Training in Action 5.2 provides an example of this involvement.

Will the training in this example transfer? According to the research, it has a very good chance. The fact that the organization is small enough that all could attend the same training at the same time and experience the same things will help the transfer process. This situation simply could not occur in a larger company.

Outcomes of Design

To develop an effective training package, it is necessary to understand the various factors that facilitate learning and transfer. This is a basic output of the design phase. Two other outputs are the identification of evaluation objectives (chapter 6) and alternative methods of instruction (chapter 7).

From the information in this chapter, you should be able to design into your training the appropriate factors to make it successful. For further guidance, look at Table 5.6, which identifies a number of assumptions about how people learn and ties them to design issues (Scherer 1984). Note that some involve specific design matters such as using force-field analysis[2] and reducing restraints to change, whereas others simply provide suggestions to the trainers during the training such as "be ready for the unexpected" and "seize teachable moments." The latter suggestions involve specific design issues. Some slack time should be built into training, since there can be a tendency to put too much into a training package. When there are opportunities to dwell on a topic that trainees have expressed interest in, it is important to have the flexibility to do this. You cannot "seize the moment" if you are already behind in material and feel you must finish it all.

Finally, focus back on the learning processes identified in Table 5.3 on page 198. As was indicated earlier, you need to consider these learning processes when designing the training. Table 5.7 (pages 215–216) provides some design considerations based on these processes.

Because evaluation objectives are derived from the training objectives, and because the needs assessment and evaluation are strongly interrelated, the next chapter will follow through on the development of the evaluation. This is the way you would proceed in the "real world," and it makes sense to present the needs assessment and evaluation as close to each other as possible in order to reinforce the relationship between the two. Evaluation issues need to be continually considered throughout, even during the needs assessment phase, which can be thought of as a pretest.

TABLE 5.6 Design Issues Related to How People Learn

Assumption	*Design Issue*
1. Learning is change.	Consider supportive measures to encourage learning.
2. Change is generally resisted.	Consider force-field analysis in your design.
3. Learning is accelerated by reduction in restraining forces.	The design needs to focus on reducing restraints rather than adding drivers.
4. People are brimming with life experience.	A major design task is to help them convert experience into learning.
5. People usually show up with unresolved self-esteem issues.	Help people feel safe and capable in the early stages of the design.
6. People are subject to gravity. They get tired holding themselves up for long periods.	Provide a comfortable setting and take a lot of breaks.
7. People have different learning styles. Some learners are interactive, some reflective; some like structure, some resist it.	A good design will allow for different styles and not be a projection of the trainer's own style.
8. Early behavior will be self-oriented. Don't expect people to work effectively on group or organizational tasks at the beginning. They are working on inclusion and psychological safety.	Hold group or organizational activities until later.

(continued)

---

[2] Force-field analysis was described in chapter 2.

TABLE 5.6   Design Issues Related to How People Learn (continued)

Assumption	*Design Issue*
9. Inclusion is the first issue. People will learn next to nothing until they feel comfortable.	Hold key learning until inclusion is addressed, and assist that process early.
10. Remember the bell curve. Expect differences on feelings of relevance, motivation to participate, ability to "process" experience, and willingness to follow directions.	Design training to address differences in the target population.
11. People are basically consistent. They do *here* what they do *there*.	Provide "here and now" facets to the design. "How is what is happening now similar/different to what happens then?"
12. A sense of community can facilitate learning. Many people learn faster and better when they feel supported by others, realize they are not alone, and see others struggling with them.	Provide opportunities for discovering "I am not alone here!" and opportunities to learn from others.
13. People learn best when they feel they have control over the pace and depth of the learning process.	Share control by allowing trainees to have input into the pace and time spent on topics.
14. Transfer of learning depends on how similar the training experiences are to the situation back home. The more similar, the easier the transfer.	Do your homework, interview, plan with participants if possible, use their own role plays or actual situations.
15. Teachable moments do occur: when you are solving a problem, facing conflict, etc.	Seize the moments when they occur and plan ways to enhance them.
16. Some stress is necessary for learning to take place—not too much, though.	Remember the stress curve: 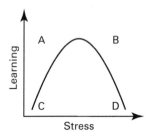
17. People pursue satisfaction of their own needs with great enthusiasm. Apathy is the result of people being asked to pursue someone else's goals.	Hook people up with their own needs early in the design. Find out why they're really coming to your event.
18. These assumptions are subject to change without notice.	Stay loose and stay in touch with your trainees and organization. Trust your instincts.

Source: Adapted from Scherer 1984.

TABLE 5.7   Training Design Considerations

Pretraining	**Attention/Expectancy**	
	Influence expectations/ attitudes of trainees.	Identify those with low expectations/poor attitudes and send to pretraining workshop to improve.
		Provide information to influence expectancies and identify positive outcomes of training.
	Demonstrate the need for training and set goals.	Do needs analysis so only relevant trainees attend training.
		Have supervisors discuss performance of trainee and set mutual goals based on future training.
		Have learning objectives distributed ahead of time.
Training	**Attention/Expectancy**	
Beginning	Create/reinforce positive attitude toward training	Allow time for suitable instructor and trainee introductions and develop a relaxed atmosphere.
		Allow for time to go through needs analysis, show learning objectives, and discuss usefulness on the job; draw example from trainees.
	Eliminate distractions	Choose site where anxiety level will be low (see classical conditioning).
		Choose proper facilities.
During	**Retention**	
	Make relevant	Continue to focus on training objectives.
		Develop links between previous learning and the new learning (activation of memory).
		Use relevant examples and offer many of them.
	Make interesting	Get trainees involved (symbolic rehearsal).
		Use relevant examples and offer many of them.
	Behavioral Reproduction/ Reinforcement	
	Encourage learning	Provide relevant practice process (including maximum similarity and/or different situations).
		Provide feedback.
Ending	**Reinforcement**	
	Be sure trainees see results of training	Provide time for examining objectives to see what was accomplished.
		Provide time to evaluate performance level accomplished and provide feedback.
	Sensitize trainees to difficulty in transfer of training	Incorporate relapse-prevention strategy.
		Provide commitment of trainer to meet with trainees to facilitate transfer.
		Develop trainee goals for transfer of training.
PostTraining	**Reinforcement**	
	Facilitate transfer	Obtain support from supervisor/peers/trainer to help trainee in transferring the training to the workplace.
		Ensure that reward systems are in line with newly trained behaviors.

The Real World of Training . . . what is wrong here

Were you able to figure out what went wrong in the two cases at the beginning of the chapter? It has to do with developing good behavioral objectives, as noted below.

CASE 1

Recall the incidents discussed in Case 1 at the beginning of the chapter. Training in troubleshooting did not transfer very well. What went wrong? Would more training help the employees become better troubleshooters? Let's re-examine the training that took place. The instructor provided a problem, and the trainees indicated the symptoms that would result from the problem. This "problem/symptom" sequence was the exact opposite of what they would be required to do on the job; see a symptom and then determine the problem. Had proper learning objectives been developed before the design of the training, the instructor would have realized his mistake. For example, consider the learning objective "Upon describing what is wrong with the system (a symptom), the trainee will be able immediately to describe all the possible problems that might cause these symptoms." Had this objective been developed before training, the type of training required would have been more obvious.

CASE 2

In Case 2, all the students followed a cycle of doing poorly on tests one, four, seven, ten, and thirteen, and much better on the other exams.

Further analysis revealed that the 32-week course was divided into five subsections, each of which had three tests. Also each subsection was taught by a different instructor. So on the very first test, the students did not know what to expect and did poorly. Once they understood what to expect on the tests, they improved on the remaining two tests. When a new instructor arrived, they prepared as usual only to find the type of test had changed; once again they did poorly. When they understood what the new instructor wanted, they did better. It was the "getting used to what the instructor wanted" that caused the cycle. Objectives were vague and students did not know what to expect. The chief instructor then developed learning objectives for all subsections, which provided guidance to both instructors and students as to what exams would be about. The problem disappeared.

Source: Mager 1975.

Key Terms

- Behavioral reproduction
- Climate
- Conditions
- Culture
- Desired outcome
- Guided discovery
- Identical elements
- Knowledge of results
- Learning objectives
- Massed practice
- Negative transfer
- Organizational outcome objectives
- Overlearning
- Part learning
- Positive transfer

- Progessive part learning
- Relapse prevention
- Sit-ins
- Spaced practice
- Standards
- Strategic knowledge development
- Symbolic encoding
- Task complexity
- Symbolic rehearsal
- Task organization
- Trainee reaction objectives
- Training objectives
- Transfer of training objectives
- Whole learning
- Zero transfer

Cases

1. Review the Multi-state Health Corporation case from chapter 2 and answer the following questions:
   a. In the implementation of the HRPS, what groups of employees are likely to need training? Think of this from a training design perspective as well as a training content perspective.
   b. For the type of training you envision for each group, what are the learning objectives? Write these in complete form.
   c. For each group of employees that will need training, what are the organizational constraints you will need to ad-

dress in the design of your training? What design features will you use to address these constraints? Be sure to address both the learning and transfer of training issues.

2. In the LEM case in chapter 2, suppose management decided to provide an outplacement workshop for management personnel who were being let go. A needs analysis indicated that what these individuals needed most was interviewing skills. How would you design a training program that would ensure trainees were interested and would get the most out of training (the focus is on the trainee)?

Exercises

1. You may have already noted that the learning objectives at the beginning of each chapter do not completely follow the three criteria we identified. They all describe the outcome in behavioral terms but do not identify the conditions or standards (these will vary with the instructor). Assume you will be the instructor for this chapter and rewrite each of the learning objectives at the beginning of the chapter in complete form. Your trainees are corporate HRD employees and you are training them on

the contents of this chapter. Additionally, write an objective for each of the other types of training objectives (trainee reaction, transfer of training, point average).

2. What is your average grade since you started your education at this institution? How hard do you work to maintain that average: 3 (very hard/hard), 2 (about average), 1 (enough to get by)? Now ask yourself why. Tie your answer into Expectancies 1 and 2 and valence of outcomes. Break into groups where

there is a mix of 1s, 2s, and 3s. Discuss what makes the person in your group a 3. Is it attractive outcomes (valence), confidence in ability (Expectancy 1), and/or belief that it will result in positive outcomes desired? From that information, is there any way you believe you could influence the 2s and/or 1s to be more motivated? What would you try to influence? Explain this in terms of Expectancies 1 and 2. How does this process relate to trainee populations in the workplace?

Questions for Review

1. What are the four types of training objectives? Why is it necessary to have objectives for all four? Who benefits from learning objectives and why?
2. What can be done long before the trainee attends training to ensure that the trainee will be motivated to learn?
3. How does knowledge of classical and operant conditioning assist us in designing effective training?
4. How would you present training material in a manner that facilitates retention?
5. If a particular task was critical to saving life (policeman shooting his gun, pilot responding to an emergency), what factors would you build into the design of training to ensure that the behavior was both learned and transferred to the workplace?
6. To help ensure transfer of training, what would you do outside the training itself? Who would you involve and how? What about the organizational structure/environment?
7. Suppose you have a group of forty employees for which you are designing a training program. These employees come from a wide range of ethnic and cultural backgrounds and also have different educational and experience backgrounds relative to the content area of the training. What training design features would you use to address these constraints?

References

Adams, J. 1987. Historical review and appraisal of research on the learning, retention, and transfer of human motor skills. *Psychological Bulletin* 101:41–74.

Ahire, S., and D. Golhar. 1996. Quality management in large vs. small firms. *Journal of Small Business Management,* April, pp. 1–13.

Anderson, J. R., and G. H. Bower. 1972. Recognition and retrieval processes in free recall. *Psychological Review* 79:97–123.

———. 1973. *Human Associative Memory.* Washington, DC: Winston.

Atwater, S. 1953. Proactive inhibition and associative facilitation as affected by the degree of prior learning. *Journal of Experimental Psychology* 46:400–404.

Baldwin, T., and K. Ford. 1988. Transfer of training: A review and directions for future research. *Personnel Psychology* 41:63–105.

Bandura, A. 1977. *Social Learning Theory.* Upper Saddle River, NJ: Prentice Hall.

———. 1991. Social cognitive theory of self regulation. *Organizational Behavior and Human Decision* 50:248–87.

Bergman, T. 1993. Job performance learning: A comprehensive approach to high performance training design. *Employment Relations Today,* Winter, pp. 399–409.

Blum, M., and J. Naylor. 1968. *Industrial Psychology, Its Theoretical and Social Foundations.* New York: Harper & Row.

Brownell, K. D., G. Marlatt, E. Lichenstein, and G. Wilson. 1986. Understanding and preventing relapse. *American Psychologist* 41:765–82.

Camp, R., P. N. Blanchard, and G. Huszczo. 1986. *Toward a More Organizationally Effective Training Strategy and Practice.* Upper Saddle River, NJ: Prentice Hall.

Cascio, W. 1995. *Managing Human Resources.* New York: McGraw-Hill Ryerson.

Cascio, W., and J. Thacker. 1994. *Managing Human Resources.* Toronto: McGraw-Hill Ryerson.

Cronbach, L., and R. Snow. 1977. *Aptitude and Instructional Methods.* New York: Irvington.

Deshpande, S., and D. Golhar. 1994. HRM practices in large and small manufacturing firms: A comparative study. *Journal of Small Business Management,* April, pp. 49–56.

Feldman, M. 1981. Successful post training skill application. *Training and Development Journal* 35:72–75.

Goldstein, I. 1980. Training in work organizations. *Annual Review of Psychology* 39: 229–72.

Hagman, J. D., and A. M. Rose. 1983. Retention of military tasks: A review. *Human Factors* 25:199–214.

Hicks, W. D., and R. J. Klimoski. 1987. Entry into training programs and its effect on training outcomes: A field experiment. *Academy of Management Journal* 30:542–52.

Hornsby, J., and D. Kuratko. 1990. Human resource management in small business: Critical issues for the 1990s. *Journal of Small Business Management,* July, pp. 9–19.

Klatzky, R. 1975. *Human Memory: Structures and Processes.* San Francisco: Freeman.

Kraiger, K., J. K. Ford, and E. Salas. 1993. Application of cognitive, skilled based, and affective theories of learning outcomes to new methods of training evaluation. *Journal of Applied Psychology* 78:311–28.

Latham, G. P., and E. A. Locke. 1979. Goal Setting: A motivational technique that works. *Organizational Dynamics* 8:68–80.

Latham, G. P., and G. A. Yukl. 1975. A review of research on the application of goal setting in organizations. *Academy of Management Journal* 18:824–45.

Lindsay, P., and D. Norman. 1972. *Human Information Processing: An Introduction to Psychology.* New York: Academic Press.

Locke, E., and G. Latham. 1990. *A Theory of Goal Setting and Task Performance.* Upper Saddle River, NJ: Prentice Hall.

Locke, E., K. Shaw, L. Saari, and G. Latham. 1981. Goal setting and task performance. *Psychological Bulletin* 90:125–52.

Mager, R. F. 1975. *Preparing Instructional Objectives.* Belmont, CA: Pitman Learning.

Mandler, G. 1954. Transfer of training as a response to overlearning. *Journal of Experimental Psychology* 47:411–17.

Martocchio, J. J., and J. Dulebohn. 1994. Performance feedback effects in training: The role of perceived controllability. *Personnel Psychology* 47:357–73.

Marx, R. D. 1982. Relapse prevention for managerial training: A model for maintenance of behavior change. *Academy of Management Review* 7:433–41.

McGhee, W., and P. W. Thayer. 1961. *Training in Business and Industry.* New York: Wiley.

McRae, C., A. Banks, A. Bures, and D. Champion. 1987. Decision making factors in small business: Training and development. *Journal of Small Business Management,* January, pp. 19–25.

Melton, A., and E. Martin. 1972. *Coding Process in Human Memory:* Washington, DC: Winston.

Naylor, J., and G. Briggs. 1963. Effects of rehearsal of temporal and spatial aspects on the long-term retention of a procedural skill. *Journal of Applied Psychology* 47:120–26.

Noe, R. A., and S. L. Wilk. 1993. Investigation of the factors that influence employees' participation in developmental activities. *Journal of Applied Psychology* 78:291–302.

Ryman, D., and R. Biersner. 1975. Attitudes predictive of diving training success. *Personnel Psychology* 28:181–88.

Saks, A., and R. Haccoun. 1996. Easing the transfer of training. *Human Resource Professional,* July/August, pp. 8–11.

Sanders, P., and J. Vanouzas. 1983. Socialization to learning. *Training and Development Journal,* July, pp. 14–21.

Schein, E. H. 1985. *Organizational Culture and Leadership.* San Francisco: Jossey-Bass.

Schendel, J. D., and J. D. Hagman. 1982. On sustaining procedural skills over a prolonged retention interval. *Journal of Applied Psychology* 67:605–10.

Scherer, J. 1984. How people learn: Assumptions for design. *Training and Development,* January, pp. 64–66.

Schmitt, M. C., and T. J. Newby. 1986. Metacognition: Relevance to instructional design. *Journal of Instructional Development* 9:29–32.

Schneider, B. 1990. *Organizational Climate and Culture.* San Francisco, Jossey-Bass.

Shiffrin, R., and W. Schneider. 1977. Controlled and automatic information processing: Perceptual learning, automatic attending and a general theory. *Psychological Review,* 84:127–90.

Stark, C. 1986. Ensuring skills transfer: A sensitive approach. *Training and Development Journal,* March, pp. 50–51.

Thacker, J., and J. Cattaneo. 1992. Survey of personnel practices in Canadian organizations. Working paper series W92-04, ISSN 07146191.

Thorndike, E. L., and R. S. Woodworth. 1901. The influence of improvement in one mental function upon the efficiency of other functions. Functions involving attention, observation, and discrimination. *Psychological Review* 8:553–64.

Tracey, B., S. Tannenbaum, and M. Kavanaugh. 1995. Applying trained skills on the job: The importance of the work environment. *Journal of Applied Psychology* 80:239–51.

Wexley, K., and T. Baldwin. 1986. Posttraining strategies for facilitating positive transfer: An empirical exploration. *Academy of Management Journal* 29:503–20.

CHAPTER 6

Evaluation of Training

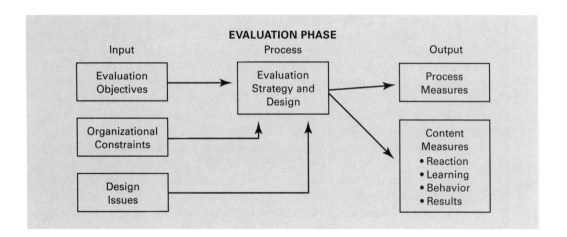

EVALUATION PHASE

Input	Process	Output
Evaluation Objectives	Evaluation Strategy and Design	Process Measures
Organizational Constraints		Content Measures • Reaction • Learning • Behavior • Results
Design Issues		

Learning Objectives

After reading this chapter, you should be able to:

- Define and describe the various types of training critera

- Describe the costs and benefits of evaluating training

- Describe the interrelationships among the various levels of training criteria

- Define, describe, and identify instances of internal and external validity

- Describe the various designs necessary to ensure internal and external validity of the evaluation

---

Training Designed to Change Behavior and Attitudes

The city of Palm Desert, California, decided to provide training to improve employees' attitudes toward their work and to provide them with skills to be more effective on the job. The two-day seminar involved a number of teaching methods including a lecture, films, role plays, and group interaction. The topics covered were conflict control, listening, communicating, telephone etiquette, body language, delegation, taking orders, and others. Throughout the two days, the value of team work, creativity, and rational decision making were stressed and integrated into the training.

Before the training was instituted, all 55 nonmanagement employees completed a paper-and-pencil questionnaire to measure both their attitudes toward the job and their perception of their job behaviors. Supervisors also completed the job behavior questionnaire for each of their employees. All 55 employees were told they would be receiving the same two-day seminar. The first set of employees (34 of them) was chosen at random.

The 21 employees who did not take the training immediately became a comparison group for evaluating the training. While the first group of employees were sent to the training, the others were pulled off the job, ostensibly to receive training, but simply took part in exercises not related to any training. Thus both groups were treated similarly in every way except for training. Both groups completed attitude surveys immediately after the trained group finished training. Six months later both groups completed self report surveys to measure changes in their job behavior. Their supervisors were asked to complete a similar behavior measure at the six-month mark as well.

The data provided some revealing information. For the trained group, no changes in attitude or behavior were indicated either by the self-report or by supervisor-reported surveys. This was also true (but expected) for the group not trained.

Source: Adapted from Miller 1990.

Was training a failure in this case? Would the training manager be pleased with these results? Was the evaluation process flawed? These are the types of issues that will be addressed in this chapter. We will be referring back to the case from time to time to answer these and other questions.

Rationale for Evaluation

Imagine a business that decided it wouldn't look at its profitability, return on investment, or productivity. You are a supervisor with this company, but you never look at how well or poorly your subordinates are performing their jobs. This is what training is like when no evaluation is conducted. Good management practice dictates that organizational activities be routinely examined to ensure that they are occurring as planned and are producing the anticipated results. Otherwise people, processes, and products or services that have gotten "off track" have no means of getting back on.

Nonetheless, many rationalizations for not evaluating training continue to exist. A late 1980s survey of 45 Fortune 500 companies indicated that all of them asked trainees how much they liked the training, but only 30% assessed how much was learned, and just 15% examined whether behavior on the job changed (Brandenberg and Schultz 1988). Other evidence from that time suggested only one company in a hundred had an effective system for measuring the impact and value of its training (McLaughlin 1986).

This attitude seems to be changing, though. By 1994 a survey of training in the United States found that for companies with 100 or more employees, 66% said they assessed learning, 62% assessed behavioral change, and 47% assessed the impact of training on organizational outcomes (Geber 1995). Why the change? A major reason is an increase in accountability for everyone. Top management is demanding evidence that training departments are contributing positively to the bottom line (Geber 1995).

On issues related to human resources, it has been suggested that Canada lags behind the United States (Cattaneo and Templer 1990). A study by McIntyre (1994) supports this finding in the area of training evaluation. A survey of companies in Canada indicates that only 30% evaluate learning, 16% evaluate behavioral change, and 5% evaluate the impact of training on organizational outcomes. This seems to be where U.S. companies were in the mid-1980s.

RESISTANCE TO TRAINING EVALUATION

Training managers can come up with a surprising number of reasons for not evaluating training. In the past, when training was often considered merely a luxury that took place only in good times, these reasons were accepted.

Nothing to Evaluate

For some, training has been seen as a luxury that was provided as a reward for good performance, or simply something that was mandated so everyone had to take their turn (Meals and Rogers 1986). The argument here is that training isn't expected to accomplish anything so there's nothing to evaluate.

The Counterargument Even in cases where training is a reward or luxury, it is designed with some goal or objectives in mind. Some type of KSA change is expected from the trainees, even if it is just that they feel more positive about their job or the company. Once this goal or objective is identified, the objectives of training can be measured. Evaluation is simply measuring the degree to which those objectives have been achieved.

No One Really Cares about Evaluating Training

The most common rationale for not conducting training evaluations is that "formal evaluation procedures are too expensive and time-consuming and no one really cares anyway." This usually means that no one has specifically asked for, demanded, or otherwise indicated that training needs to be evaluated.

The Counterargument The fact that evaluation is not specifically asked for doesn't mean that training isn't going to be evaluated anyway. Important organizational decisions (e.g., budget, staffing, performance evaluations) will be made with or without formal data on the effectiveness of training or its contribution toward organizational objectives. If no formal evaluations of training have taken place, decisions will be based upon whatever impressions the decision makers have of training. Even in good economic times, the competition for organizational budget allocations is strong. Departments that can document their contributions to the organization and the return that can be expected on the investment of new budget dollars are more likely to be granted their budget requests. The question then is not whether training should be evaluated, but rather who will do it, how it will be done, and what data will be used.

Evaluation Is a Threat to My Job

Considering that in the United States and Canada tens of billions of dollars are spent every year for training, why wouldn't companies evaluate this training? Fear of the result is one reason. Football coach Woody Hays once said he never liked to throw the forward pass because three things could happen and two of them are bad. The same could be said for evaluation. If time and money are spent on training and an evaluation determines that no learning occurred—or worse, job performance declined—tough questions will be asked. While most managers are not likely to admit this concern publicly, it is perhaps the real problem. When we use the term *evaluation,* we too often think of a single final outcome at a particular point that represents success or failure—like a report card. This type of evaluation is called **summative or outcome evaluation.** When the focus is on this type of evaluation, managers are naturally concerned about what documenting the failure of their programs will do for their careers.

The Counterargument   Evaluation doesn't have to be looked at in the context of success or failure, but rather as feedback into the system in order to modify and improve the training.

One of the authors, while trying to convince a client that the company's training should be evaluated, decided not to use the term *"evaluation."* Instead he chose the term *data tracking.* He emphasized tracking attitudes and behaviors over time and supplying feedback to the training design and trainers based on the findings. This feedback could then be used to modify training and/or organizational systems and processes to facilitate the training's success. The term *data tracking* did not have the same connotation of finality that evaluation had. Hence managers saw it as a tool for improving the likelihood of a successful intervention rather than as a pass/fail grade.

Was the evaluation in the Palm Desert case seen as summative or as a continuous improvement process? It is difficult to say without actually talking to those involved. However, if it was used for continuous improvement, assessment of the learning at the end of training would have been helpful in determining the reason transfer did not take place.

SO WE MUST EVALUATE

The arguments for ignoring evaluation of training make some sense, on the surface. However, they are easily countered when more carefully analyzed. Perhaps the biggest reason for abandoning the resistance to evaluation, however, is its benefit. This is especially true today when more and more organizations are demanding accountability at all levels. Geber (1995) noted that managers are increasingly demanding of training what has long been demanded of other departments: provide evidence of the value to the organization. Other factors influencing the need to evaluate training are the quality movement, focus on continuous improvement, and organizational cost cutting (Geber 1995).

The image of the training function, particularly that held by many line managers, has been poor. By using the same process as line managers to demonstrate accountability, you can improve the image of training. Furthermore, the technology for evaluating and even placing dollar amounts on the value of training has improved in the last several years. There is a caveat to all of this. We do not advocate a comprehensive evaluation of all training, because the value of that evaluation must be worth the cost. Sometimes the cost is simply too high.

Types of Evaluation Data Collected

In evaluation, there are two areas that can be addressed: process and outcome. Evaluation of the **process** examines how the training was designed, developed, and carried out. **Outcome** evaluation determines how well training accomplished its objectives.

PROCESS DATA

One of the authors has a cottage near a lake, and he often sees people trying unsuccessfully to start their outboard motors. In going to their assistance, he never starts by suggesting they "pull plugs" to check for ignition or "disconnect the float" to see if gas is reaching the carburetor. Instead, he asks them if the gas line is connected firmly, if the ball is pumped up, if the gear shift is in neutral (many will not start in gear), and if the throttle is at the correct position. These are process issues. He is evaluating the "process" of starting the engine to see if it has been followed correctly. If he assumed it had and tried to diagnose the "problem with the engine," he would never find it.

It is the same with training. If learning objectives were not achieved, there is no point in tearing the training program apart trying to fix it. It might simply be a process issue: the training was not set up or presented properly. In examining the training process, there are two areas to consider: process before training and process during training.

Process: Before Training

A number of steps should be taken in analyzing the processes used to develop training. Table 6.1 (page 226) identifies a number of questions that should be considered during the analysis of the training process.

First you can assess the effectiveness of the needs analysis from the documentation and/or report that was prepared. This should indicate the various sources from which the data were gathered and the KSA deficiency that was documented.

Next you can assess the training objectives. Are they in line with what was found to be deficient? Are there objectives at all levels: organizational, transfer, learning, and reaction? Are they written clearly and effectively to convey what must be done to demonstrate achievement of the objective?

Then evaluate the design of the training. For example, if trainees' motivation to attend and learn is low, what procedures have been included in the design to deal with this?

TABLE 6.1	Potential Questions to Be Addressed in a Process Analysis (Before Training)

Were needs diagnosed correctly?
- What data sources were used?
- Was a knowledge/skill deficiency identified?
- Were trainees assessed to determine their prerequisite KSAs?

Were needs translated into training objectives?
- Were all objectives identified?
- Were the objectives written in a clear, appropriate manner?

Was an evaluation system designed to measure accomplishment of objectives?

Was the training program designed to meet all the training objectives?
- Was previous learning that might either support or inhibit learning in training identified?
- Were individual differences assessed and taken into consideration in training design?
- Was trainee motivation to learn assessed?
- What steps were taken to address trainee motivation to learn?
- Were processes built into the training to facilitate recall and transfer?
- What steps are included in the training to call attention to key learning events?
- What steps are included in the training to aid trainees in symbolic coding and cognitive organization?
- What opportunities are included in the training to provide symbolic and behavioral practice?
- What actions are included in the training to ensure transfer of learning to the job?

Are the training techniques to be used appropriate for each of the learning objectives of the training?

Source: Adapted from Camp, Blanchard, and Huszczo 1986.

It is important that you examine the proposed evaluation tools to be sure they are relevant. Based on the needs assessment and resulting objectives, there should be a number of tools identified for assessing the various levels of effectiveness.

Finally, when you examine the actual training package, you should assess the areas discussed in chapter 5, especially those summarized in Tables 5.2, 5.5, and 5.6.

By evaluating these issues before training begins, you can determine any errors or omissions and correct them. If, however, you do not do so until after training has occurred, the analysis will still help you diagnose why training outcomes were or were not achieved.

Would such an evaluation have been useful in the Palm Desert case? Yes. In that situation, as it stands, we have to assume that training was not successful, but we do not know why.

Process: During Training

One of the problems with collecting only outcome data is that, when the outcomes are not achieved, it is never clear why the objectives were not achieved. Did the training that occurred reflect what was proposed, designed, and was contained in the training manual? If so, it is the design that must be changed. Or did the trainer or others in the organization make some ad hoc modifications? If this information were available in the Palm Desert case, analysis might have provided information as to why the training was not successful.

Imagine, for example, that the Palm Desert training required the use of behavior modeling, to provide practice in the skills being taught. The evaluation of outcomes shows that learning of the new behaviors did not occur. If no process data were gathered, the conclusion could be that the behavior modeling approach was not effective. What if examination of the process, however, revealed that trainees were threatened by the behavior modeling technique and the trainer allowed them to spend time discussing other issues so there was less time for this activity. Without the process evaluation, this information would not be known, and the inference might be that behavior modeling was not effective.

Examples of implementation issues to examine are depicted in Table 6.2. Here it is up to the evaluator to determine that all the techniques that were designed into the program actually took place. It is not good enough simply to determine that they occurred and the expected amount of time was allotted to each module. You must also determine that trainees actually were involved in the learning activities. As in the behavior modeling example above, the time allotted might be used for something other than behavior modeling.

Putting It All Together

"Actual" training is compared with the "expected" training to provide an assessment of the effectiveness of the training implementation. You can obtain much of the necessary information from records and reports that were developed in the process of setting up the training program. Regarding the training content, if a manual were developed it would provide an excellent source of information about what should be covered in the training. To determine what actually *was* covered, have someone moni-

---

TABLE 6.2 Potential Questions to Be Addressed in a Process Analysis (During Training)

Was there a match between trainer, training techniques, and training/learning objectives?
- Were lecture portions of the training effective?
    Was involvement encouraged/solicited?
    Were questions used effectively?
- Did the trainer appropriately conduct the various training methodologies (case, role play, etc.)?
    Were they explained well?
    Did the trainer use the allotted time for activities?
    Was enough time allotted?
    Did trainees follow instructions?
    Was there effective debriefing following exercises?
- Did the trainer follow the training design and lesson plans?
    Was enough time given for each of the requirements?
    Was time allowed for questions?

Source: Adapted from Camp, Blanchard, and Huszczo 1986.

tor the training. Videotaping, instructors' notes, and surveys or interviews with trainees can also be used. Keep in mind that when you are gathering any data, the more methods you use to gather information, the better.

When to Use It

Who is interested in the process data? As you can see in Table 6.3, this information is used primarily by the training department to determine if it is doing what it is supposed to be doing. The customers[1] of training usually aren't interested in this type of information—they are more concerned with training outcomes.

You should always try to have some process data, particularly those related to "during training," even if it is only the trainer's documentation and trainee reactions. These can be used by the trainer and other trainers to assess what seems to work and what doesn't. Sometimes you will want much more detailed process data, such as when training is to be used many times, and the information has a significant impact on the bottom line. Multiple measures of the process data increase their validity. If, on the other hand, you are setting up a half-day seminar on the new computer software, collecting process information may not be worth the cost. If you are training some new hires to work on a piece of equipment (training which has been done numerous times before) and the trainer is one of your most experienced, then process analysis is probably not necessary. If the trainer was fairly new and had never conducted this particular session before, you might want to gather process data through direct observation by a senior trainer.

OUTCOME DATA

To determine how well training has met or is meeting its goals, you need to examine the various outcomes. Kirkpatrick (1979) has identified four types of outcomes that are probably the best-known: reaction, learning, behavior, and organizational results. These outcomes are ordered: reaction outcomes come first and will influence how much can be learned; next, learning outcomes determine how much behavior can change back on the job; then behavior on the job determines how much organizational impact the training can have.

TABLE 6.3 Who Is Interested in the Process Data

Training Department
Trainer	Yes, it helps determine what works well and what does not
Other trainers	Yes, to the extent that process is generalizable
Training manager	Only if training is not successful, or if there is a problem with a particular trainer

Customers
Trainees	No
Trainees' supervisor	No
Upper management	No

Source: Adapted from Camp, Blanchard, and Huszczo 1986.

---

[1] Here, *customer* is defined as anyone who has a vested interest in the training department's work.

Reaction outcomes are measures of the trainee's perceptions, emotions, and subjective evaluations of the training experience. This is the first level of evaluation, because favorable reactions are important in creating motivation to learn. Thus reactions set a kind of upper limit on how much the trainees will learn.

Learning outcomes are measured by the requisite learning objectives and the overall training objective. The type of measurement used will depend on the measurement technology available to the evaluator and the type of learning being evaluated. Note the critical relationship between the needs analysis and evaluation. If the training process has progressed according to the model presented in this text, you will identify the method of measuring learning during the training needs analysis (TNA). At that time you measured the employee's KSAs to determine if they were adequate for job performance. The evaluation of learning should use the same measurement techniques as in the TNA. Thus the needs analysis is actually the "pretest." The amount of learning that occurs places an upper limit on the amount of change in job behavior that can occur.

Job behavior outcomes are similarly measured in a manner consistent with the TNA. Remember, during the training needs analysis you identified performance deficiencies, and you traced them to areas in which employees were behaving in a manner that was creating the deficiency. The methods used for measuring job behavior in the TNA should be used in measuring job behavior after training has been completed. Once again, the link between needs analysis and evaluation is evident. The degree to which job behavior improves places a cap on how much organizational results can improve.

Organizational results is the highest level in the hierarchy and reflects the performance deficiency identified in the TNA. It is the organizational result that often triggers reactive (as opposed to proactive) training. Here are some examples:

- High levels of scrap are being produced
- Employees are quitting in record numbers
- Sales figures have been dropping for the last two quarters
- Grievances are on the increase
- Number of rejects from quality control are rising

Putting It All Together

It has been suggested (Hamblin 1974) that only by evaluating each level in the hierarchy will one be able to understand the full effects of training. Let's examine one of the items in the above list—a high grievance rate—as it relates to the training process and the four levels of evaluation.

The needs analysis determines that the high grievance rate is a function of supervisors not managing conflict well. Their knowledge is adequate but their skills are deficient. From the needs analysis, data are obtained for later comparison with skill levels after training has been completed. Tools for evaluation are developed at this time if they are not already available from the needs analysis. Training is provided, and then participants fill out a reaction questionnaire. This measures the degree to which trainees feel positive about the time and effort they invested in the program and each of its components. Assume the responses are favorable. However, even though the trainees feel good about the training and believe they have learned valuable things, the trainer recognizes that the intended learning may not have occurred. Thus a test of conflict management skill is administered and the results are compared with pre-training data. If the results show the trainees have acquired the conflict management skills and can use them appropriately, the learning objectives have been achieved. But will these skills transfer to the job so the employees are using them in conflict situations? If we show this has occurred, then the learning has been transferred to the job. The next step is to see if the grievance rate is declining. If it is, then you could, with some level of confidence,[2] suggest that training is the cause of the decline. If you had determined that learning did not take place after training, it would not make sense to examine behavior or results, because learning is a prerequisite.

Reaction Questionnaire

What Is It   Often termed "love letters" or "happy face data" by trainers, the data collected at this level are used to determine what the trainees thought about the training. Reaction questionnaires are often criticized, not because of their lack of value, but because they are often the only type of evaluation undertaken (Saari et al. 1988; Yancey and Kelly 1990; Wexley and Yukl 1975).

Alliger et al. (1997) classified reaction questionnaires into two types: affective and utility. An **affective questionnaire** measures our general feeling about training ("I found this training enjoyable"[3]), whereas the **utility questionnaire** reflects our beliefs about the value of training ("This training was of practical value"). We will focus here on the latter type, because we believe that specific utility statements on reaction questionnaires are more valuable for making changes.

Training reaction questionnaires do not assess learning, but rather determine attitudes and opinions about the training from the trainee's perspective. A number of categories should be considered in developing a reaction questionnaire, including the relevance of training; training content, materials, and exercises; trainer(s) behavior; and the facilities.

Training relevance.   Asking trainees about the relevance (utility) of the training they have experienced provides the organization with a measure of the perceived value of the training. If most participants do not see any value in it, they will have difficulty remaining interested. Furthermore, this perceived lack of value can contaminate the program's image. Those who do not see its value will talk with others who have not yet attended training, and will perhaps suggest it is a waste of time. Self-fulfilling prophecy proposes that if you come to training believing it will be a waste of time, it will be. Even if the training really is of importance to the organization, if entering participants do not believe it is, it is not likely to achieve its objectives.

Once trainee attitudes are known, steps can be taken to change the beliefs, either through a socialization process or a change in the training itself. Think about the Palm Desert case. What do you think the trainee reactions to the training were? Might this source of information have helped to explain why no change in behavior occurred?

Training materials and exercises.   Any written materials, videos, exercises, and any other tools of instruction should be assessed along with an overall evaluation of the

---

[2] Use of the experimental designs (discussed later) will improve your confidence level.

[3] Although they are called *reaction questionnaires*, the content is often statements which the trainees respond to by circling a number that reflects the degree to which they agree or disagree.

training experience. On the basis of responses from participants, you can introduce modifications to the training to make it more relevant to participants. Another reason for doing this is that it follows the OD principle of involving trainees in the process.

The value of a reaction questionnaire can be seen in Training in Action 6.1. Here the data provided information on how to develop an orientation to empowerment. Examining the reaction questionnaire responses proved valuable for determining that

---

Training in Action 6.1

Developing an Orientation

An orientation for the introduction of an empowerment intervention was developed by a working committee at Ameritech. The orientation was to help employees understand the concept of empowerment, and why Ameritech and the Communication Workers of America had developed a joint operating agreement that included the concept.

A great deal of work went into creating the orientation. Two videos and a role play were produced in addition to other materials and methods. One video showed some trial sites where rank-and-file members were interviewed about the process. The other video showed top management and union leaders discussing the empowerment process and answering questions from a panel of workers. After the training program was complete, the working committee reviewed the content, design, and materials.

The working committee questioned the value of using both videos. Members were also concerned that the role play in the orientation would not work because many of the rank and file "were not managers" and would not like to do role plays.

At that point the consultant suggested that a reaction questionnaire be drawn up to assess what participants in a few pilot orientation sessions saw as relevant. The orientation could then be adjusted according to the findings.

The reaction questionnaire asked, "How useful was the [component being assessed] in helping you understand the empowerment concept?" The six-point scale is shown below with a sample question and the data obtained. The percentage below the question represent the distribution of the 187 respondents. Note that the percentages do not add up to 100, because some participants chose not to respond.

How useful was the Christie Handley videotape in helping you understand the empowerment process at Ameritech?

1	2	3	4	5	6
Of little use	Of some use	Useful but too much time was spent on it	Useful, helped me understand the concepts	Very useful but not enough time was spent on it.	Very useful. This module helped me a great deal to understand the concepts.
4%	10%	8%	56%	7%	14%

the Christie Handley videotape was seen by trainees as useful. It also indicated that almost three-quarters of participants perceived the role plays as useful. Open-ended responses at the end of the questionnaire asked trainees to indicate "which of the modules was most effective in helping you understand empowerment at Ameritech." Once again the Christie Handley videotape was listed by 20% of respondents and the role play by 16%.[4] Using this information, rather than trying to guess what participants would find useful, the working committee and consultant were able to configure the orientation to increase positive perceptions.

Reactions to the trainer(s). Reaction questionnaires are also useful in determining how the trainer's actions were evaluated by the trainees. Care should be taken to develop statements that specifically address the trainer's actions. General statements tend to reflect trainees' feelings about how friendly or entertaining the trainer was (halo error) rather than how well he carried out the training. Simply presenting an affective statement (Alliger et al. 1997) such as "The trainer was entertaining" would likely elicit a halo response. For this reason, it is useful to identify specific aspects of trainer behavior you wish to be rated.

Note that the questionnaire in Figure 6.1 asks the trainee to consider several aspects of the trainer's teaching behavior, allowing him to be more discriminating. Following a number of specific, behavioral statements, an overall rating, if requested, should better reflect the trainer's total performance and not be as contaminated by halo error.

Facilities. The reaction questionnaire can also contain items related to the facilities, to determine if there are things impeding the training process. Noise, temperature, seating arrangements, and even the freshness of the doughnuts are potential areas that can cause discontent. One way to approach these issues is to use open-ended questions, such as the following:

> Please describe any aspects of the facility that created problems for you during training (identify the problem and the aspect of the facility).
> "Please indicate how you felt about the following:
>   Refreshments provided
>   Ability to hear the trainer and other trainees clearly
>   Number and length of breaks

Facility questions are most appropriate if the results are going to be used to modify future training or if the facilities are likely to be used in the future for training. The more things working in the trainer's favor, the more effective training is likely to be.

The data from a reaction questionnaire provide important information that can be used to make the training more relevant, the trainers more sensitive to their strengths and shortcomings, and the facilities more conducive to a positive training atmosphere. The feedback the questionnaire provides is more immediate than with the other levels of evaluation, and therefore modifications to training can be made much sooner.

---

[4] Although this might seem low, it is not. Generally, open-ended questions are not responded to with great frequency. In this case, only about 40% responded. Furthermore, the next highest agreement for a module was only 2%. Taken in this context, the percentages are worth considering in developing the orientation.

Please circle the number that reflects the degree to which you agree or disagree with the following statements.

1 Strongly disagree, 2 Disagree, 3 Neither agree nor disagree, 4 Agree, 5 Strongly agree

1. The trainer did a good job of stating the objectives at the beginning of training.	1	2	3	4	5
2. The trainer made good use of visual aids (easel, white board) when making the presentations.	1	2	3	4	5
3. The trainer was good at keeping everyone interested in the topics.	1	2	3	4	5
4. The trainer encouraged questions and participation from trainees.	1	2	3	4	5
5. The trainer made sure everyone understood the concepts before moving on to the next topic.	1	2	3	4	5
6. The trainer summarized important concepts before moving to the next module	1	2	3	4	5

7. Overall, how would you rate this trainer (check one)

____1. Poor; I would not recommend this trainer to others.

____2. Adequate; I would recommend this trainer only if no others were available.

____3. Average

____4. Good; I would recommend this trainer above most others.

____5. Excellent; this trainer is among the very best I've ever worked with.

FIGURE 6.1 Reaction Questionnaire for the Trainer

Timing of Reaction Assessment   The timing and type of questions asked on a reaction questionnaire should be based on the information you need for evaluating and improving the training, the trainer(s), or the facility. Most reaction questionnaires are given to participants at the conclusion of training. The advantage is that the training is still fresh and the audience is captive. However, a problem with giving them at this time is that trainees may be tired after a full day of training and just want to leave. Filling out a questionnaire at this time may result in incomplete and less than valid data. In addition, the type of information you can get at this time is limited. The trainees may not know if the training is useful on the job until they have had a chance to go back to the job and try it.

An alternative is to send out a reaction questionnaire at some point (one or two months) after training. This delay gives the trainee time to see how training works in the actual job setting. However, the trainee may have also forgotten the specifics of the training, trainer behaviors, and aspects of the facilities by this time. Another problem is that the response rate may be considerably less as the respondents are no longer a captive part of the training environment.

Another approach is to provide reaction questionnaires after segments of a training program (e.g., after each day on a multiday training session). In such situations, it may be possible to modify training that's in progress on the basis of trainees' responses. Of course, this system is costlier and requires a quicker turnaround time for analysis and feedback of the data.

Regardless of how often reaction evaluation takes place, the trainer should specify at the beginning that trainees will be asked to evaluate the training and state when this will occur. Doing this not only helps to clarify trainee expectations about what will happen during training, but also acknowledges the organization's concern for how the trainees feel about the training they are receiving. It is important also that the data gathered be used. Trainees and the rest of the organization will quickly find out if you are simply gathering reactions to give the impression that you care about their reactions.

Figure 6.2 provides a list of steps to consider when developing a reaction questionnaire.

Caution in Using Reaction Measures   There is a caution regarding reaction questionnaires, particularly those that are provided some time after training with the express idea of determining the amount of training that transferred to the job. Research suggests that responses sent out some time after training tend to indicate transfer has occurred when other measures suggest it has not (Conroy and Ross 1984; Dixon 1990). Thus reaction measures should not be the only evaluation method used.

FIGURE 6.2 Steps to Consider in Developing a Reaction Questionnaire

1. Determine what you want to find out (consider training objectives).
2. Develop a written set of questions to obtain the information.
3. Develop a scale to quantify respondents' data.
4. Make forms anonymous so participants will feel free to respond honestly.
5. Ask for information that might be useful in determining differences in reactions by subgroups taking the training (e.g., young vs. old; minority vs. nonminority). This could be valuable in determining effectiveness of training by different cultures, for example, which may be lost in an overall assessment. Note: Care must be taken when asking for this information. If you ask too many questions about race, gender, age, tenure, etc., participants will begin to feel that they can be identified without their name on the questionnaire.
6. Allow space for "Additional Comments" in order to allow participants the opportunity to mention things you might not have considered.
7. Decide the best time to give the questionnaire to get the information you want.
   a. If right after training, have someone other than the instructor administer and pick up the information.
   b. If some time later, develop a mechanism for obtaining a high response rate (e.g., encourage the supervisor to allow trainees to complete the questionnaire on company time).

It is important to understand that reaction questionnaires are not likely to indicate how much is learned (Alliger et al. 1997). They do, however, provide the trainees with the opportunity to indicate how they felt about the learning. How interesting the training is will affect their level of attention and motivation. What the trainees perceive the trainer doing well and not so well is also useful feedback to the trainer. You can use this information to make decisions about modifications in the training program.

Learning

Learning objectives are developed from the TNA. The difference between the individual's KSAs and the KSAs required for acceptable job performance define the learning that must occur. The person analysis serves as the pretraining measure of the person's KSAs. This can be compared to a posttraining measure to determine if learning occurred and if any changes can be attributed to training. The various ways of making such attributions will be discussed later in the chapter. As we have noted, training can focus on three types of learning outcomes: knowledge, skills, and attitudes.

Knowledge Outcomes   Although we will focus primarily on **declarative knowledge,** it is important to remember that there are also two higher-level knowledge outcomes that training can focus on: procedural and strategic.

Declarative knowledge.   If the goal of the training was to impart some sort of factual knowledge—such as "rules covering search and seizure" or "understanding the type of question that cannot be asked in an interview"—a test can be developed to determine whether trainees have learned the knowledge. Paper-and-pencil tests are often used, one of which is the multiple-choice test. This type of test has many advantages. It is easy to administer and score and, when skillfully developed, accurately measures most declarative knowledge (Nunnally 1978). Some trainees may indicate they are not good at taking multiple-choice tests. However, evidence suggests that such tests consistently correlate highly with other forms of testing. A big advantage to multiple-choice tests is their reliability. Also, because of the number of questions you can ask, you can cover a broader range of the content than with other methods.

The major difficulty with this type of test is in the construction of the items; a complete discussion on how to write good multiple-choice questions is beyond the scope of this text, but some general rules to consider in constructing questions are found in Figure 6.3 (page 236). More comprehensive information can be found in Kropp and Hankin (1975). It may be wise to contact a local university and discuss the project with someone with the appropriate background. Even small companies with limited budgets should be able to obtain such help from a supervised graduate student anxious to get some real-world experience.

Procedural knowledge.   The second level of knowledge outcomes is **procedural knowledge.** Here the learner begins to develop meaningful ways of organizing information into mental models.[5] As was noted in chapter 4, experts develop more complex mental models for the way they organize their knowledge than do new learners, (Glaser and Chi 1989). As a result, the expert is able to access the solution strategy more quickly.

---

[5]Mental models are also known as cognitive maps, knowledge structures, and task schema.

1. Examine objectives to get a clear understanding of the content area you wish to test.
2. Write the questions in a clear manner. Shorter is better.
3. Try to choose alternatives to the correct response from typical errors made during training. Make alternatives realistic.
4. Do not consistently make the correct response longer than incorrect responses.
5. Four alternatives are usually enough. More than that takes longer to read, and it is difficult enough to write three reasonable alternatives.
6. Pretest items by giving the test to those expected to know the material. Ask them for feedback on clarity. Note any questions that many of them get wrong.
7. Give revised items to a group of fully trained (experienced) employees and a group of not trained (inexperienced) employees. The former should score very well and the later should do poorly.

FIGURE 6.3 Procedures for developing a multiple-choice test

Assessing the organization of procedural knowledge can be accomplished through a number of techniques (Flanagan 1990). The key to these testing methods is that they identify the way the trainee organizes concepts. One method uses paired comparisons to determine how the trainee sees the relationship between topics. For an example, trainees in a "train the trainer" course would be asked to indicate the relationships among a number of training concepts such as instructional design, criterion development, needs assessment, organizational analysis, and so on. Then these relationships would be compared with the relationships identified by an expert. Another method (see Figure 6.4) uses a configuration of concepts that are linked. Some of the links are blank, and the trainee must place the appropriate concepts in the blanks next to the ones it best fits with. Strategies for measuring these structures are too comprehensive to be discussed here, but for more information see Kraiger, Salas, and Cannon-Bowers (1995); Kraiger, Ford, and Salas (1993); Goldsmith, Johnson & Acton (1991); and Flanagan (1990).

Strategic knowledge. This category deals with the ability to develop and apply cognitive strategies used in problem solving. It assesses the level of understanding the trainee has about the decisions and/or choices she makes. Probed protocol analysis (Means and Gott 1988) is one assessment method. First, subject matter experts define a problem and the steps necessary to solve it. Trainees are then asked to explain step by step what they would do to solve the problem. Questions such as "Why would you do that?" "What would it mean if it did not help?" "What other test could you do?" help determine the trainees' strategies. For more information on this type of assessment, see Kraiger, Salas, and Cannon-Bowers (1995); Gill et al. (1988); and Means and Gott (1988).

One final note about cognitive (and other) tests. There is a common belief that a specific time limit needs to be given for a test. It is important to understand that speed tests provide different information than power tests (Ackerman and Humphreys

Below is a list of concepts related to road construction; use them to fill in the appropriate blank boxes in the map. Try to fill in the boxes so that related terms or concepts are clustered together. Concepts can be related because they occur at the same time, one is necessary for the other, or one leads to the other.

Each of the listed concepts is used only once. Note that some of the concepts have already been mapped for you.

CONCEPTS:

Asphalt Placement	Prime/Tack Coat	Striper
Compaction/Rolling	Rollers	Striping
Cut/Fill	Signage	Survey
Dump Truck	Site Access	Traffic
Hot Materials		

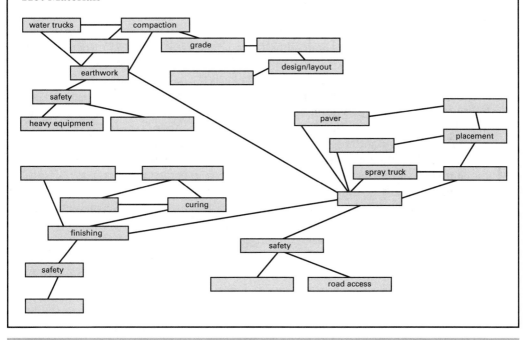

FIGURE 6.4 Test of Knowledge Organization for Civil Engineers

Source: Adapted from Hart, Kraiger, and Lamb 1996.

1990; Lord 1956). Speed tests should be given only if speed in retrieving and using information is an important job characteristic. If, however, the critical component is accuracy of retrieval and use, time limits should not be used.[6]

---

[6] It is the authors' experience, however, that in power tests some sort of time limit needs to be provided. If not, some will remain for twice the time of others to check and recheck their answers. A good approach is to indicate a general time limit (e.g., about one hour). When the time is up, ask, "How much time do you need to finish?" This is usually enough incentive for those who are simply reluctant to hand the test in.

Skill-Based Outcomes   Determining if a skill or set of behaviors has been learned is not the same as measuring whether they are used on the job. Obviously, if they are used on the job, they have been learned. However, they may be learned but not used on the job. Knowing that the skill was learned is important, particularly if it does not transfer to the job. You then know that it is a transfer of training issue, not a learning issue.

Two levels of skill acquisition are compilation (lower level) and automaticity (higher level). Most training focuses on providing the skill training at the lower level, hence evaluations tend to be at the compilation level.

Compilation.   If the training being evaluated was in swimming, it is obvious you would not give a paper-and-pencil test to determine the learning that occurred. Similarly, if you are training supervisors in interpersonal skills, a paper-and-pencil test could provide information regarding what the trainee understands about interpersonal skills, but it will not identify any interpersonal skills the trainee has.

Developing behavioral tests and standards for scoring such tests can be difficult. A number of situations need to be created in which the trainee is required to demonstrate the target skill(s). The difficulty lies in developing scoring standards. Consider the training of machinists examined by Gordon and Isenberg (1975). They noted that passing the training was more a function of the trainer running the course than of the trainees. Different trainers had different standards for passing.

To address this problem, a standardized method was needed to provide points based on criteria outlined in the training objectives. These criteria were based on tolerance requirements and finished specifications. Once these criteria were developed, trainers had clear standards from which to evaluate, and the trainer differences were eliminated. For certain skills (e.g., machining skills) a final product can be assessed by comparing what was produced to what was expected. For other skills, such as those required for conflict resolution, assessment could be done through a structured scenario in which a person acts in an angry and aggressive manner and the trainee responds using the skills taught. Using multiple raters and/or standardized forms are possibilities for scoring these types of tests. What is important in developing such tests is achieving interrater agreement. This is accomplished through standardized methods of rating that are clear to the trainer or whoever is required to conduct the testing.

Automaticity.   Skill-based training is generally evaluated at the compilation level. However, in some cases the skill must be so well learned that it can be done quickly and without much thought. For this level of skill, the evaluation would need to be much more stringent about what constitutes successful performance. One method for determining if automaticity had been reached would be a speed test in which performance had to be completed within a certain time. Emergency procedures for pilots would be an example.

Attitudes   As was noted earlier, attitudes are an important outcome of training. At the conclusion of training, it is useful to assess any changes in attitudes that were learning objectives. Numerous attitude scales are available through journals *(Personnel Psychology, Journal of Applied Psychology, Academy of Management)* and books *(Assessing Organizational Change, The Experience of Work, Boros Book of Mental Measurements)*. Developing attitude scales requires care, and you should use existing scales when possible rather than attempting to develop one. However, you may need to reword items in the survey to reflect your unique needs.

Assessing true attitude change is difficult. The primary assessment tool is a pre/post measure of responses on an attitude scale. A scale measuring "attitude toward empowerment" is depicted in Figure 6.5. A comparison of responses before and after training that indicated an increase in positive attitude toward empowerment would suggest successful training. However, there are doubts about such self-report measures, particularly if the trainees are identified. For example, the new employee might see the wisdom in hiding his dislike of team-based work after a concentrated orientation espousing the value of teams. Going to great lengths to assure respondents of their anonymity helps to ensure honesty in trainee self-reports.

Timing of Assessment of Learning   Depending on how long the training is, it might be worth assessing learning periodically throughout training, to determine how trainees are progressing. Training may need to be modified if learning is not progressing as expected.

Assessment should also take place immediately after training. If learning is not evaluated until sometime later, it is impossible to know how much was learned and

FIGURE 6.5 Example of an Attitudinal Measure

Attitudes Toward Empowerment

Please indicate the degree to which you agree or disagree with the following statements.

1 = Strongly disagree
2 = Disagree
3 = Neither agree nor disagree
4 = Agree
5 = Strongly agree

1. Empowering employees is just another way to get more work done with fewer people. (reverse scored)	1	2	3	4	5
2. Empowering of employees allows everyone to contribute their ideas to the betterment of the company.	1	2	3	4	5
3. The empowerment program has improved my relationship with my supervisor.	1	2	3	4	5
4. Empowerment has brought more meaning to my life at this company.	1	2	3	4	5
5. Empowerment interventions should be introduced in other plants in this company.	1	2	3	4	5
6. The empowerment process has been a positive influence in labor-management relations.	1	2	3	4	5

forgotten. In the Palm Desert case, the measures they took six months after training created a dilemma. Was the behavior ever learned, learned but forgotten, or was it learned but not transferred to the job?

Job Behavior Data

Once it has been determined that learning has taken place, the next step is to determine whether the training has transferred to the job. Assessment at this step is certainly more complex and is often ignored because of the difficulties of measurement.

There are a number of ways to assess job behavior. These were covered in depth in the Training Needs Analysis chapter and, in fact, the instrument used in the needs assessment should serve well as the posttest evaluation tool. The primary sources of data are interviews, questionnaires, direct observation, and archival records of performance. Questionnaires are often preferred, for several reasons:

- Opinions can be obtained about specific behaviors from a large number of employees.
- The information can be tabulated to yield a numerical response.
- Respondents are anonymous, so it is more likely that they will be honest.
- A relatively short amount of time is required to gather the data.

Because this is such a common method of evaluation, it is important to understand how to develop effective questionnaires. Figure 6.6 provides some guidelines.

Performance appraisals can also be used to document job and performance changes. As was noted in the needs analysis chapter, one very useful technique is the 360-degree performance review. If this is done on a regular basis, employees who go through training can be assessed by examining changes in their 360-degree feedback. Table 6.4 (page 242) provides the results for an individual at a large U.S. corporation. Note the discrepancy in some of the dimensions. After training, if the behavior transfers to the job, the perceptions for certain dimensions should improve as rated by others. Furthermore, if training was also designed to provide some self-analysis of the trainee's interpersonal relationship skills, the trainee's self-evaluation may go down following training.

Scripted Situations   Some recent research indicates that scripted situations may provide a better format for evaluating transfer of training than the more traditional behavioral questionnaires (Ostroff 1991). Scripted situations help the rater to recall actual situations and the behaviors related to them rather than attempting to recall specific behaviors without the context provided. The rater is provided with a number of responses that might be elicited from the script and is asked to choose the one that describes the ratee's behavior. Research suggests that this method is useful in decreasing rating errors and improving validity (Bernardin and Carlyle 1979; King, Hunter, and Schmidt 1980). An example of this method is depicted in Figure 6.7 (on page 242). As with the forced choice method of performance appraisal (Sisson 1948), it is difficult to determine which of the responses is correct. Although this is one of the reasons it is not popular as a performance appraisal tool (supervisors do not know what "good" means), in evaluating training this concern may not be as important.

Finally, if the trainer is involved in coaching some time after training, she can observe on-the-job performance of the trainee. As was discussed in the previous chapter, these sit-ins facilitate transfer (Stark 1986) and also help the trainer determine how effective the training has been in facilitating the transfer of training to the job.

1. Write simply and clearly, and make the meaning obvious.
   Bad: To what extent do supervisors provide information regarding the quality of performance of people at your level?
   Good: How often does your boss give you feedback on your job?

2. Ask one question at a time.
   Bad: Both the organization's goals and my role within the organization are clear.
   Good: The organization's goals are clear.
   My role within the organization is clear.

3. Provide discrete response options.
   Bad: During the past three months how often did you receive feedback on your work?

1	2	3	4	5
rarely		occasionally		frequently

   Good: During the past three months how often did you receive feedback on your work?

1	2	3	4	5
not once	1–3 times	about once a week	more than once a week	once a day or more

4. Limit the number of response options.
   Bad: What percentage of the time are you sure of what your compensation will be?

1	2	3	4	5	6	7	8	9	10
0–10%	11–20%	21–30%	31–40%	41–50%	51–60%	61–70%	71–80%	81–90%	91–100%

   Good: What percentage of the time are you sure of what your compensation will be?

1	2	3	4	5
0–20%	21–40%	41–60%	61–80%	81–100%

5. Match the response mode to the question.
   Bad: To what extent are you satisfied with your job?

1	2	3	4	5
strongly disagree	disagree		agree	strongly agree

   Good: To what extent are you satisfied with your job?

1	2	3	4	5
not at all	a little bit		quite a lot	very much

FIGURE 6.6 Guidelines for Writing Effective Questionnaires

TABLE 6.4   Example of 360-Degree Feedback Results

Skills Being Assessed	Very Low	Low	Average	High	Very High
Listening Skills		S	P, B	E	
Managing Conflict			S	P, B	E
Organizing			S, P	B, E	
Written Communication			S, P	B	E

S = Subordinates
P = Peers
B = Supervisor
E = Employee being assessed

Attitudes   If attitudinal change was a goal of training, you should attempt to assess how successful you were in having the attitudinal change remain once the trainee is back on the job. Assessing such attitudinal change can be accomplished through attitude surveys as discussed earlier. The same instruments used in the needs analysis and learning assessment can be used. If respondents' anonymity is ensured in such surveys, true attitudes are more likely to be reflected in the responses.

A study by Thacker and Fields (1992) of steward training provides an example of the assessment of an attitude back on the job. Training was designed to make union stewards more accessible to the rank and file by teaching them listening skills and how to interact more with the rank and file. Results indicated that when controlling for factors such as tenure as a union official and age, stewards who had received the training behaved in a more participative manner (as reported by the rank and file) and were more loyal (an attitude) to the union (self-report on a measure of union commitment). For the union, the attitude "loyalty" was as important as the behavior. Loyalty will translate into many important behaviors that might not be directly measurable, such as supporting the union's political candidates and attending union functions (Thacker, Fields, and Barclay 1990).

Timing of Job Behavior Assessment   How long you wait before assessing transfer of training depends on the training objectives. If the goal was to learn how to com-

FIGURE 6.7 Scripted Situation Item for Evaluation of a School Superintendent

The administrator receives a letter from a parent objecting to the content of the science section on reproduction. The parent strongly objects to his daughter having exposure to such materials and demands something be done. The administrator would most likely: (check one)

____ Ask the teacher to provide handouts, materials, and curriculum content for review.

____ Check the science curriculum for the board-approved approach to reproduction, and compare board guidelines to course content.

____ Ask the head of the science department for his or her opinion about the teacher's lesson plan.

____ Check to see if the parent has made similar complaints in the past.

plete certain forms, simply auditing the work on the job (pre- and posttraining) would determine if transfer had taken place. This could be evaluated rather soon after training. When learning requires more complex behavior such as problem solving or conflict resolution skills, it might take longer for the trainee to become comfortable enough with the new behavior to exhibit it on a regular basis, and longer to have others notice that the behavior has changed.

To understand this point, consider a more concrete change. Jack loses 20 pounds. First the weight loss is gradual and often goes unnoticed. Even after Jack has lost the weight, for some time people will say, "Gee, haven't you lost weight?" or "What is it that's different about you?" If this happens with a concrete visual stimuli, imagine what happens when the stimuli is less concrete and not consistent. Some types of behavioral change may take a long time to be noticed.

The training objectives should have identified the point in time at which co-workers should notice the change in behavior. Specifically asking them to assess if certain behaviors have changed makes it more likely they will notice the change. In our example, if you were asked "Did Jack lose weight?" and he had lost 20 pounds, you would more than likely notice it then, even if you had not noticed it before.

Organizational Results

The objectives of training, whether proactive or reactive, are developed to solve an organizational problem—perhaps an expected increase in demand for new customer services (proactive) or too many grievances (reactive). The fact that a problem was identified (too many grievances) indicates you had a measurement of the "organizational result." This measurement would be used to determine if there has been a change after training has been completed. Thus if it was initially determined that too many defective parts were being produced (low quality), the measurement used (number of defective parts per 100 produced) would be used again after training to assess if training was successful. This is your *organizational result.*

It is important to assess this final level, because it is the reason for doing the training in the first place. In one sense, it is easier to measure this than job behavior. Did the grievances go down? Did quality go up? Did customer satisfaction go up? Did attitudes in the annual survey get more positive? Did subordinates' satisfaction with supervision improve? Such questions are relatively easily answered. The difficult question is "Did it change because of the training?" The grievance rate may have dropped because of a successful completion of negotiations and not the training given to supervisors in how to implement the contract. Or if attitudes toward supervision were improved but everyone had just received a large bonus, the improvement might be spill-off from the bonus and not the training. This is why it is so important to gather information on all levels of the evaluation.

The links between organizational results, job behavior, and trainee KSAs should have been clearly articulated in the TNA. In this way a model is created that specifies that if certain KSAs are developed and the employees use them on the job, certain organizational results will occur. If these things happen, the model has been validated and there is some confidence that training caused these results. Thus the difficult task of specifying how training should affect the results of the organization should have already been delineated before evaluation begins. Because TNAs are not always as thorough as they should be, it often falls on the evaluator to clarify the relationship among training, learning, job behavior, and organizational outcomes. For this reason, it is probably best to focus on organizational results as close to the trainee's work unit as possible. Results such as increased work unit productivity and quality, and decreased costs, are more appropriate than increased organizational profitability, market share, and the like. Quantifying these organizational results is not as onerous as it might seem at first glance.

Timing of Assessment of Organizational Results   Consistent tracking of the organizational performance deficiencies (e.g., high scrap, number of grievances, poor quality) should take place at intervals throughout the training and beyond. At some point after the behavior is transferred to the job, you should expect improvement. Consistently tracking the performance deficiencies in the organization allows a determination of when or if this occurs.

Relationship among Levels of Outcomes

An examination of research on Kirkpatrick's outcome hierarchy concept—reaction, learning, behavior, and organizational results—shows mixed results. For example, some studies show reaction and learning outcomes to be strongly related to each other (e.g., Clement 1982). Others have indicated there is little correlation between results of reaction questionnaires and measures of learning of material (e.g., Dixon 1990). In general the findings indicate that the more removed from the actual training the outcome is, the smaller the relationship between higher- and lower-level outcomes. Figure 6.8 illustrates the hierarchical nature of the outcomes and the factors that can influence these outcomes.

The research findings make sense if one remembers that organizational outcomes generally have multiple causes. For example, productivity is affected not only by the KSAs of the employees, but also by the technology they work with, supplier reliability, interdependencies among work groups, and many other factors. Thus, while improve-

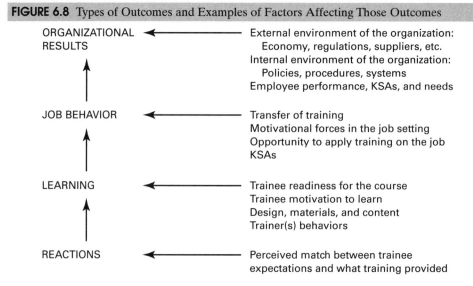

FIGURE 6.8 Types of Outcomes and Examples of Factors Affecting Those Outcomes

ORGANIZATIONAL RESULTS ◄——————— External environment of the organization:
    Economy, regulations, suppliers, etc.
Internal environment of the organization:
    Policies, procedures, systems
Employee performance, KSAs, and needs

JOB BEHAVIOR ◄——————— Transfer of training
Motivational forces in the job setting
Opportunity to apply training on the job
KSAs

LEARNING ◄——————— Trainee readiness for the course
Trainee motivation to learn
Design, materials, and content
Trainer(s) behaviors

REACTIONS ◄——————— Perceived match between trainee
expectations and what training provided

ments can occur in one area, declines can occur in another. When learning has taken place but does not transfer to the job, the issues to be concerned with are not learning, but transfer issues. What structural constraints are being placed on trainees so they do not behave appropriately? Geber (1995) describes a situation in which training in communication skills at Hutchinson Technologies, a computer component manufacturer, was not transferring to the job for some of the employees. An examination of the issue (through focus groups of workers) disclosed that some employees were required to work in cramped space with poor lighting. These conditions made them irritable and unhappy. Did this situation affect their ability to communicate to their customers in a pleasant and upbeat manner? "You bet," said their human resource representative.

Evaluating the Costs of Training

Looking at the outcomes of training is only half the battle in evaluating its effectiveness. The other half is determining if the results were worth the cost. If grievances do go down, and if the new behaviors have been exhibited and the skills have been learned, then training might be considered the cause of the reduction.[7] But many managers today might say, "So what? Was the training cost worth it?" In other words, did the benefits related to the reduction in grievances outweigh the training costs incurred? Training in Action 6.2 (page 246) shows how one training director approached this question.

There are two ways of answering the "is the training worth it" question: cost/benefit evaluation and cost-effectiveness evaluation (Cascio 1991). Some argue that the labor peace brought about by the reduction in grievances is difficult to assess but has a very high value in comparison to the cost of training. This is a **cost/benefit evaluation** because it compares the monetary costs of training to nonmonetary benefits such as attitudes and relationships. While cost/benefit analysis is important, it is possible to assess the reduction in grievances in a way that directly answers the cost-effectiveness question. **Cost-effectiveness evaluation** compares the monetary costs of training to the financial benefits accrued from training. Two ways of assessing this are calculation of the actual cost savings (based on the change in "results") and utility analysis, which examines the value of overall improvement in performance of the trained employees. The **cost savings analysis** only looks at the financial value of improvement in the problem that training was intended to correct (e.g., reduction in labor grievances). **Utility analysis** looks at all the ways in which the trainee's improved job performance will financially benefit the organization (e.g., reduced grievances, improved relations with labor force, less turnover, and so on).

Cost Savings Analysis (Results Focus). Table 6.5 (page 247) lists the common types of costs associated with training programs. These costs are compared to the savings that are realized as a direct result of improvements in the organizational problem training was designed to address. Let's look at an example.

A particular company has an average of 90 grievances a year. Seventy percent of these (63) go to the third step before settlement. The average time required by management (including HR managers, operational supervisors, etc. to deal with a grievance that goes to the third step is 10 hours. The management wages ($50 per hour on

---

[7] It is important to understand that you can never be absolutely sure of cause and effect. The examination of all four levels of evaluation provide evidence of the cause/effect, and appropriate designs (to be discussed later) enhance the level of confidence in cause/effect, but you are never absolutely sure.

| Training in Action 6.2 |

Evaluating Training at Walgreen Co.

The Walgreen Co. in Deerfield, Illinois, provides pharmacy technicians to help pharmacists behind the counter in drugstores. Pharmacy technicians are support people who interact with customers and take refill information over the phone from doctors. They are also expected to determine if generic drugs could be substituted for brand names and, if so, to ask customers if they would like the generic drug.

The pharmacists who hired the technicians were responsible for all the training—That is, until Ann Marie Laures, corporate manager for Walgreen's training department, decided that a course for these technicians might be useful. Her department designed and implemented a training package that involved 20 hours of classroom training and 20 hours of closely supervised on-the-job training. Because Walgreen has 2000 drugstores, this training would be costly, so Ann decided to determine how effective the training was.

She devised a questionnaire that asked questions such as: How speedily did the technician enter the data into the computer? How often did the technician interrupt the pharmacist with a question? How often did the technician offer generic drugs when applicable? She sent these questionnaires to pharmacists who employed some technicians who had received the training and others who had been trained in the traditional way.

In almost all cases she found that the formally trained were more efficient and wasted less time than the traditional on-the-job trained technicians. The behavior of formally trained technicians was better in all respects. She went further, however, and assessed the organizational results as well. She discovered that sales in pharmacies with formally trained technicians exceeded those where technicians were trained in the traditional manner by $9,500 annually. The cost of training was $273 per employee, which suggests the formal training was a good decision.

Source: Adapted from Geber 1995.

---

average) add $500 to the cost of each grievance ($50 × 10). In addition, union representatives spend an average of 7.5 hours at $25 per hour ($187.50) for those grievances, wages that are considered paid time as stipulated in the collective agreement. The total cost of wages to the company per grievance is $687.50. Thus the total cost for those 63 grievances that go to the third step is $43,312.50. As Table 6.6 (page 248) shows, training would cost $32,070. In the first year, the number of grievances dropped by 50%, and only eight of those went to the third step. Was training worth it? The drop in grievances suggests it was. This drop should be coupled with a more positive relationship with the union and rank and file, a benefit some would say is value enough. But the figures also indicate that the training was worth more than its cost.

TABLE 6.5   Types of Costs in Training Programs

Development Costs

All costs related to the development of the program are included, plus the cost (or proportion) of any front-end TNA and of evaluation and results tracking. The cost of all program and materials design, any computer-based programming, and any piloting of the training are also included. These costs can be amortized over the life of the program (if it is planned for more than one year) to prevent overly high costs in the first year.

Direct Costs

These are costs directly attributable to the delivery of the training program. The criteria for inclusion in this category is that if training were cancelled the day before it was to begin, the cost would not be incurred. Thus travel, materials (that could be used in the future), facilities/food and beverage (unless there is a cancellation charge), equipment rental, trainer compensation, etc. are included.

Indirect Costs

This consists of any nondevelopment item that would be incurred even if training were cancelled the day before it was to start. It would include trainer compensation for preparation, materials purchase/duplication (if not usable in the future), marketing expenses, administrative and clerical support (compensation rate for time spent on project), and any materials already sent to trainees.

Overhead Costs

These reflect the program's share of the general operating costs of the training and development department (or the business, depending on the size and nature of the organization). For a large organization with its own training department, these costs would include the program's share of the purchase and maintenance of training equipment, clerical and administrative support, training facilities, etc. For a small business that purchases the training externally, there are probably no overhead costs. On the other hand, if a training and consulting firm has developed a workshop for a client, the overhead would be considered to be the workshop's share of the normal operating expenses of the firm. Often this is calculated as a portion of revenue generated or as a fixed charge per day of training.

Participant Compensation

While participants are attending training, their salaries and benefits should be included as a cost of training. Another way to approach this is to include only the cost of replacing those employees while they are in training. Thus for a management training program lasting three days, these managers may not be replaced; other managers may be asked to assist the work unit in routine matters, and the manager attending training is expected to handle everything else outside of training time. In these cases there is no participant compensation cost because there was no organizational cost for replacing the trainee. There is, however, an opportunity cost because there are many things that didn't get done that could have gotten done if the manager were doing his regular job. There are legitimate arguments for and against including the participant compensation costs in these cases. Most organizations will have a policy on the matter.

Sixty-three grievances cost $43,312.50 prior to the training, and the eight grievances after training cost $5,500. Thus training reduced the cost of grievances by $37,812.50. Subtracting the $32,070 training costs from this leaves a savings to the organization of $5,742.50, and this is just the first year. You will note that this would be a conservative estimate, because the cost of materials, facilities, and other overhead is not included in the cost of grievances.

TABLE 6.6 Training Costs for Grievance Reduction Training	
Developmental Costs	
1. 20 days of director's time at $50,000 per year	$ 4,000
2. 5 days of trainer's time at $30,000 per year	$ 600
3. Materials	$ 1,000
Implementation Costs	
1. 5 days of trainer's time at $30,000 per year	$ 600
2. Training facility rental 5 days at $150 per day	$ 750
3. Materials and equipment	$ 2,000
4. Coffee, juice, and muffins	$ 600
5. 30 supervisors attending 5-day workshop (Average $35,000/yr.)	$21,000
Evaluation Costs	
1. 6 days of evaluator's time at $30,000 per year	$ 720
2. Materials	$ 800
Total Training Costs	$32,070

The cost-effectiveness data show that there is a $37,812.50 return on a $32,070 investment. Dividing the return by the investment produces a return-on-investment ratio of 1.179. If the ratio is exactly 1.0, the training broke even. If it is below that, it cost more than it brings back to the company. In this case we have calculated a 17.9% return on investment for the first year. Most companies would be delighted if all their investments achieved this level of return. In addition, are the nonmonetary benefits described earlier. Presenting this type of data to the corporate decision makers at budget preparation time is certainly more compelling than stating, "Thirty supervisors were given a five-day grievance reduction workshop."

Many training departments are beginning to see the importance of placing a monetary value on their training. Geber (1995) provides a number of reasons for this:

- HRD budgets are more easily justified and even expanded when HR can demonstrate it is contributing to the profit.
- There is a better commitment by trainees and their managers who become responsible for follow-up information related to return-on-investment information.
- HRD specialists are more successful in containing costs.
- Showing dollar value for training improves the image of the training department.

Training in Action 6.3 tells the story of Alberta Bell, where demonstrating the value of the training not only restored the original training, but also caused management to consider increasing it.

Because of the time and effort required to calculate the value of training, many small business managers simply do not do it. However, assessing the value of training is not an exact science and can be done more easily by means of estimates. Table 6.7 (page 250) provides a simplified approach. In his discussion of the process, Hassett

---

Training in Action 6.3

Reduction in Training Time: The Value of Demonstrating Value

Telephone company Alberta Bell of Edmonton, Alberta, was looking for ways of reducing the cost of its operations. Downsizing and cost cutting were necessary to meet the new competitive environment. One of the decisions was to reduce the entry-level training program for their customer service representatives. The two-week program was cut to one week. This would save a great deal of money by reducing the cost of training and getting service representatives out "earning their keep" earlier.

Rudy, the manager of training at Alberta Bell, wanted to assess the value of this decision. By gathering information from data already available, he calculated the average time necessary to complete a service call for those who had attended the two-week training and compared it with the average for those attending the one-week program. Those from the two-week program completed a call on average in 11.4 minutes. Those in the one-week program took 14.5 minutes. This alone represented $50,000 in lost productivity for the first six weeks of work. He further analyzed the differences in increased errors, increased collectables, and service order errors. This difference was calculated at more than $50,000. The total loss exceeded $100,000.

He presented this information to upper management. Management quickly restored the two-week training program and is considering making it longer.

Source: Adapted from Fitz-Enz 1994.

(1992) suggests that when estimates are necessary, it is useful to obtain them from those who will receive the report (usually top management). If you use their estimates, it is more likely that your final report will have credibility. Of course, larger organizations can also use this method.

Utility Analysis   In our example above, training supervisors in grievance handling reduced the total number of grievances by 50% and the number going to the third step from 63 to 8. We calculated only the cost savings of the change in third-step grievances. Utility analysis permits us to estimate the overall value to the organization of the supervisors' changes in behavior. In other words, if those trained, on average, are better performers, and better performers are worth more in dollar terms, utility analysis allows us to estimate that increased worth. A general approach to utility (Cascio 1991) is presented below:

$$\Delta U = (N)(T)(D_T)(SD_Y) - C$$

where

ΔU = dollar value of improved performance
N = number of trainees
T = time the benefits will last

D_T = difference in performance between trained and untrained groups (in standard deviation units)

SD_Y = dollar value of untrained group's performance (in standard deviation units)

C = total cost of training the trained group

Some of the variables in the equation can be directly measured whereas others must

---

TABLE 6.7 Training Investment Analysis Work Sheet

Objective:_____

Audience:_____

Returns measured over:_____ One year:_____ Other:_____

Part 1: Calculating the Revenue Produced by Training

Option A — Itemized Analysis

Increased sales:	_____	Additional sales per employee
	× _____	Revenues (or margin) per sale
	× _____	Number of employees
	= _____	Revenue Produced by Training
Higher productivity:	_____	Percent increase in productivity
	× _____	Cost per employee (salary plus benefits plus overhead)
	× _____	Number of employees
	= _____	Revenue Produced by Training
Reduced errors:	_____	Average cost per error
	× _____	Number of errors avoided per employee
	× _____	Number of employees
	= _____	Revenue Produced by Training
Client retention:	× _____	Average revenue per client
	_____	Number of clients retained
	= _____	Revenue Produced by Training
Employee retention:	_____	Average cost of a new employee (training plus lost productivity)
	× _____	Number of employees retained
	= _____	Revenue Produced by Training

Other: _____ _____

Total Revenue Produced by Training: $_____

Option B — Summary Analysis

_____ − _____ = _____

Revenue After Training	Revenue Without Training	Revenue Produced by Training

Part 2: Calculating the Return

_____ − _____ = _____

Revenue Produced by Training	Cost of Training	Total Return on Training Investment

Source: Adapted from Hassett 1992.

be estimated. For example, N, C, and D_T can be objectively determined. On the other hand, determining how long the benefits will last is really an estimate, which will be more or less accurate depending on the amount of experience the person has with training, the types of employees involved, and so on. Calculating the dollar value of the untrained group's performance falls somewhere between. It is relatively easy, for example, to determine the compensation costs. However, it is often more difficult to translate their actual performance into dollar amounts. Recall our third-step grievance example. While we know what a third-step grievance costs in management/labor compensation, we don't know the impact of those third-step grievances on the productivity of the work unit or the quality of the product/service. Thus, what is included in determining the dollar value of performance becomes a subjective decision. The final result will be an estimate of the value of the increased performance in dollars. Using the same example, an analysis of the possible utility is presented in Table 6.8.

Utility analysis is complex and beyond the scope of this text; what has been presented here is just a taste of the complexity. Cascio (1989) has developed more complicated models that account for even more factors that may affect the true financial value of training outcomes. Our purpose here is to demonstrate the difficulties of getting a true picture of the financial benefits associated with training outcomes. However, these complexities exist for any area of the business when you try to determine the effects of change. By becoming more quantitative in the assessment and description of training outcomes, training managers can put themselves on an equal footing with the other managers in the organization.

TABLE 6.8 Calculation of the Utility of the Grievance Training

Formula:	$\Delta U = (N)(T)(D_T)(SD_Y) - C$
$N = 30$	
$T = 1$ year	This is probably an overly conservative estimate
$D_T = .2$	$D_T = \dfrac{Xt - Xu}{SD\,(r\,yy)}$
	Xt = average job performance of the trained supervisors
	Xu = average job performance of the untrained supervisors
	SD = standard deviation of job performance for the untrained supervisors
	$r\,yy$ = reliability of job performance measure
	D_T is a measure of the improvement (in standard deviation units) in performance that trained supervisors will exhibit. Although obtaining the data is time-consuming (you need the performance appraisal data for supervisors, trained and untrained), the calculations can be done easily on today's computers.
$SD_Y = \$14,000$	$.40 \times \$35,000 = \$14,000$
	We used the 40% rule here: The calculation is based on 40% of the average salary of trainees (Schmidt and Hunter 1983). This and other methods to calculate SD_Y can be found in Cascio (1991).

The utility of the training based on this formula is

$30 \times 1 \times .2 \times 14,000 - 32,020 = \$51,980$

When to Use It

For whom is the outcome data? The different levels of outcome evaluation are designed for different constituencies or customers. Note in Table 6.9 that the trainer is interested in the first three levels, because they reflect most directly on her training. Other trainers may be interested in these data as well if the results have some relation to their training programs. Training managers are interested in all the information. Both reaction and learning data can be used to evaluate the trainer and also promote the program to others (when positive). When it is not positive, the training manager should be aware of this fact, because it gives him the information to intervene and turn the program around. The training manager's interest in transfer of training is to evaluate the trainer's ability to promote the transfer. Care has to be taken in using this information, because there may be many other factors operating to prevent transfer. Also, if transfer is favorable, the information is valuable in promoting the training program. This is also true for the organizational results. If the training manager is able to demonstrate positive results affecting the financial health of the company, the training department is bound to be seen as a worthy part of the organization.

Trainees are interested in seeing if others felt the same as they did in training. They are also interested in feedback on what they accomplished (learning) as well as how useful it has been to all trainees back on the job (behavior). A trainee's supervisor is interested in behavior and results, the main reason for sending subordinates to training in the first place. Upper management is interested in the results, although in some cases, where results may not be forthcoming, behavior may be the focus.

Does the interest in different levels by different customers mean you need to gather information at all levels every time? Not at all. First, a considerable amount of work is required to do this for every program offered. As with process data, it makes sense to gather the outcome data in some situations and not in others.

There is another consideration in gathering outcome data, however. Is the customer interested in the information? Although one of the major arguments for gathering the outcome data is to demonstrate the worth of the training department, some organizations have gone beyond that idea. In an examination of what she called "companies with the best training evaluation practices," Dixon (1996) noted that none of these companies (IBM, Motorola, Arthur Anderson, etc.) were evaluating training

TABLE 6.9   Who Is Interested in the Outcome Data

	Outcome Data			
	Reaction	**Learning**	**Behavior**	**Results**
Training Department				
Trainer	yes	yes	yes	no
Other Trainers	perhaps	perhaps	perhaps	no
Training Manager	yes	yes	yes	yes
Customers				
Trainees	yes	yes	yes	perhaps
Trainees' Supervisor	not really	only if no transfer	yes	yes
Upper Management	no	no	perhaps	yes

Source: Adapted from Camp, Blanchard, and Huszczo 1986.

primarily to justify it or maintain a training budget. They evaluated (particularly at the behavior and results levels) when requested to do so by the customer (top management or the particular department). This selectivity is a function of the cost in developing such evaluations. Dixon suggests that behavior and results evaluations:

- Need to be customized for each situation
- Are costly and time consuming
- Require cooperation of the customer

So, Arthur Anderson, for example, collects "results" only about 10% of the time (Dixon 1996). Motorola, on the other hand, evaluates only at the behavior level, not the results level. Executives at Motorola are willing to assume that if the employee is exhibiting the appropriate behavior, there will be a positive effect on the bottom line (Geber 1995). Training in Action 6.4 (page 254) shows how various companies are dealing with evaluation, particularly behavior and results.

Certainly all levels of data gathering are important at different times, and the training professional must be able to conduct an evaluation at every level. So when and what should you evaluate? The answer is that it depends on the organization and the attitudes and beliefs of upper management. If they perceive the training department as an effective tool of the organization and require only behavior-level evaluation, that is what you do. However, this may still require vigilance at the learning and reaction levels to ensure positive results. Darryl Jinkerson, director of evaluation services at Arthur Anderson, looks at the size and impact of the training before deciding how to evaluate it. Only those that are high profile, or where the customer requests it, will be evaluated at the results level (Geber 1995). What if training is a one-time event and there is no desire to assess individual competence (e.g., a workshop on managing your career)? Here there is simply no reason to evaluate (Sackett and Mullen 1993).

Evaluation: The Validity Issue

Once the decision to evaluate training has been made, the evaluator must become familiar with a number of issues beyond the criterion issue discussed in chapter 4. You want to be reasonably sure your findings on the effectiveness of training will be valid. After all, evaluation is both time-consuming and costly.

Let's say Sue is sent to a one-week training seminar on the operation of Windows. According to the needs analysis, she clearly did not know much about how to operate a computer in a Windows environment. After training, she is tested and it is determined she has learned a great deal. Training was effective. Perhaps—but there could also be a number of other factors that resulted in her learning how to operate in a Windows environment. She might have become interested in Windows and learned it on her own. The question is, how sure are you that the improvement was a function of the training you provided, that is, that there was *internal validity*? Once you are sure about the internal validity, how sure are you that the training will be effective for other groups who go through the same training, that is, that there is *external validity*?

We will deal with internal and external validity separately. You should be aware that these "threats" are not specific to training evaluation but relate to evaluation in general. When we discuss each of the threats, therefore, we will indicate when it is not a serious threat in the training context.

Evaluation: What Companies Are Doing

Arthur Anderson and Co. uses reaction measures for all its training. Learning is assessed about half the time, behavior less than one-third of the time, and results only 10% of the time. The "results" are evaluated only for high-profile training or where the customer requests evaluation. In one of the executive training programs for presentation skills, videotaped presentations were used to evaluate both learning and behavior. Executives were videotaped giving a presentation. This exercise served as the needs analysis to identify candidates for training. It also served as the pretest for evaluation. After the training, they were videotaped again to determine if learning took place. Six months later the executives were once again videotaped while making a presentation to a client. To measure improvement, the evaluators identified a number of the elements of a good presentation. Making good eye contact, not using nonwords *(uh, um)*, and even the type or frequency of hand movement were quantified as a means of measurement (Geber 1995).

Motorola developed a 360-degree performance appraisal process that they used as their behavior measure of leadership skills. The appraisal form is sent to the supervisors, their subordinates, and their bosses four times a year for two years, asking them to rate how frequently the supervisors display certain behaviors related to the leadership training (Geber 1995).

Texas Instruments noted that once trainees left training, it was difficult to obtain transfer of training information from them. Because of the time and expense of gathering this information, it was generally ignored. Then an automated e-mail system was developed through which trainees, after being back on the job for 90 days, were contacted and asked to complete a survey related to transfer. This system has increased the use of evaluations, reduced the time necessary to gather information, and provided a standardized process. Texas Instruments said they had already noted an improvement in the quantity and quality of participant feedback. It would seem easy enough to include an e-mail call to the trainees' supervisors for the same purpose (Overmyer-Day and Benson 1996).

FPL Nuclear uses testing to assess learning. First, however, the test serves as the needs analysis to determine who needs the training. Second, it is used as a posttest to be compared to the pretest in assessing learning. Finally the test is administered a few months after training to assess the degree of retention. If trainees do not do well on the retention test, they are provided with refresher training (Dixon 1996).

THREATS TO INTERNAL VALIDITY

Internal validity refers to the confidence you have that the results of the evaluation are in fact correct. Even when an improvement is demonstrated after training, the concern is that the change may have been for reasons other than training. To address this problem, you need to examine factors that might compromise your findings. These are called threats to internal validity.

History

History refers to the events other than training that take place concurrently with the training program. The argument is that those events could have caused learning to occur. Consider the example of Sue's computer training. Sue is very anxious to learn about computers so she buys some books and works extra hard at home, as well as attending the training. At the end of training she demonstrates she has learned a great deal, but is this learning a function of training? It might just as well be that all her hard work at home caused her to learn so much.

On a half-day training seminar, is history likely to be a concern? Not really. What about a one-day seminar or a one-week seminar? The more that training is spread across time, the more likely history could be a factor in the learning that takes place.

Maturation

Maturation refers to changes that occur because of the passage of time (e.g., growing older, hungrier, fatigued, bored). If Sue's one-week training program was so intense that she became tired, when it came time to take the posttest, her performance would not reflect how much she learned. Making sure the testing is done when the trainees are fresh would eliminate this threat. Other maturation threats can usually be handled in a similar manner, by being sure that training and testing are not so intense as to create physical or mental fatigue.

Testing

What is the influence of the pretest on learning? Suppose the pretest and posttest of KSAs were the same test. The questions on the pretest could sensitize trainees to pay particular attention to certain issues. Furthermore, the questions might generate interest, and the trainees might later discuss many of them and work out the answers before or during training. Thus learning demonstrated in the posttest may be a function not of the training but of the pretest. In Sue's case, the needs analysis, which served as the pretest for evaluation, got her thinking about all the material contained in the test. These were the issues she focused on in training. This presents less of a validity problem if pretests are given in every case and if they are comprehensive enough to cover all the material taught. Comprehensive testing will also make it difficult for trainees to recall specific questions.

Instrumentation

The problem arising if the same test is used in pretest and posttest has been noted above. If a different but equivalent test is used, however, the question is "Is it really equivalent?" Differences in the tests used could cause differences in the two scores. Also, if the rating requires judgments, the differences between pre- and posttest scores could be a function of different people doing the rating.

For Sue, the posttest was more difficult than the pretest, and even though she learned a great deal in the computer training, her posttest score was actually lower than the pretest, suggesting she did not learn anything. If the test items for both tests were chosen randomly from a large population of items, this would not be as much of a concern. For behavioral tests where raters make subjective decisions, this discrepancy may be more of a concern, but careful criteria development can help to deal with it.

Statistical Regression

There is a tendency for those who score either very high or very low on a test to "regress to the middle" when taking the test again. This phenomenon, known as *regression to the mean,* occurs because no test is perfect and there are differences as a function of measurement error. Those who are going to training will, by definition, have low scores for the KSAs to be covered in training and so will score very low on their pretest. The tendency, therefore, will be for them to regress to the mean and improve their scores, irrespective of training. In the earlier example, Sue did not know much about computers. Imagine she got all the questions on the pretest wrong. The likelihood of that happening twice is very low, so on another test she is bound to do better.

This threat to internal validity can be controlled through various evaluation designs we will discuss later. In addition, using control groups and random assignment (when possible) will go a long way toward resolving these issues.

Initial Group Differences (Selection)

In some cases, in order to provide an effective evaluation, a comparison is made between the trainees and a similar group of employees who have not been trained, called the *control group.* It is important that the control group be similar in every way to the training group. Otherwise the inherent differences between the groups may be the cause of differences after the training. Suppose that those selected for training are the up-and-coming stars of the department. After training, they may in fact perform much better than those not considered up and coming, but the problem is that they were better from the start and more motivated to improve. So if Sue was one of the highly motivated trainees, as were all her cohorts in training, they may have done better even without training.

This is not a problem if everyone is to be trained. The solution is simply to mix the two types so both the group to be trained and the control group have a mix of both types.

Loss of Group Members (Mortality)

In this situation those who did very poorly on the pretest are demoralized because of their low score and soon drop out of training. The control group remains intact. As a result, the group that has been trained does better in the posttest than the control group because the poorer scoring members have left the trained group, artificially raising their average score. The opposite could occur if, for some reason, members of the control group dropped out.

This is more of a problem when the groups are made up of volunteers. In an organizational setting, those who go to training are unlikely to drop out. Also, all department members who agree to be in the control group are a captive audience, and it is highly unlikely they will refuse to take the posttest. Although some transfers and terminations do occur to affect the numbers of participants, they are usually not that significant.

Diffusion of Training

When trainees interact with the control group in the workplace, they may share the knowledge or skill they are learning. For example, when Sue is back in the office, she shows a few of the other administrative assistants what she has learned. They are in the control group. When the posttest is given, they do as well as the trained group because they were exposed to much of what went on in training. In this case, training would be seen as ineffective, when in fact it was effective. This would be especially true if certain quotas of trainees were selected from each department. When such sharing of information reduces differences between the groups in this way, determining the effectiveness of the training could be difficult.

Compensating Treatments

When the control group and training group come from different departments, administrators may be concerned that the control group is at an unfair disadvantage. Comments such as "How come they receive the new training?" or "We all are expected to perform the same but they get the help" would suggest that the control group feels slighted. To compensate for this inequity, the managers of the control groups' department might offer special assistance or make special arrangements to help their group. For example, let's look at trainees who are learning how to install telephones more efficiently. Their productivity begins to rise, but because the supervisors of the control group feel sorry for the control group, they help them to get their work done, thereby increasing their productivity. The evaluation would show no difference in productivity between the two groups after training is complete.

Compensatory Rivalry

If the training is being given to one particular intact work group, the other intact work group may see this situation as a challenge and compete for higher productivity. Although the trained group is working smarter and improving its productivity, the control group works harder still and perhaps equals the productivity of the trainees. The result is that although the training is effective, it will not show up in the evaluation.

Demoralized Control Group

The control group could believe that it was made the control group because it was not as good as the training group. Rather than rivalry, the response could be to give up and actually reduce productivity. As a result, a difference between the two groups would be identified, but it would be a function of the drop in productivity, not the training. Even if training were effective, the test results would be exaggerated.

These threats to validity indicate how important tracking the process is in the evaluation. Just as data are gathered about what is occurring in the training, it is also useful to gather data about what is going on with the control group.

EXTERNAL VALIDITY

The evaluation has to be internally valid before it can be externally valid. If evaluation indicated that training was successful, and threats to internal validity were minimal, you would believe that the training was successful for that particular group. The next question is "Will the training be effective for the rest of the employees slated to attend training?" **External validity** is the confidence that these findings will generalize to others who undergo the training. There are a number of threats to external validity.

Testing

If the training is evaluated initially by means of pre- and posttests, and if future training does not have the pretest, it can be difficult to conclude that future training would be as effective. Those in the initial training may have focused on particular material because it was highlighted in the pretest. If the pretest is then not used, other trainees will not have the same cues. The solution is simple: Pretest everyone taking the training. Remember that pretest data can be gathered during the needs analysis.

Selection

Suppose a particular program designed to teach communication skills is highly effective with middle-level managers but when a program with the same design is given to shop-floor workers, it does not work. Why? There may be a number of reasons—perhaps differences in motivation or in entering KSAs. The important thing is that you cannot be sure that a training program that was successful with one group of trainees will be successful with all groups. Once it is successful with middle managers, you can assume it will be successful with other, similar middle managers, but if you wanted to use it to train entry-level accountants, you could not say with confidence that it would be successful (that it had external validity) until you evaluated it.

One of the authors was hired to assist a consulting firm providing team skills to a large number of employees in a large manufacturing plant. The first few sessions with managers went reasonably well; the managers seemed to be involved and learning a great deal. After about a month, training began for the blue-collar workers, using the identical processes, which included a fair amount of theory. It soon became evident that trainees were bored, confused, and uninterested. In a discussion about the problem, the project leader commented, "I'm not surprised—this program was designed for executives." In retrospect, it is surprising that lower-level managers received the training so well, given that it was designed for executives.

Reaction to Evaluation

In many situations, once the training has been determined to be effective, the need for further evaluation is deemed unnecessary. Thus some of the trainees who have gone through the program were evaluated and some were not. The very nature of evaluation causes more attention to be given to those who are evaluated. Recall the Hawthorne Studies, which have indicated the power of evaluation in an intervention. The Hawthorne Effect is explained by the following (Goldstein 1991):

- Taking the training was a novelty for the trainees.
- The trainees felt themselves to be special because of being singled out for training.
- The trainees received specific feedback on how they were doing.
- The trainees knew they were being observed, so they wanted to perform to the best of their ability.
- The enthusiasm of the instructor inspired the trainees to perform at a high level.

Whatever the mechanism, there is no doubt that those who receive more attention may respond better as a function of that attention. As with the other threats to external validity, when you change the way groups are treated, you jeopardize the training's external validity.

Multiple Techniques

In clinical studies, a patient receives Dose A. It does not have an effect, so a month later she receives Dose B, which does not have an effect, so she receives Dose C and is cured. Did Dose C cure her? Perhaps, but it could also be that it was the combination of A, B, and C that had the required effect. The use of multiple techniques could influence training when some component of the training is changed from one group to the next. For example, a group received one-on-one coaching, then video instruction. The members did poorly after receiving the coaching but excelled after receiving the video instruction, so video instruction became the method to train future employees. It was not successful, however, because it was the *combination* of coaching and video instruction that had resulted in initial success.

WHAT DOES IT ALL MEAN?

It is useful to have an understanding of the above issues in order to understand why it is difficult ever to suggest with certainty that training or any other intervention is the cause of any improvement. There is never absolute certainty regarding the internal or external validity of a training program. Careful consideration of these issues, however, and use of well-thought-out designs for the evaluation can improve the likelihood that training, when shown to be effective, is in fact effective (internal validity) and will be effective in the future (external validity). This information is useful for assessing training and, equally important, helps you assess evaluations of outside vendors.

Evaluation Design Issues

A number of texts provide excellent information on appropriate designs for conducting evaluations (Cook, Campbell, and Peracchio 1990; Cook and Campbell 1979; Campbell and Stanley 1963). Unfortunately, many of their recommended designs are impractical in most organizational settings. Finding the time or resources to create a control group is difficult at best. Getting approval to do pretests on control groups takes away from productivity time and is difficult to justify.

Scientifically valid research designs are difficult to implement, so organizations often use evaluation designs that are generally not acceptable to the scientific community (Camp, Blanchard, and Huszczo 1986). This does not mean you cannot have some confidence in your results. As you will note below, although some research designs are less than perfect, there are ways of improving them and addressing the threats to validity. The two designs most often used, and most criticized by scientists, are the posttest only and the pretest/posttest methods (Wexley and Latham 1981).

BASIC DESIGNS

Posttest Only

The posttest-only method occurs when training is provided (represented by X) and then a posttest is given (represented by $T2$). The design is represented as X $T2$.

There are problems with the posttest-only design, and in certain instances (discussed below) it is not a recommended choice. There are, however, times when the method is completely acceptable. As Sackett and Mullen (1993) have noted, evaluation has two possible goals: to determine if change has taken place, and/or to determine if a level of competence has been reached. If the latter is the only goal of the evaluation, a posttest-only design should suffice. If, for example, there are legal requirements to have everyone in the company who handles hazardous waste understand what to do in an emergency, presumably any training that is developed need only provide a test at the end to be assured that all trainees have reached the required level of knowledge. As more companies are required to be ISO 9000 (or equivalent) certified, it will be increasingly important to prove that employees have the required skills. As a result, certification will become the goal of employee training, and in that case the posttest only will suffice.

We have frequenlty mentioned the value in doing needs analysis. If you have done a needs analysis, you already have pretest data, and so the posttest-only design becomes moot. Posttesting automatically provides you with a pretest/posttest design.

Furthermore, there may be archival data to serve as the pretest. Performance appraisals, measures of quality, and the like might allow for some pre–post comparison. Although such historical data may not be ideal, it could provide some information as to the effectiveness of training. Alternatively, you could identify an equivalent group and provide its members with the same posttest, thereby turning the design into a posttest only with control group (see below). Suddenly you have a much more meaningful design.

The posttest-only design as it stands is problematic for assessing change. There could be a number of other competing causes for the change, as Table 6.10 suggests. Nevertheless, we would agree with Sackett and Mullen (1993) that any evaluation is better than none. Gathering any pretraining information that might suggest that the level of KSAs prior to training was lower than in the posttest would help to bolster the belief that training was effective.

Pretest/Posttest

The other method used frequently by organizations is the pretest/posttest design. Using the same representations as above (and adding $T1$ to represent the pretest), this design is expressed as $T1\ X\ T2$.

The criticism of this method is that without a control group, it is difficult to determine the impact of training on any changes that occur. A number of threats to validity remain (see Table 6.10). Although you can demonstrate that KSAs have changed, you are not able to say that training is responsible for those changes. For example, you may have been training a group of machine operators to operate new drill-press machines. Pretesting the trainees revealed that none knew how to operate the machine. After a three-day training session, a posttest showed that, on average, the trainees were able to operate the machine correctly 85% of the time. A big success? Not if the supervisor of the work group says that the ones without training can operate the machines correctly 95% of the time by reading the manuals and practicing on their own. There could be many reasons why those who did not go to training were better on the job. Perhaps they already knew how to operate the machine. Perhaps a manufacturer's representative came and provided on-the-floor training to them. Or it could be that your training somehow slowed down the learning process. Therefore the prevailing wisdom is that a control group is necessary.

TABLE 6.10   Sources of Invalidity

	Internal								External			
	History	Maturation	Testing	Instrumentation	Regression	Selection	Mortality	Interaction of Selection and Maturation, etc.	Testing	Selection	Reactive to Evaluation	Multiple Techniques
Posttest Only (no control group)	−	−		−		−	−			−		
Pretest/Posttest (no control group)	−	−	−	−	?	+	+	−		−	−	?
Posttest Only (with control group)	+	+	+	+	+	+	+	+	+	+	?	?
Pretest/Posttest (with control group)	+	+	+	+	+	+	+	+	−	?	?	?
Time Series Design	−	+	+	?	+	+	+	+	−	?	?

Note: In the tables, a minus indicates a definite weakness, a plus indicates that the factor is controlled, a question mark indicates a possible source of concern, and a blank indicates that the factor is not relevant.

It is with extreme reluctance that these summary tables are presented because they are apt to be "too helpful" and to be depended upon in place of the more complex and qualified presentation in the text. No + or − indicator should be respected unless the reader comprehends why it is placed there. In particular, it is against the spirit of this presentation to create uncomprehended fears of, or confidence in, specific designs.

Source: Adapted from Campbell and Stanley 1963.

In many instances using a control group is simply not an option. Does this mean you should not bother to do anything? Absolutely not. In fact, it is better to do something than nothing. Sackett and Mullen (1993) note that we have tended to focus on the negative aspects of the preexperimental designs rather than examine ways of using them most effectively when other options do not exist. The pre-/post-no-control group at least establishes that changes did take place. The questions regarding internal validity of these findings can be explored in other ways (Cook and Campbell 1979).

Sackett and Mullen (1993) suggest that simply examining available information can help determine if there were extraneous occurrences that might have caused the improvement in learning. History can be examined through interviews with the trainees. Maturation can usually be ruled out for adults, given that training is not generally very long. The point is that evaluation designs provide a mechanism for measuring the threats to validity, but simple investigation into the likelihood of these threats may be all that is needed. This method may be particularly relevant for the small business, where the size makes it easier to identify potential threats.

Internal Referencing Strategy   Another way of dealing with the lack of a control group is **internal referencing strategy (IRS).** Haccoun and Hamtiaux (1994) provided support for this design that includes using relevant and nonrelevant test questions in the pre- and posttest. Here's how it works.

Both pretests and posttests contain questions that deal with the training content as well as questions that deal with related content not trained. In the pretest, trainees will do poorly on both sets of questions. On the posttest, if training is effective, improvement should show only for the trained items. The nonrelevant items serve as a control. In their research on the IRS, Haccoun and Hamtiaux noted that the results obtained from the IRS design were identical to those obtained when a control group was used.

Many of the threats to internal validity do not exist with the IRS, because with no control group to react in an inappropriate manner, issues such as diffusion of training, compensatory treatment, compensatory rivalry, and others are not a concern. The only threats are history, maturation, testing, statistical regression, and instrumentation.

As has been noted, history can be investigated through examinination of the time frame in which training occurred. Any events that may have had an influence on the trainees could be assessed as to their potential impact. Also, given that the relevant and nonrelevant items are similar in nature in the IRS, any historical event should affect both types of items in a similar manner.

Maturation issues can be dealt with by ensuring that the training is designed to keep trainees interested and motivated, and to prevent them from becoming tired or fatigued.

The reactive effect of testing can be dealt with if parallel tests are used. *Parallel tests* are tests that cover the same content but do not use identical questions. This technique does lead to another potential problem (instrumentation), which can be addressed. If all trainees receive a comprehensive pretest, this is not an issue.

Instrumentation is a concern when two different tests are used. If a large pool of items are developed from which test items can be chosen at random, the result should be equivalent tests.

Once again it is important to note that in any evaluation you can never be 100% sure that training caused the improvement. This design is not suggested to take the place of more stringent designs, when they are practical. It is appropriate, however, when the alternative is posttest only, or nothing. Again, some control is better than none at all.

One final note. The IRS design can be used to determine improvement in KSAs, but Haccoun and Hamtiaux (1994) advise it has a tendency to show that training is not effective when in fact it is. In other words, the training must provide a substantial improvement from pretest to posttest in order for it to be detected.

MORE COMPLEX DESIGNS

There are two factors to consider when developing a sound evaluation design: control groups and random assignment.

The **control group** is a group of similar employees who do not receive the training. It is used to determine if changes that take place in training also take place for those who do not receive training; any change could be a function of training or some other factor. Including a control group helps to determine whether the difference in pretest and posttest scores is due to the training or some other factor.

Random assignment is the assignment of employees to either the control group or the training group by chance, to ensure that the groups are equivalent. It is more applicable to experimental laboratories than to applied settings such as in training, for two reasons. First, given the small number of employees placed in one group or the other, the theory of randomness is not likely to hold true. When we split a group of 60 employees into two groups of 30, it is quite likely that there will be real differences within the two groups. Random assignment works well when there are multiple groups of 30, or when the total number of subjects is very large (e.g., 500).

Second, it is unlikely that the organization can afford the luxury of randomly assigning employees to each group. The work still needs to be done, and managers would want some control over who will be in training at a specific time. For this reason, it makes more sense to match employees as best you can so the two groups have representative sampling. Below are discussed a number of designs that have control groups. We believe that assigning trainees through representative sampling is a more effective way of obtaining equivalent groups, although it must be pointed out that the assessments of the designs that have control groups (see Figure 6.10) assume random assignment.

Posttest Only with Control Group

Posttesting only with a control group is represented by the following:

Trainee Group (representative sampling) X $T2$

Control Group (representative sampling) $T2$

As is noted in Figure 6.10, this design and the following one are equivalent in terms of dealing with internal validity, but remember that information in the figure is based on random assignment.[8]

If for some reason a pretest has not been conducted or if you did not provide a pretest to a control group at the beginning of training, you can compare the trainees with a control group using a posttest-only design. Differences in test scores noted between the groups (trainees doing better) will provide evidence of the success of the training. There is a tendency to downplay the effectiveness of this design because there is no pretest to assess equivalence of the groups before training. If the training and control groups were large enough to result in effective random assignment, you will be more confident of the findings (see Table 6.10). True randomness, however, is not ensured in a single set of trained and control employees. In this situation, **representative sampling,** matching employees on specific variables such as tenure, age, educational background, and other features will be more likely to provide equivalent groups, although one way to be more confident of equivalence is use of a pretest.

Pretest/Posttest with Control Group

The expression for pretest/posttest with a control group is:

Trainee Group (representative sampling) $T1$ X $T2$
Control Group (representative sampling) $T1$ $T2$

This is one of the more favorable designs for eliminating threats to internal validity. If random assignment was possible, all the threats to internal validity would be dealt with (see Table 6.10). The issue here is how equivalent the two groups are, given they were divided through representative sampling. A pretest can determine this. If the pretests of both groups are equivalent, you have one more piece of evidence that the groups are equal, and posttest differences (if the trained group obtains higher scores) will suggest that training was successful.

---

[8] What we are saying is that we believe the best way to obtain equivalence of the two groups is to use representative sampling. However, we cannot be sure that this will result in true equivalence. Therefore, although Figure 6.10 indicates that the designs deal with internal validity issues, they do so only to the degree the groups are in fact equivalent.

Threats to external validity related to having a control group are still a concern (compensatory treatments, rivalry, etc.). These might be managed by explaining to both groups the need for a control group and by treating the control group no differently except for the training. Reactive effects to testing can be dealt with by simply testing all those to follow, so that any cues that are provided will be provided to everyone. When a TNA is conducted, this will occur anyway. Careful test construction and administration will reduce concerns about trainees learning only answers to the test questions. If the test is causing trainees to focus on certain material, there will be no problem as long as all receive the pretest. The reactive effect to being in the training is another concern that must be dealt with. Treating the control group in a similar manner as the trainees (except for the training) will be a difficult task, and the Hawthorne Effect could have an impact on the external validity of the training. Again, this does not mean the situation is hopeless, just that trainers and training directors must be diligent in their efforts to develop sound practices to alleviate these threats the best they can.

Time Series Design

The time series design is represented by:

Trainee Group $T1$ $T2$ $T3$ $T4$ X $T5$ $T6$ $T7$ $T8$

This design uses a series of measurements before and after training. In this way, the likelihood of internal validity threats such as testing or regression to the mean are very small (see Table 6.10). Also, when everyone attends training at the same time (a one-shot training program), this design can be used whether the number is large or small. It can still be argued that because no control group is used, history (internal validity) and many external validity concerns are not addressed. But recall that in applied settings, the goal is to be as sure as you can about the results, given organizational constraints. If enough measures are taken pre- and posttraining to deal with fluctuations in performance, the change after training is certainly suggestive of learning.

In instances where the training will be provided to everyone at the same time, there is little room for elaborate designs, and the time series design becomes especially useful. If you gather data over a number of periods before and after training (and if they indicate training was successful), you can be more certain about the impact of training than had you simply done a pretest/posttest on the group. Remember, in an applied setting you will never be absolutely sure of the impact of training, but taking care to use the best possible design (considering constraints) is still better than doing nothing at all.

To make this design more powerful, consider adding a control group, expressed by:

Trainee Group $T1$ $T2$ $T3$ $T4$ X $T5$ $T6$ $T7$ $T8$
Control Group $T1$ $T2$ $T3$ $T4$ $T5$ $T6$ $T7$ $T8$

In this way, you are able to deal with the concern regarding history. External validity issues are still a concern.

Multiple Baseline Design
Multiple baseline design is represented by:

Trainee Group A	T1	T2	T3	X	T4	T5	T6	T7	T8	T9	T10 . . .
Trainee Group B	T1	T2	T3	T4	T5	X	T6	T7	T8	T9	T10 . . .
Trainee Group C	T1	T2	T3	T4	T5	T6	T7	X	T8	T9	T10 . . .
Trainee Group D	T1	T2	T3	T4	T5	T6	T7	T8	T9	X	T10 . . .

In this design, multiple measures are taken much as in time series, but each group receives the training at a different point in time. Each untrained group serves as a control for the trained groups. Issues related to external validity are dealt with, especially if Groups A through D represent all those to be trained. All will eventually be treated similarly, so concerns related to external validity are significantly reduced. Here the ability to say that changes measured by the test are due to the training is very strong. If each group improves after its training, it is difficult to argue that something else caused the change.

Solomon 4 Group
Once again, in this design caution must be given as we use representative sampling, and the value of the design is based on equivalence of the four groups. The Solomon 4 group is a very thorough design in that it deals with all the concerns related to internal validity. It also deals with the reaction effect of the pretest. This design is represented as follows:

Group 1 (representative sampling)	T1	X	T2
Group 2 (representative sampling)	T3		T4
Group 3 (representative sampling)		X	T5
Group 4 (representative sampling)			T6

If you used this design, you would be able to confirm that pretesting did not have an effect on training success. On the basis of this information, you could suspend pretesting with the assurance that doing so would not affect the training success. As was noted earlier, however, for the required complexity it simply makes sense to use the pretest consistently.

When this design is used, you can make a number of assertions based on the findings. First, if T2 > T1 and T4, and if T5 > T6, and if T5 > T3, then the strength of your inference that training resulted in improvement is high. If T6 is equal to T1 and T3, then history and maturation are not the cause of any improvement. If T2 and T5 are equal and both are higher than T1, then the reactive effect of testing is not a concern.

WHAT DESIGN TO USE
Determining the true impact of training requires an investigation into the validity of evaluation results. A number of methods are available, and the more complex the design, the more valid the results. There are, however, other considerations when you

are deciding on an evaluation design. Innovation can provide good substitutes when the best is not possible. Consider the multiple baseline design above. This is a powerful design and certainly is a possibility if a number of employees need to receive the training over time. However, what if multiple measures were not possible? The following design would address many of the same concerns, and although it is not as elaborate, it certainly deals with many of the validity issues. If pretest scores are all comparable, and posttest scores indicate an improvement, these results are a strong argument for showing training was responsible.

Trainee Group A	*T1*	*X*	*T2*					
Trainee Group B			*T1*	*X*	*T2*			
Trainee Group C					*T1*	*X*	*T2*	
Trainee Group D							*T1*	*X*	*T2*

We have already mentioned that most organizations do not evaluate all training at all levels. Furthermore, even when evaluating training, many organizations do not use pretest/posttest or control groups in a manner that would eliminate many of the threats to validity. Dixon (1997) indicated that of the companies she investigated in her article "New Routes to Evaluation," only one, Arthur Anderson, used designs that would deal with many of the validity issues. Other companies, including IBM and Johnson Controls, follow such procedures only when asked by particular departments or higher-level management, or when they can defray some of the high cost of developing reliable and valid tests by marketing the final product to other organizations (Dixon 1997). The demand for certification in some skills (primarily because of ISO 9000 and others' requirements) has created a need for these types of tests.

When you are evaluating training, if using control groups and or pretesting is not possible, remember there are other investigative methods for assessing the likelihood that factors other than training account for any change in KSAs. By understanding the issues related to internal and external validity, you will be able to make good decisions regarding the design used in training evaluation.

What About the Small Organization?

For the small business owner, sending employees to training that is not effective could significantly affect the company's financial health. Consider the owner who is constantly terminating employees because they are unable (or unwilling) to do the job properly. They all receive training and most but not all turn out to be ineffective. Why? If training is being evaluated, you could rule out the training itself as the problem and move to other possibilities. If training is not evaluated, however, perhaps employees are lost because the training is not effective and only the very brightest manage to pick up the required skills.

The small business owner might think it is not necessary to evaluate training because he will know it was effective if he sees changes on the job after training. Actually this is probably true; in a small business you would soon know if recently trained employees are performing at the expected level. However, if training is a significant cost to the owner, evaluating learning before and after training can still be of value. After all, the trainees may be learning on-the-job, and the training may not be adding anything to their KSAs.

Much of the training in a small business is on-the-job training. In such cases evaluation is often simply an assessment of the trainee's ability to learn. Examining the training process is not considered. As we will discuss in the next chapter, on-the-job training requires trainer skills just as does any other training. Simply placing a new employee with an experienced employee and expecting the experienced one to train is not wise. It can be worthwhile to evaluate the process of training that goes on, as well as the outcomes, especially if the position is at a lower level where, because of turnover or promotion, a rather high number of employees receive training.

Because a small business may have one or two employees who need training, there may be a feeling of hopelessness when it comes to using a training design to determine training success. White, Rosenthal, and Fleuridas (1993) suggest **single-case designs,** which are often used in the lab, to evaluate the training provided to professional counselors; there is no reason this design cannot also be used by managers to evaluate training when the number of employees is small.

The single-case design uses data from one individual and makes inferences based on that information. To deal with issues of validity, the multiple baseline approach could be used. Suppose two supervisors need to be trained in active listening skills. Because the business is small, both cannot attend training at the same time. Using a predetermined checklist developed for evaluating the training, you count the number of active listening phrases each of them uses in conversations with you. Take several measures over three or four weeks. Then one supervisor is sent to training. Continue monitoring the active listening after the person returns. Did the number increase for the trained supervisor and not the other supervisor? Now the second supervisor is given training, after which you continue monitoring her conversations. If both employees improved after training, you can infer that the training was effective. Although this approach is suggested for the small business, it is also useful in any sized organization where there are very few trainees.

The movement to quality standards such as ISO 9000 has created a need for certification in a number of areas. Although the standards do not suggest how to evaluate training, they do specify that the organization must maintain training records and periodically evaluate training. Below is an excerpt from the QS 9000 requirements manual.

> Training records can be diplomas, certificates, licenses, experience, resumes . . . .
> The standard does not suggest any specific method for evaluating training effectiveness. A popular method is annual review of training . . . . Results of the review are recorded and are used as feedback for revising and updating the training program. Another method is periodic assessment of individual employees . . . .
> (*QS 9000 Requirements* 1995)

Certification can become both the documentation and evaluation of training, something that might explain why becoming certified is so popular (see Training in Action 6.5 on page 268).

David Alcock of Canadian Plastics Training Center in the Toronto area says that although not many of the center's clients request an evaluation of training, he has noted such requests are on the increase. Most of the center's clients are small injection-molding businesses. The need for certification seems to be the driving force behind the necessity to evaluate. Canadian Plastics Training conducts standardized injection-molding training on its own site and provides a skill-based evaluation. A trainee

---

Training in Action 6.5

QS 9000 Audit

Carol works for a small automotive supplier and is preparing for its QS 9000 audit in a few weeks. QS 9000 is a quality assurance program similar to ISO 9000. It requires documenting of a great many issues regarding how the company goes about its business.

Carol says that QS 9000 does not demand that the company conduct formal evaluations of its training. She continues, "But we must train relevant employees in statistical process control (SPC), blueprint reading, and other skills. In an audit, an auditor can ask one of our employees questions related to SPC, and the employee better know the answer. If she does not, we better have a reason why. So evaluation is a good idea; we simply don't have the time or resources to do all the evaluation of training we would like."

To deal with the training, she says, "We have one of our employees sent out to training—for example, SPC training. That person becomes our expert and trains others as required. Do we formally test them on SPC? No. We do have reaction questionnaires to see how well they liked the training. We also have in place a performance review process that identifies areas of behavior that should emerge from the training. Supervisors are asked how often the trainee has been seen performing SPC behaviors (or other trained skills)."

She goes on to say, "We do have specific certification requirements for operating forklifts, and for that we test people; it is a safety issue. I worked in a much larger organization before this, and there we had a much more comprehensive evaluation of training, but we also had a great many more resources. Here I think we are moving forward in our thinking about training and evaluation, and QS 9000 has been a driving force behind that push."

---

who passes the skill-based test becomes certified as an injection molder. In many cases, employees are sent by their company for this training, but some employees pay their own way to improve themselves.

One reason these small companies do not evaluate is the cost. For in-house training done by Canadian Plastics Training, a late 1997 cost of evaluation for 20 employees to be trained to a higher-level classification was $25,000. Many small companies simply do not have those resources. Another issue noted by Mr. Alcock has to do with what the evaluation would be used for. For example, suppose a unionized shop wants to upgrade the skills of the workforce. Sending them to training would have the union's blessing. Evaluating the learning, on the other hand, might be met with a great deal of resistance. The union leadership and rank and file might be very concerned about the company knowing how well the employees did on a test. Would the results be used to get rid of some employees? If not, what is the purpose of the evaluation? Convincing the union that evaluation is a way of assessing the effectiveness of training might be difficult to do, depending on the relationship between union and management. Training in Action 6.6 shows what one small company is doing.

Training in Action 6.6

Training and Evaluation at Scepter Manufacturing

"ISO makes training mandatory," says Don Villers, plant manager of the 160-employee Scepter Manufacturing plant in Scarborough, Ontario. "We train everyone from the shop floor to the front office." The plant was ISO 9002 certified in 1994, and since then has gone beyond the ISO training requirements.

In the company's rating system supervisors are required to rate each of their employees on a scale from 1 to 10. An employee must reach 10 to be certified at that level and to be eligible for promotion. The rating system is not seen as punitive, but developmental. It is used as a needs analysis to identify skill deficiencies, then as a learning measure, and finally as a transfer of training measure.

What about results? According to Villers, "Defective parts have dropped from 5% to .1%. Scrap has also dropped 50%." He attributes this success primarily to training. As a result of the success, the training budget is ten times the $6,000 per year the company spent three years ago.

Source: Adapted from LeGault 1997.

Much of the discussion above is related to the evaluation of learning. The exception is on-the-job training, where learning and behavior tend to blend together. What about results in this case? After reading the article on Scepter Manufacturing (LeGault 1997), one of the authors called Mr. Villers to ask how he knew the drop in scrap and defective parts (results) was a function of training. His reply: "We are a small company, and it is the only thing that we changed." He makes an important point related to the examination of results in small businesses. When you do training, evidence of the impact can be much faster. Also it should be easier to rule out threats to validity, without the need for the more complex designs.

Summing It All Up

We began this chapter discussing the importance of a comprehensive evaluation. We end it suggesting that a comprehensive evaluation is not always necessary. With the understanding of validity and design issues, you now realize the difficulties that surround evaluation. It can be complex and in many cases costly. For this reason, we have suggested throughout this chapter that evaluation is useful and important but not necessary at all levels all the time. Furthermore, good detective work can, in some cases, replace complex designs in assessing the validity of evaluation.

The decision as to what training should be evaluated and at what levels will be easier if the organization is proactive. By examining the strategic plan, you will be able to identify those areas of training that require evaluation and the extent to which you need to evaluate. Without such direction, the training department will need to identify its mission and goals as best it can and work from there to determine the training that needs to be evaluated. Even for a large organization, it is simply not practical to evaluate everything. Thus all organizations need to determine what training they need to evaluate and how they will do so.

Palm Desert continued

The Palm Desert case at the beginning of the chapter provides an example of an effort to evaluate using a control group and pre/post design. Even here, however, there are problems in the way evaluation was managed. One issue is that learning was not assessed. Only behavior change was assessed six months after training. We know the training did not transfer, but we don't know why. If it did not transfer because it was never learned in the first place, what was the reason? It may be that there was simply too much material to learn in a one-day seminar. Examining the process of developing the training might have revealed this problem, and the training could have been revised before it was implemented. For a small organization, the training was obviously a major undertaking, and a more comprehensive training evaluation might have been more advisable.

Key Terms

- Affective questionnaire
- Control group
- Cost/benefit evaluation
- Cost-effectiveness evaluation
- Cost savings analysis
- Declarative knowledge
- External validity
- History
- Internal referencing strategy (IRS)
- Internal validity
- Job behavior outcomes
- Learning outcomes
- Maturation
- On-the-job training
- Organizational results
- Outcome
- Procedural knowledge
- Process
- Random assignment
- Reaction outcomes
- Representative sampling
- Single-case designs
- Strategic knowledge
- Summative or outcome evaluation
- Utility analysis
- Utility questionnaire

Cases

CASE 1

You run Tricky Nicky's Carpet Cleaning Co., which cleans carpets for businesses. On average, one carpet cleaner can clean six offices in the working hours from 6:00 P.M. until 3:00 A.M. You have 100 cleaners currently working for you and they work 250 days per year. A recent analysis of the rework that must be done finds that, on average, one in every six carpets cleaned is not up to your standards. Because of Nicky's "Satisfaction Guarantee," when a carpet does not make the standard, it is redone immediately at no extra cost to the business.

The profit on a cleaning is $20. You pay your cleaners $15 per hour. When you reclean a carpet, you lose $20 in employee time.

Your training manager has done a needs assessment regarding this issue at your request. He reported that half the employees are not reaching the standard one in nine times, and the other half are not meeting the standard two in nine times, for an average overall of one in six ($[1/9 + 2/9]/2 = 1/6$). The needs assessment also indicated that the cause was a lack of KSAs in both cases.

The training manager proposes a training program that he estimates will reduce the recleaning by half, to 1 in 12. The training would take four hours and could handle 20 employees per session.

Costs associated with the training:

Developmental Costs (assume 250 working days in a year)

20 days of training manager's time for development at $40,000 per year	$3,200
Miscellaneous	800

Direct Costs

4 hrs per session at $40,000 per year (trainer)	$400
Training facility	500
Material and equipment	2,000
Refreshments	600

Employee salaries (Nicky decides to do this on a Saturday and pay his employees an extra $5 per hour as overtime) $20 per hour per employee

Lost profit (none as they are training on overtime)

Indirect Costs

Evaluation of training	
10 days of training manager's time	1,600
Material and equipment	600
Clerical support—20 hours at $10 per hr	200

CASE QUESTIONS

1. How much does the recleaning cost Nicky per year? Show all mathematical calculations.

2. If everyone is trained, how much will the training cost? How much if only the group with the most errors is trained? Show all mathematical calculations.

3. What is the cost savings of the training if everyone is trained? What is the cost benefit? Show all mathematical calculations.

4. Should both groups be trained or just one with the most recleanings? Show all mathematical calculations.

5. Let's back up and assume we're still at the needs analysis stage. Assume that employees had the KSAs needed to clean the offices effectively. What other factors might you look at as potential causes of the recleaning problem?

CASE 2 QUESTIONS

1. In chapter 5 you identified training that needed to be done in the MHC case, and developed learning objectives for that training. Describe how you would go

about evaluating that training. Given the information in the case, indicate how you would evaluate whether the training you designed accomplished its objectives. Be sure to indicate the evaluation design(s) you would be using as well. Provide a rationale for both your measures and your design(s).

Exercises

1. Examine the reaction questionnaire your school uses. Is it designed to rate the course content and/or to rate instructors? Does it meet the requirements of a sound reaction questionnaire? Why or why not? Explain how you would improve it (if possible).

2. Break into small groups, each group containing at least one member who has received some type of training in an organization. Interview that person on what the training was designed to teach, and how it was evaluated. Did the evaluation cover all the levels of outcomes? How did the trainee feel about that?

Devise your own methods for evaluating each of the levels based on the person's description of the training.

3. Assume you are the manager of the training department of a large organization. Four employees are enrolled in a training course (assume it is this course). You are aware that for the course there are reaction questionnaires and tests (to measure learning) done at the school. Design a method for assessing the transfer of training to your department. What about a measure of organizational results?

Questions

1. What is the relationship among Kirkpatrick's four levels of evaluation? Would you argue for examining all four levels if your boss suggested you should look only at the last one (results) and that if it improved, you would know that training had an impact?

2. What is the difference between cost/benefit analysis and cost-effectiveness analysis? When would you use each and why?

3. What is the difference between cost-effectiveness analysis and utility analysis. When, if ever, would you use utility rather than cost effectiveness? Why?

4. Assume you were the training manager in the Westcan case (in chapter 4). How

would you suggest evaluating the training, assuming they were about to conduct it as suggested in the case? Be as specific as you can.

5. Of all the designs presented, which one would you consider to be most effective for dealing with the internal and external validity issues while also being practical enough to convince an organization to adopt it? If your design involved random assignment, how would you accomplish this? If your design left many of the threats to validity unchallenged, how would you argue that this condition is acceptable?

References

Ackerman, P. L., and L. G. Humphreys. 1990. Individual differences theory in industrial and organizational psychology. *Handbook of Industrial and Organizational Psychology. 2d ed.* 2:223–82.

Alliger, G. M., S. Tannenbaum, W. Bennett, H. Traver, and A. Shotland. 1997. Meta analysis

of the relationship among training criteria. *Personnel Psychology* 50:341–57.

Bernardin, H., and J. Carlyle. 1979. The effects of forced choice methodology on psychometric characteristics of resultant scales. Paper presented at the annual meeting of the Southern Society of Philosophy and Psychology.

Brandenberg, D., and E. Schultz. 1988. The status of evaluation of training: An update. Presentation at the National Society of Performance and Instruction Conference, April, Washington, DC.

Camp, R. R., P. N. Blanchard, and G. E. Huszczo. 1986. *Towards a More Organizationally Effective Training Strategy and Practice.* Upper Saddle River, NJ: Prentice Hall.

Campbell, D. T., and J. C. Stanley. 1963. *Experimental and Quasi-experimental Designs for Research.* Chicago: Rand-McNally.

Cascio, W. 1989. Using utility analysis to assess training outcomes. In *Training and Development in Organizations,* edited by I. Goldstein. San Francisco: Jossey-Bass.

———. 1991. Applied psychology in personnel management. 4th ed. Upper Saddle River, NJ: Prentice Hall.

———. 1995. *Managing Human Resources.* 4th ed. Upper Saddle River, NJ: Prentice Hall.

Cattaneo, R., and A. Templer. 1990. Strategic contrasts: A comparative analysis of two examples of human resource management effectiveness. Proceedings of the Annual Conference of the Administrative Sciences Association of Canada. Vol 11. Whistler, B.C. pp. 25–34.

Clement, R. W. 1982. Testing the hierarchy theory of training evaluation: An expanded role for trainee reactions. *Public Personnel Management Journal* 11:176–84.

Conroy, M., and M. Ross. 1984. Getting what you want by revising what you had. *Journal of Personality and Social Psychology* 47:738–48.

Cook, T. D., and D. T. Campbell. 1979. *Quasi-experimentation: Design and Analysis Issues for Field Settings.* Chicago: Rand-McNally.

Cook, T. D., D. T. Campbell, and L. Peracchio. 1990. Quasi Experimentation. In *Handbook of Industrial and Organizational Psychology,* 2d ed., vol. 1, edited by M. D. Dunnette and L. M. Hough, pp. 507–620. Palo Alto, CA: Consulting Psychologists Press.

Dixon, N. 1990. The relationship between training responses on participant reaction forms and post test scores. *Human Resource Development Quarterly* 1(2):129–137.

———. 1996. New routes to evaluation. *Training and Development,* May, pp. 82–85.

———. 1997. Personnel communication, July 9. Associate Professor, George Washington University, Department of Administrative Sciences.

Fitz-Enz, J. 1994. Yes you can weigh training's value. *Training,* July, pp. 54–58.

Flanagan, D. L. 1990. Techniques for eliciting and representing knowledge structures and mental models. Unpublished manuscript. Naval Training Systems Center, Orlando, FL.

Geber, B. 1995. Does your training make a difference? Prove it! *Training,* March, pp. 27–34.

Gill, R., S. Gordon, J. B. Moore, and C. Arbera. 1988. The role of conceptual structure in problem solving. In Proceedings of the Annual Meeting of the American Society of Engineering Education. Washington, DC: American Society of Engineering Education.

Glaser, R., and M. Chi. 1989. Overview. In *The Nature of Expertise,* edited by M. Chi, R. Glaser, and M. Farr. Hillsdale, NJ: Erlbaum.

Goldsmith, T. E., P. J. Johnson, and W. H. Acton. 1991. Assessing structural knowledge. *Journal of Educational Psychology* 83:88–96

Goldstein, I. L. 1991. Training in work organizations. In *Handbook of Industrial and Organizational Psychology,* 2d ed., vol. 2, edited by M. D. Dunnette and L. M. Hough, pp. 507–620. Palo Alto, CA: Consulting Psychologists Press.

Gordon, M. E., and J. F. Isenberg. 1975. Validation of an experimental training criterion for machinists. *Journal of Industrial Teacher Education* 12:72–78.

Haccoun, R., and T. Hamtiaux. 1994. Optimizing knowledge tests for inferring learning acquisition levels in single group training evaluation designs: The internal referencing strategy. *Personnel Psychology* 47:593–604.

Hamblin, A. C. 1974. *Evaluation and Control of Training.* New York: McGraw-Hill.

Hart, P., K. Kraiger, and T. Lamb. 1996. Summative evaluation of civil engineering 350: Civil engineering 448 and curriculum tests. Interim Technical Report for period June 1 to August 30.

Hassett, J. 1992. Simplifying ROI. *Training,* September, pp. 53–57.

King, L., J. Hunter, and F. Schmidt. 1980. Halo in a mulitdemential forced choice performance evaluation scale. *Journal of Applied Psychology* 65:507–16.

Kirkpatrick, D. L. 1979. Techniques for evaluating training programs. *Training and Development Journal* 33(6):78–92.

Kraiger, K., J. K. Ford, and E. Salas. 1993. Application of cognitive, skill based and affective theories of learning outcomes to new methods of training evaluation. *Journal of Applied Psychology* 28(2):311–28.

Kraiger, K., E. Salas, and J. Cannon-Bowers 1995. Measuring knowledge organization as a method for assessing learning during training. *Human Factors* 37:804–16.

Kropp, R., and E. Hankin. 1975. Paper and pencil tests for evaluating instruction. In *Evaluating Training Programs,* edited by D. Kirkpatrick. Madison, WI: American Society of Training and Development.

LeGault, M. 1997. In house training that gets results. *Canadian Plastics,* February, pp. 14–18.

Lord, F. M. 1956. A study of speed factors in tests and academic grades. *Psychometrika* 21:31–50.

McIntyre, D. 1994. *Training and Development 1993: Policies, Practices and Expenditures.* Toronto: The Conference Board of Canada.

McLaughlin, D. J. 1986. The turning point in human resource management. In *Strategic Human Resource Management,* edited by F. K. Folkes. Upper Saddle River, NJ: Prentice Hall.

Meals, D., and J. W. Rogers. 1986. Matching human resource management to strategy. In *Strategic Human Resource Management,* edited by F. K. Folkes. Upper Saddle River, NJ: Prentice Hall.

Means, B., and S. Gott. 1988. Cognitive task analysis as a basis for tutor development: Articulating abstract knowledge representations. In *Intelligent tutoring systems: Lessons learned,* edited by J. Psotka, L. Massey and S. Mutter. Hillsdale, NJ: Erlbaum.

Miller, S. 1990. Effects of municipal training on employee behavior and attitudes. *Public Personnel Management* 19:429–40.

Nunnally, J. C. 1978. *Psychometric Theory.* New York: McGraw-Hill.

Ostroff, C. 1991. Training effectiveness measures and scoring schemes: A comparison. *Personnel Psychology* 44:353–74.

Overmyer-Day, L., and G. Benson. 1996. Training success stories. *Training and Development,* June, pp. 24–29.

Saari, L., T. Johnson, S. McLaughlin, and D. Zimmerlie. 1988. A survey of management training and education practices in U.S. companies. *Personnel Psychology* 41:731–43.

Sackett, Paul R., and E. J. Mullen. 1993. Beyond formal experimental design: Towards an expanded view of the training evaluation process. *Personnel Psychology* 46:613–27.

Schmidt, F. L., and J. E. Hunter. 1983. Individual differences in productivity: An empirical test of estimates derived from studies of selection procedure utility. *Journal of Applied Psychology* 68:407–14.

Sisson, E. 1948. Forced choice: The new army rating. *Personnel Psychology* 1:365–81.

Stark, C. 1986. Ensuring skills transfer: A sensitive approach. *Training and Development Journal,* March, pp. 50–51.

Thacker, J. W., and M. Fields. 1992. Evaluation of steward training: Did it do what you wanted it to. Published in Proceedings of the 44th Annual Meeting of the Industrial Relations Research Association. New Orleans, January.

Thacker, J. W., M. Fields, and L. Barclay. 1990. Union commitment: An examination of antecedent and outcome factors. *Journal of Occupational Psychology* 63:17–20.

Wexley, K. N., and G. P. Latham. 1981. *Developing and Training Human Resources in Organizations.* Glenview, IL: Scott, Foresman.

Wexley, K., and G. Yukl. 1975. *Organizational Behavior and Industrial Psychology: Readings with Commentary.* New York: Oxford University Press.

White, L., D. Rosenthal, and C. Fleuridas. 1993. Accountable supervision through systematic data collection: Using single case designs. *Counselor Education and Supervision* 33:32–37.

Yancey, G. B., and L. Kelly. 1990. The inappropriateness of using participants reactions to evaluate effectiveness of training. *Psychological Reports* 66:937–38.

Training Methods

Learning Objectives

After reading this chapter you should be able to:

■ Describe the various formats, purposes, procedures, strengths, and limitations of the following training methods:

- Lectures and lecture/discussions
- Computer-based training (CBT)
- Games and simulations
- On-the-job training (OJT)

■ Describe:

- The types of learning objectives for which each method is most suited
- The impact of the method on the learning process

■ Identify:

- The various audiovisual options
- Their value as standalone training or enhancements to the above methods
- Their respective strengths and limitations

275

Video-Based Sales Training at Motorola

Each year Motorola creates a master training plan for its sales force that is driven by business objectives. The plan takes into account the company's strategic plans, business objectives, and operational tactics for each product. The initial plan is developed and then reviewed and critiqued by senior management, the different divisions, the marketing function, and a training council. The input from these stakeholders is synthesized into a master training plan that has been agreed to by all the important stakeholders.

Designers of video-based sales training at Motorola first ask the question, "What outcomes do we want from salespeople as a result of the training?" Answers to this question become the specific learning objectives of the video training. Once the training content has been designed, the videos are produced by an outside company that has been retained by Motorola for this purpose. A video training module takes from three to six months to produce. Professional actors are used and live video is shot in plants, at customer's offices, and other locations, as well as in the studio.

Videos are used to train sales representatives in the following areas:

Product information

- New products and system descriptions
- Product applications
- Competitive product analysis

Critical changes in policy and procedures. For example:

- Changes in compensation plans
- Sales contests

Market information

- Market updates
- Customer profiling
- Location shots

  Product usage in customer settings such as computer integrated manufacturing applications

Sales techniques

- Review/reinforce/supplement skills developed during live courses
- Model desired behavior in specific situations
- Model undesirable behavior for critique/coaching

After production, videos and study guides are shipped to salespeople according to their need for the training. As many as a thousand sales representatives may get a video training module. The sales representatives then engage in self-study by reading supplementary materials that accompany the video, watching the video, and following directions. When a salesperson believes she has mastered the material, she completes an exam at the end of the study guide, then calls a toll-free number and transmits the results.

Salespeople who successfully complete a module receive positive reinforcement through the annual "Make the Grade" recognition program. Results from the module exams are also factored into performance and merit reviews as well as promotional opportunities. Those who fail the exam are asked to go through the video and study guide again before retaking the module exam. If a salesperson fails an exam twice, the sales manager is notified.

Excepted from Honeycutt, McCarty and Howe 1993.

Overview of the Chapter

This chapter and chapter 8 address instructional methods in different ways. This chapter provides a basic understanding of the methods' components and variations; their strengths and limitations in terms of cost, suitable learning objectives, and other factors; and characteristics of the training group for which the method is best suited.

Chapter 8 addresses training program development and implementation issues, as well as tips for using the various instructional methods. That chapter also addresses how the various methods relate to, and complement each other. For example, this chapter will tell you about the lecture method, and the next chapter will tell you how to conduct a lecture. At the end of this chapter we will compare the ability of the different training methods to develop knowledge and skills, or influence attitudes.

Matching Methods with Outcomes

Because the various instructional methods differ in their ability to influence knowledge, skills, and/or attitudes, it is important to understand the strengths and weaknesses of a method in each of these three learning areas. However, before moving into that discussion, a brief review of the KSA definitions might be helpful. Refer to the definitions in chapter 1 if you need more detail.

Knowledge can be acquired at three distinct levels: declarative, procedural, and strategic. *Declarative knowledge* is the person's store of factual information, *procedural knowledge* is the person's understanding about how and when to apply the facts, and *strategic knowledge* is used for planning, monitoring, and revising goal-directed activity, including learning.

Skills are a person's ability to carry out specific tasks such as operating a piece of equipment, communicating effectively, or implementing a business strategy. Skills combine knowledge of "what" to do "when" with the ability to do it. Two levels of skill acquisition are *compilation* (lower level) and *automaticity* (higher level), reflecting differences in the degree to which the skill has become a routine or automatic behavior pattern.

Attitudes are employee beliefs and/or opinions about objects and events and the positive or negative feelings associated with them. Attitudes affect motivation levels, which in turn influence behavior.

What might be the knowledge, skill, and attitude objectives in the Motorola case? Many training programs have learning objectives in more than one area. When they do, they need to combine several training methods into an integrated whole, because no single method can do everything well. The various methods can be divided into cognitive and behavioral approaches, and trainers must understand the strengths and weaknesses of each.

Cognitive methods provide verbal or written information, demonstrate relationships among concepts, or provide the rules for how to do something. These stimulate learning through their impact on cognitive processes and are associated most closely with changes in knowledge and attitudes. Though these types of methods can influence skill development, it is not their strength. Conversely, **behavioral methods** allow the trainee to practice behavior in a real or simulated fashion. They stimulate learning through behavior and are best used for skill development and attitude change. Thus either behavioral or cognitive learning methods can effectively be used to change attitudes, though they do so through different means. Cognitive methods are best for knowledge development and behavioral methods for skills. What strengths do you think Motorola's video-based training had for developing a sales representative's knowledge? How about skills and attitudes? What are the problems you see with using videotapes for developing sales skills? Do they have an advantage over just reading about how to sell? Are they as good as having a trainer who can answer questions and provide feedback? Let's look at the various training methods to see what they do well and not so well.

The Lecture

Nearly all training programs have some lecture component. The lecture is best used to create a general understanding of a topic or to influence attitudes through education about a topic. In its simplest form, the lecture is merely telling someone about something (Broadwell 1980). Do you think the Motorola videos contained any lecture components? Even though a lecture is videotaped, it is still a lecture. When the trainer starts training by telling the trainees the objectives, the agenda, and the process that will be used in training, she is using the lecture method.

Several variations in the lecture format allow it to be more or less formal or interactive (Brown 1978; Bligh 1974). The clearest difference is the role trainees are expected to play. The lecture, by itself, does not include trainees interacting with the trainer. Adding discussion and a question-and-answer period invites the trainees to be more interactive in the learning process.

STRAIGHT LECTURE/LECTURETTE

The **straight lecture** (Broadwell 1980) is an extensive oral presentation of material by the lecturer while the trainee attempts to absorb the information. A good lecture is well organized and begins with an introduction, which lays out the purpose of the lecture, the order in which topics will be covered, and any rules about interrupting the lecture for things like questions and opportunity for clarification. The introduction is followed by the main body of the lecture, the topic content. These topic areas too should be logically sequenced so that trainees are prepared for each topic by the content of the preceding topics. The lecture should conclude with a summary of the main learning points or conclusions. Because lectures require long periods of trainee inactivity, a shorter version of a lecture, the **lecturette,** is often used. It has the same characteristics as the lecture but usually lasts less than 20 minutes.

During a straight lecture or lecturette, the trainee does little except listen, observe, and perhaps take notes. Even when done well, this is not a very effective technique for learning. However, it is useful when a large number of people must be given a limited amount of information in a relatively short period. The lecture should not contain too many learning points, because trainees will forget information in direct proportion to the amount of information provided. This means shorter lectures are usually better. However, longer lectures can be effective if the length is due to examples and clarifying explanation.

A major concern about the lecture method is that it does not allow the trainees to clarify their understanding or correct misunderstandings. When the only training objective is to acquire specific factual information, often better learning can be achieved at less cost by putting the information into text. Printed text and video can reach a larger number of people less expensively than a lecturer can. Lectures typically require paying for the trainer, facilities, and other expenses each time they are presented. Also the trainees can review the printed or video training material as often as they need for retention. In addition, because they can read or view the material at their leisure, lost productivity due to training is minimized. The only added value provided by the lecture is the credibility the lecturer can give to the material by his or her personal presence and the attention he commands through his presentation skills.

DISCUSSION METHOD

The **discussion method** uses a lecturette to provide trainees with information that is supported, reinforced, and expanded on through interactions both among the trainees and between the trainees and the trainer. This added communication gives it much greater power than the lecture. Higher-level knowledge objectives, such as principle learning and problem solving, can be achieved by using logically sequenced lecturettes, each followed by discussion and questioning.

The discussion method provides a two-way flow of communication. Knowledge is communicated from trainer to trainees, and understanding is conveyed by trainees back to the trainer. Verbal and nonverbal feedback from trainees enables the trainer to determine if the material has been understood. If it has not, the trainer may need to spend more time on this area or present the information again in a different manner.

Questioning can be done by both the trainees and the trainer. When the trainees volunteer questions, they are demonstrating they have been thinking about the content of the lecture. When the trainer asks questions, he stimulates thinking about the key areas that are important to know. Asking and responding to questions are trainer skills that will be discussed in the next chapter. For now the point is that questioning (by trainees or the trainer) and discussions are beneficial because they enhance understanding and keep trainees focused on the material. Furthermore, discussions allow the trainee to be actively engaged in the content of the lecture, an activity that improves recall and future use.

STRENGTHS AND LIMITATIONS OF LECTURE AND DISCUSSION

In examining a method's strengths and limitations we will focus on four major issues:

- The cost in both financial and other resources required to achieve the training objective(s)

- How much control the trainer has over the material that will be covered
- The type(s) of learning objectives addressed
- How the method activates different learning processes (i.e., attention, retention, and behavioral reproduction)

Cost

In the Motorola case, the company determined that it was more efficient to use video-based training than to provide salespeople with classroom-style lectures and discussions. However, this is not always the case. Developing and implementing lectures or lecturettes and their associated discussion/question periods are relatively inexpensive. The financial costs typically are associated with the following:

- Developing content and organization
- Compensation of trainer and trainee time spent in training
- The training facility for the program
- Travel, lodging, and food for the trainer and trainees

Straight lecture and discussion methods are among the most time-efficient, with discussion slightly less efficient. They require less time to develop than other methods and typically require less time to cover a specified amount of material. Of course, the more questions and discussion allowed, the greater the amount of time required. As has been mentioned, if the training objective focuses on factual information and interaction is not important, a written or video presentation is likely to be more efficient and equally effective. The advantage of the lecture is that it guarantees that everyone is exposed to the information. Other methods rely on trainees' self-reports. For example, in the Motorola case, the employees were supposed to watch the video prior to taking the exam. However, they didn't have to. Of course the exam serves as a check that they at least know the important aspects of the material.

Control of Material and Process

Straight lectures and lecturettes provide a high degree of trainer control over the training process and content. The material covered is predetermined by the trainer, as are the processes used to present the material. The trainees have little if any influence other than whatever involvement was allowed in the TNA and program design process. However, as the training becomes more interactive, control shifts more to the trainee. Trainee questions or answers to questions shape the content of what is covered. The group dynamics help to shape the processes used by the trainer in presenting the information.

For example, the order in which issues arise is determined partly by the lecture content and partly by the types of questions raised and the results of the discussion sessions. Discussions can move into tangential areas that are not specifically addressed in the lecture material but are of interest to the trainees. Almost everyone has experienced the classroom discussion that wanders into interesting but irrelevant areas as a result of a well-placed question to the instructor about his favorite topic.

As the objectives for knowledge acquisition increase (i.e., Gagné's types), the amount of two-way interaction required for learning must also increase. For example, higher-level learning such as principle learning and problem solving require more discussion and questioning. An advantage of increasing trainee participation in the content is that it increases the amount that is learned. A disadvantage is that it decreases trainer control over what is learned and increases the time required for learning. Thus, if time or control of content are important, the amount and types of trainee questions and discussions need to be limited. Since discussion and questions can be limited or cut off, the trainer still maintains a greater control of content and process relative to other methods.

Learning Objectives (KSAs)

The lecture is most useful when trainees lack declarative knowledge or have attitudes that conflict with the training objectives. The discussion method is more effective than the straight lecture for learning higher-order knowledge such as concepts and principles. It is possible for the trainee to develop some degree of procedural knowledge via this method, though other methods (e.g., computer- and video-based training, and simulations) are generally more effective. Since discussions provide only information (not opportunities for behavioral reproduction), they should be used only for knowledge or attitudinal objectives.

If the training objective is skill improvement, the discussion method is not appropriate. However, training objectives often include both knowledge and skill development. That is, the knowledge is a prerequisite for the skill. For example, the training objective may be to improve managers' ability to conduct effective meetings. But first the managers would have to know the components of effective meetings (facts) and when and how to use them (procedures). While the lecture/discussion method may be appropriate for meeting the factual and some of the procedural objectives, you should address the skill development objectives through methods that allow the trainees to practice conducting meetings.

The discussion method is more effective than the straight lecture at producing attitude changes. Because attitudes consist of a person's beliefs and feelings about an object or event, they are especially vulnerable to new learning. The lecture, and especially the discussion, can change employee attitudes by providing new insights, facts, and understanding. This is illustrated in Training in Action 7.1 on page 282.

Learning Processes

We will use the social learning theory model to describe the effect of the various instructional methods on different learning processes. If you want to review these learning processes (attention, retention, and behavioral reproduction), they are found in chapter 3 and specifically Figure 3.6 on page 111.

The lecture and discussion methods are very good at capturing trainee attention, at least in the short term. They have some strength in the area of retention, especially the discussion method. However, neither is good at facilitating behavioral reproduction, except to create attitudes that are supportive of the desired behavior.

Table 7.1 (page 283) lists the basic components of the lecture/discussion. These will be discussed more fully in chapter 8, but are presented here to show the impact each component has on the various learning processes.

Attention   Done properly, the lecture attracts and maintains the attention of trainees. In fact, of the three learning processes (attention, retention, and behavioral reproduction), attracting attention is what the lecture does best. The various ways of accomplishing this are described in chapter 8. For now, it is enough to think about how a typical lecture is set up.

Training in Action 7.1

Changing Managerial Attitudes about Problem-Solving Teams

An automobile parts manufacturer was planning to implement employee problem-solving teams. A training needs analysis of middle- and first-level managers showed that managers were resistant to these proposed changes in the work design that would give hourly employees more authority in making decisions. Of the many reasons for this resistance, two of the most common were "These are decisions we are supposed to be making" and "This will reduce the need for managers. Some of us will lose our jobs."

The training was designed to give these managers the KSAs necessary to function in the new team-based system. A portion of the lecture/discussion was devoted to addressing concerns about reducing managerial positions. It was explained that the company did not intend to lay off or terminate any managers as a result of this change but would reduce the size of the managerial workforce through attrition.

Another part of the discussion addressed the change in duties and responsibilities of first-line managers. It was explained that they would have new duties and responsibilities replacing those that were transferred to the hourly problem-solving teams. These new responsibilities—facilitating team problem solving and decision making, serving as liaison between the team and other parts of the organization, acquiring resources for the team, doing long-range planning, and so forth—had been incorporated into a new performance appraisal. First-line managers would no longer be evaluated in those areas that would be handled by the problem-solving teams.

During the discussion sessions following the lecture the managers expressed fears and concerns that had not been addressed. The trainer was able to address these issues either directly, by indicating other parts of the training program that dealt with those issues, or by indicating that she would bring someone in to address the issues at the next session.

These lecture, discussion, and questioning periods made it clear to trainees that no manager would be terminated because of this new system. While they were losing some responsibilities, they were gaining others. Because their performance reviews would be based on the new responsibilities, clearly they needed to develop the necessary KSAs.

A subsequent survey of these managers showed that they had a significantly more positive attitude about the problem-solving team concept than before training.

The trainees are all facing the lecturer. He is in the brightest light and is the only one speaking. Everything is done to focus attention on him.

Although it can be easy to gain the attention of the trainees at the start, one of the limitations, especially of longer lectures, is that trainees' attention can wander. A good lecturer will speak at about the rate of 125 words per minute, but the average

TABLE 7.1 Basic Lecture/Discussion Components and Effects on Learning	
Lecture/Discussion Components	*Learning Process Affected*
1. Orientation	
Presenting information so that trainees understand the direction in which the lecture is headed and the organization for getting there	Attention
2. Enthusiasm	
Presenting information in a manner that conveys the topic's importance and inherent value	Attention
3. Variety	
Using voice, gestures, various components listed in this table, and audiovisual aids	Attention Rentention: Symbolic coding
4. Logical organization	
Presenting information in a logical order and providing logical transitions between topic areas	Retention: Cognitive organization
5. Providing explanation	
Describing facts, concepts, and principles in a clear and easily understood manner	Retention: Symbolic coding Cognitive organization
6. Giving directions	
Providing instructions in a manner that allows trainees to understand what they are to do and how to do it	Retention: Cognitive organization Symbolic rehearsal
7. Illustrating	
Providing clear, interesting, and relevant examples of how information can or has been applied (both correctly and incorrectly)	Attention Retention: All areas
8. Comparing and contrasting	
Articulating the similarities and differences, advantages and disadvantages, etc. of relevant topic areas	Attention Retention: Cognitive organization
9. Questioning and discussing	
Seeking information from the trainees regarding their comprehension and their content-related ideas and stimulating the trainees' thought processes (e.g., Socratic questioning)	Attention Retention: All areas
10. Summarizing	
Highlighting important concepts covered in a manner that links the topics/ideas together	Retention: Cognitive organization

person processes information at a rate equivalent to 400 to 500 words a minute. Thus a trainee's attention can fluctuate dramatically over the course of just a one-hour lecture. Attention begins to decline after 15 to 20 minutes and begins to pick up again only near the end (Johnstone and Percival 1976; Lloyd 1968; Maddox and Hook 1975). This phenomenon is a primary reason for the use of lecturettes. Questions and discussion, if properly managed by the trainer, act to heighten attention and refocus thought processes.

Retention   Retention involves the processes of symbolic coding, cognitive organization, and symbolic rehearsal. The strongest link in this method's retention process is the first step of symbolic coding. A *symbolic coding* system is provided during the lecture when the trainer is describing, explaining, and illustrating the learning points. The words and images she uses are her way of symbolically coding the meaning of the material. These are interpreted by the learner and translated into the learner's own symbolic coding scheme. The challenge for the trainer is to present the material in a way that the trainer's and learner's symbolic codes have the same meaning. The discussion/question segment of the training helps to align the trainee's symbolic coding with the training objectives. Reproducing the content of the training in written form (an outline at a minimum) facilitates the trainee's symbolic coding process and, ultimately, his recall of the information at a later date (e.g., back on the job). Using visual aids will facilitate the trainee's coding process by providing additional cues such as graphics and text. The more varied the stimuli used to present the same material, the more accurately the information is coded.

Organizing the coded information into already existing or new cognitive structures is what social learning theorists call *cognitive organization.* The organization of information determines the ease of recall and how appropriately it is used when it is recalled. When trainees become actively engaged in integrating concepts and principles into their cognitive structures, the cognitive organization process is facilitated. Discussion and questioning allow them to clarify their understanding of the information and organize it appropriately. Better cognitive organization occurs when the trainees are free to discuss various aspects of the new knowledge and its relationship to already existing knowledge and to question the trainer about actual or hypothetical situations where they might use the knowledge.

The lecture or lecturette may stimulate some thinking about how to apply the new knowledge, which is *symbolic rehearsal.* While the trainer can and should make suggestions about how the knowledge could be applied, these suggestions are not as powerful as the trainee imagining how it is applicable to her specific situation. Properly managed, the discussion/question session can facilitate this symbolic rehearsal. For example, as a trainer you might ask the trainees to think about ways in which the knowledge could be used in their work area and write their ideas down on a flip chart. You could then organize the trainees into small groups and have each individual report his or her thoughts to the group. You might say to the group members, "As you listen to others describe how they could apply this knowledge, imagine you were applying it that way in your work area. When the person is finished, discuss the application idea and how it would apply in your area." This process would not only surface misunderstandings and possibly clarify them, but would assist in the cognitive organization of the information. The primary value, however, would be that each trainee was getting a chance to mentally practice (i.e., symbolic rehearsal) using the new knowledge in a variety of ways and situations.

Behavioral Reproduction   The lecture/discussion approach does not provide for practicing actual behaviors, so it is not appropriate for skill development objectives. Although it might be valuable for developing the knowledge base required to learn a skill, or developing attitudes that support using the skill, it is not useful in developing the skill itself.

Training Group Characteristics

The Trainees For a lecture to be effective, trainees should be at about the same general level of intellectual ability and have about the same level of related content knowledge. If the trainee group is widely divergent in either of these areas, you will have a difficult time aiming the lecture at the appropriate level of understanding. If the lecture is otherwise an appropriate method, the best approach is to train the groups separately.

The discussion method allows more diversity in a training group, because the discussion period provides an opportunity for more active learning. Trainees who learn better in a more active mode have the opportunity to do so. Trainees also have the opportunity to learn from their peers as they participate in the discussion and ask questions.

Size of Training Group Straight lectures or lecturettes can be given to groups ranging from just a few to hundreds of trainees. The discussion method, however, places restrictions on the size of a class. In general, it should be small enough to allow all trainees ample opportunity to participate in discussions and questioning. The appropriate size will depend on the complexity of the material and the amount of time allocated. The more complicated the material, the more questions that will arise and the more discussion that will be needed, and therefore the fewer the number of trainees that can be accommodated. Alternatively, more time could be allocated to accommodate more trainees. It is important to remember, however, that no amount of extra time will compensate for too many trainees. The dynamics of large groups make it difficult or impossible for all to participate in a meaningful way. When trainees cannot participate meaningfully, they will inevitably become less involved and withdraw their attention.

Computer-Based Training

With the increasing demand for higher levels of employee knowledge and skill, HRD departments are faced with providing training to more and more employees. Many companies are implementing computer-based training (CBT) as an alternative to classroom-based training. Some of the reasons for this are demonstrated in the following beliefs many companies hold about CBT (*Personnel Journal* 1995):

- Reduces trainee learning time
- Reduces the cost of training
- Provides instructional consistency
- Affords privacy of learning (errors can be made without embarrassment)
- Allows the trainee to master learning
- Is a safe method for learning hazardous tasks
- Increases access to training

To understand why these beliefs may or may not be valid, you first have to understand what CBT is and how it works. **Computer-based training** is so varied in its form and application that it is hard to describe in concise terms, but it can be broadly defined as any training that occurs through the use of a computer (Gordon 1994). Under this definition, CBT goes by many different names; Table 7.2 (page 286) lists some of these with a brief description.

TABLE 7.2	Names and Descriptions of Computer-Related Training Aids
PI	Programmed instruction (PI) provides computer-based programs consisting of text, graphics, and perhaps multimedia enhancements that are stored and connected to one another electronically. Material to be learned is grouped into chunks of closely related information. Typically, the trainees are presented with the information in the chunk and then tested on their retention of it. If they have not retained the material, they are referred back to the original information. If they did retain it, they are referred to the next chunk of information to be learned. PI may be computer based but it is also found in printed material and interactive videos.
CBT	Training provided in part or whole through the use of a computer. Computer-based training is the term most often used in private industry and the government for training employees using computer-assisted instruction.
CMI	In computer-managed instruction (CMI) the computer is used for administrative functions such as registration, record keeping, scoring, and grading.
ICAI	When the computer-based training system is able to provide some of the primary characteristics of a human tutor, it is often referred to as an intelligent computer-assisted instruction (ICAI) system. This is a more advanced form of PI. Expert systems are used to run the tutoring aspect of the training, monitoring trainee knowledge within a programmed knowledge model and providing adaptive tutoring based on trainee responses.
ITS	Intelligent tutoring systems (ITS) make use of artificial intelligence to provide tutoring that is more advanced than ICAI type tutoring.
Simulations	Computer simulations provide a representation of a situation and the tasks to be performed in the situation. The representation can range from identical (e.g., word processing training) to fairly abstract (e.g., conflict resolution). Trainees perform the tasks presented to them by the computer program, and the computer program monitors their performance.

Most CBT has its roots in **programmed instruction (PI),** though PI can be used without a computer. There are significant differences between PI and the other computer-based training methods, but PI principles are the basis on which these other techniques operate. Table 7.3 describes these principles while at the same time providing an example of the PI approach. By working sequentially through the questions, you can get a feel for how this method works and what principles of learning are used.

PI is a method of self-paced learning managed by both the trainee and the learning system (e.g., computer program). CBT applies PI techniques within a computerized format to create the learning experience. However, PI can also come in book, tape, interactive video, or other formats. We will focus on the computerized application, but keep in mind that the principles are the same regardless of format. In the mid-1980s CBT was a fairly novel idea. Today it is becoming a mainstream approach, with 66% of leading edge companies using it to some degree (*Training and Development* 1998). However, it is not appropriate for all types of training needs or situations.

TABLE 7.3   Programmed Instruction for PI

Learning Stem	Questions	Instructions
1. Many people think it is impossible to learn without making a large number of errors. Because *trial-and-error learning* is time-consuming and creates frustration in the learner, most people don't like this method. After making a large number of errors, people begin to *lose their desire* to learn. Many trainers feel that if learning is carefully *pro-grammed* to occur in a specific manner, people can learn without making a large number of errors.	1.a Learning by making a number of errors until the right response is discovered is called: 1.b What is likely to happen to people's desire to learn when they must use the trial and error method? 1.c When the material to be learned is pre-pared so that the trainee makes few errors, it is said to have been carefully:	Compare your answers with those below: 1.a Trial and error learning 1.b It decreases 1.c Programmed If your answers closely match those above, go on to section 2. If not, reread section 1, paying close attention to the italicized concepts. Then answer the questions again.
2. Programmed instruction (PI) operates on the principle that if *learning is programmed to occur in small steps,* few errors will occur. Another principle of PI is that if trainees are *given immediate feedback* regarding the appropriateness of their response, they will learn more quickly and complete a greater amount of material.	2.a If the goal is to reduce the number of trainee errors before the material is learned, how should learning be programmed? 2.b To increase the amount learned and the speed of learning, when should feed-back be given?	Compare your answers with those below: 2.a In small steps 2.b Immediately If your answers closely match those above, go on to section 3. If not, reread section 2, paying close attention to the italicized concepts. Then answer the questions again.
3. Trainee learning is enhanced if the trainee is active in the learning process. PI asks trainees to *respond to questions, putting the trainee in an active learning mode.* Because trainees learn at different rates, *they will learn best if they can move through the material at their own pace.* PI allows people to learn at their own pace. Finally, *frequent review of material helps trainees retain* the material for longer periods of time.	3.a Programming questions into the material enhances learning because it places trainees into a(n) _____ mode of learning. 3.b At what pace should trainees move through the material to be learned? 3.c Frequent review of material results in:	Compare your answers with those below: 3.a Active 3.b Their own pace 3.c Longer retention of the material If your answers closely match those above, go on to section 4. If not, reread section 3, paying close attention to the italicized concepts. Then answer the questions again.
4. In summary, PI allows trainees to learn more material, more quickly, and retain it longer with less frustra-tion by: (1) programming small learning steps resulting in fewer response errors,	4.a What are five prin-ciples that PI uses to improve the ease, amount, speed, and retention of learning? 4.b PI increases the trainees' desire to	Compare your answers to those below: 4.a (1) Small learning steps (2) Frequent and active response by the trainee

(continued)

TABLE 7.3 Programmed Instruction for PI *(continued)*

Learning Stem	Questions	Instructions
(2) requiring frequent active responses by the trainees, (3) providing immediate feedback to trainee responses, (4) allowing trainees to move through the material at their own pace and (5) frequently reviewing the material.	learn by reducing the number of _____ the trainee is likely to make.	(3) Immediate feedback (4) Self-paced learning (5) Frequent review 4.b Response errors. If your answers closely match those above you have successfully completed the section on PI. If not, review section 4 again.

STRENGTHS AND LIMITATIONS OF CBT

Costs

Arguments have been made both supporting and criticizing the cost effectiveness of CBT. Because of the wide variety of CBT methods and applications, it is best to look at the factors that make CBT more or less cost effective in particular situations. Developing a CBT program from scratch is a labor-intensive process requiring knowledge and skills in learning, programming, and computer systems. Therefore it is a costly process. The software development typically requires significant lag time between when the need is identified and completion of the CBT program. This lag time is a limitation, because many training needs require relatively immediate attention. On the other hand, for certain types of training, the benefits of the CBT approach can outweigh the costs and lag time. The costs of developing and implementing a CBT program are related to the following factors:

- Number of trainees taking the course per year
- The cost of wages per hour for trainees while they are taking the course
- The cost of wages per hour for course developer
- The amortized cost of hardware to support the CBT
- The amortized cost of software used in the CBT
- Hours needed to complete the CBT program
- Hours needed to develop CBT course content
- The stability of the course content

In general, the development cost of CBT is higher than that of other techniques, although video and interactive video are fairly comparable. These costs are not usually justified for a small number of people. Eurich (1990) has reported that one hour of CBT instruction averages about 200 hours of development time. Of course, the more material, the higher the cost of developing the course material.

Hardware costs can also be prohibitive if hardware has to be purchased just for the training. For example, purchasing 20 computers or creating a 20-station network can cost as much as $85,000. If the computers will have other uses, however, their cost can be amortized across all uses and only the proportion allocated for the CBT program is assigned as a cost of the program. The same may be true for software. If the branching programs or expert systems have additional uses in the company, the costs can be spread across all uses. Nonetheless, because CBT requires each trainee to interact individually with the program, dedicated computer stations must be available for training, so start-up costs can be higher than with most other forms of instruction. However, this expense may be offset by the fact that trainees appear to learn the same amount of material faster with CBT than with other methods (Wexley 1984). For larger numbers of trainees, the savings realized by shortening the training time can be substantial.

Control of Material and Process

Perhaps the most important advantage of CBT is its control over the content of the material, method of presentation, and movement of the trainee through sequentially structured learning episodes based on previous trainee responses (Kearsley 1984). If it is also a CMI system, the learner's progress is automatically recorded. Each trainee can move quickly through material that is already familiar or easily grasped. As the learner finds the material less familiar or more difficult, the CBT provides more instruction, tutoring, and explanation. The pace of learning is controlled by the interaction between the software and the trainee.

Typically, no trainer is present to deal with adverse trainee reactions to the materials or format, or to address questions the trainee may have. Pilot testing of the CBT attempts to identify these issues and incorporate appropriate segments into the CBT to deal with them. For example, at periodic intervals the program may query the trainee about his or her reaction to the material. On the basis of the trainee's response, the presentation is altered. However, this feature adds considerably to the cost of the program and is a very difficult, if not impossible, task.

The CBT software determines the content and process of the training. If the material is properly developed, this method ensures that each set of prerequisite KSAs is mastered before the learner moves on to the next level. It also ensures that each topic area is covered. These features can be advantageous or disadvantageous compared with instructor-based training. The advantages are that it ensures consistency of topic coverage and topic mastery across all trainees. Sometimes, however, it is necessary to diverge from prescribed topic areas to heighten trainee interest or improve understanding. A live trainer could identify when such divergence is necessary; a software program can only present what it is programmed to present.

The trainee control problems associated with this approach might decrease its desirability for some situations. Because CBT is often used as a standalone method, there is no control over who is actually going through training.

A few years ago a professor of an introductory MBA accounting course decided to use a CBT program to teach the basic accounting principles. Each student was provided with his or her personal password to sign on to the system. Students could complete their lessons at their convenience, as long as they completed the ten modules within a three-week period. The modules were linked so that the students had to complete module one before they could begin module two, and so on. According to the records generated by the program, everyone had completed all the modules by the end of the third week. At this point the professor began his lectures and discussions about contemporary accounting practices. It soon became clear that many of the students didn't understand the basic principles. Further investigation revealed that a number of students had recruited others to use their password and complete their CBT modules. The professor abandoned the CBT approach the following year.

Would the same thing happen in an organization where certain training has been mandated (e.g., safety, sexual harassment) and the trainees are not particularly motivated to complete it? Might this also occur if rewards were attached to completing the training but not to actually using the KSA on the job? For example, employees in "pay for knowledge" systems have been known to divide the training among the members of the group so that one or two people complete the training for all the other members. If there are concerns about who is completing the training, you will need to develop additional control mechanisms to ensure that the trainees are completing the CBT themselves.

Learning Objectives (KSAs)

CBT is best used as a method for enhancing trainees' declarative and, in particular, procedural knowledge base. It can also be useful in developing some types of strategic knowledge, teaching some types of skills, and influencing attitudes. CBT can enhance the trainee's declarative knowledge through repeated presentation of facts, using a variety of formats and presentation styles. It can do an excellent job of describing when and how to apply the knowledge to situations relevant to the training objectives. It can develop procedural knowledge by providing opportunities to apply this knowledge to various simulated situations. CBT can document the appropriateness of the trainee's application and provide additional practice modules to improve areas of weakness.

Skill development is possible but more limited with CBT. The degree to which CBT is able to duplicate the environment and actual workplace situations will determine its usefulness in developing skills. For some situations, the CBT can create task simulations that are highly consistent with the actual job. For example, CBT software that trains employees in the use of word processing, spreadsheet, and other computer-based software can easily replicate situations they will face when back on the job. Conversely, it is very difficult to develop skills that require the use of natural language (e.g., interpersonal or conflict resolution skills) or psychomotor development (e.g., athletic skills) using CBT (Eberts and Brock 1988; Goldstein 1993). These skills typically involve interaction between two or more people or between a person and an object in a dynamic environment. Developing these skills requires trainees to engage in the interaction and receive immediate feedback about their performance. It is extremely difficult for computers to simulate these situations realistically. For instance, CBT can't accurately simulate a real person interacting with the trainee. Just trying to capture all the oral and nonverbal behavior that people are capable of in responding to a particular statement is a monumental task.

Quite a number of computer-based multimedia games attempt to simulate careers, such as being a business owner or a scientist, but the problem is that they can respond only in a narrow manner. Imagine playing the role of a job interviewee. You might want to ask the interviewer about the job expectations. Unless its a very sophisticated system, you will have to do so by using the keyboard, mouse, or some other device, so you aren't really engaging in the interaction as it would normally occur. Second, the program will accept only certain symbols. In real life you might say, "What are the standards that will be used to judge my performance?" but the program might not accept these terms. It would respond with some cue indicating that the message was not understood. You would have to keep trying different ways of saying the same thing until you used something the software was able to interpret. In real life there are a lot of ways of saying the same thing, and meaning is conveyed from sender to receiver with more fluidity than between computer software and a person.

What does all this mean? It means that CBT can be a useful tool in developing skills that are related to operating or using a computer. It can also help trainees learn about skills, such as interpersonal skills. However, it is not as good as other methods at helping the trainee actually develop those skills through practice and feedback. On the positive side, it can enhance skill development by providing information and even a model of how to behave in a particular situation. However, it won't be able to observe the person and provide feedback on such things as standing too close when talking to someone or not maintaining good eye contact.

Attitudes and motivation can be influenced through CBT in much the same ways as lectures and audiovisuals influence these cognitive structures. The factual relationships among objects and events and the consequences of particular courses of action can be portrayed in many ways with CBT technology. Thus, how objects, events, and their relationships are perceived can be altered by the material presented in the CBT. However, the opportunity to experience or interact personally with the objects and events is limited by CBT's ability to simulate reality. As a result, the emotional or affective side of attitudes may not be activated. In addition, human interaction is not available when CBT is used as a standalone method. Trainees do not have the opportunity to discuss their attitudes with others while a trainer monitors, directs, and reinforces the discussion to support the desired attitude(s). This may be one reason many adult learners prefer CBT to be combined with some form of instructor-based training (Goldstein 1993).

Learning Process

Attention   CBT is generally seen as more interesting and motivating than instructor-based training such as the lecture and discussion. Trainees cite reasons such as feeling less threatened by the machine and their control over the pace of instruction (Ganger 1990; Hannafin 1984). In addition, CBT can integrate audio and visual effects that draw the learner's attention to the material, as will be discussed in the audiovisual section. For these reasons, CBT is very good at capturing and retaining trainee attention.

Retention   Certainly the CBT method provides many cues that can be used in the symbolic coding process. Textual, auditory, and oral cues can be integrated to allow trainees to use those that fit best with their learning style for coding the content of the training (Gagné 1977). Because CBT can use a wide range of audiovisuals (AVs), it can be very effective in facilitating trainees' symbolic coding. Cognitive organization is also assisted by the AV aspects of the CBT. This methodology provides its own organization of the material that may or may not correspond to the trainees' cognitive structures. However, it does break each learning segment down into small steps, making it easier to integrate. Through the accumulation of these small steps and their repetition until mastery has occurred, CBT is able to shape the cognitive organization of the trainee in the desired manner. The ease with which the trainee is able to do this will depend on how closely the organization of the CBT matches the cognitive organization of the trainee.

Symbolic rehearsal is a cornerstone of the CBT approach. Each learning segment is presented until mastery occurs. The CBT first moves trainees through mastery of the facts and then provides application segments in which the trainees apply the facts to specific situations. Trainees must imagine themselves in the situation and apply their knowledge to that situation; they then respond and receive immediate feedback on the appropriateness of their response. For example, suppose trainees were learning to take photographs. The CBT would provide a simulated situation such as the inside of a room, artificial lighting, and objects that are closer or farther away and would provide a description of what should be photographed. The trainees would then indicate the camera settings for taking the picture. The CBT can even provide feedback that shows what would have happened in a real situation. Using the photography example, the CBT program could show what kind of photograph would have been produced. It allows each trainee to continue to practice while providing immediate feedback, until she has mastered the simulation. This type of symbolic rehearsal borders on behavioral reproduction and is very valuable for retaining the material.

Behavioral Reproduction   Unless the material to be learned involves direct interaction with computers or software, it is very difficult to provide behavioral reproduction through CBT. The photography example above is not true behavioral reproduction because the trainee isn't using a real camera or a real scene. CBT is good at teaching what should be done and providing symbolic rehearsal, but is very limited in teaching how to do it. Behavioral reproduction that requires natural language interaction or psychomotor skill development (e.g., handling customer complaints or welding a pipe) is generally not possible with CBT. However, advances in virtual reality might make these possible in the future.

What CBT does well is model appropriate behavior and provide simulations in which the trainee can apply her knowledge. These components will facilitate the development of skills but don't provide the opportunities actually to reproduce the desired behavior and receive feedback. For example, CBT can be used to learn a foreign language. The trainee can learn the meaning of words, their correct usage, and even how to replicate the appropriate pronunciation, but he will not learn to use the language conversationally until he actually interacts with someone in the language and receives feedback.

Training Group Characteristics

Typically, only one trainee can use a computer station at a time. Thus the number of trainees that can be trained at the same time is limited by the number of stations. However, because the training is available virtually all the time, this is not much of a problem unless a great number of trainees must be trained in a short period. If the CBT is on a CD or floppy disk, then trainees can take it home or anywhere they have access to a computer.

CBT takes into account many differences in trainee readiness, so there are relatively few trainee limitations for CBT. Trainees must be able to read and understand the text and AV components of the CBT. Some people are initially uncomfortable working with CBT as a standalone method (Goldstein 1993). In addition, while computers and software have become much easier to operate, there are still those who are unfamiliar with and intimidated by them. Computer KSAs are prerequisites for trainees going through CBT, so if you are considering this method, be sure to assess the trainees' reading levels, computer literacy, and attitudes about CBT. You can address these issues with some type of pretraining orientation or preparation program.

Games and Simulations

Training games and simulations are designed to reproduce or simulate processes, events, and circumstances that occur in the trainee's job. Trainees can thus experience these events in a controlled setting where they can develop their skills or discover concepts that will improve their performance. Equipment simulators, business games, in-basket exercises, case studies, role plays, and behavior modeling are examples of this technique. We will discuss each of these techniques separately and then describe the strengths and limitations of simulations in general.

EQUIPMENT SIMULATORS

As the name suggests, **equipment simulators** are mechanical devices that require trainees to use the same procedures, movements, and/or decision processes they would use with equipment back on the job. Simulators such as these have been developed to train airline pilots (Killian 1976; Mecham 1994), air traffic controllers (Killian 1976; Parsons 1972), military officers (Erwin 1978), taxi drivers (Edwards, Hahn, and Fleishman 1980), maintenance workers (Fink and Shriver 1978), telephone operators (Barrett, Benko, and Riddle 1981), ship navigators (Paffet 1978), and product development engineers (Slack 1993).

It is important that the simulators be designed to replicate, as closely as possible, the physical aspects of the equipment and operating environment trainees will find at their job site. This resemblance is referred to as the **physical fidelity** of the simulation. In addition, psychological conditions under which the equipment is operated (time pressures, conflicting demands, etc.) must also be closely matched to what the trainees experience on the job. This similarity is called **psychological fidelity.** Training in Action 7.2 (page 294) describes what can happen when the fidelity of the match between simulation and work setting is less than adequate. The events described in this example were reported by a new sales clerk trainee; although there may be some perceptual distortions, it was nevertheless his reality.

The literature on sociotechnical approaches to organizational development provides guidelines for the design/redesign of equipment (Davis 1973; Walton 1975). HRD professionals engaged in the design of simulators should involve those who will be using the equipment and their supervisors in its design and pretesting. Their input helps reduce potential resistance to the equipment and, more important, increases the degree of fidelity between the simulation and the work setting. In Training in Action 7.2,

---

Sales Simulation

Twenty-five retail sales clerk trainees were learning how to operate the company's electronic sales register system. The trainees each stood in front of a sales register which was actually an older model that had been refitted to serve as a training device. On a screen facing each trainee, a video depicted a customer. On the counter in front of the trainee, the items the customer was purchasing were automatically brought forward on a conveyer belt. The trainee entered key strokes to activate the register for a new sale, picked up each item, and scanned it into the register. When all the items were entered, the trainee entered more key strokes to total the sale. Then the conveyer brought forward either cash, a check, or a credit card, simulating the customer's payment choice, and the trainee had to enter the appropriate key strokes. If cash was used, the cash drawer opened, and the clerk was to deposit the payment and remove the correct change. Credit cards were scanned and automatically debited. Payment by credit card or check also required the customer's identification to be documented. Once payment was received, any change and the receipt were to be given to the customer (simulated by placing it in a bin on the counter). The items were then bagged and given to the customer (again placed in the bin).

This might have been a pretty good simulation. Unfortunately, when the trainees were placed at the real registers the next day, things were quite different. First, the registers were a newer model and some of the keys were in different places. Second, there were people standing impatiently in line. Some wanted to purchase items and others needed help with merchandise or wanted to know the location of items in the store. The clerks not only worked the register but also had to interact with the customers. The scanner wouldn't read some customers' credit cards. Some customers argued about the price of items, insisting they were on sale for a lower price than the scanner indicated. Some customers, after their items were totaled, decided they didn't want one of the items or wanted additional items. Needless to say, the simulation training wasn't seen as being very helpful and many considered it to have lowered their capabilities. They felt they made many key stroke errors because of the training. If they had just learned on the job, they wouldn't have had to unlearn portions of the previous day's training.

---

if trainers had brought in experienced sales clerks or their supervisors to pilot the simulation, they would have immediately identified the fidelity problems, which could then have been corrected.

BUSINESS GAMES

Business games are simulations that attempt to represent the way an industry, company, or subunit of a company functions. Typically, they are based on a set of relationships, rules, and principles derived from theory or research. However, they can also reflect the actual operations of a particular department in a specific company. Trainees are provided with information describing a situation and are asked to make decisions about what to do. The system then provides feedback about the impact of their decisions, and they are asked to make another decision. This process continues until some predefined state of the organization exists or a specified number of trials have been completed. For example, if the focus is on the financial state of a company, the game might end when the company has reached a specified profitability level or when the company must declare bankruptcy.

Many business policy simulations examine the total organization but some focus on the functional responsibilities of particular positions within an organization (e.g., marketing direction, human resource executive). These latter types are often called *functional simulations.* Because the differences between the two types of simulations are rather trivial except for the focus and scope of the game, we group them together. A wide variety of business games and simulations are available. A good source for exploring them or learning how to develop your own game is the Association for Business Simulations and Experiential Learning. Its publication *Developments in Business Simulation and Experiential Learning* describes new business games and simulations. The association also sponsors an annual conference in which new exercises, games, and simulations are demonstrated and discussed.

Business games involve an element of competition, either against other players or against the game itself. Some of the purposes for which business games have been developed and used are listed below (Dakin and Wood 1995; Kaplan, Lombardo, and Mazique 1985; Groth and Phillips 1978; Goudy 1981; Zemke 1982):

- Strengthen executive and upper management skills
- Improve decision-making skills at all levels
- Demonstrate principles and concepts
- Integrate separate components of training into an integrated whole
- Explore and solve complex problems in a safe, simulated setting
- Develop leadership skills
- Improve application of total quality principles and develop skill in using quality tools

Games that simulate entire companies or industries provide a far better systems perspective than other training methods. They allow trainees to see how their decisions and actions influence not only their immediate target but also related areas. Training in Action 7.3 (page 296) describes one such simulation. The choice of criteria will depend on the nature of the game and the goals of the training.

IN-BASKET TECHNIQUE

The **in-basket technique** provides trainees with a packet of written information and requests, such as memos, messages, and reports, that would typically be handled in a given position such as a sales manager, a staff administrator, or an engineer. This popular quasi-simulation focuses primarily on decision making and allows an opportunity for both assessing and developing decision-making KSAs. Generally, the trainees are given a role (usually a type of job) to play, a description of the role, and general information about the context. They are then given the packet of materials that make up

---

Training in Action 7.3

The People's Express Simulator

A simulation has been developed based on People's Express, an airline company that existed in the 1980s. It was eventually acquired by a competitor but made quite a splash in the business news for a while. It was a start-up passenger airline that managed to capture a significant market share in just a few years. It was one of the first airlines to offer deep discount air travel, with friendly but no-frills service.

The simulation can be played individually or by several people adopting different top management decision-making roles. The game begins with the decisions to be made after the company's first year in business. The player(s) must decide how much money to invest in new aircraft, new employees, quality/services, and marketing. The game utilizes industry and economic statistics from the time periods involved to determine the effect of the players' decisions. The game is played for a specified number of years or until specified financial criteria are reached (positive or negative).

If only a single player is involved, the game can be used to demonstrate the integrated nature of decision making in this business. Too much money invested in new aircraft means not enough trained staff to work the aircraft, higher payroll and training costs, and lower service levels. Too much investment in marketing may outstrip capacity, wasting a portion of the marketing investment, creating unnecessarily high costs and resulting in lower demand in the future (due to turning away customers and lower service). The player must find the right balance between investments in these four critical areas. When multiple players are involved, the learning can also focus on how to reach consensus decisions, and the importance of sharing information and strategies across functional areas.

---

the in-basket and asked to respond to the materials within a certain time period. After all the trainees have completed the in-basket, a discussion with the trainer follows, in which the trainee describes the rationale for her decisions. The trainer provides feedback, reinforcing decisions made appropriately or having the trainee develop alternatives for those made inappropriately.

A variation on the technique is to run multiple, simultaneous in-baskets in which each trainee receives a different but interrelated set of information. The trainees must interact with one another to gather all the information necessary to make an appropriate decision. This activity allows development of communication, as well as decision-making skills. It also includes elements of role play and business games training.

In-baskets are best at developing procedural and strategic knowledge. This knowledge is translated into decisions, so decision-making skills are also enhanced. These are primarily cognitive rather than behavioral skills. Typically, the trainee's decisions are simply written down. A few in-basket exercises require the trainee to "call" someone and communicate the decision or request additional information, such as in multiple, simultaneous in-baskets. In these cases, interpersonal skills can also be developed.

CASE STUDY

Case studies attempt to simulate decision-making situations that trainees might find on the job. The trainee is usually presented with a written (or videotaped) history, key elements, and the problems of a real or imaginary organization or subunit. The written case study can be from a few pages to 100 or more. A series of questions usually appears at the end of the case. The longer ones provide a great deal of information that has to be examined and assessed for its relevance to the decisions being made. Others require the trainee to conduct research to gather the appropriate information. The trainee must then make certain judgments and identify possible solutions to the problem.

Typically, trainees are given time to digest the information individually. If time permits, they are also allowed to collect additional relevant information and integrate it into their solution. Once individuals have arrived at their solutions, they may meet in small groups to discuss the different diagnoses, alternatives, and solutions that have been generated. Then the trainees meet with the trainer, who facilitates and directs further discussion.

Cases reflect the typical situation faced by most managers: incomplete information about many of the factors related to a decision. The trainer should convey that there is no single right or wrong solution (Argyris 1980) but many possible solutions. The learning objective is to have trainees apply known concepts and principles and discover new ones. Their solutions are not as important as their understanding of the advantages and disadvantages that go along with the solution. The trainer must guide the trainees in examining the possible alternatives and consequences without actually stating what they are.

A variation of case study is the **incident process,** in which trainees are given only a brief description of the problem (Pigors and Pigors 1987) and must gather additional information from the trainer (and perhaps others) by asking specific questions. Since managers gather most of their information from questioning and interacting with others, this activity is felt to simulate a manager's work more closely. In all case study methods, the information sorting and gathering process can be as much a learning focus as the nature of the problem being worked on. In such instances the focus is on understanding the criteria that separate relevant from irrelevant information and learning where and how to gather relevant information.

The decision-making aspects of the case study are focused primarily on developing strategic knowledge. The information-gathering aspects are skill development, since trainees actually perform this activity. However, feedback about information-gathering skills is generally not as heavily emphasized as the trainees' ability to analyze and make decisions.

ROLE PLAY

The **role play** is an enactment (or simulation) of a scenario in which each participant is given a part to act out. Trainees are provided with a description of the context— usually a topic area, a general description of a situation, a description of their roles (e.g., their objectives, emotions, concerns), and the problem they each face. For example, the topic area could be managing conflict and the situation might revolve around scheduling vacation days with the two parties in conflict being the supervisor and subordinate. The problem could be that the subordinate wants to take his vacation the first week in August and the supervisor knows a big project is coming due on that date. Once the participants have read their role descriptions, they act out their roles by interacting with one another.

The degree to which the scenario is structured depends on the goals of the training. **Structured role plays** provide trainees with more detail about the situation as well as more detailed descriptions of each character's attitudes, needs, opinions, and so on. Sometimes structured role plays even include a scripted dialogue. This type of role play is used primarily to develop interpersonal skills such as communication, conflict resolution, and group decision making.

Spontaneous role plays are loosely constructed interactions in which one of the participants plays himself while the other(s) play people with whom the first trainee has interacted in the past (or will in the future). This type of role play focuses on attitudes and is typically used to develop insight into one's own behavior and its impact on others rather than to develop specific skills.

In a **single role play,** one group of trainees role-plays for the rest, providing a visual demonstration of some learning point. Other trainees observe the role play, analyzing the interactions and identifying learning points. While this format provides a single focus for trainees and feedback from a skilled observer (the trainer), it does have some disadvantages. Those chosen to act as the characters may experience acute embarrassment at being the center of attention. They also don't have the advantage of watching others perform the roles. In addition, they may not play the roles in a manner that clearly portrays the behaviors that are the focus of training. Having people other than trainees act out the role play eliminates these problems but adds some cost to the training.

A **multiple role play** is the same as a single role play except that all trainees are in groups, with each group acting out the role-play simultaneously. Following the role play, each group analyzes the interactions and identifies learning points among themselves. Each group may report to the others a summary of its analysis and learning. This format allows a rich discussion of the issues, because each group will have played the roles somewhat differently. It also reduces the amount of time required to complete the process but may reduce the quality of feedback as well. Trainees are generally reluctant to provide negative feedback to peers. Even if they are willing, they may not have the experience or expertise to provide constructive feedback. Videotaping the role play is another option. The tape could be used by the trainee for self-evaluation, and the trainer could examine them between sessions and provide individual feedback.

The **role rotation** method begins as a single role play. After the characters have interacted for a period of time, the trainer will stop the role play and discuss what has happened so far and what can be learned from it. Then different trainees are asked to exchange places with some, or all, of the characters. These trainees then pick up where the others left off. This format allows both a common focus for all trainees (except those in the role play) and demonstrates a variety of ways to approach the roles. It keeps trainees more active than the single role play and allows feedback from a skilled observer. However, it requires the progress of the role play to be frequently interrupted, creating additional artificiality. Again, trainees may be inhibited from publicly critiquing the behavior of their fellow trainees and may be embarrassed to play a role in front of everyone else.

BEHAVIOR MODELING

Behavior modeling uses the natural tendency for people to observe others to learn how to do something new. This technique is most frequently used in combination with some other technique. For example, the modeled behavior is typically videotaped and then watched by the trainees. We have included it in the games/simulation section because once the trainees have observed the model, typically they practice the behavior in some form of role play or other simulation. However, the behavioral modeling process itself is distinctly different from these methods. The steps in behavior modeling training are described by many authors (e.g., Huegli and Tschirgi 1980; Goldstein 1993; Wexley and Latham 1991; Sims and Manz 1982). Although there are minor differences among the various models, they can be summarized as follows:

1. Define the key skill deficiencies.
2. Provide a brief overview of relevant theory.
3. Specify key learning points/critical behaviors to watch for.
4. Have an expert model the appropriate behaviors.
5. Have trainees practice the appropriate behaviors in a structured role play.
6. Have the trainer and other trainees provide reinforcement for appropriate imitation of the model's behavior.
7. Have the trainee's supervisor reinforce appropriate demonstration of behavior on the job.

Behavior modeling differs from both role plays and simulations by first providing the trainee with an understanding of what the desired skill level looks like. This method is based on Bandura's social learning theory and obviously is focused on developing behavioral skills. However, steps 2 and 3 reflect the cognitively oriented learning features of the technique and steps 5 to 7 the behaviorist/reinforcement theory features.

A training module composed of all seven steps is developed for each skill to be learned. An overview module should also be provided, as well as a separate workshop for those who will supervise the trainees back on the job. An example of this type of training is a package called "Interaction Management," consisting of more than a dozen two-hour modules and an introductory overview module. It also includes a two-day workshop for the trainees' managers, focusing on the managers' reinforcement of appropriate behaviors back on the job. A portion of the workshop uses behavior modeling as well.

Behavior modeling is useful for almost any type of skill training. It has been used for training in interpersonal skills, sales training, interviewee and interviewer training, safety training, and many other areas (Burke and Day 1986; Decker and Nathen 1985; Huegli and Tschirgi 1980; Latham and Frayne 1989; Smith 1976). One method of behavior modeling makes extensive use of video modeling and feedback. The trainee first observes the behavior being performed by a model and then attempts to reproduce the behavior (step 5) while being videotaped. Through split screen devices, the model and the trainee can be shown side by side, and the trainee can see exactly where his performance needs to be improved. In this approach, the trainee can see not only what should be done, but also what should *not* be done.

STRENGTHS AND LIMITATIONS OF G/S

While there are a variety of formats for games and simulations, they have many common strengths and limitations. When a specific format differs from others in this regard, we will discuss it separately. Otherwise, our discussion of strengths and limitations applies to all formats.

Costs

The development costs of games and simulations vary from format to format. In general, equipment simulators are the most expensive to develop, but cost will depend on the nature of the equipment that is simulated. For example, millions of dollars are spent on aircraft simulators used to train commercial and military flight officers. On the other hand, retail clerks and bank tellers can be trained on the actual equipment they will use on the job, which can be moved back and forth from training to the job site. If the development costs of your equipment simulators are quite high, you might immediately dismiss this approach. However, you should look at the cost in relation to feasible alternatives and their outcomes. This may show the simulator to be cost effective. One alternative to an equipment simulator is on-the-job training, although this might not work for some types of training. For example, pilot trainees taking test flights will not be exposed to all the possible situations they might encounter in flying thousands of hours a year, so the trainees would not learn from this method as much as they could from a simulator. Certainly the company wouldn't want to place the aircraft and crew in dangerous situations, yet pilots will need to know how to respond in such situations. In addition, the cost of "flying" a simulator is a very small fraction of the cost of flying an actual aircraft, which entails fuel, ground personnel, fees, and other expenses. Thus the total costs of using the simulation can be lower than alternative methods, even when the cost is quite high.

At the low end of development costs are role plays. A wide range of role plays have already been developed and published, including instructions and suggestions for their use (e.g., *Organizational Behavior Teaching Journal* and textbook publishers). Many of these are free. If you want to develop your own, tailored to your company's needs, you can do so at little cost. Business games and simulations are somewhat more complicated, thus usually more expensive than role plays. The development cost of games and simulations varies widely depending on their complexity and equipment requirements. Multimedia or computer-based presentations will be more expensive (see earlier discussion of these methods). Like other simulations, they have the advantage of being reusable, so the cost can be amortized across the number of trainees. Behavior modeling costs can range from moderately low to high, depending on the format used. Using an expert to model the desired behavior live (e.g., welding two plates together) simply involves the cost of the model. Since the model is typically an employee of the company, the cost is just the lost production while the expert is modeling. Using professional actors as models, as you might for interpersonal skills training, will add to the cost but may be worth it in terms of improved quality. Use of live models is more expensive than using videotaped models because the cost is incurred each time the model is used. Videotaping the model allows the videotape to be used again but adds the cost of creating it. Professionally developed videos can be fairly expensive and will be discussed more fully in the audiovisual section of this chapter.

The degree of flexibility built into the simulation or game will determine its cost effectiveness. For example, a cockpit simulator that is programmable and otherwise able to reflect the characteristics of many different aircraft or changes in aircraft will be more cost effective than one that can simulate only one type of aircraft. The same is true of business games and other types of simulations. A game or business simulation that is programmed to create different economic situations and business conditions will have a wider audience base and a longer useful life than one that doesn't.

The cost of making mistakes while in training must be factored into the cost/benefit decision when you compare methods. One of the primary strengths of games/simulations is that they allow trainees to develop and practice skills in a safe setting. Mistakes in business decisions can be financially disastrous. Mistakes in equipment operation can cause damage to the equipment and physical harm to the operator and others. Mistakes in interpersonal behavior can also result in financial losses to the company through lost customers, resentful employees, misinterpreted instructions, and the like. These mistakes may result in psychological harm to the trainee in terms of lowered self-esteem and confidence, increased defensiveness, and other negative effects. Simulations and games allow trainees the opportunity to develop their skills in a situation where the costs of making a mistake are low or nonexistent.

Control of Content and Process

When games and simulations are used, the content of what is learned and the processes used in learning are influenced by both the trainer and the trainee. The game or simulation provides a set of information that focuses on a particular content area. The People's Express Simulator (Training in Action 7.3), for example, focuses on integrating business decisions across functional areas to improve company profitability and growth. Games and simulations also provide instructions and guidelines that strongly influence the learning processes. So, by selecting an existing game or simulation or developing a new one, the trainer exerts control over the learning content and process. Many games and simulations are structured so that situations occur in a predetermined order, providing the trainer with greater control over both content and process. This is desirable if all trainees will be exposed to the same situations back on the job. Arrest procedures for police or machine maintenance and troubleshooting for equipment operators are examples. Other games and simulations allow the situation to change according to how trainees respond. Here the trainee has greater influence on what is learned and how. These types of games and simulations are useful when trainees must learn how to deal with a wide range of situations and how to apply general principles. Business and financial planning, decision making, and military battle tactics are areas where these types are particularly useful.

Once the game or simulation has been chosen, the trainer can exert control over learning processes by instructing trainees on how they should proceed through the game/simulation and providing additional learning activities. Unfortunately, trainers sometimes use games and simulations without developing structured preparatory and follow-up learning experiences. Often they do this with the rationale of allowing the trainees an opportunity to be more spontaneous and active in the learning process. However, without the proper preparation, orientation, and follow-up activities, trainees will learn less than they could and may miss important concepts entirely. Their perception might then be that the exercise was fun and entertaining but irrelevant.

The format providing the least built-in structure is the unstructured role play, in which only a general set of guidelines is given to the participants beforehand. How the trainees interact while playing out their roles is under their control. Although the trainer controls the choice of situation and roles, the trainees control how they are carried out. By asking the role players to focus on certain steps in the learning process, such as saying, "First try to identify the cause of the conflict, and then try to generate win–win alternatives," the trainer exerts more influence. In the case of role plays, reduced structure allows the trainees to imagine the situation as it might occur on the job. The potential danger is that it may be so unstructured they don't take their roles seriously or they are unable to imagine how it could possibly apply to their job.

Cases provide more structure, particularly in setting the situation (i.e., characteristics of the organization). However, the trainees' process of analyzing the case is largely internal or influenced by the interaction within the training group. Through the manner in which the trainer facilitates discussion of the case, she is able to exert more or less control over what trainees learn and how.

Equipment simulators generally provide the most structure. They must replicate the physical and psychological characteristics of the equipment and the environment in which it is operated. The simulator itself controls the content and process of learning. To the extent that the simulation is programmable, the trainer can manipulate the content. The trainer can also influence the focus of learning somewhat through instructions. Trainees have some control over what is learned by the responses they make. For example, one pilot trainee might experiment with different thrust, flap, and rudder alignments while in the simulator whereas another may use only the alignments he has been told are proper. The first pilot learns what happens under a variety of alignments, the second learns only what happens under the proper alignments.

Learning Objectives (KSAs)

Games/simulations provide opportunities to learn through concrete experiences that requires both theory and application. Theory provides the general principles that guide action. Application provides the opportunity to test those principles and understand them at a behavioral level, not just as abstract intellectual knowledge. As the philosopher Confucius said, "I hear and I forget. I see and I remember. I do and I understand."

Some types of knowledge enhancement and attitude change are achievable through games and simulations, but usually supplemental methods are required. In general, games and simulations do not attempt to provide declarative knowledge—some initial level of declarative and procedural knowledge is assumed. Games and simulations provide a context in which this knowledge is applied. If the focus of training is specifically on declarative or procedural knowledge acquisition, games and simulations are not the most effective methods. If, however, you want the trainee to understand how the knowledge should be applied and to develop strategies for doing so, one or more of the game or simulation formats is a good choice for developing procedural and strategic knowledge while also developing skills. Take the example of a business game in which several teams of trainees compete for product market share. The game makes some assumptions about the knowledge trainees have about basic marketing strategies (e.g., product, pricing, promotions, and location). It allows them to apply their knowledge and see the consequences of that strategy. The intent is not to teach what the components of marketing strategy are, but rather how to apply them in an integrated fashion. In the course of the game, trainees may learn more about each of the components and learn new principles about the relationships among the components, but this learning occurs as a result of, or in conjunction with, their ability to develop and implement an integrated marketing strategy. In the process they learn new strategies for problem solving, and enhance their strategic knowledge.

There are many reasons why games and simulations do a good job of developing skills. First, they simulate the important conditions and situations that occur on the job. Second, they allow the trainee to practice the skill. Finally, they provide feedback about the appropriateness of their actions. Each of the formats has particular types of skills for which it is most appropriate.

- Equipment simulators obviously are best at teaching people how to work with equipment.
- Business games are best for developing business decision-making skills (both day to day and more strategic) and for exploring and solving complex problems.
- The in-basket technique is best suited to development of strategic knowledge used in making day-to-day decisions.
- Case studies are most appropriate for developing analytic skills, higher-level principles, and complex problem-solving strategies. Because trainees do not actually implement their decision/solution, its focus is more on the "what to do" (strategic knowledge) than on the "how to get it done" (skills).
- Role plays provide a good vehicle for developing interpersonal skills and personal insight, allowing trainees to practice interacting with others and receiving feedback.

Role playing is an especially effective technique for creating attitude change (Solem 1960; Fazio and Zanna 1981). It allows trainees to act out behavior that reflects their attitudes and to experience others' reactions as well as their own feelings about the behavior. This experience and feedback allow the trainee to make appropriate attitudinal adjustments. As an old role-playing saying goes: "Seeing's believing, but feeling's the truth." Although trainees may see the logic of a principle through a lecture and see its application in a video or CBT, they are able to feel its personal value only when they use it themselves.

Learning Process
Attention   One of the strengths of games and simulations is their ability to gain the attention of the learner. A potential drawback is that it may focus attention away from the learning objectives. The active learning process used by these training methods is generally more compelling to trainees than sitting through a lecture or reading a text. In most games and many simulations, the aspect of competition against oneself or others increases attention and enthusiasm. Many also have clever gimmicks that

capture trainees' interest, but these can also distract trainees from the real objectives of the training. Sometimes trainees get so engrossed in the competition or "figuring out" the gimmick that they fail to learn the principles or develop the skills the game/simulation was intended to produce. That is why it is important for trainers to build modules into the training that prepares trainees to use the game or simulation by identifying the desired learning outcomes. Modules might also be planned for breaks during the simulation to capture learning that has occurred and to refocus trainees on the learning objectives. In general, a debriefing module should always be included so that trainees can reflect and elaborate on what they have learned.

Another important factor affecting trainee attention is the credibility of the game or simulation. When it does not realistically represent the key characteristics of the trainees' job, trainees will not take it seriously and will give it less attention. Consider a role play or simulation designed to improve union/management problem solving. It asks trainees who are members of union/management committees to work on resolving certain issues. If these issues are, in reality, already contractually mandated in the company, both sides have to pretend that part of the labor contract doesn't exist. Since it does exist, trainees are likely to consider the training irrelevant and not take it seriously.

Retention   Games and simulations are best at developing trainees' skills in applying or using knowledge. The assumption, then, is that the factual and procedural knowledge needed to play the game or use the simulation has already been provided, and so this information exists as symbolic codes in the trainees' cognitive structure. Games or simulations don't do a very good job of teaching facts or procedures, but they are very good at enhancing factual and procedural knowledge through the repeated recall and use of the information during the training. Thus they serve to refine and reinforce symbolic coding. Games and simulations focus primarily on the cognitive organization and symbolic rehearsal processes. Because the trainee must use many different areas of knowledge to complete the game or simulation, it allows the trainee to see connections and relationships between different bodies of knowledge. Learning these new connections and relationships allows trainees to solve problems and develop strategies for achieving goals. Most games and simulations require trainees to engage in symbolic rehearsal by having them plan out their action steps and anticipate their consequences.

Behavioral Reproduction   Of course, the real strength of games and simulations is their focus on learning by doing. Creating realistic situations in which trainees can apply their knowledge to goal-directed actions and receive fairly immediate feedback is critical for skill development. For games and simulations behavioral reproduction is a significant part of the learning process. In order for the desired learning to occur, the training design must include feedback to the trainees about their actions. This requirement follows from the principles of reinforcement and shaping discussed in chapter 3.

TRAINING GROUP CHARACTERISTICS

Equipment simulators are typically used by one person at a time. This provides an advantage in that differences in trainee readiness can, to some extent, be addressed. As with all games and simulations, however, trainees must possess the prerequisite knowledge and skill to make effective use of the method. Equipment simulators do limit the number of trainees who can be trained on the device. This becomes a problem when a large number of trainees must be trained in a short period of time.

Business games and simulations, including behavior modeling, typically use small groups ranging in size from three to eight trainees. Differences in trainee characteristics can be both an advantage and disadvantage, depending on the goals of the training. Differences in content knowledge or experience can be an advantage if one of the goals of training is to increase the awareness of how different people approach the situation. In a business game or simulation, for example, constructing a group of trainees from different functional areas of the business allows each trainee to learn how decisions in their area affect other areas. Thus, all trainees learn a more integrative framework for decision making. On the other hand, such groups generate more conflict and require more time for discussion and decision making. Other differences in content knowledge can be more troublesome. When some trainees in the group are more knowledgeable of basic business concepts than others, they can become irritated at having to educate the rest of the group. They see others as getting a lot more out of the training than they are. In general, it is best to make sure that groups are formed so that everyone has relatively the same level of basic knowledge. However, this will depend on the training objectives. Having more knowledgeable trainees educate those less knowledgeable may be your method of choice. The point is that the trainer must take care to identify how trainee group composition matches the training objectives.

On-the-Job Training

The most frequently used training method, especially in smaller businesses, is to use the more experienced and skilled employees, whether co-workers or supervisors, to train less skilled and experienced employees. This **on-the-job training (OJT)** takes many forms and can be supplemented with classroom training. Instruction by co-workers or supervisors at the job site often occurs on an informal basis and is characterized by the following:

- It has not been carefully thought out or prepared.
- It is done on an ad hoc basis with no predetermined content or process.
- No objectives or goals have been developed or referred to during training.
- The trainers are chosen on the basis of technical expertise, not training ability.
- Trainers have no formal training in how to train.

Formal OJT programs are quite different. They are typically conducted by employees who have been identified as having superior (not necessarily the best) technical knowledge/skills and who can effectively use one-on-one instructional techniques. Since conducting one-on-one training is not a skill most people develop on their own, organizations with formal OJT programs provide "train the trainer" training for these employees.

Formal OJT programs should have a carefully developed sequence of learning events. Learning is usually achieved through the following steps:

- The trainee observes a more experienced and skilled employee (the trainer) performing job-related tasks.

- The procedures and techniques used are discussed before, during, and after the trainer has demonstrated how the job tasks are performed.
- When the trainer determines that the trainee is ready, the trainee begins performing the job tasks.
- The trainer provides continuing guidance and feedback.
- The trainee is gradually given more and more of the job to perform until he can adequately perform the entire job on his own.

The generalized instructional process described above is formalized in more detail as the **job instruction technique (JIT).**

JOB INSTRUCTION TECHNIQUE (JIT)

Gold (1981) noted that the JIT, developed during World War II, was still one of the best techniques for the implementation of OJT. It continues to be a standard in evaluating OJT programs. The technique uses a behavioral strategy with a focus on skill development, but there are usually some factual and procedural knowledge objectives as well. JIT consists of four steps—prepare, present, try out, and follow up—as shown in Table 7.4.

TABLE 7.4   JIT Instruction/Learning Sequence

Basics of Instruction	*Social Learning Processes Activated*[a]
Prepare	Attention and motivation
• Break down the job.	
• Prepare an instruction plan.	
• Put the learner at ease.	
Present	Attention
• Tell.	Retention:
• Show.	Symbolic coding
• Demonstrate.	Cognitive organization
• Explain.	
Try Out	Retention: Symbolic rehearsal
• Have the learner "talk through" the job.	
• Have the learner instruct the supervisor on how the job is done.	
• Let the learner do the job.	Behavioral reproduction
• Provide feedback, both positive and negative.	Reinforcement
• Let the learner practice.	
Follow Up	
• Check progress frequently at first and provide feedback.	Behavioral reproduction Reinforcement
• Tell the learner whom to go to for help.	
• Gradually taper off progress checks.	

[a] From *Social Learning Theory,* Figure 3.6 (page 111).

Prepare

Preparation and follow up are the two areas that are most often ignored in OJT programs. Preparation should include a written breakdown of the job. The person responsible for the OJT may believe that, because he knows the job very well, there is no need to prepare a written documentation of it. To ignore this step, however, is to miss seeing the job through the eyes of the trainee. If the trainer knows the job very well, there are probably many things he does without thinking, and as a result they can be overlooked in training. A systematic analysis and documentation of the job tasks will ensure that all the points are covered in the training.

The next step is to prepare an instructional plan. First, the trainer must determine what the trainee already knows. The person analysis portion of a needs assessment provides this information. If a TNA has been completed, the trainer will need to review these data. If not, checking personnel records and interviewing the trainee are ways of determining what the trainee knows and what training should focus on.

Finally, putting the trainee at ease is just as important in OJT as it is in the classroom. You must take care to create a comfortable learning atmosphere. One way to accomplish this is to provide the trainee with an orientation to the OJT/JIT learning process. This may or may not be provided by the JIT trainer. In this orientation you should help trainees understand their role and the role of the trainer in the process. The importance of trainee listening and questioning should be emphasized. Familiarizing trainees with the steps in the JIT process will reduce their anxiety because they will know what to expect.

Present

The four activities of this stage are tell, show, demonstrate, and explain (Gold 1981). First, tell and show. As the trainer you would provide an overview of the job while showing the trainee the different aspects of the job. You are not actually doing the job, but pointing out where buttons are pushed, where materials are located, where to stand, and so on. When this is completed, you would demonstrate how to do the job and explain why it is done in that manner. If the job has many components or is complex, you should cover only one segment at a time, in the same order in which they occur when the job is performed. During the demonstration you would indicate why the procedure is performed in that particular way, emphasizing key learning points and important safety instructions.

Try Out

Before actually trying the behaviors, the trainee should be able to explain to the trainer how to do the job. This step provides a safe transition from watching and listening to doing (symbolic rehearsal). The trainee then attempts to perform the job and the trainer is able to provide instant feedback. The trainer should consider that any errors that take place are probably a function of the training, not the trainee. With this in mind, the focus will be on improving the method of instruction rather than on the inability of the trainee to comprehend. In any case it is useful to allow the trainee to learn from mistakes, provided they are not too costly. Allowing the trainee to see the consequences of using an incorrect procedure, such as having to scrap the product, reinforces the use of the correct procedures. Such an occurrence becomes a form of negative reinforcement, since using the correct procedures avoids the scrap. The trainer can help by questioning the trainee about his actions while the trainee is performing the job and by guiding him in identifying the correct procedures.

Follow Up

There is a tendency for informal OJT programs to consider training completed after the previous step. This is not the case. The trainer must check the trainees' work often enough to prevent incorrect or bad work habits from developing. It is important that trainees feel comfortable asking for help during these initial solo efforts. The trainer should take every opportunity to reinforce trainees in areas where they are performing well. As trainees demonstrate proficiency in the job, progress checks can taper off until eventually they are eliminated.

APPRENTICESHIP TRAINING

Apprenticeship training, another form of OJT, is one of the oldest forms of training. Its roots date back to the Middle Ages, when skilled craftsmen and tradesmen passed on their knowledge to others as a way of preserving the guilds (similar to unions) they belonged to. There are many similarities in today's North American apprenticeship programs. Apprenticeship programs are partnerships between labor unions, employers, schools, and the government. Most apprenticeships are in skilled trade and professional unions such as for boiler engineers, electrical workers, pipe fitters, and carpenters. In general, an apprenticeship program requires about two years of on-the-job experience and 180 hours of classroom instruction, though requirements vary from program to program (*National Apprenticeship Training Program* 1987). Journeymen provide the training on the job, and adult education centers and community colleges typically provide the classroom training. An apprentice must be able to demonstrate mastery of all required skills and knowledge before being allowed to graduate to journeyman status. These programs are regulated by governmental agencies, which also set standards and provide services.

COACHING

Coaching is the process of providing one-on-one guidance and instruction to improve knowledge, skills, and work performance. Usually, coaching is directed at employees with performance deficiencies, but it can also be used as a motivational tool for those performing adequately. While co-workers can be coaches, especially in team-based organizations, more typically it is the supervisor who acts as coach. One analysis suggests that in the past supervisors spent, on the average, only about 10% of their time coaching subordinates, but in today's organizations they typically spend more than 50% of their time in such activities (Finnerty 1996). Although there are many different models of how the coaching process works, the format generally follows the outline below. This outline looks at the process from the coach's perspective.

1. Understand the trainee's job, the KSAs and resources required to meet performance expectations, and the trainee's current level of performance.
2. Meet with the trainee and mutually agree on the performance objectives to be achieved.
3. Mutually arrive at a plan/schedule for achieving the performance objectives.

4. At the work site, show the trainee how to achieve the objectives, observe the trainee perform, then provide feedback. This is similar to JIT.
5. Repeat step 4 until performance improves.

As can be seen, coaching is similar to JIT, involving one-on-one instruction in how to perform a task. A key factor in the learning process is the interpersonal relationship between the coach and the trainee.

While coaching is clearly a skill-focused method, it can also be used for knowledge development (e.g., facts and procedures), although other methods are better for transmitting knowledge. Like the OJT trainer, the coach must be skilled both in how to do the task(s) and in how to train others to do them. HRD professionals typically don't perform the role of coach (unless they are coaching other HRD professionals). Rather, they train supervisors in the coaching process and develop the supervisors' interpersonal skills to make them more effective.

Mentoring is considered to be a form of coaching in which an ongoing relationship is developed between a senior and junior employee. The purpose of mentoring is to provide the more junior employee with guidance and a clear understanding of how the organization goes about its business. Whereas coaching focuses on the technical aspects of the job, mentoring focuses more on improving the employee's fit within the organization. Thus coaching emphasizes skill development, and mentoring emphasizes attitude development. Generally, mentoring is conducted only for management-level employees, though in some cases it has been applied at lower levels. In the past mentoring was primarily an informal activity, but it has become formalized in many organizations. The concerns about untrained OJT trainers discussed earlier apply to mentoring as well.

TRAINING THE TRAINER FOR OJT

For OJT programs to be effective, the trainers must be motivated to serve in the training role, be skilled as trainers, and have the interpersonal skills necessary to interact effectively with those they train (Rothwell and Kazanas 1994). The components for training the trainer should include the following:

- The company's formal OJT process (e.g., JIT), the policies and support provided by the organization
- Interpersonal skills and feedback techniques
- Principles of adult learning

Trainers' normal job responsibilities should be reduced while they are training others. Some reduction in productivity must be anticipated and built into job expectations. As with any other job assignment, performance as a trainer should be evaluated periodically with feedback and appropriate reinforcement.

STRENGTHS AND LIMITATIONS OF OJT

OJT is clearly a useful method for skill enhancement, since trainees are applying their knowledge in the actual job situation. Thus transfer of training occurs naturally. An additional benefit is that the OJT process will provide new employees with a rapid orientation to how the company operates. It also has the potential of developing more positive relationships among older and new employees and between supervisors and their subordinates.

A major concern in OJT is the competency of the trainer. The trainer must possess the technical competence, the training competence, and the motivation to train. Without all these characteristics, training is not likely to be successful. In addition, the organization must provide the trainer with enough time away from his regular job to do the training. This accommodation not only leads to better training, but demonstrates the organization's commitment to its OJT program.

Cost

OJT has some clear cost advantages if it is done effectively. Trainees and trainers are both at the job site performing job activities. Though neither the trainee nor the trainer will be producing at full capacity, they are at least producing something. With other techniques, neither the trainer nor the trainee is engaged in producing the organization's products or services while training is going on. Also there are no expensive training materials to purchase such as simulators, games, or computer-based training modules. All the materials are part of the normal work equipment.

OJT also speeds up the learning process. There is no delay between training and its application to the work situation. In addition, there is evidence that one-on-one training produces faster learning that is more resistant to forgetting (Gordon, Morgan, and Ponticell 1995). The more efficient the training, the less costly it is.

One cost concern in implementing OJT is the cost of training the trainers. Unlike other methods, for a start-up OJT system most if not all of the trainers will need training. In addition, while other methods have one trainer for many trainees, this method uses one-on-one training. The drop in productivity due to having the more skilled employees conducting training must be added into the cost. In addition, companies should expect some increased waste, breakage, and downtime due to inexperienced trainees operating the equipment.

Control of Content and Process

The content and process of learning in OJT is controlled primarily by the trainer during the "prepare" and "present" stages of training. As training progresses to the "try out" and "follow-up" stages, the trainee and trainer jointly control the content and process. This occurs because it is the trainee's actions that determine what the next learning module will be. The training moves as quickly or as slowly as necessary for the trainee to master the learning. Thus, if the trainee is in the "talk through" portion of trying it out and misses some steps, the trainer might again demonstrate how the job is done. If the trainee is able to "talk through" the steps correctly, the trainee might be ready to move to the "instruct the trainer" portion. However, if the trainee said, "You know, I was just guessing on some of those steps," the trainer might repeat the "talk through" portion until the trainee felt confident he knew all the steps.

Learning Objectives (KSAs)

The primary focus of OJT is skill development, but since we have discussed this aspect previously, we will not deal with it here except to say that OJT is a good method of developing skills. OJT can also enhance the knowledge base of trainees and influence their attitudes. Through discussions with the trainer and through questioning and restating of techniques, the trainee can learn factual and elementary procedural information. However, classroom techniques and individual reading assignments are more efficient and do a better job of developing this type of knowledge. Advanced procedural knowledge and strategic knowledge are better developed through experiential learning like OJT. This occurs through a combination of observation and discussion as well as through physical interaction with the equipment, materials, and other accoutrements of the job.

The attitudes new employees hold about their job and their company come from observing and interacting with others. OJT provides a great opportunity to get employees off on the right foot by clarifying the norms, expectations, and culture of the work unit. Of course, accomplishing this will depend on the ability of the OJT trainer to convey these appropriately to the trainee.

On a final note, if knowledge acquisition is required to perform the job, OJT techniques should be supplemented with other techniques that are more suited to knowledge acquisition. Apprenticeship training is a good example. For skilled trades, it is important to develop the skills of the trade; however, certain knowledge is a prerequisite for that skill development. That is why a significant amount of classroom training is also required as a part of the training. Computer-based training, role playing, reading texts, manuals, and other techniques can all be combined successfully with OJT.

Learning Process

Trainees are likely to be relatively more attentive and more motivated during OJT, since it is easier to see a direct relationship between the training and job performance. Verbal and visual stimuli direct attention to key learning points. Periods of active practice require the trainee to attend to what they are doing and what is being said, thus increasing the learning potential.

The visual, auditory, and tactile cues in OJT assist in the symbolic coding process, providing many relationships among objects and actions in the work environment. Through observation, practice, and discussion, the trainee cognitively organizes these relationships into easily recalled patterns of behavior.

By asking the trainee to describe the steps in the operation (before letting the trainee perform the operation), the trainer is facilitating the symbolic rehearsal process. The trainee must imagine himself going through the operations as he describes the procedures.

Behavioral reproduction, of course, is a strong point of this method. The trainee practices small portions of the operation until they are mastered and then moves on to larger portions until his command over the tasks that make up the job have reached the level needed to perform the job alone.

Audiovisual Enhancements to Training

Audiovisuals (AVs) can be useful enhancements for meeting all three types of training objectives (K, S, and A) and are easily applied to any of the other methods discussed. **Audiovisual aids** consist of any physical, mechanical and/or electronic media used to provide or assist instruction. Typically they are used as a supplement to other methods of training, rather than as a standalone means of instruction, though some are effective training devices by themselves.

The range of AV alternatives is quite large, from simple chalkboard or whiteboard text and images to interactive multimedia presentations. They can be grouped under the headings of static or dynamic media. **Static media** are presentations of fixed text or images such as printed matter, overhead transparencies, pictures/slides, and computer-generated projections. An AV is considered static if the material presented is stationary. **Dynamic media** create sequentially moving stimuli. That is, the information is presented in a continuously moving progression from a beginning to an end. Audiotapes and videotapes, computer-generated presentations, and moving film are examples.

STATIC MEDIA

Static media are generally not suitable for training as a standalone method. Rather they are used to augment and enhance other methods, in particular the lecture method, but they are adaptable to other training techniques as well.

Newsprint/Charts and Posters

Newsprint, charts, and posters display information through words and/or images. They range from handmade, with felt markers and newsprint, to professionally prepared, glossy prints. The advantage of these presentations is that they can be posted on walls or other vertical surfaces so the information is visible to trainees while other training methods are in use (e.g., lecture, role plays, video). For example, these media are frequently used to post an outline of the day's training and to display procedural steps related to the training material. They allow trainees to place the material that is presented at any time in the program to be put in the context of the total program. Figure 7.1 shows a poster that could be used during conflict resolution training. It might be left up during the entire training so that trainees are constantly reminded of the six steps the training focuses on.

Posters and charts the trainer knows will be used during training should be prepared before training and checked for accuracy. The credibility of the training and the trainer will suffer if errors exist on these materials.

Projected Text and Images

In the past, the two methods of projecting text or images for simultaneous viewing by an audience were photographic slides and overhead transparencies. Today there are also computer-generated projections. *Photographic slides* are simply photographs of training-related text, graphics, or actual equipment. They require the subject matter to be prepared and photographed, the film to be developed, and the slides to be mounted and ordered in the correct sequence.

Creating *overhead transparencies* requires text and images to be transferred to the transparency material (generally clear acetate). This can be done by hand with transparency markers, but the result is not usually professional looking and can damage the credibility of the training. Computer-generated text and images as well as those copied from printed matter can be pasted together to create attention-getting and informative overheads. This can be done through a variety of mechanical devices, but usually a fairly advanced computer system and image scanner are required.

Computer-generated projections are more sophisticated than overhead transparencies. Many popular office software packages contain "presentation" software components that allow you to create projections, discussion notes, and other training aids you can integrate into the presentation. Microsoft and Corel are two com-

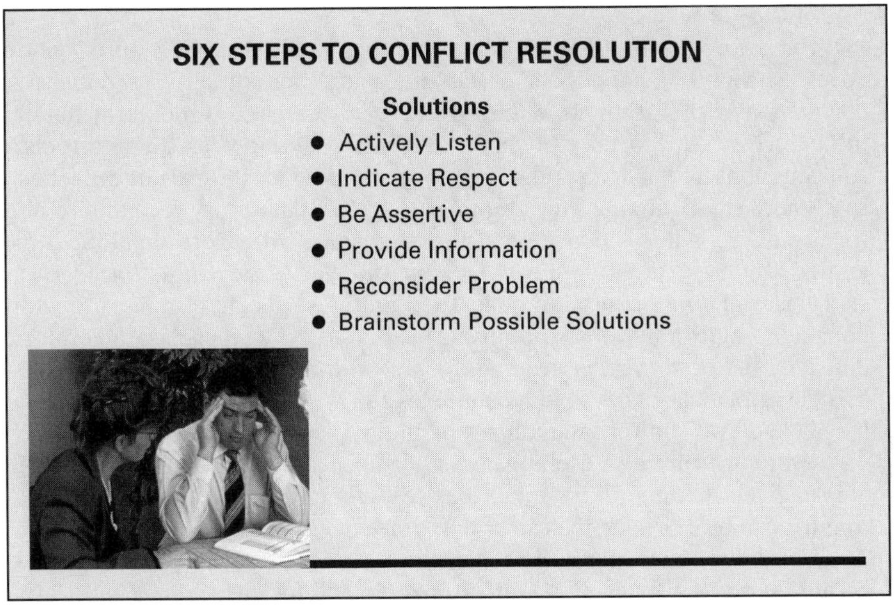

FIGURE 7.1 Example of a Poster That Might Be Used in Conflict Resolution Training

panies that produce such programs. Once the projections have been created and placed in proper order, they can be downloaded onto a floppy disk or stored on the hard drive. During the training itself, the trainer will require a computer, a high-intensity overhead projector, and a liquid crystal display (LCD) unit. The computer communicates the image to be projected to the LCD unit, and the projector projects an enlarged image from the LCD unit onto a large screen. Several manufacturers have integrated the projector and LCD units into a single machine that will also project video images. The presenter can control the display of the projections with a mouse, clicking to move from one projection to the next, or he can time the presentation so that the image automatically advances to the next projection after a specified period of time.

Each of these methods has the same purpose: to focus trainees' attention on specific content. In addition to displaying information, projections can aid the trainer in moving systematically through the components of the training. This feature is especially useful in training methods where the interaction between trainer and trainees may cause the trainer to lose his place; the trainer can simply look to the projection being displayed to get back on track.

DYNAMIC AUDIOVISUAL METHODS

Dynamic AVs include audio-only tapes, moving film, videos, and computer-generated presentations. Dynamic visuals can also serve as aids to enhance other methods of training. However, unlike static visuals, these methods can be and frequently are used as the sole method of training.

Audio-Only Tapes

The *audiotape* has the same characteristics as the straight lecture. The only differences are that the audiotape is exactly the same each time it is used and it has no accompanying visual stimulus. While advances in video and computer-generated presentations have reduced the popularity of audio-only tapes as training tools, there are still situations in which an audio-only tape could be used to advantage. They are effective where the content of the training is primarily auditory recognition and/or auditory response. Almost fifty percent of companies with more than 50 employees use audiocassettes in their training (*Training and Development* 1998). One obvious instance is when the material to be learned requires specific responses to auditory cues. Telephone and radio operators of all types (e.g., 911 emergency operators, taxi dispatchers, and customer service line operators) can receive beneficial training through audiotape playback that closely simulates the work environment. Learning a foreign language is also a fairly common use of audiotapes.

Audiotapes are also useful when other forms of training are not available. For example, given the amount of time sales representatives spend in their cars, audiotape training can be a productive use of that time.

Thus advantages of this approach over the lecture are its portability and ability to be reused both for training additional people and for easy review and clarification by trainees. Also if it is important that all trainees receive exactly the same information, an audiotape will be better than a lecture.

Moving Film and Videos

Videos and *motion picture* film are good ways of both showing and telling trainees how to do something. They can present conceptual or factual information by integrating narration with visual illustrations, graphics, and animated depictions. These media are relatively portable and generally can be made available to trainees at their convenience. It's clear these media have many advantages. No wonder 96% of companies with 50 or more employees used videotapes for training (*Training and Development* 1996), making them second only to classroom instruction.

Videos in particular have been used as a standalone training technique. A video, like a lecture, is a one-way communication system, but with the disadvantage of no discussion/question session. A number of firms have used video to enhance training in ways similar to those described in Training in Action 7.4. However, the use of interactive video technology is becoming more widespread, allowing some degree of two-way interaction. This type of training is very similar to computer-based training.

The advent of widespread video recording and playback capability has reduced the use of film. Many of the most frequently viewed training films have been transferred to the video format. The ease of use, both in developing the product and presenting it during the training, makes video superior to film in almost every instance. However, if there is an already existing film that can be of value in training, by all means use it.

Computer-Generated Dynamic Presentations (CGDP)

With the ability to project computer screen images onto a large screen and the increasing ability to digitize sound and image electronically, the computer is rapidly becoming a critical training tool. Multimedia software allows computers to store, modify,

---

Training in Action 7.4

Using Video in Catalog Sales Training

Here are two examples of how videos have been used to train employees working in the catalog department of two very different types of organizations.

The Boston Museum of Fine Arts mails out catalogs of museum reproductions on a seasonal basis. They use seasonal and temporary labor to help keep costs low, but this practice requires constant training of new personnel. To meet this need, they commissioned Creative Video Design to produce a training video for their telephone order takers. The video demonstrates how to greet the customer, how the phone system works, how to log on to the computer, enter the order, etc. Another video was developed for the warehouse personnel demonstrating how to read and interpret inventory and shipping slips.

Talbots is a women's fashion merchandiser with hundreds of stores and a large catalog sales department. To make sure their catalog employees understand Talbots' total operations, and particularly the way the catalog department works, they have developed a series of videos. One provides a video tour of the catalog and store distribution center to new employees. Another video traces how a piece of clothing listed in their catalog makes its journey from the customer's order to delivery to the customer's home. Having a full understanding of the operations helps catalog salespeople give better service and advice to their customers.

Source: Summarized from *Catalog Age,* January 1994, p. 59.

---

and reconfigure sound and image as well as text to create nearly any combination of audio and visual presentation. Developing a computer-generated dynamic presentation (CGDP) does require considerably more hardware and software knowledge than do the presentation software packages discussed earlier. The development process is similar to that of producing a video but also includes converting all the components into digital media. As with video productions, it is advisable to use professionals to ensure the quality of the presentation.

STRENGTHS AND LIMITATIONS OF AUDIOVISUALS

Static AVs are one-way communication techniques and should rarely if ever be used as standalone training tools. The only exception is printed material such as books or pamphlets; these can by used alone if the material is simple and straightforward. This use typically occurs as self-study materials and not as part of a formalized training program. Because static media cannot demonstrate how to use the material, answer questions, or allow for interaction between the trainee and trainer, their value is greatest as a supplement to other methods. Because they are generally not appropriate as a standalone training method, we will compare static visuals with each other and with dynamic audiovisual methods.

Cost

Static AVs   An advantage of static visuals is their lower development costs. These range from low (overhead transparencies, flip charts, and computer-generated projections) to moderate (photographic slides and professionally prepared posters). Implementation costs, on the other hand, range from low (flip charts and overhead transparencies) to high (computer-generated projections). The high implementation cost is entirely due to the cost of equipment. Overhead projectors are relatively inexpensive (several hundred dollars), slide projectors are slightly more, and computer image projection requires a relatively sophisticated system, which can range from $3,500 to $10,000. Of course, all this equipment is amortized across the training sessions in which it is used, so even the most expensive projection devices may be only a minor factor in the total cost of training.

Static visuals are reusable, so a trainee who didn't understand it the first time can look at it again and again. It isn't necessary, however, for the trainee to use the original materials. For a minimal cost, overhead transparencies and computer-generated projections can be copied to paper and given as handouts (slides are more expensive to convert). Doing this will help to address any moderate to small differences in learning readiness among trainees.

Computer-generated overhead transparencies and projections have a unique advantage because they are stored electronically. Any given display can be modified relatively easily by adding or removing text and images, reducing the cost of program modifications or adaptations. Slides, on the other hand, would have to be completely redone. For example, assume you have produced 30 photographic slides for training human resource clerks in the proper procedure for processing a worker's compensation claim. It is not likely these slides would be much use in training supervisors about how to handle a workplace accident, even though worker's compensation claims are closely related. If computer-generated overheads or projections had been used, the original projections could be easily modified to delete irrelevant material and include the new material. Likewise, if six months later the government rewrites the worker's compensation laws, you will probably need to replace most of the slides for the HR clerks rather than modifying the existing slides. Technological advances in computer imaging and projection have made slides less and less viable as static visual aids.

Dynamic AVs   Using a professional video production company is expensive. A completed video can cost from $700 to $1,200 per minute (Honeycutt, McCarty, and Howe 1993) or more, but it is often worth the cost because of the professional appearance of the video. Even developing in-house videos is fairly expensive, given the cost of labor, equipment, and so on. Developing an original CGDP can require even higher up-front costs than producing a video, because each component of the multimedia package must be developed, then digitized and integrated into a coherent, logically flowing package. The cost of development is lowered if the training components can be developed digitally in the first place.

Although the up-front cost is high, the per-person cost of producing a video can be low if the trainee population is large enough. Videos, film, and CGDP are portable and reusable. Videos and computer-generated dynamic presentations are easily and cheaply duplicated. Therefore, they can be seen by different trainees in different places at any time, and they can be seen many times by the same trainee. This is valuable for refresher courses or for trainees who learn at a slower pace. Because of their reusability, the development cost can be spread over a large number of trainees, reducing the per-trainee costs.

When they are used for standalone training, the biggest advantage of videos and CGDPs is that trainees can view/study at their convenience. This cability can have a significant cost and time savings with regard to the trainees' and trainers' travel. For example, ADC Communications estimated it would cost about $150,000 to bring the company's 60 salespeople to the Minneapolis headquarters for a week of sales training (Honeycutt, McCarty, and Howe 1993). By using standalone video training, this cost was eliminated. Since most employees have a VCR and television at home, there is little equipment for the company to buy. The company should, however, provide on-site equipment for those employees who do not own the equipment or whose home environment is not conducive to learning. CGDP does not have this equipment cost advantage, since the necessary hardware and software cannot be assumed to be widely owned by employees.

Finally, if employees view the tape at home or on free time at work, the productivity savings are substantial. If trainees must travel more than 200 miles to get to a centralized training location, they will have lost not only their productivity for the time they were at training, but also one or two days of travel time.

One way to cut the cost of video training is to rent or buy a video from commercial producers. A large number of commercially available training videos cover a wide variety of topics. Also videos and films produced primarily for entertainment can be used effectively in training. For example, one of the authors has used segments of the classic film *Twelve Angry Men* (a film about a jury's deliberations during a criminal trial) to illustrate the problems and benefits of consensus decision making. Small portions of the movie *Falling Down* have been used to illustrate various risk factors and warning signs for workplace violence. Television broadcasts can be used in a similar fashion. For example, textbook publishers are now accompanying some of their textbooks with videocassettes containing segments of news programs and TV specials that relate to the content of the text.

Equipment costs vary across the media used. Film requires a projector and screen for presentation, and a video requires a VCR and television. Videos can also be projected onto large screens with a video projector. The technology is rapidly improving, and state-of-the-art projectors (costing about $4,000) can display large-screen images. This capability overcomes one of the disadvantages of the TV video, which is that only a small group of trainees can easily see it at the same time.

Control of Material and Process

Static AVs   Generally computer-generated projections are more easily controlled by the trainer than are other static visuals. The sequence of projections can be structured so material is displayed only when the presenter begins to discuss it. Text can be programmed to fade into and out of the projection with a click of the mouse. The mouse can also be used to point to or highlight particular parts of the projection. Finally, there is no need to worry about slides or overheads getting out of order, being upside down, and the like. Because the whole visual presentation is contained on a single floppy disk, it is more easily transportable than slides or overheads.

While computer-generated projection has many advantages, it also has a major disadvantage: It suffers all the potential problems of computer technology. Hard drives crash at inopportune times, floppy disks aren't readable by the operating system, viruses abound, and software and disk formatting compatibility issues must be solved. To avoid most of these problems, you can carry your own portable computer to the training site, but make sure a compatible backup is available. Of course, carrying a laptop reduces the convenience of having to carry only a single floppy disk.

Dynamic AVs   The disadvantage of acquiring a commercially made video is that the information may not be specific to your company or your training content but rather must appeal to the largest audience. When you use such videos, you will likely need to augment them with additional training relevant to your trainees. You control the content and process of learning through selecting the video and creating the supplemental materials.

The portability of dynamic audiovisuals means that trainees can take them off the shelf and use them when convenient. To this extent, the learning process is controlled by the trainee. However, watching a training video or multimedia presentation at home allows for many distractions. The process with which training occurs is completely in the hands of the trainee, since she can stop the presentation whenever she likes and do something else. Thus the desired level of learning may not be attained.

When video and CGDP are used as standalone techniques, the content and presentation format are controlled, but not the manner in which the trainee goes through the material. Particularly with video, the trainee may fast-forward over parts he doesn't understand or is bored with. Thus evaluating learning is particularly important when this training technique is used.

Learning Objectives (KSAs)

Appropriately prepared and displayed audiovisuals will enhance almost any training and are especially effective for techniques in which the trainee is less active, such as lecture/discussion and some types of CBT. However, the nature of the learning objective will determine which type of audiovisual is most appropriate.

Knowledge   Both static and dynamic AVs facilitate the trainee's knowledge development through their ability to activate or enhance learning processes. They focus trainee attention and provide visual stimuli that aid symbolic coding and cognitive organization. They are also useful for highlighting cues that will stimulate appropriate recall. AVs are most effective at enhancing declarative knowledge but can also be useful in developing procedural knowledge. Dynamic audiovisuals are more suited than static AVs for developing procedural knowledge, because they are able to model the steps required to perform the task and display a variety of situations in which the task is appropriate.

Skills   Static presentation of information is not very useful for skill building. They do not lend themselves to facilitating development or the practice of skills. Dynamic presentations, however, can be very useful in skill development and practice. For example, foreign language audiotapes use this approach. Dynamic audiovisuals can also make it easier to simulate the work environment. In police departments, for example, a film or video is used to place the trainee in the position of searching a building for an armed and dangerous suspect. The trainee must make decisions about what to do in a variety of situations such as the sudden appearance of objects and people, or entering a room with a closed door, and so on.

Another audiovisual technique increasingly being used is videotaping the trainee's performance during practice and using the video as feedback for skill improvement. While dynamic AVs can provide good models and instructions for skill development, usually they are not capable of providing feedback, so they should not be used as standalone methods. Interactive videos and CGDP provide the exceptions to this rule.

Attitudes   Static and dynamic AVs, used in conjunction with other techniques, can facilitate attitude change by visually clarifying the relationships among objects and events that are the basis of trainee opinions and evaluations. For example, the Domtar plant in southern California used static visuals to display the consequences of not following correct safety procedures. This manufacturer of construction products used graphic displays of eye injuries in a safety training program to develop positive attitudes about wearing safety goggles. It also used pictures of employees working on various equipment with some wearing and some not wearing safety goggles; trainees were asked to identify the potential hazards to the individual in each picture. The process allowed the trainees to make the proper links between wearing the goggles and protecting themselves from injury. It is interesting to note that this plant won many safety awards from both the company and the state. The ability to provide visual documentation of the relationship between objects and events is a powerful source of learning and attitude change. Beliefs such as "wearing goggles is uncomfortable and unnecessary" are often reinforced by cognitive distortions and rationalization. Statements like "If you're careful, you don't need goggles" and "I'm too experienced to get an eye injury" are examples of the kind of rationalizations heard at the Domtar plant. The trainer's words alone may not be sufficient to change attitudes. Visual displays allow the trainees to see that their distortions and rationalizations are inaccurate, making a change in attitudes easier to accomplish. Dynamic AVs can produce even more powerful images, because the connection between objects, actions, and consequences can be made even more explicit.

Learning Process
Attention   The phrase "a picture is worth a thousand words" reflects the importance of visual representation in the learning process. Static visuals provide the trainee with a visually based message, even if the image is simply enlarged text. Visual stimuli focus the trainee's attention when they represent a change in the environment. No matter how professional, a trainer's voice and image become familiar to the trainees after a period of time. When this occurs, it becomes easier for the trainee's attention to wander. The periodic presentation of new visual stimuli activates the attention process. If the visuals are consistently similar in format (e.g., all text, black print, same font size) they too will lose their ability to attract attention. Combining graphic images, charts, and text and varying color to highlight key learning points will add zest to the training and maintain trainee attention. With dynamic audiovisuals the dynamic nature of the presentation itself attracts attention, since it is constantly changing.

The trainer should be careful that all AVs are integrated with the content of the training. When they have little relationship to the content, they become distracting and can actually reduce learning. This can also occur if the trainer doesn't manage the presentation of the visuals properly, such as placing transparencies on the projector incorrectly, standing in front of the screen, or otherwise interfering with the normal viewing of the visual. Trainees often begin to attend to the trainer's management of the presentation rather than to the content of the presentation, thus reducing learning.

Retention   Because different trainees learn more or less effectively through different media, the use of AVs provides additional modalities for learning. When several media are used to convey the same message, the message is more easily coded for storage and has more reference points. In general, visual communications are absorbed more quickly and retained for a longer time than auditory messages. Visual images are also more readily coded symbolically and recalled in their original form (Gagné 1977).

The symbolic coding process is enhanced when pictures or graphic images provide visual cues that supplement or complement auditory or written cues. Combining cues from different senses results in more accurate symbolic coding and thus better retention (Gagné 1977). If a variety of images are shown, all pertaining to the same issue, trainees will have a wider base of common cues to use in storing the information. Audiovisuals also are extremely good for demonstrating events and effects not usually observable or noticed. For example, enlarged images of tiny or microscopic objects are useful in many training settings. In the safety training example discussed earlier, trainees were able to see the effects of not wearing goggles. Since eye injuries are often not easily observable, the visual projections used in the training allowed the trainees to see what actually happened to the eye and what damage very small bits of material can do. By making objects and effects visible, symbolic encoding becomes much easier.

Cognitive organization can be facilitated by graphic images that demonstrate how the training relates to familiar concepts. Pictorially representing these relationships makes integrating the new with the old easier than using verbal descriptions alone. Integration is likely to be easier and faster if the trainer is able to represent visually both the old cognitive organization and the new, showing the changes required. To the degree that the trainees' cognitive structures are different from each other, creating visual representations of them all is difficult. However, this can be accomplished by having the trainees develop pictorial representations of their cognitive organization on flip charts. They can then use these to compare with the new organization being presented. For example, suppose jobs in a work group have been redesigned because of a change in how the product is produced. During training you could have trainees map out how the old job was performed. Then, after presenting the new work procedures, you could then compare the old with the new and identify the areas where the new KSAs provided by the training will be needed.

Using AVs in training provides a common reference for all trainees. When you ask the trainees to "picture this" or "imagine you are . . . ," each trainee may hold a different image, but when you provide the image, they all receive the same sensory cues. When the trainees later recall the image, the frame of reference will be similar for all. Though there will be differential loss of information and detail across trainees, the basis of the recalled information is the initial image you provided.

AVs can be somewhat useful in aiding symbolic rehearsal. They provide visual cues that trainees can use to practice hypothetical applications of the training material. This works in much the same manner as behavioral reproduction, described be-low. The difference is that in symbolic rehearsal the trainees are only imagining them-selves applying the new learning. The AVs can help to create the context in which the symbolic rehearsal takes place as well as providing cues to assist in the symbolic re-hearsal (as in guided discovery).

Behavioral Reproduction   AVs can be used to enhance the learning of a new be-havior. By illustrating what to do, AVs can provide a model of how to perform. This is usually accomplished best with dynamic AVs. Static or dynamic AVs can also be used to provide the appropriate cues for when to perform. For example, sometimes cue cards are given to trainees when they are practicing new behaviors. These aids need to be present and visible when the new behavior is first being practiced. In the training facility, supplying these cues shouldn't pose a problem. However, to allow opportuni-ties for reproduction outside the training environment, the visual images must be eas-ily portable. Many training programs provide pocket- or wallet-sized cards (static vi-sual aid) to help trainees in practicing the new material back on the job. As we mentioned earlier, videos and CGDPs are portable but require equipment that may not be compatible with the trainee's work station (particularly line employees). What AVs are not able to do is observe the trainee's performance and provide appropriate feedback. Thus, while AVs can enhance behavioral reproduction, they have strong limitations as standalone tools for this type of learning.

The big advantage of CGDPs is that each component of the training can have the audiovisual format that is best for meeting the objectives of that component. Some of these multimedia packages are now interactive, allowing the trainee to respond to questions and even pose questions, and thereby in some ways eliminating the one-way communication limitation of standard videos and static AVs. With interactivity comes two-way communication, though the limitations discussed earlier about the quality and type of interaction should be kept in mind.

Limitations for Learning

The principal limitation of static visuals is that they are typically not standalone learning tools. They are best used as enhancements to other methods. Because they are static, they have difficulty capturing the full range of material that is dynamic. While it is possible to capture the essence of some types of dynamic material, such as the "steps in conflict resolution" or "tips for providing constructive feedback," dy-namic audiovisual media will generally do this more easily and with higher quality. Except for the most sophisticated dynamic AVs (i.e., interactive CGDP), they are un-able to adapt to differing characteristics of the trainees or the situation. It is a "one-size-fits-all" technique. If trainees do not have the KSAs to learn from the AV, they won't learn no matter how many times they reuse it.

Trainee Characteristics

Obviously the trainees must be able to understand the AVs. This point may sound fairly trivial, but it is often overlooked and is likely to occur more than is commonly believed. For example, the poster in Figure 7.1 assumes the trainees can read. If the trainees are managers, this is a pretty safe assumption. However, if they are line em-ployees in an assembly plant, there could be problems. Not only must trainees be able to read, they must understand the terms. Even all managers may not know what the trainer means by "actively listen," "assertive," or "reconsider the problem." Displaying this poster without defining all the terms might create confusion for the trainees. The issue of understandability applies to all AVs, static and dynamic.

When there are wide differences in trainee readiness levels, AVs aimed at the highest level of KSAs may not be understandable to those at the lower level. If they are aimed at the lowest level, they will seem unnecessary and boring to those at higher levels. If a dynamic AV is being used as a standalone program, it is probably best to provide separate training AVs customized to the readiness levels of each group.

A Summary of Method and Learning Objective Match

We have discussed in some depth the ability of the various training methods to address different KSA learning objectives. However, it is useful to have a summary of what each method does well. This is provided in Table 7.5. Please note that this table represents a general guide and more specific information is provided in the relevant

TABLE 7.5 Training Method Effectiveness at Meeting KSA Objectives

	GOAL OF TRAINING					
	Knowledge			*Skills*		*Attitudes*
Training Methods	*Declarative*	*Procedural*	*Strategic*	*Technical*	*Interpersonal*	
Lecture						
Straight	3	2	1	1	1	3
Discussion	4	3	2	1	1	4
Computer Based	5	4	3	2[a]	2	3
Simulation/ Cases						
Equipment	1	3	2	5	1	2
Case Study	3	2	4	2	2	3
Business Game	2	3	5	2	2[b]	2
In-Basket	1	3	4	1	2[c]	2
Role Play	1	2	2	2	4	5[d]
Behavior Modeling	1	3	3	4	5	3
OJT						
JIT	3	5	4	4	2	5
Apprentice	5	5	4	5	2	5
Coaching	3	5	4	4	4	5

Scale: 1 = not effective
2 = mildly effective
3 = moderately effective
4 = effective
5 = very effective

[a] This rating is for general technical skills. For some specific skills (i.e., computer software) the rating would be a 5.
[b] If the business game is designed for interpersonal skills, this would be a 4.
[c] If multiple in-baskets were used this rating would be 3.
[d] Specifically role reversal.

sections of this chapter and chapter 8. While learning objectives are a critical factor in designing a training program, other factors such as cost, control of training content, and learning processes also need to be taken into account. As the table notes, most of the methods are at least mildly effective in more than one area, and a particular learning objective can be met by more than one method. You may need to make trade-offs between effectiveness at meeting the learning objective and the cost of the method or the time required to develop it into a usable training program. These issues are discussed in the next chapter.

Key Terms

- Apprenticeship training
- Audiovisual aids
- Behavior modeling
- Behavioral methods
- Business games
- Case studies
- Coaching
- Cognitive methods
- Computer-based training (CBT)
- Discussion method
- Dynamic media
- Equipment simulators
- In-basket technique
- Incident process
- Job instruction technique (JIT)

- Lecturette
- Mentoring
- Multiple role play
- On-the-job training (OJT)
- Physical fidelity
- Programmed instruction (PI)
- Psychological fidelity
- Role play
- Role rotation
- Single role play
- Spontaneous role plays
- Static media
- Straight lecture
- Structured role plays

Case Analysis

Training for Customer Service Specialists

As a part of the president's initiative to remove "barriers to learning" at regional Midwestern University, an analysis of student services operations was conducted. That analysis revealed that the barriers deemed most important by students were those that would delay or prevent them from registering for classes. These fell into three areas:

- Resolving issues relating to fines accrued over the previous terms (e.g., library, parking, late fees).
- Accurately completing forms and meeting processing deadlines for financial aid in time to enroll in classes.
- Acquiring appropriate advising so that they enrolled in the right classes (avoiding the problems associated with drops and adds).

As a result of this analysis, the university decided to create a new position called Customer Service Specialist (CSS). The job description is presented below.

Classification Specification

Supersedes: New Classification

Title: Customer Service Specialist Grade: PT08

General Summary

Supervise, support, monitor, and assist with the continuous improvement of the work unit's customer service functions and related operational activities. Ensure quality customer service both in person and over the telephone. These activities require a working knowledge of the work unit's program policies, procedures, and regulations as well as an understanding of other departments and systems that interface with the work unit's activities.

Essential Duties

Personally provide and ensure that customer support staff provide positive customer service practices throughout the work unit, including: greeting departmental customers in person or over the telephone, identifying their needs, obtaining necessary and appropriate information, and processing customer requests in a manner that will best meet the needs of the customer.

Monitor and ensure that customers perceive that customer service support staff treat them with courtesy, respect, tact, and a sincere desire to meet their needs.

Provide mediation and resolution to customer complaints and requests within delegated authority limits and consistent with departmental policies.

Communicate to customers the departmental policies and procedures related to their needs, and provide customers with appropriate forms and instructions.

Design and implement systems to ensure that forms turned in by customers are the appropriate forms for their service request and that they are complete and, where possible, accurate.

Work with the appropriate departmental administrator to identify the training needs of designated support staff in the work unit who provide direct customer service. Where appropriate, provide on-the-job training and coaching. Work with the designated department administrator to identify appropriate training experiences for customer service support staff.

Recruit, interview, and make recommendations in the hiring of customer support staff.

Identify processes and procedures in the department that are causing problems for groups of customers (not individuals) and work with department management toward their improvement. Where authorized, implement improvements in systems, processes, and procedures that will increase the customer satisfaction capability of the department.

Develop and maintain a network of contacts with other university departments that commonly interface with the work unit.

Interact with other university departments to resolve a customer's problem or meet the customer's needs.

Interpret and reconcile account records related to area of assignment.

Receive, read, and interpret correspondence and determine proper handling.

Perform other related duties as assigned.

Supervision Received

Supervision is received from designated departmental administrator.

Supervision Exercised

Supervision may be exercised, as determined by the appropriate departmental administrator, over customer service representatives, clerical support staff, and student support staff in the work unit who provide direct customer service.

Qualifications

Ability to read, write, interpret instructions, and perform basic arithmetic, and communicate orally and in writing at a level typically acquired through the completion of an associates degree, is necessary.

Personal computing skills sufficient to utilize word processing and/or spreadsheet applications, and to perform file management and data input/retrieval functions are necessary. Knowledge of specific software applications and university information systems utilized in the work unit assigned is desirable.

Supervisory skills needed to provide direction to subordinates, monitor and manage subordinate performance, plan, organize and coordinate the customer service activities are required, and supervisory experience is desirable.

Preference is given to those who have mastered basic customer service and problem-solving skills listed below:

- The ability to communicate accurately and pleasantly with customers (across a wide diversity of cultural backgrounds) is necessary in order to identify customer needs and solve customer problems.

- The ability to communicate moderately to highly complex policies, procedures, and regulations and to ensure understanding of these while working under pressure (e.g., handling several requests at the same time) is required.

- Effective problem-solving abilities are required to: (1) identify and prioritize customer service problems, (2) conduct a root cause analysis to determine the cause(s) of a problem, (3) develop a range of alternatives that will remove the cause(s) of a problem, (4) identify the alternatives that are most effective, and (5) develop an implementation plan for carrying out the alternative selected.

- Effective conflict management skills are required (e.g., defuse emotionally charged situations, clearly identify issues, clearly communicate procedures for resolving the issue, working with the customer to develop a resolution acceptable to the customer and the work unit).

- Knowledge and understanding of university, state, and federal policies, systems, procedures, and regulations as they pertain to the work unit's ability to meet customer needs and to areas of the university that interface with the work unit in meeting those needs.

Those hired without the above competencies will undergo training prior to assuming job responsibilities. During the training period these individuals will be considered temporary employees. Upon successful completion of the training, the classification will be changed to permanent. Failure to complete training successfully will result in termination of employment or reassignment to another position, at the discretion of the university.

Working Conditions

Work is performed in a typical office environment.

After the position was posted and advertised, 25 applicants were selected. Unfortunately, only 7 of these were assessed as having the desired level of problem-solving and customer service knowledge and skills.

CASE QUESTIONS

You have been given the challenge of designing the training program for the temporary CSS employees who must complete training before they become permanent CSS employees.

1. What are the training objectives for the CSS training program? Indicate how these are tied to the KSA requirements. Assume that all trainees need KSAs in all areas listed in the relevant portion of the job specification.
2. Based on the training objectives provide a training agenda, indicating the time allocated and order of modules in your program.
3. For each module, describe what the module is supposed to accomplish and the training methods you will use to accomplish it. Provide your rationale.
4. How will you evaluate whether each person in your training program has mastered the knowledge and skill levels needed to perform as a CSS? Describe the types of questions you would ask of those supervising the CSS employees graduating from your program.

Exercises

1. Your instructor will assign you (or your group) one of the methods from the chapter. Contact the HRD department of a local business. Indicate that you are learning about training and would like to know if they use the method in their training programs. If so, ask if you can schedule a time to observe the method being used. If they don't use the method or if you are unable to observe it, try another company until you are successful. While observing the method, take careful notes about how it is used. On a date specified by your instructor the class will report their observations.

2. In small groups develop a role play. First determine the objective of the role play. It should be a very limited objective that can be achieved in 15 to 20 minutes. Then develop all aspects of a role play that will achieve your objective.

3. You have 10 minutes to think about the best classroom-based learning experience you have had and to list the things that made it such a good experience. When the 10 minutes are up, you will have 10 additional minutes to think of the worst classroom-based learning experience you have ever had and list the factors that made it such a bad experience. At the end of this time the instructor will ask you to share your experiences.

4. Use the Internet to identify the types of games and business simulations that are available. From your research select four of these that have different learning content objectives. Prepare a one- to two-paragraph description for each.

Questions for Review

1. Supervisors often resist taking on the role of coach. What can organizations do to encourage supervisors to be effective coaches?

2. Go through the different instructional methods and sort them into those you think would be most useful in training someone on the technical aspects of the job and those that would be most useful in the more social aspects of their job. Provide the rationale for your decisions.

3. Why are classroom-based training programs (lecture/discussion, role play, games, etc.) used so much more than individualized approaches to training? Do you think this choice is appropriate?

References

Argyris, C. 1980. Some limitations of the case method: Experiences in a management development program. *Academy of Management Review* 5:291–98.

Barrett, G., T. Benko, and G. Riddle. 1981. Programmable simulator speeds operator training. *Bell Laboratories Record* 59(7):213–16.

Bligh, D. 1974. *What's the Use of Lectures?* Middlesex, England: Penguin Education.

Broadwell, M. 1980. *The Lecture Method of Instruction.* Englewood Cliffs, NJ: Educational Technology Publications.

Brown, G. 1978. *Lecturing and Explaining.* New Fetter Lane, London: Methuen and Co.

Burke, M., and R. Day. 1986. A cumulative study of the effectiveness of managerial training. *Journal of Applied Psychology* 71:232–45.

Dakin, S., and G. Wood. 1995. Learn TQM principles using jumbled proverbs. *Quality Progress,* October, pp. 92–95.

Davis, L. 1973. Evolving alternative organizational designs: Their sociotechnical bases. *Human Relations* 30:261–71.

Decker, P., and B. Nathen. 1985. *Behavior Modeling Training: Principles and Applications.* New York: Praeger.

Eberts, R. E., and J. F. Brock. 1988. Computer-based instruction. In *Handbook of Human-*

Computer Interaction, edited by M. Helander. Amsterdam: Elsevier.

Edwards, D., C. Hahn, and E. Fleishman. 1980. Evaluation of laboratory methods for the study of driver behavior: Relations between simulator and street performance. *Journal of Applied Psychology* 62:559–66.

Erwin, D. E. 1978. Psychological fidelity in simulated work environments. *Proceedings of the American Psychological Association,* Toronto, Canada.

Eurich, N. P. 1990. *The Learning Industry: Education for Adult Workers,* Lawrenceville, NJ: Princeton University Press.

Fazio, R., and M. Zanna. 1981. Direct experience and attitude-behavior consistency. In *Advances in Experimental Social Psychology,* edited by L. Berkowitz. New York: Academic Press.

Fink, C. D., and E. L. Shriver. 1978. Simulators for maintenance training: Some issues, problems and areas for future research. *AFHRL Technical Report.,* Brooks Air Force Base, Texas, 78–127.

Finnerty, M. 1996. Coaching for growth and development. In *The Training and Development Handbook,* edited by R. Craig. New York: McGraw-Hill.

Gagné, R. 1977. *The Conditions of Learning.* New York: Holt, Rinehart & Winston.

Ganger, R. E. 1990. Computer based training works. *Personnel Journal* 69(9):85–91.

Gold, L. 1981. Job instruction: Four steps to success. *Training and Development Journal,* September, pp. 28–32.

Goldstein, I. L. 1993. *Training in Organizations,* 3d ed. Pacific Grove, CA: Brooks/Cole.

Gordon, E. E., R. Morgan, and J. Ponticell. 1995. The individualized training alternative. *Training and Development,* September, pp. 52–60.

Gordon, S. E. 1994. *Systematic Training Program Design.* Upper Saddle River, NJ: Prentice Hall, p. 197.

Goudy, R. 1981. Two years of management experience in two challenging weeks. *ABA Banking Journal* 73(6):74–77.

Groth, J., and C. Phillips. 1978. What would you do if a crisis hit your firm? *Management World* 7(3):12–16.

Hannafin, M. J. 1984. Guidelines for using locus of instructional control in the design of computer assisted instruction. *Journal of Instructional Development* 7(3):6–10.

Honeycutt, E. Jr., T. McCarty, and V. Howe. 1993. Sales technology applications: Self-paced video enhanced training: A case study. *Journal of Personal Selling and Sales Management* 13(1) (Winter): 73–79.

Huegli, J., and H. Tschirgi. 1980. Preparing the student for the initial job interview: Skills and methods. *American Business Communication Association Bulletin* 42(4):10–13.

Johnstone, A., and F. Percival. 1976. Attention breaks in lectures. *Education in Chemistry* 13:273–304.

Kaplan, R., M. Lombardo, and M. Mazique. 1985. A mirror for managers: Using simulation to develop management teams. *Journal of Applied Behavioral Science* 21:241–53.

Kearsley, G. 1984. *Training and Technology.* Reading, MA: Addison-Wesley.

Killian, D. 1976. The impact of flight simulators on U.S. Airlines. *American Airlines Flight Academy,* Fort Worth, TX.

Latham, G., and C. Frayne. 1989. Self-management training for increased job attendance: A follow-up and replication. *Journal of Applied Psychology* 74:411–16.

Lloyd, D. 1968. A concept of improvement of learning response in the taught lesson. *Visual Education,* Winter, pp. 23–25.

Maddox, H., and E. Hook. 1975. Performance decrement in the lecture. *Educational Research* 28:17–30.

Mecham, M. 1994. Cathay refines approach to simulator training. *Aviation Week and Space Technology,* January 17, pp. 35–37.

National Apprenticeship Training Program. 1987. Washington: Employment and Training Administration: Department of Labor.

Paffet, J. A. 1978. Ships' officers use simulators to learn vessel operation. *Minicomputer News* 4(8):11–13.

Parsons, H. M. 1972. *Man-Machine System Experiment.* Baltimore: Johns Hopkins Press.

Personnel Journal, 1995. Interaction has its attraction. July, pp. 27–28.

Pigors, P., and F. Pigors. 1987. The case method. In *Training and Development Handbook: A Guide to Human Resource Development,* edited by R. Craig. New York: McGraw-Hill, pp. 414–29.

Rothwell, W., and H. Kazanas. 1994. *Improving on-the-Job Training.* San Francisco, Jossey-Bass.

Sims, H., and C. Manz. 1982. Modeling influences on employee behavior. *Personnel Journal* 61(1):58–65.

Slack, K. 1993. Training for the real thing. *Training and Development,* May, pp. 79–89.

Smith, P. 1976. Management modeling training to improve morale and customer satisfaction. *Personnel Psychology* 29:251–59.

Solem, A. R. 1960. Human relations training: A comparison of case studies. *Personnel Administration* 23:29–37.

Training. 1995. Industry report: trends. October, p. 61.

Training and Development. 1998. The 1998 ASTD state of the industry report. January, pp. 35–37.

Walton, R. 1975. From Hawthorne to Topeka and Kalmar. In *Man and Work in Society,* edited by E. Cass and F. Zimmer. Van Nostrand Reinhold, Co.

Wexley, K. N. 1984. Personnel training. *Annual Review of Psychology* 35:519–51.

Wexley, K., and G. Latham. 1991. *Developing and Training Human Resources in Organizations.* 2d ed. New York: HarperCollins, pp. 88–90.

Zemke, R. 1982. Can games and simulations improve your training power? *Training* 19(2):24–31.

CHAPTER 8

Development and Implementation of Training

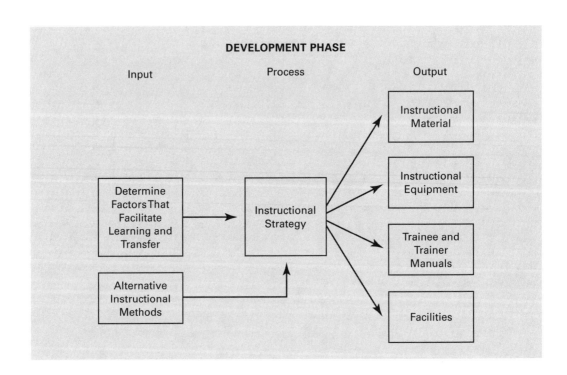

DEVELOPMENT PHASE

Input   Process   Output

Determine Factors That Facilitate Learning and Transfer

Alternative Instructional Methods

Instructional Strategy

Instructional Material

Instructional Equipment

Trainee and Trainer Manuals

Facilities

Learning Objectives

After reading this chapter, you will be able to:

- Describe what is required to be an effective lecturer

- Describe how to choose or develop instructional material for training

- Be able to develop, or know where to find appropriate material for the instructional method you wish to use

- Examine a room and determine if it meets training requirements

- Choose the most effective seating arrangement based on the nature of the training

- Choose appropriate AV for a given training objective and method

- Describe what is required in developing different training methods

- Describe the key considerations in implementing different training methods

---

Jack Goes to Training

Jack is a 43-year-old machinist who has worked for Scanton Industries for 23 years. It seems that there is constantly something new to learn, and Jack is getting nervous about his job. The nervousness grew last week when he saw a new batch of equipment arrive. It looked something like the machinery he uses now, but it was hooked up to computers. Bill, his foreman, said, "It looks like you'll be going back to school for a couple of days, Jack. You're going to have to learn how to program your work into the computer." Jack smiled but felt sick to his stomach. He was always good with his hands, but he had never done well in school.

All Jack thought about all weekend was the training he had to go to. He fell asleep Sunday night thinking about it. He was awakened by the phone at 7:00 o'clock the next morning. It was Bill telling him training had been switched from the local training center downtown to the local school, because of a sudden strike at the training center. The school was the only place available on short notice.

As Jack walked up the steps of the local school, he felt sick to his stomach again. He entered the hall and then the classroom. Everything was similar to what he remembered about school, except now each desk had a computer on it. Even the smell was the same, and it brought back memories. Some were good—the guys getting together between classes—but most were bad—being yelled at, taking tests, and doing poorly. As he sat in the wooden chair in the very back where he used to sit, he looked out the window and began to daydream, just as he had in high school.

The other 20 trainees were quietly sitting around. All of them seemed as nervous as he was. Suddenly someone burst through the door.

"Hi, my name is Jason Reston. I'm your instructor for this course. You're here to learn some basic computer skills and how to program the various machinery that you will be using at work. I realize you come from different companies and will operate different machines, but the process for all of them is similar." Jack was back from his daydream. Well, here we go, he thought.

"First I am going to show you how to get signed on and into the program you will be running . . . ."

At lunch Jack and Murray, who sat next to him in class, went to a local deli. "Are you keeping up?" Jack asked.

"Are you kidding? Are we going to be tested on this stuff?" asked Murray.

"I have no idea. If we are, I'm dead" said Jack.

The afternoon went slowly. The trainer simply gave an instruction and the trainees entered the information into the computer, then he gave another and they entered that.

"How are we supposed to remember all this?" Murray whispered.

The second day was worse. On a couple of occasions Jack was jolted out of his daydream while staring out the window.

"Jack," yelled Jason, "Are you with us? . . . "

It was 3:00 on the second afternoon when Jason announced that they would be tested to see what they had learned. Jack looked at the test questions. Was he that stupid? He did not even understand many of the questions. Would he lose his job if he failed this test? He could almost hear his boss yelling at him, "You are fired, get out, get out. . . ."

This case is an example of how not to conduct training. The anxiety Jack was feeling about going to training was exacerbated by the training room and the training itself. As we go through the chapter, think about what you would have done to make the training more conducive to adult learning.

Instructional Methods

As Table 7.5 showed, most of the training methods discussed in chapter 7 are at least mildly effective in more than one area. Chapter 7 provided information on each method to help you decide which would be best suited to meet various goals of training. This chapter will provide information about how to actually develop or locate material necessary for the method chosen. Finally, we will discuss the procedure for implementing the training.

LECTURE

As Table 7.5 noted, when the TNA reveals a deficiency that is at least partially due to a lack of knowledge or to attitudes that are in conflict with the desired behavior, the lecture may be an appropriate component of the training. Since a **lecture** is designed to transmit information, it is applicable only when addressing knowledge or attitudinal objectives.

The first rule of the effective lecture is to lecture in a manner that facilitates two-way communication. Unless you are there simply to provide some basic information (e.g., the new benefits package), you need two-way communication, not the style used by Jason Reston in the preceding case. Two-way communication is accomplished through the discussion method, which includes questioning.

Questioning

Questioning is a powerful tool, because it can help trainees discover for themselves answers to questions that are likely to be asked. The question also provides feedback about whether trainees are perceiving the information correctly and helps to provide common understanding. There are a number of types of questions with which trainers should be familiar.

Closed-Ended versus Open-Ended Questions   The **closed-ended question** asks for a specific answer. "What are the five strategies for dealing with conflict?" "What is the next step in the procedure?" This type of questioning is useful when you wish to assess learning or review previous material.

The **open-ended question** requires no specific response. In this case, there is no wrong answer—you are generally seeking an opinion. "What do you think about this method of problem solving?" "How would you approach this issue?" "What did you learn from that exercise?" Questions such as these are useful for obtaining trainee involvement, to generate discussion, and to demonstrate that the trainer is willing to listen to trainees' point of view.

Both types are useful. Consider closed questions when you wish to regain control of the discussion or to assess that specific points have been learned. Use open-ended questions when you wish to relax the trainees or explore their beliefs and opinions about issues. If Jason Reston had used some open-ended questions, they might have helped the trainees relax.

Overhead versus Direct Question   An **overhead question** is a question, either open- or closed-ended, directed at the whole group rather than one person in particular. They are nonthreatening, because they do not require any particular person to respond. If no one responds, however, tension could mount. This type of question is useful when you have a high level of involvement, which you might have already generated using open-ended "overhead" questions. If only a few trainees are answering the questions, it is wise to revert to the direct question.

The **direct question** is asked of a particular trainee. It is used to draw out nonparticipators and obtain differing points of view. As any trainer knows, there are often a few trainees who will willingly answer any and all questions. If this continues, many trainees will tire of hearing from the same few trainees and will withdraw. Keeping everyone involved in discussions is an important skill required of an effective trainer. Once trainees see that answering a question is a safe and rewarding experience (they are not ridiculed, they are praised for responding), overhead questioning will result in most of them being willing to answer questions.

Relay versus Reverse Question   The trainer, when asked a question, reasks the question of the group. This is called a **relay question.** The trainer is asked, "How would this concept work in a unionized shop?" The trainer would respond, "An interesting issue. Does anyone have any ideas?" This type of question allows the trainer to hear other points of view before having to share hers. It can lead to interesting discussions about the issue that probably would not otherwise have come up.

The **reverse question** is similar, except you state the question back to the person who asked it. Responding to the same question you might say, "Interesting question Bill. Your area is unionized; how do you think it would work there?" This is best used when the trainer believes that the questioner really wants to provide his point of view but is hesitant. The reverse question allows him the opportunity to do this. Be careful in redirecting a question back to the questioner though. If you overuse it, you could inhibit trainees from asking a question for fear of having to answer it themselves.

Encouraging Trainee to Respond

Asking questions is only half the equation. Trainees need to respond. Broadwill and Dietrich (1996) provide some interesting tips on how to encourage responses. First, do not rush to fill the silence. Trainers seem to have less tolerance for silence than do trainees. Sometimes waiting them out will work. Second, ask them to write out an answer. Say, "Pick up your pens and write down a few reasons why workers are not motivated." Then allow them time to do this. Broadwill and Dietrich report that trainees are much more willing to read what they have written than answer off the top of their head. This method also allows the trainer to ask specific trainees to respond as the pressure of the "unknown" question is gone. A variation would be to ask trainees to share their responses with one or two other trainees and come up with a common answer. This technique further diffuses the accountability.

To facilitate the involvement of trainees, set the tone early. At the beginning of training you will notice a certain amount of tension and reluctance to get involved. The ice-breaker is an excellent method of encouraging participation. It also helps trainees to get to know each other and thereby feel more comfortable.

Ice-breaker   An **ice-breaker** is a game or exercise that gets trainees involved in meeting and talking with others. It is designed to be fun but at the same time generates energy that will transfer to the rest of the training. Would this have been a useful way for Jason Reston to have started his training? We believe so. The major reason given for not using an ice-breaker is that it takes up too much time. Jolles (1993) suggests this is a mistake. He likens it to the tortoise and hare story. Without the ice-breaker, training starts off fast, but, because of the lack of "getting to know others" and making discussion a legitimate part of training, it loses the race.

The choice of ice-breaker depends on the size of the group. If it is not too large, you can have trainees break into triads (if possible, set these up ahead of time so group members do not know each other). Each trainee interviews one member of the triad, with the third as an observer. The questions should be simple but should help to get to know the person. For example:

Their name (for obvious reasons)

Organization they are from and title (learn about the type of work they do)

How long in present job (learn about their experience)

What they like best about their job (learn about work person)

What their hobbies are (learn about home person)

Once the interviews have been conducted, each trainee in turn introduces the interviewed person to the total group. This exercise gets everyone talking to the total group, provides information on trainees, and releases a great deal of the tension.

Listening

In order to be effective, the trainer must have good listening skills. Good listening is difficult, for several reasons.

- We are able to process information much faster than someone speaks, and so we have opportunities to do or think of other things.
- We often believe we know what the person is going to say, so we interrupt to respond.
- We believe that speaking, not listening, is where the power and control are.

Listening therefore requires practice. Active listening is a method developed by Carl Rogers in clinical counseling. It involves three steps:

1. Listening carefully to what is said
2. Summarizing in our mind what was said
3. Feeding this summary back to the individual

You will find that doing this helps keep you focused, but more important, it confirms to the speaker (and all other trainees) what has been said, leaving little room for misunderstandings. Training in Action 8.1 provides an example of active listening.

Other Techniques for Maintaining Interest

Effective questioning and listening will assist greatly in obtaining and maintaining trainees' interest, but there are other things trainers can do.

Training in Action 8.1

Active Listening

Dialogue between trainer and trainee at the training workshop on decision making:

Trainee:	This is training in decision making but I am in sales. What I want to know is how will this training help me?
Trainer:	You want to know how this training will help you improve your sales.
Trainee:	No, not necessarily in sales . . . just help me do my job better.
Trainer:	So you would like to know what the benefits of this training are and how these benefits will help you do your job.
Trainee:	Yes, that's right.

Move Around While Talking   This does not mean to pace methodically back and forth, but it does mean get out from behind the podium. If you must use a podium, move away from it from time to time. In fact, if you can, stay away from it altogether. Moving around while lecturing gives the impression that you are comfortable with the material. If you approach trainees from time to time, talking specifically to them, you set a friendly atmosphere. The movement also requires trainees to follow you with their eyes, preventing the "glazed stare" that can occur if the trainer is stationary.

Use Nonverbal Communication   Everyone sends out **nonverbal cues** all the time. The important thing is to send the correct cues. Keep eye contact on a trainee who is asking a question; do not turn your back and walk away while he is talking. Nod your head when a trainee is answering a question, and keep eye contact. Also, maintain eye contact with the trainee group while you are talking to them. Avoid talking to the overhead projector, the image on the screen, or your notes. Don't fold your arms. Doing this suggests that the discussion is over or that you are displeased.

The key to nonverbal behavior is to convey enthusiasm about the information you are discussing. If the enthusiasm is real rather than feigned, your nonverbal expressions will likely show this. Think of the last time you passionately argued a point of view. Were your arms out in front of you and your palms up? Perhaps you were moving your hands up and down in short gestures. Or were your arms folded across your chest?

But what if you are not enthusiastic about the material you must present? You can certainly come to feel this way after having presented the same material a number of times. What do you do? First you must realize how important enthusiasm is to effective training. Recall training sessions in which you have been the trainee. It is easy to distinguish the good from the not-so-good trainer. The good invariably was enthusiastic. Now psych yourself up. Tell yourself you must generate enthusiasm. Give yourself reasons to be enthusiastic about the material. Remember, the trainees have not been through the material as many times as you have. So, starting off enthusiastically will be infectious, for both the trainees and you.

Get Rid of Dysfluencies   **Dysfluencies** are those "and uh," "like," "um" space fillers that are injected into speech. Everyone uses them occasionally, but some use them far too often. This usually happens when a trainer is nervous or unsure of himself. It becomes immediately noticeable and trainees tend to focus on these utterances rather than the material. Videotaping your lectures, or simply asking others to inform you when you use them, can help you get rid of them.

Provide Variety   Recall from chapter 7 that trainees' attention begins to decline after 15 to 20 minutes of lecture (Johnstone and Percival 1976; Lloyd 1968; Maddox and Hook 1975). Be sure, therefore, to provide breaks, activities, and the like to keep trainees interested in what you are saying. Keeping a watchful eye on the trainees can signal time for a break. Even a five-minute stretch can help. Exercises or games[1] are also valuable for gaining and maintaining interest.

---

[1]Not to be confused with business games discussed earlier.

Exercises/games.   Introducing exercises or games that are fun and interesting is an excellent method for gaining attention and creating motivation. They are especially useful if they provide an entree to or an example of the training objective. It is important that these tools be used with a clear and definite purpose. We emphasize this point because of the experience of a colleague at a training workshop a few years ago (see Training in Action 8.2 on page 338).

A number of models incorporate exercises into the learning process (Palmer 1981). One such model is exhibited in Figure 8.1 on page 339. This model, which is a modification of an earlier Pfeiffer and Jones model (1980), allows the trainees to experience first-hand a process related to the current training, then to hear some information about the topic and compare what they did with what they learned. Then they process the new information, generalize it to their situation, and attempt to apply it in a more relevant situation. Let's examine this process more closely.

Experience.   The learning experience begins with some sort of activity that ties into the training topic. In this way, all trainees share a common experience from which to begin. This first experience should not be too closely related to the actual work setting.

Consider training managers to be better interviewers. One of the objectives is to teach them to be able to develop appropriate interview questions. The first thing you will probably realize is that most managers already believe they are good interviewers. How do you convince them training is necessary? To emphasize the importance of sound question development, the exercise (experience) could be that they have been asked to help a committee select the new leader of a scout troop. Trainees have 10 minutes to develop their own interview questions. Then they could meet in small groups and develop an overall list of questions, and the rationale for each. This is posted on newsprint and discussed.

Lecturette.   The second step is for the trainer to provide some information (e.g., concepts and principles) related to the topic at hand. This can be in the form of lecture, film, and so on.

In our example, a lecture would describe how to develop interview questions related to job requirements. Here it is important to examine the job to determine what is needed rather than simply making up questions that sound good.

Processing.   The trainees have had an experience and been provided with information regarding the same topic. Now have them work in small groups to discuss what they did using the new information they have received.

In our example, the groups would analyze the questions they had developed and answer the question, "What criteria did we use to determine these questions?" Another question might be, "How are these questions related to the job of scout leader?" Then each of the small groups could report to the total group what they discovered about how they developed interview questions.

Generalizability.   At this point it is important that the trainees see how the learning is relevant to situations outside the training. Pfeiffer and Jones (1980) note that the key question to ask here is "So what?" You want the trainees to consider how this new information fits with the things they do back on the job. From the analysis and learning that took place, trainees should infer that there might be a better way or immediately generalize the situation to other similar situations.

Using Games in Training

A few years ago Helen went to a seminar that was heralded as an advanced seminar in process consultation. She went so far as to call the instructor to be assured that it would be advanced, not "an introduction to."

At the seminar Helen soon realized that although the other 11 attendees had a great deal of experience as trainers, they were not at an advanced stage of process consultation. It was also evident that the trainees were from a number of prominent companies across the United States. About halfway through the five-day seminar they were put in two groups to learn about the different ways of intervening in a team's process. After receiving the information, the two groups were told to go off separately and develop a game for training the other group.

Each of the participants in Helen's group told of a game he or she had used in previous training and how much everyone had liked it. Helen suggested developing a role play whereby they could demonstrate the various components of process intervention. One of the other trainees said, "No one likes role plays."

"That's right," agreed another, and the group moved on to the more enjoyable games they had been discussing. When they finally decided they would play the spider web game, Helen asked how they would tie the training into the game. Unanimously, they said that it was not necessary.

"The professor did not say we needed to do that" was the reply. "The game is to get the group interested in training. We'll move to the training after the game is finished" was another reply. Helen insisted that they somehow tie the game to the process consultation training they had been given, and reluctantly two of the group worked with her to accomplish this.

Back in the training room, the other group went first, getting Helen's group to play a game. After the game was completed, the professor asked, "But how does this tie into the training?" They all looked puzzled, and everyone in Helen's group looked at her rather sheepishly. When it was their turn, Helen's group did tie the training to the game but the professor commented, "It looks like you first decided on what game you wanted to play, then tried to fit the training into the game; it should be the other way around. First think what are you trying to accomplish, then find a game to meet that requirement."

The point to this story is that exercises and games that do not tie into the training objective are a waste of valuable training time. Although games are fun, their major value is in their ability to reinforce the learning while providing a break in the routine.

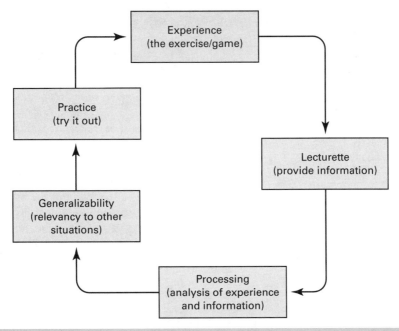

FIGURE 8.1 Experiential Learning Model

In our example, the trainees might decide that the use of job-related information for developing interview questions for all jobs would be appropriate.

This would be an opportunity to provide another lecturette on how to examine a job to determine the relevant questions to ask.

Practice. The trainees receive another task similar in nature so they are able to practice the newly found skill. Note that in this step, the task should be more closely related to the actual job.

In our example, the trainees could be asked to develop interview questions for selecting someone for their job.

Specific Behaviors to Avoid

The ideas presented above will help enormously in developing a lecture that provides the appropriate atmosphere for adult learning. For specific things to avoid when in front of the trainees, and suggestions on how to avoid them, see Table 8.1 on page 340.

COMPUTER-BASED TRAINING (CBT)

Computer-based training is very effective for declarative knowledge. If declarative knowledge is the goal of training and there are a large number of trainees, the value of looking at CBT is obvious. Once the CBT is developed, trainees can complete the training at their own pace, on their own time (if desirable), and from different locations around the country. Forlenza (1995) notes that CBT can automate the repetitive components of training just as machines do in manufacturing. CBT can handle the

TABLE 8.1 Typical Lecture Presentation Errors and Ways to Avoid Them

Errors	Ways to Avoid
Talking with back to trainees while writing on board or flip chart.	Don't talk and write at the same time. Have flip charts prepared ahead of time when possible. If considerable board work is required, use overhead transparencies.
Using highly technical words, unfamiliar jargon, or complex sentences.	If technical words or jargon must be used, provide definitions. Simplify the language and sentences so meaning is clear. Pilot test at least part of the lecture with an audience similar to the trainees.
Providing examples or asides without much relevance to the trainees.	The lecturer doesn't have to provide all the examples. Ask trainees to provide some of the examples or illustrations. In preparing the lecture, go to the supervisors of the trainees to get examples that are relevant.
Reading rather than lecturing.	Prepare an outline of points to be covered rather than a word-for-word script. Be very familiar with each point on the outline so that you are able to talk about it without reference to notes.
Speaking in a monotone.	Listen to TV and radio commentators, paying close attention to when and in what way they change their tone and the pitch of their voice. Practice fluctuating the tone and pitch of your voice on tape and in everyday conversation. Use pauses in your lecture so you can think about how you want to say something.
Making distracting gestures.	Videotape a lecture you are giving, and observe your gestures. If they are distracting or irritating to you, the trainees probably feel the same way. Some gestures are useful and keep trainee attention. Don't stand stiff as a board either. The gestures you use are habits and can be practiced out or in.
Leaving overhead projector on with no transparency or an irrelevant transparency.	Get in the habit of glancing at the overhead projection as you are talking about the material it displays. When you are at the end of the material, you will see that it is time to turn the overhead off.
Losing your place in the lecture.	This happens most frequently because your notes are too detailed and you can't find your place. Another technique is to check off topics you have completed.

knowledge-based training, while classroom training and OJT can deal with the hands-on practice. CBT can also be used to teach procedural knowledge and some skills (computer).

If Choice Is to Use It

In developing a CBT program, you need to consider three factors: self-pacing, level of interactivity, and level of sophistication of the multimedia (*Training* 1993). **Self-pacing** allows trainees to choose the topics they wish to study, the difficulty level, and the rate of instruction. **Level of interactivity** refers to the program's ability to allow trainees to respond to questions. The **sophistication of the multimedia** in this context refers to the relationship between the audio and video portions of the program.

TABLE 8.2 Points to Consider in Development of CBT		
Factor	*High If*	*Low If*
Self-pacing	• The pace of the program is entirely controlled by the learner. • Trainees can select menu options to determine the order of modules. • Trainees can skip lessons or segments at will and can exit the program from any screen. • Additional practice and more in-depth material are available upon request.	• The only way to control the pace of the presentation is by using the Enter key. • It is not menu-driven, i.e., the trainee can't select a particular lesson segment or skip segments. • Trainees can exit the program only at certain points.
Interactivity	• Trainees' responses follow instructional segments. • The program tests skills and judgments, not just facts. • The orderly sequence of topics is apparent to the learner.	• The program has long, uninterrupted lesson segments that offer no chance for the trainee to ask or answer questions. • The program tests recall instead of skills. • Segments do not build on one another. • The learner's answers are tagged right or wrong with no further explanation.
Multimedia	• The voices are distinct and natural. • A voice provides program instructions so that the trainee doesn't have to read them. • Sound and visuals reinforce one another. • Visuals use color and motion to reinforce the audio message and illustrate the idea presented.	• The sound or visuals are of poor quality. • There is no direct connection between the audio and visual material (the sound is limited to irrelevant music, for example). • The sound is restricted to a voice saying, "You are correct" or "Try again." • The visuals don't reinforce instructional points.

A good CBT system should rate high on all three factors. Table 8.2 provides a checklist for ensuring that it does.

If the decision is to purchase a CBT program, it is often useful to integrate the CBT into your organization. Integration requires developing discussions around how the CBT is related to the problems and issues your organization deals with, and/or providing examples of the relationship. The more generic the CBT, the less it will cost, but the more difficult it might be to integrate into your organization, so it may be more cost effective to choose a program that is industry (or topic) specific (Blumfield 1997). Even then, you need to be careful to integrate the CBT into the organizational setting by having trainees meet to discuss its applicability.

This is not to suggest, however, that company specific is always necessary, as can be seen in Training in Action 8.3 on the following page.

The High Cost of Multimedia Training

The software developer was extolling the virtues of multimedia training. "It will alter the learning landscape for the next millennium," he said to 200 training executives at a Boston conference. Rick Corry, newly appointed training executive from Owens Corning, listened with mild annoyance. He had recently been told by one of these people that they would develop a nice CD-ROM training program for Corning for $150,000. The software developer went on to say that Corry's division would not be able to share it with other business units in Owen Corning. In fact, the corporation would not even have the copyright on the program for two years, during which the developer could sell it to anyone else it chose to.

When the speaker asked if there were any questions, Corry looked at all the others in the audience, and said, "I'm just wondering, why don't we get together and share what we have and fund what we need? After all, most companies have similar training needs in a number of areas: basic sales skills, time management, leadership skills, interpersonal skills." The room went silent. The speaker did not say a word. As the session ended, Corry was surrounded by training executives and collected 27 business cards from people who wanted to explore the idea.

From that encounter came a consortium of large noncompeting manufacturing companies; it is called LearnShare. One of its goals is to develop partnerships with vendors of multimedia training, "but in a manner that is as good for us as it is for them," said Corry. With the consortium's combined revenues of over $100 billion and 2.2 million employees, they are likely to have some real clout with vendors.

One of LearnShare's first objectives was to determine how similar the training needs across the different companies were. LearnShare conducted a survey in all nine companies of the training material that was not related to processes or products. The result: 74 percent of the training was addressing the same needs. In other words, diversity training is diversity training no matter where it's taught.

The companies are already sharing nonmultimedia training information and programs. Furthermore, they are sharing training space. Motorola, for example, is letting managers at Owens Corning who are stationed in the Pacific Rim sit in on some training Motorola is conducting in its facility there.

How about multimedia training? LearnShare is in discussions with Wilson Learning, a major vendor, about splitting the cost of developing a multimedia training program. LearnShare would get the program, and Wilson would have the rights to market it elsewhere. Wilson is interested and discussions continue.

Source: Adapted from Blumfield 1997.

GAMES AND SIMULATIONS

When you choose a method of training for a KSA, you need to think about the constraints of that format. Sometimes two methods are similar in what they are able to train (e.g., case study and business game) but time constraints permit only one to be used.

Equipment Simulators

If technical skills in the operation or maintenance of equipment are the focus of training, one of the best instructional methods is the **simulator.** As we noted in chapter 7, simulators have long been used in the training of pilots, air traffic controllers, and other positions where errors on the job could be very serious. These simulators are very expensive to develop, but because errors on the job could be deadly, the expense is necessary.

The simulator can occupy the bulk of the training time. Tasks can be attempted on the simulator, feedback can be provided, then it is back on the simulator. Learning by doing is the major focus here. At the same time, the instructor can be available to provide continuous and instant feedback.

If Choice Is to Use It   Simulators can be used for most psychomotor skills training, but care must be taken in the development of a simulator. There might be a tendency to use out-of-date machinery. Who would want to use a brand-new piece of machinery for training when it could be on the shop floor and have a direct impact on productivity? This was in fact part of the problem in Training in Action 7.2 in chapter 7. What is often not understood is the need to have the exact machinery for proper transfer of training. After all, if the skills do not transfer well, productivity is lost.

Also the simulation must include all the features of the real situation (fidelity). Imagine a pilot learning how to fly a simulator that did not have a wind factor built in. Suppose in landing a real plane the pilot lines up with the runway and heads straight in, as taught, and suddenly there is a 30 mph crosswind. This is the type of thing that happened in Training in Action 7.2. Suddenly there were customers with different requests and events that were simply not part of training.

The simulation should first require the skills to be displayed without any interference from other factors such as wind in the case of the pilot and customers in the case of the clerks. Once the trainee has acquired the basic skills, however, the outside factors need to be introduced in the training.

BUSINESS GAMES/IN-BASKET/CASE STUDY

As Table 7.5 suggests, if training is to focus on cognitive skills, the case study, business game, and in-basket are all appropriate methods. It is important to note, however, that they are not meant to be standalone techniques but are used to enhance a training program. We will say more about this later.

Because each method differs in a number of ways, we will discuss the requirements for each separately.

Business Game

The use of **business games** in training is on the rise (Faria 1989), possibly because most of them are computer based. Generally the trainer has the master program, and trainees have their own disk with information related to their business and its environment. Trainees make decisions about what they wish to do and enter this information on a disk, which is given to the trainer. Data from all trainees are entered into the trainer's computer, and the computer generates feedback, which is then provided to the trainees. Computer-based business games typically have from 50 to 100 pages of information that trainees need to read and become familiar with.

There are two types of games: intercompany and intracompany. The intercompany games require trainees to compete in a marketplace. The more complex games require decisions on where to build factories, what product to advertise, the level of quality of the product, how many salespeople to hire, how to pay them, and so on. Trainees are assigned to teams who compete against one another in the simulation game. As a result, the decisions made by each team have an impact on the overall environment they all share.

Intracompany business games require teams or individuals to represent different functional areas in a single company. The process is similar to that of the intercompany, but without the competition.

The general method of instruction is to have trainees read the complete manual, then meet in teams to discuss a strategy and make the decisions. The team decisions are transferred to the trainer[2] (game administrator), who tabulates the decisions from all the teams and returns the results to the teams. These teams reexamine the information in light of the previous decisions and make another decision. This process continues over a number of decisions. Faria (1997) has suggested that a minimum of 12 decisions need to be made in order to have trainees benefit from the exercise: The first four provide trainees with a general understanding of the game and how the various factors interact, the second four provide a framework for competing, and in the final four, strategic decisions are made with enough knowledge to be meaningful. After the final decisions are in and results tabulated, trainees meet to discuss the results and the criteria they used in making their decisions.

A long period of time is required to complete all the decisions and conduct meaningful discussion afterwards. This would be very difficult to use in a one-day workshop. Training over a number of days or weeks would be ideal for business games. Another possibility would be to alternate portions of the training (lecture mode) with trials on the simulation, continuing in this way to the end of the game, at which point a general discussion would take place. If the training is to take place over a number of sessions, you need to make sure the trainees are interested enough in the game to take the preparation time between sessions necessary to make informed decisions. Faria (1997) has found that trainees often become very involved in these simulations, spending a great deal of time determining their strategies.

If Choice Is to Use It   If you decide to use a business game, you have a good chance of finding a relevant one, because they focus on a wide range of topics, including marketing, accounting, finance, and general management. It is still important, however, to be sure that the game fits the learning objectives.

The simulation game requires a great deal of time to incorporate into training effectively. First you need to provide the knowledge base required to operate in the simulation. Then there must be time for the trainees to familiarize themselves with the simu-

---

[2]In organizations that have computer networks, the trainee can input the data directly into the network, where the trainer accesses it directly.

lation. Some of this can be done concurrently with providing the operating knowledge. Then the game begins. Discussion sessions can take place at particular times during the playing of the game, but the main session would take place at the end. At this point you must take the time to be sure everyone is fully debriefed on how the game has proceeded and encourage discussion about what was learned. It is useful to have teams or individuals present to the rest of the trainees the decisions they made and the results from those decisions. In these discussions a great deal of learning can take place.

In-Basket

If learning objectives focus around prioritizing, organizing and planning, and decision making, the in-basket can be an appropriate training tool. The **in-basket** is composed of a number of memos, phone messages, and other written requests typically found in an office "in-basket." The trainee must read and respond to them, in writing, in a limited amount of time (1 to 3 hours). The exercise requires the trainee to make decisions about a number of issues and to organize and plan his schedule for when he begins his new job (see Training in Action 8.4 on the next page).

The process follows a standard format (see Training in Action 8.4). Once the trainees have completed the in-basket, the trainer can conduct a general discussion about the way particular decisions were made and the criteria that were used. For example, the trainer may ask trainees what strategies they used to prioritize the information, asking questions such as, "What criteria did you use to determine which person to contact first when you finally arrived on the job?" "How did you determine in what order to address all the issues?" Then discussion can become more specific and address how trainees responded to actual items: "What did you do about the complaint that was three weeks old?"

The advantages and disadvantages of the various approaches would be highlighted in this discussion. During or immediately following the discussion you would provide instruction covering alternative approaches to making the various types of decisions. Conclude with a discussion of the lessons learned and how these can be applied on the job.

Although the in-basket takes relatively little time to complete, it can still cut into valuable training time. Unless it is a multiple, or simultaneous, in-basket, it is useful to have trainees complete it prior to coming to training or as an evening assignment (if training is longer than one day). In these cases the time constraints are removed. Also if you have the time to examine trainees' in-basket decisions before the training session, you can develop meaningful questions regarding their responses. You could even meet with each trainee before the formal training to provide individual feedback. At the training session an overall group discussion could then take place.

It can take as much as half a day to complete the in-basket and the discussion that follows. This could be reduced to about two hours if the in-baskets were completed before training. However, providing individual feedback will take longer. We suggest this be done separately in one-on-one sessions, prior to the group discussion.

If Choice Is to Use It   In-baskets are not as readily available as simulations. One reason may be that they are relatively easy to develop yourself; simply examine someone's in-basket for the material.[3] Take papers from the in-basket, including filler material that

---

[3]The information needs to be obtained from in-baskets of the job being trained for. Items could actually be taken from a number of in-baskets as long they were all from the job in question.

Training in Action 8.4

Typical Instructions for an In-Basket Exercise

SALESPERSON IN-BASKET
Instructions for Participant

Your name is Lee. You have been with Bennett Corporation for $1^1/2$ years and are a salesperson in the business machines marketing force on the East Coast. A position opened up in the mid-west region a few weeks ago when the salesman, John Quitt, left the company and his customers without notice. The other salespeople in your new office have tried to cover the calls that have come in from the accounts you are to be assuming. Obviously, they have not been able to handle all the calls, so you have some catching up to do. You are not to be transferred to fill this opening for one week, but the company has flown you out to the mid-west office to go through your predecessor's in-basket, which has become quite full. It is Sunday evening, April 13, and no one else is in the office. In 75 minutes you must leave to catch a plane to the Eastern Region Training Center, and you will not be able to be contacted for the week you are there.

Read through the items and decide on a course of action. It is imperative that you respond immediately since you will not be back for a week. All responses must be in writing so you can leave them for the other office personnel. Responses may include letter writing, memos to others and/or yourself, scheduling meetings, making phone calls (outline what is to be discussed), etc. You may write your responses on the same memo you received, or the memo pad provided for you. Writing paper is also provided if you wish to write a letter. Be sure to attach any memos or letters to the appropriate item. You have never been to the mid-west and have never met any of your new co-workers.

An organizational chart and calendar are provided for your reference. Remember, you have only 75 minutes to go through your in-basket.

Remember: Every action you take or plan to take *must* be in writing. If you can't write it down, the assessor will have *no way* of assessing your performance.

IT IS ADVISABLE TO READ THROUGH THE ENTIRE IN-BASKET BEFORE TAKING ANY ACTION.

Time Table
5 minutes   Read instructions
75 minutes   Read and respond to in-basket items.

*** Please do not proceed until told to do so. ***

requires no action (flyers, memos copied to the person, etc.) and follow the standard scenario (Training in Action 8.4). Use the trainee's current position as the position in the scenario. To provide the stress of real-life management, the amount of information that needs attention should be more than can be expected to be completed in the allotted time. To determine appropriate actions that should be taken, choose high performers in the job in question and ask them what they would do. The attraction of the in-basket is that it is developed from real information from the trainees' organization.

Case Study

The general method of instruction for the **case study** is to have each trainee read the case and develop answers to the questions provided. If there are enough trainees to form small groups, the next step would be for these small groups to meet and discuss the case. Incorporating the different perspectives of each trainee, the group again answers these same questions. Then all trainees meet with the trainer and discuss the case, focusing initially on the posed questions. Answers to these questions can lead to different areas of the case. The trainer will have a list of his own questions to ask depending on where the discussion goes.

The trainer facilitates the group discussion, keeping the communication climate open while ensuring that the focus is on important learning points. The trainer acts as a catalyst by calling on trainees for opinions and encouraging others to confront aspects of a position they do not support. An important part of being a trainer is deflecting requests from trainees to give the trainer's "solution" to the case.

Suppose problem analysis is the skill being trained. Here it is important that the trainer allow the case to go in the direction the trainees wish to take it, as long as they are pursuing a problem and analyzing it. The trainer must guide the trainees in examining the possible alternatives and consequences of each of their solutions. This is a guided discovery approach and the trainer's solution is irrelevant to that process; in fact, it hinders it.

Sufficient time must be made available for individuals to read and analyze the case alone, in small groups (optional), and then as a total group. This could all be done in one day, but, especially if the case were long, little time might be left to do anything else. If there are several training days, especially if the training is off-site and trainees are staying at a hotel, structured assignments can be built into the evenings. Doing this reduces the downtime of the training day. Of course, you always have the option with a one-day training period to provide the case and ask that trainees read it and answer provided questions ahead of time. However, this technique is advisable only when you can be sure everyone will in fact read it ahead of time. Trainees are more likely to read the case if they realize they will be required to meet in small groups to discuss it.

If Choice Is to Use It   If the decision is to use a case, a wide variety are available from various sources. Harvard cases are perhaps the best-known, although in Canada the University of Western Ontario has many available. These cases are often based on real organizations that have gone through some difficult times. The advantage of "real" cases is that you can enrich the case with up-to-date information from the organization, as well as "what the outcome of the case really was" and how it affected the company. If the decision is to use an already written case, it is important to make your selection carefully. The case must reflect the objectives of the training. For example, if the training is in advanced marketing mix analysis, the trainer must be sure the case is complex enough to allow such learning to take place.

Writing a case requires a special skill, and if you can locate one that fulfills the objective, it is probably preferable to use it. However, there are advantages to writing the case yourself. First, you can write it with the learning objectives in mind and, therefore, make it truly relevant. Second, there is a real opportunity to assist with transfer of training by writing about the trainees' own organization (Argyris 1980). The issues will be relevant to the training objectives and to the trainees personally. Engel (1973) provides a guided process for writing a case.

ROLE PLAY/BEHAVIOR MODELING

If the goal is to train in interpersonal skills, the two favored methods are the role play and behavior modeling. Both these methods require interaction between trainees. When assigning dyads or triads to work together, do not pair up trainees who work together on the job. There are two reasons: first, the trainees might have a difficult time being serious, and second, roles could create animosity if there are already problems between the two trainees.

Role Play

The **role play** usually starts with a one- or two-page description of what the trainees are to do. Role plays are reasonably easy to develop, and real problems and issues that exist in the organization can be used. They can be strategically placed throughout training to provide not only the skills practice but also a change of pace.

Feedback is an important component in the role play. As we noted in chapter 7, there are tradeoffs depending on the method of feedback. Sometimes the trainer has one set of trainees do the role play and provides feedback to them, with the help of the other trainees. This method places a great deal of stress on the trainees doing the role play, because all eyes are on them. The other major concern here is that the role play is designed to provide learning by doing. In the above scenario, not everyone is "doing" (although we also do learn vicariously). An alternative is to have trainees rotate through the role-play position. The problem of stress still persists, however, and a great deal more time is required. One way to provide feedback to everyone more quickly is to have skilled observers available to observe the role plays and provide feedback, but this can be costly.

A method to consider is setting the trainees up in groups of three: the person creating the situation (initiator), the person who will respond using the skills, and the observer (who will provide feedback). Provide three sets of role plays that are different but have the same learning points. Also provide sheets of "learning points to look for" regarding the three role plays. Now each of the trainees will have the opportunity to be in each of these three positions. Of course, the trainees will not be as skilled as the trainer, and the feedback will not be as comprehensive. This approach reduces the amount of time required to complete the process, but the disadvantage is in the quality of feedback. Trainees are generally reluctant to provide negative feedback to peers, and even if they are willing, they are not experts, so feedback may not be accurate. Nevertheless, if it is set up with clear instructions and an understanding of the requirements, this can be an excellent learning tool. Each trainee is able to practice the skills, see how the skills work on them (as the initiator), and watch and provide feedback (as the observer). It may be useful to have the instructor and two volunteers run through exactly what is required (using a different role play) before starting. Videotaping of the role play is another option that could be used. The tape can be used by the trainee to self-evaluate, it can be used by peers in small groups to evaluate each other, and/or the trainer could examine the tapes between sessions and provide individual feedback.

If Choice Is to Use It   Role plays are available in many textbooks and from other sources, but they are also reasonably easy to write. The advantage of writing them is that you can often tailor them to the trainee population. Many trainees complain that the role play is too artificial. One solution might be to have trainees write their own. In the first session (several sessions are necessary to do this) trainees would have the opportunity to do some predetermined role plays. Using these role plays as a model, they write one based on their own experience.

Consider the following situation. Arnold is learning conflict resolution skills. Training to date has provided him with the opportunity to role play a few different situations where he has used the conflict skills being taught. To make the role plays more meaningful, the trainer asks trainees to write their own role play for the next training session. She specifies that the role play should be a situation the trainee has experienced, a conflict situation he did not handle very well.

Generally there are two roles written in a role play, the initiator (the person who starts the interaction) and the responder (the person who responds, using the relevant skills). Arnold thinks about past situations where he has had a conflict with others and decides to write about the time he had a disagreement with Chris, his office manager, about their computer software. He writes up the background that led to the conflict and what Chris had said to him.[4] This will be the role-play write up for the initiator when he goes back to training. He will give it to a fellow trainee to role play and he will respond. He does not need to write up the responder's role because he was the responder and knows what the situation was. Hopefully the exercise will give Arnold an opportunity to respond in a more productive manner using the skills he is learning.

It is important not to make the role plays too complex or confusing. Wohlking (1976) noted three common problems with the written role play:

- Problems to be dealt with in the role play are not generally handled at the trainees' level in the organization. Thus the level of generalizability to the job is reduced.
- Roles are often incomplete or misleading, creating confusion.
- The script creates too many conflicts that cannot be resolved in the time allowed for the role play.

There are also some concerns about the trainees' involvement in the role play. For some trainees the role play can be considered "fun" but not real, so generalizability to the job is lessened. Others find it stressful to act out a role with others watching. Table 8.3 (page 350) provides tips on how to develop and present a role play.

Depending on the method used in providing feedback, the time frame for completing a set of role plays could be from one hour to one day. Preparing for the role

---

[4]Arnold should use the role plays he has already participated in during training as outlines for how to write the role play. Also Table 8.3 provides some relevant information.

TABLE 8.3 Tips for Developing and Presenting Role Plays

Developing

- Carefully create your characters to prove your point. Provide two characters who are going to clash in exactly the way you want. For example, use one player to force another either to use the skills you've taught or to illustrate what happens when those skills aren't used. Don't write a script (unless you are teaching rote responses), but provide detailed background on characters' habits, attitudes, goals, personalities, and mood, as well as on the business restrictions that motivate or restrain them.
- Use role playing to illustrate one key problem. Don't try for more than one topic or you will diffuse the impact and distract the learners with too much information.

Presenting

- Take the time to introduce the situation. Give trainees enough background to understand what's at stake. Then assign the roles.
- Both the role plays and the discussions can get off the topic. To prevent this, make sure participants understand your instructions. For example, tell them, "The customer service representative must (1) use the customer's name three times; (2) organize, clarify, and confirm the nature of the customer's problem; (3) empathize with the customer; and (4) offer to do something for the customer." If you plan to use observers to provide feedback, have each of them use an observation sheet to look for key behaviors and to respond to key aspects of the performance.
- If the role play gets off the topic, stop the performance and ask, "What are the problems here? Why isn't the conversation moving in the right direction?" Be assertive to ensure that they stay in character and on the topic.
- After the performance, always discuss what happened. This is when learning takes place. Ask questions of each player, and have the group advise the players. Encourage discussion. Challenge them with alternatives: "What would have happened if . . . ?"

Source: Adapted from Mitchell 1993.

play (along with a demonstration) could take 20 to 30 minutes. With a large number of trainees, and each trainee role-playing in front of the rest, it could take the complete day. If the trainees are divided into groups of three, each trainee could do a role play, then return to the larger group and discuss the feedback with everyone in about two hours. If the role plays were videotaped, feedback could also be provided by the trainer at a later time. This system would be especially effective in a multiple-day training session off-site, where individual feedback sessions could be scheduled after dinner.

Behavior Modeling

The two differences between **behavior modeling** and role play are that in behavior modeling, (1) technical skills as well as interpersonal skills can be trained and (2) the trainee views a demonstration of how to perform before being asked to perform. Specific learning points should be identified, so the trainee recognizes what must be done. Developing a video that depicts the learning points is critical to this method. Although you could use a live model, the video is better for two reasons. First, it will be an accurate, standardized depiction of the required behavior. You can redo it until it is exactly the way you want. Using a live model leaves room for variations or inappropriate behaviors. Second, you can insert into the video script learning points and the steps being followed. These allow the trainee to see the behavior and the specific point it is highlighting at the same time.

In ideal behavior modeling, trainees watch the video of the model, perform the behavior, watch a videotape of their own performance (if videotaped), and finally receive feedback on their behavior. This takes a great deal more time than the role play. If videotaping is used, the number of concurrent sessions that can take place is limited by the number of video cameras and VCRs available. Also a sufficient number of trainers must be available to provide feedback.

For maximum effectiveness, everyone must receive the practice and feedback, which, no matter how it is done, will require a great deal more time than the role play. You will need to consider this factor in scheduling the training.

If Choice Is to Use It   The difficulty in developing behavior modeling scenarios is the video requirement. A number of videos are available, but it is important to preview them before purchase, because the quality varies considerably (Hequet 1996). Developing your own video is also a possibility, but cost, your ability to make a professional product, and the time needed may rule out that option.

Table 8.4 (page 352) provides a number of suggestions if the decision is to use behavior modeling.

ON-THE-JOB TRAINING

On-the-job training (OJT) is the preferred method for many organizations, especially the small business. It is an appropriate approach in large companies as well where there are only a few trainees at one time.

Job Instruction Training

Chapter 7 indicated that **job instruction training (JIT)** was one of the effective structured approaches to delivery of OJT. Of the four steps in JIT—prepare, present, try out, and follow up (see Table 7.4 on page 306)—the first and last seem to be ignored most often in a traditional OJT process.

If Choice Is to Use It   You might ignore the preparation step because you are not aware of what needs to be done. To facilitate your awareness, Table 8.5 (page 353) provides an example of the preparation step for the job of press feeder. If it looks similar to the operational analysis in the chapter on needs assessment, it is. If an operational analysis has been completed, the majority of the work outlined in Table 8.5 will have already been done.

The follow-up step may be ignored because it is simply not considered important. This step, however, is critical to ensure that the trained skills continue as they were taught. During the try-out step the trainee may have demonstrated his capabilities in doing the job, but as with anything freshly learned, short-cuts, poor work habits, and incorrect procedures can creep into performance. By periodically dropping by to follow up, you can catch such performance discrepancies and correct them before they became habitual. Following up becomes less important as the trainee's performance becomes consistently acceptable.

Structured OJT is very effective when done properly and supported by the organization. Rothwell and Kazanas (1990) provide seven steps that will help ensure successful OJT (see Table 8.6 on page 354).

TABLE 8.4   Things to Consider for Implementing Behavior Modeling

- Carefully select the trainer/program administrator who will set up and conduct the sessions. He or she must be skilled and experienced with this technique.
- Carefully consider whether this technique will meet your needs within your constraints of time and money. Unless you can identify specific skill deficiencies, present a positive model of the appropriate behavior, provide the time for each trainee to practice the behavior under the watchful eye of the trainer, and arrange for reinforcement from the manager of each trainee back on the job, you probably shouldn't select this technique.
- Identify real skill deficiencies in advance of training and involve the potential trainees and their bosses in this process. This activity will gain the key people's attention and their ownership of the objectives of the training sessions.
- Break the skills into small behaviors. Build a module around each small behavior and progress one step at a time, starting with a simple behavioral element, in order to gain confidence.
- Do not emphasize more than seven learning points during any one training module.
- Models used to demonstrate the correct way of behaving/handling a certain situation should have sufficient status to be credible yet easy for the trainees to identify with.
- Using a videotape of a model performing the correct behavior ensures that all groups of trainees will see a positive example and may reduce costs since it is reusable. However, this advantage may be negated, since it is difficult to find a model and a situation likely to be highly relevant and identifiable across diverse groups of trainees.
- Before trainees actually practice the desired behavior, have them verbalize the behavioral cues demonstrated by the model and then have them visualize their pending performance. Decker (1982) found that doing this does not enhance trainee reactions to the training process but does improve generalization and use of the behaviors in new situations.
- A supportive climate that encourages experimentation must be established for the practice sessions. Emphasis on positive reinforcement rather than criticism increases self-confidence and learning.
- After each session, some behavior modeling experts provide a wallet-sized card that outlines the key learning points and critical steps. This acts as a security blanket for the trainees so they can feel assured they will know the crucial features as they attempt to apply the training back on their jobs.
- Conduct a review session after several modules have been completed in order to reinforce the learning points and to demonstrate the progress that has been attained by the trainees.
- Manage the consequences of attempting the newly trained behaviors in the actual job situation. Work with the managers of the trainees to ensure that they set attainable goals for their subordinates, remove obstacles that may prevent trainees from attempting the new behaviors, and provide incentives for such attempts.

Source: Camp, Blanchard, and Husczco 1986.

Apprenticeship

Apprentices spend a required amount of time in a classroom as well as in the workplace. The length of classroom training and on-the-job training varies from job to job. An apprentice cook, for example, requires one year of OJT and a week of classroom training, whereas a mold maker requires four years of OJT with three eight-week classroom sessions (Apprentice Information 1995).

If Choice Is to Use It   Although formal apprenticeship programs are strictly controlled by the Department of Labor, there is nothing stopping an organization from setting up its own informal apprenticeship programs. The journeyman rank you pro-

TABLE 8.5 Job Breakdown Sheet for OJT

Dept: Metal Decorating   Prepared by J. Smith
Job: Feeder Pressman   Date: June 8

Main Steps	*Key Points*	*Tools/Equipment Material*	*Safety Factors*
Part I (Start of shift)			
1. Check level of fountain solution and refill if necessary	Ask pressman which solution to use. Scratch mark shows minimum and maximum capacities	All solutions kept in metal containers in storeroom	Do not spill on walkway
2. Check level of varnish in wet varnish machine and refill if necessary	Check card for type of material being used and determine amount of thinner necessary to obtain proper viscosity	Same as #1	Very volatile and flammable
3. Wash sponges, bucket, and gum containers	Use same thinner as in #2	Same as #1	Do not wash in enclosed area because of fumes
Part II (Start a new bundle in press)			
1. Request lift driver to bring over new bundle	Do not wait until bundle on press is almost finished		
2. Check new bundle to be sure it is the correct one and is in good condition	Pull the job ticket and check order number; examine top sheets and sides and corners of bundle	Leather-palmed gloves	Always wear gloves when handling sheets to prevent cuts
Part III (Whenever press is stopped)			
1. Lower elevator with bundle on it and cover with master sheet	Lower only until top of bundle is at a convenient height	Leather-palmed gloves	Wear gloves
2. Unless otherwise instructed by pressman, wet plate on front unit	Be sure entire plate is wet; dry spots can oxidize and damage plate	Use sponges and clear water	Be sure press is clear before wetting plate

Source: Adapted from Gold 1981.

vide your employees upon successful completion will not be transferable to other organizations, but you can take advantage of the process nonetheless.

Try to find and examine a comparable job that has an apprenticeship program, and use it as a model. The classroom training is usually at a local community college, school of technology, or similar institution. Apprentices are usually off the job for

TABLE 8.6 Steps You Can Take for Better OJT

1. Establish policy.

Prepare a written description that puts the organization "on the record" as supporting structured OJT and makes a commitment to it. Make sure that the purpose of structured OJT is spelled out and is related to the company's other HRD efforts.

2. Establish accountability.

Make clear who is primarily responsible for OJT. Write it into their job descriptions. Then ensure that part of their performance evaluation is based on how well they carry out this responsibility.

3. Review precedents.

Make a few calls to find out what other organizations in your industry are doing about structured OJT. Do they provide training on the subject? If so, to whom? For how long? What is the course content? What cost savings can be traced to it? Use this information in efforts to design your program. It will also be useful in case your attempts to improve structured OJT in your organization come under attack. Nothing quiets critics faster than pointing out that "our competitors—or excellent firms in the industry—are doing it!"

4. Design and routinely conduct training on the principles of structured OJT.

Supervisors and experienced workers are the most likely ones to conduct structured OJT in the workplace. In most organizations, they do not know how to do it. Teach them how and then sit back and take credit for the fantastic results!

5. Provide specialized support for line managers who use structured OJT.

In most organizations, certain jobs are common entry points for employees. Design "off-the-shelf" lesson plans, job aids (checklists, procedures manuals, and training manuals), individualized learning contracts, and individualized training progress report forms for those jobs. They will save time and effort while improving the quality of structured OJT. Making that kind of support available enhances OJT by providing users with the tools to do it—and makes the HRD department a real partner with line management in improving structured OJT.

6. Avoid turf battles.

Begin efforts to improve OJT on a small scale, in work units where supervisors or managers are supportive. Use your successes there as a springboard to other units and to additional resources.

7. Consider literacy skills.

Do not assume that employees—or, for that matter, supervisors—are highly literate. Indeed, take advantage of efforts to improve OJT to assess performance problems that can be traced to literacy issues.

Source: Adapted from Rothwell and Kazanas 1990.

their classroom training, but in designing your own you might be able to arrange night school classes, classes on the weekend, or some combination of the two. Correspondence school training has been known to be substituted for the classroom training.

Before venturing out to develop your own apprenticeship program, check with local government agencies regarding the programs available. Given that government is usually willing to help pay for the classroom training part of the apprenticeship program, it may be advantageous to make your program official.

Coaching

The main difference between **coaching** and traditional OJT is that in coaching the supervisor continues to analyze the subordinate's performance, plan mutually acceptable action, create a supportive climate, and motivate the subordinate to improve

(Orth, Wilkinson, and Benfari 1987). Effective coaching requires a relationship between the coach (supervisor, peer) and player (employee) that motivates the employee to seek help from the coach in order to be a better performer (Evered and Selman 1989). This means the role of the supervisor must change from controlling to collaborating.

Just as a needs assessment should be undertaken before it is decided that training is required, the supervisor should examine some basic issues before assuming that coaching is needed. Figure 8.2 outlines the basic questions the supervisor should ask. Note the similarity to Figure 4.2 (page 130) in the needs analysis chapter.

If Choice Is to Use It   Once it is decided that coaching is necessary, the five steps laid out in chapter 7 should be followed. Skills required to be an effective coach are similar to those for an effective trainer (that should be no surprise). Good questioning techniques, active listening skills, and good feedback skills all must be used when coaching.

Mentoring is a form of coaching, except that mentors are not the mentored person's supervisor but rather are at a higher level in the organization—usually a senior manager mentors a junior manager. In the past, mentoring has been quite informal, but some organizations have formalized the process (Kram 1985). Phillips-Jones (1983) has identified features of successful mentoring programs. First, as in any organizational intervention, top management must truly support it. Allowing mentoring activities to take place on company time is one way of sending the signal that they are important. Mentoring needs to be integrated into the overall career development process. There should be internal access to training and development programs and materials to supplement mentor/mentee activities.

FIGURE 8.2 Assessment of Need for Coaching

Question		Response
Are there obstacles in the system that prevent effective performance?	→ Yes →	Remove obstacles or revise expectations
Do negative consequences follow good performance?	→ Yes →	Change the consequences
Do positive consequences follow poor performance?	→ Yes →	Change the consequences
Is the employee aware that improvement is expected?	→ No →	Provide proper feedback
Does the employee know how to improve?	→ No →	Train or coach
Could the employee improve performance if he wanted to?	→ Yes →	Coach

Insist that the mentor program be voluntary. Forcing managers to take part in mentoring activities will do more harm than good. A reluctant mentor cannot provide the interest and motivation needed to assist someone in the organization.

Assign mentors to mentees. Most formal mentor programs require a nominating procedure. Mentees are nominated by their supervisor and matched by the director of training to a mentor. It is a good idea to allow for switching, particularly if a match does not seem to be working.

Keep each phase of the program short. Six-month cycles are enough time for a mentor to help her mentee in a significant manner while not being tied indefinitely to the mentee (given that the choice of mentee was not hers). If the mentor finds the process successful, they will sign up for another stint.

Provide an orientation for mentors and mentees. This is a formal process by which they can meet and hear about what has worked in the past, and the role expectations for both in the mentoring relationship.

The mentors should be allowed to do their mentoring in a manner congruent with their style, not be forced to follow a strict format. The orientation can provide some successful past mentors, who could describe how they took on the role. Presenting a few different approaches will reinforce that it is not necessary to follow a specific process.

Finally, it is important to monitor the mentoring process. This monitoring is critical to its success. Have specific check points where you survey both parties about the progress of the mentee. This could be in the form of a meeting to discuss what has happened, a request for mini-reports on progress, or simply phone calls to ask how the process is working. Use this information to highlight successful mentoring relationships in company newsletters and other communications. This publicity will keep individuals motivated and keep the program visible. Plotting the career paths of mentees is another method of showing the success of the program.

TRAINERS FOR OJT

Apprenticeships use journeymen to train apprentices; coaching uses supervisors to improve subordinates' job skills and knowledge. OJT in general uses co-workers and supervisors as trainers. None of these people started out to be a trainer and likely none has formal training in how to be an effective trainer. Thus, any company that uses OJT should carefully consider the cost benefit of providing train-the-trainer training. In chapter 7, we discussed the types of training OJT trainees should receive. Other issues related to OJT trainers are discussed below.

Selecting OJT Trainers

The best trainer isn't necessarily the person who can do the job the best. The best trainer is the one who has a good command of the job and who can interact effectively with others. Obviously, the trainer must understand and be able to perform the job well, but unless that person can also communicate her knowledge to others in a supportive manner, little learning will take place. If those selected to be OJT trainers don't have these skills, training the trainer is indicated.

Motivating the OJT Trainer

Not only do trainees need to be motivated to learn, trainers need to be motivated to train. Trainers should also recognize the necessity of closely observing the trainee to ensure adequate skill development and to prevent the trainee from causing damage to equipment and property or injury to self or others. For this to happen, OJT trainers must be rewarded for spending the time training as well as for doing their job. There are a number of ways to do this, but the important thing to remember is that someone who is training another employee should not be expected to perform at the same level of productivity as someone who is not. Some rewards must be provided for giving effective training. Think back to the proper process of OJT. It requires the trainer to methodically go through the steps of particular tasks and then have the trainee do the same. This requires time, which will take away from the productivity possible if the trainer was doing his own job.

One way to motivate the OJT trainer would be to have a different (higher) classification for someone who was training employees. This would provide prestige (and perhaps more money) for the position. At the same time the measure of performance for the trainer could be how well the trainee performs at the end of the formal OJT. Here, the motivation would be to turn out good trainees, rather than maintaining the trainer's level of performance. If this is not done, and trainers are expected to perform at a similar level as nontrainers, then the result might well be what happened at a food service and vending company. They used experienced vending machine service route drivers to train new route drivers. The company had a history of very high turnover of trainee drivers. It attributed this to the nature of the job, the low starting wage, and the hours required. The arrival of a new human resources manager led to a reexamination of this problem. Discussions with current trainees and trainees who had voluntarily terminated their employment in the recent past revealed that some of the trainers would do all the easy work (restocking the machines) and make the trainees do the "dirty" work (performing maintenance on the machines). Others wouldn't let the trainees do any of the work because it "slowed them down." Since the drivers were paid on the basis of the number of machines they serviced, rather than on an hourly rate, they were essentially doing the training for free.

The Small Business

OJT is the training method of choice for the small business. Many small businesses use peer training because they have no budget for training in any formal way. The value of following the procedures outlined in JIT, whether the supervisor or a peer is to be the trainer, cannot be overemphasized. An up-front investment of time to train the OJT instructor and prepare the proper plan will ensure an optimal return on investment. Research suggests that structured OJT such as that described in JIT can get workers up to speed on their jobs in half the time regular training takes (Filipczak 1996).

Another important consideration is choosing the instructor. You need to choose an employee who has a solid work ethic and correctly models the appropriate behaviors you want emulated. Remember that trainees will probably go to these trainers for help and other general information. These trainers will likely become de facto mentors to the trainee. Although these issues are important for any size organization, the impact on a small company will be greater, so these issues are more crucial. Of course apprenticeships are also excellent ways for small businesses to obtain a skilled workforce.

Audiovisual Enhancements

Identifying the appropriate type of media for each part of training is important to the development of the training program. If audio or audiovisual tapes need to be developed, a longer time frame and/or a larger budget (if they will be produced by a professional) will be necessary. Table 8.7 shows advantages and disadvantages of the various audiovisual methods.

TABLE 8.7			
	Audiovisual Aid	*Advantages*	*Disadvantages*
S T A T I C	Charts/Poster	Ability to develop lists with trainees enhances group interaction; can post and refer to during training; use in lighted room	Difficult to view from a distance; bulky to transport
	Overheads	Able to overlay systems, flowcharts, etc.; easy to use; can see from a distance; use in lighted room	Can be distracting; projector can block view
	Computer-Generated Overheads	Able to develop flashy visual aids; use of color and control of points (one presented at a time); easily modified; easily controlled	Flashy presentation could distract from training; rely heavily on technology
D Y N A M I C	Audiotapes	Can learn at any time (even traveling to work); reusable	Single sensory input, no interaction
	Film and Video	Can demonstrate appropriate behavior; good for receiving personal feedback; can present and integrate conceptual information; some commercially available are reasonably priced and appropriate	High material cost; very high development cost; need to dim lights; store-bought not specific to company
	Computer-Generated Dynamic Presentation	Can be very flashy presentations; use of color and sound provide different stimuli for obtaining interest	Same as computer-generated overheads

STATIC MEDIA

Whether you're using a poster, newsprint, chart, or overhead, you need to be aware of certain rules when you're developing these static media. The biggest mistake made in using this medium is cramming too much information on the one poster, sheet, or overhead.

Newsprint, Charts, Posters

Newsprint is probably the most often used aid in adult training. You can list learning objectives on it and post it on the wall for everyone to see throughout the training. During the training session you can generate lists related to the topic being trained, which is an excellent method for encouraging participation. These trainee-generated lists can be displayed on the walls of the training room to refer to as necessary.

Trainers can also prepare lists ahead of time. Depending on how they are prepared, these could be considered posters or charts. Guidelines for creating newsprint information (as well as posters) are similar to those for overhead preparation (see Table 8.8 below). Print in large (3 inch) letters using a wide-tipped marker. Keep the number of points to six or seven, and keep them brief.

Overheads

Most word processors are able to develop large print suitable for **overheads,** and photocopy machines or printers can transfer the image to a transparency. The advantages of the overhead are that it is used in a fully lighted room, and it is possible to build (overlay) a model or other visual aid. As an example, consider training on how to put together a piece of machinery. The first transparency would be the base. Each piece to be added could be on a separate transparency and you would "build" a model of the machine with successive overlays as you spoke. If the training was on how to complete forms, you would place a copy of the form on the overhead and write on the transparency to show the proper procedures. Similarly, you can place blank transparencies on the overhead and write on them as the discussion creates relevant points.

When you are making transparencies ahead of time, it is useful to have them framed with cardboard. This keeps them from sticking to each other or sliding off the table. Also number them so they will not be out of order when you are training. Table 8.8 provides some guidelines for developing transparencies.

Slides

Slides can provide a clearer look at things. Close-up enlargements of parts can present details not otherwise seen. The slides can be synchronized with an audiotape so the presentation is fully automated.

TABLE 8.8 Guidelines for Producing Transparencies

For each transparency:
- Present one idea or concept
- Print in large letters (1/4–1/2 inch type, larger if by hand)
- 6 or 7 lines with 6 to 8 words per line
- Use color for impact

Computer-Generated Projection

Computer-generated projections are similar to overhead transparencies, but they can be presented in a more sophisticated manner using various software packages. They have the advantage of combining art, photographs, and other graphic images with text. They also make your presentation more professional and give it pizzaz.

Resources Needed

The resources required differ according to the visual media used. Charts and posters simply require vertical surfaces where they can be attached and a method of attachment (masking tape is an old favorite of trainers). However, resources for producing these visual aids can range from simple paper and markers to the cost of a graphic designer and professional printer.

Creating overhead projections may require several types of equipment. However, the simplest way is to create the material on a computer and then print directly to the transparency. A color ink-jet printer allows you to create professionally looking overhead transparencies. You will have to purchase special color transparency film for the ink-jet printer unless you have a color laser printer or a color copier that processes transparency film. Using overhead transparencies requires an overhead projector.

Creating computer-generated projections requires a computer of sufficient capability to handle the presentation software. For the computer-generated projections you need a computer and an integrated LCD/projector machine.

Projection media require a projection surface, usually a screen, but occasionally an off-white wall, free of objects, can be used. The projection area must be capable of being darkened so the images are clearly visible.

Planning for Using Static Visuals

For effective static visuals, the room setup must allow easy viewing by all trainees. Seating should be arranged to allow a clear path for the projector's beam, and the projector should not block the trainees' view of the screen. Line of sight should also be clear for newsprint information. Here are some additional considerations:

1. Rehearse the presentation using the static visuals on the equipment in the room where training will occur. Doing so will reveal all the things you had forgotten about as well as the things you didn't know (e.g., the circuit breaker for the outlet won't handle the computer projection unit and the video equipment at the same time).
2. Bring extra equipment accessories. Extra projector bulbs, cables, extension cords, and easels should be at the training facility before training begins. Remember, Murphy's Law applies to trainers too. In fact, for trainers there is the following addendum: The more important the event, the more likely things will go wrong. Extra precautions are always wise.
3. Arrive at the training site early and check that all equipment is in working order. Make sure visuals are ready to operate when training starts (correct order, right side up, computer-generated projections ready, etc.).
4. If you are using computer-generated projections, bring along a set of traditional overheads (transparencies) for emergencies.

Protocol

When you use static visual aids, keep these points in mind:

- When using an overhead, place the pointer on the overhead rather than pointing at screen; doing this allows you to keep your focus on the trainees.
- Turn off the overhead when it's not in use.
- Keep the line of sight to visual aids clear by placing the aid in a strategic location.
- Do not talk to the visual aid, but face the trainees. Turn to the visual aid to identify a point, then turn back to the trainees.
- When a visual aid is no longer being discussed, remove it.
- When you write on newsprint, try as much as possible to continue to face the trainees; do not stand in front of the easel or face it.

Trainee's Manual

Although not generally considered a static visual, the trainee's manual is an important guide to the training. To keep the trainees' interest and their complete involvement in discussions, you will find it useful to provide notes on all the information that you will be presenting. The trainees then will be able to pay more attention to what you and others are saying and doing, rather than being concerned about taking notes. The manual often includes all lecture materials, learning points, and supplemental readings. It also includes any exercises and some blank sheets for jotting down notes and lists in small group meetings.

The best holder for the manuals is a three-ring binder so the trainee can add information as training continues. It is sometimes better to keep certain information from the trainees until it is time to use it. Exercises are an example of material that should be held back. You do not want trainees being distracted from the current topic by trying to figure out various problems ahead of time.

Instructor's Manual

The instructor's manual provides all the information that is in the trainees' manual, as well as information on what the trainer needs to do and how to do it. It is a visual aid for the trainer. The format is to have the lecture notes (and other material provided to the trainees) on the right-hand page, and the instructions for the trainer on the left-hand page. Instructions range from when to generate lists on newsprint, to what some of the expected information on the list might be and how to respond. For an example page from an instructor's manual see Table 8.9 on the following page.

DYNAMIC MEDIA

Audiotapes

The **audiotape** is generally considered a standalone type of training. Like the straight lecture, it provides information. If you use the audiotape as a presentation, then the same rules that apply to presenting a good lecture apply to the audiotape.

Audiotapes can also be used for taping the actual sounds, or recreating the sounds required for training. For example, if you were training mechanics to understand the different sounds a transmission makes when it is healthy versus damaged, you might

TABLE 8.9   Sample of Instructor's Manual

Instructor's Notes	Time Schedule	Points to Be Covered	Reference

INSTRUCTOR'S NOTES

Moving forward: A role play

Purposes

1. Develop an understanding of how management (if you are union) or union (if you are management) felt about QWL involvement. (Role Reversal).

2. Provide some insight into what the next step should be if one wishes to pursue a QWL effort.

3. Demonstrate that there are a number of concerns about moving forward in a QWL effort and the importance of addressing these concerns.

Instructor preparation

• This role play is designed for small groups of 8 people each (4 union and 4 management). Since the total number of participants in a given orientation will vary, you will probably have some unequal groups.

Your objective should be to divide the groups so the total number in each group will be roughly the same.

Introduce role play and give instructions

Role play: Instructor preparation

• While the role plays are underway, the two instructors should be circulating among the various groups to give assistance as needed or to observe dynamics.

• Be sure to keep watch on the time and to give a notice when there are 5 minutes left to go.

• When time is up, ask for volunteers to tell:
  • How far they got
  • What decisions they made
  • How they felt (Role Reversal)
  • What they learned

MOVING FORWARD: A ROLE PLAY

Hand out ten cards, color coded for union and management

Up until now, we have been concerned with discussing what QWL is, some advantages regarding getting involved and so on. But where do you go from here? If you decide to get involved in QWL, what's the next step?

With this next exercise, we hope to help you find the answer to some of those questions and at the same time have some fun. We are going to do this by letting each group answer the question: *"Where do we go from here?"*

We are also going to give everyone in the group a role to play. How many here have role-played before? . . . WAIT FOR SHOW OF HANDS.

I am sure each of you can vouch for how realistic and interesting role plays can be once you get going.

Each group will be made up of 4 union representatives and 4 management representatives. We would ask that you take a role *opposite* to the position you hold in the organization. In other words, if you a union person, take a management role, and if you are a management person, take a union role.

Role Play

We have just handed out cards with these names written on them.

POINT TO PREPARED EASEL

Role Play		Prepared
Management (Green)	Union (Blue)	Easel
Lynn	Pat	
Jan	Jamie	
Tony	Lee	
Kelly	Fran	

TABLE 8.9 Sample of Instructor's Manual (continued)

Instructor's Notes	Time Schedule	Points to Be Covered	Reference

Post role play discussion

Who would like to tell us how far they got in the project?

How many completed all the points on the chart?

What did you come up with?

Anybody come up with something different that they would like to share?

So what do you think the purpose of this exercise was?

What did you learn by participating in the role play?

• If in Role Reversal someone comments about seeing the other point of view, *pick up on that*. Emphasize that it's important to understand *perception*. How people see things is affected by their position, and it's important to try to understand where the other person is coming from.

• If someone says they didn't get very far or it's really a complicated issue, *pick up on this* and emphasize that it takes a long time to get QWL going and we can't expect them to accomplish too much in this short a time. Many meetings of longer duration are spent to get a QWL project going.

Also regarding complexity, suggest that it is a difficult thing to implement and one must be patient and realize that it is not an easy exercise. Implementation of a QWL project does take a lot of hard work—which can be at times frustrating (as you no doubt noted on this exercise).

So if you are a management employee, choose a card with names written in blue; if union, choose green names. This will give you one of the opposite roles.

If your table does not have an equal number of union and management individuals, then choosing an opposite role will not be possible, so just take a role similar to your position in the organization (management or union). Take the appropriate card and place it in front of you now.

Any questions so far?

Before we begin, there are a few points I would like to cover about the role play (TURN TO NEXT EASEL PAGE)

ROLE PLAY

DO'S	• BE YOURSELF	Prepared Easel
	• IMPROVISE OR MAKE UP FACTS THAT ARE NOT COVERED IN THE ROLE	
DON'TS	• DO NOT GO BACK AND READ ROLE ONCE YOU BEGIN	
	• DO NOT ASSUME SOME OTHER PERSONALITY	

First (point to easel), be yourself. Most people are very good at acting if they make up their own lines. So act like you would in any situation.

Second (point to easel), improvise as necessary. If a question is brought up that is not covered in the roles, make up an appropriate answer consistent with your role. Use your own experiences and beliefs to help you in this.

tape the sounds from actual problem transmissions senior mechanics have worked on. Once developed, the audiotape could be used to teach trainees to recognize the different sounds an automobile transmission makes and what they mean. The same audio could also be used for testing trainees.

Moving Film and Videos

We tend to recall "stories" much better than general information. Well-told stories tend to get our attention and are more easily encoded into memory (Sneed 1992). In developing a video, you will face two issues: developing the story to catch the attention of the trainees, and the process of putting the story on video.

First, when you construct a story line, there are five elements to include (Sneed 1992): (1) A person (main character), has (2) a problem or conflict. The person (3) experiences an intervention/insight that (4) changes the main character, and (5) creates a new order. If you follow these rules in setting up your story, you will be successful. Table 8.10 describes the points to consider in developing the story.

The second issue is the development of the video. Developing a training video is not just a matter of getting a video camera and a blank videocassette. In the first step, called *storyboarding,* you write exactly what will happen in the story, paying particular attention to the points outlined in Table 8.10. Once the story has been developed, you are in the preproduction stage, and you need to acquire the resources you need to produce the video. These activities would include such things as preparing the props and set, casting the parts, arranging for costuming, identifying necessary equipment and crew, and so on. Scheduling for the shooting should take into account rehearsals, the order in which scenes need to be recorded, and finally the actual days and times for recording. Once the scenes have been recorded, the various segments need to be edited and integrated into the final product. If you don't have a substantial background and experience in video production, the final product is likely to have an unprofessional appearance.

Computer-Generated Presentations

If you decide to develop computer-generated AVs, you can certainly enhance the credibility of training, especially if there is a great deal of lecture required. To develop a good system will require a portable computer (if you need to go off-site, for example) and software to run the system.

A number of programs are available that can do the job. Once you have put all the information on the disk, you need to conduct a trial run to become comfortable operating it during training.

Planning for Using Dynamic Media

A rule of thumb to use for adequate trainee viewing (whether static or dynamic visuals are used) is one foot of trainee distance from the screen for every inch of screen size. Thus, for a 32-inch TV screen the maximum distance trainees should be from the screen is about 32 feet. Unless the room is wired and the TV adaptable to external speakers, sound volume can also become a problem. Adequate volume for those who are 7 feet from the TV will be too low for those who are 32 feet away, and making the sound adequate for those who are furthest away can make it too loud for those in the front. One solution is to create a semicircle around the TV, although this limits the number of people who can be comfortably seated.

TABLE 8.10 Points to Consider in Creating a Story for a Video

Have one main character
- must be realistic (not perfect)
- have a problem, but otherwise successful

The problem
- character has a major problem
- can be personal struggle in his mind, or an actual problem with another employee
- must build tension with this problem, character should come close to disaster (e.g., threaten to fire her)

Intervention/insight
- character gains insight from
    mentor: Obi Wan Kenobi in *Star Wars*
    dream: Ghosts in *A Christmas Carol*

Too much story/too little story
- the general consensus is that if the story introduces too much extraneous material and too many actors, the points get lost
- the other extreme is not enough story so trainees do not really understand why things are happening. Solid storyboarding will assist in preventing this.

Use of humor
- humor can actually assist recall. For this reason, if you use humor, make sure the humor comes from the learning points. This way when trainees recall the joke they recall the learning point.

Learn from others
- examine video developed by professional

Source: Adapted from Sneed 1992.

Learning to operate the equipment is also more difficult than with the other methods. Little skill is required to operate an overhead or slide projector. Significantly more skill is required to operate the computer or the image projection equipment and to load the software and get it ready to run properly. Finally, most projection equipment built prior to 1995 required dimming the lights so low that the atmosphere was more conducive to sleeping than learning. However, new technology has solved that problem.

As with anything mechanical, it is important to try the system before training begins. Arrive early to check out all the equipment. Be sure remote controls for lights, video, and so on are operating and you understand how they work. Put the equipment through a trial run. Have a backup for any video or disk that will be used. Video machines do eat tapes, and disks do crash. Most training facilities have more than one VCR and computer, which are critical if an important part of training requires their use. Find out where the extra VCR is kept, and carry a portable computer as a spare. If that is not possible, have backup overheads. Breakdowns do happen.

Protocol

When you are using dynamic visual aids keep these points in mind:

- Turn off the TV/computer or other visual aids when you are not using them.
- Keep the line of sight to visual aids unblocked. If the group is large, use two TVs placed in strategic locations connected to the single VCR.

- When you are talking about or discussing an issue (even for a short time) between film clips, turn the lighting up. Do not attempt to discuss issues in a semidark or dark room.

Facilities

An important part of any training program is the environment. The best training is of little value if it is conducted where there are distractions, uncomfortable seating, difficulty in seeing audiovisual presentations, or similar problems. Attention to these issues, therefore, is critical. This issue was briefly discussed in chapter 5 in the section on eliminating distractions.

THE TRAINING ROOM

Whether you design your own training facility or simply go off-site to train, you need to consider many factors in making your training room a learning-friendly environment. The following describes the type of training room that is ideal for most types of training.

It is best if the room has no windows. Windows can distract the trainees, as was evident in the case at the start of the chapter. Jack was easily distracted from the training for many reasons, but the window gave him a way to avoid the training. If the room does have windows, be sure they have shades or curtains you can close. Light coming through the windows can create glare as well as be distracting. The walls should be blank, not decorated with pictures or painted in bright fancy colors. Beige is a nice neutral color. Lighting should be adjustable so it can be dimmed for overheads, video presentations, and the like and be made brighter for the lecture, discussions, and exercises. The room should be close to square in shape. Rectangular rooms limit the type of seating arrangements possible. A rule of thumb is to avoid a training room whose length exceeds its width by more than 50 percent (Davis and Hagman 1976). The room should be carpeted and have a sound-absorbing ceiling.

Ideally, if the training is off-site, you would want assurances that the walls are reasonably soundproof, especially if dividers separate the room. If it is your own facility, ensure that soundproofing is built into the room. It would also be desirable to have nearby breakout rooms that were soundproofed.[5]

The room should be equipped with its own temperature control, and the heating/cooling fans should be quiet. This point may sound trivial—after all, who would build a training room with noisy fans? The problem is that contractors are good at building buildings but do not specialize in any particular type. When the new University of Windsor Business School was being built, a team of faculty members provided input into the design of the classrooms. This helped tremendously in the development of user-friendly classrooms, but the team didn't think about fan noise. The result: one of the few complaints about the new building is fan noise. When the fans are on, it becomes very difficult to hear students asking or answering questions.

Under the heading "nice to have," consider the following. Newer training rooms have tracks built onto the wall and going completely around the room. These tracks have

---

[5]Breakout rooms are small rooms near the main training room where small groups can work on exercises without distractions.

a slot into which newsprint paper can be pushed, allowing for the hanging of charts and posters anywhere in the room. Whiteboards are sometimes built into the walls at strategic locations. Built-in consoles that control lighting, audiovisuals, and computers provide easy access to the operation of these training aids. They often come with a remote control so trainers can operate the lights and AVs from wherever they are standing.

If AVs are built into the facility, make sure they are situated so that all trainees are able to view and hear them. Also make sure that they are not built into places where the equipment itself blocks sight lines.

Furniture

Be sure to have tables and chairs rather than student desk-chairs. Tables should be movable so they can be set up in any configuration (see below). An ideal table size is 5 feet long and $2^1/_2$ feet wide. This size allows two people to sit comfortably on one side. Many configurations are possible by arranging the tables. Putting two tables together makes a 5-foot square where eight people can hold a group discussion.

Chairs should be padded and cloth covered (not vinyl), be equipped with castors, and be able to swivel. Trainees will be required to sit for extended periods of time, and comfort is important. In addition to providing overall comfort, the swivel and castors allow for ease of movement when trainees must form small groups or turn and work with another trainee. Armrests are also preferred. Being able to lean back and rest your arms creates a relaxing environment, conducive to learning.

Furniture Setup

The seating arrangements depend on the type of training that will be conducted. The typical configurations are classroom, U-shape, conference, and circle. The arrangement determines the degree of formality and where the attention is focused. It also affects the level of two-way communication (Chaddock 1971). To appreciate this point, consider the two extremes, circle and classroom (Figure 8.3 A and B on page 368). The classroom style (B) places the focus on the trainer and limits two-way communication between trainees, because the trainees are all facing one direction.[6] When a trainee sees such a setup, her role is clearly defined in her mind: she is there to listen. Now consider the circle. Here the focus is evenly distributed, there is no single person being looked at. A trainee sees this style and his role is also defined; he will be a part of the discussion. Furthermore, this lack of focus makes it easier for trainees to debate and discuss issues among themselves.

For providing employees with information on the company's position regarding sexual harassment, the classroom configuration may be appropriate. Here the goal is to provide information, and the focus should be on the trainer. Most two-way communication will be question-and-answer exchanges between trainer and trainee. Now suppose the goal is to train managers to deal with sexual harassment. A circle is chosen, because the goal is to generate discussion about managers' experiences and discuss ways of handling them. In the circle, trainees face one another and the trainer is "one of the members" of the circle, with equal focus on all. Another obvious difference between these two configurations is that with the classroom, a larger number of trainees can be accommodated.

---

[6]If no tables are used, more trainees can be accommodated. This arrangement is called the theater style.

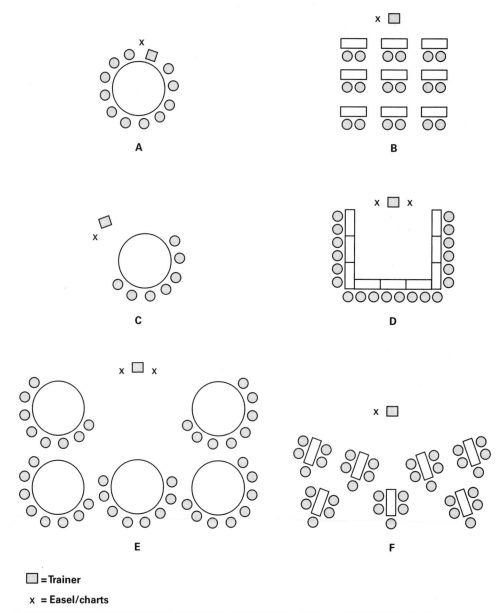

☐ = Trainer

x = Easel/charts

FIGURE 8.3 Different Seating Arrangements for Training

There are a number of modifications of these two extremes. The semicircle (Figure 8.3C) encourages trainee discussion, allowing trainees to be face-to-face when the trainer is not talking. In this situation the trainer would stand when presenting information and sit with the trainees to encourage discussion.

Perhaps the configuration used most often is the U-shape (Figure 8.3D). It is similar to the semicircle but allows for a larger group of trainees. The U-shape allows focus to be on the instructor, a fair amount of face-to-face with others for discussion, and the ability to have a reasonably large group (30 to 35 trainees), although with a larger group the U itself can become too large. The trainer must be careful not to move too deeply into the U and cut off those at the end. Also if flip charts are used, two sets may be needed to make reading them easy for all participants, particularly if the number exceeds 30. Placing the charts at the open end of the U and slightly inside (see Figure 8.3D) ensures that you will not be blocking the view and all participants can easily see the material.

In a slightly different version trainees sit at round tables in a semicircle (Figure 8.3E). This arrangement facilitates easy switching from lecturette to small group exercises or discussions. Figure 8.3F is similar but with rectangular tables. The other advantage of these configurations is that they set up small groups who can interact, making the training less threatening at the beginning.

OFF-SITE TRAINING FACILITIES

While there is a certain pride in having your own training facilities, they can be expensive, and even when you have a choice, there are several advantages to off-site training.

First, being off-site provides more assurance that trainees will not be interrupted. It is simply too easy to contact the trainee if she is on the same floor or even in the next building.

Another advantage is the change of pace it offers. Going to a hotel or conference center is not the same as going to work. Many trainees will associate staying in a hotel with vacation (unless they are traveling salespersons). This change of pace is even more important if there is a great deal of stress associated with the job. Recall the discussion of classical conditioning. Regular pairing of work with stress will result in a feeling of stress upon arrival at the workplace. Off-site training in this situation might be more amicable to the learning process. However, choose the off-site facility with care. Remember Jack and his training at the old school?

Going off-site also allows the trainer to choose a facility compatible with the needs of the particular training event. If breakout rooms, a classroom, U-shaped setup, or all three are required, you can choose the location that best fits the requirements.

The Trainer

TRAINER KSAs

It is useful to examine the KSAs of an effective trainer, presented in Table 8.11 (page 370). Note that many of the requirements are similar to those suggested for an effective lecturer. This is so because almost all training has a lecture component.

Just how much knowledge of the subject matter does the trainer need to have? The level of knowledge depends on the complexity of the subject matter. Highly technical subject matter requires a high level of such knowledge. Is the high level of knowledge more important than being a skilled trainer? Perhaps that is not the correct question, because both subject matter knowledge and trainer skills are important. We know that trainer skills are critical to effective training, so the better question is,

TABLE 8.11 Knowledge, Skills, and Attitudes Required of an Effective Trainer

Knowledge

    Subject matter

    Organization

    Adult learning process

    Instructional methods

Skills

    Interpersonal communication skills

    Verbal skills (ability to explain clearly)

        • Active listening

        • Questioning

        • Providing feedback

    Platform skills (ability to speak with inflection, gesture appropriately, and maintain eye contact)

    Organization skills (ability to present information in logical order and stay on point)

Attitudes

    Commitment to organization

    Commitment to helping others

    High level of self-efficacy

"Which is more advisable, to train the trainer in the technical skills or to train the expert in training skills?" The answer, especially if the subject matter is highly technical or complex, is the latter.

It is also useful to have some knowledge of the organization and trainees. Such knowledge increases the credibility of the trainer and helps her answer questions that come up regarding integrating the training back into the workplace.

Although most of the knowledge and many of the skills required of a trainer are trainable, it would be best to be able to begin with individuals who already possessed the attitudes identified in Table 8.11, because attitudes are more difficult to change.

TRAINER CREDIBILITY

The credibility of the trainer will have a significant impact on the effectiveness of training, so it is important to create a positive first impression and maintain it throughout the training.

First Impression

It has often been said of the "selection" interview that the favorable (or unfavorable) impression a job candidate makes is made in the first few minutes. The same could be said of the impression the trainer makes on trainees. Because this issue is so critical to effective training, the first few minutes need to be managed well. In the case at the beginning of the chapter, what kind of first impression do you think Jason Reston made? Did he establish any credibility with the trainees? Did he demonstrate a concern for their needs? Did he seem approachable?

What should a trainer wear for training? The answer is: You must know your audience. If you are unsure, ask. In many situations a business suit is a safe bet. If you are training accountants who all come to work in conservative business attire, you had better do the same. This same attire, however, could distance you from some other groups. If you are training line workers from a manufacturing plant, you may wish to dress more casually and not wear the uniform of management. Remember, you want the trainees to perceive you as someone able to help them in their job. To gain this credibility, you need to dress appropriately. Appropriate dress for training line workers might be casual dress—tasteful casual, but casual nevertheless.

What is equally important is that the clothes fit well, shoes are shined, and accessories match what you are wearing. This "first impression" will help establish your credibility.

Experience

The credibility of the trainer is also determined by his credentials: where he comes from and what he has done. For example, one very successful trainer told us about one of his first training assignments, at the age of 23, as part of a corporate training staff. The course was called "Nonfinancial Motivation Techniques." The trainees were first-line supervisors with an average of six years' experience in their positions and over ten years with the company. Ten minutes into the first training component (the lecture), one of the older trainees raised his hand and said, "Sonny, have you ever supervised a group of unskilled laborers?" The answer, of course, was no, but he qualified it with the fact that he had supervised white-collar employees. Several knowing smirks around the room made it clear that the trainer's credibility had been destroyed. Throughout the rest of the program, trainees were inattentive, lethargic, and occasionally rude. This trainer learned early on that trainer credibility is a key factor in the effectiveness of the lecture technique.

How could the trainer have handled that situation more effectively? One thing he could have done was set the context of the training at the beginning. He could have said something like the following: "I will be presenting a number of nonfinancial techniques that you might be able to use to motivate your employees. These are techniques that have worked for other supervisors in a variety of situations. First, I will explain the technique and then we will discuss how it might work for you or how it might be adapted to work for you. You know your work units better than anyone else, so I'm counting on everyone to help identify ways these techniques can be applied."

A trainer does not need to have the same work experience as the trainees to be effective. However, he needs to be seen as having something worthwhile to offer. Here the trainer is offering some new ideas and his expertise in facilitating the discussion of these ideas, but—and this is important—he is not dismissing or diminishing the expertise of the audience. What he is saying is, "Let's merge our separate areas of expertise to arrive at something we both want (more motivated employees)."

Acknowledging the differences in experience at the beginning of training is also important. This allows the trainees to see that the trainer is aware of the differences and is taking them into account. One way to do that in the situation just discussed would have been to say, "My experience has been supervising white-collar employees. How do you think the motivations of these employees differ from those you supervise?" After some differences are noted, the trainer might then ask, "At one time, most of you were unskilled workers. What were the things that motivated you when you were an unskilled worker?" This question would allow the supervisors to see that while individuals may differ in the things that motivate them, there are general categories of motivators that go across all individuals. The questioning process allows the trainees to test their assumptions and learn through self-discovery.

Integrated Instructional Strategy

The information presented in this book comes together in the instructional strategy used for a training program. The strategy is compiled in a written document, often called a program development plan, detailing the methods, materials, equipment, facilities, and trainers for the training program. There are a variety of systems for documenting the strategy (program management timing charts, technical reports, etc.). Our purpose is to indicate what should be included in the documentation, rather than the form it should take. Important issues to address in your strategy are discussed below.

CONTENT: LEARNING POINTS

A **learning point** is an important piece of information that must be learned in order for the trainee to accomplish the learning objective. Each objective will provide specific information as to what needs to be learned. Consider this learning objective: "Solder 20 feet of 1/2-inch copper pipe, using elbows and unions, in 20 minutes or less with no leaks." In order to ensure no leaks, the trainee must pay specific attention to the cleaning of the copper pipe, the proper heating of the pipe, and correct application of the solder. These would be learning points, which the trainer would need to be sure the trainee mastered.

METHOD OF INSTRUCTION

We have discussed a variety of training methods from which you can choose. As we have noted, each method has strengths and weaknesses. Many of them, such as role play, behavior modeling, and case study, are not meant to be standalone methods but rather facilitate learning by providing alternative mechanisms for providing practice.

Although the method's effectiveness in meeting the learning objective should be the major criteria for selection, other considerations are costs, time needed to develop, and time allotted in the training session. If cost, for example, inhibits your ability to use the best method, you need to choose a different method that meets the budget but still provides the practice needed. Literacy of the workforce is another issue you may need to consider. Methods such as programmed instruction and computer-based instruction rely on trainees' ability to read and understand. If they are not skilled in this area, alternative approaches need to be considered, particularly if reading is not an important skill for the job.

FACILITIES, MATERIAL AND EQUIPMENT, TRAINERS
Facilities

If you have your own facility, be sure it is available and reserve it. If you are going off-site, then you can be selective as to the design of the room. If breakout rooms are necessary or different seating arrangements (lecture, small-group discussion) are required, be sure the site can accommodate your needs. If there are dividers to other rooms, inquire about the events scheduled next to you. Attending a training session when there is a motivational speaker or sales rally next door can be very distracting. If nothing is scheduled, get assurance that the booking office will be sensitive to your concerns if they book the rooms next to yours. Check the soundproofing of the panels that separate the rooms. Avoid booking rooms that lead directly to the kitchen unless you know they are soundproofed.

Materials and Equipment

Document all the material you will need such as text, overheads, and the like, and time frames for their completion. If you are developing material, be sure to provide sufficient time to have it prepared properly. At off-site locations be sure you order the equipment and anything else being provided by others far enough in advance. If you can afford it and there is time, have important charts, posters, and easel sheets professionally printed.

Trainer

How do you choose the trainer? One of the most commonly cited reasons for training not being effective is its lack of relevance to the trainee's situation. Comments such as "The training is great but it will not work in our plant," "You do not understand the problems we have," "My boss is the one who should be here, he makes the decisions" indicate the concern trainees perceive as to the transferability of the training to their job.

To deal with this issue, Curry (1977) suggests training middle managers as trainers. Doing so will alleviate most of the above concerns, but Curry does point out there are potential problems doing this. The fact that the middle manager may be the supervisor of some of the trainees could dampen these trainees' enthusiasm for training.

Larger organizations can overcome this problem simply by not involving managers in training people who directly report to them. Smaller organizations would have to assure such trainees that they will be treated the same as others. As long as trainees did not perceive any different treatment, the word would soon get out that this system was okay. Another concern is the potential that the middle manager may spend too much time on the organization and its issues rather than on the training topics. Solid training objectives would help to prevent this.

Another way to develop a successful training program is probably not used enough because of the cost. That is to use a seasoned trainer (e.g., outside or internal consultant) and a manager to team-teach the training program. The two could work from each other's strengths. Another advantage of this approach is that the manager receives good on-the-job training on how to be an effective trainer.

THE STRATEGY

With the above information, the strategy can now be articulated. For each objective, a number of things need to be identified: facilities and configuration, learning points, methodology for training, equipment and material required. Table 8.12 (page 374) provides a useful outline that should serve as a guide for completing the instructional strategy. This will help you systematically examine what is required and what sequence (if there is more than one objective) makes the most sense. As each learning objective is considered (along with its learning points), the most effective configuration of methods, material and equipment, facilities, and trainers is determined.

TABLE 8.12   Components of Instructional Strategy

Program Development Plan
Name of Program: Pipe Fitting I
Target Population: Apprentices who have successfully passed the gas fitters exam
Overall Training Objective: Trainees will be able to examine a work project and with appropriate tools; measure, cut, thread, and install the piping according to standards outlined in the gas code.

Learning Objective	*Learning Points*	*Method*	*Material and AV*
1. Using a tape measure, determine the length of and number of pipes necessary to connect the furnace to the gas meter in a manner that meets the gas code	1. Take into account the extra length necessary because of threading 2. Take into account that length is reduced by different fittings, e.g., street elbow, union, elbow, etc. 3. How to construct appropriate drop for furnace	Lecture and simulation	Trainee manual Overhead projector Assortment of 1-inch and 3/4-inch fittings; elbows, street elbows, and unions Mock meter and furnace setup Tape measure, note pads
2. Use threading machine to cut and thread length of pipe required	1. Length of thread required 2. Importance of cutting and reaming, measuring, and use of threading machine oil	Lecture and simulation	Trainee manual VCR and TV Threading tape Threading machine Steel pipe Oil Tape measure

Facility and configuration:

Trainer:

Measures to assist transfer:

Method of evaluation:

In Table 8.12 the lecture method will provide the cognitive information and the simulation will provide actual practice. If the training is to teach supervisors how to deal effectively with conflict, the methodology might be lecture or discussion to provide information, depending on the sophistication of the group, and role play or behavior modeling to provide practice.

Once you have established the methods to be used and the sequencing of the training, it is necessary to determine time frames for each of these activities. In most cases time is limited, and the inexperienced training developer tends to have too much material to cover. Always allow for a reasonable amount of time for discussion and interaction. This is where most of the learning occurs.

Based on the type of training that will be taking place, you need to decide on the training facility and the seating configuration. Having this information clearly documented improves the likelihood that mistakes will not be made. There could be a problem if the training required a great deal of face-to-face interaction among the trainees but the training facilities were too small to accommodate this.

Mechanisms that will be used to ensure transfer need to be documented so that it is clear what is expected to occur once training is completed. Generally, you expect transfer of training to occur, but often little is done to ensure that it does. When no one person is responsible, the feeling of responsibility is diffused and transfer is soon forgotten.

Similarly, it is important to indicate the methods that will be used in evaluating the training, along with time frames. Once again, having this information clearly outlined will help to ensure that it will happen.

After the program development plan has been carefully constructed and agreed on, the next step is to obtain or develop the instructional material, instructional media, and equipment as discussed earlier in the chapter. By methodically completing the program development plan and using it as a guide, you should be able to identify and develop everything required for training.

THE ALTERNATIVE TO DEVELOPMENT

There are a number of reasons why an organization may choose not to develop its own course. A small business may not have the resources; large companies may not have many individuals to train or simply may have too many other projects in the works. In such situations there are alternatives. You can either hire a consultant to use one of their prepackaged programs, or look to outside seminars for the training.[7]

The Consultant

If the training you need is not specific to your organization, but more generic (e.g., conflict management, interviewing skills, or computer skills), you can find a consultant who has a training package that can be adapted to fit your needs. The other extreme is to use the consultant's prepackaged program without any alterations, reducing the overall cost.

The advantage to prepackaged programs is that they are ready to go. The disadvantage is that they are not specific to your company. This tradeoff may be more acceptable for a session on conflict resolution than a session on team development. In fact, many prepackaged programs can be used to supplement a company's own program. They can be less costly than hiring a consultant, but some are still very expensive. Some consulting firms have prepackaged programs and also provide training for your trainers. This adds to the cost, but the training is usually very good. If a great deal of training will be taking place in your organization, this option may be worth the extra expense if it is amortized over a number of sessions.

---

[7]One other option which we will not discuss is the hiring of a consultant to do all the work, from needs analysis to evaluation. This is the most expensive alternative, and would result in a program tailored to your needs much as if you did it all yourself. This might be a consideration if you had a specific training requirement, did not have the time yourself, and/or did not have the expertise in house.

In deciding whether to use a consultant there are many questions to consider[8]:

- How many employees are to be trained, and will they need constant retraining?
- Is there an advantage to having a neutral third party involved (e.g., union–management cooperative ventures)?
- Is there a rush to get the training done?
- Do you have the expertise in-house?

If the decision is to use a consultant, make sure you consider the following:

- Ask for references, ask who they have trained, and be sure to follow up on this information (consultants vary in their expertise).
- Determine how much the consultant knows about your industry.
- See what the training objectives look like in some of their training packages.
- Find out how the consultant evaluates her success in training.
- Make sure you know who you will be getting to do the work. Often you meet the salesperson, not the person who will do the training.

Outside Seminars

The outside seminar is training offered from time to time at local hotels, conference centers, and universities. These seminars are the least expensive and best alternative if you have only a few employees to be trained. If you have a minimum of 10 to 12 individuals to be trained, these seminars may be in-house. In-house seminars can be tailored to your organization for a moderate extra cost. They can also include an evaluation component.

When choosing a seminar, consider the following factors:

- What are you attempting to train? Skills require practice, and seminars often are large and cannot include practice sessions.
- Is there any form of evaluation? (There seldom is.)
- How focused are the training objectives?

You should also send someone to preview the seminar and report back on its potential value.

If you decide to purchase training, assess how it fits into the overall training strategy. Many companies are implementing team training because it is "the thing to do." Spending money on team training simply because others are doing it will only waste money. Training should be seen as a mechanism to support the organization's mission and goals. There must be other mechanisms in place to support the training if it is to transfer effectively.

ALTERNATIVES FOR THE SMALL BUSINESS

Jack Zenger, president of the Times Mirror Training Group in California, has found that there is significantly more interest in training by small business. Hiring a consultant or purchasing prepackaged training may be the answer for the small business,

---

[8]These suggestions, and the suggestions related to using a consultant, also apply to the hiring of a consultant to do all the work (needs analysis to evaluation).

which in many cases simply does not have the resources to develop its own training. In doing so, it is important for the small business to follow the suggestions on choosing a consultant or packaged training.

Small businesses could also examine the feasibility of developing a consortium of small businesses that could all use the same training. LearnShare, mentioned earlier, discovered that 74% of their training was not specific to a particular organization's process or products (Blumfield 1997). The same should be true of small companies. Why not take advantage of this commonality and work together to identify training needs and share in the cost of developing or purchasing relevant training? Small businesses often belong to industry-specific associations. These provide a venue for discussing this idea to determine level of interest. Even if a consortium is too complex a project to consider, what about purchasing a few prepackaged training programs? If a small business located three other companies with similar training interests, they could save 75 percent of the cost.

Western Learning Systems of California is a variation on the consortium idea. It developed a number of courses for larger companies but retained the copyright. It was then able to market these courses to small companies at a more affordable rate. A small company purchases a membership with Western Learning and can send employees to various training sessions. The cost is $189 per employee, a saving of about $100 per person (Filipczak 1994).

Another inexpensive way to train in some areas is to have those who require training read a particular book, then have a discussion group on the topic. It can be led by the person most knowledgeable about the subject. One company that was preparing for ISO certification had the group of employees read a book written by one of the quality gurus, Philip Crosby. They would read a chapter, then meet and discuss it. The manager would prepare some questions in advance to keep the discussion going (Filipczak 1996). Earlier we argued how important trainee involvement in training is for adult learning. These discussion groups are the epitome of involvement. It should be noted that at this company the informal training turned into a more formal training program after this initial orientation.

Although this method does not follow all the criteria we suggest for an effective training program, it might more than compensate by motivating its participants. There is no one best way to train, especially when you consider the cost benefit for various training alternatives. Training in Action 8.5 (page 378) provides examples of various methods being used by small businesses.

Finally, there are resources small businesses can use to expand their training capabilities. The U.S. Chamber of Commerce has a federation of programs and services division. Canada's equivalent is the Federal Business Development Bank. These are places where small business can obtain help in fulfilling their training needs. The federation of programs, for example, has as its objective "to provide low-cost training to small businesses." The vice president, Roger Jask, did a needs analysis of the type of training required to keep small businesses alive, and from this analysis he developed a number of self-study courses that can be purchased for about $20 each. Exercises are included, and at the end of each chapter there is a test that the trainee completes and sends to Jask to be scored. Also, at the end of the text a test is given in a similar manner. Passing the course earns the trainee a certificate indicating successful completion (Filipczak 1996).

Training in Action 8.5

The Small Business: What Is It Doing?

Brenda Schissler, president of Staffmasters, a small temporary service provider in Lousiville, has ten permanent employees. Each of them specializes in a topic (e.g., safety) and goes to outside seminars to gain relevant knowledge. Upon return, each is responsible for teaching the others about the particular issue (Filipczak 1996).

Kevin O'Brian is the Quality Assurance person responsible for ISO standards at Rivait Machine Tools Inc., a 14-person operation in Windsor, Ontario. Basically one type of work is done at Rivait Machine, so instead of providing training in the procedures required, they developed a "job aid," which is a checklist of tasks. The employee goes through the list, checking off each task as he completes it, then moving to the next task. This way training, except at the basic level, is not necessary (O'Brian 1997).

You do not have to be big to win prestigious awards, but you do need training. Custom Research Inc. is a market research company based in Minneapolis. Each of its 105 employees received a minimum of 130 hours of training in 1995. In 1996 it became the first professional service company and the smallest company ever to win the Malcolm Baldrige National Quality Award (Zemke 1997).

Steve Braccini, president of Profastener, a small business in California with about 150 employees, suggests that it is a good idea to send two rather than only one employee to a specific type of training. If you send only one, his view of what took place might be skewed. By sending two and having them discuss the training with each other, you ensure a common understanding. Braccini believes this system results in a better overall product. Braccini makes one other important point: He always has these employees attend a "train the trainer" course before going on any training (Filipczak 1996).

Implementation

At this point you are ready to implement your instructional strategy. This phase of the training model is depicted on page 379. Outputs from the development phase are brought together in a training program. However, before your training program is ready for general use, typically two steps should be undertaken: a dry run and a pilot (Abella 1986). The former is a "first test" of new material; here the training package may not be presented in its entirety. The latter is the first full-blown presentation of the training using finished materials.

DRY RUN

The **dry run** is conducted to test the effectiveness of the training program in a very controlled setting. For a good dry run, use potential trainees. Those chosen for the dry run should be hand-picked according to their diverse backgrounds (be sure to have

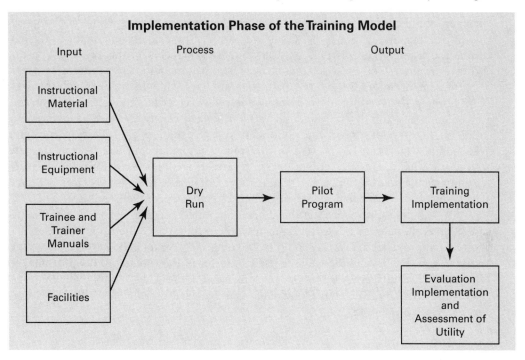

Implementation Phase of the Training Model

Input — Process — Output

Instructional Material

Instructional Equipment

Trainee and Trainer Manuals

Facilities

Dry Run

Pilot Program

Training Implementation

Evaluation Implementation and Assessment of Utility

some content experts), their general supportiveness of the value of training, and their willingness to provide feedback.

If there are not enough potential trainees to have a group go through the dry run, choose more seasoned employees or, if necessary, some of the design team and managers involved in developing the training. The trainer should preferably be someone who has been involved in the training design and development.

The dry run may not require that all the training modules in the program be tested. If you have previously used a specific exercise, case, or role play with similar participants, the dry run for this exercise may simply involve the participants' reading the exercise and providing feedback as to its relevance. Working through the exercise and full discussion may not be necessary. Other exercises, particularly newly developed ones, probably require the participants to go through the full process.

It is important to have a list of questions for participants after each exercise or module you test. For example, after participants have completed a role play, you may wish to determine if the situation is realistic for this organization. If it is not, future trainees may dismiss the training as being irrelevant. Other questions you may wish to ask are: Was the information contained in the exercise clear enough to do the exercise? Were the instructions clear? Was the time allocation too long or too short?

Feedback from the dry run needs to be examined and the training revised where applicable. Then it is time for the pilot program.

PILOT PROGRAM

The **pilot program** is different from the dry run in that trainees are there to be trained. This will be a full-fledged program. The dry run should have refined the training to the degree that there should not be any major glitches. Trainees for the pilot program should also be chosen carefully: You do not want anyone who is not support-ive of training, and who may be disruptive. You still may need some input to further refine the training and disruptions would not be conducive to this process. You do, however, want a good cross-section of those who will be in the later training sessions.

In the pilot program, the three main goals are to provide the trainees with the rele-vant training, to assess further the timing and relevance of modules and various train-ing components, and to determine the appropriateness, clarity, and flow of material. In addition, in the pilot session you will obtain from the trainees valuable responses and viewpoints, which can be inserted in the trainee's manual, and will help guide new trainers in what to expect. Another goal is to provide an opportunity for future instruc-tors to attend and experience the training firsthand. Finally, the pilot program will pro-vide valuable feedback to designers regarding effectiveness of the training.

After the pilot, revisions that have been identified need to be completed. One fi-nal note: Although this pilot program should help to improve the program, examina-tion and appropriate revisions should be ongoing. As we explained earlier, evaluating training goes far beyond the training itself. Transfer of the training to the job, plus or-ganizational results, are the primary reasons for training. Thus training will continue to be modified until desirable outcomes can be reliably achieved. The evaluation process is a continuous one.

TIPS FOR TRAINERS

A number of good tips for lecturing were featured earlier in the chapter. The lecture is often a component of training and may need to be occasionally reviewed. The fol-lowing tips relate to other issues trainers should be aware of in order to deliver an ef-fective training session.

Preparation

The trainer needs to arrive early and be sure everything is in order. Check seating arrangements and make sure materials have arrived. All equipment should be work-ing and, more important, you should know how to operate it. All overhead projectors, for example, are supposed to have a spare bulb inside, but is it there? All videos have a standard mode of operation, but is the remote working, and do you understand it? Is there enough flip chart newsprint? As trainer, you need to be sure everything is ready to go before the trainees arrive, otherwise you can lose your credibility before you get started.

The Beginning of Training

Once you have everything ready to go, it is time to begin greeting trainees. Small talk with individuals before the session will help make them comfortable and, in turn, will facilitate discussion once the training begins.

Starting on time is important. Recall the reinforcement theory discussed in chap-ter 3. If those who arrive late discover training has not begun, the belief is reinforced that showing up on time is not necessary. A late start also punishes those who do ar-rive on time. For the rule of starting on time to be effective, however, you need to ob-tain commitment from the trainees (see below).

Although starting on time is important, very few trainers we know start exactly on time the first day. Most trainers allow for some tardiness the first day when trainees may not know exactly where the training room is or simply did not give themselves enough time to get to the location. A good practice is to start training with an ice-breaker—an exercise that allows for those who arrive a little late to fit right in with little disruption.

Trainees may have different expectations about what the training will be about and have come for various reasons. After an ice-breaker, it is useful to ask trainees what they expect to get from the training. You simply ask each person or have small groups develop lists to present to the larger group. These expectations are written on newsprint for future reference. You can indicate to the trainees which of the points mentioned are a part of the training. For any points that are not part of the training design, you may offer to try and fit them in[9] if they are appropriate. If not, explain why they are not appropriate for this training session. You should also promise to go back to the list periodically to be sure all things that you promised to cover were in fact covered.

Following or concurrently with this introductory step, go through the agenda to indicate what will be happening over the duration of the training. Trainees should be told how breaks will be distributed and how messages to them will be handled. One way to determine these things is to ask for a short discussion regarding the rules that will be set down for the training period. In this way, the trainees abide by these rules because they helped develop them. If you want to expedite the process, you can prepare a set of suggested rules, and explain why they are useful, and ask the trainees for any suggestions to modify, add, or delete from the list. At this point the rule of starting on time can be discussed and decided upon.

Setting the Tone

Dress As was suggested earlier, be sure to dress appropriately. If appropriately means business attire, however, you may want to loosen up after the training gets underway. The trainees need to feel comfortable, and if many show up wearing suits, you can signal the more relaxed nature by removing your jacket or loosening your tie if you are wearing one. You might say, "I think I need to loosen up a bit; please feel free to do the same." For training spread over several days, you might at some point on the first day have the trainees decide on an appropriate dress code.

The Podium One of the authors was hired to assist a consultant in training the automobile workers in a new plant. The consultant had hired a number of local people because of the size of the project. Because concurrent training sessions were taking place, we all had opportunities to observe each other. One trainer was in the habit of sitting behind a table while talking to the trainees, another stood behind a podium, and the rest stood and moved around a lot, going back to their notes only occasion-

---

[9]The authors have found that most of the time the points raised by trainees are already included in training. This is especially true when an effective needs analysis has been conducted.

ally. Which procedure is best? Again it depends. Standing behind the podium or sitting at a desk may be acceptable if there is primarily one-way communication. This may not be the most effective style for training adults, however, where two-way communication is important. In these cases any barriers (desk, podium) impede the communication process. Additionally, if the trainees did not have a good experience in their early school years, seeing someone sitting behind a desk and teaching them might evoke the traditional school setting and cause them to feel uneasy about the training. Being out in front of a desk or podium and moving around helps make the trainer look more accessible and open to input. In any event, the two-way communication is much more important in the lecture/discussion method, whereas for the straight lecture a podium is perfectly acceptable.

Listening and Questioning

Contrary to what you might think, it is more important for a trainer to have good listening and questioning skills than presentation skills. This is not to demean presentation skills, but rather to stress the importance of listening and questioning. The techniques discussed earlier cannot be emphasized too strongly. If you are using the lecture/discussion method, use the experience and information provided by the trainees. Control the urge to tell them continually of *your* experiences. Remember that trainees relate to one another and their experiences more than to yours.

Providing Instructions

It is important to provide clear instructions with each exercise you plan to use. Many role-play exercises are wasted because trainees don't understand exactly what is expected. Oral instructions certainly need to be provided, but a handout containing identical information is also useful for trainees to refer to. Even then, it is helpful to provide an example of what you expect. Once the exercise has begun, it's too late. It is discouraging to both the trainer and trainees if the trainees are confused and embarrassed because they misunderstood what they were supposed to be doing.

Dealing with Different Trainees

A successful trainer needs to understand how to deal with the various types of trainees he might encounter. Some need to be encouraged to become more involved in discussion, while others are far too involved.

Quiet Trainee   We have already discussed methods for encouraging quiet trainees to become more involved (small group discussions, writing their answers first), and these are usually successful. But what if they do not work? If you have a number of small-group discussion sessions, one way to encourage the quiet trainee is to ask each group to rotate the person who is responsible for reporting back to the larger group. The quiet trainee will then have a turn reporting to the larger group, increasing his participation. However, too much pressure to become involved is not a good idea. If the quiet person is speaking up during the small-group sessions, he is providing input. Do not attempt to get these trainees to participate at an equal level to others if they are not so inclined. Doing so can create too much tension in the environment. If what we have already proposed has not significantly changed the quiet trainee's behavior, forget it.

Talkative Trainee   The talkative trainee is usually far more of a problem than the quiet one. No matter what question you ask, he has an answer. Usually the answer involves a long story, and soon other trainees are rolling their eyes and tuning out. The trainer loses the trainees' attention, and valuable training time is wasted on irrelevant stories. You need to tone down their input, but not embarrass anyone. One thing to try is asking others for their opinion. Say something like, "We have been making Lex do all the work here so far—how about someone else responding?" Or use the direct questioning technique to get the focus away from the talkative trainee. You can also talk to the talkative trainee in private, suggesting that you appreciate her comments but are concerned that others are not participating as much as they should. In this context, asking the talkative trainee to hold back on her participation usually works.

Angry Trainee   Some trainees who come to training simply do not want to be there. They will set out to ruin the session for everyone. You need to deal with such trainees early on before they disrupt the class. One of the authors was training line workers in team concepts and, although the union executive and most union members were supportive of the training, some were violently opposed. In the first session one of these trainees said, "I really do not want to be here; this training is management propaganda designed to weaken the union." The author's response was, "I have heard that said before; how do others feel about the training?" At that point a number of others indicated support for the training and, although the angry trainee did not participate very much in the rest of the training, he did not disrupt it either.

   If in such a situation the trainer found that most of the trainees felt the same way, then it would be wise to spend some time discussing the issue, because such an attitude will certainly affect training. The important thing here is to focus on how training can be a benefit to them. One way to accomplish this is to ask trainees to identify ways they would be able to use the training.

The Comedian   This trainee is a gift and a curse. He is a gift because if his jokes work, and if they are not put forth too often, they will do wonders to set a positive tone. Laughter is good medicine, and a comedian is able to provide it. The potential curse is in the nature and frequency of the jokes. Many jokes these days are inappropriate. In some cases it is difficult to know what is offensive, and you do not want to have even a small number of trainees feel that a particular joke was offensive. Also if the comedian does get a lot of laughs, she is likely to continue to joke around. This can disrupt the timing of the sessions and put the trainer behind.

   So what to do? If the joking gets out of hand or some jokes are inappropriate, you can talk with the comedian at a break. Indicate a concern that some of the humor is offensive to some of the trainees or is distracting from the focus of training. In doing this, you need to indicate appreciation of the comedian's intention to contribute to the training, but reach an agreement about how often the jokes can be offered and what type of jokes are acceptable. Doing this should be enough to curb such behavior.

Jack Goes to Training

Get up . . . . Get up, you're going to be late for the training!

"Huh," grunted Jack. "What time is it?"

"It's 7:30 and you have to go downtown to the training center today, remember?" said his wife.

Wow, what a dream, thought Jack as he walked up the steps of the training center, feeling a little nervous. The training room was not at all like a schoolroom. No windows, no blackboards. As he entered the room, he was approached by a nicely dressed man who said, "Hi, my name is Doug. Welcome to the training center. Have you ever been here before?" The name tag indicated Doug was the trainer. He seems like a nice guy, thought Jack.

"There's some coffee and doughnuts over there—help yourself." said Doug. This might even be enjoyable, thought Jack, although he still felt a little apprehensive.

With introductions out of the way and the objectives and agenda explained, Doug summed up by saying, "So at the end of the two days you will be expected to take a set of specifications and program them into the machine. Are there any questions?"

"So there are no tests," said Jack.

"Well," responded Doug, "that is the test."

Jack was a bit confused, "But that is what we do at work—I don't see it as a test. A test is where I have to write down an answer to some question you pose about all this stuff."

"There are no paper-and-pencil tests, just behavioral tests," said Doug.

Suddenly it was lunchtime. Jack thought, "It was true, time does go fast when you are having fun. This sure isn't like school." All 23 trainees went to another room where lunch was served.

"I can't believe it. This is nothing like I expected," said Ron. Ron was the fellow that Jack had to interview and introduce to the group in what was called an ice-breaker. That ice-breaker sure did a lot to get me relaxed and actually interested in the training, thought Jack.

Ron continued, "I always did poorly in school and was petrified about coming here." Jack responded, "Me too."

Ron said, "I like the idea of his periodically giving us minitests. Gives us an idea of how we are doing and provides us with extra help if we are falling behind."

"Tests . . . oh yeah, I find it hard to consider them tests. They're hands-on, exactly what we will do on the job," said Jack.

Later Jack thought, "Wow, it's already over."

"Nice job, Jack. You are now certified on this piece of equipment," said Doug.

"Hey, Ron," said Jack, "do you believe how much fun learning can be?"

Ron agreed. "Doug was great. He kept getting our input and tying our experiences to the new stuff we had to learn. I never thought I would say this, but I would like to get more training like this."

"You bet," said Jack. "I still can't believe how great this was—especially after the dream I had."

Key Terms

- Apprentices
- Audiotape
- Behavior modeling
- Business games
- Case study
- Closed-ended question
- Coaching
- Computer-based training
- Direct question
- Dry run
- Dysfluencies
- Ice-breaker
- In-basket
- Job instruction training (JIT)
- Learning point
- Lecture
- Level of interactivity
- Mentoring
- Newsprint
- Nonverbal cues
- On-the-job training (OJT)
- Open-ended question
- Overhead question
- Overheads
- Pilot program
- Questioning
- Relay question
- Reverse question
- Role play
- Self-pacing
- Simulator
- Sophistication of the multimedia

Case Analysis

Jim worked as a laborer for a gas utility in Winnipeg, Manitoba. When the opportunity came to apply for a backhoe/front-end-loader operator job, he was very excited. Three people had applied. To select the one who would get the job, the company asked each of them to actually go out and work on the backhoe for a day. Jim realized that he did not have a chance for the job, because he had never even driven a tractor let alone used a backhoe. When he went out, he did not know how to start the tractor, and one of the other backhoe operators who was getting his machine had to show him. He managed through the day and, to his surprise, did better than the others. He was given the job.

On his first day at the new job, one of the other backhoe operators showed him where to check the hydraulic fluid and said, "These old Masseys are foolproof. You will be okay." Jim taught himself how to dig a hole by trial and error. He initially believed that the best way was to fill the bucket as much as possible before emptying it. He would wiggle the bucket back and forth until it was submerged and then curl it. When it came out of the hole, the earth would be falling off the sides. This was not so difficult after all, he thought. He cut through his first water line about two weeks after starting his new job. Having to go into a deep hole after it had been full of water did not make the crew very happy. After he cut through his third water line, the crew chief pulled him aside and said, "You are taking too much earth out with each bucket so you don't feel the bucket hitting the water line; ease up a bit." Water lines were usually 6 to 8 feet down, so Jim would dig until about 5 feet and then try to be more careful. It was then he pulled up some telephone lines, which were only about 3 feet deep.

Realizing there was more to operating a backhoe than he first thought, he sought out Bill Granger, who was known to have broken a water line only twice in his 15 years. It was said he was so good he could dig underneath the gas lines—a claim that Jim doubted. Bill said you need to be able to feel any restriction. The way to do that was to have more than one of your levers open at the same time. Operating the bucket lever and the boom lever at the same time reduces the power and causes the machine to stop rather than cut through a line of any type. Jim began to do this and still broke water lines, but there was a difference now. He knew immediately that he had broken one; he could feel the extra pull, whereas in the past he found out either by seeing water gushing up or by hearing the crew chief swearing at him. He was getting better. Jim never did become as good as Bill Granger. In fact two years later he applied for another job as gas repairperson and was promoted. The interesting thing is that the training as a gas repairperson was not much better.

CASE QUESTIONS

1. What are the potential costs to this lack of training? Why do you think the company operated in this manner?

2. What type of training would you recommend: OJT, classroom, or a combination? Describe what the training might entail.

3. What type of training environment would you provide?

4. Who would you get to do the training and why?

5. Would you consider purchasing a training program for backhoe operators? Provide your rationale.

Exercises

1. Check the room where your class meets. Does it meet the requirements of a good training room? What additions would make it more amenable to effective training?

2. Assume you are in training on conflict resolution. Think of a situation where you got in an argument with someone, and write up the role of the person with whom you were in conflict. Follow the instructions in the chapter. Do not forget you need to write the role of the other person, not you, because you will play yourself. Show the role to a classmate and ask him or her to play it. As you play your part, try to behave differently than you did in the original confrontation. Although you do not have any training in the area of conflict resolution, simply try to remain calm and not turn the situation into a confrontation. Now debrief; how did it go? Was the role play useful in helping you practice being calm? Ask the classmate if the role you wrote could have been better in terms of providing information as to how the classmate should have acted.

3. In a small group each person takes turns getting up and giving a three-minute impromptu speech (on anything). Have someone designated as the bell ringer. Each time you use a dysfluency (*uh, and uh, um,* etc.) the bell ringer will hit a glass with a spoon (or make some other sound). Keep score for each person. Now over the next few weeks have friends tell you when you use these dysfluencies, and try to reduce them. Then get together with your group and redo the exercise. Note the improvement?

4. In small groups choose someone who has worked in a particular job. Interview the person to determine the job requirements, and develop a procedure for providing OJT for the job.

Questions for Review

1. You are asked to deliver a two-day workshop for managers on effective feedback skills. It is focused primarily on performance reviews. There are 100 managers who need to be trained. Describe what the content of the training would entail, methods you would use (e.g., lecture, case study, role play) and the instructional media and equipment you would want. Why? Also what type of room setup you would want. Why? Indicate how many sessions you would need for this number of managers. Why?

2. Describe the various types of questioning and when they are used.

3. What is the difference between role play and behavior modeling? When would you use one versus the other?

4. Describe the proper method for preparing and conducting OJT.

References

Abella, K. 1986. *Building Successful Training Programs.* Reading, MA: Addison-Wesley.

Apprentice Information. 1995. *Ontario Training and Adjustment Board.* Toronto: Queens Printer.

Argyris, C. 1980. Some limitations to the case method: Experience in a management development program. *Academy of Management Review* 5:291–98.

Broadwill, M., and C. Dietrich. 1996. How to get trainees into the action. *Training,* February, pp. 52–56.

Blumfield, M. 1997. Learning to share. *Training,* April, pp. 38–42.

Camp R., P. Blanchard, and G. Huszczo. 1986. *Toward a more organizationally effective training strategy and practice.* Upper Saddle River, NJ: Prentice Hall.

Chaddock, P. 1971. How do your trainers grow. *Training and Development Journal,* March, pp. 2–7

Curry, T. 1977. Why not use your line managers as management trainers? *Training and Development Journal,* November, pp. 43–47.

Davis, I. K., and J. Hagman. 1976. What is right and wrong with your training room environment. *Training,* July, p. 28.

Decker, J. J. 1982. The enhancement of behavioral modeling training of supervisory skills by the inclusion of retention processes. *Personnel Psychology* 35, pp. 323–332.

Engel, H. 1973. *Handbook of Creative Learning Exercises.* Houston: Gulf.

Evered, R., and J. Selman. 1989. Coaching and the art of management. *Organizational Dynamics* 18(2):16–32.

Faria, A. J. 1989. Business games: Current usage levels. *Journal of Management Development* 8:59–65.

———. 1997. Personal communication.

Filipczak, B. 1994. Training consortia. *Training,* August, pp. 51–57.

———. 1996. Training on the cheap. *Training,* May, pp. 28–34.

Forlenza, D. 1995. Computer based training. *Professional Safety,* May, pp. 27–29.

Gold, L. 1981. Job instruction: Four steps to success. *Training and Development Journal,* September, pp. 28–32.

Hequet, M. 1996. Video shakeout. *Training,* September, pp. 46–50.

Johnstone, A. H., and F. Percival. 1976. Attention breaks in lectures. *Education in Chemistry* 13:273–304.

Jolles, R. 1993. *How to run seminars and workshops.* New York: Wiley.

Kram, K. 1985. Improving the mentoring process. *Training and Development Journal,* April, pp. 40–43.

Lloyd, D. H. 1968. A concept of improvement of learning in the taught lesson. *Visual Education,* pp. 23–25.

Maddox, H., and E. Hook. 1975. Performance decrement in the lecture. *Educational Research,* 28:17–30.

Mitchell, G. 1993. *The Trainers Handbook.* New York: AMACOM.

OBrian, K. 1997. Personal communication, Rivait Machine and Tool, Oldcastle Ontario, July 24.

Orth, C. D., H. E. Wilkinson, and R. C. Benfari. 1987. The manager's role as coach and mentor. *Organizational Dynamics* 15(4):66–74.

Palmer, A. 1981. Models of behavioral change. In *The 1981 Annual Handbook for Group Facilitators,* edited by J. E. Jones and J. W. Pfeiffer. San Diego: University Associates Press.

Pfeiffer, J. W., and J. E. Jones. 1980. *The 1980 Annual Handbook for Group Facilitators.* San Diego: University Associates Press.

Phillips-Jones, L. 1983. Establishing a formalized mentoring program. *Training and Development Journal,* February, pp. 38–42.

Put SPIMM in your CBT. 1993. *Training,* February, pp. 12, 14.

Rothwell, W., and H. Kazanas. 1990. Planned OJT is productive OJT. *Training and Development Journal,* October, pp. 53–56.

Sneed, L. 1992. Making your video tell a story. *Training,* September, pp. 59–63.

Wohlking, W. 1976. Role playing. In *Training and Development Handbook,* edited by R. L. Craig. New York: McGraw-Hill.

Zemke, R. 1997. The little company that could. *Training,* January, pp. 59–64

CHAPTER

9

Management Development

Learning Objectives

After reading this chapter you will be able to:

- Identify and describe the roles and responsibilities of managers at different levels in the organization

- Identify and describe the general competencies and characteristics of effective managers

- Describe the important organizational factors that determine which managerial characteristics are desirable at a given time and situation

- Describe how management training needs can be influenced by changes in organizational strategy

- Describe how to gather and feed back data as part of the management development person analysis

- Describe the unique development needs of technical managers

- Identify the various sources and types of training related to management development

---

LINDA WACHNER TAKES THE REINS AT WARNACO

In 1986 Linda Wachner took over Warnaco, a manufacturer of women's lingerie, which had been in financial difficulty. Wachner's goal was to take the company public and ensure its profitability in a hostile, competitive market and fairly stagnant economy. She knew she had to make radical changes to restore the company to competitiveness. Since that time, the company has gone public, the stock has risen 75% above its initial offering, the debt has been cut by 40%, sales have increased by 30%, earnings before taxes have increased by 140%, and operating cash flow has almost doubled. Wachner has had an unrelenting focus on the company's performance. Her own financial situation is closely tied to the company's, since she owns 10% of the stock.

As she is the only female CEO of a Fortune 500 company, her leadership has been carefully scrutinized. Wachner combines energy, drive, and enthusiasm with hard-core fiscal management. She maintains a focus on the customer and has high demands for her employees. Her employees view her as a tough boss, and often feel that she expects too much. Although her "do it now" philosophy focuses on responding to customer preferences in the short and long run, she has also been able to reap considerable savings from cost cutting. For example, she reduced the corporate staff from 200 to 7. Some say that Wachner does not do a good job of managing people because of her single-minded focus on company profitability. She is unrelenting in getting to the point and requiring her colleagues to do the same.

"Have I yelled at meetings? No question. Do I think I've ever hurt anybody? I hope not. Look, I just want people to be good and I put enormous pressure on everyone to get this company moving in the right direction," she says. "I know I push very hard, but I don't push anybody harder than I push myself. Last year I traveled 200 days visiting stores, plants, and so on."

At the same time, she motivates her workers with her praise of their work. She visits the stitch room almost daily, picking up and examining the fabric, lace, and trim the seamstresses are working on. "These are to die for," Wachner declares with a supremely satisfied smile as she holds up a garment. "Beautiful. Just beautiful." Maintaining the grueling schedule may be difficult for employees, but Wachner emphasizes creating an environment where employees have a high energy level and focus on a common goal. Her determination has created a hard-as-nails image—but a style that gets the job done.

Why Focus on Management Development?

We have already discussed in detail the training process and a great many training techniques. Why is it important to single out managers for special consideration? Don't the processes and techniques we've already discussed apply to them? In short, yes, they do apply. However, there are several reasons for examining this part of the organizational community in more detail.

MANAGERS GET A LOT OF TRAINING

One of the most frequently reported types of training over the last several years is management skill development (Froiland 1993; *Training and Development* 1993; *Training* 1994, 1995, 1996). It is one of the three most frequently used types of training provided by companies. This is true across every industry from financial and banking institutions to manufacturing to communications to utilities. Management training becomes more important as the organization increases in size, but not dramatically. Eighty-two percent of firms with fewer than 500 employees report management development programs, compared with 92% of those with 10,000 or more employees (*Training* 1996). Thus whether large or small, and regardless of industry, management training is seen as a vital part of improving organizational performance. Any training professional needs to understand a part of the business that is in such demand. However, the main reason for understanding this area of HRD is that managers are critical to the success of the company.

MANAGERS ARE ACCOUNTABLE FOR SUCCESS

Managers carry a different and more complex burden for ensuring the success of the enterprise than nonmanagers. Thinking back to the case that opened this chapter, ask yourself how much responsibility Ms. Wachner has for the success of Warnaco relative to other employees. As others have observed, the business environment leading into the next century is expected to place even more demands on management. Managers will have to deal with a labor pool that is shrinking in terms of the skilled and educated and that is becoming increasingly diverse. At the same time, more technologically sophisticated systems are being implemented (Cascio and Zammuto 1987; Offerman and Gowing 1990). It is management that is responsible for ensuring that employees have the knowledge and skills required to perform their jobs and that diversity is seen and used as a strength rather than a focus for divisiveness. In fact, it is management's responsibility to ensure that all systems and resources are appropriately integrated so the organization can achieve its objectives. It's no wonder that companies place a high priority on developing the KSAs of their managers.

THE MANAGER'S JOB IS COMPLEX

Another, and perhaps the most important, reason to examine management development closely lies in the nature of managerial effectiveness. What makes an effective manager is more complex and difficult to ascertain than with most other targets of training and development. Thus it is more difficult to assess needs, to develop training content and methods and, most certainly, to evaluate the effects of training. Do you think Ms. Wachner is a good manager at Warnaco? What criteria are you using? Would everyone agree with those criteria?

A good training process first develops an understanding of the employee's training needs before designing the training program. For management development this is not an easy task. Typically, a manager's effectiveness is determined by how well his unit meets its objectives. However, determining his training needs from the performance of the unit is problematic. A complex alignment of many factors influences the unit's performance, and the manager can affect these factors in many ways. For example, Ms. Wachner's organization has been successful. Would she be just as successful in a different company in a different industry? To understand a manager's development needs, you must first understand the context in which the manager and the unit operate. This includes the strategic direction of the organization, the technology of the manager's unit, the human and financial resources available to the unit, and the unit's structure in relation to the rest of the organization.

Information about the context in which the manager must operate can be collected from an organizational analysis. An operational analysis would identify the managerial competencies required to create the appropriate match between the organization's strategy and the unit's structure, resources, and technology so the unit is able to achieve its objectives. To identify the manager's developmental needs, her attitudes, knowledge, skills, and behavioral styles would have to be compared with the competencies required for the job, the job in this case being the management position in that particular unit. Determining all this is difficult enough, and it becomes even more difficult when you realize there are many ways for a manager to go about achieving the unit's objectives. Just identifying a manager's developmental needs is a complex task filled with ambiguities. Identifying or developing a training program to meet those needs is just as difficult and ambiguous.

Our Approach to Management Development

It is only after the managerial process is understood that appropriate needs analysis can occur. This understanding is also required for the trainer to be able to select the instructional strategy that will best meet the manager's developmental needs. Although we will identify some sources from which training programs can be acquired or developed, that is not the focus of this chapter. One reason is that there are literally thousands of programs available; a book could be written on that topic alone (and probably would sell quite well). New management development programs are developed frequently, older ones fall out of favor and then many years later may suddenly reemerge as a "favored" approach.

The focus of this chapter is on increasing your ability to determine management development needs. Our philosophy is that the educated consumer makes wiser choices. Understanding the match required between managers and their organizational context provides two long-lasting benefits to the training professional:

1. An increased ability to determine a manager's development needs
2. An increased ability to assess accurately the appropriateness of a particular training program for meeting those needs

Thus we will provide an integrated framework (a model, if you will) for assessing managerial behavior within the organizational context. Again, doing so takes a systems perspective—looking at the manager within the unit within the organization.

General Overview of the Managerial Job

It is a well-established principle of management that the effectiveness of particular styles, behaviors, and traits is contingent on other organizational variables (Howell, Dorfman, and Kerr 1986). That is, a successful managerial approach in one situation can easily be unsuccessful in another. This being the case, how can general statements be made about managerial duties and responsibilities across industries? Actually, there is no real contradiction here. The general activities carried out by managers seem to have more similarities than differences (Campbell et al. 1970). However, the frequency, the relative importance, and the manner in which these behaviors are performed differ greatly between organizations, even within the same industry. The first task is to understand the general makeup of the managerial job. Once this is accomplished, we can turn our attention to some of the contextual factors that determine the frequency and style in which these activities are performed.

MANAGERIAL ROLES

Much of the research on managerial activity has been integrated into general roles that can be "customized" to fit into a particular management position in a particular organization (Mintzberg 1975). Figure 9.1 illustrates the relationships among these roles, which form an integrated whole in which each role affects the others. One implication of this model is that managers must have not only the KSAs required to perform each role, but also the KSAs required for their integration. While individual managers may give more or less importance to a particular role, eliminating or neglecting one role has direct consequences on the performance of other roles, and hence on managerial effectiveness.

Mintzberg defined a manager as anyone who is in charge of an organization or one of its subunits. The manager's roles derive directly or indirectly from the formal authority and status granted to the position. The nature of the activities required of each role is described in Table 9.1 on page 394.

There have been less systematic but more flavorful descriptions of day-to-day managerial work, as listed below (Mintzberg 1975; Sayles 1979):

- Engaging in brief, varied, and discontinuous activities
- Accommodating an unrelenting pace of activity
- Performing numerous regular duties, as well as handling the exceptions in their own as well as their subordinates' routine
- Making decisions on the basis of judgment and intuition
- Providing subordinates with a clear understanding of their job and its boundaries (yet jobs overlap and boundaries are blurred)

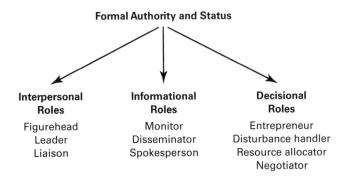

FIGURE 9.1 Mintzberg's Managerial Roles

TABLE 9.1 Description of Managerial Roles

Roles	Activities
Interpersonal	
Figurehead	Meeting the routine, obligatory, social and legal duties required of the head of a unit. Examples: attendance at social functions, meeting with politicians, buyers, or suppliers
Leader	Maintaining, developing, and motivating the human resources necessary to meet the needs of the unit
Liaison	Developing and maintaining a network of individuals outside the unit in order to acquire information and action of benefit to the unit
Informational	
Monitor	Searching for and acquiring information about the unit and its environment so that the manager becomes an information center for the unit and the organization. Derives from liaison and leader roles
Disseminator	Distributing selected information to others within the unit or organization, some of which has been transformed through integration with other information
Spokesperson	Distributing selected information to others outside the unit regarding plans, values, activities, etc. of the unit and conveying the appropriate image of the unit
Decisional	
Entrepreneur	Proactively developing and adjusting the unit to take advantage of existing opportunities or meet anticipated threats in the environment. Actions are based on inferences and conclusions drawn from the evaluation and integration of information gathered in the monitor role
Disturbance Handler	Reacting to meet the immediate demands of the unit. Examples of demands: a wildcat strike, loss of a major customer
Resource Allocator	Evaluating and choosing among proposals; integrating and authorizing activities and resource utilization
Negotiator	Bargaining to acquire the resources to meet the needs of the unit and organization

- Recognizing that routine and standardization are required to achieve efficiency but often must be sacrificed to create change; feeling comfortable doing either
- Needing controls and valid information, yet knowing that controls reduce information validity
- Regarding rules and standards as important constraints that must be observed, but acknowledging they are often inconsistent and making decisions about which must be ignored to meet others

From the descriptions of managerial activity above and from Table 9.1, it is clear that managers operate in a dynamic internal environment where they must constantly act to meet the challenges of new circumstances. Managers of subunits must not only adapt to new circumstances themselves, but also coordinate their actions with other subunits that are also adapting. There is typically little time for careful planning and reflection. When careful planning has occurred, it often won't reflect new circumstances that have arisen since the plan was developed.

Managers must have at their fingertips the knowledge and skills necessary to meet these challenges as soon as they arise. This is not to say that careful planning and reflective analysis are not necessary in organizations. It is just that managers don't often have the time for this important activity. That is why so many organizations have staff units whose job it is to provide the manager with recommendations based on careful planning and thoughtful reflection. A typical manager, however, must quickly be able to diagnose a situation, develop an appropriate response, see that it is implemented, and move on to the next task. To do this, the manager must understand the organization, its strategies and capabilities, how his unit fits into the puzzle, and how his behavior will influence events. The next section addresses many of these issues.

ORGANIZATIONAL FACTORS

Managerial context refers to the alignment of an organization's environment, strategy, structure, and technology as described in chapter 2. These factors play a significant role in determining which managerial KSAs are necessary. Although many of the KSA requirements may be the same across organizations, different organizational contexts will require the KSAs to be used more or less frequently and in varying manners (or styles). The organizational analysis portion of a managerial needs analysis should carefully consider the factors discussed here and their relation to managerial requirements. You may wish to review Figure 2.2 (page 38) and the related material in chapter 2 to refresh your understanding of organizational context.

INTEGRATING STRATEGY, STRUCTURE, AND TECHNOLOGY

Organizations seek to maximize the integration of strategy, technology, structure, and human resources through their design. Managers must monitor and manage these interactions within their unit to ensure their unit's activities are integrated with the strategic direction and technological base of the organization. This integration is depicted in Table 9.2.

As discussed in chapter 2, the market leader organization will have a more uncertain environment thus requiring more nonroutine technologies. Rapid changes in technology create high levels of complexity in organizations that are driven by technology; which market leaders typically are. In these organizations, interactions among the factors that affect efficiency and effectiveness create ambiguity and uncertainty. As a result, less job specialization, more coordination, and more decentralized decision making are the strategy. On the other hand, recall from chapter 2 that the cost leader strategy is more effective in environments with greater certainty. This type of strategy calls for more routinized technology, more centralized decision making, and

TABLE 9.2   Strategy, Technology, and Structure Integration

	Market Leader	*Cost Leader*
Technology	Nonroutine	Routine
Structure:		
Design	Organic	Mechanistic
Decision making	Decentralized	Centralized

reduced organizational complexity. These various strategies have direct implications for the skills, traits, and styles of managers within these different organizations.

Whereas a corporation or strategic business unit (SBU) faces an array of environmental forces, the individual subunit will face only a portion of those forces directly and must respond appropriately to these direct forces. While the subunits must support the organization's strategy, effective management practice for a subunit will vary according to its own environment and its role in the overall strategy. However, on a general level, the environment of the subunits will tend to reflect the organization's strategic environment.

General Characteristics of Managers

We pointed out in the chapter on needs assessment that an employees' duties and responsibilities must be understood to determine the KSAs required to perform those tasks. Much of the management development literature, unfortunately, suggests that evidence of managerial effectiveness in one organization can be applied to other organizations. Whether this is true or not will depend on the similarity of the organizational context; remember our caution about copying other organizations without understanding the theory behind their practice. Nevertheless, this literature does identify many managerial characteristics that seem to be necessary for most managers.

The characteristics we will discuss are, like managerial roles, very general in nature and are thought to be applicable across most organizations. Later we will provide a model you can use to integrate these general characteristics into various organizational contexts. As we review the empirical literature on managerial characteristics that are predictive of success, remember that the criteria used to determine "effectiveness" or "success" vary considerably across studies. We accept that some aspect of effectiveness or success was found to be associated with these characteristics. Certainly, the frequency with which they are reported in the literature gives support to their organizational utility in certain contexts.

MANAGEMENT STYLES

A wide variety of management style theories attempt to demonstrate the relationship between managerial behavior and the situation in which that behavior occurs (Wexley and Latham 1991). We do not intend to explore each of these, but there is at least one common thread running through the vast majority. Style seems to be related to two dimensions of leader behavior: employee-oriented and task-oriented (Karmel 1978; Schein 1980). These styles have been further differentiated by path–goal theory and its related research (House 1971; House and Mitchell 1974; Keller 1989; Mathieu 1990).

Employee-oriented styles require higher levels of interpersonal skills (discussed in the next section) and are reflected in either participative or supportive managerial actions. A **participative style** emphasizes involving subordinates in decision making, particularly in how they go about achieving their task. A **supportive style** is characterized by friendliness, empathy, and concern for meeting employees' needs.

Task-oriented styles, which require fewer human and more technical skills, are reflected in directive and achievement-related managerial actions. In the **directive style,**

subordinates are given instructions about what to do, how to do it, and when it should be done. The **achievement style** emphasizes goal setting and high performance expectations for subordinates.

CATEGORIES OF MANAGEMENT CHARACTERISTICS

In addition to a manager's style, which represents her actual behavior, factors related to the manager's cognitive makeup also affect her effectiveness. The research we examined[1] can be organized into four major categories: conceptual knowledge/skill, technical knowledge/skill, interpersonal knowledge/skill, and personal traits. These categories are not independent of each other. Your personal traits influence your interpersonal skills and both will have some effect on how you carry out technical and conceptual activities. Most likely it is the integration of all four categories into a whole that determines the degree of success a manager will have. Unfortunately, there is little the research literature can tell us about how successful managers integrate these characteristics. Nonetheless, it is both convenient and useful to consider them separately for the time being.

Conceptual Knowledge and Skills

Conceptual knowledge and skills refer to the mental abilities required to analyze and diagnose complex situations and make appropriate decisions. They are essential and common to all (or nearly all) management positions. Listed below are some of the more frequently cited examples of the requirements in this category:

PLANNING AND DECISION MAKING
- Knowledge of decision-making alternatives and skill in their use
- Setting priorities
- Forecasting events
- Integrating organizational policies, procedures, and objectives
- Adapting to legal, social, and political environment

ORGANIZING
- Developing appropriate organizational structures
- Coordinating separate but interrelated activities
- Scheduling activities to reach time, efficiency, and quality goals
- Allocating resources to maximize return on investment

CONTROLLING
- Knowing how to apply various control systems
- Developing control systems

---

[1] Primary and secondary research we examined which have led us to the conclusions in this section are: Andrews 1967; Bass 1990; Bennis and Nanus 1985; Birch and Veroff 1966; Bray 1973; Bray and Grant 1966; Bray, Campbell, and Grant 1974; Brown and Karagozoglu 1993; Byham 1980; Gutpa 1984; Gutpa and Govindarajan 1984; Howard and Bray 1988; Karmel 1978; Katz 1974; Kirkpatrick and Locke 1991; Kouzes and Posner 1988; Luthans, Hodgetts, and Rosenkrantz 1988; McCauley, Lombardo, and Usher 1989; McClelland 1961, McClelland and Boyatzis 1982; McClelland and Burnham 1976; Minor 1975; Niehoff and Romans 1982; Porter and McKibbin 1988; Schein 1980; Smith and Harrison 1986; Starcevich and Sykes 1982; Thornton and Byham 1982; Zaleznik 1970.

- Developing and supporting initiatives
- Developing policy, procedures, and objectives

Technical Knowledge and Skills

Technical knowledge and skills are necessary to carry out the operations of a particular functional area (e.g., marketing, engineering, human resources). For example, advertising, direct sales, and consumer psychology are areas where technical knowledge and skills are expected in a marketing manager. Also included in this category are general technical knowledge and skills required for managing any organizational unit. The most frequently mentioned of these are financial analysis, budgeting, managerial accounting, and marketing goods and services.

Interpersonal Knowledge and Skills

Interpersonal knowledge and skills, often called "human" skills, refers to the ability to work with, understand, and motivate others, both individually and in groups. As Mintzberg's research indicates, managers spend most of their time interacting with others. It is primarily the manager's interpersonal skills and knowledge of human behavior that will determine her success in influencing others and developing information networks. Examples of knowledge and skill elements in this category are:

- Understanding individual differences
- Motivating subordinates
- Developing subordinates
- Building a work team and providing team leadership
- Managing conflict constructively
- Adjusting behavior to fit situational demands (behavioral flexibility)
- Presenting a position in a compelling fashion (persuasion)
- Listening effectively
- Awareness of social cues
- Maintaining objectivity in social situations

Personal Traits

Personal traits are not knowledge and skills, but rather qualities of the manager as a person. In some ways you could think of them as attitudes, but they are considerably more complex. A personal trait is a relatively permanent predisposition to behave in a particular way. Early leadership studies consistently failed to identify personality traits that predict successful leaders (Bass 1981), but research over the last fifteen years has found certain measurable characteristics that seem to be predictive of future success as a manager. You should remember that personal traits may change markedly over the course of a manager's career. Those discussed here were characteristic of early career stages and were associated with managers' success over the long term. However, the causal relationship is far from clear.

Earlier work by McClelland and his colleagues identified four need states that are predictive of effective and ineffective managers. We will focus on three: Need for Achievement (nAch), Need for Power (nPow), and Need for Autonomy (nAut). Those high in nAch possess a strong desire to assume personal responsibility, wish to receive concrete feedback on task performance, and have a single-minded preoccupation with task accomplishment (McClelland 1961). Those high in nAut have a strong desire to work independently. For situations where they work alone, they prefer to control their own pace and procedure and not to be hampered with excessive rules (Birch and Veroff 1966). These individuals tend to resist working in groups and have a need to be personally responsible for outcomes. Those high in nPow have a strong desire to lead, influence, and control the people and things around them (McClelland and Burnham 1976).

More recently, Kirkpatrick and Locke (1991) have discussed these need states in terms of two general characteristics they term *drive* and *leadership motivation*. **Drive** includes nAch as well as ambition (Howard and Bray 1988), energy (Kouzes and Posner 1988), and tenacity (Bass 1990). **Leadership motivation** relates primarily to nPow and distinguishes between a need for institutional power, which is directed toward organizational goals, and a need for personal power, which is focused on personal goals (McClelland and Boyatzis 1982; Minor 1978). Institutional power needs are related to more successful managers and personal power to less successful managers and nonmanagers. The research also shows that those high in nPow (institutional), moderately high in nAch, and moderate to low in nAut are generally the most effective managers (Andrews 1967; Zaleznik 1970). In addition, likableness, resistance to stress, and career orientation have been found to be predictive of future success.

We have said that one common thread running through the management style literature was the the existence of two general styles of management. A second common thread is that leaders/managers must adapt their style to fit different situations. A manager's ability to be **flexible** or **adaptable** with respect to style of management has been shown to be a predictor of success (McCauley, Lombardo, and Usher 1989; Smith and Harrison 1986; also see Wexley and Lathum 1991). This characteristic is found in the literature as both a personal trait and a skill. Regardless of which, it is clearly a necessary component for long-term success as a manager. However, it may be required more in certain kinds of organizations than in others.

INTEGRATING MANAGERIAL ROLES AND CHARACTERISTICS

When you examine the roles managers must perform and the characteristics needed by effective managers, you will see it becomes possible to match characteristics with roles. Table 9.3 (page 400) depicts such an integration. For example, performing obligatory ceremonial duties (figurehead) will almost certainly require awareness of social cues, oral communication skills, and behavioral flexibility. The manager's personal traits, particularly likableness and resistance to stress, are likely to influence how they respond to those situations; conversely, it is not likely that a manager's technical or conceptual knowledge/skill will be much of a factor in this role. Using similar logic, we have matched characteristics with roles.

Although this table can serve as a heuristic device in relating a manager's knowledge, skills, and traits to various aspects of managerial jobs, it is important to remember that the precise nature of the roles and requisite managerial characteristics will differ from organization to organization and even within the same organization. In particular, the evidence is reasonably conclusive that the importance of the various roles, and consequently the associated knowledge and skills, differs from level to level within the organization's hierarchy.

TABLE 9.3 Managerial Roles and Associated Management Characteristics

Managerial Role	Conceptual	Technical	Interpersonal	Personal
Interpersonal				
Figurehead			yes	yes
Leader	yes		yes	yes
Liaison	yes		yes	yes
Informational				
Monitor	yes	yes		yes
Disseminator	yes	yes	yes	
Spokesperson	yes	yes	yes	
Decisional				
Entrepreneur	yes	yes	yes	yes
Disturbance handler	yes	yes	yes	yes
Resource allocator	yes	yes	yes	yes
Negotiator	yes		yes	yes

Roles, KSAs, and Management Level

Lower-level managers primarily supervise and coordinate the work of nonmanagers. They are usually in daily contact with their subordinates and peers and are responsible for the day-to-day operations of their unit. They depend primarily on their interpersonal and technical skills to get the job done (Coleman and Campbell 1975). Their roles are primarily leader, monitor, disseminator, disturbance handler, and negotiator. Usually other roles, requiring greater levels of conceptual skills, are made unnecessary because rules, policies, procedures, and upper management decisions have taken their place.

Middle managers coordinate the activities of lower-level managers. The manager in the middle (or sometimes the muddle, as they like to say) must perform the roles of liaison, spokesperson, resource allocator, and entrepreneur as well as most of the roles performed by the lower-level manager. Interpersonal skills remain important, but technical skills decrease in importance. Conceptual skills become somewhat more important.

Top managers coordinate the activities of the organization through their middle managers. Conceptual skills are of primary importance at this level, particularly the entrepreneurial role. Informational, liaison, and figurehead roles become more predominant, and the focus of the other roles changes from inside to outside the organization.

Although organizations in general place higher priority on certain types of managerial KSAs at different levels in the organization, the discussion above is not especially helpful in identifying the job requirements of managers in a specific organization. Each organization will have its own context and specific expectations of managers within that context. Thus while it is generally helpful to know that supervisors typically are expected to rely on their technical more than their conceptual knowledge and skills, the relative importance will depend on the organizational context.

Integration: Strategies and Management Characteristics

The research on organizational environment, strategy, structure, and technology can be combined with the leadership research to provide some general prescriptions for what managerial characteristics will be effective at the two extremes of the strategy continuum. In the most general sense, effective managers have been said to possess technical, interpersonal, and conceptual skills (Katz 1974). The leadership research adds the concepts of personal traits and style. Below we will examine each of these factors and assess the degree to which they are more or less relevant in market and cost leader organizations. Table 9.4 provides a summary of this discussion.

TECHNICAL COMPETENCE AND CONTEXT

Research indicates that technical competence is an important foundation for effective management (Bennis and Nanus 1985; Smith and Harrison 1986). Both market and cost leader strategies require managers with high levels of technical competence, but the technical sophistication required of market leaders is much greater since they are operating on the leading edge of technology. They are also required to employ many technologies capable of significant flexibility in application, making their technologies more complex and less predictable. Thus in Table 9.4 market leader organizations are rated higher in the need for managers with technical skills.

INTERPERSONAL COMPETENCE AND CONTEXT

The market leader strategy uses a more organic, less formalized design, which requires the manager to interact more with higher-level managers, subordinates, and peers. These interactions are critical to coordinating activities within and between units. In cost leader organizations the centralization of decision making and the formalization of rules, procedures, and policies decrease the importance of many of the

TABLE 9.4   Strategy—Managerial Characteristics Integration

	Market Leader	*Cost Leader*
Skills		**Skills**
Technical	More sophisticated and nonroutine	Less sophisticated and routine
Interpersonal	Higher	Lower
Conceptual	Higher	Lower
Traits		**Traits**
Drive	High	High
Flexibility	Higher	Lower
Leader motive	High	High
Style		**Style**
Participative	Higher	Lower
Supportive	No difference	No difference
Achievement	Higher	Lower
Directive	Lower	Higher

interpersonal skills. These characterizations reflect a relative difference in the two types of organizations and should not be construed in an all-or-none fashion. Effectiveness in human skills has generally been shown to differentiate between successful and unsuccessful managers (Brown and Karagozoglu 1993; McCauley, Lombardo, and Usher 1989; Kirkpatrick and Locke 1991), but logic would suggest it is more likely to do so in market leader organizations, where considerably more interaction is required (see Table 9.4).

CONCEPTUAL COMPETENCE AND CONTEXT

Again, because of the routine technology, mechanistic design, centralized decision making, and formalized coordination systems, the cost leader organization, by design, has reduced the importance of managerial conceptual skills except at the higher levels of the organization. Market leader organizations, on the other hand, require managers with greater conceptual skills at all levels, because of their more complex organization and the need to reduce barriers to creativity. There is agreement that technical skills are more important at lower-level management positions, conceptual skills more important at higher levels, and human skills important at all levels. What we are saying here is that conceptual skills are more important at all levels in the market leader compared to the cost leader organization.

Studies have generally supported the notion that interpersonal and conceptual skills are more predictive of managerial success than are technical skills (Luthans, Hodgetts, and Rosenkrantz 1988; McCauley, Lombardo, and Usher 1989; McClelland and Burnham 1976; Porter and McKibbin 1988). This, of course, makes sense if technical activities decrease in frequency as one moves from lower to higher management positions. The more effective managers are those who are able to handle the increasing demands of human and conceptual problems. In addition, individuals are typically hired or promoted to management positions on the basis of their technical competence at lower levels, so these skills are less likely to differentiate effective from ineffective performers. Particularly in technical units, new employees are rarely hired on the basis of interpersonal skills or ability to conceptualize complex organizational systems. When they are promoted to managerial positions, they are likely to need development in these areas.

PERSONAL TRAITS AND CONTEXT

For nearly all of the traits we have examined we found no compelling evidence or logic to suggest that managers high in these traits will be more or less effective in any particular organizational context. The only trait variable likely to be more useful in one organization than the other is flexibility. Because market leader organizations face more ambiguity and change than cost leaders, the manager with higher levels of adaptability would likely be more effective than one who was less flexible. This point is reflected in Table 9.4.

MANAGEMENT STYLE AND CONTEXT

Of the two employee-oriented styles, only the participative style would be expected to show differences in effectiveness based on strategy. Our logic suggests that participative styles are more effective in market leader organizations. Obviously, a decentralized structure promotes higher levels of participation in decision making. In the technical units of the market leader organization, this issue is especially important, because innovation and creativity are facilitated by multiple inputs and synergistic outcomes. In addition, because of the nonroutine nature of the technology, decisions relating to a particular area of that technology require the input of those most familiar with it.

We found compelling reasons for the participative style to be less effective in the cost leader organization. Here the decisions are more centralized. The jobs are well defined by the routine technology, policy, procedures, and the structure. There would be very few reasons or opportunities for employees to participate in decisions that would meaningfully affect their job. Remember, we are talking about an organization at the extreme end of the continuum. Even here, we are not saying there would be no participation, only that its value to the organization would be less.

We could find no logic to support the notion that a supportive style would be more or less effective in either organizational context. Although employees are likely to be somewhat different in organizations at opposite ends of the strategy continuum, we find no justification for postulating differences in need for friendliness, empathy, or concern from their managers. Our belief, supported by much of the research, is that this style is effective in nearly all organizations.

For the task-oriented styles, there are clear structural reasons to suggest differences in the effectiveness of the achievement versus directive styles. For the market leader, the achievement style is more effective. This type of organization requires managers to reduce some of the ambiguity of their unit's task. The organization's task—to quickly identify and place in the market new products or significant modifications of old products—creates ambiguous expectations, and the achievement-oriented manager clarifies goals, parameters, and performance expectations. In the cost leader organization, goals and expectations are well understood and standardized, so there is little need for the manager to exert effort in this area; in fact, subordinates are likely to see such behavior as redundant and negative.

Some amount of directive behavior will be useful in the market leader organization to the extent that it clarifies responsibilities and expectations. However, the detailed direction of who will do what, how, and when is contrary to the structural and technological systems of the market leader. For the cost leader, however, it is clearly important for the manager to monitor and ensure that the right people are doing the right things at the right time. In addition, the cost leader's design uses a centralized system in which operations are driven from the top. It is the manager's responsibility to ensure that changes in expectations are accurately conveyed to subordinates and that subordinates comply with the direction in a specific manner. We view the directive style as being more effective in the cost leader organization. Still, managers in such organizations must be discriminating in how it is applied. High or adequately performing employees in this organization may find additional direction from the manager irritating. Conversely, in the market leader organization employees may come to desire direction from their managers because of the absence of well-defined structure in their jobs. Nevertheless, the design of this organization favors the achievement style over the directive: providing employees with goals and objectives and giving them the autonomy to figure out the best way to achieve them (see Table 9.4).

The relationships described here between strategy and manager characteristics are generalizations, as are the relationships described between strategy, structure, and technology. Any given organization that has adopted a market leader strategy will have some routine as well as nonroutine technologies. The point is that they will have a greater preponderance of nonroutine technologies than if they had chosen a cost leader strategy. Likewise, the managerial characteristics related here to organizational strategy indicate the characteristics that will be effective when the structural and technology characteristics of that strategy are present. Perhaps the most appropriate use of Table 9.4 is at the organizational subunit level. If the subunit is structured in ways consistent with the strategy, the managerial characteristics associated with the strategy are likely to be more effective. Consideration could be given to using this table in developing a managerial needs assessment where the organizational context of the manager's unit can be measured.

Management Development Implications

What is suggested from the model just presented is that a key to effective management is knowing the context in which you are operating, knowing what is required of you in order to create the best match with the context, and having the KSAs to do what is required. Thus management development programs should, in general, provide training programs that address these issues.

UNDERSTANDING CONTEXT

The most obvious implication of the context/management characteristics model is that effective managers must be able to adapt themselves and their unit to the needs of the organization, and to do this they must have a clear understanding of the organization's strategy and their unit's part in the strategy. It is only with this understanding that managers can use their personal characteristics most effectively. Thus an important part of all management development programs should be the clarification of the organization's situation, its strategy for coping with the situation, how the various units fit into the strategy, and how the training program relates to these things. Too often management development programs try to provide managers with skills, knowledge, styles, and traits without an understanding of the context in which they are to be applied. In the worst case the development is inappropriate for some units, and in the best case, in those units where the development is appropriate, the managers don't understand why it's appropriate.

SELF-AWARENESS AND DIAGNOSTIC SKILLS

Once managers understand what is needed from their unit and why, it is important that they understand how their own characteristics influence the activities within their unit and its relationships with other units. This understanding requires skills in self-awareness and diagnosis. To increase self-awareness, managers need to have access to the basic data required to diagnose cause–effect relationships between their behavior and other's actions.

Diagnostic skills are necessary to identify why gaps exist between what is expected of the unit and what actually occurs. The manager must be able to create the appropriate match between her behavior and (1) the structure/design of the unit, and (2) the characteristics of the subordinates. Doing this requires the ability to diagnose the existence and cause of mismatches. Self-awareness and diagnostic skills are the basic requirements for managerial adaptability to changing conditions.

Of course an alternative is to place managers in situations that match their characteristics (a leader–match approach; Fiedler and Chemers 1974, 1976). Although this approach may be effective in the short run, there is no guarantee that things will remain stable. It is preferable to try to develop these basic adaptability skills in all managers. However, for selecting new managers, particularly in technical areas, it would seem best to select those who most closely match the organizational context of the unit they will manage; they will likely be effective in the short term and their adaptability skills can be developed for the long term.

Once a manager understands the organizational context within which her unit operates and has acquired the adaptability skills of self-awareness and diagnosis, she is ready for the appropriate development of knowledge, skills, and styles. For this, a managerial person analysis is required.

THE MANAGERIAL PERSON ANALYSIS

Certainly, identifying the required KSAs for a managerial job is difficult. Assume you have already completed this task and now you must determine if the managers in unit A have the required KSAs. How would you go about determining a manager's style, his traits, and how he interacts with peers, subordinates, and superiors? One method gaining considerable popularity is the 360-degree feedback (360-DF) described in chapter 4. This requires a sample of those with whom the manager interacts to fill out an anonymous questionnaire about the manager. The responses are then analyzed and graphed to provide feedback to the manager. The results can show where general agreement lies among subordinates, peers, and superiors concerning how the manager "comes across." These data, combined with the data from the unit's operations and other measurement tools, can then be used to identify areas of development for each manager. It can also be used during training to help the manager identify the cause–effect relationships between his behavior and others' reactions. The manager, of course, should be involved in identifying his areas of strength and weakness. If the manager is not involved, something like what happened in the Training in Action 9.1 (page 406) is likely to occur.

This multiple-source feedback should be used only for development purposes, not for formal performance evaluations or for pay, promotion, or termination decisions. If it is, the responses of those filling out the questionnaire are likely to change. Those who are friends will inflate the manager's score, rivals (peers and some of the superiors) will lower their ratings somewhat, and the staff support person the manager has been complaining about will cut him to the bone. However, the research shows that when assessment occurs for developmental purposes, the validity of personal characteristics measurement is enhanced by the inclusion of supervisor, co-worker, subordinate, and customer ratings (Waldman, Yammarino, and Avolio 1990).

Though 360-DF often results in positive comments about the manager, it can also provide powerful, uncomfortable, and surprising information. In addition to the characteristics discussed in this chapter, 360-DF provides feedback about a number of other personal characteristics that typically do not show up in the research on management effectiveness. For example, one manager learned that he stood too close to

Training in Action 9.1

Fast Track??

A major drug company chose one of its finance officers to attend a customized leadership program at the University of Pennsylvania's prestigious Wharton School, which cost the company over $24,000 for the five-week program. The finance officer went off to training assuming that he was being put on the fast track; after all, only a few executives were picked for this program every year. Instead, the company saw this as the last chance to improve the executive's interpersonal skills. After returning from the training, and two lateral moves later, he left the company. "Nobody was straight with me before I took the course," said the executive. "My bosses were looking for a changed man, but I wasn't any kinder or gentler. If anything, I suppose I was more aggressive, which to them, I guess, was more abrasive."

Constructed from information reported in *The Wall Street Journal,* September 10, 1993, p. R-6.

people when talking to them and that little bits of saliva would fly out of his mouth when he spoke—not a good combination for a manager looking to advance his career. After feedback, he stood farther back and started speech therapy. Another manager, the head of Nestle's Perrier operation, found out that when he moved from head of sales and marketing to the CEO position, people changed their interpretation of his behavior. His temper and occasional "public whippings" of senior managers had previously been tolerated and seen as demonstrating forceful management, but when he became CEO and acquired authority to fire anybody, his behavior became frightening and managers stopped coming to him with problems and ideas (O'Reilly 1994).

Because of the sensitive nature of the data, feedback must be carefully handled by the training professional to ensure that the manager sees it as "legitimate" and constructive. The most difficult comments to accept are those about interpersonal skills such as "untrustworthy," "poor listener," "uses poor judgment." These are seen as core competency skills and nearly every manager assumes he is strong in these areas. The Center for Creative Leadership estimates that only about a third of all managers accurately predict how others view them. Another third have inflated views of their talents. For these managers, the most surprises await, because subordinates almost always rate them the least effective (O'Reilly 1994). For some hard-core control-oriented managers it sometimes takes massive doses of feedback before the message finally sinks in. Many will attempt to dismiss the results as inaccurate, inappropriate, or irrelevant. The training professional's job is to help the manager come to terms with and accept the results. When results are consistent (e.g., most people rate the manager in the same way), it will be more difficult for him to explain them away. The most important part of the feedback agent's job is helping the manager understand that his intentions are not the same as other people's interpretation of his behavior. Once the manager has made this association, he can then begin to explore what he might do differently to achieve the results he desires.

Sources of Knowledge/Skill Acquisition

The most obvious source of management training is the organization itself. However, most companies use a combination of internal and external sources to provide their managers with the appropriate mix of developmental opportunities. A survey of training managers (*Training and Development* 1998) showed 93% of the companies providing both internal and external training to supervisors and middle managers, and 63% providing such training for executives. Only about 15% of the firms said they developed internal courses for executives, while over 60% did so for middle managers and supervisors. These numbers tell us that very few firms rely only on internal training resources, especially for upper-level managers and executives. Those involved in management development must be familiar with training and development opportunities outside their organization as well as being able to develop useful programs internally.

The following sections explore some of the more frequently discussed alternatives in the literature. This does not imply an endorsement of any particular source. Rather we present them to demonstrate the variety of sources that are available.

EXTERNALLY BASED TRAINING

Executive and management education programs at universities provide knowledge and skills of a general nature. These programs cover the range of management issues from traditional MBA programs to building strategically effective organizations. Other sources of management development activities are training companies, consultants, and professional associations. They supply a wide variety of training activities ranging from broad-based, general-application programs to those that are narrowly focused on limited areas of skill and knowledge.

When the education is narrowly focused, dealing with specific topics such as project management, team building, financial analysis, or effective communication, the managers typically stay in residence at the training site for a few days to several weeks. When the focus is broader, dealing with general management domains (e.g., executive MBA programs), the manager likely attends training for a few hours to a few days periodically over periods of up to 24 months. Typically, the goal of broad-based programs is generic skill or content learning rather than job specific. Personal insight is generally not a goal; classroom-based methods tend to be used rather than games and simulations (Hall 1986). Personal insight and job-specific KSAs are more typically addressed in the narrow focus programs.

The principal advantages of externally based programs are as follows:

- They expose managers to the current thinking and theory in management.
- They remove organizational constraints in exploring new approaches.
- They allow interchange of ideas among managers from different organizational backgrounds.
- They cost less per person than internally developed programs.

Problems that have been noted with externally based programs include:

- Inability to relate content to company-specific approaches
- Inconsistency of instructor effectiveness (some are excellent, others poor) and an inability of the contractor to choose the instructor (this is more an issue with executive MBA programs than with residential programs)

- Inability to specify expected company outcomes as a result of the training
- Extended time away from the job
- Failure of the manager's company to provide on-the-job reinforcement of concepts and skills
- Inability to control the content of the training; the company can choose the course or program, but not the content

Despite these concerns, most companies see externally based management programs as valuable tools. About 49% of companies utilize university-based residential or executive MBA programs, and most of these companies use some form of external short course (*Training and Development* 1998). The primary reasons for utilizing these programs are credibility of the organization offering the program, the nature of the program topic areas, and the belief of the manager that it will meet her needs.

CORPORATE UNIVERSITIES

In an attempt to overcome some of the deficiencies of university-based education while maintaining many of its advantages, large corporations have created their own internal "universities." Phillips Petroleum, General Electric, IBM, Motorola, McDonald's, and Xerox are just a few of the nearly 400 companies that have analyzed the characteristics of university-based versus external, nonuniversity-based formal educational programs for managers and found that they could do better internally (Eurich 1985; Starcevich and Sykes 1982). The primary reasons are as follows:

- The organization understands its own approach to management and can convey it better to its managers.
- Managers can obtain job-specific knowledge and skills.
- The company can ensure quality instruction.
- Because of the organization's size, the courses are cost effective.

Public and private universities draw a wide range of managers to their management development programs. The diversity of backgrounds and interests requires that the concepts and methods taught must be general in nature so as to be applicable across most situations. Although students are usually encouraged to apply these concepts and methods to their own organization, there is little the faculty can do to make them transfer this knowledge to their jobs.

The corporate university, on the other hand, can integrate the technical, conceptual, and interpersonal skills within the context of their organization's strategy, structure, and technology. The company can control and shape the curriculum to meet its own needs and values, can provide the same content to everyone, and can schedule instruction to be convenient for the organization and the trainee.

There are, however, problems attached to the corporate university approach. Matching the curriculum to the needs of the organization remains a difficult task. Pressures within the organization may discourage training in some areas or using certain methods while encouraging others. Although this situation reflects the political reality of the organization, it limits the organization's ability to develop new and more effective approaches. In addition, costs may actually be higher than for externally developed programs. Phillips, for example, found its costs to be about 50% more than for similar external training and education (Camp, Blanchard, and Huszczo 1986).

It should be emphasized that this approach is possible only for large organizations. It is neither practical nor feasible for small- to moderate-sized businesses to create their own university. These organizations will have to rely on public and private universities as well as other external training and development suppliers.

Regardless of whether training is provided internally or through external sources, the training department should attend to the match between the content of the training and the context within which the managers are to use it. The following questions should be carefully explored before a particular program of management development is adopted:

1. Do the program outcomes meet an identified need?
2. Will the learning that results from the training be supported on the job?
3. Will behavior resulting from the training conform to the organization's policies, procedures, and norms?
4. Will the individuals receive any personal benefit from the training?
5. What is the cost/benefit ratio of the approach compared with that of alternative approaches?

Another important point is the evaluation of such training. It is one thing to train managers and discover that the training is of little or no value. It is quite another to continue to do so, wasting training dollars and credibility year after year.

TYPES OF MANAGEMENT DEVELOPMENT PROGRAMS

A description of the full diversity of management development approaches and techniques is beyond the scope of this chapter. However, we have identified a variety of programs and techniques that are associated with the competencies of effective management described earlier. We are not necessarily advocating the use of any of these but are simply providing a glimpse of the diversity available. Those wishing to probe deeper into this area might begin with the references provided.

Knowledge/Skills Development: Conceptual

There is a variety of ways to develop conceptual skills in managers. These include:

1. Management/business games, simulations, and case studies (see chapters 7 and 8).
2. On-the-job training: Included in this are mentoring, coaching, job rotation, understudy training, and junior boards. Mentoring and understudy training are similar in that the manager works closely with a senior manager to develop or improve skills. The mentoring relationship was discussed briefly in the training methods chapter. Understudy training occurs when the manager is assigned as an assistant or adjunct to the senior manager; she learns by observing the senior manager and completing assignments of gradually increasing complexity and responsibility. Junior boards combine simulation and on-the-job training techniques. A junior board of directors is created composed of promising middle-level executives, who are given critical issues relating to the company's business and asked to provide senior management with recommendations (Mintzberg 1975; Roberts 1974).
3. Decision making: Situations are diagnosed to determine the appropriate approach to making a decision. For example, Vroom and Yetton provide a model

in which the manager learns the relevant situational variables that determine whether the decision should be made by the manager alone, delegated to a group of subordinates, or handled somewhere in between (Vroom and Yetton 1973; Vroom and Jago 1988). Another approach to decision making is rational manager training, which uses simulations to develop managers' problem-solving and decision-making skills. A unique feature of this approach is the use of actual situations in the company for analysis, identification, and elimination of potential problems. Unsolved as well as already solved problems are used for knowledge and skill development (Kepner and Tregoe 1975). Related to this is the conference method, in which the focus is on group rather than individual problem solving and decision making (Maier 1963, 1982). Much of the current quality improvement and quality management training has its grounding in these approaches (e.g., Scholtes 1988).

4. Managerial roles: This approach, based on Mintzberg's (1975) model discussed earlier, is aimed at providing managers with an understanding of what they are doing and why. Through self-observation and understanding of one's roles, effectiveness is said to be increased. A related approach, the incident technique (Pigors and Pigors 1987), utilizes critical incidents from the organization, asking managers to identify the facts needed to address the incident. Doing so develops the skills especially needed to perform the monitoring and disturbance handler roles.

Knowledge/Skills Development: Technical

Technical training, especially professional skills training, is often purchased from outside sources. About 60% of companies acquire this type of training from outside vendors (*Training and Development* 1998).

1. Degree and certification programs: Degree programs in business and technical disciplines provide the technical foundation for most managers. In addition, technical knowledge and skills specific to a particular discipline can be developed through external suppliers such as professional associations and through certificate training programs. For example, the Society for Human Resource Management in the United States and the Human Resources Professionals Association of Ontario, in Canada, provide training programs which prepare human resource managers to take the certification exam. Other professional disciplines (e.g., accounting, finance, engineering) have similar types of programs. Professional associations also provide opportunities for continual learning through workshops and seminars.

2. Workshops and seminars: These are offered over a wide range of topics and by a wide range of providers (e.g., universities, professional associations, consultants, training companies). Larger companies prefer internally developed workshops and seminars, because they have the resources to acquire high-level instructors and develop the appropriate training materials. These programs are also more easily tailored to fit the specific needs of the company.

Interpersonal and Management Style

We have combined these approaches because it is difficult to separate management style from interpersonal skills. In fact, management styles are often addressed in training through emphasizing one or more interpersonal skills.

1. Interactive skills training: This approach uses simulations and feedback from observers to provide trainees with ways of interacting more effectively with others. It is an approach that makes managers more aware of how their behavior influences the way others perceive them and react to them (Rackham and Morgan 1977).

2. Leader match training: This program, based on Fiedler's contingency model of leadership, trains managers to diagnose their situation and themselves determine the best fit (Fiedler, Chemers, and Mahar 1976). Since Fiedler proposes that a manager's personal characteristics are relatively unchangeable, the training provides ways of manipulating the situation to match the strengths of the manager. Thus, in this approach interpersonal skills are not modified, but rather the manager is shown how to create the situation for which his style is most appropriate.

3. Grid management: The two most important managerial characteristics in this approach are the manager's concern for work outcomes and her concern for people (note the parallel here with "employee and task orientation"). The proposition here is that managers who have strong concerns in both of these areas are the best managers. Training focuses on developing the manager's ability to display these characteristics simultaneously. While the manager must respond to different situations with the appropriate behavior, it is the value orientation associated with both a strong concern for people and task that guides the manager's behavior (Blake and Mouton 1985; Yukl 1989).

4. Workshops and seminars: Again, these are offered over a wide range of topics and by a wide range of providers. These programs typically focus on a particular skill area such as communication, managerial style, leadership, or team facilitation.

Developing Personal Traits

Development of personal traits can be a part of many management development programs. A few programs that focus specifically on trait development are listed below.

1. Role motivation: The object of this program is to develop six motivational states in managers: favorable attitude toward authority; desire to compete; assertiveness; desire to exercise power; desire for distinctiveness; and a sense of responsibility. These motives help them deal with employee work deficiencies and meet organizational criteria for effectiveness (primarily in large organizations). It includes development of interpersonal skills but focuses primarily on self-examination and development of internal values (Minor 1978).

2. Need for achievement: A program of self-study, goal setting, and case analysis, this is designed to provide managers with an understanding of their need for achievement and development of that need so that it is focused on constructive behavior. This approach has yielded the best results for small business owners, particularly at the early stages of their careers (McClelland 1961; McClelland and Burnham 1976; Miron and McClelland 1979).

3. Transactional analysis: This approach deals primarily with the orientation of the manager when interacting with subordinates. It suggests that unhealthy relationships within the work group arise from adult (manager) to child (subor-

dinate) interactions rather than adult to adult. The training focuses on self-awareness and improving the manager's ability to develop adult-to-adult relationships with subordinates and superiors (Berne 1964; Harris 1969).

The Special Needs of the Technical Manager

Technical managers have usually received academic training in their technical disciplines with little, if any, exposure to the study of organizational behavior and management processes. Organizations appear to have relied on the premise that an individual with technical expertise can acquire organizational and managerial skills, knowledge, and expertise on his own. Shuman (1989) has shown that for technical managers, the management of unit morale, esteem, autonomy, and goal congruence were the primary predictors of subordinate turnover attitudes. Training managers report that the content areas where training is most needed are managing people, strategic planning, decision making, and human resource management (Saari et al. 1988). It is apparent, then, that a deeper understanding of the technical manager's developmental needs would be useful, along with a systematic approach to meeting those needs. Unfortunately, companies do not often seem inclined to determine the needs of their managers in general, much less their technical managers. For example, a survey of management training and education practices in the United States (Saari et al. 1988) showed that management needs assessments were conducted by only 27% of the companies. The most frequent approach to management development was on-the-job training.

The literature indicates that technical experts' performance as managers is deficient in the following areas (Bettman 1987):

1. Having a willingness to reduce the focus on technical issues in favor of organizational and managerial issues
2. Understanding and using organizational priorities, requirements, and processes in decision making
3. Developing and maintaining interpersonal relationships with subordinates that generate their trust and confidence
4. Communicating with superiors, subordinates, and colleagues in an understandable, efficient, and positive manner
5. Managing conflict among subordinates constructively so their efforts are integrated to achieve the organization's goals

HISTORY AND EXPERIENCE

Technical professionals' skills, knowledge, and interests are generally related to things rather than people. Their education and training typically place them in solitary exercises and emphasize individual accomplishment. They are hired because of their expertise at manipulating and controlling things. If they advance and are rewarded, they do so because they have been good in the world of defined cause-and-effect relationships in their specialized field, and perhaps in their quantitative management of time, labor, and financial resources. Once the technical manager is moved into higher levels of management, she is called upon to function in a multidisciplinary environment, attending to political, organizational, and business issues for which her history and education have not prepared her.

SKILLS

The effective technical/professional has, by definition, developed strong technical skills within her discipline. However, a great many technical employees have little education or background in the traditional management activities of planning, organizing, and controlling (Badriu 1987; Eckerson 1989; Ford and Kleiner 1987). Just as important, the training and experience of the technical professional has not developed the interpersonal (human) skills or the conceptual adaptability needed for managing people and organizations (Badriu 1987; Eckerson 1989; Lennark 1988).

TRAITS

We have said that research indicates that those high in nPow (institutional rather than personal), moderately high in nAch, and moderate to low in nAut are the most effective managers. Unfortunately, technical professionals can generally be characterized as being high in nAch and nAut (Badriu 1987; Rosenbaum 1991). From the Kirkpatrick and Locke perspective, we can say that their drive is perhaps too high because their focus on task accomplishment prevents them from being attentive to the effects they are having on others. Furthermore, their nPow, or leadership motivation, is typically based in the personal rather than the institutional domain. Their loyalties lie in their profession rather than their organization, and they see recognition from their peers as more valuable than recognition from their organization. Fortunately these need states appear to be changable through training (Miron and McClelland 1979).

LEADERSHIP STYLE

The technical professional has typically had no leadership training and is likely to mirror the styles used by his manager, or the personal style that has worked successfully up to the point of receiving the promotion. Unfortunately, these are not the most appropriate models if the promotion requires managing the work of others. The technical professional's past has emphasized a "best" methodology and a "right" answer. Ambiguities are eliminated and politics ignored. As a result of high loyalty to the profession, they remain heavily involved in the technology of the work they are managing and see themselves as the experts (that is why they were promoted, after all). As the experts, they make all the important technical decisions, and when they delegate they provide specific instructions about the tasks to be performed. The directive leadership style fits comfortably with their past training (i.e., technical degrees, graduate studies), their past experience (e.g., running a lab), and their own self-image (Bettman 1987; Ford and Kleiner 1987). Many of the general requirements for successful managers are not typically inherent in technical professionals who are promoted into management positions. If these individuals happen to work in market leader organizations, they will have even fewer of the required characteristics.

STRATEGIES FOR DEVELOPMENT
OF TECHNICAL MANAGERS

Technical experts can learn to be effective and productive managers, provided both the organization and the experts themselves recognize the need to change and adapt to the realities of new requirements. Organizations must address the question of why it is essential that the technical experts be given managerial roles and what the expectations are for those roles. The organization can then develop a rationale for placing managerial components into the technical experts' job descriptions and assign jobs with an increasing degree of those managerial components. The model presented earlier for integrating organizational strategy, structure, technology, and managerial characteristics is at least a good starting point.

The technical expert needs to receive counseling to understand fully that the focus on technical issues will decrease. He also needs to recognize the potential risk of falling behind in technical expertise because of the shift to a managerial job.

The organization needs to establish a performance review program specifically oriented toward technical experts who have been assigned an increasing managerial responsibility. The objective is to assess continually her managerial training needs in order to enhance the potential for success as a manager. Finally, it is important in these instances to evaluate training to be assured that (1) the technical expert learns appropriate behavior, (2) the technical expert transfers the behavior to the job, and (3) the organizational structure facilitates this transfer. If this is done, the technical expert can indeed become the effective manager necessary in today's competitive environment.

Key Terms

- Achievement style
- Adaptability/flexibility
- Conceptual knowledge and skills
- Corporate universities
- Directive style
- Drive
- Employee-oriented styles
- Executive/management education
- Interpersonal knowledge and skills

- Leadership motivation (nPow)
- Managerial context
- Managerial style
- Participative style
- Personal traits
- Supportive style
- Task-oriented styles
- Technical knowledge and skills
- Technical manager

Case Analysis

Will Teams Work?

An automobile parts manufacturer (APM) was attempting to institute employee problem-solving teams to improve quality. This action had been strongly encouraged by its biggest customer, a major automobile manufacturer. The competition in the original equipment manufacturing (OEM) business is especially fierce. The major automobile manufacturers (Ford, GM, Chrysler, Toyota, Honda, etc.) are demanding high-quality parts at extremely low costs, and they are playing one supplier against the other in order to force the OEM industry to meet their standards.

A training needs analysis of middle- and first-level production managers was conducted. These managers were responsible for the operation of the parts production system, a system that is highly mechanized and somewhat automated. The labor force in this area is primarily high school graduates, but many have less education. The managers' responsibility prior to the change was to ensure that the hourly workers did their jobs in the proper manner and that the right amount and type of parts were produced to meet the production schedule.

The TNA showed that these managers had low technical knowledge because they had been hired to monitor the hourly employees. They didn't really understand the machinery and equipment and had never operated it. Most of them use a confrontational style in dealing with their subordinates because they feel that if they took a gentler approach, the unionized workforce would take advantage of them. They were all selected on the basis of their high need to control their environment, high need to achieve, and willingness to work with others to get the job done. These traits still characterize this group of managers.

CASE QUESTIONS

1. What is the managerial context in which these managers will be operating? Do you think training designed to help managers understand the context they will be operating in will be helpful? Why or why not?
2. What types of competencies should be developed in the management training? Give your rationale.
3. What types of training should be used to provide the different competencies? How long will it take to provide this training? Give your rationale.
4. What are the alternatives to management development? Do you think one of these alternatives should be used? Why or why not?

Exercises

1. Bring a recent article (no more than a year old) that identifies KSAs that will be critical for managers in the immediate future. Be prepared to discuss the article and its management development implications in small groups or with the entire class.
2. Interview two managers with at least two years of management experience. One manager should come from a company whose strategy is toward the cost leader side, the other toward the market leader side. If possible they should both be in the same functional area. Determine the management development they have received from their company. Determine how satisfied they are with the development they have received so far. Bring this information back to class and be prepared to share it with others, providing an analysis of how consistent these two experiences are with what the text proposes.
3. Research the Internet to see what the best companies do in management development. What are the similarities? Are there any major differences? Bring this information to class and be prepared to discuss it.
4. How does management education prepare a manager for her role? What are the ways in which management education occurs? Do some seem better to you than others? Why or why not? Can other forms of training substitute for management education? Why or why not?
5. Interview a manager with five or more years of experience. Record the manager's current position, previous positions, and education. Identify the manager's roles and responsibilities. Afterwards, answer the following:
   a. How do the roles and responsibilities compare to those described in the text?

b. Identify the KSAs required to meet this manager's roles and responsibilities.

c. How have the manager's previous experience and education prepared him for his current roles and responsibilities?

References

Andrews, J. 1967. The achievement motive and advancement in two types of organizations. *Journal of Personality and Social Psychology* 6:163–68.

Badriu, A. 1987. Training the IE for a management role. *Industrial Engineering,* December, pp. 18–23.

Bass, B. 1981. *Stogdill's Handbook of Leadership: A Survey of Theory and Research.* Revised and expanded. New York: Free Press.

Bass, B. 1990. *Handbook of Leadership.* New York: Free Press.

Bennis, W., and B. Nanus. 1985. *Leaders: The Strategies for Taking Charge.* New York: Harper and Row.

Berne, E. 1964. *Games People Play.* New York: Grove Press.

Bettman, R. 1987. Technical Managers Mismanaged: Turnover or Turnaround? *Personnel Journal* 66, pp. 64–70.

Birch, D., and J. Veroff. 1966. *Motivation: A Study of Action.* Monterey, CA: Brooks/Cole.

Blake, R., and J. Mouton. 1985. *The Managerial Grid III: The Key to Leadership Excellence.* Houston: Gulf Publishing.

Bray, D. 1973. New data from the management progress study. *Assessment and Development* 1:3.

Bray, D., R. Campbell, and D. Grant. 1974. *Formative Years in Business: A Long-Term AT&T Study of Managerial Lives.* New York: Wiley.

Bray, D., and D. Grant. 1966. The assessment center in the measurement of potential for business management. *Psychological Monographs* 80:1–27.

Brown, W., and N. Karagozoglu. 1993. Leading the way to faster new product development. *The Executive* 7:1.

Byham, W. 1980. Starting an assessment center. *Personnel Administrator* 25(2):27–32.

Camp, R., P. Blanchard., and G. Huszczo. 1986. *Toward a More Organizationally Effective Training Strategy and Practice.* Upper Saddle River, NJ: Prentice Hall, pp. 285–86.

Campbell, J., M. Dunnette, E. Lawler III, and K. Weick, Jr. 1970. *Managerial Behavior, Performance, and Effectiveness.* New York: McGraw-Hill.

Cascio, W., and R. Zammuto. 1987. *Societal Trends and Staffing Policies,* Denver: University of Colorado Press.

Coleman, E., and M. Campbell. 1975. *Supervisors: A Corporate Resource.* New York: AMACOM.

Eckerson, W. 1989. Techies need training for management roles. *Network World,* April 10.

Eurich, N. 1985. *Corprorate Classroom: The Learning Process.* Princeton, NJ: Carnegie Foundation for the Advancement of Teaching.

Fiedler, F., and M. Chemers. 1974. *Leadership and Effective Management.* New York: Scott Foresman.

Fiedler, F., M. Chemers, and L. Mahar. 1976. *Improving Leadership Effectiveness: The Leader Match Concept.* New York: Wiley.

Ford, B., and B. Kleiner. 1987. Managing engineers effectively. *Business,* Oct.–Dec., pp. 49–52.

Froiland, P. 1993. Who's getting trained? *Training,* October, pp. 53–65.

Gutpa, A. 1984. Contingency linkages between strategy and general manager characteristics: A conceptual examination. *Academy of Management Review* 9:399–412.

Gutpa, A., and V. Govindarajan. 1984. Business unit strategy, managerial characteristics, and business unit effectiveness at strategy implementation. *Academy of Management Journal* 27:25–41.

Harris, T. 1969. *I'm OK You're OK.* New York: Harper & Row.

House, R. 1971. A path-goal theory of leadership. *Administrative Science Quarterly,* September, pp. 321–38.

House, R., and T. Mitchell. 1974. Path-goal theory of leadership. *Journal of Contemporary Business,* Autumn, p. 83.

Howard, A., and D. Bray. 1988. *Managerial Lives in Transition: Advancing Age and Changing Times.* New York: Guilford Press.

Howell, J., P. Dorfman, and S. Kerr. 1986. Moderating variables in leadership research. *Academy of Management Review,* 11, pp. 88–102.

Karmel, B. 1978. Leadership: A challenge to traditional research methods and assumptions. *Academy of Management Review,* July, pp. 477–479.

Katz, R. 1974. Skills of an effective administrator. *Harvard Business Review,* Sept.–Oct.

Keller, R. 1989. A test of the path-goal theory of leadership with need for clarity as a moderator in research and development organizations. *Journal of Applied Psychology,* April, pp. 208–12.

Kepner, C., and B. Tregoe. 1975. *The Rational Manager: A Systematic Approach to Problem Solving and Decision Making.* New York: McGraw-Hill.

Kirkpatrick, S., and E. Locke. 1991. Leadership: Do traits matter? *The Executive* 5:2.

Kouzes, J, and B. Posner. 1988. *The Leadership Challenge: How to Get Things Done in Organizations.* San Francisco: Jossey-Bass.

Lennark, R. 1988. The Cost Engineer as Manager. *Cost Engineering* 30 (September):9.

Luthans, F., R. Hodgetts, and S. Rosenkrantz. 1988. *Real Managers.* Cambridge, MA: Ballinger Press.

Maier, N. 1963. *Problem Solving Discussions and Conferences.* New York: McGraw-Hill.

———. 1982. *Psychology in Industrial Organizations,* 5th ed. Boston: Houghton-Mifflin.

Mathieu, J. 1990. A test of subordinates' achievement and affiliation needs as moderators of a leader's path-goal relationships. *Basic and Applied Social Psychology,* June, pp. 179–89.

McCauley, C., M. Lombardo. and C. Usher. 1989. Diagnosing management development needs: An Instrument Based on How Managers Develop. *Journal of Management* 15:3.

McClelland, D. 1961. *The Achieving Society.* New York: Van Nostrand.

McClelland, D., and D. Burnham. 1976. Power is the Great Motivator. *Harvard Business Review* 54:2, pp. 100–110.

McClelland, D., and R. Boyatzis. 1982. Leadership motive pattern and long-term success in management. *Journal of Applied Psychology* 67, pp. 737–43.

Miner, J. 1978. Twenty years of research on role-motivation theory of managerial effectiveness. *Personnel Psychology* 31:739–60.

Mintzberg, H. 1975. The manager's job: Folklore and fact. *Harvard Business Review* 53(4): 49–61.

Miron, D., and D. McClelland. 1979. The impact of achievement motivation training on small businesses. *California Management Review,* Summer, pp. 13–28.

Niehoff, M., and M. Romans. 1982. Needs assessment as step one toward enhancing productivity. *Personnel Administrator,* May, pp. 35–39.

Offerman, L., and M. Gowing. 1990. Organizations of the future: Changes and challenges. *American Psychologist* 45:95–108.

O'Reilly, B. 1994. 360 feedback can change your life. *Fortune,* October, p. 17.

Pigors, P., and F. Pigors. 1987. Case Method. In *Training and Development Handbook: A Guide to Human Resource Development,* edited by R. Craig. New York: McGraw-Hill.

Porter, L., and L. McKibbin. 1988. *Future of Management Education and Development: Drift or Thrust into the 21st Century?* New York: McGraw-Hill.

Rackham, N., and T. Morgan. 1977. *Behavior Analysis in Training.* Maidenhead, England: McGraw-Hill.

Roberts, T. 1974. *Developing Effective Managers.* Stratford-upon-Avon: Edward Fox and Son.

Rosenbaum, B. 1991. How to lead today's technical professional. *Training and Development Journal,* 44, pp. 100–101.

Saari, L., T. Johnson, S. Mclaughlin, and D. Zimmerle. 1988. A survey of management practices in U.S. companies. *Personnel Psychology* 41:731–43.

Sayles, L. 1979. *Leadership: What Effective Managers Really Do and How They Really Do It.* New York: McGraw-Hill.

Schein, E. 1980. *Organizational Psychology.* 3d ed. Upper Saddle River, NJ: Prentice Hall.

Scholtes, P. 1988. *The Team Handbook: How to Use Teams to Improve Quality.* Pittsburgh: Joiner & Associates.

Shuman, J. 1989. Technical supervision and turnover among electrical engineers and technicians. *Group and Organizational Studies,* December.

Smith, K., and J. Harrison. 1986. In search of excellent leaders. In *The Handbook of Strategy,* edited by W. Guth. New York: Warren, Gorham & Lamont.

Starcevich, M., and J. Sykes. 1982. Internal advanced management programs for executive development: The experience of Phillips Petroleum. *Personnel Administrator,* June, pp. 27–33.

Thornton, G., and W. Byham. 1982. *Assessment Centers and Managerial Performance.* New York: Academic Press.

Training. 1994. "Industry Report," October.

Training. 1995. "Industry Report," October.

Training. 1996. "Industry Report," October.

Training and Development. 1993. Leading questions, March, 12–14.

Training and Development. 1998. State of the industry report, January, 22–43.

Vroom, V., and A. Jago. 1988. *The New Leadership: Managing Participation in Organizations.* Upper Saddle River, NJ: Prentice Hall.

Vroom, V., and P. Yetton. 1973. *Leadership and Decision Making.* Pittsburgh: University of Pittsburgh Press.

Waldman, D., F. Yammarino, and B. Avolio. 1990. A multiple level investigation of personnel ratings. *Personnel Psychology* 43:811–35.

Wexley, K., and G. Latham. 1991. *Developing and Training Human Resources in Organizations.* 2d ed. New York: HarperCollins.

Yukl, G. 1989. *Leadership in Organizations.* Upper Saddle River, NJ: Prentice Hall.

Zaleznik, A. 1970. Power and politics in organizational life. *Harvard Business Review,* 48:47–60.

Index

A

Abella, K., 378
Abilities, 5
    See also Knowledge/skills/abilities (KSAs)
Academic Directory of Programs in HRD, 25
Academy of Management, 238
Accommodation, 98, 114–115
Accountability, 391
Achievement, need for, 411
Achievement management style, 397
Ackelsberg, R., 50, 51
Ackerman, P. L., 236
Active listening, 200, 335
Acton, W. H., 236
Adams, J., 204
ADC Communications, 317
Affective questionnaire, 230
Ahire, S., 211
Alcock, D., 172, 267
Alderfer, C., 86, 87
Alliger, G., 232, 235
American Assembly of Collegiate Schools of Business
    (AACSB), 44
American Society for Training and Development
    (ASTD), 25
Analysis. *See* Evaluation of training; Needs analysis;
    Organizational analysis
Anderson, A., 203
Anderson, J. R., 200, 201
Anderson Consulting, 73
Andrews, J., 399
Angry trainees, 383
Anticipatory learning, 112
Apprenticeship training, 308, 352–354
Arbera, C., 236
Argyris, C., 348
Arlow, P., 50, 51
Arthur Anderson, Co., 253
Automaticity, 6, 238
Assessing Organizational Change (Seashore), 161, 238
Assessment, 239–240, 242–244
    See also Evaluation of training; Needs analysis;
        Organizational analysis
Assimilation, 98

Attention/expectancy
    audiovisual (AV) enhancements to training, 319–320
    computer-based training, 291
    design, training
        attracting attention, 199–200
        distractions, eliminating, 199
        pretraining, 215*t*
    games and simulations, 303–304
    lecture, the, 281–283, 283*t*
    social learning theory, 112
Attitudes
    audiovisual (AV) enhancements to training, 319
    computer-based training, 291
    defining, 6–7, 277
    evaluation of training, 222
    expected performance, 146
    job behavior outcomes, 242
    role play, 303
    scales, attitude, 238–239, 240*f*
    writing a learning objective, 187–188
AT&T Universal Card Service, 73
Audiotapes, 314, 361, 364
Audiovisual (AV) enhancements to training
    advantages/disadvantages, 358*t*
    characteristics, training group, 321–322
    computer-based training, 291–292
    costs, 316–317
    dynamic media, 312–318, 361, 364–366
    knowledge/skills/abilities, 318–319
    learning processes, 319–321
    materials and exercises, 317–318
    Motorola, 276–277
    range of AV alternatives, 311–312
    static media, 312–313, 313*f,* 359–361
Ausubel, D. P., 110
Automaticity, 6, 238, 277
Avolio, B., 405

B

Badriu, A., 413
Baldwin, T., 204, 208–210
Baltes, P. B., 114
Bandura, A., 94, 111, 200, 207
Banks, A., 212
Banks, M., 18, 172

NOTE: A *t* following a page number indicates tabular material and an *f* following a page number indicates a figure.

Barclay, L., 242
Barnard, W., 114
Barrett, G., 293
Bass, B., 157, 398, 399
Beatty, R., 153
Behavioral reproduction
  audiovisual (AV) enhancements to training, 321
  computer-based training, 292
  design, training, 202–203, 215*t*
  games and simulations, 304
  lecture, the, 283*t*, 284
  social learning theory, 113
Behaviorist approaches to learning
  cognitive approaches contrasted with, 96–99, 97*t*
  methods, training, 278
  modeling, behavior, 299–300, 350–351, 352*t*
  practice, 191
  tests, 161
  See also Gagné's learning types
Belmont, J., 117
Benedict, M. E., 153
Benfari, R. C., 355
Benko, T., 293
Bennett, W., 232, 235
Benson, G., 254
Benson, R., 52
Bergman, T., 209
Bernardin, H. J., 153, 240
Bettman, R., 412, 413
Bias, 151–152
Bible, R., 52
Biersner, R., 194
Birch, D., 399
Blake, R., 411
Blanchard, P. N., 158, 195, 206, 259, 352, 408
Blum, M. L., 149, 151, 152, 204
Blumenthal, R., 51, 52
Blumfield, M., 341, 342, 377
Bobko, P., 94
Bojyatzis, R., 399
Borkowski, J., 117
Boros Book of Mental Measurements, 238
Boulton, W., 39
Bower, G. H., 200, 201
Bower, J., 36
Braccini, S., 378
Bracker, J., 50, 172
Brandenberg, D., 223
Briggs, G., 204
British Airways (BA), 2–3, 9, 20, 21
Broadwell, M., 278, 334
Brock, J. F., 290
Brookfield, S., 117
Brown, A., 117
Brown, C., 32–33
Brown, G., 278
Brown, W., 402
Brownell, K. D., 207
Brundage, D., 114
Bruner, J. S., 96
Buchele, R., 51
Budgets, 11–12, 190

Bures, A., 18, 172, 212
Burke, M., 299
Burnham, D., 399, 402, 411
Burns, T., 40
Business games, 294–295, 303, 305, 343–345
Butterfield, E., 117

C

Calantone, R., 51
Cameron, K. S., 44
Cammann, C., 182
Camp, R., 158, 195, 206, 259, 352, 408
Campbell, D., 259
Campbell, J., 393
Campbell, M., 400
Canadian Plastics Training Center (CPTC), 172, 267, 268
Cannon-Bowers, J., 236
Capital resources, 133
Carlyle, J., 240
Carnevale, A., 58
Carrol, S., 163
Carter, N., 58
Cascio, W., 128, 156, 192, 203, 245, 249, 251, 391
Case studies
  analytic skills, developing, 303
  implementation of training, 347–348
  management development, 414–415
  methods, training, 323–326
  needs analysis, 176–179
  planning, strategic, 74–77
  simulating decision-making situations, 297
Casner, J., 171
Catalog sales training, 315
Cattaneo, J., 211
Cattaneo, R., 223
Cavalier Tool & Manufacturing, 52
Cavanaugh, J., 117
Center for Creative Leadership, 406
Centralization in the HRD organization, 57–58
Certification programs, 267–268, 410
Chaddock, P., 367
Chaining, 104–105
Chamber of Commerce, U.S., 377
Champion, D., 18, 172, 212
Chandler, A., 36, 38
Change
  fighting. *See* Resistance to change/learning
  model, steps in a generic planned, 63*f*
  process, 35
  stage and ISO 9000 procedures, 14
Characteristics, training group
  audiovisual (AV) enhancements to training, 321–322
  computer-based training, 292–293
  games and simulations, 304–305
  lecture, the, 285
  See also characteristics of managers *under* Management development
Charts, 312, 359
Chemers, M., 405, 411
Chi, M., 235

Chief executive officers (CEOs), 167–169, 212
Chuvala, J., 7
Classical conditioning, 100–102, 197–198
Clement, R. W., 25, 244
Cleveland, J. N., 156
Climate, organizational, 210–211
Closed-ended questions, 333
Clothes, 381
Coaching, 308–309, 354–356, 355*f*
Coast Guard, U.S., 73
Cognitive approaches to learning
    behaviorist approaches contrasted with, 96–99, 97*t*
    cognitive organization, 112, 284, 318, 320
    conceptual knowledge and skills, 397–398, 402, 409–410
    methods, training, 278
    tests, 160–161
    See also Declarative knowledge; Gagné's learning types; Procedural knowledge; Social learning theory; Strategic knowledge
Coleman, E., 400
Comedian, the, 383
Compensating treatments, 257
Compensatory rivalry, 257
Competencies, development of professional, 25, 26*t*, 27–28, 47–48, 71–72
Competitive strategy, 36–37, 56–57
Compilation, 6, 238, 277
Complexity, 39
Computer-based training (CBT)
    aids, names and descriptions of training, 286*t*
    beliefs companies hold about, 285
    computer-generated dynamic presentations, 314–321, 364
    costs, 288–289, 342
    declarative knowledge, 339–340
    interactivity, 340, 341*t*
    knowledge/skills/abilities, 290–291
    learning processes, 291–293
    materials and exercises, 289–290
    programmed instruction, 286, 286*t*–288*t*
    projected text and images, 312–313, 360
    self-pacing, 340, 341*t*
    sophistication of the multimedia, 340, 341*t*
Concept learning, 108–109
Conceptual knowledge and skills, 397–398, 402, 409–410
Confrontation meeting, organizational, 64–65
Conroy, M., 234
Consensus, 158, 160*t*
Constraints, organizational, 189–191, 190*t*
Consultants, 17, 375–376
Contamination, criterion, 150–152
Content and process, control of, 301–302, 310
Content validity, 152
Context/management characteristics model, 404
Control group, 256, 257, 262–264
Cook, J., 161
Cook, T. D., 259
Core technology, 40
Corporate universities, 408–409
Corry, R., 342
Cost leader organizations, 37, 45, 56, 403

Costs of training
    audiovisual (AV) enhancements to training, 316–317
    computer-based training, 288–289, 342
    cost/benefit and cost-effectiveness evaluation, 245
    cost savings (results focus), 245–247
    estimates, using, 248–249, 250*t*
    games and simulations, 300–301
    grievance reduction, 248*t*, 251*t*
    lecture, the, 280
    monetary value on training, placing a, 248
    on-the-job training, 310
    types of costs, 245
        development, 247*t*
        direct costs, 247*t*
        indirect, 247*t*
        overhead, 247*t*
        participant compensation, 247*t*
    utility analysis, 249, 251, 251*t*
    value of demonstrating value, 249
    Walgreen Co., 246
Crawford-Mason, C., 84
Credibility, trainer, 370–371
Criterion measures
    contamination, 150–152
    deficiency, 150
    defined, 148
    developing, 152–153
    relevancy, 150
    reliability, 148–149
    validity, 148–150
Cronbach, L., 193
Cultural/ideological issues, 63
Culture, organizational, 57, 211
Curry, T., 373
Customer service representatives (CRSs), 8, 323–326
Custom Research, Inc., 378

D

Dakin, S., 295
Data sources
    gathering TNA data, 161–162
    operational analysis, 138*t*–139*t*
    organizational analysis, 134, 135*t*–136*t*, 138*t*–139*t*
    person analysis, 154*t*–156*t*
    process data, 225–228, 226*t*–228*t*
    See also Outcome evaluation
David, F., 41
Davis, L., 293
Day, R., 299
Dayal, I., 137
Decision autonomy, 41
Decker, J. J., 352
Decker, P., 299
Declarative knowledge
    audiovisual (AV) enhancements to training, 318
    computer-based training, 339–340
    criterion measures, 152
    defining, 5–6, 277
    expected performance, 145
    outcome data and evaluation of training, 235
    paper-and-pencil tests, 160

Defensiveness and resistance to learning, 115
Deficiency, criterion, 150
Degree programs, 410
Deming, W. E., 84
Demoralized control group, 257
Deshpande, S., 18, 211
Design, organizational, 40–41
Design, training
  behavioral reproduction, 202–203, 215*t*
  constraints, organizational, 189–191, 190*t*
  evaluation of training
    control group, 262–264
    internal referencing strategy, 261–262
    multiple baseline design, 265
    posttest-only method, 259–260
    pretest/posttest, 260–261
    random assignment, 262–264
    Solomon 4 Group, 265
    time series design, 264
    what design to use, 265–266
  exercises and questions for review, 217–218
  knowledge/skills/abilities, 183, 192
  learning, facilitation of
    trainee, focus on the, 192–198
    training design, focus on, 198–203, 198*t*, 202*t*,
      213*t*–214*t*
  learning objectives, 183
  motivation of trainee, 193–197
  needs analysis, 173–175
  outcomes of, 212–213, 213*t*–216*t*, 216–217
  strategic knowledge, 202*t*, 203
  training processes model, 21*f*, 22
  transfer, facilitation of
    organizational intervention, focus on, 209–212
    training design, 203–208
Devanna, M., 36, 63
Development
  costs, 247*t*
  criterion measures, 152–153
  discrepancy, 153
  distinguished from education and training, 7
  phase and training processes model, 22, 24, 331
  See also Management development; Methods,
    training; Organizational development;
    Planning, strategic
Developments in Business Simulation and Experiential
  Learning, 295
DeVito, J., 49
Diagnostic and planning interventions (Macro),
  64–65, 66*f*
Diagnostic skills, 404–405
Dick, W., 110
Dietrich, C., 334
Diffusion of training, 257
Direct costs, 247*t*
Directive management style, 396–397
Direct questions, 333
Discipline Without Punishment (Grote), 92
Discrimination learning, 106–108
Discussion method, 279
Disseminator role, 394*t*
Distinctiveness, 158

Distractions, eliminating, 199
Disturbance handler role, 394*t*
Division of labor, 41
Dixon, N., 234, 244, 252, 253, 266
Dobbins, G., 157
Dobyns, L., 84
Dorfman, P., 392
Doverspike, D., 156
Dowling, M., 39
Dress, 381
Drive, 399
Dry run, 378–379
Duker, J., 51
Dulebohn, J., 207
Duncan, B., 39
Dunnette, M., 5, 6, 393
Duty to accommodate, 146
Dynamic media
  audiotapes, 314, 361, 364
  computer-generated dynamic presentations,
    314–315, 364
  costs, 316–317
  defining, 312, 313
  materials and exercises, 318
  moving film and videos, 314, 364
  planning for using, 364–365, 365*t*
  protocol, 365–366
Dysfluencies, 336

E

Ebert, R., 18
Eberts, R. E., 290
Eckerson, W., 413
Economic conditions influencing training strategies,
  55–56
Education, 9
Edwards, D., 293
Electronic information systems, 50
Elliot, S., 39
Employee-oriented management style, 396
Encoding, 201
Engel, H., 348
Entrepreneur role, 394*t*
Environmental uncertainty, 38–39, 44
  See also External environment, an organization's;
    Internal environment, an organization's
Equipment simulators, 293–294, 302, 303, 343
Errors, 151, 340*t*
Eurich, N. P., 288
Evaluation of training
  attitudes, 222, 238–239, 240*f*
  cases, 270–272
  company practices, 253–254
  costs, 245–249, 247*t*–248*t*, 250*t*–251*t*, 251
  criterion measures, 147–153
  data collected, types of
    outcome data. *See* Outcome evaluation
    process data, 225–228, 226*t*–228*t*
  design issues, 259–266
  exercises and questions for review, 272
  learning objectives, 221
  objectives, training, 189

performance data, 158–161
rationale for, 222–225
small businesses, 266–269
strategic knowledge, 236–237
summary, 269–270
training processes model, 22, 23–24
validity, 254–259
See also Needs analysis
Evered, R., 355
Executive and management education programs, 407
Exercises/games and lecturing, 337–339
See also Games and simulations
Existence needs, 86
Expectancy theory, 92–94, 194–197
Expectations toward training, 194
Expected performance and job analysis
attitude, 146
criterion measures, 147–153
declarative knowledge, 145
duty to accommodate, 146
knowledge, 115–116
skill requirements, 146
Experience of Work, (Cook), 161, 238
Experimentation component of a learning
organization, 49
External environment, an organization's
components of, 38
economic conditions, 55–56
environmental uncertainty, 38–39, 44
law and regulations, 55
selection of a training strategy, 53, 54*f*
strategies, external, 42–44
system and, interactions between, 19–20
technology, training, 55
training, externally based, 407–408
training providers, 54–55
External validity, 257–259
Extinction, 90

F

Facilities
furniture, 367
integrated instructional strategy, 372–373
off-site training, 369
seating arrangements, 367–369, 368*f*
training room, 366–367
Facility questions, 232
Failure, learning from, 56
Farh, J., 157
Faria, A. J., 343, 344
Farren, C., 115
Fazio, R., 303
Federal Business Development Bank (FBDB) in
Canada, 173, 377
Feedback, 162, 207
Feldman, M., 208
Fiedler, F., 405, 411
Fields, M., 32–33, 242
Figurehead role, 394*t*
Filipczak, B., 13, 357, 377, 378
Fink, C. D., 293
Finnerty, M., 308

Flanagan, D. L., 236
Fleishman, E., 5, 293
Fleuridas, C., 267
Follow-up to facilitate transfer of training, 210
Fombrun, C., 36, 63
Force-field analysis, 65, 66*f*
Ford, B., 413
Ford, J., 5, 152, 206, 236
Ford, K., 204, 209
Ford automotive parts manufacturing system, 69–70
Forlenza, D., 339
FPL Nuclear, 254
Frayne, C., 299
Froiland, P., 391
Functional simulations, 295
Furniture, 367

G

Gagné, R. M., 96, 99, 110, 320
Gagné's learning types, 99, 100*t*
concept learning, 108–109
discrimination learning, 106–108
principle learning, 109–110
problem-solving, 110
shaping and chaining, 102–105, 103*f*
signal learning, 100–102
stimulus-response learning, 102
verbal association learning, 105–106
Gainer, L., 58
Games and simulations
behavior modeling, 299–300, 350–351, 352*t*
business games, 294–295, 303, 305, 343–345
case study, 297
characteristics, training group, 304–305
content and process, control of, 301–302
costs, 300–301
equipment simulators, 293–294, 302, 303, 343
in-basket technique, 295–297, 303, 345–347
knowledge/skills/abilities, 302–303
learning processes, 303–304
role play, 297–299, 348–350, 350*t*
Ganger, R. E., 291
Garvin, D., 48
Geber, B., 223, 225, 245, 248, 253
Gecas, V., 94
Geddie, C., 115
General Electric, 408
Generalizability, 337
Gill, R., 236
Gillette, T., 7
Gilmere, J., 7
Gilmore, F., 51
Gioia, D. A., 153
Gist, M., 94
Glaser, R., 235
Goal setting, 197–198, 207–208
Gold, L., 306, 307, 353
Goldsmith, T. E., 236
Goldstein, I., 193, 258, 290, 291, 293, 299
Golhar, D., 18, 211
Gordon, E., 118, 310
Gordon, M. E., 238

Gordon, S., 236
Gott, S., 236
Goudy, R., 295
Gowing, M., 391
Goyindarajan, V., 37
Graf, P., 96
Grid management, 411
Grievances and evaluation of training, 245–248, 248t, 251t
Griffin, R., 18
Griffith, G. A., 114
Grote, D., 92
Groth, J. C., 295
Group characteristic bias, 151
Growth needs, 86–88
Gudmundson, D., 51
Guided discovery, 201
Gutpa, A., 37

H

Haccoun, R., 208, 261, 262
Hahn, C., 293
Halo effect, the, 151
Hamblin, A. C., 229
Hamtiaux, T., 261, 262
Hankin, E., 235
Hannafin, M. J., 291
Hansen, K., 13
Harris, M. M., 157
Harrison, J., 399
Hassett, J., 248
Hawthorne Effect, 258
Hepworth, S., 161
Hequet, M., 351
Herbert, G., 156
Hewlett-Packard, 43, 56
Hicks, W. D., 209
History as a threat to internal validity, 255
Hodgetts, R., 402
Holt, D., 18
Honeycutt, E., Jr., 277, 317
Hook, E., 283, 336
Hornsby, J., 18, 211
House, R., 396
Howard, A., 44
Howe, V., 277, 317
Howell, J., 392
HR. *See* Human Resources (HR) department
HRD. *See* Human Resource Development (HRD) departments
Huegli, J., 299
Human Resource Development (HRD) departments
  alternatives, strategic training
    manager/intermediary, 59–61, 60f
    mixed, 61–62
    primary provider, 58–59
  centralization and training environment, 57–58
  competencies, development of professional, 25, 26t, 28, 47–48
  learning organization, the, 48–50
  outcome, focus on, 7
  strategy, developing a, 53–57

See also Planning, strategic; *individual subject headings*
Human Resource Information System (HRIS), 34, 159
Human resources, 133
Human Resources (HR) department
  competitive strategy, 56–57
  increased importance of, 44–46, 45t, 46f
  training as part of, 14–18, 15f
  See also Planning, strategic; *individual subject headings*
Humorous trainees, 383
Humphreys, L. G., 236
Hunger, J., 50
Hunter, J., 240
Huszczo, G., 158, 195, 206, 259, 352, 408

I

IBM, 408
Ice-breaker, 334–335
Identical elements, 206
Implementation of training
  dry run, 378–379
  exercises and questions for review, 386–387
  facilities, 366–369
  integrated instructional strategy, 372–378
  pilot program, 379–380
  tips for trainers
    beginning of training, 380–381
    different trainees, dealing with, 382–383
    dress, 381
    instructions, providing, 382
    listening and questioning, 382
    podium, the, 381–382
    preparation, 380
  trainers
    credibility, 370–371
    experience, 371–372
    knowledge/skills/abilities, 369–370, 370t
  training processes model, 22, 24
  See also Methods, training
In-basket technique, 295–297, 303, 345–347
Incident process, 297
Incongruities in organizational environment, 132
Incumbents and analyzing a job, 139, 140t
Indirect costs, 247t
Individual differences related to learning, 117–119, 192–193
Institute for Social Research at the University of Michigan, 161
Instruction. *See* Implementation of training; Integrated instructional strategy; Methods, training
Instructions, providing, 382
Instrumentation as a threat to internal validity, 255–256
Integrated instructional strategy
  alternative to development
    consultants, 375–376
    seminars, outside, 376
    small businesses, 376–377
  facilities, 372–373

learning points, 372

management development, 395–396, 395*t*, 399–400, 400*t*, 401*t*

materials and exercises, 373

method of instruction, 372

organizational development, 72

strategy, 373–375, 374*t*

trainers, 373

Integrated personnel systems, 9

Intelligent computer-assisted instruction (ICAI), 286*t*

Intelligent tutoring systems (ITS), 286*t*

Interactive skills training, 340, 341*t*, 411

Internal environment, an organization's

change and resistance, levels of internal, 67–68

competitive strategy, 56–57

culture, organizational, 57

internal strategies, 42–44, 48–50

obstacles in the system, 163

organizational analysis, 133–134

organizational development, 62–64

See also Structure, organization; Technology

Internal referencing strategy (IRS), 261–262

Internal validity, 254–257

International Organizational for Standardization (ISO), 14

See also ISO 9000 series of standards

Interpersonal knowledge and skills, 398, 401–402, 410–411

Isenberg, J. F., 238

ISO 9000 series of standards, 14, 52, 53, 267, 269

J

Jackson, S., 37

Jago, A., 410

Jamison, D., 36

Jannisse, R., 52

Jinkerson, D., 254

Job aid, 163

Job behavior outcomes, 229, 240, 241*f*–242*f*, 242–243, 242*t*

Job-duty-task, 141–142, 142*f*

Job instruction technique (JIT). *See* On-the-job training (OJT)

Job performance, 85–86

See also Motivation and performance; Performance appraisals

Johnson, P. J., 236

Johnson, T., 230, 412

Johnstone, A., 283, 336

Jolles, R., 334

Jones, J. E., 337

Journal of Applied Psychology, 238

K

Kaplan, R., 295

Karagozoglu, N., 402

Kargar, J., 51, 52

Karmel, B., 396

Katz, D., 19

Kavanaugh, M., 210, 211

Kaye, B. L., 115

Kazanas, H., 309, 351, 354

Kearsley, G., 289

Keats, B., 50, 172

Keller, R., 396

Kelly, L., 230

Kendall, C., 117

Kepner, C., 410

Kerr, S., 392

Khan, R. L., 19

Killian, D., 293

Kimble, G. A., 102

King, L., 240

Kirkpatrick, D. L., 228

Kirkpatrick, S., 402

Klatzky, R., 200

Kleiner, B., 413

Kliener, A., 48

Klimoski, R. J., 209

Knowledge

declarative, 5–6

procedural, 6

strategic, 6

Knowledge predictor bias, 152

Knowledge/skills/abilities (KSAs)

audiovisual (AV) enhancements to training, 318–319

changing objectives and strategies, 35

computer-based training, 290–291

defining, 4–7

design, training, 183, 192

education and training, distinction between, 9

games and simulations, 302–303

growth needs, 87, 88

internal referencing strategy, 262

job performance, 85–86

lack of basic, 45–46

lecture, the, 281

links between job behavior and trainee, 243–244

management development, 393, 395, 400, 409–410

motivation to learn, 115–116

needs analysis, 127, 129

needs translated into training objectives, 184–185, 185*t*

on-the-job training, 310–311

proactive TNA, 165

process data, 225

relevant, 9

resistance to change, 68

results, organizational, 243

self-efficacy, 95

strategic knowledge, 203

task-oriented approach, 144*t*, 145

trainees controlling their learning, 117

trainers, 369–370, 370*t*

See also Declarative knowledge; Procedural knowledge; Strategic knowledge

Knowles, M. S., 97, 116, 117

Konz, A., 166

Kraiger, E., 236

Kraiger, K., 5, 152, 206

Kram, K., 355

Kropp, R., 235

Kuratko, D., 18, 211

Kuri, F., 173

L

Landy, F., 137
Lang, J., 51
Large businesses, 17–18
Latham, G. P., 99, 188, 197, 200, 207, 259, 299, 396, 399
Lawler, E., 161
Lawler, E., III, 393
Laws and regulations, 55, 191
Leadership, 394*t*, 399, 411, 413
Learning
    audiovisual (AV) enhancements to training, 319–321
    behaviorist *vs.* cognitive approaches, 96–99, 97*t*
    case analysis, 129–133
    computer-based training, 291–293
    definitions for, 4, 95–99
    design, training, 192–203, 198*t*, 202*t*, 213–214*t*
    exercises and questions for review, 124–125
    failure, learning from, 56
    Gagné's learning types, 99–110, 100*t*
    games and simulations, 303–304
    individual differences related to, 117–119, 192–193
    integrated instructional strategy, 372
    knowledge, 5–6
    lecture, the, 281–284
    motivation. *See* Motivation and performance
    needs analysis, 126, 229
    objectives. *See* Knowledge/skills/abilities (KSAs);
        learning objectives *under individual subject
        headings*
    on-the-job training, 305–308, 306*t*, 311
    outcome data and evaluation of training, 229, 235–240
    overlearning, 205–206
    social learning theory, 111–113
    theories, 83–84
    what is, 95–96
    whole *vs.* part, 204–205
    Wilderness Training Labor, 81–83
    See also Resistance to change/learning
Learning organization, the, 48–50
LearnShare, 342, 377
Lecture, the
    characteristics, training group, 285
    costs, 280
    discussion method, 279
    errors and ways to avoid them, 340*t*
    knowledge/skills/abilities, 281
    learning processes, 281–284
    materials and exercises, 280–281
    needs analysis, 332
    questioning, 333–334
    response and interest, encouraging trainee
        dysfluencies, 336
        exercises/games, 337–339
        ice-breaker, 334–335
        listening, 335
        move around while talking, 336
        nonverbal communication, 336
        variety, providing, 336
    straight lecture, 278–279

Lee, E. F., 94
LeGault, M., 12, 269
Leibowitz, Z. B., 115
Leifer, R., 41
Lengnick-Hall, M. L., 118
Lennark, R., 413
Levine, E. L., 153
Levy, P., 157
Lewin, K., 65
Liaison role, 394*t*
Lichenstein, E., 207
Lindsay, P., 200
Lippitt, G., 25
Listening, 200, 335, 382
Lloyd, D., 283, 336
Locke, E. A., 94, 188, 197, 200, 207, 402
Lockheed Corporation, 7
Lombardo, M., 295, 399, 402
Longenecker, C. O., 153
Lord, F. M., 237
Luthans, F., 402

M

Maddox, H., 283, 336
Mager, R. F., 185
Mahar, L., 411
Maier, N., 410
Malcolm Baldrige National Quality Award, 378
Management by objectives (MBO), 159
Management development
    case analysis, 414–415
    characteristics of managers
        conceptual knowledge and skills, 397–398, 402
        integrating managerial roles and characteristics, 399–400, 400*t*, 401*t*
        interpersonal knowledge and skills, 398, 401–402
        personal traits, 398–399, 402
        styles, management, 396–397, 402–404
        technical knowledge and skills, 398, 401
    context, understanding, 404
    exercises and questions for review, 415–416
    integrating strategy/structure/technology, 395–396, 395*t*
    learning objectives, 389
    managerial context, 395
    overview of training in organizations, 1, 10–11
    person analysis, 405–406
    responsibilities, 10–11, 25
    roles, managerial, 393–395, 394*t*, 400*t*
    self-awareness and diagnostic skills, 404–405
    sources of knowledge/skill acquisition
        corporate universities, 408–409
        externally based training, 407–408
    technical manager, 412–414
    types of programs
        knowledge/skills development (conceptual), 409–410
        knowledge/skills development (technical), 410
        personal traits, 411–412
        style, interpersonal and management, 410–411
    why focus on, 390–392
Manager/intermediary strategy, 59–61, 60*f*

Manual, trainee's and instructor's, 361, 362*t*–363*t*
Manz, C., 94, 299
Market follower organizations, 37
Market leader organizations, 37, 403
Marlatt, G., 207
Marquardt, M., 50
Marshall, C., 2
Marsick, V., 117
Martin, E., 200
Martocchio, J. J., 207
Marx, R. D., 207
MASCO Corp., 62
Maslow, A. H., 86
Massed practice, 204
Materials and exercises
    audiovisual (AV) enhancements to training, 317–318
    computer-based training, 289–290
    integrated instructional strategy, 373
    lecture, the, 280–281
    reaction outcomes, 230–231
Maturation as a threat to internal validity, 255
Mazique, M., 295
McCarty, T., 277, 317
McCauley, C., 399, 402
McClelland, D., 398, 399, 402, 411, 413
McCormick, E., 145
McDonald's, 408
McDonough, E., III, 41
McEnery, J., 157, 158
McGhee, W., 129, 131, 205
McGill, M., 48
McKay, D., 18
McKibbin, L., 44, 402
McLagen, P. A., 25
McLaughlin, S., 230, 412
McRae, C., 212
Meals, D., 223
Means, B., 236
Mecham, M., 293
Mechanistic design, 40
Melton, A., 200
Memory, activation of, 200–201
Mental models component of a learning organization, 49
Mentoring, 309, 355
Methods, training
    audiovisual (AV) enhancements to training, 311–322, 358–366
    case analysis, 323–326, 347–348
    computer-based, 285–293, 339–342
    exercises and questions for review, 327, 386–387
    games and simulations, 293–305, 343–351
    integrated instructional strategy, 372–377, 395–396, 399–401
    learning objectives, 275, 330
    lecture, the, 278–275, 332–339
    Motorola, 276–277
    on-the-job training, 305–311, 351–358
    outcomes matched with methods, 277–278
    summary, 322–323, 322*t*
    See also Implementation of training;
        Knowledge/skills/abilities (KSAs)

Michalak, D. F., 163
Miles, R., 37, 38
Miller, S., 222
Minor, J., 399, 411
Mintzberg, H., 41, 171, 393, 410
Miron, D., 411, 413
Mirvis, P., 161
Mission, organizational, 36, 132–133
Mitchell, G., 350
Mitchell, T., 396
Mixed strategy, 61–62
Monitoring training, 228, 394*t*
Moore, J. B., 236
Morgan, R., 118, 310
Morgan, T., 411
Mortality as a threat to internal validity, 256
Motion picture film, 314, 364
Motivation and performance
    computer-based training, 291
    design, training, 193–197
    expectancy theory, 92–94
    knowledge/skills/abilities, 85–86
    leadership, 399
    needs analysis, 86–88
    reinforcement theory, 88–92
    resistance to change/learning, 114–117
    self-efficacy, 94–95
    social learning theory, 111–112
    trainers, 357, 411
Motorola, 253, 276–277, 408
Mouton, J., 411
Mullen, E. J., 254, 259–261
Multimedia, sophistication of the, 340, 341*t*
    See also Computer-based training (CBT)
Multiple baseline design, 265
Multiple-choice test, 235, 236*t*
Multiple role play, 298
Multiple techniques as a threat to internal validity, 259
Multistate Health Corporation (MHC), 31–33, 74–77, 167–169
Murphy, K. R., 156

N

Nadler, L., 25
Nathen, B., 299
Naylor, J., 150–152, 204
Needs analysis
    cases, 176–179
    designing and appropriate training program, 173–175
    exercises and questions for review, 179–180
    framework for conducting a, 129–131
    gathering TNA data, 161–162
    learning objectives, 126
    learning processes, 229
    lecture, the, 332
    motivation and performance, 86–88
    operational analysis, 136–153
    organizational analysis, 131–136
    outcomes of TNA, 162–164
    overview of training in organizations, 9–11

Needs analysis *(continued)*
  person analysis, 153–161
  proactive TNA, 165–169, 171
  reactive TNA, 169–171
  small businesses, 172–174
  training processes model, 22–23
  why conduct a, 127–129
  See also Evaluation of training
Need to know, 116
Negative reinforcement, 89–91
Negative transfer, 203
Negotiator role, 394*t*
Newby, T. J., 203
Newsprint, 359
Newstrom, J. W., 118
Noe, R. A., 209
Nonroutine technology, 40
Nontraining needs, 162–164
Nonverbal communication, 336
Norman, D., 200
Nunnally, J., 152, 235

O

Objectives, training
  advantages of, 188–189
  design, training, 23
  developing clear, 164
  identifying, 185–186
  needs translated into, 184–185, 185*t*
  standards, 187
  types of, 185*t*
  writing good, 186–188
  See also Knowledge/skills/abilities (KSAs)
O'Brian, K., 378
OD. *See* Organizational development
Offerman, L., 391
O'Neal, H., 51
On-the-job training (OJT)
  apprenticeship training, 308, 352–354
  coaching, 308–309, 354–356, 355*f*
  content and process, control of, 310
  costs, 310
  job instruction technique, 306–308, 307*t*, 351–352,
    354*t*
  knowledge/skills/abilities, 310–311
  learning processes, 305–308, 306*t*, 311
  small businesses, 357–358
  trainers
    motivating, 357
    selecting, 356
    training, 309
Open-ended questions, 333
Open-systems model
  environment and the system, interactions between,
    19–20
  training processes model, 21–24
Operant conditioning, 88–89, 197
Operational analysis, 136
  analyzing the job
    how many to ask, 139
    how to select, 140
    incumbents, 139, 140*t*

  task-oriented approach, 141–143, 143*f*, 144*t*, 145
  what is the job, 137
  what to ask about, 141
  where to collect data, 141
  whom to ask, 137
  worker-oriented approach, 141, 141*f*
  data sources, 138*t*–139*t*
  defining a, 130
  expected performance, 145–153
  proactive TNA, 166–167
  reactive TNA, 169
Opportunity bias, 151
O'Reilly, B., 406
Organic design, 40
Organizational analysis
  data sources, 134, 135*t*–136*t*, 138*t*–139*t*
  defining a, 129–130
  internal environment, 133–134
  mission and strategies, 132–133
  performance discrepancy, 131
  proactive TNA, 165–166
  reactive TNA, 169
  resources, 133
Organizational Behavior Teaching Journal, 300
Organizational confrontation meeting, 64–65
Organizational development (OD)
  change and resistance, levels of internal, 67–68
  change process, 35
  diagnostic and planning interventions, 64–65
  internal systems, support from, 62–64
  overview of training in organizations, 13
  techno-structural interventions, 65–67
  and training, 68–73
Organizational outcome objectives, 185, 185*t*, 229,
    243–244
  See also Outcome evaluation
Orientation for introducing an empowerment
    intervention, 231
Orth, C. D., 355
Oskamp, S., 5, 6
Ostroff, C., 240
Outcome evaluation
  defining, 24
  design, training, 212–213, 213*t*–216*t*, 216–217
  four types of outcomes, 228–229
  job behavior outcomes, 240, 241*f*–242*f*, 242–243,
    242*t*
  learning processes, 229, 235–240
  methods matched with outcomes, 277–278
  reaction outcomes, 230–235
  relationship among levels of outcomes, 244–245,
    244*f*
  results, organizational, 243–244
  when to use it, 252–254, 252*t*
Overhead costs, 247*t*
Overhead questions, 333
Overhead transparencies, 312, 359, 359*t*
Overlearning, 205–206
Overmyer-Day, L., 254
Overview of training in organizations
  British Airways, 2–3
  budgets, 11–12

competencies, development of professional, 25, 26*t*, 27

effectiveness, maximizing, 3–4

exercises and questions for review, 28

ISO 9000 series of standards, 14

management responsibilities, 10–11

needs of organization and employees, 9–11

open-systems model, 19–24

organizational development, 13

structure of training organizations, 14–18, 15*f*

terminology, 4–9

Owens Corning, 50, 159, 342

P

Paffet, J. A., 293

Palicsar, A., 117

Palmer, A., 337

Paper-and-pencil tests, 160–161, 235

Participant compensation, 247*t*

Participative management style, 396

Pavlov, I. P., 101

Payne, R., 156

Pearce, J., 41

Pearson, J., 50

Peer support, 209–210

People's Express, 296

PepsiCo, 56

Peracchio, L., 259

Percival, F., 283, 336

Performance appraisals

pros and cons, 153

self-ratings, 157–158

selling, 10

succession planning, 190

supervisor ratings, 153, 156–157

360–degree performance review, 158

See also Expected performance and job analysis; Motivation and performance

Performance data

behavioral tests, 161

cognitive tests, 160–161

consensus, 158, 160*t*

distinctiveness, 158

proficiency tests, 160

surveys, 161

work planning and review, 159

Performance discrepancy (PD), 131, 153, 169–171

Performance ratings, bias in, 151

Perkins, D., 48

Perrow, C., 40

Personal mastery component of a learning organization, 49

Personal traits, 398–399, 402, 411–412

Person analysis

data sources, 154*t*–156*t*

defining a, 130

management development, 405–406

performance appraisals, 153, 156–158

performance data, 158–161

proactive TNA, 167–169

reactive TNA, 169

Personnel Psychology, 238

Peterson Paper Products, 129–133

Pfeiffer, J. W., 337

Phillips, C., 295

Phillips-Jones, L., 355

Phillips Petroleum, 408

Photographic slides, 312

Physical fidelity, 293

Piaget, J., 96, 114

Pigors, F., 297, 410

Pigors, P., 297, 410

Pilot program, 379–380

Pilot training, 202–203

Pinto, P. R., 25

Planning, strategic

case analysis, 74–77

constraints, organizational, 190–191

dynamic media, 364–365, 365*t*

exercises and questions for review, 77

external and internal factors, 38–41

HR and HRD influences on competitive strategy, 44–50

HRD's role in supporting strategy, 53–62

internal and external strategies, matching, 42–44

learning objectives, 30

mission, organizational, 36

Multistate Health Corporation, 31–33

overview, 33–35

proactive and reactive strategy, 41–42

small businesses, 50–53

static visuals, 360

steps in a generic planned-change process, 63*f*

strategy, 36–37

See also Organizational development (OD)

Podium, the, 381–382

Political issues, 63

Ponticell, J., 118, 310

Porter, L., 44, 402

Positive reinforcement, 89, 91

Positive transfer, 203

Postaudit stage and ISO 9000 procedures, 14

Posters, 312, 313*f,* 359

Posttest-only method, 259–260, 263

Posttraining, 216*t*

Practice, conditions of

massed *vs.* spaced practice, 204

overlearning, 205–206

whole *vs.* part learning, 204–205

Preaudit stage and ISO 9000 procedures, 14

Pretest/posttest design, 260–261, 263–264

Pretraining, 215*t*

Primary provider strategy, 58–59

Principle learning, 109–110

Proactive strategy, 41–42

Proactive TNA

operational analysis, 166–167

organizational analysis, 165–166

person analysis, 167–169

reactive *vs.,* 171

Probed protocol analysis, 236

Problem-solving, 22, 49, 110, 282
Procedural knowledge
  audiovisual (AV) enhancements to training, 318
  criterion measures, 152
  defining, 6, 277
  outcome data and evaluation of training, 235–236, 237*f*
Process, training as a. *See* Training processes model
Process data and evaluation of training, 225–228, 226*t*–228*t*
Process mapping stage and ISO 9000 procedures, 14
Process theories of motivation
  expectancy theory, 92–94
  reinforcement theory, 88–92
Profastener, 378
Proficiency tests, 160
Programmed instruction (PI), 286, 286*t*–288*t*
Progressive part training, 205
Projected text and images, 312–313, 360
Psychological fidelity, 293
Pugh, D., 156
Punishment, 90, 91, 162, 163

Q

QS 9000 requirements, 267, 268
Questioning, 333–334, 382
Quiet trainees, 382

R

Rackham, N., 411
Randolf, W., 41
Random assignment, 262–264
Raytheon, 56
Reaction outcomes
  caution in using reaction measures, 234–235
  defining, 229
  facility questions, 232
  materials and exercises, 230–231
  relevance, training, 230
  trainers, reactions to, 232
  when to measure reaction, 233–234
Reactive strategy, 41–42
Reactive TNA, 169–171
Readiness to learn, 116
Reelcraft industries, 52
Regression to the mean, 256
Reinforcement systems
  design, training, 215*t*
    classical/operant conditioning, 197–198
    posttraining, 216*t*
  motivation and performance, 88–92
Relapse prevention strategy, 207, 208*t*
Relatedness needs, 86
Relay questions, 334
Relevancy, 9, 116–117, 150, 230
Reliability, 148–149
Resistance to change/learning, 113
  defensiveness, 115
  evaluation of training, 223–224
  motivation and performance, 114–117
  problem-solving teams, 282

role play, 191
  three levels of change, 67–68
Resource allocator role, 394*t*
Resources, 133
  See also Materials and exercises
Results, knowledge of, 207
Results, organizational, 229, 243–244
Retention
  audiovisual (AV) enhancements to training, 320
  computer-based training, 291–292
  design, training, 215*t*
    memory, activation of, 200–201
    symbolic coding, 201
    symbolic rehearsal, 201–202
  games and simulations, 304
  lecture, the, 283*t*, 284
  social learning theory, 112–113
Reverse questions, 334
Rewards, 162, 210
Reynolds, A., 50
Riddle, G., 293
Rivait Machine Tools, 52, 378
Rivero, J. C., 37
Roberts, C., 48
Rogers, J. W., 223
Role(s)
  managerial, 393–395, 394*t*, 400*t*
  motivation, 411
  play, 191, 297–299, 303, 348–350, 350*t*
  rotation, 298–299
Rosenbaum, B., 413
Rosenkrantz, S., 402
Rosenthal, D., 267
Ross, M., 234
Ross, R., 48
Rossett, A., 58, 70, 73
Rothwell, W., 309, 351, 354
Routine technology, 40
Rummler, G., 127
Ryman, D., 194

S

Saari, L., 188, 197, 200, 230, 412
Sackett, P. R., 254, 259–261
Saks, A., 208
Salas, E., 5, 152, 206, 236
Sales simulations, 294
Samsung, 50
Sanders, P., 194
Sarri, L. M., 99
Sayles, L., 393
Scales, attitude, 238–239, 240*f*
Scepter Manufacturing, 12, 269
Schacter, D., 96
Schaubroeck, J., 157
Schein, E., 211, 396
Scherer, J., 213
Schissler, B., 378
Schmidt, F., 240
Schmitt, M. C., 203
Schneider, B., 166, 210
Schneider, C. P., 87

Schneier, C., 163
Scholtes, P., 410
Schuler, R., 37
Schultz, E., 223
Scranton Industries, 331–332
Scripted situations, 240, 242*f*
Seashore, S., 161
Seating arrangements, 367–369, 368*f*
Selection as a threat to internal/external validity, 256, 258
Self-awareness, 404
Self-directed training delivery systems, 50
Self-efficacy, 94–95, 116, 207
Self-managed barrier removal, 164
Self-managed work groups (SMWG), 69–70
Self-pacing, 340, 341*t*
Self-ratings, 157–158
Selman, J., 355
Seminars, 376, 410, 411
Senge, P., 48
Shaping, 100, 102–104, 103*f*
Shared vision component of a learning organization, 49
Shaw, K., 188, 197, 200
Shaw, R., 48
Sherman, R., 52
Shimamura, A., 96
Shotland, A., 232, 235
Shriver, E. L., 293
Shuman, J., 412
Signal learning, 100–102
Similarity, maximizing, 206
Sims, H., 94, 153, 299
Simulations, 286*t*, 290–291, 305
    See also Games and simulations
Single-case designs, 267
Sit-ins, 210
Size of training group, 285
Skills
    audiovisual (AV) enhancements to training, 318–319
    defining, 5
    evaluation of training, 238
    expected performance and job analysis, 146
    two levels of skill acquisition, 6, 277
    See also Knowledge/skills/abilities (KSAs)
Skinner, B. F., 89, 91, 97
Slack, K., 293
Slides, 359
Slocum, J., 48
Small businesses
    alternatives to developing training program, 376–377
    defined, 18
    evaluation of training, 266–269
    ignoring, 18
    needs analysis, 172–174
    on-the-job training, 357–358
    planning, strategic, 50–53
    transfer of training, 211–212
Smith, B., 48
Smith, K., 399
Smith, P., 299
Sneed, L., 364, 365

Snow, C., 37, 38
Snow, R., 193
Social learning theory
    attention, 112
    behavioral reproduction, 113
    motivation, 111–112
    retention, 112–113
Solem, A. R., 303
Solomon 4 Group, 265
Spaced practice, 204
Speed tests, 237
Spokesperson role, 394*t*
Spontaneous role plays, 298
Squire, L., 96
Stability, 39
Staffmasters, 378
Stalker, G., 40
Standards, 187, 267–268
    See also ISO 9000 series of standards
Starcevich, M., 408
Stark, C., 210, 240
Static media
    advantages/disadvantages, 358*t*
    charts, 312, 359
    computer-generated projection, 360
    costs, 316
    manual, trainee's and instructor's, 361
    material and processes, control of, 317–318
    newsprint, 312, 359
    overheads, 359
    posters, 312, 313*f,* 359
    projected text and images, 312–313
    protocol, 361
    resources needed, 360
    slides, 359
Stimulus-response learning, 100, 102
Stone, N., 44
Straight lecture, 278–279
Strategic knowledge
    defining, 6, 277
    design, training, 202*t*, 203
    evaluation of training, 236–237
Strategy, organizational, 36–37, 53–57
    See also Integrated instructional strategy;
            Organizational development (OD);
            Planning, strategic
Strickland, B., 115
Structure, organization
    decision autonomy, 41
    defining, 40
    design, organizational, 40–41
    division of labor, 41
    overview of training in organizations, 14–18, 15*f*
    techno-structural interventions, 65–67
    training organizations, 14–17
Structured role plays, 298
Student registration office, 8
Subsystem within the organizational system, training
        as a, 20*f*
Succession planning, 165, 190
Supervisor ratings, 153, 156–157
Supervisor support, 209

Supportive management style, 396
Surveys, 64, 161
Sykes, J., 408
Symbolic coding, 112, 201, 284, 318
Symbolic rehearsal, 113, 201–202, 284, 292
System and the environment, interactions between, 19–20
Systems thinking component of a learning organization, 49

T

Talkative trainees, 383
Tannenbaum, S., 131, 210, 211, 232, 235
Task complexity, 204
Task organization, 204
Task-oriented approach
  assessment procedure followed by computer firm, 144*t*
  critical importance of tasks, determining, 142, 143*t*
  directive and achievement-related actions, 396, 403
  job-duty-task, 141–142, 142*f*
  knowledge/skills/abilities, 145
Task structure, 106, 107, 107*t*
Team approach/building, 11, 49, 147, 282
Technology
  constraints, organizational, 191
  core, 40
  games and simulations, 293–305
  interventions, techno-structural, 65–67
  management development, 398, 401, 410, 412–414
  training, 55
  See also Computer-based training (CBT)
Tell and sell approach, 10
Templer, A., 223
Tests
  attitude scales, 238–239, 240*f*
  behavioral, 161
  cognitive, 160–161
  surveys, 161
  validity, threats to internal/external, 255, 258
  See also Evaluation of training; Needs analysis
Texas Instruments, 253–254
Thacker, J., 192, 203, 211, 242
Thayer, P. W., 129, 131, 205
Theory, a few words about, 83–84
Thomas, J., 137
Thompson, J. D., 40
Thorndike, E. L., 88, 157
360–degree performance review, 158, 242*t*, 253, 405
Tichey, N., 36, 63
Time series design, 264
Timing of assessment of
  job behavior, 242–243
  learning, 239–240
  results, organizational, 244
Toby, J., 161
Total Quality Management (TQM), 211
Tough, A., 116
Tourgh, W., 114
Tovar, R., 58
Tracey, B., 210, 211

Trainees controlling their learning, 116–117
  See also individual subject headings
Training, 70
Training and Development (Froiland), 391, 407, 408, 410
Training, 7
  and organizational development, 13, 68–73
  strategy, 12–13, 53–57
Training needs analysis (TNA). *See* Needs analysis
Training processes model, 21*f*
  development phase, 24
  evaluation phase, 23–24
  implementation phase, 24
  needs analysis phase, 22–23
  problem-solving processes, 22
Training stage and ISO 9000 procedures, 14
Transactional analysis, 411–412
Transference of knowledge component of a learning organization, 49
Transfer of training
  climate and culture, 210–211
  defining, 203
  goal setting, 207–208
  objectives, training, 185, 185*t*
  peer support, 209–210
  practice, conditions of, 204–206
  relapse prevention strategy, 207, 208*t*
  results, knowledge of, 207
  reward systems, 210
  similarity, maximizing, 206
  small businesses, 211–212
  supervisor support, 209
  Texas Instruments, 253
  three possibilities, 203
  trainer's support, 210
  vary the situation, 206–207
Transparencies, overhead, 312, 359, 359*t*
Traver, H., 232, 235
Tregoe, B., 410
Tschirgi, H., 299
Two-way communication, 333

U

Ultimate criterion, 149–150
Usher, C., 399, 402
Utility analysis, 249, 251, 251*t*
Utility questionnaire, 230

V

Validity, 150, 254
  content, 152
  invalidity, sources of, 261*t*
  reliability and, relationship between, 148–149
  threats to external, 257
    Hawthorne Effect, 258
    multiple techniques, 259
    selection, 258
    testing, 258
  threats to internal
    compensating treatments, 257
    compensatory rivalry, 257

demoralized control group, 257
diffusion of training, 257
history, 255
instrumentation, 255–256
maturation, 255
mortality, 256
regression, statistical, 256
selection, 256
testing, 255
ultimate criterion, 152–153
Variability in situations, 206–207
Variety, providing, 336
Vasey, J., 137
Verbal association learning, 105–106
Veroff, J., 399
Video-based training, 276–277, 314
See also Audiovisual (AV) enhancements to
training
Villet, J., 58
Vroom, V., 410

W

Wachner, L., 390
Waldman, D., 405
Walgreen Co., 246
Walker, J. W., 25
Wall, T., 161
Walton, R., 293
Warnaco, 390
Warr, P., 161
Weick, K., Jr., 393
Westcan, 127, 175
Western Learning Systems, 377
Westmeyer, P., 116
Wexley, K., 208, 210, 230, 259, 299, 396, 399
Wheelen, T., 50

Whetten, D. A., 44
White, L., 267
Wilderness Training Labor, 81–83
Wilk, S. L., 209
Wilkinson, H. E., 355
Williams, J., 157
Williamson, D., 14, 52
Willis, S. L., 114
Wisnia, S., 14
Wohlking, W., 349
Wood, G., 295
Woodward, J., 40
Work Planning and Review (WP&R), 157, 159
Workshops, 410, 411

X

Xerox, 50, 408

Y

Yager, E. G., 163
Yammarino, F., 405
Yancey, G. B., 230
Yanouzas, J., 194
Yetton, P., 410
Ypsilanti Ford Plant, 69–70
Yukl, G. A., 131, 188, 230, 411

Z

Zaleznik, A., 399
Zammuto, R., 391
Zanna, M., 303
Zemke, R., 295, 378
Zero transfer, 203
Zimmerlie, D., 230, 412
Zola-Morgan, S., 96